Double-Edged Diplomacy

STUDIES IN INTERNATIONAL POLITICAL ECONOMY
Stephen D. Krasner and Miles Kahler, General Editors
Ernst B. Haas, Consulting Editor

Double-Edged Diplomacy

International Bargaining and
Domestic Politics

EDITED BY

Peter B. Evans, Harold K. Jacobson,
Robert D. Putnam

UNIVERSITY OF CALIFORNIA PRESS

Berkeley   Los Angeles   London

University of California Press
Berkeley and Los Angeles, California

University of California Press, Ltd.
London, England

Copyright © 1993 by
The Regents of the University of California

Library of Congress Cataloging-in-Publication Data

Double-edged diplomacy: international bargaining and domestic
politics / edited by Peter B. Evans, Harold K. Jacobson, Robert D.
Putnam.
    p. cm.—(Studies in international political economy; 25)
    Includes bibliographical references and index.
    ISBN 0-520-07681-8 (alk. paper).—ISBN 0-520-07682-6 (pbk.:
alk. paper)
    1. International relations—Case studies. 2. Diplomacy—Case
studies. 3. Political science—Case studies. I. Evans, Peter B.,
1944–   . II. Jacobson, Harold Karan. III. Putnam, Robert D.
IV. Series.
JX1395.D65 1993
327'.0722—dc20   92-23297
                                           CIP

Printed in the United States of America

9 8 7 6 5 4 3 2

The paper used in this publication meets the minimum requirements of
American National Standard for Information Sciences—Permanence of
Paper for Printed Library Materials, ANSI Z39.48-1984 ♾

CONTENTS

PREFACE

This book was conceived in the course of a project on domestic politics and international relations conducted at the Center for Advanced Study in the Behavioral Sciences in Stanford, California, during 1988–89. Harold Jacobson and Robert Putnam proposed the project. David Cameron and Peter Evans joined as sponsors, and the four of us collectively led the project.

Tracing the lineage of intellectual works, however, is never uncomplicated. The project might not have occurred, and certainly would not have taken the form that it did, had not Robert Putnam written "Diplomacy and Domestic Politics: The Logic of Two-Level Games."[1] This piece became the point of departure for the Center project and ultimately for this book. Putnam's article was an outgrowth of the book that he wrote with Nicholas Bayne,[2] which in turn was an outgrowth of his experiences on the staff of the National Security Council during the Carter Administration. The other three project leaders also had long-standing interests in the interaction between domestic politics and international relations: Cameron's stemmed from his study of comparative electoral systems; Evans' from his perspective on development and dependency; and Jacobson's from his interest in international cooperation. Over the years, Jacobson and Putnam had intermittent conversations on the topic.

The Center project considered two basic questions: first, whether Putnam's insights and generalizations could be applied to negotiations that included non-Western countries; second, whether they could be applied to negotiations about other topics than economic issues. Beyond seeking answers to these questions, we wanted to explore the extent to which Putnam's metaphor or model could be developed, enhanced, and expanded.

During the year at the Center, we and other fellows met regularly in a bimonthly seminar. In these sessions we sought to evaluate Putnam's metaphor or model by considering it in the light of other theoretical perspectives. To test whether it had broader applicability, we convened two workshops at the Center during the fall of 1988. Some twenty scholars were invited to present synopses of other types of international negotiations and to assess the explanatory power of Putnam's ideas in the context of the cases that they had studied.

By early 1989, based on the experience of the seminar and the workshops, we were convinced that the project could yield a useful book, and we set about to constitute a team. The editors of this book and the authors of its chapters, most of whom had participated in one or both of the workshops, came to be the team. Because of other commitments, David Cameron decided that he could not be part of the team. We first met as a group at the Center for Advanced Study in the Behavioral Sciences in July 1989. Each participant presented a preliminary version of her or his chapter. We began the task of harmonizing the chapters: defining terms so that they could be used consistently and creating a template that would shape the empirical chapters in a common manner. Through this process we collectively determined the directions of our work and the character of the book.

The Palo Alto meetings, like those that followed, provided numerous examples of the synergy that intense collaboration can add to scholarship. As the group developed a shared vocabulary and a shared sense of important puzzles, new insights emerged that were genuinely collective products. For example, John Odell used his account of U.S. negotiations with Brazil to spark a debate about when domestic conflict helps a nation's bargaining position and when it hurts. After a wide-ranging discussion, Lisa Martin suggested that both threats and promises require domestic ratification, an idea that other participants further refined. The final formulation of this insight—and of many others reflected both in individual chapters and in the Introduction and Conclusion of this volume—owed much to the creativity and generosity of the group in exchanging constructive suggestions with one another.

We next met as a group on Cape Cod for a week in June 1990. This meeting concentrated on the contribution of the book to the development of theory. We discussed fully developed versions of all the chapters, with special attention to what would go into the Introduction and Conclusion. By the late fall of 1990 the chapters were assembled as a book manuscript, and we were ready to show our product to the outside world. Final revisions, designed to take readers' reactions into account, were made in the summer and fall of 1991.

The Ford Foundation generously provided funds to support our work, both on the project at the Center for Advanced Study in the Behavioral Sciences and for subsequent stages. This book would not exist without this financial help. We especially acknowledge the support of Gary Sick and Stanley Heginbotham, then at the Foundation, whose insights and enthusiasm were indispensable to the project.

During 1988–89 the Center for Advanced Study in the Behavioral Sciences was responsible for the administration of the project; after that it was administered by the Center for Political Studies of the University of Michigan's Institute for Social Research. Both institutions provided impeccable support, leaving the editors and authors free to concentrate on the substance of the work. As the project progressed, Barbara Opal, of the Center for Political Studies, became its administrative manager. Her organizational abilities and dedication were essential ingredients in the project's completion.

Our debts are many. Beyond the Ford Foundation and the two centers, we benefited greatly from the knowledge and wisdom of participants in the bimonthly seminars and the fall 1988 workshops at the Center for Advanced Study in the Behavioral Sciences, and from those who have read and commented on the manuscript. We particularly want to thank Gabriel Almond, David Baron, Richard Brody, Bruce Bueno de Mesquita, Matthew Evangelista, Jeffrey Frieden, Alexander George, Judith Goldstein, Peter Gourevitch, Joanne Gowa, Lloyd Gruber, Stephan Haggard, Keisuke Iida, John Ikenberry, Stephen Krasner, Robert Lawrence, Robert Litwak, Timothy McKeown, Ronald McKinnon, Sylvia Maxfield, James Morrow, Condoleezza Rice, Norman Schofield, Nancy Tuma, Robert Ward, Stephan Weatherford, Hans Weiler, and John Zysman. We are grateful to Naomi Schneider of the University of California Press, who has been a gentle but firm and patient and wise editor.

The book is a team project. We collectively accept responsibility for its shortcomings and share credit for whatever merits it may have.

Peter B. Evans
Harold K. Jacobson
Robert D. Putnam
March 1992

NOTES

1. Robert D. Putnam, "Diplomacy and Domestic Politics: The Logic of Two-Level Games," *International Organization* 42 (Summer 1988): 427–460 (reprinted as the Appendix to this volume).

2. Robert D. Putnam and Nicholas Bayne, *Hanging Together: Cooperation and Conflict in the Seven-Power Summits*, rev. ed. (Cambridge, Mass.: Harvard University Press, 1987).

ABBREVIATIONS

AAA	Agricultural Adjustment Act
AEA	American Electronics Association
AGPM	French Association of Maize Producers
AIOC	Anglo-Iranian Oil Company
AMEX	American Export Airlines
ASU	Arab Socialist Union
BAe	British Aerospace
BITU	Bustamante Industrial Trade Union (Jamaica)
BOAC	British Overseas Airways Corporation
CAB	Civil Aeronautics Board (U.S.)
CAP	Common Agricultural Policy
CDU	Christian Democratic Union (Germany)
CBEMA	Computer and Business Equipment Manufacturers Association
COG	chief of government
CSU	Christian Social Union (Germany)
DRAM	Dynamic Random Access Memory chips
EC	European Community
EFA	European Fighter Aircraft project
EFF	extended Fund facility (IMF)
EPC	Economic Policy Council
EPROM	Erasable Programmable Read-Only Memories
Eximbank	Export-Import Bank
FDP	Free Democratic Party (Germany)
FMLN	Farabundo Martí Front for National Liberation (Salvadoran guerrillas)
FMS	Foreign Military Sales (U.S. legislation)
FRG	Federal Republic of Germany
FSLN	Sandinista National Liberation Front
GATT	General Agreement on Tariffs and Trade
GDP	gross domestic product

PART 1

Introduction

Introduction
Integrating International and Domestic Theories of International Bargaining

Andrew Moravcsik

In the midst of the Great Depression, plagued by the common scourges of unemployment, bankruptcy, and debt, the leading industrial nations met in London for the 1933 World Economic Conference. The most critical issues of modern international economic cooperation were all on the table: exchange-rate stability, trade barriers, external debt, and macroeconomic coordination. Despite a common crisis of unprecedented proportions and a well understood set of technically feasible solutions, domestic forces in various countries—notably the divergence of economic ideologies on the part of national central bankers, and the obstinacy of the French peasantry—torpedoed the negotiations. This momentous failure led to even greater monetary instability, stagnant trade, the repudiation of debt, and deepening depression, all of which contributed to the success of fascism in Germany and, ultimately, the outbreak of World War II.

A half-century later, the lessons of the Depression were receding into the past. But though the economic crisis was less acute, the same countries were negotiating similar issues. In 1986, for example, the United States threatened to block one billion dollars in agricultural imports from Europe—a transatlantic trade sanction of unprecedented size—if proposed European Community (EC) barriers against imports of American feed grains were not retracted. As in 1933, the French government gave uncompromising support to its farmers, who would have been the major beneficiaries of the EC regulation. Yet this time the French government was unable to act on its own. Trade policy was coordinated by the European Commission in Brussels, but the U.S. government undermined EC support by carefully targeting major farm products of its members—olives for Italy, cognac for France, whiskey and gin for Britain, cheese for the Netherlands—a strategy that led journalists to dub the affair "the Yuppie War." The European Commission attempted to support the French position, calling for a counterthreat, but these efforts were resolutely blocked by the others, and the issue was quickly settled on American terms.

During the last two decades of its existence, the Soviet Union gradually opened up to the West. Yet the policies pursued by Soviet leaders from Brezhnev to Gorbachev posed paradoxes for those who saw the Soviet Union as a purposive, calculating state reacting to external incentives. In the 1970s, Brezhnev pursued an inconsistent policy of reconciliation in Europe and rivalry in the Third World, until, with the war in Afghanistan, the second part of the policy overwhelmed the first. Barely a decade later, Gorbachev adopted a quite different strategy, opening to the West while pursuing a policy of unilateral Soviet concessions worldwide. Both Brezhnev's adventurism and Gorbachev's accommodation find explanations in Soviet domestic politics. In order to reap the gains of Western economic cooperation, Brezhnev had to placate domestic hard-liners with aggression in Africa and Asia. Gorbachev, whose situation was more dire, pursued an opposite policy, seeking to use massive unilateral concessions to gain the Western economic aid needed to carry out *glasnost* and *perestroika*.

These three episodes in twentieth-century diplomatic history share one important characteristic common to many international negotiations: the statesmen involved simultaneously calculated the domestic and international implications of their actions. The outcomes in each case would be inexplicable without an analysis of the paradoxical interactions between domestic and international politics.

Robert Putnam has sought to capture this quality of international negotiations with the metaphor of a "two-level game."[1] In Putnam's metaphor, statesmen are strategically positioned between two "tables," one representing domestic politics and the other international negotiation. Diplomatic tactics and strategies are constrained simultaneously by what other states will accept and what domestic constituencies will ratify. To conclude a negotiation successfully, the statesman must bargain on these two tables, both reaching an international agreement and securing its domestic ratification.

Putnam's metaphor suggests a set of fundamental concepts, questions, and assumptions that help structure an analysis of international negotiations. The first section of this essay situates the two-level-games approach among existing efforts to link domestic and international politics theoretically. The second section summarizes the eleven case studies in this volume, including the three described above; explains the criteria by which they were selected; and presents the hypotheses about international negotiations as a two-level game that are explored in these cases.

INTEGRATING THEORIES OF DOMESTIC AND INTERNATIONAL POLITICS

The Level-of-Analysis Problem

Explanations of interstate relations have traditionally been categorized according to their "level of analysis." The level of analysis tells the investigator where to look for the causes of state behavior by classifying competing explanations (or independent variables) according to the units in which they are conceptualized.[2] The most widely employed schema, introduced in the 1950s by Kenneth Waltz, distinguishes three levels of analysis: international-level (or "systemic") explanations look to a state's position in the international system; domestic-level explanations look to the society, culture, and political institutions of individual nation-states; and individual-level explanations look to the personal or psychological characteristics of individual statesmen. The two-level-games project is concerned with all three levels, although in this section I will focus primarily on the international and domestic levels.[3]

International explanations assume that nation-states are unitary actors responding to external incentives. Nineteenth-century diplomatic historians spoke of the "primacy of foreign policy"; today, political scientists describe the state as a "billiard ball." The most venerable theory of international relations, dating from Thucydides and Machiavelli, is the Realist approach, which stresses the preeminent role of power in international relations. In recent years, international or systematic explanations have been most closely associated with "neo-Realist" heirs to this approach, above all Kenneth Waltz. But the argument, associated with such liberal thinkers as Norman Angell and Cordell Hull, that international interdependence renders war obsolete, is another such international or systemic theory.[4] In both theories, outcomes shift only in response to changing external constraints, not domestic changes.[5] "The internal attributes of states," one theorist has observed, "are given by assumption rather than treated as variables."[6] Specifically, states are assumed to have stable and broadly similar domestic preferences, decision-making procedures, and abilities to extract resources from society. They are distinguished only by their relative position in the international system.

Domestic explanations, by contrast, locate the determinants of foreign policy and international relations within the nation-state itself. State behavior does not respond to the international system; it constitutes it. Faced with common challenges, states may react very differently. This view traces its roots back to a number of sources, including the liberal tradition of Immanuel Kant, John Stuart Mill, and Woodrow Wilson, who stressed that in democratic polities, foreign policies, like internal policies, are subject to domestic debate and deliberation.[7]

Current domestic theories can be divided into three subcategories, according to the source of domestic policy posited by the analyst.[8] First, "society-centered" theories stress pressure from domestic social groups through legislatures, interest groups, elections, and public opinion.[9] Second, "state-centered" domestic theories locate the sources of foreign policy behavior within the administrative and decision-making apparatus of the executive branch of the state. Cybernetic limitations on decision-making, governmental elite ideologies of free trade or anti-Communism, and bureaucratic procedures have been used to reinterpret such classic subjects of Realist historiography as the Peloponnesian War, Bismarckian imperialism, and the NATO alliance.[10] Third, theories of "state-society relations" emphasize the institutions of representation, education, and administration that link state and society. The liberal claim that democracies do not make war on one another is based on one such theory.[11]

Among international relations theorists, it is widely recommended that analysts stick to a single level of analysis. Some, like J. David Singer, argue that different levels of analysis are mutually exclusive, asserting that "one could not add these two types of statements [systemic and domestic causes] together to achieve a cumulative growth of empirical generalizations."[12] Others concede that domestic factors may be important, but tend to be empirically intractable.[13] As we shall see, a majority of international relations theorists recommend that the analyst give priority to international explanation and employ theories of domestic politics only as needed to explain anomalies.

Yet only a limited set of real-world problems in international relations lend themselves to this sort of analysis. As I seek to demonstrate in the following section, pure international theories, while attractive in principle, tend to degenerate under the collective weight of empirical anomalies and theoretical limitations into explanations that include domestic factors. In the language of Imre Lakatos, whose writings on the philosophy of science have been widely invoked as a heuristic model for social-scientific theory-building, the tendency for international explanations to use an increasing number of ad hoc variables is one of the hallmarks of a "degenerating" research program ripe for revision. As a result, empirical studies formulated at a single level of analysis, international or domestic, are increasingly being supplanted by efforts to integrate the two.[14]

The Limitations of Pure Systemic Theory

Even the purest systemic theories concede the existence of domestic politics, but they maintain that it can be captured within stable assumptions about the nature of states. Both Realist and Liberal interdependence variants of systemic theory customarily assume that states are (at least boundedly) rational actors, that they have stable preferences across outcomes, and that they possess a fixed ability to mobilize domestic bargaining resources. If these three aspects of state behavior are held constant, systemic theorists argue, domestic politics can be reduced to an intervening process, a "transmission belt" or "black box," through which international imperatives are translated into state policies. In this view, the causes that account for different international outcomes are found in the international environment, even if the mechanisms by which those causes influence state policy are domestic. Thus, for example, although the U.S. military buildup under the Reagan Aministration was due in a proximate sense to policy choices made through the U.S. political process, Reagan's election and the decisions that followed might be interpreted as a predictable national response to perceptions of a more threatening international environment. International explanations are thus compatible with complex patterns of domestic decision-making in which actors deliberate the alternatives, as long as it can be shown that rational adaptation to the external environment is likely to be the ultimate result.

In short, all sophisticated theories of international relations, domestic and international, tend to concede that domestic actors are active participants in foreign policy-making. The question that divides them is whether the observed domestic behavior can best be accounted for by using international or domestic *theory*.

While systemic approaches may appear to banish debate over the influence of domestic politics, controversy is inevitably reintroduced by the need to justify the particular assumptions made about the nature of the actors. To eliminate domestic politics from consideration, restrictive analytic assumptions about the nature of domestic politics must be made. While making such assumptions is legitimate, indeed indispensable, social-scientific practice, such assumptions must approximate underlying reality to the extent necessary to justify their use.[15] For a systemic theory to be useful, it is not essential that the state actually be unitary, but it must function in important respects, both domestically and internationally, as if it were. These "as if" assumptions about domestic politics should be subjected, like other elements of theories, to theoretical criticism and empirical scrutiny. They are always disputable.[16]

With these caveats in mind, the construction of pure systemic theories of international relations is an abstract possibility. In practice, however, such arguments are surprisingly rare. Despite their claims, most systemic theorists shy away from actually making the restrictive assumptions required to reduce domestic politics to stable assumptions about the nature of states. The most celebrated attempt is Waltz's structural realist theory, outlined in his *Theory of International Politics*. Waltz specifies maximization of the probability of state survival as the preeminent interest of the state—although he concedes, as an empirical matter, that the aims of states are "endlessly varied," and the pursuit of survival is not "a realistic description of the impulse that lies behind every act of state."[17] Nonetheless, Waltz argues that states act *as if* they seek security, because survival is "a prerequisite to achieving any goals that states may have, other than promoting their own disappearance as political entities." Thus, states "at a minimum, seek their own preservation, and at a maximum, drive for universal domination."[18] Under these assumptions, Waltz predicts the constant possibility of war, the formation of balances of power, and the stability of bipolar systems.

The indeterminacy in the assumptions about state motives greatly weakens Waltz's theory, however, since the domestic factors underlying the variation in preferences between defensive and aggressive states threaten to become the major explanation of the incidence of war and patterns of power-balancing. At best, the domain of Waltz's theory must be limited to that subset of relations involving at least one regime that defines its interests in a potentially hostile way; more likely, systemic theory becomes an altogether unreliable guide, since in the absence of any hint how to go about deriving the variance in the goals of states from the international system, the result in *any* specific case is indeterminate without an examination of domestic politics.

Systemic theories of international political economy are plagued by the same fundamental indeterminacy regarding the nature of the actors, and hence the same tendency to degenerate. Consider three examples. After empirical tests failed to confirm the early claims of "hegemonic stability theory," which derived the hegemon's preference for a liberal world economy from its external power position, the theory was reformulated (as we shall discuss in more detail later) to accord more autonomy to domestic politics.[19] Postwar American liberals reformulated nineteenth-century liberal thought, arguing that the predicted pacific effects of economic interdependence will be observed only among *democratic capitalist* states. The claims of early Marxist "dependencia" theorists, who stressed external constraints on Third World development, were supplanted by those who stress the autonomous role of domestic institutions and coalitions in shaping the responses of less developed countries (LDCs) to the world economy.[20]

As these examples suggest, few truly international theories have been advanced, and even fewer empirically confirmed.[21] Systemic theorists, whether in security studies or international political economy, are thus faced with a dilemma. They can maintain the purity of the international level of analysis by radically limiting their theories to those areas where restrictive assumptions hold, or they can seek systematic ways to integrate domestic politics into systemic approaches. Each alternative challenges one of the major justifications for privileging systemic theory: the former undermines its comprehensiveness, the latter its parsimony. As Waltz conceded, over three decades ago: "The partial quality of each image sets up a tension that drives one toward the inclusion of the others."[22] Factors highlighted by systemic theories are certainly *necessary* to any satisfactory account of international affairs, but doubts have grown that these astringent theories are, by themselves, *sufficient* to the task.

Thus the question facing international relations theorists today is not *whether* to combine domestic and international explanations into a theory of "double-edged" diplomacy, but *how* best to do so. Before turning to the two-level-games approach, the next section analyzes progress that has been made so far in efforts to combine domestic and international theories.

Domestic Politics as the Source of Residual Variance

In seeking to integrate domestic and international politics, most systemic theorists retreat to the metaphor of domestic politics as an "imperfect" transmission belt that introduces deviations from rational response to external imperatives. Many theorists favor this approach because it continues to privilege systemic theory, while permitting domestic politics to enter the analysis as an independent, but clearly secondary, influence on policy. Robert Keohane maintains that international explanations should serve as the "first cut" of any analysis: "an international-level analysis . . . is neither an alternative to studying domestic politics, nor a mere supplement to it. . . . On the contrary, it is a *precondition* for effective comparative analysis. Without a conception of the common external problems, pressures, and challenges, . . . we lack an analytic basis for identifying the role played by domestic interests. . . ."[23] In this view, domestic politics is an intervening variable that introduces residual variance around the predictions of systemic theory. Residual variance can be introduced by relaxing any of the three fundamental assumptions: rational decision-making, a fixed ability to mobilize domestic resources, and stable preferences across different domestic regimes.

Relaxing the Assumption of Rationality.   The view that states calculate their responses to systemic imperatives imperfectly has a long pedigree. Democratic governments, because of their non-unitary nature, have long been criticized for their failure to pursue rational policies. Tocqueville criticized their endemic inability to "fix on some plan" and "coordinate the details of some great undertaking."[24] Sharp criticisms of democracy's persistent departures from rationality gives the work of Morgenthau and Kennan much of its normative edge and popular appeal. Kissinger condemns the rigidity of modern bureaucratic structures designed to "manage" foreign policy, while Morgenthau observes that in democracies "the need to marshal popular emotions to the support of foreign policy cannot fail to impair the rationality of foreign policy itself."[25] Realist historians view "American policy-makers as rational, sober individuals with a valid understanding of the requirements of the international power situation, who act contrary to U.S. national interests because they are swayed by social or domestic political pressures."[26]

In his writings on foreign policy, Waltz concurs with classical Realists that domestic institutions have a direct effect on the ability of a nation to respond "quickly" and "pragmatically" to international problems. Systemic explanations account for the "pressures" that create a "range of likely outcomes," but not "how, and how effectively, the units of the system will respond to those pressures and possibilities." For this reason, he concludes, "structure is certainly no good on detail."[27] Unlike Tocqueville and Morgenthau, however, Waltz believes pluralistic democracies like the United States, stabilized by their broader roots in domestic society, to be more capable of acting "effectively and responsibly in the world" than the more centralized parliamentary system of the United Kingdom or the authoritarian system in the Soviet Union.[28]

Even studies of misperception, organizational decision-making, and uncertainty in foreign policy that are ostensibly critical of Realist theory often inadvertently pay homage to it by treating such factors as departures from a norm of rational adaptation to the system, rather than as independent causes. Allison's bureaucratic theories, Krasner's statist approach, and Jervis's theories of misperception are all designed, at least in part, as explanations of the reasons why foreign policy diverges from the "national interest."[29]

Relaxing the Assumption of Constant Mobilization Capability. Alongside its role as a source of irrational decision-making, domestic politics is often viewed by systemic theorists as a factor influencing the ability of states to mobilize (or extract) resources. In pure systemic theory, statesmen are assumed to be able to mobilize whatever domestic resources, institutional or material, are necessary to achieve vital foreign-policy objectives. In relaxing the assumption, however, variations in domestic circumstances become part of the specification of bargaining capability. Statesmen must make tradeoffs between domestic and international goals. Once again, there is a long tradition of including the ability of leaders to mobilize domestic society in the specification of "power." Morgenthau, for example, did not limit national power to material factors: "National character and, above all, national morale and the quality of government, especially in the conduct of foreign affairs, are the most important, but also the most elusive, components of national power."[30] Michael Barnett has recently rehabilitated this tradition, arguing that the relationship between national security and domestic political economy is best understood by examining "state strategies for mobilizing those financial, productive, and human resources considered necessary for national security."[31] Michael Mastanduno, David Lake, and G. John Ikenberry have recently proposed the model of a Janus-faced "Realist state" with a competitive international face and an extractive, self-legitimating domestic face.[32] Similarly, strategic trade theory and "post-dependency" analyses of bargaining between multinational firms and LDCs both stress the importance of a state's ability to extract and commit long-term resources as an important aspect of international economic bargaining.[33]

Relaxing the Assumption of Stable State Preferences.   As was noted in the previous section, variance in state preferences poses the most fundamental challenge to international explanations. In a pure systemic account, as Duncan Snidal points out, domestic politics can be captured within "simple assumptions about . . . preferences."[34] International theorists have employed domestic theories in their work to account for deviations from their international predictions. Morgenthau, Wolfers, and other classical Realists criticized proponents of domestic ideologies—nationalist, pacifist, or otherwise—for encouraging moralistic and overambitious national goals. "Moderation in policy," Morgenthau declared, "cannot fail to follow moderation of moral judgment."[35] Kissinger contended that the predictions of state behavior from the Realist model become indeterminate when "domestic structures" are unstable or are based on "incommensurate notions of what is just."[36]

Like their Realist counterparts, pure Liberal interdependence theories also tend to degenerate into explanations that permit an increasingly important role for independent domestic factors as sources of residual variance. The "second-image-reversed" approach provides domestic micro-foundations for Liberal interdependence theory on which more precise predictions can be based. Scholars in the "second-image-reversed" tradition, including Peter Gourevitch, Ronald Rogowski, Peter Katzenstein, and Helen Milner, argue that distributional coalitions (and even institutions) form in response to their relative economic position in world markets—their "production profile," in Gourevitch's terminology.[37] This approach was initially designed to explain coalition formation in comparative politics, but is increasingly being extended to explain policy formation in foreign economic policy.

For most second-image-reversed theorists, domestic politics is more than a transmission belt for international impulses. For Rogowski, international factors only account for the patterns of domestic coalitions, while domestic theories influence the outcomes of intercoalitional conflict.[38] Milner argues that states support sectorial interests, but that when sectors are divided, the outcomes of inter-firm conflicts become unclear. In Katzenstein's account of the rise of democratic corporatism in small European countries, international economic crisis and domestic social structures interact.[39] In his study of late nineteenth- and early twentieth-century U.S. trade policy, which draws on both second-image-reversed and mercantilist elements, David Lake identifies the "national trade interest" with the executive branch of the government, while domestic interest groups are viewed as forces that impede the executive from pursuing the common good. He concludes that international factors explain overall tariff levels, while domestic theories explain the distribution of tariffs across sectors.[40]

More recently, some scholars have taken the move to accommodate residual variance in state preferences to its logical extreme by linking purely *domestic* theories of state preferences with *systemic* theories of interstate bargaining.[41] "Given state interests, whose origins are not predicted by the theory, patterns of outcomes in world politics will be determined by the overall distribution of power among states," as one literature review summarizes the position.[42] The practice of using domestic factors to account for variance in national interests, while retaining international theories of bargaining, has been rediscovered by younger scholars in security studies—particularly to explain international aggression. While some of the theories considered earlier assumed that domestic factors account for residual variance in state preferences, these theories are more radical, arguing that the variance in state preferences is almost entirely due to differences in domestic arrangements.

In his study of alliance formation in the Middle East, for example, Stephen Walt modifies the Realist paradigm by arguing that states do not balance against power, but rather against threats. The factor Walt relies on most heavily to explain threats is "perceived intentions," which he discusses largely in terms of domestic political factors. Indeed, in some of his examples, the "threat" to a government stems not from a foreign military menace but from a domestic fifth column attracted by the ideology of a foreign state.[43] In a similar vein, Jack Snyder and Stephen van Evera trace destabilizing military policies to a cultish belief in the value of an aggressive strategy.[44] The beliefs in Wilhelmine Germany, for example, that potential adversaries were aggressively inclined, the faith in a bandwagoning theory of alliance formation, the assumption that empires were valuable assets, the conviction that war was socially desirable, and outright nationalism all bolstered the bias toward aggressive policies and contributed—through a systemic logic—to the breakdown in the balance of power and the outbreak of World War I. Beneath all these factors, according to van Evera, lies "the extraordinary influence of professional European militaries on civilian opinion, and the social stratification of European societies"—effects that were particularly important in late-developing undemocratic states like Germany and Russia.[45] Consistent with the assumption of rational state action, each of these scholars employs domestic politics to account for state interests, and then relies on classical balance-of-power reasoning to draw the systemic consequences. This raises the intriguing question of whether any of these theorists can still claim to be Realists. Indeed, this position seems almost to reverse the "residual variance" approach by asserting the priority of (largely domestic) theories of preference formation over systemic theories of strategic interaction and bargaining—a view more properly associated with Liberalism.[46]

Similar attempts to combine domestic and international theories can be found in studies on international political economy. Consider the intellectual trajectory of "hegemonic stability theory," the claim that the predominance of a single great power, such as the United States after World War II, is the decisive factor in overcoming collective action problems blocking the formation of liberal international economic regimes. Initial variants proposed by Charles Kindleberger, Stephen Krasner, and Robert Keohane implied the possibility of a strong version of the theory, in which the interests of governments, as well as their bargaining power, are determined by their position in the international political system. In short, hegemonic states can be assumed to be liberal. Accordingly, most of these authors sought correlations between hegemony and liberalization. Yet the strong version of hegemonic stability theory was almost immediately called into question, even by its originators, who invoked domestic factors as parallel influences on policy. Krasner's path-breaking study invokes domestic "leads and lags" to explain anomalies in half the time periods studied. Kindleberger undermines the systemic variant by challenging the analysis of nineteenth-century Europe as a period of British trade hegemony, and by stressing U.S. policy *failure* in the 1930s. In different ways, David Lake, Duncan Snidal, and Keohane all challenge the assumption that domestic constituencies in hegemonic countries must necessarily provide international stability or liberal economic institutions as predicted. John Ruggie, observing that hegemonic powers like Nazi Germany and the post–World War II Soviet Union imposed restrictive orders, suggested that domestic factors are required to explain the substantive content of policy. In a look back at nearly two decades of research, it is thus difficult to find studies that employ a purely systemic variant of hegemonic stability theory—yet, with the partial exception of Lake's study of U.S. trade policy, domestic factors have yet to be integrated theoretically into such explanations.[47] Recent analyses of European integration, of OECD financial regimes, and of the Anglo-Chinese negotiations over Hong Kong, stress the domestic sources of state interests, while employing international theories to account for bargaining outcomes.[48]

Criticisms of the "Residual Variance" Approach.   The sequential use of theories drawn from different paradigms provides one solution, often a useful one, to the problem of combining domestic and international theories. But it is open to at least three important criticisms.

First, the decision to begin with systemic, as opposed to domestic, theory is essentially arbitrary. Systemic theories are not inherently more parsimonious, nor more powerful, nor more precise than their domestic counterparts.[49] Nor is Keohane's contention that "we must understand the context of action before we understand the action itself," and thus systemic theory provides a necessary "analytical basis" for analyzing domestic influences, decisive.[50] As suggested above, the converse may be more true: domestic politics provides the analytical basis for analyzing international factors. In the absence of a compelling theoretical argument or clear empirical evidence from studies that assess domestic and international explanations on an equal basis, the grant of priority to systemic theories simply introduces an unwarranted bias into the body of empirical research conducted in international relations.

Second, by privileging international-level theories and bringing in domestic factors only as needed, this approach tends to encourage ad hoc interpretations rather than explicit theories about the interaction between domestic and international politics. There is little theoretical justification for the divisions between international and domestic theory drawn in the explanations described above, nor can there be, since the two bodies of theory are derived separately. Rather than calculating domestic and international interests simultaneously, such theories often make inconsistent assumptions about the rationality or preferences of statesmen, who are assumed to respond sometimes to external incentives and sometimes to internal incentives. Moreover, without a broader theoretical framework, the analyst is left without guidance about *which* domestic influences to emphasize. The result may be a haphazard checklist of possibly relevant domestic "factors," ranging from national character to class structure to constitutional law.

Third, the sequential use of domestic theories of interest and international theories of bargaining, even where domestic factors are treated as prior to systemic ones, is at best incomplete, since, with only a few contemporary exceptions, such explanations have ignored the influence of domestic factors *on international bargaining.* As the classical Realists were already aware, the effects of domestic factors are not limited to the process of interest formation, but affect strategy and bargaining outcomes as well. To fill this gap, the two-level-games approach, to which we now turn, presents a framework for analyzing the combined impact of domestic and international factors on international bargaining.

Two-Level Games: Statesmen and Interactive Bargaining

The two-level-games approach begins by assuming that statesmen are typically trying to do two things at once; that is, they seek to manipulate domestic and international politics simultaneously. Diplomatic strategies and tactics are constrained both by what other states will accept and by what domestic constituencies will ratify. Diplomacy is a process of strategic interaction in which actors simultaneously try to take account of and, if possible, influence the expected reactions of other actors, both at home and abroad. The outcome of international negotiations may depend on the strategy a statesman chooses to influence his own and his counterpart's domestic polities. By exploiting control over information, resources, and agenda-setting with respect to his own domestic polity, the statesman can open up new possibilities for international accord or bargaining advantage. Conversely, international strategies can be employed to change the character of domestic constraints, as in the case of "synergistic issue linkage," which Putnam defines as an international deal that creates "a policy option . . . that was previously beyond domestic control."[51] The statesman can also target policies directly at domestic groups in foreign countries, seeking allies "behind the back" of his international counterpart.

The image of the executive as "Janus-faced"—forced to balance international and domestic concerns in a process of "double-edged" diplomacy—stands in sharp contrast to the images that privilege either the demands of domestic political constituents or the systemic logic of the national interest. Taken alone, either the international or domestic view may remove real initiative and discretion from the chief executive. In domestic, "constituency-driven" models, leaders become passive political registers, summing the franchise-weighted vectors of domestic interests and moving in the indicated direction; while in international, "systemic" models, chief executives must respond to the manifest dictates of the international system. The international and domestic logics are elegant and parsimonious in their own terms, but, as we have seen, they are often tricky to combine. The assumption of this project is that if the two logics do not correspond, an area of autonomy is created in which the chief executive must choose how to reconcile them. "Statesmen in this predicament," writes Putnam, "face distinctive strategic opportunities and strategic dilemmas."[52]

The theoretical propositions suggested by the two-level-games metaphor will be examined in a later section. For now, it is important to note that this framework is quite compatible with much in the existing approaches examined above. From the Liberal interdependence school comes the important insight that rising levels of trade and investment are eroding de facto sovereignty, so that the achievement of domestic policy goals increasingly requires interstate negotiations.[53] From the "second-image-reversed" approach comes the notion that the "national interest" is defined in terms of the differential impact of international agreements on specific domestic actors. Perhaps the closest antecedent is Classical Realism (and more recent theories of the "Realist state"), in which the statesman mobilizes domestic society to achieve international objectives.

Yet the two-level-games approach differs from previous theories in three essential respects. First, it is a theory of international bargaining. As we have seen, most attempts to integrate domestic factors into systemic theory have focused on the formation of national preferences. One might say that the two-level-games approach seeks to do for interstate bargaining what the second-image-reversed approach did for interest formation. (As such, the two may be complementary). In other words, complex patterns of interdependence do not simply constrain statesmen, as the interdependence school argued, but also create new possibilities for creative statecraft. In this sense, despite the inclusion of domestic politics, it has much in common with Realist theory, which also focuses on the determinants of bargaining power.[54]

The second departure from previous theory concerns the emphasis on the statesman as the central strategic actor. The stateman's choice of strategy is assumed to be an important element in international negotiations. Informed by rational-choice theory, the two-level-game approach offers the analyst guidance as to which domestic "factors" are likely to be most crucial, and thus seeks to move the discussion of the domestic determinants of foreign policy beyond the stage of ad hoc checklists. The two-level-games approach invites us to explore within a single framework the implications of different specifications of the principal-agent relation between the polity and the statesman, and different specifications of the statesman's interests. These include the Classical Realist view of a statesman faced with domestic constraints on mobilization; the view, more consistent with a Liberal approach, that the statesman is a pure "agent" of society, seeking to maximize domestic political support; and finally, the notion of statesmen seeking to realize personal goals. One unexpected byproduct of the latter concept may be renewed interest in explanations that stress the individual psychology and political skill of statesmen—"first-image" explanations, according to Waltz's typology.

Such theories have fallen into disuse—but by mapping more precisely the areas of structural constraint and autonomy surrounding the statesman, the two-level-games approach may permit their more rigorous application and evaluation.

The third and most distinctive departure from previous theory is that the statesman's strategies reflect a simultaneous "double-edged," calculation of constraints and opportunities on both the domestic and international boards. The two-level-games approach recognizes that domestic policies can be used to affect the outcomes of international bargaining, and that international moves may be solely aimed at achieving domestic goals. This differentiates the model from approaches, including those examined above, in which two sets of constraints—domestic interests and international bargaining—are treated as superimposed; these might be termed "additive approaches." The two-level-games framework offers convenient language in which to express the theoretical claims of additive approaches, and they are explored in a number of the case studies in this volume. But the most theoretically distinctive element in the two-level-games approach is its typology and analysis of strategies for simultaneously exploiting both levels in a bargaining situation. There are times when, as Putnam observes, "clever players will spot a move on one board that will trigger realignments on other boards."[55] Because of its stress on the interaction between the two levels, we term this sort of analysis an "interactive approach."

INTEGRATING THEORY AND EVIDENCE

The Cases To Be Studied

The empirical research in this volume comprises a series of paired comparisons of international negotiations, described in more detail below. These cases were selected in order to evaluate the utility of the framework across a wide range of strategic situations, issue areas, and historical epochs. A reader of Putnam's initial article might object that a majority of the examples cited were drawn from bargaining about economic cooperation between advanced industrialized democracies in the postwar period—a subset of international negotiations often believed to be biased toward domestic theories by the preponderance of economic issues and positive-sum situations.

To counteract this potential source of bias, and to strengthen confidence in the empirical generalizations drawn from the data, a more diverse set of cases were selected.[56] Cases were taken from the diplomacy of dictatorial and democratic, developed and developing, countries. Some investigate prewar or immediate postwar diplomacy, as well as more recent events. Of the eleven case studies, four analyze extremely conflictful negotiations over security and territorial issues, and three explore particularly difficult issues in North-South relations. There are numerous examples of zero-sum coercive bargaining, and threats and counterthreats, in both economic and security affairs. This inclusion of conflictual negotiations in the set of cases to be investigated enabled the project to extend the two-level-games approach well beyond the more cooperative domain addressed in Putnam's initial essay, and provided the basis for some of the most important theoretical advances in this work. In particular, special attention was given to the implications of domestic politics for the credibility of international threats.

Throughout, the method of "structured, focused comparison" was employed, whereby a standardized set of questions about the process and outcomes of negotiations was posed about a series of case studies.[57] The participants then related the authors' findings to potential generalizations about two-level interactions. In this sense, the case studies are designed to support a preliminary assessment of the validity of assumptions and hypotheses drawn from the two-level framework.

Each of the paired case studies described below employs theories expressed within the two-level-games framework to account for two dimensions of negotiated outcomes: (1) success or failure in reaching agreement, and (2) the distribution of gains and losses. The first dimension, success or failure, is defined in terms of agreement on deliberately coordinated policies that is negotiated, ratified, and implemented, whether or not the agreement has the ultimate consequences anticipated by the parties and regardless of how the costs and benefits of the agreement were shared among the participants. Each chapter contains at least two paired cases: one success and one failure. Deliberate policy change (or deliberate policy continuity, if that is what the agreement calls for) may be recorded explicitly, as in a formal treaty, but it may also involve tacit coordination. This measure of success includes implementation, thereby capturing the possibility of "involuntary defection," when a nation reneges on an agreement over the opposition of its statesman. In examining the second dimension of negotiations, its distributional effects, each author seeks to determine which nation is favored by the distribution of costs and benefits and how the outcome is related to the preferences of the statesmen and domestic constituencies.

Four case studies examine enduring issues of high foreign policy: (1) East-West conflict in Central Europe; (2) NATO nuclear policy; (3) Franco-German collaborative arms procurement; and (4) the Arab-Israeli dispute.

Jack Snyder applies the two-level-games approach to the explosive legacy of the Potsdam settlement: the East-West conflict over Berlin. In analyzing the paradoxical shifts in East-West bargaining from Stalin to Gorbachev, Snyder contrasts the two-level-games approach to both a Realist analysis based on the "security dilemma" and a domestic analysis that locate the sources of interstate conflict in the demands of domestic interest groups or alliance partners. While both security concerns and domestic pressures offer plausible explanations for the stalemate of the Stalin and Khrushchev periods, the two must be examined together to account for the paradoxical policies of Brezhnev, who pursued detente in Europe while placating domestic groups with adventurism in the Third World, and Gorbachev, whose policies of unilateral international concessions can only be understood as part of an epochal effort at domestic reform.

Conflict is prevalent within alliances, as well as between them. Richard Eichenberg demonstrates that the bewildering twists and turns of the most contentious issue in NATO over the past two decades—the stationing of U.S. missiles in Germany—can only be fully understood with reference to the reverberation between the rhetoric of American presidents and the responses of German citizens. The well-publicized failure of Chancellor Schmidt and President Carter to agree on a NATO policy created a turbulent swell of popular pressure for compromise. No sooner was agreement reached, however, than President Reagan launched a campaign of anti-Soviet rhetoric that inflamed German public opinion against implementation of the agreement. A few years later, when Reagan reversed U.S. policy again to support the radical "double zero" arms-reduction agreement with the USSR, the same German public could be exploited to his advantage, since it blocked efforts by Chancellor Helmut Kohl to mobilize opposition to the agreement. In 1989 the positions were reversed again, as President Bush called for the modernization of NATO missiles and Kohl was able to exploit the same public sentiment as an excuse for not supporting the American initiative.

France and Germany, rivals for two centuries, have become models of military cooperation. Yet my examination of three Franco-German negotiations over the past two decades to establish collaborative manufacture of sophisticated armaments finds that cooperation does not preclude competition. Although each country stood to save tens of billions of francs and Deutschemarks on each collaborative project, only the negotiations over combat helicopters were crowned with success, while discussions about battle tanks and fighter aircraft ended in failure. Despite the common presumption that the traditional Realist concern with autarky leads military planners to defend autarkic arms procurement, the military supported all three agreements. In the cases of fighters and tanks, however, they were overruled by domestic arms producers, whose efforts to maintain their position as independent arms exporters in an oligopolistic global market carried the day. More recently, European governments have responded to these failures by adopting a sophisticated two-level strategy designed to undermine the powerful monopolistic position of their domestic arms producers.

In the violent history of the Arab-Israeli dispute, the Camp David accords stand out as a turning point. Janice Stein reveals that this momentous agreement turned on a unique conjuncture in domestic politics—a simultaneous economic crisis in Egypt and political crisis in Israel. Although negotiations had failed just six months previously, these crises created a brief window of opportunity for agreement. Following Sadat's dramatic speech before the Knesset in Jerusalem, which transformed Israeli public opinion, American financial aid offered the means to carry out economic reform in Egypt. Carter's own willingness to underwrite almost any agreement stemmed from the hope that an agreement would bolster his own flagging domestic support.

Three case studies examine the relevance of the two-level-games model to issues in North-South relations: (1) the Carter human rights policy in Argentina and Guatemala; (2) U.S. policies toward Panama and Nicaragua; and (3) International Monetary Fund (IMF) stabilization agreements in Jamaica and Somalia. All three are cases of coercive diplomacy, in which the ability to "ratify" a threat (that is, to win adequate domestic support for implementing the threat) becomes a critical concern of statesmen.

Lisa Martin and Kathryn Sikkink contrast two cases in which the Carter Administration threatened to terminate foreign aid unless notorious violators of human rights—the governments of Argentina and Guatemala—permitted international monitoring. Paradoxically, the more powerful and autonomous of the two, Argentina, succumbed to U.S. pressure, while tiny Guatemala, heavily dependent on American military aid, successfully resisted it. Martin and Sikkink argue that an explanation of this anomaly must recognize that President Videla of Argentina was surreptitiously employing U.S. pressure to help reshape his own governing coalition, while the Guatemalan elite stood firm against American pressure. Moreover, Congressional limitations on the ability of the Carter Administration to compromise rendered U.S. threats against Argentina more credible than those against Guatemala.

In his comparison of the most prominent Central American security issues of the late 1970s—the Panama Canal Treaty and the emergence of the Sandinista government in Nicaragua—Robert Pastor explores the reasons for the success and failure of U.S. initiatives in the region. Once again, international security concerns alone are inadequate to explain the divergent outcomes. The success of the Panama Canal Treaty negotiations, Pastor concludes, reflected the skill of both Carter and Torrijos in manipulating their domestic constituencies, while Reagan's attempts to fund the "contra" insurgency against the Sandinista government were blocked by an intransigent Congress. The contrast between Carter and Reagan also illuminates the theoretically crucial distinction between cases in which the statesman's own preferences in the international negotiations are more moderate than those of his constituents, and cases in which the statesman's preferences are more hawkish.

The conditions imposed by the IMF on its borrowers constitute a lightning rod for criticism by developing countries of what is widely perceived as exploitation by the North. Miles Kahler's study of IMF stabilization programs in Jamaica and Somalia demonstrates that domestic constraints on LDC governments, over which the IMF has little control, undermine its seemingly dominant position. While access to finance would seem to give the IMF the upper hand, domestic instability and the uncertainty concerning implementation in LDCs limit its ability to monitor and enforce its conditions. Conversely, leaders can bolster their domestic popularity by standing up to the IMF. Kahler also analyzes the effects of the "domestic politics" of the IMF itself on these negotiations, illustrating how the internal workings of intergovernmental organizations can be understood within the two-level-game framework.

Four cases range across more than half a century of international economic conflicts among advanced industrial or newly industrializing states: (1) the attempt by Europe and the United States to stem the tide of the Great Depression at the World Economic Conference of 1933; (2) postwar Anglo-American discussions over the creation of airline and oil regimes; (3) Japanese-American trade disputes in construction and semiconductors; and (4) U.S. conflicts with Europe and Brazil over agriculture and computers.

In one of two case studies from the first half of this century, Barry Eichengreen and Marc Uzan reexamine perhaps the most momentous failure in the long history of international economic cooperation: the World Economic Conference of 1933, where the leading industrial nations of the world failed to negotiate a coordinated response to the Great Depression. The result was greater monetary instability and deepening depression, which contributed to the success of fascism in Germany and elsewhere. Eichengreen and Uzan demonstrate that a particular pattern of domestic factors—economic ideologies, interest group pressures, and the structure of representative institutions—obstructed agreement on several possible packages of mutually beneficial trade and monetary measures.

The foundations of the current international economic institutions were laid between 1945 and 1950. Helen Milner takes us back to a period when the political organization of two vital international market sectors, oil and airline services, was in the process of formation. In the case of oil, private firms successfully opposed government regulation and formed instead a private cartel; while in the case of airlines, an intergovernmental regulatory regime was created. Milner demonstrates the importance of domestic political factors, including the unity of industrial sectors, the side-payments provided by governments to domestic groups, and the nature of domestic institutions. She concludes that even the strongest governments have difficulty dissuading firms from entering into advantageous private international arrangements.

Few sectors have been spared in the controversies over the U.S.-Japanese trade relationship in the 1980s. In his comparison of the labyrinthine politics of bilateral disputes over semiconductors and construction, Ellis Krauss seeks to explain why negotiations led to very different outcomes in the two cases, despite important similarities in the negotiating processes and contexts. In the semiconductor case, an apparent agreement collapsed in acrimony when Japanese domestic actors (firms) "defected," leading to major U.S. retaliation; whereas in the construction case, agreement was reached and implemented, despite (or rather, because of) the unusually intimate relations between the Japanese construction industry and the Japanese political leadership. Krauss argues that these differing outcomes cannot be explained simply by either domestic or international analysis alone, but require a closer examination of the two-way links between negotiators and constituents on each side of the international table, as well as of tacit and explicit transgovernmental alliances. These cases illustrate that domestic interest groups do not merely respond passively to potential agreements negotiated between the governments, but instead seek to manipulate (and are manipulated by) government leaders and agencies, and that their influence on international negotiations depends importantly on these strategic considerations.

John Odell turns to two other sources of trade disputes in recent decades: the EC's Common Agricultural Policy (CAP) and the protection of domestic high-tech "infant industries" by newly industrializing countries. In two controversies in the 1980s examined by Odell—Brazilian programs to support their domestic computer industry, and new EC limitations on U.S. feed-grain exports to Spain and Portugal—the U.S. government threatened retaliation if the offending policies were not rescinded. The paradoxical outcomes of these disputes—the powerful EC complied fully, while Brazil made only minor adjustments—turned, according to Odell, on the extent to which domestic groups would "ratify" threats, which decisively affected their credibility. U.S. feed-grain farmers were more than ready to support sanctions, even at the expense of retaliation against U.S. farm products, while IBM and other U.S. computer multinationals were much less ready, concerned as they were about their large stakes in Brazil. Thus, while Brazil found a powerful domestic ally in the United States, the EC did not, and was eventually forced to settle on American terms.

Moving from Metaphor Toward Theory

These eleven sets of paired comparisons are used to evaluate the two-level-games approach, which can be understood as metaphor or as theory.[58] As metaphor, Putnam's approach provides a general framework for describing international negotiations. The two-level-games metaphor views the relationship between domestic and international politics through the eyes of the statesman.[59] "Each side is represented by a single leader or 'chief negotiator' "—referred to in this volume as a statesman or "chief of government" (COG). For expository purposes, Putnam divides the process of negotiation into two stages: the bargaining phase, in which statesmen bargain to a tentative international agreement; and the ratification phase, in which domestic constituents in each country decide, formally or informally, whether to ratify and implement the agreement. The ratification process is thus the "crucial theoretical link" between domestic and international politics—although in reality, as Putnam makes clear, the international and domestic "phases" are intertwined and simultaneous, as expectations and unfolding developments in one arena affect negotiations in the other arena.[60] Each state is assumed to have a "win-set," defined as the set of potential agreements that would be ratified by domestic constituencies in a straight up-or-down vote against the status quo of "no agreement." With increases in the benefits of an agreement or the costs of no agreement, the win-set expands. The statesman acts as the agent for the polity, but is constrained only by the win-set—that is, by the nature of the agreements that the domestic polity would ratify.

In order to generate empirical hypotheses about state behavior, Putnam's two-level-games metaphor requires more restrictive definition. It is essential to specify the preferences of and constraints on the major actors. Three essential theoretical building blocks are needed: specifications of domestic politics (the nature of the "win-sets"), of the international negotiating environment (the determinants of interstate bargaining outcomes), and of the statesman's preferences. (Note that these three influences on policy correspond to Waltz's three levels of analysis.) The editors of this volume did not impose common specifications on the various authors. Due to the paucity of rigorous deductive work capable of supporting empirical research, no attempt was made to develop formal models of two-level games.[61] Instead, the project stressed the inductive generation of hypotheses and generalizations, encouraging the authors to work within the framework to develop and make explicit their own specifications of these elements. The authors were also encouraged to educe from the case studies their own theoretical and conceptual insights into the dynamics of successful and unsuccessful domestic/international negotiations.

Nonetheless, the analyses do share considerable theoretical common ground. Guided by the initial article by Putnam and a series of discussions among project participants over several years, the authors focused on a set of convergent questions and hypotheses about the interaction between domestic and international politics. The following sections introduce some hypotheses about the three key points of theoretical concern—domestic constraints, international constraints, and the preferences of the statesman—that are explored in the case studies of this volume.

The Manipulation of Domestic Constraints.   Under what conditions are statesmen able to act independently of constituent pressures? How can statesmen employ issue linkage and side-payments to alter domestic constraints? How do interest-group configurations, representative institutions, and levels of uncertainty affect the strategies of statesmen?

In the two-level-games framework, the most fundamental constraint on the statesman is the size of the win-set, which in turn depends on a number of domestic factors, including the distribution of domestic coalitions, the nature of representative institutions, and the domestic strategies employed by statesmen. The two-level-games approach assumes that domestic coalitions form on the basis of an assessment of the relative costs and benefits of negotiated alternatives to the status quo, and that the basis of these assessments remains constant throughout the analysis.[62] The domestic constraints on policy-makers depend not only on group calculations of interests, but on their political influence. "What counts [domestically] is not total national costs and benefits, but their incidence, relative to existing coalitions and proto-coalitions."[63]

The two-level-games approach suggests that the statesman can gain influence in a number of ways. The most fundamental is by exploiting his or her freedom to act autonomously within the domestic win-set. The influence of social groups rests ultimately on their role in the ratification process, and the underlying preferences of social groups regarding "up-or-down" ratification rarely constrain the statesmen to a single outcome. As long as the statesman remains within the win-set, he or she can manipulate the precise terms of agreements toward a personally preferred outcome. Conversely, the exclusive power to negotiate internationally, and to submit items for domestic ratification, affords the statesman a tacit veto over any agreement, to be exercised simply by refusing either to negotiate in earnest or to submit any accord for ratification.

  Statesmen may also achieve ratification of provisions previously outside the win-set by linking them to more popular provisions. The two-level quality of linkage is particularly striking when the statesman attempts to gain approval for an important domestic measure by linking it to an attractive international agreement, or vice versa—a tactic Putnam refers to as "synergistic issue linkage."[64]

An even more interesting possibility is that statesmen will adopt strategies to reshape the domestic win-set. While the underlying preferences of domestic groups are assumed to be constant, the win-set reflects many other relevant characteristics of the domestic polity, including the nature of institutions, information, and patterns of mobilization and issue linkage, which (unlike the underlying interests of domestic groups) are here treated as variables, not constants. Statesmen may sometimes alter the outcome of the ratification process by manipulating these more contingent constraints. Statesmen may shape the formal and informal ratification procedure (e.g., voting rules, status of the agreement under separation of powers, party discipline, agenda-setting, issue linkage) or alter the domestic balance through side-payments, enforcement of party discipline, selective mobilization of political groups, or manipulation of information about the agreement. Perhaps the most radical method of altering domestic constraints is to implement a broad program of social or institutional reform. In general, the greater the statesman's control over these instruments, and the lower the cost of exercising such control, the greater his or her ability to shape the final agreement.[65]

In this volume there can be found many examples of strategies designed to alter the size of the domestic win-set. Two instances of synergistic issue linkage are Gorbachev's scheme to link domestic restructuring in the Soviet Union to an external bargain combining Soviet withdrawal from Eastern Europe and Western economic assistance, described by Jack Snyder; and Sadat's remarkably similar calculation about the Camp David agreement, analyzed by Janice Stein. Richard Eichenberg demonstrates how Reagan's manipulation of the symbols and rhetoric of nuclear deterrence had a long-term and largely unexpected impact on the West German win-set regarding nuclear deployments. The Carter Administration's strategic approval of public works projects during the ratification of the Panama Canal Treaty, described by Robert Pastor, demonstrates the use of side-payments. Both Gorbachev, in Snyder's account, and European procurement officials, in my armaments case study, attempted to restructure the economy in order to undermine the power of special-interest groups that obstruct international agreements.

These cases (and others) allow us to explore the varying efficacy of such strategies.

The phenomenon most distinctive of the two-level-games approach is what Putnam termed *synergy*, in which international actions are employed to alter outcomes otherwise expected in the domestic arena. By setting the international agenda, joining international regimes, or linking issues in international negotiations, statesmen have the power to shape the way in which issues are decided domestically. Just as the European Monetary System has been interpreted as an important lever to increase the credibility of domestic monetary discipline, for example, so the European defense planners in my study of armaments procurement seek to precommit domestic firms to collaborative research-and-development and market-sharing arrangements in the hope of decisively altering the domestic balance of power.

A variant of this tactic is what we term *COG collusion*, in which statesmen exchange political assets in order to strengthen the prestige of the opposing statesman vis-à-vis his or her domestic constituency. Clearly, this is one theme underlying recent East-West relations (as described by Snyder), in which Gorbachev sought to use high-profile diplomacy with the West to enhance his domestic prestige. Another example (described by Ellis Krauss) is the tacit cooperation between American and Japanese bureaucrats to open the Japanese construction industry to international competition.

Several factors might be expected to have a direct effect on the ability of statesmen to manipulate domestic constraints and to act independently: the concentration of domestic groups; the extent to which they are informed about the agreement; the effects of a precommitment; and the domestic institutions for ratification. On the basis of Olsonian collective-action analysis, it seems reasonable to expect that concentrated groups that are disadvantaged by an agreement—such as the interwar French farmers described by Barry Eichengreen and Marc Uzan, or the multinational business interests analyzed by John Odell—will become both intransigent and influential opponents of agreement. Conversely, the more diffuse the costs and benefits of the proposed agreement, the more possibilities for statesmen to target swing groups and gain their support at relatively low cost. As Schattschneider describes in his classic account of the 1934 Reciprocal Trade Agreements Act, an expansion in the mobilized public can be particularly advantageous if it can be selectively used by the statesman.[66] The most extreme case is a "Bonapartist" strategy of provoking a foreign-policy crisis to bolster the domestic popularity of the regime, exemplified by the temptation facing Miles Kahler's LDC leaders to defy the IMF. Yet the cases also allow us to explore the conditions under which the converse strategy might be plausible, as in the peace initiatives of Sadat and Gorbachev, launched to gain the international support needed to overcome otherwise insurmountable domestic problems.

Uncertainty about the content of an agreement may increase the ability of a statesman to manipulate public perceptions by selectively releasing information. In cases where gains and losses are clear, certain, and focused on concentrated groups, the room for creative statecraft is diminished, and tangible side-payments would probably be necessary.[67] The differential importance of information in the two-level-games approach also has implications for the temporal course of negotiations. We might expect statesmen to have a great deal of control over the initiation of negotiations and the setting of a negotiating agenda; less control over the domestic conditions under which the ratification vote is taken; and no direct control over the final vote itself. Accordingly, domestic mobilization around an issue tends to increase over the course of a negotiation, thereby decreasing the autonomy of the statesman. This hypothesis can be explored, for example, in the decade-long series of negotiations over the stationing and removal of nuclear missiles in Germany traced by Richard Eichenberg.[68]

The flexibility of the institutions through which ratification takes place can be decisive. Helen Milner, for example, asks whether executive discretion to negotiate an agreement as either a treaty or an executive agreement was a key distinction between the postwar oil and airline negotiations. Lisa Martin and Kathryn Sikkink extend this line of inquiry, proposing a tripartite typology of ratification procedures—*approval, authorization,* and *acquiescence.* Approval denotes ex post ratification; authorization denotes a priori ratification, as with fast-track provisions for Congressional ratification of trade bills; and acquiescence denotes an agreement which needs no formal ratification, and against which hostile domestic groups must initiate specific action. The more restrictive the ratification procedure, they hypothesize, the less autonomy is left to the statesman.

Domestic Politics and International Bargaining. How do domestic constraints affect the success and distributional effects of international bargains? What sorts of manipulation of domestic and foreign win-sets permit statesmen to achieve international gains? Do domestic factors affect the ability to make credible threats, as well as the ability to conclude agreements?

Putnam's article is based on the proposition that the outcome of international negotiations reflects the size of the domestic win-sets. Putnam also advances two corollary propositions about the relationship between domestic constraints and bargaining power. The first proposition is that larger win-sets increase the number of potential agreements and decrease the probability that nations will defect from those they make. This renders international agreement more likely, ceteris paribus. He goes on to distinguish *voluntary defection*, in which a unitary state led by a statesman fails to ratify or to implement an agreement; and *involuntary defection*, in which domestic groups override or subvert an agreement supported by a statesman.[69] The second proposition, which Putnam draws from Thomas Schelling, is that the relative size of the respective domestic win-sets will affect the distribution of the joint gains from the international bargain. Assuming that both sides have an interest in reaching agreement, a differential in the relative size of the win-sets shifts the distribution of costs and benefits in favor of the player with the more constrained win-set. While the traditional view is that internal divisions weaken a state's bargaining position, the two-level-games approach suggests that divisions may under some circumstances strengthen it.

In seeking to reshape domestic constraints to promote his favored policies, the statesman may either constrict or expand the win-set. A strategy of *"Tying Hands"* attempts to *constrict* the domestic win-set. The rationale for adopting this strategy is to induce the opposing statesman to compromise at a point closer to the first statesman's preferences—a practice that runs counter to the normal expectation that the statesman will preserve the maximum possible level of executive autonomy. Statesmen who adopt the second strategy, *"Cutting Slack,"* attempt to *expand* the domestic win-set to accommodate an international agreement that might otherwise be rejected.

The exploitation of asymmetrical information is once again a key issue. For example, does asymmetrical knowledge about ratifiability permit a negotiator to use deliberate misinformation as a negotiating tactic? It seems plausible that under conditions of high uncertainty, statesmen may gain a negotiating edge by deliberately exaggerating to opposing negotiators the tightness and inflexibility of domestic constraints. There is anecdotal evidence that this strategy is often attempted, but little evidence on whether it often succeeds. One hypothesis would be that the more open the regime, the less uncertainty about domestic ratifiability exists, and the less credible disinformation would be. The cases examined here—some involving pluralist democracies of various sorts, for example, and others involving authoritarian regimes of various sorts—enable us to make some preliminary judgments about the circumstances under which uncertainty may be exploited for strategic purposes.[70]

A statesman also faces an interesting set of strategic alternatives with respect to foreign win-sets. Unless the statesman is opposed to all agreements, there is almost always an incentive to expand the opposing win-set, since this simultaneously increases the probability both of an agreement and of reaching a more advantageous one. Given the lack of direct control over internal institutions and agendas in foreign countries, statesmen have more limited means of influencing foreign win-sets than domestic ones. Nonetheless, policies aimed at foreign polities are common.

A common strategy, of course, is to raise the cost of no-agreement to key constituents on the other side, thus rendering even unfavorable agreements relatively more attractive. Beyond this familiar use of threats (and the strategy of COG collusion described earlier), there are several other interesting strategic possibilities. Statesmen can *target linkages or side-payments* by offering specific benefits to particularly powerful domestic constituencies or swing groups in a foreign country. Targeting becomes particularly delicate in negotiations where multinational interests are involved, since the same domestic actor may appear on both domestic boards—witness the role of IBM in the U.S.-Brazilian negotiations over computers analyzed by Odell. A second tactic to alter domestic constraints in a foreign country is *reverberation*, which occurs when actions by one country alter the expectations about an agreement held by domestic groups in a foreign country. Reverberation may result from deliberate attempts at persuasion ("suasive reverberation" or "suasion")—a striking example examined here is Sadat's sensational visit to Israel—or it may be the unintended result of public reaction to the course of the negotiations. One hypothesis that can be explored in our cases is that negotiations over public goods, such as security, will be more subject to strategies based on reverberation, whereas private (or "privatizable") goods will more appropriately evoke a strategy of targeting or side-payments.

In coercive bargaining, in which threats are employed, the relationship between domestic constraints and bargaining leverage is more resistant to simple generalization. The two-level implications for a state *receiving* a threat have long been evident in the literature: a threat broadens the win-set by raising the cost of "no-agreement." Moreover, the more powerful the domestic groups targeted by the foreign threat, and the more vulnerable they are to it, the more effective that threat. But the two-level implications for the state *making* threat have heretofore received far less theoretical attention.[71] The two-level-games approach implies that the credibility of a threat depends in part on the assurance that it would be carried out, which increases with the extent of domestic support for executing the threat. The more powerful the groups disadvantaged at home by a threat, the less credible and sustainable it will be. The credibility of a grain embargo, for example, is inversely proportional to the power of domestic agricultural interests. In other words, *threats, like promises, must be ratified.*

This proposition was not addressed in Putnam's original article, but emerged from discussions in this collaborative project.[72] This hypothesis becomes particularly relevant in cases of coercive bargaining like some of those included in this volume. A comparison of the cases analyzed by Pastor and by Martin and Sikkink on U.S. relations with Latin America, for example, allows us to explore whether (and how) Reagan's threats against the Sandinistas were undermined by Congressional opposition, whereas Carter's threats against Videla in Argentina were made more credible by Congressional attitudes. Yet the relationship between the ratifiability of an agreement and the ratifiability of a threat remains unclear. One hypothesis might be that the two vary inversely: a narrowing of the win-set on potential agreements would be correlated with increased credibility of threats. Another set of hypotheses links the credibility of a threat with the distribution of domestic interests in the state making the threat: for example, the more concentrated and influential the domestic interests which would bear the *costs* of enacting a threat, the lower the threat's credibility; whereas the more concentrated and influential the interests that would *benefit* from enacting a threat, the greater its credibility. These hypotheses are articulated and explored in several individual chapters, especially the comparative study of U.S.-Brazil and U.S.-EC trade sanctions by Odell.

The Preferences of the Statesmen.   How do the preferences of the statesman influence the choice of strategies and the outcome of negotiations?

Since the two-level-games approach posits the partial autonomy of the statesman, two-level analysis requires a specification of the statesman's preferences. A rational statesman will employ available "double-edged" strategies only if they further his or her own aims. The set of agreements preferred by the statesman to the status quo may be termed the statesman's "acceptability-set." These preferences may reflect: (1) the statesman's interest in enhancing his domestic position, perhaps by pursuing the median domestic interest; (2) an effort to mobilize an optimal response to international imperatives, regardless of domestic factors (much as the Classical Realists portray it); or (3) individual policy preferences about the issues in question, perhaps stemming from idiosyncratic "first-image" factors like past political history or personal idealism. The strongest incentive for initiating international agreements, exemplified by Sadat's high-stakes gamble on peace with Israel, would be a statesman's perception that resources available domestically were insufficient to resolve a politically untenable situation, and that synergistic linkages at the international level might provide additional leverage—a cooperative twist on the classic argument about Bonapartist motivations for war.

Rather than inquiring into the origins of the statesman's preferences, the essays in this volume take them, like the preferences of his constituents, as given. The focus of the analysis is instead on the strategic incentives created by certain configurations of the "acceptability-set" relative to the domestic "win-set." The possible configurations can be divided into three categories: the statesman-as-agent, the statesman-as-dove, and the statesman-as-hawk.[73] In the case of the "statesman-as-agent," the statesman's acceptability-set reflects the interests of the median domestic group and is encompassed by the domestic win-set. In the case of the "statesman-as-dove," the acceptability-set lies at least partially outside the domestic win-set and *closer* to the opposing win-set. In the case of the "statesman-as-hawk," the acceptability-set lies at least partially outside the domestic win-set, but *further* from the opposing win-set than the set of agreements ratifiable domestically.

In the case of the statesman-as-agent, there is no conflict between the statesman and society. The statesman has little incentive to expand the win-set, although he or she may seek to contract it to gain an international negotiating edge. Statesmen are more likely to attempt to expand the win-set ("cut slack") when they are doves or hawks, or when they favor agreement for its own sake, independent of its content. An example is Jimmy Carter's willingness to back any agreement that could be signed by Begin and Sadat, as described by Stein. When both statesmen are doves, incentives are created for COG collusion. A striking example of collusion between statesmen against their domestic polities is found in the European armaments cooperation I examined, in which governments have instituted long-term policies with the goal of undermining domestic resistance to cooperation in the future. Another example of collusion between two statesmen-as-doves may be the Panama Canal negotiations between Carter and Torrijos.

The relationship between the preferences of the statesman and the credibility of threats is more complex. One intriguing hypothesis is that threats are most credible when delivered by a statesman-as-dove or statesman-as-agent, since the statesman can convincingly portray herself or himself as restraining a rabid domestic constituency that would surely ratify the threat—whereas a statesman-as-hawk (Reagan in Nicaragua?) risks issuing international threats that will not be backed up at home. Also, it may be that once a statesman enters into a negotiation, the personal costs of no-agreement (in terms of prestige and reputation) may increase, rendering agreement more attractive and hence more likely.

Strategies Employed by Domestic Groups. Can domestic groups adopt two-level strategies? What is the role of transnational alliances in international negotiations?

Although this project focuses primarily on the possibilities for action by statesmen, it is worth noting that the two-level-games model also implies that domestic groups have opportunities to develop similar strate-

gies and counterstrategies. A "transnational alliance," for example, occurs when domestic groups in more than one country agree to cooperate
or exchange political assets in order to prevail over other domestic
groups or over governmental opposition. Bureaucracies and other state
actors can also act as interest groups and form a "transgovernmental
alliance," as Krauss describes in his cases of U.S.-Japan trade negotiations.[74] Finally, domestic groups may seek to strengthen or undermine
the domestic support of a foreign chief executive.

Although the hypotheses derived from the two-level-games approach,
which see the statesman as intermediary between international and domestic politics, are not theoretically incompatible with transnational alliances, the two are often alternative explanations for similar phenomena,
with one focusing on the statesman as the key strategic player and the
other on societal actors. In a two-level-games analysis, a transnational or
transgovernmental alliance would be likely to form only when private
groups were opposed by their own state—i.e., when the statesmen are
hawks.[75] Cooperation between domestic groups in different countries is
less likely when the statesmen are doves, since the interests of the opposing sides would be likely to diverge. The opposition of IBM, a multinational corporation with interests in both the United States and Brazil, to
U.S. trade sanctions, in Odell's study of a dispute over computers, provides an interesting example of a transnational force opposing state policies.

The alternative two-level strategies available to the statesman and to
domestic actors are summarized in the typology below. They fall into
four categories: reshaping the domestic win-set; reshaping the foreign
win-set; transnational alliances; and actions by domestic groups to undermine a foreign leader. One can think about these strategies as discrete
means of connecting the two boards.[76] As the diagram suggests, these
strategies exhaust the possibilities for two-level action.

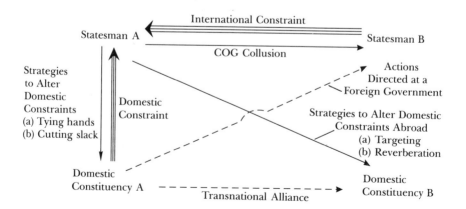

CONCLUSION

The goals of this project are modest. Eleven case studies are used to carry out "plausibility probes" regarding existing hypotheses about two-level games, and to seek new hypotheses. At a minimum, the cases help to "map the universe" of two-level-games phenomena, both by expanding the number of documented causal chains between international and domestic politics and by extending the model to areas where its implications have yet to be explored. The result will be a greater body of empirical generalizations about two-level games, which constitute a promising starting point for those developing formal models or systematic empirical studies of the interaction between domestic and international politics. Such empirical generalizations drawn from case studies are, at least, an "indispensable first step" in the transition from metaphor to social-scientific theory.[77]

Among the theoretical implications not fully appreciated in the original formulation of the two-level-games approach, but explored in more detail here, are the autonomy that an individual statesman can gain by exploiting the role of gatekeeper; the role of domestic support in issuing credible threats; the role of asymmetrical information about domestic politics in international negotiations; and the importance of the distinctions among statesman-as-hawk, statesman-as-dove, and statesman-as-agent. Another important theoretical byproduct of the study is that it challenges us to revisit the level-of-analysis problem, throwing into relief the many instances in which the levels collapse into one another. The two-level-games approach joins a number of other theoretical responses in a general consensus that we need to move toward more complex syntheses of domestic and international explanations. The resulting framework may permit a more systematic integration of domestic ("second-image") and individual ("first-image") influences on foreign policy into systemic theory.

The most distinctive empirical contribution of the two-level-games approach lies in its analysis of conditions under which an enterprising statesman gains bargaining advantages by employing strategies that are "double-edged," exploiting domestic and international politics simultaneously. Each of the case studies herein takes up this issue. Many of the empirical findings, more extensively reported in the Conclusion, are striking. The cases suggest that theories based on a single level of analysis are frequently insufficient to account for important phenomena in world politics. The domestic process of ratification and the concentration of social interests influence international bargaining possibilities. Threats, like agreements, must be ratified. The significance of informational asymmetries appears to depend on the nature of the domestic regimes. Diplomacy between advanced industrial democracies is transparent, so that democratic statesmen find it difficult to mislead their negotiating partners about domestic constraints. Among nondemocratic regimes, uncertainty may play a more prominent role than elsewhere. Domestic constraints vary in the course of negotiations, tightening as the concrete provisions of an agreement become more clear. Statesmen often find it easier to launch negotiations than to gain domestic ratification for the resulting agreements.

With the spread of democratic regimes throughout the globe, the effect of domestic politics on foreign policy can only increase. The most important area in which systemic theory enjoyed widespread acceptance—the bipolar conflict between the U.S. and the USSR—is being transformed. Yet it would be naive to believe that the international politics of the new era will be harmonious. Complex patterns of conflict and cooperation will emerge, reflecting not only the calculation of geopolitical advantage or constituency pressures, but also the complex interaction between them.

The Program on International Politics, Economics, and Security (PIPES) at the University of Chicago provided a congenial intellectual and logistical environment in which to write this essay. For suggestions and comments, I am grateful to Anne-Marie Burley, James Caporaso, David Dessler, Peter Evans, Stephan Haggard, Ted Hopf, Harold Jacobson, Robert Keohane, Lisa Martin, Robert D. Putnam, Thomas Risse-Kappen, Kamal Shehadi, Duncan Snidal, Jack Snyder, Fareed Zakaria, two anonymous reviewers, and members of the Chicago/PIPES Colloquium and Harvard Domestic-International Interactions Project.

NOTES

1. Robert Putnam, "Diplomacy and Domestic Politics: The Logic of Two-Level Games," *International Organization* 42 (Summer 1988): 427–460, reprinted in the Appendix to this volume.

2. See Kenneth N. Waltz, *Man, the State, and War: A Theoretical Analysis* (New York: Columbia University Press, 1959); and J. David Singer, "International Conflict: Three Levels of Analysis," *World Politics* 12 (April 1960): 453–461, and "The Level-of-Analysis Problem in International Relations," *World Politics* 14 (October 1961): 77–92.

3. For a useful discussion of the relationship between domestic and international explanations, see Christopher H. Achen and Duncan Snidal, "Rational Deterrence Theory and Comparative Case Studies," *World Politics* 41 (January 1989): 164–165. The number of levels and their relative utility is neither preordained nor arbitrary, but can and should vary according to the analytic purpose at hand. Waltz introduced the classic three levels of analysis. J. David Singer and Arnold Wolfers reduce these to two: the international system and the national state for Singer, and the system and the individual for Wolfers. Robert Jervis

adds a fourth: bureaucratic process. James Rosenau discerns five, dividing the domestic level into state, society, and intermediating institutions. See Waltz, *Man, the State and War*; Singer, "The Level-of-Analysis Problem"; Arnold Wolfers, "The Actors in International Politics," in Wolfers, *Discord and Collaboration* (Baltimore: Johns Hopkins University Press, 1962), pp. 3–24; Robert Jervis, *Perception and Misperception in International Politics* (Princeton, N.J.: Princeton University Press, 1976), p. 15; James Rosenau, "Pre-Theories and Theories of International Politics," in R. Barry Farrell, ed., *Approaches to Comparative and International Politics* (Evanston, Ill.: Northwestern University Press, 1966), p. 43.

4. Richard Rosecrance, *The Rise of the Trading State: Commerce and Conquest in the Modern World* (New York: Basic Books, 1986); Dale Copeland and Duncan Snidal, "Economic Interdependence and War" (paper presented at the Program on International Politics, Economics, and Security, University of Chicago, 21 February 1991).

5. For critical reviews of this literature and a move toward integrating domestic and international factors, see Fritz Mayer, "Bargains Within Bargains: Domestic Politics and International Negotiation" (Ph.D. dissertation, Kennedy School of Government, Harvard University, May 1988); Putnam, "Diplomacy and Domestic Politics" (see Appendix to this volume, pp. 464–465 n. 43).

6. Robert O. Keohane, "Theory of World Politics: Structural Realism and Beyond," in Keohane, ed., *Neo-Realism and Its Critics* (New York: Columbia University Press, 1986), p. 165.

7. See Andrew Moravcsik, "Liberalism and International Relations Theory," *Harvard CFIA Working Paper* (Cambridge, Mass.: Harvard University, 1992).

8. For a useful analysis, see G. John Ikenberry, David A. Lake, and Michael Mastanduno, "Introduction: Approaches to Explaining American Foreign Economic Policy," *International Organization* 42 (Winter 1988): 1–14.

9. Important works on the domestic politics of security policy include James Rosenau, ed., *Domestic Sources of Foreign Policy* (New York: Free Press, 1967); Charles Hermann, Charles Kegley, and James Rosenau, eds., *New Directions in the Study of Foreign Policy* (Boston: Allen and Unwin, 1987); John Lewis Gaddis, *Strategies of Containment: A Critical Appraisal of Post-War American Foreign Policy* (New York: Oxford University Press, 1981), extended to the Reagan era by Fareed Zakaria, "The Reagan Strategy of Containment," *Political Science Quarterly* 105 (Autumn 1990): 373–396. On foreign economic policy, see E. E. Schattschneider, *Politics, Pressures, and the Tariff* (New York: Prentice-Hall, 1935); John Mark Hansen, "Taxation and the Political Economy of the Tariff," *International Organization* 44 (Autumn 1990): 527–552.

10. Characteristic theoretical statements include Graham Allison, *Essence of Decision: Explaining the Cuban Missile Crisis* (Boston: Little, Brown, 1971); John Steinbruner, *A Cybernetic Theory of Decision: New Dimensions in Political Analysis* (Princeton, N.J.: Princeton University Press, 1974); Judith Goldstein, "Ideas, Institutions, and American Trade Policy," *International Organization* 42 (Winter 1988): 179–217; and Stephen Krasner, *Defending the National Interest: Raw Materials Investments and U.S. Foreign Policy* (Princeton, N.J.: Princeton University Press, 1976). For analyses of the Peloponnesian War as a battle between competing

domestic ideological factions, Bismarck's imperialism as an attempt to maintain a viable domestic coalition, and the NATO alliance as an attempt to reassure Western publics, see, respectively, James Nolt, "Social Order and Threat: Thucydides, Aristotle, and the Critique of Modern Realism" (mimeo., University of Chicago, 1990); Hans-Ulrich Wehler, *Bismarck und der Imperialismus* (Cologne: Kiepenhauer und Witsch, 1969), and Christoph Bertram, ed., *Defence and Consensus: The Domestic Aspects of Western Security* (London: International Institute for Strategic Studies, 1983).

11. On domestic intermediating structures in the area of security studies, see Michael Doyle, "Kant, Liberal Legacies, and Foreign Affairs," *Philosophy and Public Affairs* 12 (Summer and Fall 1983): 205–235 and 325–353; Henry Kissinger, "Domestic Structures and Foreign Policy," *Daedalus*, Spring 1966: 503–529; Stephen Van Evera, "Why Cooperation Failed in 1914," in Kenneth Oye, ed., *Cooperation Under Anarchy* (Princeton, N.J.: Princeton University Press, 1986), pp. 80–117. On their role in foreign economic policy, see Peter J. Katzenstein, *Between Power and Plenty: Foreign Economic Policies of Advanced Industrial States* (Madison: University of Wisconsin Press, 1978).

12. Singer, "The Level-of-Analysis Problem," p. 29. But Singer hints elsewhere in the same article that a framework combining domestic and international explanations is possible.

13. Achen and Snidal, "Rational Deterrence Theory," p. 166.

14. I am indebted to Kamal Shehadi for his wide-ranging literature review entitled "Domestic-International Links" (Domestic-International Politics Seminar, Harvard University, 10 May 1990).

15. See Achen and Snidal, "Rational Deterrence Theory," pp. 154 and 164–165.

16. Timothy McKeown, "The Limitations of 'Structural' Theories of Commercial Policy," *International Organization* 40 (Winter 1986): 45. Indeed, disputes over assumptions mark good scientific practice, both because they provide independent evidence of a theory's validity and because they help maintain the proper vigilance against omitted variable problems, particularly in qualitative analysis. For an intriguing introduction to some of the philosophical issues, see James D. Fearon, "Counterfactuals and Hypothesis Testing in Political Science," *World Politics* 43 (January 1991): 169–195.

17. Kenneth N. Waltz, *Theory of International Politics* (Reading, Mass.: Addison-Wesley, 1979), pp. 91–92. In another context, Waltz, following Wolfers, adds that when "preservation of the state is not in question, national goals easily fluctuate between the grandiose and the frivolous" (Waltz, *Foreign Policy and Democratic Politics: The American and British Experience* [Boston: Little, Brown, 1967], p. 16).

18. Cited in Keohane, "Theory of World Politics," p. 173, advancing a criticism similar to that offered here.

19. This was already clear in Stephen D. Krasner, "State Power and the Structure of Foreign Trade," *World Politics* 28 (April 1976): 317–347.

20. The following progression is representative: Andre Gunder Frank, *Capitalism and Underdevelopment in Latin America: Historical Studies of Chile and Brazil,*

rev. ed. (Harmondsworth, Eng.: Penguin, 1971); Henrique Cardoso and Enzo Faletto, *Dependency and Development in Latin America* (Berkeley: University of California Press, 1979, but published earlier in Spanish); Immanuel Wallerstein, *The Capitalist World Economy: Essays* (Cambridge, Eng.: Cambridge University Press, 1979), chaps. 1, 4, 9, 14, and 18; Peter Evans, *Dependent Development: The Alliance of Multinational, State, and Local Capital in Brazil* (Princeton, N.J.: Princeton University Press, 1979); Stephan Haggard, *Pathways from the Periphery: The Politics of Growth in the Newly Industrializing Countries* (Ithaca, N.Y.: Cornell University Press, 1990).

21. For an overview, see John A. Vasquez, *The Power of Power Politics: A Critique* (New Brunswick, N.J.: Rutgers University Press, 1983).

22. Waltz, *Man, the State, and War*, p. 230.

23. Keohane, "The World Political Economy and the Crisis of Embedded Liberalism," in John Goldthorpe, ed., *Order and Conflict in Contemporary Capitalism* (Oxford: Clarendon Press, 1984), p. 16. There is "something particularly satisfying both about systemic explanation and about the structural variant of it" (Keohane, "Theory of World Politics," p. 193). See also Keohane, "The Theory of Hegemonic Stability and Changes in International Economic Regimes, 1967–1977," In Keohane, ed., *International Institutions and State Power: Essays in International Relations Theory* (Boulder, Colo.: Westview Press, 1989), p. 80.

24. Alexis de Tocqueville, *Democracy in America* (Garden City, N.Y.: Anchor Books, 1969), pp. 226–230.

25. Kissinger, "Domestic Structures"; Hans Morgenthau, *Politics Among Nations: The Struggle for Power and Peace*, 3rd ed. (New York: Knopf, 1963), p. 7; see also pp. 143–148. Arnold Wolfers observes that "by establishing the 'normal' actions and reactions of states in various international situations, the states-as-actors model sets a standard on which to base our expectations of state behavior and deviations. At the same time, a far more complex model is required if our expectations are to become sufficiently refined and realistic to take into account at least the predispositions of typical categories of decision-makers" (Wolfers, "The Actors in International Politics," p. 17).

26. Deborah Welch Larson, *Origins of Containment: A Psychological Explanation* (Princeton, N.J.: Princeton University Press, 1985), p. 8.

27. Waltz, *Theory of International Politics*, p. 70, see also pp. 60–72.

28. Waltz, *Foreign Policy*, pp. 307–308, 310–311.

29. Graham Allison, *Essence of Decision*; Stephen Krasner, *Defending the National Interest*; for analyses of the misperceptions and consistent departures from rationality common to those in policy-making roles, see Jervis, *Perception and Misperception*, pp. 28–31; Larson, *Origins of Containment*. For an attempt to model domestic and international influences on decision-making much criticized for its lack of deductive micro-foundations, see Richard Snyder, H.W. Bruck, and Burton Sapin, *Foreign Policy Decision-Making: An Approach to the Study of International Relations* (New York: Free Press, 1962).

30. Morgenthau, *Politics Among Nations*, p. 206. For a classic view, see Otto Hintze, "Military Organization and the Structure of the State," in Felix Gilbert, ed., *The Historical Essays of Otto Hintze* (New York: Oxford University Press, 1975).

31. In "High Politics Is Low Politics: The Domestic and Systemic Sources of Israeli Security Policy, 1967–1977," *World Politics* 43 (July 1990): 561, Barnett concludes that "the Janus-faced state is alive and well and living in the domain of national security policy."

32. Mastanduno, Lake, and Ikenberry, "Toward a Realist Theory of State Action," *International Studies Quarterly* 33 (December 1989): 457–474. This analysis, while remaining quite abstract, attempts to draw the international implications of different state structures.

33. Klaus Stegemann, "Policy Rivalry Among Industrial States: What Can We Learn from Models of Strategic Trade Policy?," *International Organization* 43 (Winter 1989): 73–100; Chalmers Johnson, *MITI and the Japanese Miracle: The Growth of Industrial Policy, 1925–75* (Stanford, Calif.: Stanford University Press, 1982); Evans, *Dependent Development.*

34. For a concise, insightful discussion from which the quotation is taken, see Duncan Snidal, "IGOs, Regimes and Cooperation: Challenges for International Relations Theory," in Margaret Karns and Karen Mingst, eds., *The United States and Multilateral Institutions: Patterns of Changing Instrumentality and Influence* (Boston: Unwin Hyman, 1990), p. 340.

35. Morgenthau, *Politics Among Nations*, p. 11; see also p. 563 and chaps. 21 and 22. The destruction of the older intellectual and moral consensus and its replacement with a form of aggressive nationalism, Morgenthau argued, undermined the balance of power and made possible virulent forms of conflict such as the Cold War and total war.

36. Kissinger, "Domestic Structures," pp. 261–262.

37. The phrase "second-image-reversed" was coined by Peter Gourevitch, and is elucidated in his *Politics in Hard Times: Comparative Responses to International Economic Crises* (Ithaca, N.Y.: Cornell University Press, 1986). See also Ronald Rogowski, *Commerce and Coalitions: How Trade Affects Domestic Political Alignments* (Princeton, N.J.: Princeton University Press, 1989); Peter Katzenstein, *Small States and World Markets: Industrial Policy in Europe* (Ithaca, N.Y.: Cornell University Press, 1985); and Helen Milner, *Resisting Protectionism: Global Industries and the Politics of International Trade* (Princeton, N.J.: Princeton University Press, 1988).

38. Another alternative is to endogenize domestic factors by demonstrating that they result from previous international bargains—the most notable attempt being neo-functionalist regional integration theory. Similarly, following Rogowski, one might argue that the GATT regime has stimulated exports and thus created its own domestic support. Such explanations are intriguing, but tend to predict the stability of existing regimes, rather than regime creation or policy change.

39. See Peter Katzenstein, *Small States and World Markets: Industrial Policy in Europe* (Ithaca, N.Y.: Cornell University Press, 1985). Katzenstein concludes that "the democratic corporatism of the small European states is a response to international pressures" in the 1930s and 1940s (p. 192), but he also argues that successful adaptation was dependent on the existence of a "tradition of accommodative politics dating back beyond the 19th century" (p. 35), based on "a weak landed nobility, relatively strong urban interests, a divided Right, a moderate Left, no

revolutionary break with the past; and . . . proportional representation" (p. 189). Jeff Frieden and Lisa Martin reminded me of this element of complexity in Katzenstein's account.

40. David Lake, *Power, Protectionism, and Free Trade: International Sources of U.S. Commercial Policy, 1887–1939* (Ithaca, N.Y.: Cornell University Press, 1988). For similar arguments, see Stephen Krasner, *Structural Conflict: The Third World Against Global Liberalism* (Berkeley: University of California Press, 1985).

41. For an argument that the determinants of state interests and of bargaining outcomes ought to be kept separate, although the determination of national interests does not necessarily require a domestic theory, see Andrew Moravcsik, "Disciplining Trade Finance: The Origins and Success of the OECD Export Credit Arrangement," *International Organization* 43 (Winter 1989): 174–176.

42. Keohane, "Theory of World Politics," p. 183.

43. Stephen Walt, *Origins of Alliances* (Ithaca: Cornell University Press, 1987), pp. 265–266.

44. In the literature, this offense–dominance factor is sometimes considered an attribute of military technology and sometimes an attribute of domestic polities. These authors tend to treat it as the latter. See Jack Snyder, "Conclusion," in Robert Jervis and Jack Snyder, eds., *Dominos and Bandwagons* (New York: Oxford University Press, 1991), p. 285.

45. Van Evera, "Why Cooperation Failed in 1914," pp. 83–95.

46. Andrew Moravcsik, "Is Anybody Still a Realist?" (unpublished paper delivered before the Domestic-International Politics Seminar, Harvard University, 10 May 1990). Per an agreement that analysis of preference formation should precede consideration of strategic interaction, thus granting priority to Liberal theory, see Moravcsik, "Liberalism and International Relations Theory."

47. Stephen Krasner, "State Power and the Structure of Foreign Trade"; David Lake, "The State and American Trade Strategy in the Pre-Hegemonic Era," *International Organization* 42 (Winter 1988): 33–58; Keohane, "Theory of World Politics," p. 183; Duncan Snidal, "The Limits of Hegemonic Stability Theory," *International Organization* 39 (Autumn 1985): 207–232. John Gerard Ruggie, "Continuity and Transformation in the World Polity: Toward a Neo-Realist Synthesis," *World Politics* 35 (January 1983): 261–285.

48. Andrew Moravcsik, "Negotiating the Single Act: National Interests and Conventional Statecraft in the European Community," *International Organization* 45 (Winter 1991): 19–56; Moravcsik, "Disciplining Trade Finance"; Bruce Bueno de Mesquita, David Newman, and Alvin Rabushka, *Forecasting Political Events: The Future of Hong Kong* (New Haven, Conn.: Yale University Press, 1985).

49. A full discussion of this claim would take us beyond the boundaries of this chapter. The existence of parsimonious domestic theories, such as the Liberal argument that democracies calculate interests in a more broad-based way and hence do not provoke great-power war, undermines Realism's claim of uniqueness. For suggestive evidence that Realist theories generally lack explanatory power, see Vasquez, *The Power of Power Politics*.

50. Keohane, "Theory of World Politics," p. 193.

51. Putnam, "Diplomacy and Domestic Politics" (Appendix, p. 448).

52. Ibid. (Appendix, p. 459).

53. Richard N. Cooper, *The Economics of Interdependence: Economic Policy in the Atlantic Community* (New York: Columbia University Press, 1968). This is similar to what Putnam calls "synergistic issue linkage."

54. I thank Anne-Marie Burley for discussions on this point. More generally, see Robert O. Keohane and Joseph S. Nye, Jr., *Power and Interdependence: World Politics in Transition* (Boston: Little Brown, 1977); Moravcsik, "Liberalism and International Relations Theory," pp. 37–38.

55. Putnam, "Diplomacy and Domestic Politics" (Appendix, p. 437).

56. This is a "most different" comparative strategy. The cases were not deliberately selected so as to highlight obvious two-level effects. Nonetheless, selection bias may stem from the fact that the cases that attracted investigators tended to be those that engender highly publicized domestic controversy. One might expect two-level-games phenomena to be more prevalent in such situations, as statesmen seek to manipulate the domestic polity for a marginal advantage to assure successful negotiations, or to employ two-level strategies (unsuccessfully) to forge domestic consensus.

57. For a thorough discussion of this method, see Alexander George, "Case Studies and Theory Development: The Method of Structured, Focused Comparison," in Paul Lauren, ed., *Diplomacy: New Approaches in Theory, History, and Policy* (New York: Free Press, 1979), pp. 43–68.

58. On the distinction between metaphor and theory, see Duncan Snidal, "The Game *Theory* of International Politics," in Kenneth Oye, ed., *Cooperation Under Anarchy*, pp. 29–30 and 34–36.

59. Putnam betrays considerable suspicion of those who employ "state strength" as an independent variable. Yet the two-level-games metaphor is in fact indebted to their insights. Putnam criticizes the institutionalists for their focus on autonomous state behavior, yet the "relative autonomy" of the COG emerges as a key consideration in this analysis ("Diplomacy and Domestic Politics" [Appendix, pp. 456–459]). A major advantage of Putnam's metaphor over previous approaches, however, is that it encourages the analyst to derive "relative autonomy" from strategic considerations, such as the size of the win-set, the nature of the ratification process, and the relative positions of the preferences of statesman and domestic constituency. Autonomy is seen not merely as an enduring characteristic of the state, nor of the statesman, but also as a result of an issue-specific ratification process, which can place strict limits on executive prerogatives.

60. Putnam, "Diplomacy and Domestic Politics" (Appendix, pp. 438–439).

61. In drafting this chapter, a search was made for detailed formal models that might clarify the issues of two-level games, beyond the heuristic use of models employed here. While formal models may eventually generate unique, testable two-level propositions about nested negotiations, they have not done so to date—nor is there evidence that they could have provided unique insights on which to base detailed empirical analysis. The problems of two-level games closely resemble those that arise in the spatial modeling of legislative behavior. Yet according to a recent survey by an important advocate of such applications,

neither testable nor counterintuitive propositions have emerged out of the deductive work carried out in formal legislative studies between 1979 and 1988, although the existence of precise institutional rules expedites theorizing to a far greater extent than in almost any international negotiations. See Keith Krehbiel, "Spatial Models of Legislative Choice," *Legislative Studies Quarterly* 13 (August 1988): 312–313. (Krehbiel has subsequently performed some empirical analysis on simple propositions drawn from competing theories of legislative organization: Krehbiel, *Information and Legislative Organization* [Ann Arbor: University of Michigan Press, 1991].) For this project, therefore, the use of game theory as heuristic, rather than as a formal model, appeared more promising. For examples, see George Tsebelis, *Nested Games: Rational Choice in Comparative Politics* (Berkeley: University of California Press, 1990); and Martin and Sikkink in this volume.

62. In other words, subnational actors (which in any particular case may be interest groups, political parties, ethnic groups, bureaucratic agencies, or even influential individuals) are the fundamental actors designated by the model. These calculations of group costs and benefits are particularly complex when there is more than one alternative to no agreement. Under these circumstances, an alternative favored by less than a majority (or plurality) can be ratified, so long as a majority prefer it to no-agreement (Putnam, "Diplomacy and Domestic Politics," Appendix, pp. 445–446).

63. Ibid., p. 451.

64. Ibid., p. 448.

65. The division beween manipulable and nonmanipulable constraints raises some difficult issues. The notion that statesmen can persuade their constituents to change their utility functions, implied in Putnam's article, would seem to stretch the concept of a domestic constraint. It might better be understood as the manipulation of information under conditions of uncertainty or domestic incentives. If the domestic polity is viewed as merely a passive constraint, then domestic politics could be subsumed within an *ex ante* specification of state preferences and bargaining power, thus permitting a unitary-actor analysis of bargaining. If, on the other hand, the two-level-games approach is extended to permit domestic actors to develop their own strategies vis-à-vis the statesman (as is done in a number of the case studies that follow), then domestic politics becomes a true game, rather than merely a set of manipulable constraints on the statesman.

66. Schattschneider, *Politics, Pressures, and the Tariff.*

67. The promise of safeguards, exemptions, adjustment assistance, and accompanying domestic measures in economic negotiations may permit the executive to redistribute the costs and benefits of an international agreement or to create uncertainty about its eventual costs and benefits. It is difficult to measure the resources available to a statesman to manipulate the polity, but the popularity of the government may be one useful proxy: the more popular the government, the more autonomy it is likely to enjoy vis-à-vis domestic forces.

68. Anne-Marie Burley and Abram Chayes remind me that in iterated negotiations, interest groups will learn over time to mobilize in early stages of the negotiations.

69. Putnam, "Diplomacy and Domestic Politics" (Appendix, p. 440). The notion of involuntary defection makes sense only in a two-level-games framework that distinguishes between the statesman and society.

70. This influence may be either deliberate or unintentional. For a skeptical view regarding the credibility, and hence the efficacy, of attempts to deceive an opposing country about domestic constraints, see Bruce Bueno de Mesquita and David Lalman, "Domestic Opposition and Foreign War," *American Political Science Review* 84 (September 1990): 747–765. Within the project, this hypothesis was introduced in my chapter on armaments collaboration.

71. For a detailed empirical study that stresses the extent to which constituents are willing to bear the costs of threats, see Bruce Jentleson, *Pipeline Politics: The Complex Political Economy of East-West Energy Trade* (Ithaca, N.Y.: Cornell University Press, 1986). For a cogent theoretical discussion of the opportunity costs of wielding power—which does not, however, examine the sources of domestic political constraints—see David Baldwin, *Economic Statecraft* (Princeton, N.J.: Princeton University Press, 1985), pp. 119–130.

72. John Odell and Lisa Martin were particularly responsible for this formulation of the proposition.

73. These terms were suggested by Robert Putnam.

74. A transnational or transgovernmental alliance should be strictly distinguished from a situation in which groups find themselves on the same side of an issue without explicit coordination ("a transnational coalition"), or where a change in interests or expectations arises out of direct interactions between domestic groups, leading to the formation of a coalition.

75. Of course, collusion between two dovish statesmen might be thought of as a special kind of transnational alliance.

76. If one relaxed all the constraints at once, then the two-level game would be intractable, and we eschew that approach. Tsebelis (*Nested Games*, pp. 9–10) justifies a similar procedure by arguing that it is necessary in order to reduce the problem to "manageable dimensions."

77. Achen and Snidal, "Rational Deterrence Theory," p. 167.

PART 2

Security Issues

2

Dual Track and Double Trouble
The Two-Level Politics of INF

Richard C. Eichenberg

This chapter examines the two-level diplomacy of NATO's intermediate nuclear force (INF) posture. It covers the period between 1977, when Chancellor Helmut Schmidt forced the INF issue onto NATO's agenda, and 1988, when the INF "double-zero" treaty, which completely eliminated this class of missile, was agreed to by the West German government and ratified by the U.S. Senate. The focus is primarily U.S.–West German relations, since the crucial intra-Alliance diplomacy on this issue was carried out between these two countries. After an initial round of hesitation, the United States became the strongest advocate of missile deployment, and of course it was the United States that provided the missiles, and later negotiated their removal with the Soviets. Chancellor Schmidt is widely seen as the originator of NATO's INF modernization program, and throughout NATO's controversy over the issue West Germany was the crucial "deployment" country.

Four outcomes are examined here:

1977: Disagreement between President Jimmy Carter and Chancellor Helmut Schmidt on the question of how to react to changes in the European nuclear balance.

1979: Agreement between Carter and Schmidt on NATO's 1979 "dual-track" decision to deploy INF while negotiating arms limitations with the Soviets.

1983: Ratification/Implementation of the 1979 decision, in the form of a vote by the West German Bundestag to proceed with deployment.

1988: Agreement between President Ronald Reagan and Chancellor Helmut Kohl on the "double-zero" elimination of INF, accomplished in the INF Treaty of 1987.

Movement toward agreement and/or disagreement that occurred within each of these four episodes will also be examined. My central argument is that the primary determinant of agreement was the size of the domestic win-set. When win-sets were large, as was the case in 1977, chiefs of government (COGs) were free to pursue personal preferences, for the number of ratifiable approaches was correspondingly large. In the language of this volume, the COGs' acceptability-sets lay fully within their domestic win-sets—virtually any of their preferred outcomes could be ratified—giving Carter and Schmidt great flexibility in their diplomacy. In the 1977 episode, this flexibility led to a clash of incompatible leadership preferences and resulted in disagreement.

In the three subsequent episodes, the domestic win-sets were shrinking as a result of the domestic polarization that followed the INF decision, and the crisis atmosphere in East-West relations. Leaders on both sides were therefore required to accommodate dissent, both among their own constituents and in the domestic ranks of their negotiating partners. Otherwise, they risked disagreement—or failure to implement—on an issue that had become a crucial test of Alliance cohesion. Domestic win-sets had become smaller than the COGs' acceptability-sets—there were now fewer ratifiable approaches in the win-set than options considered acceptable by the COGs. Ironically, it appears that there was more overlap between what their respective constituents wanted than between the preferred outcomes of the two leaders—a classic case of COGs-as-hawks. In each of these three cases, COGs moved away from personal preferences in their attempts to remain within or broaden their own win-set or that of their opposite number. In each case, agreement resulted.

Thus the episodes in this chapter differ from other cases in this book in that Level I agreement often resulted *because* of shrinking domestic win-sets, and not in spite of them. I attribute this outcome to two considerations that affect the calculations of chief negotiators. First, failure to agree on important issues within a valued international institution (in this case NATO) carries domestic costs that are far higher than the costs of failure to agree on individual issues. Second, for chief negotiators who are vulnerable domestically, international agreement represents a potential source of general domestic support.

I also believe that variations in agreement and disagreement in the INF case cannot be explained by systemic factors. Broadly speaking, the issue before the actors was the question of how to respond to a shift in the nuclear balance of power. Systemic theory would predict that a deterioration in the balance of power would bring agreement on the part of Alliance partners on the need to deal with it. Yet the initial reaction of the partners in this case was disagreement. Although agreement later occurred, the determining factors were not systemic in nature, and periods of disagreement often preceded these outcomes. I contend that domestic factors explain this variation.

FROM DUAL TRACK TO DOUBLE ZERO: A BRIEF HISTORY

INF became an issue for the NATO Alliance as a result of Soviet weapons deployments and the treatment of European nuclear forces in the U.S.-Soviet Strategic Arms Limitations Talks (SALT).[1] In 1976, the Soviets began deploying the SS-20, a mobile, multiple-warhead missile of intermediate range that represented a considerable improvement to their older SS-4 and SS-5 missiles. For NATO, one possible response to the Soviet deployment would have been cruise missiles, which were then under development in the United States. Perhaps not surprisingly, in 1976 the Soviets proposed a ban on cruise-missile testing in the SALT talks, and throughout the subsequent negotiations the Soviets attempted to limit deployment of cruise missiles or transfer of the technology to American allies.

Disagreement: Schmidt's 1977 Speech

Chancellor Schmidt expressed his concern about the INF balance to President Gerald Ford during the summer of 1975. Ford promised Schmidt that INF would be taken up in the SALT II negotiations, but only after the American elections of 1976, in which Ford faced a challenge from Ronald Reagan, a vehement critic of SALT. Schmidt later reported that he was satisfied with this assurance, citing his personal trust in Gerald Ford and his understanding of Ford's domestic political requirements.[2]

Schmidt continued his entreaties on the INF issue after the election of President Jimmy Carter in 1977. In his memoirs, Schmidt reports that during the course of 1977 it became clear to him that Carter had no intention of bringing the SS-20 into the SALT negotiations. In July 1977, Schmidt argued for inclusion of INF in the SALT process during a meeting with Carter in Washington, but he later observed that his request to Carter and his advisers "fell on deaf ears."[3] In September, Schmidt reports that he

> took considerable time to make Brzezinski understand the strategic situation of my country . . . in which the political threat posed by the rapidly growing force of SS-20's played the major role. The success of my efforts was small. Brzezinski's view was that all of this was really not Bonn's problem, but America's. Were Bonn to be subjected to pressure by the SS-20, the United States was capable of meeting it with its strategic nuclear force . . . and like Brzezinski, Carter showed absolutely no understanding for my worries.[4]

The American side of the story is much the same. Brzezinski agrees that he saw no need for a response to the SS-20, given the robustness of the American nuclear deterrent.[5] In fact, the American government attempted to dissuade the Europeans of the need for an INF solution. In mid-1977, the Administration dispatched Leslie Gelb, then Director of Politico-Military Affairs in the U.S. State Department, to Europe to argue against any NATO deployment to counter the SS-20, citing verification problems in arms control and the fear that such a deployment would "decouple" European security from the United States.

These encounters led Schmidt to the least charitable interpretation of American intentions: "Washington was pursuing the goal of reducing only the strategic threat to American territory, without letting consideration of European security interests get in the way."[6] Frustrated with the lack of American responsiveness on the INF issue, Schmidt went public with his disagreement in October 1977 in a speech to the International Institute for Strategic Studies (IISS). In that speech, Schmidt warned that the stabilization of the U.S.-Soviet arms race in the SALT process, while laudable, could threaten European interests: "Strategic arms limitation confined to the United States and the Soviet Union will inevitably impair the security of the West European members of the Alliance vis-à-vis the Soviet military superiority in Europe if we do not succeed in removing the disparities of military power in Europe parallel to the SALT negotiations."[7]

Schmidt's speech was interpreted for exactly what it was: a public declaration that the United States and West Germany could not agree on an approach to the related problems of INF and SALT. The disagreement was all the more remarkable for the fact that it was expressed publicly.

Agreement: The 1979 Dual-Track Decision

The initial result of Schmidt's speech was continuing U.S.-West German disagreement on the issue. One month after the speech, Secretary of State Vance argued in Congressional testimony that he saw no need for new nuclear weapons in Europe, given the deterrent effect of U.S. bombers based in Britain and the increased number of submarine-based warheads allotted to NATO's commander. That same fall, David Aaron of the National Security Council staff traveled to Europe to argue against NATO INF deployments.

During 1978 and 1979, however, the positions of the U.S. and West German governments were reversed. In the spring and summer of 1978, the U.S. government moved to respond to European concerns. After the NATO Summit in May, Carter called for a response to the SS-20, linking NATO modernization with arms control. In July, Carter approved Presidential Review Memorandum 38 (PRM 38), which called for an interagency study of the INF issue. By September the resulting plan to modernize NATO's INF received cabinet-level approval. By early 1979, when Carter and Schmidt (together with French President Giscard D'Estaing and British Prime Minister James Callaghan) met at the Guadeloupe Summit, agreement seemed complete. All four leaders agreed on the need to modernize NATO's INF while proceeding with arms-control negotiations.

As Garthoff notes, the U.S. government had not merely reversed its opposition to an INF deployment. It had become an enthusiastic supporter: "A successful campaign for NATO consensus on a new LRTNF [Long-Range Theater Nuclear Forces] deployment initiative now became a major goal of American policy. . . . Accordingly, throughout 1979 the United States actively led—and sometimes drove hard—the Alliance members to reach agreement."[8]

As these comments suggest, the American endorsement of the deployment decision brought with it the paradox that Europeans now seemed hesitant. Helmut Schmidt's intentions were one source of their doubts. During 1979, Schmidt seemed to edge away from the impending NATO decision, raising fears in Washington that he would defect. A first source of concern had been Schmidt's handling of the issue at the Guadeloupe Summit, which Carter characterized as "very contentious."[9] At Guadeloupe, Schmidt agreed on the need for the decision, but he also called attention to his domestic difficulties by noting that the proposed decision "would not fall on undivided opinion in my country."[10] For this and other reasons, he enumerated a series of restrictions on Germany's participation in the decision and deployment, which he later repeated in a report to the Bundestag. In a speech to the Social Democratic Party's parliamentary group one month before the December decision, Schmidt hinted that NATO might forgo deployment provided "that the Soviets get rid of much of what they had produced."[11] In light of these actions on Schmidt's part, Brzezinski speculated that "Whether Schmidt would hold firm was open to question."[12]

However, despite hints of discord and perhaps even defection, growing pressure from the Soviets, and the beginnings of domestic discontent in West Germany, plans for the decision went forward throughout 1979. By the fall, an integrated plan for the deployment of ground-launched cruise missiles and Pershing II ballistic missiles, together with arms-control negotiations, was approved by NATO's consultative bodies. On December 12, 1979, the NATO Council unanimously approved this "dual-track" decision.

AGAINST ALL ODDS:
RATIFICATION AND IMPLEMENTATION, 1980–1983

Ratification and implementation of the dual-track decision were thrown into serious doubt almost immediately. One reason was the dramatic deterioration in the international climate that began with the Iran revolution and hostage crisis and continued with the Soviet invasion of Afghanistan and, later, the imposition of martial law in Poland. With the SALT II Treaty withdrawn from consideration, and the Carter Administration moving both to sanction the Soviets and to build up its own military forces, the sense of crisis was palpable, and it increased even more with the accession of the Reagan Administration, with its calls for military superiority, a delay in arms control, and sanctions against the "evil empire."

Public concern brought tremendous pressure on governments to preserve some semblance of détente. Nuclear weapons became the symbol of these desires. In the United States, the freeze movement became the focus of anti-nuclear activism in the public and within the Congress. Public opinion polls showed that as much as 70 percent of the American public supported the freeze. In Western Europe, NATO's dual-track decision became the target of an intensive anti-nuclear campaign. In West Germany, the anti-nuclear Green Party grew to parliamentary strength on the basis of its opposition to INF, and all parties were forced to deal with anti-nuclear sentiment within their ranks. Depending on the wording of the polls, 40 to 65 percent of the German public opposed deployment. From the perspective of polls and protests, then, by at least 1982 there was serious question whether any West German government could ratify the deployment decision in the face of intense domestic opposition. Even if it did, could it remain in power to implement the decision?

These pressures caused serious strains in U.S.-West German relations, at times calling into question the consensus that had been developed around the dual-track decision. The most serious dispute arose during 1980, as Chancellor Schmidt moved to preserve detente and arms control in reaction to President Carter's behavior following the Soviet invasion of Afghanistan. Schmidt incurred the ire of the Americans in part because of his aggressive efforts to preserve detente, as in his trip to Moscow in April of 1980—seen in Washington as a sign of weakness or perfidy. But the most serious threat to implementation of the dual-track consensus came in Schmidt's calls for a moratorium on NATO deployments. Although Schmidt's offer was rather moot (NATO would not be ready to deploy in any case until 1983), it infuriated the American administration, which already doubted his willingness and ability to stick to the decision.

When Schmidt repeated his moratorium idea to his party's annual congress in June 1980, it led to a truly bitter confrontation between the President and the Chancellor at the Venice economic summit.[13] Even so, Schmidt traveled to Moscow once again in July, where he persuaded the Soviets to enter negotiations on INF.

Schmidt's relations with President Reagan were surprisingly smooth, despite the latter's well-known rejection of detente and arms control. Even so, Schmidt brought persistent pressure on Reagan to overcome the opposition to arms control that was implicit in the President's statements and explicit in the desires and actions of his lieutenants.[14] In a meeting with the President-elect, and later during the first months of the Reagan Administration, Schmidt sought reassurances that negotiation would in fact take place. In early 1981, he tied Reagan to a publicly announced date for the beginning of negotiations. As the negotiating positions were developing, it was the West German government which introduced the notion of a "zero option" into NATO's deliberations and pressed for its adoption in Washington. As one German scholar has argued: "If at the beginning of 1980 the West German government's energies were directed toward compelling the Soviets to negotiate, a year later it worked with the same energy for the resumption of talks by the U.S."[15]

Paradoxically, the "single-zero" option that President Reagan presented to the Soviets was not the preferred option of the new German administration headed by Chancellor Helmut Kohl, for his Conservative coalition (especially its right wing) was convinced of the need for some INF to maintain a graduated nuclear deterrent, and it feared that the zero option would reinforce the public's anti-nuclear sentiments, which could lead to complete denuclearization in Europe.[16] Nonetheless, in the face of domestic sentiment favoring negotiation, and a desire to maintain harmony with Washington, the new Kohl government endorsed the zero negotiating position. Even so, as domestic opposition continued—many critics of INF opposed the single-zero position precisely because they judged it to be a ploy to block agreement—the Kohl government soon began urging Washington to show flexibility. Thus, during 1983, the year of German elections as well as the planned beginning of NATO's deployment, the West German government urged the Americans to accept an "interim solution" above zero, and Kohl later urged both governments to seek a speedier agreement, perhaps on the basis of the famous "walk in the woods" agreement that both the American and Soviet governments had rejected in 1982.[17] And in fact, in late 1983 the American government did introduce an interim solution to the negotiations, but it too was rejected by the Soviets. In late November, with no negotiated agreement in sight, the coalition government of Helmut Kohl sought and received the endorsement of the Bundestag to implement the deployment. Missiles began arriving in West Germany the next day.

Agreement: The 1987 Double-Zero Treaty

The commencement of NATO's deployment marked the beginning of a hiatus in U.S.-Soviet negotiations that was largely unbroken until the accession of Mikhail Gorbachev to the leadership of the USSR. Although the United States and the Soviet Union did agree in January 1985 to resume talks on strategic and intermediate nuclear forces—and to begin talks on space weapons—it was Gorbachev who initiated a series of concessions and proposals that culminated in 1987 with the "double-zero" INF Treaty.

The outlines of agreement occurred at the Reykjavik Summit, where Reagan and Gorbachev agreed on the eventual elimination of all nuclear missiles, regardless of range. Perhaps responding to the fears of their advisers and allies, both leaders later backed off this position, but Gorbachev nonetheless continued to offer concessions that Washington could not refuse. In spring 1987, for example, he offered a zero solution for both short-range and intermediate-range INF. By the spring of 1987, most obstacles to a U.S.-Soviet INF Treaty had been cleared.[18]

Paradoxically, the last remaining obstacle was the resistance of some West Germans to this "double-zero" solution. German doubts, expressed both in public statements and in press reports of government deliberations, were confusing and contradictory as well. What the entire INF episode had concealed was the variety of opinion within West Germany, and especially within the Conservative coalition of the Christian Democratic Union (CDU) and Christian Social Union (CSU), on the role of nuclear weapons in NATO defense. The Gaullist or military-strength wing of the Conservatives had always had doubts about any zero option. Put another way, they continued to favor the arguments originally put forth to support the INF decision: that NATO needed to maintain the INF rung in the flexible response ladder of deterrence. The ability of INF to strike Soviet territory was fundamental to this purpose.

The Kohl government had accepted the zero option as a negotiating position because of the need for domestic support, the desire to accommodate an American government that favored the proposal, and the apparent belief that the Soviets would never accept it. Once Gorbachev did accept the zero solution for INF and added his willingness to cancel short-range INF as well (an issue which NATO had not yet discussed), the Gaullists' objections emerged once again. Throughout the spring of 1987, the Conservative coalition was shaken by a debate over whether or not to accept Gorbachev's proposal, a debate made all the more delicate by President Reagan's obvious enthusiasm for double zero. Throughout this debate, the Conservatives rehearsed familiar issues in NATO's strategy of flexible response: the fact that "double zero" would restrict NATO to weapons of a range that would be used on German soil; the fear that double zero, together with the peace movements and the "spirit of Reykjavik," would lead to complete denuclearization in NATO; and the fact that double zero would remove a deterrent without addressing the problem of Soviet conventional superiority. For these reasons, members of the Conservative wing offered a number of alternatives, including a "zero-plus" position in which NATO would retain some INF, the modernization (not elimination) of shorter-range INF, and even a threat to reconsider NATO membership.[19]

Chancellor Kohl shared some of these reservations, but he had long ago committed his government to at least the single zero on INF. The outstanding question was whether his government would assent to the second zero on short-range INF, a question that remained unresolved for six weeks as the German coalition debated the issue. Only after pressure had built from Washington did the Kohl government assent to "double zero," but the lack of enthusiasm was evident, for Kohl added the condition that the agreement exclude a number of nuclear-capable (Pershing IA) missiles that were under the control of the Bundeswehr (although the warheads were not). When the Soviets then insisted that double zero could not go ahead without a German agreement to do away with their missiles, Kohl once again relented.

Thus, three months after Gorbachev's double-zero offer, the last intra-Alliance obstacle to the INF Treaty was cleared. With ratification by the U.S. Senate in May 1988, dismantling and destruction of the missiles could begin.

Recapitulation: Variations in Agreement and Disagreement

One of the puzzles of the U.S.-German politics of the INF issue is that, despite the fact that the balance of power was deteriorating throughout the period from 1977 to 1987—the Soviet deployment of SS-20's began with 10 in 1977 and reached 441 by 1986—the level of agreement and disagreement on how to respond to the deployment varied considerably. Initially (1975), Gerald Ford and Helmut Schmidt agreed rather amicably to shelve the issue. By 1977, however, Schmidt was moved by his disagreement with the Carter Administration to issue a strongly worded public dissent. During 1978 and 1979, the American and German roles reversed, with the Americans pushing strongly for missile deployment and the West Germans appearing to brake. Yet agreement was ultimately reached at the end of 1979.

Obviously, since the balance of power was deteriorating throughout this period, systemic factors cannot explain these variations in the level of agreement. I believe that the primary factors affecting the level of agreement were domestic—the size of win-sets. In the United States, leadership of NATO and strength vis-à-vis the Soviets became important political needs for Jimmy Carter and affected his win-set for the SALT II Treaty (and re-election). Carter added an INF deployment to his acceptability-set, and moved actively to meet German concerns. In the meantime, domestic pressures within West Germany forced Schmidt to emphasize arms control rather than deployment. In the end, the two were able to agree because NATO's dual-track decision allowed Carter to emphasize strength (deployment) and Schmidt to emphasize detente (negotiation). Agreement resulted *because* of shrinking win-sets and not in spite of them.

At first glance, the subsequent outcomes of the case appear to confirm a systemic interpretation. In 1983, as the nuclear balance worsened, West Germany did indeed respond by ratifying and implementing the deployment that was designed to right the balance. In 1987, the Germans accepted the double-zero treaty because it corrected the imbalance through arms control.

I contend that the systemic interpretation overlooks the impact of domestic factors. In 1983, the deployment was ratifiable in West Germany only because the United States agreed first to negotiate with the Soviets and later to show flexibility in the negotiations. This flexibility on the part of the American administration represented a shift from its initial preference, and it was the result of domestic pressure within the United States as well as in West Germany. In fact, some officials in Washington and Bonn saw no win-set for deployment unless negotiations showed some progress. Finally, in 1987, important elements of the West German ruling coalition opposed the treaty on precisely the military grounds that a systemic explanation would emphasize as the determinant of agreement. In the end, the German government accepted the treaty because the alternatives did not fall within its win-set. In summary, in 1983 and 1987, U.S.-German agreement occurred in spite of rather than because of changes in the balance of power. And once again, domestic polarization (shrinking win-sets) forced leaders toward agreement rather than disagreement.

THE STAKES:
THE IMPACT OF DOMESTIC INTERESTS ON INF

The primary issues in the INF case were whether and how to respond to a perceived shift in the nuclear balance of power. Unlike economic

and many security issues, the INF question did not involve material interests. In fact, the financing and procurement of the missile systems were
of minor importance. Rather, what was most at stake in the INF issue
were questions of ideology and strategic beliefs on the roles of force and
statecraft—deterrence and detente—in the pursuit of national security.
As the debate unfolded, this question became the focal point of competition between competing coalitions and institutions for control of party
policy and government itself.

Ideological debate on security issues has a long-standing tradition in
West Germany. Social Democrats have generally favored the idealist or
liberal argument that balance of power and deterrence are the causes
of conflict rather than its solution. As a result, the SPD has a legacy of
support for international law, arms control, and detente approaches to
peace that rely on negotiation, trade, and interdependence rather than
a balance of power. The Conservative parties (CDU and CSU), in contrast, built an image as the partisans of military strength, and their anti-
Communism produced an additional measure of skepticism of detente.

Although the politics of security in the United States are sometimes
characterized as provincial or idiosyncratic, the post-Vietnam security
debate is actually similar in substance to the West German, but its origins
are more recent, arising from debates about the utility and morality of
force in the Vietnam War. As several scholars have argued, the debate in
the United States in the post-Vietnam era shifted from the old isolationist
arguments about whether to participate in world affairs to a new set of
debates that pit a "liberal" coalition favoring detente and interdependence approaches against a "conservative" coalition that favors the balance of power and interventionist approaches of the Cold War. Of
course, given the heterogeneity of American parties, this debate crossed
partisan lines, but in substance the "force versus statecraft" debate was
much the same as in Europe.[20]

In both the United States and West Germany, these debates were
dormant for most of the 1970s. In Europe, *Ostpolitik* combined with
NATO's Harmel Doctrine, which joined deterrence and detente in official Alliance policy to bridge the competing approaches of left and right.
In the United States, the Vietnam settlement, detente, and arms control
of the early 1970s accomplished much the same sort of truce between
competing coalitions. In both Europe and the United States there was
political support for military strength, so long as it occurred parallel to
detente; detente was tolerated as long as it was pursued on the basis of
military strength.

However, the deterioration of East-West relations in the aftermath of
the 1979 invasion of Afghanistan reactivated the debate, and nuclear
weapons became the central issue. The important feature of the INF

issue is that it broke down the deterrence/detente compromise and polarized domestic actors along party, ideological, and institutional lines. Actors became adamantly attached to the mutually exclusive alternatives of deployment or negotiation. In West Germany, the polarization occurred both between and within political parties. As the SPD reverted to its traditional "negotiate first" position, it caused conflict not only with the CDU, but also between its own radical and moderate wings. Conversely, as the CDU pushed the "deploy first" position, it risked losing support from moderates who supported negotiation. And of course, all parties faced the competition of the Greens, who offered an undiluted anti-nuclear platform and threatened to complicate the delicate mathematics of electoral coalitions. Thus the ideological debates triggered by the INF issue engendered a competition for power and control within parties as well as for control of government and policy.

American parties are less homogeneous, but the security debate between liberals and conservatives polarized in much the same fashion. Especially after the Reagan military build-up and the President's hesitant approach to arms control, liberals of both parties (and in the peace movements) began a legislative and budgetary battle to change the Administration's policies. This debate also found expression in the institutional competition between Congress and the President. Not only were the security coalitions competing for public sentiment and votes, they were also competing for institutional control over security and arms-control policy.

Thus, while the INF case does not offer the neat set of material interests that characterize economic issues (where domestic winners and losers are easier to identify), there are nonetheless distinct political and ideological issues that divided domestic actors and institutions and framed their competition. I interpret the increasing polarization of German and American domestic coalitions as an erosion in the size of win-sets. During the period of detente and arms control that characterized the 1970s, there were many potentially ratifiable approaches to national security policy that would meet the Harmel-type formula on which domestic coalitions could agree. In fact, during the 1970s NATO did pursue arms control just as its members increased defense spending at a very healthy pace. However, as the international climate deteriorated and the INF issue came on the table, domestic actors polarized to incompatible ideological positions. The number of ratifiable approaches in this context is obviously smaller. As I argue in subsequent sections, the impact of this polarization—shrinking win-sets—was bound to affect diplomacy, for in both the United States and West Germany political institutions provide many opportunities for the "votes" of citizens and party activists to be counted.

THE IMPACT OF DOMESTIC FACTORS
ON COG NEGOTIATING STRATEGIES

In this section I describe the negotiating preferences of the four chief exec tives involved in this case by casting them in terms of the debate over deterrence and detente described in the previous section. With the possible exception of Helmut Schmidt, each of the chief executives defined his acceptability-set in terms of a preference for deterrence or detente—the deployment or negotiating track of NATO's decision. Yet each was also forced to shift from this initial preference to a position that more closely matched the domestic win-set. In three of the four episodes under study, the shift led to agreement.

Disagreement: 1977

President Jimmy Carter began his administration with a clear preference for negotiation. He had campaigned on a platform of reducing military spending, and by canceling the B-1 bomber and deferring production of neutron weapons, he reinforced his image as an arms-control President. In addition, he sought to differentiate his administration from the *realpolitik* of the Nixon/Kissinger team, and he made the negotiation of deep cuts in the SALT II Treaty one of the highest priorities of his new administration. Given the priority of U.S.-Soviet arms control to Carter's preferences, he resisted Schmidt's requests to place INF on the SALT agenda, for it would complicate a negotiation that was already overburdened with difficult and controversial issues. Modernization of INF was clearly outside of Jimmy Carter's acceptability-set.

Helmut Schmidt's preferences lay squarely in support of the Harmel formula. Throughout his career, he had placed great emphasis on the need for *both* deterrence and detente, and a close reading of his 1977 speech reveals that he did not preclude arms control as a solution to the INF imbalance. Indeed, the speech was motivated precisely by his desire to see INF inserted into the SALT process. Nonetheless, because of the prominence of the 1977 speech and its emphasis on the imbalance of military power, Schmidt became irretrievably identified as a proponent of deployment first—and in any case, his insistence on dealing with the INF issue led to disagreement with Carter throughout 1977, and to his well-publicized speech in which he expressed this disagreement.

Why could the two most important leaders of the Alliance not agree on a response to a shift in the balance of power? Seen in the context of the entire INF episode, the explanation appears to lie in the domestic political strength of the two leaders. In subsequent controversies over INF, leaders were forced to shift their positions to solidify their own domestic consensus as well as the domestic base of their opposite number.

In 1977, however, both Carter and Schmidt were quite strong domestically. Neither saw any need to build domestic strength throughout international diplomacy; nor was either leader under pressure to accommodate the domestic needs of the other.

One reason is that the INF issue was not yet salient in either country. In 1977, the mixture of detente and military strength that defined the Harmel formula was still the guiding principle of East-West relations. In Alliance deliberations, nuclear weapons issues had taken a back seat to the conventional modernization envisioned in NATO's long-term defense program. There was little if any public debate on European security issues. In the United States, Carter's popularity was extremely high. In early 1977, he still enjoyed the support that derived in part from his refreshing style and in part from the relief of the post-Watergate era. In fact, Carter's net public approval rating in early 1977 was 62 percent![21]

Like Carter, Schmidt had just been elected, and he also derived popularity from having replaced a tarnished administration (Brandt had resigned in 1974 over a spy scandal). Security and nuclear weapons issues were hardly noticeable on the German agenda. The Green Party had not yet adopted the peace platform as its centerpiece, and in any case its public support was still below 1 percent. And although Schmidt was known as a tough-minded pragmatist who usually braked the reforms of his more progressive party colleagues, it was precisely this competence that earned him wide acclaim as he steered the Federal Republic of Germany through the recession of 1975. In many circles, Schmidt's FRG was known as the "model" for Western societies, making him the most popular German politician and increasing his value and prestige within his party.

In summary, during 1977 neither Carter nor Schmidt faced the pressure of upcoming elections. Security issues in general were overshadowed by economic issues on the public agenda, and European security issues were hardly discussed at all. Both politicians were at the peak of their political power. In this situation, they faced no need to compromise, and they therefore placed their own preferences first. Since their acceptability-sets were incompatible, the likelihood of agreement was slim.

Agreement: 1979

This situation changed drastically during 1978. It is the paradox of the Carter Administration that the President won election on his mildly dovish platform at precisely the time that important elements of his constituency—in the public and in Congress—were growing wary of the Soviets and thus more interested in a policy of military strength. Support for increased defense spending had been rising since 1976. In fact, in 1976 the segment of the American public favoring an increase in defense spending outnumbered those who favored cuts for the first time during the 1970s, and support for increased defense continued to rise during the late 1970s. Public approval of the President's handling of the Soviet Union collapsed during 1977 and 1978, just as the public grew more supportive of protecting American allies, more hostile toward the Soviets, and more pessimistic about American military strength. Finally, by the beginning of 1978, the President's public-approval rating had fallen from 62 percent to 17 percent.[22]

Although the INF issue was not salient to the American public, the related issues of SALT and INF were coming under closer scrutiny in Congress. For example, according to Raymond Garthoff, Senator Henry Jackson, by far the most important Senate contact (and critic) on arms-control issues, began urging Europeans to express their INF concerns to the Americans, and an adviser to Jackson and his assistant Richard Perle criticized the SALT negotiations because they drove a wedge between the United States and its allies.[23]

Thus, quite early in the Carter Administration, the President came under generalized pressure to shift his policies from his preference for negotiation over strength. He was also pressured to respond to European concerns about INF. Pressure came from his staff as well. In his memoirs, Brzezinski reveals portions of his confidential weekly summaries for the President. In late 1977, Brzezinski wrote to Carter that the "public perception of your foreign policy is that it is 'soft.' . . . You should consider taking some 'tough' decisions, i.e., European security, the neutron bomb. . . ." In early 1978, he wrote to the President that "A president must not only be loved and respected, but also feared. I suggest that you try to dispel the impression that you and the administration are too cerebral by picking some controversial subject and acting with anger and roughness to demonstrate that no one can pick a fight with the U.S. If we do not do this soon, Begin, Brezhnev, Vorster, Schmidt, Castro, and Qaddafi will thumb their noses at us."[24]

Carter did not immediately accept this advice, for it was in March 1978 that he deferred production of the neutron bomb after pushing the European allies to accept it. However, that decision served to reinforce Carter's image of weakness, and it was one reason that his staff now urged him to get behind a NATO deployment decision that would demonstrate his strength and cast him in the role of Alliance leader—badly needed in light of the polls and the prospects for Congressional ratification of SALT. In short, Carter's switch on INF was part of his broader attempt to shore up his domestic position as the public and Congress grew wary of the Soviets and critical of the President's policies. The

President calculated that neglect of INF was becoming more costly in terms of domestic politics, so he shifted his acceptability-set accordingly.

Helmut Schmidt was also coming under domestic pressure, especially during 1979. Members of his own party began criticizing Schmidt's position on nuclear weapons, especially his apparent willingness to accept the neutron bomb and INF, and this debate became public for the first time during 1979. The Green Party, now moving to the peace issue, edged up in the polls to 4 percent, perilously close to the 5 percent threshold that would bring representation in the Bundestag.

These pressures explain Schmidt's rhetorical shift during 1979 to an emphasis on the negotiating track. Nonetheless, the criticism was relatively mild—there was not yet a peace movement—and Schmidt remained very strong domestically and within his own party. In fact, his popularity continued to rise throughout 1978 and 1979, reaching 50 to 60 percent even as the NATO decision approached. As we will see below, Schmidt also took steps to challenge critics of his policy. In the end, although he had wavered in his rhetoric, Schmidt was able to keep the bargain that he had wrested from Jimmy Carter, in part because of his political strength and his value to his party, in part because he had used that strength during 1979 to ensure that the decision gave equal emphasis to the arms-control track that was an essential component of his winset. Thus, it was Carter's shift away from his initial preference that paved the way for agreement, a shift that was due to the related requirements of Alliance leadership and domestic politics. Schmidt's shift was rhetorical, but it protected his flank and maintained domestic support for the agreement.

Ratification and Implementation: 1980–1983

The key question during this period was whether NATO's deployment decision could be ratified and implemented at the end of 1983. In West Germany, both Helmut Schmidt and his successor (in October 1982) Helmut Kohl began with preferences favoring deployment. Schmidt continued in his belief that both the deployment and negotiating tracks were necessary, while Kohl reflected the strong support for deployment that derived from his party's traditional emphasis on military strength, nuclear deterrence, and loyalty to Washington.

These preferences came under heavy pressure. Opposition to the deployment, apparent in large public protests, was confirmed by polls that indicated a broader public unease. In the crisis atmosphere of early 1980, the Germans' fear of war rose dramatically. Majorities in all parties opposed any interruption of arms negotiations after the Soviet invasion of Afghanistan. Depending on the poll, large minorities and even majorities opposed the INF deployment, and support for NATO itself experienced a sharp decline. The Green Party, now organized explicitly on an anti-INF platform, doubled its support to 8 percent in 1982.[25] In the midst of the turmoil, both Schmidt and Kohl faced national elections (in 1980 and 1983, respectively).

Both leaders responded to these domestic pressures by shifting to a rhetorical emphasis on negotiation and even by shifting to positions that were short of their initial preferences. Schmidt worked furiously to protect the negotiating track throughout his last two years in office, by floating his moratorium proposals and by personally pressuring both Moscow and Washington to negotiate. Kohl signed onto Reagan's zero proposal in 1981, despite his party's traditional attachment to flexible nuclear response, and during 1982 and 1983 he pressured Washington to show progress on negotiations, even if that meant deserting the zero option.

Ronald Reagan, of course, had been elected on a platform that put an absolute priority on military strength before negotiation. Indeed, in both his comments and his actions, Reagan made it clear that the rebuilding of strength was a necessary prelude to arms-control negotiations. And of course, Reagan's priorities received almost unquestioned support during 1981—in the Congress as with the public. Although INF was still not a major public issue in the United States at this time, by implication the consensus on his policy of strength represented an endorsement of the President's announced intention to delay arms-control negotiations or scrap them altogether. Indeed, given his own rhetoric and that of his aides, it seems fair to say that negotiated arms agreements were not initially within Reagan's acceptability-set.

Nonetheless, Reagan's preferences were soon challenged by shifting constituent preferences. The most visible source of criticism came in the freeze movement; but as in Europe, public opinion also reflected the anti-nuclear mood. Virtually all polls on the freeze found majority support during 1981–1983, and freeze resolutions on the ballots in the 1982 midterm elections were overwhelmingly successful. Public approval of Reagan's handling of the Soviet Union had been quite high (55 percent) in 1981, but by 1983 it dropped to the low point of his administration. Whereas public support for defense spending reached its highest level in the history of the Gallup Poll in 1981, only one year later it had dropped by 40 percentage points to the level of the early 1970s. Finally, Reagan's public-approval rating turned negative in early 1982 and continued to decline throughout 1983.[26]

The pressure on Reagan was increased by Congressional activism on defense and arms-control policy. Freeze resolutions in both House and Senate were one indication of congressional pressure; but in addition, congressional critics threatened to usurp the President's authority by withholding funding for the MX missile or legislating a "build-down" of strategic arms. The MX was all the more important for its symbolism in Europe: were the United States to cancel the MX, how could the Europeans be expected to hold firm on INF? As the pressure grew during 1982, the President's political advisers began worrying that lack of progress on arms control could threaten the President's re-election.[27] As a result of these domestic pressures, Strobe Talbott later argued, "the principal negotiations throughout 1983 were not between the U.S. and the Soviet Union, but between the White House and the Congress."[28]

Pressure came from Europe as well. Of course, Schmidt and Kohl had reported their domestic troubles to Washington and pressed for progress in negotiation—otherwise ratification and deployment would be threatened. Their problems were confirmed by analysis in Washington. During the INF debate, the American government increased the frequency of its public opinion polling in Europe. During 1981 and early 1982, for example, it conducted seven surveys of German opinions on the INF issue. In the fall of 1982, Paul Nitze, the chief American INF negotiator, cited these polls to support his argument that the United States should show more flexibility by backing away from Reagan's zero proposal. At a meeting in the State Department, Nitze said:

> We have a political problem in Europe. A considerable percentage of European public opinion is not satisfied with our zero-zero position and would be satisfied with an outcome that left us with zero on our side. . . . There's another percentage of the European population that doesn't hold out any hope for zero-zero, but might be satisfied if we seem to be exploring an equitable solution above zero. The first thing we've got to do is start exploring these solutions, so that it becomes more likely that the requisite percentage will support deployment.[29]

What Nitze was arguing, in effect, was that ratification of the deployment would not be in the win-set of European governments unless a negotiating position other than the zero option was pursued—precisely the argument that was made by Kohl during 1982 and 1983. Schmidt had made a similar argument to Reagan in late 1980 and early 1981 when he persuaded the President to begin negotiating immediately.

As it turns out, Reagan's shift toward arms control was successful. As Table 1 illustrates, West German public attitudes relaxed after Reagan's announcement in November 1981 that INF negotiations would begin, and especially after the United States presented a draft treaty reflecting the zero option in February 1982. The German public's fear of war dropped considerably, support for NATO rose once again after dropping in 1981 and 1982, and polls on U.S.-German relations indicated an endorsement of the American government's more moderate course.

TABLE 1.   West German Public Opinion on Security Issues

	1. *Fear War*	2. *Support NATO*	3. *U.S.-German Relations:*			4. *INF:*	
			Improving	Deteriorating		Oppose	Accept
1977	21%	72%	—	—	3/81	40%	55%
1980	35	80	—	—	7/81	26	57
1981	42	42	9%	42%	10/81	32	50
1982	28	48	5	43	12/81	40	42
1983	28	74	—	—	1/82	47	51
1984	22	77	23	5	2/82	39	50
					4/82	29	58

Table 1 shows *partial* responses to four separate survey questions:
(1) Respondents were asked to rate their fear of war on a scale from 0 (least probable) to 100 (most probable); no. 1 shows the percentage who rated the probability of war from 50 to 100. *Source:* Commission of the European Communities, *Eurobarometre: Public Opinion in the European Communities* no. 22 (Brussels: December 1984), p. A19.
(2) Respondents were asked if they thought NATO essential to German security; no. 2 shows the "net support" for NATO—that is, the percentage supporting NATO minus the percentage who did not support NATO. *Source:* Richard C. Eichenberg, *Public Opinion and National Security in Western Europe* (Ithaca, N.Y.: Cornell University Press, 1989), table 4.5.
(3) Respondents were asked if U.S.-German relations had improved, deteriorated, or stayed the same in comparison to a year earlier. *Source:* Hans Rattinger, "The Bundeswehr and Public Opinion," in Stephen Szabo, ed., *The Bundeswehr and Western Security* (London: Macmillan, 1990), p. 107.
(4) Respondents were asked if they opposed INF unconditionally, accepted it unconditionally, or accepted it only if arms talks were to proceed; the latter two responses have been combined in no. 4. *Source:* Eichenberg, *Public Opinion and National Security*, table 5.1.

Most important, opposition to the deployment itself declined during 1982.

In summary, if implementation in late 1983 was possible only because of the relaxation in public attitudes, this relaxation was in turn due to the shift in negotiating positions exhibited by Washington during 1981 and 1982. Faced with both his own domestic problems and the knowledge that domestic opposition in Europe threatened INF ratification, Reagan moved first to negotiate and then to introduce flexibility into his position. Both Schmidt and Kohl moved to rhetorical positions that placed a priority on negotiations—a shift for both leaders. The deployment went ahead not because the public perceived it as a correction to the balance of power, but because the public could tolerate it so long as it took place in the context of negotiation. As had been the case in earlier episodes, shrinking win-sets forced leaders to seek agreement on the basis of positions (preferences) they had earlier rejected. Once again domestic politics, by pressuring the leaders toward more accommodating positions, worked to favor Level I agreement rather than hinder it.

Agreement: 1987-88

As noted earlier, the final paradox of the INF case is that the zero option, offered by Reagan to mollify the arms controllers in Europe and America, later became the cause of the final U.S.-German dispute on INF. When Gorbachev accepted the zero option for INF in 1987, and added his offer of a second zero on short-range INF, he challenged the historical preference of important elements of the conservative wing of the ruling CDU for some nuclear deterrence based on INF. Kohl shared some of these reservations, but he eventually assented to Reagan's obvious preference for double zero, and in the process he also agreed to remove the German missiles that for the Conservatives were the last remaining symbol of flexible nuclear response.

Once again, the determining factors were domestic. If the nuclear protests of preceding years had not provided sufficient evidence, opinion surveys now showed that the German public favored both zero options by overwhelming margins (Table 2). The option of banning INF enjoyed the support of almost 90 percent of the public, and when faced with the choice of accepting Gorbachev's additional zero on short-range INF or deploying weapons of this type—which NATO did yet not have—the Germans reacted with predictable negativism.

Reagan's preferences were clear. He had taken great pride in offering

TABLE 2.   Public Opinion on the Single and Double Zero Options, May 1987

	Attitudes Toward Single Zero		
	Britain	France	Germany
Favor	65%	71%	89%
Oppose	24	24	9
Don't know	11	5	2
	Attitudes Toward a Second Zero		
	Britain	France	Germany
Ban all short-range missiles	46%	52%	73%
Retain right to build own	42	27	12
Don't know	12	21	15

NOTE: The first group of responses refers to the zero option on intermediate-range INF only. The second responses refer to the second zero on short-range INF contained in Gorbachev's 1987 proposal; NATO could accept his offer or decide to build its own short-range INF missiles, not then in the inventory.

SOURCE: Dennis M. Gombert, *West European Publics Favor Eliminating INF Missiles* (Washington, D.C.: Office of Research, U.S. Information Agency, May 20, 1987), tables 1 and 2.

his zero proposal. Moreover, in 1986 and 1987, as the final negotiations with the Soviets and the West Germans were taking place, he once again found himself in need of a political success to shore up his domestic weakness. In the wake of the Iran-Contra affair and the Reykjavik Summit, Reagan's popularity had plunged once again. In the spring of 1987 his net approval rating was barely positive; and although Reagan did not face re-election in 1988, he had his party's prospects and his own legacy to consider.

For this reason, the Reagan Administration pushed Kohl quite hard to override the objections in his party and accept double zero. In a visit to Brussels in early 1987, Secretary of State George Shultz described the alternatives:

1. Accept double zero.
2. Reject *any* zero option and proceed with INF deployments.
3. Accept zero on INF, but reject zero on short-range INF and proceed to deploy new NATO missiles of this type to match the Soviets.

As the survey results in Table 2 make clear, only the first option had any support within West Germany. In fact, Shultz could not have done a better job in describing the parameters of Kohl's win-set.

THE STRATEGIC BEHAVIOR OF CHIEFS OF GOVERNMENT

Leaders have two alternatives when faced with an eroding domestic consensus. They can challenge constituents and attempt to build support for their own preferences—in effect expanding the win-set. Alternatively, they can shift their acceptability-sets in the direction of constituent preferences. In the four episodes examined here, both challenge and adaptation are revealed, but Ronald Reagan exhibited a third variant: he wrapped a challenge in the cloth of a shift in policy.

Helmut Schmidt is the clear example of a leader who, through a number of mechanisms, challenged his constituents to support his policy. One of his stratagems was to use international diplomacy to create positive domestic reverberation that would solidify his win-set. As the INF decision approached in 1979 and he faced criticism from within his own party, Schmidt traveled both to Washington and to Moscow to tie down support for negotiation on INF. At home, he argued that it was only through participation in the INF decision that West Germany could bring such pressure. In fact, after the SALT II Treaty was shelved in the U.S. Senate, Schmidt reminded his party that the INF negotiations were the only remaining forum of active superpower arms control. In early 1981 he traveled to Washington to secure Reagan's public commitment to a specific date for opening negotiations. Throughout 1980 and 1981,

Schmidt forcefully reminded the Americans that it was only through negotiations that German domestic support for deployment could be maintained, and at home he reminded his party that it was only by sticking to deployment that the Americans could be tied to arms-control negotiations. When this strategy began to fail, Schmidt threatened to resign. The threat to resign was also used by Foreign Minister Genscher to his own party convention. In summary, Schmidt actively manipulated international diplomacy and his own considerable value to his party to shore up his win-set. Through 1982, it was a successful strategy.

Jimmy Carter and Helmut Kohl were forced to redefine their acceptability-sets rather than challenge the changing preferences of constituents. In Carter's case, the shift was both clear and dramatic, as he (and Brzezinski) accepted the arguments of advisers and senators that an American response to European concerns was required. In 1987, Kohl's acceptance of the double-zero treaty required him to override some of his own doubts, but more important, it also required him to override the views of fellow conservatives who were critical of the treaty. Nonetheless, the decision allowed him to keep in tune with the clear preference of the public and the majority sentiment in his party.

Ronald Reagan managed simultaneously to challenge his critics and adjust to the clear shift in domestic preferences. As criticism mounted in the American public and Congress, as well as in European public opinion, Reagan was pushed to reverse his opposition to arms control or risk defeat on his budget and legislative control of arms-control policy. In Europe, implementation of the INF deployment was at risk. The announcement of the zero option in late 1981 served to defuse the opposition, but it was a double-edged adjustment in policy, for neither the drafters of the proposal nor most outside observers thought that the Soviets would ever accept it. Indeed, most students of the period agree that the proposal was designed specifically to mollify the American freeze movement and the European peace movements without risking agreement. The ultimate irony of the zero-option proposal is that it was targeted strategically at domestic and European audiences in an attempt to solidify the win-set for arms deployments—but because it reverberated so positively on the German audience, it defined Kohl's win-set in such a way as to preclude any future deployment above zero.

COG STRATEGIES OF ACCOMMODATION AND COERCION

One of the interesting features of the INF case is the demonstration that leaders modulate their strategies not just to influence their own constituents, but also to take account of—or advantage of—the domestic constraints on their opposite numbers. As they do domestically, leaders face the choice of either challenging a negotiating partner to change his position or accommodating a difference in approach—but the unique feature of bargaining in the two-level context is that leaders attempt to manipulate the domestic situations of their opposite numbers in the negotiating process.

An example of accommodation occurred in 1975, when Schmidt agreed to delay the inclusion of INF in the SALT talks because of Gerald Ford's expressed desire to keep SALT off the agenda during the 1976 election campaign. Similarly, the shift in Ronald Reagan's arms-control strategy was designed specifically to accommodate Schmidt and Kohl in the face of the German public's uneasiness about INF and the lack of progress in arms control. Indeed, the European opposition became an ally to members of the Reagan Administration (such as Nitze) who argued first that negotiations must begin, and later that flexibility on the zero option was required to insure German implementation of deployment.

Helmut Schmidt's behavior reveals several instances of attempts to create reverberation that would change the stance of his negotiating partners. The IISS speech is perhaps the best example. Of course, the motivations for the speech were well grounded in Schmidt's policy differences with Carter, but he chose an audience of elite strategists and defense analysts to deliver the message. Elsewhere, Schmidt explains in detail his appreciation for both the views and the influence of the American foreign policy "establishment" represented in such institutions as the Council on Foreign Relations and the gathering of influentials at Bohemian Grove. For Schmidt, one of the satisfying characteristics of the American foreign policy establishment was its traditional support for the coupling of American and European security.[30] Thus, it seems fair to assume that Schmidt was attempting to mobilize the American establishment in support of his view that Carter was neglecting European interests in the SALT negotiations.

Later in 1979 and in 1980, Schmidt again took account of Carter's domestic problems when he pushed for progress on the negotiating track and strove to tie Washington to a continuation of dialogue with the Soviets after the invasion of Afghanistan. Indeed, when Carter and Brzezinski criticized his actions, Schmidt confronted them at the Venice Summit and secured Carter's endorsement of his planned trip to Moscow. As he later said:

> On the way to Venice, politically I felt good. Above all I understood that, for reasons of domestic politics, Jimmy Carter was far more dependent on my goodwill than I on his, for his prestige at home and in the world had been damaged—and mine had not.[31]

Ronald Reagan was less severe in pushing the double-zero treaty on Helmut Kohl, but his actions certainly suggest that he was aware of the narrow range of the latter's win-set. In fact, when Secretary of State Shultz traveled to Brussels to describe possible responses to Gorbachev's double-zero offer, he was both setting the agenda and reminding his German colleagues that only double zero lay within the German win-set. In the end, Kohl had been the victim of double targeting: by Gorbachev, who was doubtless aware that double zero was the most popular option in German domestic politics; and by Reagan, who initiated the original zero option and warmly embraced Gorbachev's double zero.

THE ROLE OF INSTITUTIONS

One purpose in analyzing negotiations as a two-level process is to explore the impact of domestic institutions on the prospects for international agreement. Are there institutional features that increase the impact of domestic factors on international strategies? If so, do they increase or decrease the prospects for international agreement? The INF case clearly demonstrates that institutional factors condition the impact of domestic variables on negotiating positions, for in both West Germany and the United States specific institutional features increased the impact of domestic variables and required leaders to shift their positions.

West Germany operates under a system of qualified proportional representation, in which parties gain representation in the Bundestag when they surpass 5 percent of the popular vote. As a result, minority voter sentiment is important in West Germany, because minor parties may compete successfully at the margins of the major parties' vote. With four major parties competing in elections, even marginal changes in votes can change coalition dynamics. As a result, elections can become an important "ratification" event. Both national elections and frequent region (*Länder*) elections serve this role. Thus, once citizens are mobilized on an issue, governments must pay attention to voter opinion.

Not surprisingly, political parties play a crucial role in this process of mobilizing voter sentiment or, in the contrary view, of responding to that sentiment. Indeed, given the electoral dynamic noted above, they must do so to survive. Thus, political parties play an important direct role, for the ebb and flow of their poll standing or electoral strength provides an informal reading on "ratification" questions. Moreover, there are other institutional contexts in which ratification is tested. The annual party conventions are particularly important, for they debate and decide the party's position on major issues. Recall that it was at the party conventions that Schmidt and Genscher issued threats to resign to maintain their parties' support for the dual-track decision.

Other actors do participate in the process, but they are dominated by the dynamics of party government. For example, ministers and ministries have predictably parochial views, but these are overshadowed by party and coalition concerns at the cabinet level. An interesting example of this dynamic was provided by the shifting tone of ministry views under the Schmidt and Kohl governments. Under Schmidt, the Defense Ministry—controlled by the SPD—favored the pro-negotiation emphasis of the SPD, and the Foreign Ministry—controlled by the Free Democratic Party (FDP)—attempted to pull government policy toward firm support for negotiation and solidarity with the Americans. Later, under the Kohl government, these roles switched: the Defense Ministry, now under a CDU minister, emphasized nuclear deterrence and thus skepticism of double zero, while the FDP Foreign Ministry pushed negotiation and acceptance of the zero options. Thus, in Germany's parliamentary system, ministers' first loyalty is to the party. This example also illustrates the impact of coalition politics. The FDP traditionally plays a "balancer" role in German politics, resisting SPD and CDU attempts to push government policy toward the ideological extremes.[32]

The INF debate in Germany is replete with illustrations of the impact of these institutions. The mobilization of public sentiment (most of it negative) was itself sufficient cause for parties and governments to re-examine their negotiating positions. In addition, the rise of the Green Party to parliamentary strength threatened to stalemate government in Bonn; for so long as the traditional parties refused to coalesce with the Greens, there was the prospect that no combination of parties would command a parliamentary majority. Of course, this threat created incentives to shift toward the concerns of Green voters, evident not only in the SPD, which had to protect its flank on the left, but also in the FDP, whose parliamentary representation could be threatened were the Greens to reduce their vote.

Significantly, three out of the four shifts in the German position occurred very close to elections. In 1980, Schmidt floated his moratorium and pushed for detente just before his party's conference in the run-up to the May election. In 1982, Kohl pushed for negotiating flexibility as he faced his first electoral test in 1983. And in 1987, while Kohl had just won re-election, the margin had been narrow, and as the double-zero debate unfolded, his party and coalition were torn by dissension as local elections approached.

In the United States, the importance of voter sentiment is also institutionalized in the electoral process. Once an issue has mobilized the level of concern that was evinced in the 1980s, both President and Congress must be attentive to the electoral consequences. And while parties are less homogeneous than is the case in Europe, the competition for voters occurs nonetheless. Moreover, international negotiations are influenced by an additional institutional feature: the congressional power of the purse and its right to ratify international agreements. Thus, just as candidates for Congress and the presidency must acknowledge voter sentiment for electoral reasons, the two institutions also compete for control over budgetary and negotiating policies in the arms-control field.

Both public sentiment and institutional competition played a role in the evolution of the American position on arms control generally, and INF specifically. Both Carter and Reagan changed positions on INF (albeit in different directions) as voter assessments of their handling of arms-control issues shifted. From 1977 to 1978, when Carter shifted to a position of strong endorsement of an INF deployment, his popularity rating had declined by over 60 percentage points, and other polls showed disapproval of his handling of the Soviets. Between 1981 and 1982, when Reagan shifted to a position of flexibility on the INF negotiations, his popularity rating had dropped by 43 percentage points, and public evaluations of his Soviet policy had reached a low point.

The intervention of Congress is also crucial to the American side of the INF story. Carter placed a very high priority on ratification of the SALT II Treaty; but as the negotiations progressed, his own image of weakness, together with Congressional criticisms of his negotiating position, put ratification in doubt. In this context, European support for SALT II would be crucial, a connection that Senator Jackson brought to Carter's attention. Reagan later faced the same sort of pressure in the opposite direction. Faced with increasing congressional intervention in the arms-control process, through limitation of MX funding and legislation on the "build-down," Reagan was forced to speed up arms-control negotiations. His flexibility on INF was part of this broader shift. In summary, the institutional power of Congress forced Carter and Reagan to seek positive reverberation through international negotiations.

Can we generalize about the importance of these institutional features on international negotiating strategies? One obstacle to generalization arises from the nature of the issue. Obviously, public opinion, elections, and legislative intervention are of potential importance in any democracy. The question is when and why they have an impact, and on this score the INF issue may be the exception rather than the rule. After all, INF was part of an intensive polarization of East-West relations and domestic politics. As I have argued, the contours of the debate were truly fundamental, invoking age-old ideological debates on questions of war and peace. The international climate approached a level of crisis that was reminiscent of the most intense early periods of the Cold War. In such times, and on such an issue, perhaps we should be surprised were domestic factors *not* to have an impact.

One way to address this question is through a comparison of the institutions and negotiating positions of other NATO countries. All NATO countries faced the same crisis atmosphere of the early 1980s, and all experienced some degree of domestic polarization on the INF issue. One fact about the INF issue that is often overlooked is that, while anti-nuclear and anti-INF sentiment reached as high as 50 percent in all countries, there was considerable variation in governments' responses. In France and Great Britain, for example, Margaret Thatcher and François Mitterrand remained solidly behind the 1979 decision and the implementation of the decision in 1983. In Belgium and the Netherlands, in contrast, governments first delayed agreeing to the decision and later added qualifications when they ratified and implemented the decision.[33] West Germany, as we have seen, falls somewhere in the middle: although it accepted and ratified the decision without qualification, this occurred only after leaders shifted their positions to take account of domestic opposition.

These variations are rooted in domestic institutions. In Britain and France, the preferences of chief executives are most insulated from those of constituents. In Britain, of course, there is little chance that minority sentiment will have an impact on election outcomes, for the single-member, "first past the post" electoral system precludes parliamentary representation of minorities—a fact not lost on the major parties. In France, the dominance of the presidency allows for great independence in foreign affairs, and while parliamentary representation is proportional, this occurs only after a two-round, run-off system in which smaller parties are eliminated. Finally, in both Britain and France, there is a culture of executive dominance in which the independence of the executive in foreign affairs is enshrined in informal, but effective, norms.[34]

Belgium and the Netherlands are governed through pure proportional representation. Of course, this insures the representation of minority views, but more important, it sensitizes the larger parties to the necessity to compete for popular sentiment. Small shifts in votes can mean victory or defeat for a party or coalition. On an issue like the INF debate, governments oppose popular sentiments at their peril.[35]

In summary, a broader comparative perspective does indeed suggest that institutional patterns mediate two-level politics. In systems of greater executive dominance, the preferences of chief negotiators are more likely to persist, for the pressures of minorities pose little threat. In more "populist" systems, chief negotiators must be attentive to the development of popular attitudes, and thus dynamics of party institutions and electoral competition are likely to have an impact on Level I positions.

CONCLUSIONS AND EXTENSIONS

One obvious conclusion that emerges from the INF case is that domestic factors influence international negotiating positions in ways that illustrate the utility of viewing international bargaining as a two-level process. Presidents Ford, Carter, and Reagan all reacted to the INF issue on the basis of their own domestic considerations as well as the domestic situations of their German negotiating partners. Chancellors Schmidt and Kohl behaved similarly. There is also evidence that the leaders behaved strategically, targeting their moves to challenge or accommodate negotiating partners by manipulating the domestic environment of their opposite numbers or by shifting policies to take account of shrinking win-sets at home and abroad.

The link between domestic politics and international agreement in the INF case also leads to some important observations concerning the impact of international institutions on two-level politics and the general domestic political value of international agreements. Agreement on INF was important domestically not merely on the merits of the issue. In fact, in the United States, INF was never really perceived as fundamental to American security; and even in the earliest phases of the issue in West Germany, it was not controversial or even particularly salient. Rather, the domestic value of harmony on INF derived from its symbolic importance as an issue of institutional management. In this case, the institution was the NATO Alliance. Once the very existence of NATO became tied to INF, the domestic importance of the latter increased. Disagreement on INF could threaten the Alliance itself, an outcome that would carry very high costs domestically, given the value placed on NATO as an institution. Put another way, the cost of no-agreement and even disharmony on INF was far higher than the cost of disagreement on this particular weapons system. For this reason, successful management of the INF issue became a domestic political necessity. Failure to do so would leave leaders responsible for the weakening or disintegration of an important international institution. As a result, leaders sought Level I agreement by shifting toward options that lay within their own shrinking win-sets and within the win-set of their opposite number.

In addition, the INF case illustrates the more general value of international agreement to leaders whose domestic base has been weakened. For example, Carter, Schmidt, Reagan, and Kohl all experienced an erosion of their domestic support, in part because of INF, but also as a result of other factors—especially economic factors. In every case, these leaders shifted their position on INF to enhance the prospects for agreement and thus to enhance their domestic position. Note also that this generalization is supported by the exception: in 1977, both Carter and Schmidt were very strong domestically, leaving them free to express their incompatible preferences.

For two important reasons, this analysis of the role of international institutions in two-level diplomacy should be pursued. First, it suggests an interesting avenue for comparative inquiry: Do patterns of two-level politics vary across issue areas? Does the presence of a broader institutional investment affect the two-level dynamic? Second, the importance of institutions might help us predict the future pattern of agreement and disagreement in the Western Alliance. Given the collapse of the Soviet Union and the Warsaw Pact, the value of NATO as an institution has arguably declined. If so, the domestic political cost of disagreement within the Alliance has also declined, and one would predict a correlative decrease in the domestic value of successful Alliance management. As a result, leaders should prove less willing to accommodate the domestic situation of their partners, for the value of positive reverberation from compromise and agreement will now be lower.

Finally, it is worth noting that the iterative nature of the INF negotiation is one of the most important aspects of this case, both substantively and methodologically. As we have seen, many Level I actions were taken in response to Level II factors. These Level I actions in turn affected future domestic win-sets, which of course influenced subsequent Level I actions. One of the virtues of studying these four "sub-cases" is precisely that we can see the iterative dynamics of strategic action, domestic reverberation, and subsequent action. And of course, even in the absence of iterative reverberation, by analyzing a series of outcomes that include both agreement and disagreement we can draw stronger generalizations than would be achieved by studying a single case. Thus, by studying the four primary episodes in the decade of the INF controversy, we could compare the lack of domestic pressures on Schmidt and Carter in 1977 to their presence in later episodes, a comparison that led to the conclusion that the absence of domestic pressure leaves leaders free to negotiate on the basis of personal preferences, leading in this case to disagreement. In the subsequent cases, domestic pressures from constituents who were more favorable than their leaders to the Harmel formula of deterrence *and* detente forced the leaders toward mutual accommodation.

The iterative nature of the case also shows that targeting and reverberation can have outcomes that are unpredictable, for both the theoretician and the policy-maker. The most prominent example is the paradoxical (implicit) alliance between Ronald Reagan and the anti-nuclear forces in West Germany. Between 1981 and 1987, Reagan's rhetoric became increasingly anti-nuclear: in his announcement of the zero option; in his SDI project; and in his joint decision with Gorbachev at Reykjavik to eliminate all nuclear weapons. By most accounts, Reagan's rhetoric was a combination of conviction and strategic targeting. On the one hand, there seems no doubt that Reagan was sincere in his conviction that nuclear deterrence was fundamentally immoral, or that in any case the most appropriate approach to arms control was to do away with entire classes of weapons.

On the other hand, especially in the case of the INF zero proposal, there is no doubt that Reagan's advisers saw an opportunity to simultaneously ensure ratification of deployment and preclude an undesired agreement with the Soviets. As we have seen, however, the "anti-nuclear" alliance had fundamental implications. Because it reverberated so strongly with the German audience, it restricted Kohl's win-set when the 1987 double-zero treaty was negotiated, and in this the American government achieved its goal. Nonetheless, when Reagan was succeeded by George Bush in 1989, the anti-nuclear rhetoric exacted a price. Seeking to avoid yet another "third zero" on the shortest-range (tactical) nuclear weapons not covered by the treaty, the Bush Administration sought to secure European agreement on a modernization plan. Kohl and Genscher, however, had had enough. They first criticized the plan—causing yet another Alliance spat on INF—and later managed to delay the issue by securing American assent to the need for further study. Ultimately, with the collapse of the Warsaw Pact in 1989 and 1990, the Alliance agreed to drop the plan. Throughout this latest episode, it was clear that Kohl and Genscher saw no domestic win-set for modernization of shortest-range missiles. That narrow win-set was only the latest reverberation of Reagan's zero-option rhetoric of previous years.

I am grateful for the many comments and suggestions offered by the editors of this volume and by my fellow contributors. I also thank Jay P. Greene for research assistance and for an especially penetrating commentary on the chapter, and Robert Art, Jeffrey Boutwell, Ivo Daalder, Alexander George, David Spiro, and Gregory Treverton, who read the chapter and made suggestions for improving it.

NOTES

1. Unless otherwise cited, the chronological details of this case are drawn from the following works: Thomas Risse-Kappen, *The Zero Option: INF, West Germany, and Arms Control* (Boulder, Col.: Westview Press, 1988); Ivo Daalder, *The Nature and Practice of Flexible Response* (New York: Columbia University Press, 1991); Raymond Garthoff, "The NATO Decision on Theater Nuclear Forces,"

Political Science Quarterly 93 (1983): 317–346; Zbigniew Brzezinski, *Power and Principle: Memoirs of a National Security Adviser* (New York: Farrar Straus Giroux, 1985); Jeffrey Boutwell, *The German Security Dilemma* (Ithaca, N.Y.: Cornell University Press, 1990); and Helmut Schmidt, *Menschen und Mächte* (Berlin: Siedler Verlag, 1987).

2. Schmidt, *Menschen und Mächte*, p. 210.

3. Ibid., pp. 225–226.

4. Ibid., p. 230.

5. Brzezinski, *Power and Principle*, pp. 307–308.

6. Schmidt, *Menschen und Mächte*, p. 226.

7. Cited in Risse-Kappen, *The Zero Option*, p. 23.

8. Garthoff, "The NATO Decision," p. 204.

9. Jimmy Carter, *Keeping Faith: Memoirs of a President* (New York: Bantam Books, 1982), p. 235.

10. Schmidt, *Menschen und Mächte*, p. 232.

11. Risse-Kappen, *The Zero Option*, pp. 40, 47.

12. Brzezinski, *Power and Principle*, p. 308.

13. Described by the participants, in: Carter, *Keeping Faith*, pp. 535–539; Brzezinski, *Power and Principle*, pp. 309–311; and Schmidt, *Menschen und Mächte*, pp. 255–264.

14. The standard sources on American arms-control policy in this period are two books by Strobe Talbott: *Endgame: The Inside Story of SALT II* (New York: Harper and Row, 1979), and *Deadly Gambits: The Reagan Administration and the Stalemate in Nuclear Arms Control* (New York: Knopf, 1984).

15. For the best account of the development of the zero option, see Risse-Kappen, *The Zero Option*, pp. 67–84; the quote is from p. 66. The matter is also discussed by Schmidt, *Menschen und Mächte*, p. 333.

16. The initial Reagan "zero-option" proposal differed from the "double zero" that was later negotiated in the INF Treaty because it did not include shorter-range INF missiles.

17. Risse-Kappen, *The Zero Option*, pp. 93–95.

18. Ibid., pp. 116–150.

19. This description of the CDU's debate on double zero draws heavily on Risse-Kappen's excellent account, ibid., pp. 124–143.

20. The literature on this subject is voluminous. For a particularly insightful treatment, see Eugene Wittkopf, *Faces of Internationalism: Public Opinion and American Foreign Policy* (Durham, N.C.: Duke University Press, 1990). For a comparison of coalitions in the United States and Western Europe, see Richard C. Eichenberg, *Public Opinion and National Security in Western Europe* (Ithaca, N.Y.: Cornell University Press, 1989), pp. 209–216.

21. This figure is from the standard Gallup question which asks respondents if they approve or disapprove of the President's performance. The figure cited in the text is "net approval"—that is, the difference between approval and disapproval of the President. I am grateful to James Stimson for providing these data.

22. The figures on public support for defense spending are from the standard Gallup question, which asks if defense spending should be increased, de-

creased, or kept the same, taken from the *Gallup Reports*, various issues. Public opinion on the President's handling of Soviet policy is described in Miroslav Nincic, "The United States, the Soviet Union, and the Politics of Opposites," *World Politics* 40 (July 1988): 465. Other data on security issues during this period are drawn from William Schneider, "Peace and Strength: American Public Opinion on National Security," in Gregory Flynn and Hans Rattinger, eds., *The Public and Atlantic Defense* (Totowa, N.J.: Rowman and Allanheld, 1985), pp. 325, 328, 333.

23. Garthoff, "The NATO Decision," p. 200; and Talbott, *Endgame*, p. 142.

24. *Power and Principle*, pp. 560–561.

25. German polls on the INF issue are reproduced in Eichenberg, *Public Opinion*, chap. 4. Poll figures on the Chancellor's popularity and party strength are from a collection of Allensbach surveys in the Zentralarchiv für Empirische Sozialforschung, University of Cologne, ZA Study 800, to which I am grateful for providing the figures.

26. Data on public support for the freeze are taken from Schneider, "Peace and Strength," pp. 347–349. Other figures in this paragraph are taken from Nincic, "The Politics of Opposites," p. 461; and *Gallup Reports*, various issues.

27. For details on the increasing public and congressional pressure, see Talbott, *Deadly Gambits*, pp. 244, 247, 267, 300–307.

28. Ibid., p. 302.

29. Cited in ibid., p. 163.

30. Schmidt had long been associated with the Council on Foreign Relations, and had twice been a guest at Bohemian Grove. In his memoirs, he laments the decline in the influence of the American foreign policy establishment, with specific reference to the Carter and Reagan administrations: *Menschen und Mächte*, pp. 264–281.

31. Ibid., p. 255.

32. The switch in ministry positions is described in Risse-Kappen, *The Zero Option*, pp. 92–93.

33. On Dutch and Belgian actions, see ibid., pp. 102–103. A detailed description of the domestic debate in each country is provided by Leon Sigal, *Nuclear Forces in Europe: Enduring Dilemmas, Present Prospects* (Washington, D.C.: Brookings Institution, 1983).

34. On Britain, see Hugh Heclo and Aaron Wildavsky, *The Private Government of Public Money* (Berkeley: University of California Press, 1974).

35. For a more detailed analysis of the interaction of public opinion, electoral institutions, and executive culture on the INF issue, see Eichenberg, *Public Opinion*, pp. 235–241; on the more general interrelation of domestic factors and state structures, see Thomas Risse-Kappen, "Public Opinion, Domestic Structure, and Foreign Policy in Liberal Democracies," *World Politics* 43 (July 1991): 479–512.

3

The Political Economy of Security Agreements
The Linked Costs of Failure at Camp David

Janice Gross Stein

INTRODUCTION

At a summit meeting organized by Jimmy Carter at Camp David in September 1978, Egypt and Israel agreed to a framework for peace in the Middle East. To explain the process and substance of the agreement, this chapter addresses two separate but analytically linked questions. It assesses, first, the impact of enfranchised domestic players as well as international constraints on the negotiation of a security agreement in a hostile international environment. This formulation of the question conceives of leaders as constrained in their negotiating behavior by the interaction of strategic and domestic variables.

The chapter also looks more broadly at domestic economic and political variables. In this second line of inquiry, leaders are conceived as active rather than passive agents who are not only constrained by their domestic political economies and security environments but actively attempt to reconfigure them.[1] I contend that identifiable linkages between strategic threat and crises in domestic political economies shaped leaders' bargaining strategies. As the process of negotiation proceeded, and crises in their domestic political economies intensified, leaders "learned" and changed their preferences to focus on absolute loss. Driven primarily by their focus on loss—principally in Egypt, but in Israel and the United States as well—leaders attempted to reshape linked sets of domestic and security variables. This shared focus on the adverse consequences for security and their domestic political economies of a failure to agree explains the timing and substance of agreement between the two adversaries.[2]

This interpretation of agreement differs from that offered by "structural realists" in several important ways. It challenges the contention that the international structure determines state behavior and argues that through their behavior leaders shape that structure as well. It also disputes the proposition that agreement can be explained largely by the international distribution of capabilities. It argues instead for the inclusion of domestic economic and political as well as strategic variables in an interactive analysis that specifies the linkages leaders identify between these two sets of variables, the conditions under which they make these linkages, and their impact on the leaders' bargaining behavior. Finally, it disputes the Realist emphasis on relative gains and examines the impact of absolute loss on agreement.

The insufficiency of structural realist explanations is demonstrated by their inability to solve two major puzzles. From their analysis of the relative decline of Soviet and Egyptian capabilities in the region, Realists infer a shift in the pattern of Egyptian alignment, first to a tighter alliance with the Soviet Union and then away from the Soviet Union to the United States. Similarly, they deduce a pattern of greater dependence by Israel on the United States, given the relative decline in Israel's economic and military capabilities after the October War in 1973. Together, neo-realists argue, these two changes converged to create the structural preconditions for agreement between Egypt and Israel mediated by the United States.[3]

This analysis is insufficient in two important respects. It cannot explain the shift between the stalemate of November 1977, when President Sadat aborted the multilateral negotiations, and the agreement reached in September 1978. The relative changes in capabilities identified by Realist arguments were present when the parties began to explore the possibility of agreement in January 1977, but they failed to agree that autumn. Objective measures of relative capabilities, however, may not tap changes in leaders' estimates of their positional strength. If President Sadat, who at Camp David made most of the concessions necessary to achieve agreement, had become increasingly pessimistic about Egypt's capacity to manage its security crisis, then the agreement requires little explanation. Realist arguments would provide a parsimonious explanation, and the puzzle would virtually disappear. There is no evidence, however, that Egyptian subjective estimates of their relative capabilities varied. During this period, President Sadat did not display increasing pessimism about Egypt's military option; on the contrary, during the negotiation process he threatened to revert to belligerency.

Equally important, these arguments cannot explain the kind of agreement that was reached.[4] They cannot explain the substantial shift in President Sadat's acceptability-set, in comparison to his opening bargaining position, or the distribution of costs and benefits among the parties. If changes in the patterns of power and poles of alignment are insufficient to explain either agreement or its substance, we must look to other interpretations.

In this chapter I argue first that opening bargaining strategies can best be explained by the intersection of crises in domestic political economies and threats to security. Both Egypt and Israel, but particularly Egypt, faced domestic crises and threatening strategic uncertainties which were amplified by their simultaneity. At the onset of negotiations, the intersection of these two sets of factors defined the bargaining space of leaders in both Egypt and Israel. Particularly in Egypt, economic and political problems at home delimited the set of strategies that could be used internationally, while uncertainty about security defined the strategies used to manage domestic problems.

From this perspective, domestic and international factors are conceived as superimposed constraints in an additive game. The constraints which defined the bargaining space at the onset of negotiations, moreover, were not constants, but varied as the process of bargaining proceeded. Throughout the process, each leader played two games at a time—at the international table together, and at the domestic table at home. In large part because of the intensifying crisis in its domestic political economy, Egypt in particular could not use strategies at one table which compromised its strategy at the other. The strategies it developed had to be effective simultaneously at both the international and domestic tables.

Leaders not only saw overlapping constraints, but also identified synergistic linkages between the two sets of factors. Egypt in particular identified tangible benefits from a security agreement which would permit political and economic restructuring at home. Because leaders saw the issues as synergistically linked, any agreement that was reached at one table had consequences for the other.[5] Their expectation of synergy created not an additive but an interactive game which defined their bargaining strategies.

Finally, in this chapter I argue that even though Egypt and Israel were adversaries, the substance of the agreement can best be explained by their growing focus primarily on absolute loss, defined through the linkages between domestic and security factors. I suggest further that the risk propensities of leaders changed as crises in their domestic political economies intensified and the bargaining process imposed costs on the participants over time. At the point of agreement, estimates of absolute loss were in large part a function of high estimates of the linked political, economic, and security costs of no-agreement.

THE AGREEMENT AT CAMP DAVID

On September 17, 1978, at Camp David, Prime Minister Menahem Begin of Israel and President Anwar el-Sadat of Egypt signed a two-part agreement on a framework for peace in the Middle East. They agreed to conclude within three months a bilateral peace treaty which would require Israel to withdraw completely from the Sinai Peninsula, with appropriate security arrangements, and Egypt to establish full diplomatic relations with Israel. They also agreed to a framework for autonomy on the West Bank and the Gaza Strip; the creation of a self-governing authority by Israel, Egypt, Jordan, and mutually acceptable representatives of the Palestinians; the withdrawal of Israel's military forces to specified security locations; and a transitional period of five years to determine the final status of the West Bank and Gaza. Final negotiations on the peace treaty between Egypt and Israel were not completed until March 26, 1979, when a treaty was signed at the White House. The first phase of the negotiations on autonomy for the West Bank and Gaza ended inconclusively, and this part of the agreement was never implemented.

This chapter examines only the agreement at Camp David and its subsequent ratification by the People's Assembly in Cairo and the Knesset in Jerusalem. I contend that, in large part because both leaders were confident of their capacity to restructure or circumvent domestic opposition, neither shaped his bargaining strategy at Camp David to meet the anticipated opposition of those within domestic political institutions who had to ratify the agreement.

MODELING THE PROCESS OF BARGAINING AND AGREEMENT

The bargaining process that led to Camp David stretched over a period of 20 months, and can be divided into two analytically distinct phases. A multilateral process began soon after President Carter took office in January 1977 and included Israel, Egypt, Jordan, Saudi Arabia, Syria, the Palestine Liberation Organization (PLO), the Soviet Union, and the United States. When the parties got to the table at Camp David, only the United States, Egypt, and Israel remained. Indeed, one of the principal functions of the process over time was to eliminate those parties who threatened to obstruct a negotiated agreement.[6] Two critical points in this process can be identified: no-agreement in November 1977, when the multilateral search for a comprehensive settlement of the Arab-Israel conflict failed; and agreement in September 1978, when Egypt and Israel agreed to a bilateral settlement and a framework for peace in the Middle East.

Modeling the process that led to agreement at Camp David is complicated by the presence of a powerful and active third party, the United States, which also played simultaneously at an international and domestic table. Bargaining can be conceived as a multilateral process or, more properly, as two simultaneous two-level games: one between Israel and the United States, and the second between Egypt and the United States.

There was very little direct negotiation between Israel and Egypt at Camp David or, with the exception of the brief period between November 1977 and January 1978, in the 20-month process preceding the meeting. Consequently, win-sets in the United States were relevant at both tables.[7]

Although the domestic strategies of Israeli and Egyptian leaders were directly relevant to their negotiations at the table with the United States, each set of leaders paid attention to the domestic politics that shaped strategy at the other table, where simultaneous negotiations were ongoing. In modeling the agreement at Camp David, it is important to capture the simultaneous linkages across and under the two sets of tables.

This chapter maps the security and domestic constraints at the outset of negotiations, traces their impact through to these two critical points, and explores the strategies leaders in Egypt and Israel designed to address the two sets of constraints simultaneously. It also examines the synergistic linkages leaders identified, and their attempts to reshape these constraints, both domestic and international, to facilitate agreements that would feed back to ameliorate domestic crises and create new coalitions at home and abroad.

THE STRUCTURE OF DOMESTIC AND SECURITY INTERESTS:
OPENING BARGAINING POSITIONS

When President Sadat considered going to the table in January 1977, he sought a comprehensive but phased settlement of the Arab-Israeli conflict. Although he gave primacy to a full withdrawal of Israel's forces from the Sinai, a second critical minimum was agreement on the general principles of the rights of the Palestinians to self-determination and Israel's commitment to withdraw from Arab territories captured in 1967. These critical minima were consistent with Egypt's definition of its domestic, regional, and international interests and strategies.

Even before President Nasser's death in 1970, Egypt began tentative experiments with an open-door investment policy in order to address the growing crisis in the economy, which was badly exacerbated by the punishing defense expenditures for preparations to regain the territory lost in the 1967 war. Under President Sadat, Egypt first tightened its alignment with the Soviet Union in an effort to secure additional economic and military resources, but by 1972 ruptured this relationship and made tentative overtures to the United States. In 1973, student and worker demonstrations, rapidly falling foreign-exchange reserves, and pessimism about the prospects of diplomacy mediated by the United States converged to persuade President Sadat that the only alternative to an intolerable economic and strategic status quo was a limited war with Israel.[8]

In the aftermath of the politically successful but militarily disastrous war in 1973, Egypt reoriented its strategies at home and abroad. In April 1974, the regime circulated the October Working Paper, which defined the public sector as necessary but inefficient and gave new importance to the role of the private sector.[9] The new economic strategy of quasi-liberal experimentation, *al-infitah al-iqtisadi*, was consistent with Sadat's regional strategy: closer reliance on Arab oil-producing states and an end to confrontation with traditional regimes. Sadat looked to the oil-producing states to provide the capital and investment to push the Egyptian economy forward.

Political liberalization was more timid. The October Working Paper reaffirmed the regime's commitment to limited liberalization, particularly to an end to the capricious exercise of power. In July 1975 the National Conference of the Arab Socialist Union, the only official authorized party, sanctioned the formation of "platforms" which would give voice to competing political tendencies within the party.[10] On March 15, 1976, President Sadat endorsed the formation of three fixed platforms, within the limits of the alliance of working forces which reserved 50 percent of the seats for workers and peasants.

The three platforms began to prepare for the first comparatively free legislative elections, quickly scheduled for the autumn of 1976. The results of the election in November changed little in the political configuration. The center scored an overwhelming victory: it won 80 percent of the seats and crushed the opposition.[11] The aggregate vote for the center, however, masked important socio-political weaknesses and sources of opposition to the regime. The industrial areas and the public-sector working class, disadvantaged by the policy of economic liberalization, represented a relatively large negative vote for the regime; the more industrial the area, the lower was the vote for the center.[12]

Egypt's international strategy was consistent with its strategy of limited economic and political liberalization at home and rapprochement with traditional oil-producing states in the region. President Sadat relied heavily on the United States to mediate between Egypt and Israel to secure the withdrawal of Israel's forces from the territories it had occupied in 1967. In the years following the October War, Sadat had expanded the gains he had made through a process of phased disengagement with Israel and was reluctant to risk these limited gains in renewed warfare. He was persuaded that the intersecting security and economic crises Egypt faced could be resolved only if the United States were to compel Israel to withdraw from the territories it had occupied in 1967. Any agreement would have to go beyond the Sinai to include the other Arab belligerents if Egypt were to retain the support of the oil-producing states for its domestic economic needs.

In the wake of the October War, international, regional, and domestic economic strategies were complementary: Egyptian labor plus Arab capital and Western technology would ameliorate the growing crisis at home, and the United States would ameliorate the security crisis which imperiled foreign investment and drained the economy through the high level of defense spending. Not only were the three strategies complementary, they were interdependent: liberalization of the economy and receptivity to investment from Arab oil-producers made Egypt more attractive to the United States as a regional partner, and reliance on the United States to resolve the Arab-Israeli conflict made Egypt more attractive to conservative oil-rich economies.

Israel's opening bargaining position was substantially different from that of Egypt. Prime Minister Yitzhak Rabin sought as a critical minimum a bilateral peace treaty with Egypt, with full normalization of relations and complete demilitarization of the Sinai Peninsula in return for a phased withdrawal. On the future of Gaza and the West Bank, Rabin had very limited flexibility: in April 1974, he had assured factions within his own party as well as his coalition partners that a national referendum would be held when the status of the West Bank was negotiated. Consequently, Rabin sought to minimize any linkage between the two sets of issues. Israel's opening bargaining strategy was consistent with intersecting domestic, regional, and international constraints.

Israel faced an intensifying economic and political crisis in early 1977. Defense spending had grown rapidly in the wake of the October War, the balance-of-payments deficit had soared, and inflationary pressures were acute, particularly among the urban poor who were the principal supporters of the leading opposition party, the Likud, led by Menahem Begin.[13] The Labor Party, the pivotal party in all Israel's coalition governments since the creation of the state, had been badly discredited by its poor performance in the opening hours of the October War. The government in office during the war had resigned and was replaced by a weak and badly divided government led by Yitzhak Rabin, a former Chief of Staff whose roots within the party were shallow. Prime Minister Rabin had little authority over his cabinet and was constantly subjected to challenge by his colleagues who had independent bases of support within the Labor Party. In Israel, in early 1977, a looming economic crisis was exacerbated by an acutely weak political leadership.

Rabin favored a bilateral phased agreement with Egypt for regional as well as domestic reasons. Israel's military leadership and some of its civilian leaders were now persuaded that deterrence, based on superior military capabilities, was necessary but insufficient to prevent another war. A necessary complement to deterrence was an agreement with Egypt that would fracture the Arab coalition by removing Egypt as a potential participant in a future round. Israel's regional and domestic strategies were consistent: the Prime Minister hoped to reduce the threat to Israel's security by fracturing the Arab coalition through bilateral agreement with Egypt and, in the context of a reduced threat, control defense spending and inflation and reduce the soaring deficits.

The United States was critical to the success of both strategies. It had played an essential role in brokering two disengagement agreements between Israel and Egypt in the past three years. In order to induce the parties to cooperate, the United States had functioned as monitor, insurer, and guarantor, and as financier through the extensive side-payments it had made to Israel in both cases.[14] Prime Minister Rabin was persuaded that without extensive American involvement, agreement between Egypt and Israel was unlikely.

From the outset, President Carter was deeply committed to a comprehensive settlement of the Arab-Israel conflict in all its aspects. This strategy was consistent with international and regional American interests and domestic economic interests, but only in part with important political interests. Carter engaged to avoid an anticipated crisis rather than to manage an existing one. He was deeply concerned about the adverse economic and strategic consequences of renewed war in the Middle East and attached high priority to development of a comprehensive energy policy at home.[15]

However, the domestic constituency of the President was heterogeneous. His advisers and important senior bureaucrats favored a comprehensive settlement, while many in the corporate sector wanted an active and vigorous attempt by the President to prevent another war, with all its anticipated consequences. The American Jewish community, however, with close links to the Congress, supported only a settlement that would be acceptable to Israel's leaders. The push toward a comprehensive settlement was consistent with international, regional, economic, and some but not all domestic interests in the United States.

THE FAILURE TO AGREE: NOVEMBER 1977

These opening positions in January 1977 shaped the bargaining strategies of the United States with both Egypt and Israel, as well as with other regional players, as Washington struggled to organize, jointly with the Soviet Union, a multilateral conference in Geneva to negotiate a comprehensive settlement of the Arab-Israeli conflict. That effort ended when President Sadat aborted the process by deciding unilaterally to travel to Jerusalem to address Israel's Knesset. Why did Sadat terminate the multilateral process?

Two sets of variables are critical to the explanation. First, in Egypt the domestic political and economic crisis intensified in the first nine months of 1977, shortening the time available for a negotiated agreement. On the night of January 17, official prices on subsidized commodities were increased by administrative decision, without consultation, debate, or vote by the Assembly.[16] Immediately, Egypt experienced its worst riots in 25 years: from Aswan to Alexandria, workers in the urban and industrial areas demonstrated with the police and government as their primary target; the army was forced to fire on demonstrators, and a curfew was imposed. Although the increased cost of basic commodities was the spark, the political weakness of the regime among urban residents, industrial workers, and public-sector employees, along with the artificially large majority of the center and complaints about the fairness of the election, combined to produce an acute political crisis.

President Sadat quickly attempted to shore up the legitimacy of his regime by organizing a nationwide referendum. At the same time, the experiment in political liberalization contracted as Sadat attacked the left, which he held responsible for the riots, and rehabilitated the right as a counterweight.[17] The changing political and economic context made even more imperative an agreement brokered by the United States and exclusion of the Soviet Union from the diplomatic process.

Second, and closely related, the preliminary process of negotiation reduced uncertainty about the bargaining ranges of important participants and, in so doing, made clear to President Sadat the obstacles to a comprehensive multilateral settlement. He identified important obstacles both among his Arab allies and in the domestic politics of Israel and the United States. At the same time, participation in the process of negotiation imposed costs and further elevated the losses of no-agreement to Egypt. Sadat decided in consequence that a dramatic change in strategy was necessary both to remove the constraints imposed by his Arab allies and to enlarge the domestic win-sets of the newly elected Prime Minister of Israel, Menahem Begin, and President Carter, through what Putnam calls "suasive reverberation."

As the process of consultation to prepare the Geneva Conference proceeded, Sadat became increasingly convinced that a unified Arab delegation would obstruct progress and that Syria would exercise a unitary veto on a settlement.[18] To force the pace of negotiation, Sadat could see no alternative but to break free of the constraints imposed by his Arab allies and substitute himself as the "agent" of Arab interests.

There were, of course, potential costs regionally to such a dramatic shift in strategy. Foremost among them was a decline in capital investment and aid from the oil-producing countries. But Arab aid to Egypt, which had reached a peak of 1,264 million dollars in 1974 in the aftermath of the October War, had declined to 625 million dollars in 1976.[19]

The economy continued to deteriorate rapidly in 1977. In the absence of a settlement, defense expenditures remained at approximately 50 percent of total GNP, and Egypt continued to forgo the estimated one billion dollars of revenue from the oil fields in the Sinai. Egypt desperately needed a resolution to the security crisis; only if this was resolved would Egypt receive the material, factories, and food, quickly and cheaply on predictable terms, which were needed to revitalize the economy. Only the United States could meet these needs. The cost of the loss of Arab support was dwarfed by the losses imposed by the absence of an agreement.

A STRATEGY OF "SUASIVE REVERBERATION"

During the process of preliminary bargaining, Sadat had also learned a great deal more about the domestic obstacles to an agreement in Israel and the United States. In May, elections in Israel resulted in the formation of a narrow coalition government led, for the first time in Israel's history, by the Likud Party and Menahem Begin.[20] In the past, Likud had been consistently unwilling to consider any territorial concessions on the West Bank.

In considering a dramatic personal address to Israel's Knesset, Sadat hoped to create a constituency for negotiation with Egypt in Israel and expand Begin's win-set. The Egyptian President also hoped to influence American public opinion and help President Carter compensate for his self-professed political weakness.[21] Although the decision met with considerable opposition from Sadat's senior advisers in Cairo, the President had considerable autonomy as a result of the deep divisions among institutional interests.[22] President Sadat deliberately chose a strategy designed to reverberate in Israel and the United States.

Sadat's strategy of "suasive reverberation" succeeded brilliantly.[23] Egyptian demands for withdrawal from captured Arab territory were unchanged, but Israel's leaders and public paid attention to the deed rather than to the words. In large part through this single, dramatic act, Sadat changed Israel's incentives to negotiate. Why did the strategy succeed in reshaping domestic constraints in Israel?

First, the initiative was irreversible: once the President of Egypt traveled to Jerusalem, he could not undo the deed. Because it could not be reversed, the action was treated as a valid indicator of Egyptian intentions rather than as a signal that could be manipulated.[24] Israel's leadership and public recognized the irreversibility of the action and, consequently, gave it great weight.

Second, the substantial political cost to President Sadat of breaking the long-standing Arab taboo of not treating directly with Israel was also apparent to Israel's leaders. Dissension within the Egyptian government was pronounced, and a tidal wave of criticism from the Arab world engulfed the Egyptian leader. Israel's leaders reasoned that Egypt's President would not incur such heavy costs were he not sincere.[25]

Third, Sadat's arrival in Jerusalem challenged the most important set of beliefs about Arab goals among Israel's leadership and public. A broad cross section of Israelis had assumed that Arab leaders were unrelentingly hostile, so much so that they were unprepared to meet Israel's leaders face-to-face. Once these core beliefs were shaken, it became easier for Israelis to revise associated assumptions and expectations.

Fourth, President Sadat spoke over the heads of Israel's leadership directly to Israel's public and, indeed, to the American public. With his flair for the dramatic, he created the psychological and political symbols which would mobilize public opinion to press their more cautious and restrained leaders. In so doing, he removed constraints on leaders in Israel and the United States and created political inducements to action. Sadat's action reverberated through multiple audiences and multiple constituencies.

When the bargaining resumed in January 1988, the number of participants was reduced to three, the constraint of the Arab coalition was eliminated, and new constituencies in Israel were mobilized and prepared to press their leaders to reach an agreement. In the United States, some of the domestic constraints operating on President Carter had been reduced and his win-set correspondingly enlarged.

CAMP DAVID: THE ABSOLUTE COSTS OF NO-AGREEMENT

The rapidly intensifying political and economic crisis in Egypt; the structure of the bargaining process, in which the future relationship with the United States had become one of if not the most important assets at stake for both Egypt and Israel; and the costs already invested in the negotiations, in the context of the changed configurations of domestic interests in both Israel and the United States, together led leaders in the three countries, and particularly in Egypt, to focus on the absolute and linked costs of no-agreement. This focus explains the timing and the substance of the agreement at Camp David.

By the time Sadat, Begin, and Carter arrived at Camp David, the boundaries of the negotiation had been narrowed and the agenda delimited. The process of preliminary bargaining had eliminated a comprehensive settlement of the Arab-Israeli conflict from the agenda.[26] At issue were a bilateral peace treaty between Egypt and Israel, with normalization of relations; the removal of Israel's settlements from the Sinai; the scope of the demilitarization of the Sinai Peninsula; an agreement on the general principle of the right of the Palestinians to self-determination; and the linkage between normalization and the future of the Palestinians.[27] On almost all the specific issues on the table, the final agreement at Camp David was closer to Israel's than to Egypt's preferences.[28] What explains this outcome?

In the months that followed President Sadat's visit to Jerusalem, the political and economic situation deteriorated further.[29] To counter the growing political power of the religious right, Sadat encouraged the resurgence of the nationalist Wafd Party, which strongly supported the return of the Sinai. The crisis in the Egyptian economy was also apparent by the spring of 1978. The IMF refused to approve long-term investment in Egypt, because of increased budget deficits, and demanded fundamental economic reforms. Sadat responded to the intensifying economic and political crisis with wide-scale repression and yet another attempt at political restructuring.[30] He attempted to strengthen the political weight of the technocratic and managerial leadership to balance the growing political effectiveness of the opposition to a peace treaty within established institutions, particularly the military, and to counter the appeal of the religious right and the left.[31]

It can be argued that the growth of opposition from both the left and the right, and their shared opposition to an agreement with Israel, narrowed Sadat's win-set. Given the centralization of power in the presidency, however, the impact of growing opposition was rather to widen President Sadat's acceptability-set—the terms he was prepared to accept in order to get an agreement. As Ismail Fahmy, the former Foreign Minister noted, "If you disagreed with Sadat, you collapsed."[32] The President controlled opposition through dismissal and repression, and through the rotation of senior political leaders to prevent the coalescence of opposition. At the same time, the growing economic crisis dramatically increased the economic and political costs of failure. Whereas President Sadat had considered an agreement on the Sinai and a resolution of Egypt's security crisis merely desirable at the outset of negotiations in January 1977, by the summer of 1978 agreement was imperative. Failure to reach an agreement would not only shift Egyptian strategy away from a negotiated agreement and toward an unwanted war, it would defeat economic strategy at home.[33] At Camp David, Sadat focused overwhelmingly on the absolute and linked costs of failure.[34]

Although the deterioration of Israel's political economy was not as dramatic, it was nevertheless considerable. In the summer of 1977, the new Likud government had introduced a strategy of economic liberalization, based on a laissez-faire monetary policy designed to stimulate exports and encourage foreign investment. The government allowed the pound to find its own level in foreign-exchange markets, eliminated currency controls, and drastically reduced subsidies for exports and basic commodities. By the spring of 1978, exports and foreign investment had increased. Nevertheless, because the government did not accompany its strategy of economic liberalization with a reduction in government spending, the rate of inflation increased dramatically.[35] Public opinion polls suggested that the issue of inflation was now more important to the voters than any security issue.

Compounding the absolute costs of failure for both Egypt and Israel was the bargaining structure at Camp David. After the first day, the process of negotiation was almost exclusively bilateral, between the United States and either Egypt or Israel. This pattern accurately reflected the underlying structure of the relationship among the three participants: Egypt and Israel both competed for the support and resources of the United States. The high value both sides attached to the support of the United States was partly a function of the structure of bargaining, but more fundamentally it reflected the importance of the United States to both their political economies and their security.

American diplomatic, military, and economic support was essential to Israel because of its international isolation and its dependence on American aid.[36] Prime Minister Begin's principal constraint was not in Israel but in the White House. Egypt's future relationship with the United States was even more central to Sadat's calculations. President Sadat placed a very high valuation on American support in his estimate of absolute loss if no agreement were reached.[37] Tahseen Bashir, his spokesman, recalled that immediately prior to his departure from Cairo to Camp David Sadat anticipated failure. The President was pessimistic about Israel's willingness to make concessions on the Palestinian issue and consequently prepared Egyptian officials for a massive information campaign that would hold Israel responsible for the failure to reach an agreement.[38] On the eleventh day at Camp David, however, when the Egyptian President threatened to end the negotiations, Carter warned Sadat that if he left, "It will mean an end first of all to the relationship between the United States and Egypt."[39] The support of the United States was essential to Egypt to achieve its domestic and security objectives: the strategy of economic liberalization depended critically on American aid, investment, and technology transfer, and resolution of the crisis with Israel depended on the active participation and commitment of the United States. It was the threat of these linked losses if no agreement were reached that persuaded Sadat to broaden his acceptability-set and accept the proposed agreement on the West Bank and the Gaza Strip.

The political costs of the extensive preliminary bargaining that had preceded Camp David added to the already high estimates of loss in

Egypt and Israel, and led President Carter to focus on the costs of failure. Sadat had already paid a heavy price among his Arab allies for his participation in the negotiations. In Israel, one of the important parties in the governing coalition had fractured, in large part over the slow pace of the negotiation process, and a vigorous peace movement in Israel was organizing large public demonstrations.[40] Sadat's strategy of "suasive reverberation" had generated considerable political pressure within Israel for an agreement.

The prospect of domestic political loss was most salient, however, for President Carter, as he considered his alternatives in the face of the ongoing stalemate between Egypt and Israel in the summer of 1978. Carter had invested heavily, both in time and in political capital, with little visible return, and was willing to risk a great deal to avoid the estimated high costs of a failure to agree. Agreement of any kind was a political necessity.[41] On July 30, Carter made the high-risk decision to invite Begin and Sadat to a summit meeting at Camp David. Driven by the high costs of failure, Carter abandoned his own preferences for an agreement and enlarged his acceptability-set to include any agreement that was acceptable to the two leaders from the Middle East. The terms of the agreement were no longer important; any agreement acceptable to the two leaders would be broadly acceptable to the multiple constituencies in the United States. In so broadening his acceptability-set, President Carter removed the constraints imposed by the heterogeneity of his constituency.

At Camp David, all three leaders focused on absolute loss, although to varying degrees. Although it is impossible analytically to measure the relative magnitudes of estimates of absolute loss across the three leaders, intuitively the evidence suggests a rank ordering of Sadat, then Carter, and finally Begin. Sadat focused overwhelmingly on the costs of a failure to agree and the attendant loss of American support; such a loss would compromise his fundamental economic, political, and security objectives. Carter focused heavily on the adverse political consequences of no-agreement, which were magnified by the costs of the heavy political investment in the preceding 18 months. Begin, whose estimate of the adverse domestic political consequences of failure was considerably lower, nevertheless focused on the absolute strategic and economic costs to Israel's relationship with the United States if Israel were held responsible for the failure to agree. At Camp David, this shared focus on the losses that flowed from synergistic linkages transcended almost all of the specifics on the table and drove the process of negotiation through the obstacles to agreement. The relative magnitude of emphasis on absolute loss explains why Sadat and Carter moved to meet the critical minima set by Begin.

RATIFICATION OF THE AGREEMENT:
THE MANIPULATION OF DOMESTIC CONSTRAINTS

There was important opposition to the Camp David agreements within both Egypt and Israel. President Sadat managed the process of ratification by restructuring yet again the central elements within the government that he appointed, and Prime Minister Begin adroitly manipulated the procedures of ratification to circumvent the opposition within his own party.

In Egypt, the anticipated opposition to the agreement from the Ikhwan, former members of the Free Officers, Nasserites, and the left materialized immediately. In the People's Assembly, members of professional syndicates and industrial leaders with close ties to the military worried about the economic consequences of isolation from the Arab world. To neutralize the opposition, President Sadat appointed Mustapha Kamil, the former Secretary of the Arab Socialist Union (ASU) and a prominent member of the technocratic elite, as Prime Minister, and to prevent the possibility of a cohesive government that could unite against the President in the future, dismissed Kamil's close ally, Muhammad Abd el-Ghani Gamassy, as Minister of War. As his replacement, Sadat chose Kamal Hassan Ali, a well-known officer and a friend of Mubarak. In so doing, the President bolstered morale and support for the peace process within the military.[42]

President Sadat moved swiftly to reap the benefit of political restructuring. He announced the appointment of Khalil as Prime Minister on October 2, defended the Camp David agreement to the People's Assembly the next day, and swore in the new cabinet on October 5. The new cabinet formally approved the agreement on October 10, and the People's Assembly did so four days later.

The ratification of the agreement in Israel was effected through a similar strategy, despite the fundamental differences between the two political systems. In Israel's system of proportional representation, effective opposition frequently comes from within the coalition, and even more from well-organized factions within the pivotal party in the coalition, rather than from the official opposition. Within the Likud, however, smaller parties and factions within the pivotal party in the coalition, Herut, were less well institutionalized, with fewer resources and weaker relationships to independent clienteles than their counterparts in the Labor coalition. This was a function both of their historic evolution and of their very recent ascension to power.[43] To counter the far more serious opposition from factions within Herut, Begin decided to depart from normal political practice and refused to submit the agreement to Herut institutions for approval.

The Prime Minister made ratification of the Camp David agreements a national rather than a party issue.[44] At the same time, he released his coalition members from normal party discipline in the voting in the Knesset. In so doing, he simultaneously neutralized some of the opposition from party interests and further emphasized the national consequences of the decision. Begin correctly anticipated the support of the Labor opposition, even though some of its members considered the security provisions in the Sinai inadequate and preferred territorial concessions on the West Bank to the proposed arrangements for autonomy, which they feared would be the precursor to an independent state. Nevertheless, they too faced an issue of overriding national importance.

To assure ratification of the agreement, Begin bypassed his party's political caucus as well as the influential Foreign Affairs and Security Committee of the Knesset, accelerated cabinet consideration, and requested that the Knesset schedule an early debate. After eight hours of acrimonious debate, the cabinet approved the agreement by a vote of 11 to 2, with 4 abstentions, and on September 27, after a protracted and bitter debate, the Knesset approved the agreement by a vote of 89 to 19, with 17 abstentions.

Both Sadat and Begin, for different reasons, were confident of their capacity to manipulate domestic coalitions and institutions. The highly centralized political system in Egypt made a strategy of political manipulation relatively easy for Sadat. Begin exercised strong although not complete control of his party and correctly anticipated that the formal opposition would counter the opposition within his party. By denying his party its unofficial but traditional role, he transformed approval of the agreement into a nonpartisan national issue and assured ratification. In large part because both were confident of their capacity to restructure or circumvent domestic opposition, neither leader shaped his bargaining strategy at Camp David to meet the anticipated opposition of those within domestic political institutions who had to ratify the agreement.

CONCLUSION

Analysis of the structures and strategies that led to agreement at Camp David is suggestive of two sets of related propositions. The first set examines the impact of win-sets on the negotiation of security issues in a hostile international environment. Analysis of this case suggests that strongly autonomous leaders are unlikely to be constrained in their negotiating behavior by their domestic win-sets, even when formal ratification of an agreement is required. Both Sadat and Begin were confident, correctly so, of their capacity to expand the size of their win-sets through manipulation of domestic coalitions and procedures. They were confident in large part because of their autonomy which derived either from a highly centralized political system or from undisputed authority as a party leader. President Carter was far less autonomous than his two counterparts, even though he faced no formal ratification process. Only in his case can the broadening of his acceptability-set be traced directly to the impact of the constraints imposed by a heterogeneous constituency on a leader with low autonomy.

A second, somewhat unexpected, observation is that leaders were unable to use their win-sets as a bargaining resource. President Carter, for example, explicitly tried to manipulate the narrowness of his win-set to extract concessions from Egypt and Israel. Israeli Foreign Minister Dayan exploited the attempt to gain concessions from Carter; and President Sadat, concluding that Carter was embattled and weak, aborted the preferred American strategy of negotiation.[45] When President Sadat attempted to increase his bargaining advantage by referring to the concerted opposition among Egyptian officials to an agreement with Israel, Prime Minister Begin dismissed this contention as implausible, given Sadat's autonomy and authority. In this case, neither the size of the win-set nor the scope of autonomy appear to be systematically related to bargaining advantage.

Finally, although leaders did not succeed in manipulating their own win-sets as bargaining resources, they did succeed in manipulating the domestic win-sets of the others. As we saw, during the process of bargaining that preceded Camp David, President Sadat learned a greater deal about the domestic constraints in the United States and Israel and, through a strategy of "suasive reverberation," successfully reshaped the win-sets of the other two leaders. In so doing, he increased the incentives of Israel's leaders to reach agreement with Egypt, as well as the political costs of failure, and eased the political process of ratification. Insofar as the strategy of suasive reverberation simultaneously expanded win-sets and increased the political costs of failure in both the United States and Israel, it contributed significantly to agreement.

The second set of propositions defines domestic variables more broadly and relates crises in the domestic political economy to leaders' risk-propensities and strategic behavior in a hostile international environment. Analysis of this case points to the positive relationship between the intensifying crisis in the Egyptian political economy, an unstable and threatening security environment, and agreement. It suggests that in a context of uncertainty about security and a political-economic crisis, a bias toward agreement on security issues in a hostile international environment is partly a function of the capacity of an agreement on security to effect structural transformations at home.

In this case, Egyptian behavior is best fitted to this proposition and indeed is better fitted over time as the negotiations proceeded. An agreement became more imperative over time because of Egyptian expectations of synergistic linkages between the agreement and their capacity to reconfigure their domestic political economy through a strategy of economic and political liberalization. The proposition fits less well with Israel's behavior only in one respect: Israel's strategy of economic liberalization was somewhat less ambitious in its implications for the reconfiguration of their domestic political economy. Nevertheless, the adverse economic consequences which they anticipated from a failure to agree would have badly compromised a strategy already in difficulty.

The argument needs an important qualification. Leaders' preferred strategies of domestic reconfiguration may critically affect their assessment of synergistic linkages. In the 1960s, when Egyptian leaders attempted to reconfigure their political economy in a hierarchical command structure, even though they depended heavily on international resources to effect that transformation, they were strongly biased against agreement and chose to manage their security crisis through confrontation. It was only when Egypt turned toward a strategy of economic and political liberalization that its leaders focused on the importance of reducing the intensity of the security crisis, as a prerequisite to successful liberalization, and on the linked costs of no-agreement.

The argument depends on specification of the causal sequence of domestic and security variables in the process toward agreement. It gives primacy to political and economic variables, broadly defined, and their impact on behavior on security issues. It is extraordinarily difficult, however, to disentangle the impact of the two sets of variables when security and domestic crises intersected, as they did in the case of Egypt. Two indirect streams of evidence are suggestive, however, about the sequencing of domestic and security variables in this process toward agreement.

Indirectly, there is no evidence of covariation between President Sadat's estimate of Egyptian military capabilities from 1977 through to Camp David and his acceptability-set. After the October War, Sadat began seriously to explore agreement as an alternative to war, to resolve the crisis with Israel as well as to ameliorate the economic crisis at home. The lessons learned from the last war, however, can be treated as a constant rather than a variable throughout the period under analysis, when Sadat's acceptability-set varied substantially. Moreover, from the onset of negotiations through to their conclusion, Egyptian military capabilities did not decline nor did President Sadat display increased pessimism about Egypt's military option. The crisis in Egypt's political economy, however, did intensify dramatically during the process of negotiation.

More directly relevant, in both cases of domestic reconfiguration in

Egypt—first toward a command economy in the 1960s and then toward a liberalized political economy in the 1970s—efforts at domestic restructuring preceded the changes in behavior on security issues.[46] If this is indeed the correct sequencing, the *kind* of domestic reconfiguration Egyptian leaders attempted appears, at least indirectly, to have shaped their evaluation of alternative strategies of conflict management. It did so by delimiting the kinds of international strategies that would create the synergistic linkages they needed at home.

The causal path between domestic and security variables cannot be established with confidence on the basis of this kind of evidence. With further research, it may be possible to specify relationships among different patterns of domestic reconfiguration, anticipated synergistic linkages with strategies of conflict management in a hostile international environment, and a bias against or toward agreement on security issues. Evidence from this case suggests, on the one hand, that attempts at economic and political liberalization were accompanied by the anticipation of synergistic linkage and a bias toward the reduction of an intense conflict with an adversary. Attempts to reconfigure the political economy within a command structure, on the other hand, were associated with a bias toward confrontation of an adversary.

Analysis of this case suggests as well that the synergistic linkages between agreement and domestic reconfiguration were largely independent of the terms of agreement at the international table. Egyptian leaders most closely reflected this expectation, although Israel's leaders did so as well. Put bluntly, Egyptian and Israeli leaders anticipated synergistic linkages from the *fact* of, rather than the terms of, the agreement at Camp David. This was so in large part because of the special role of the United States as monitor, guarantor, insurer, and financier of any agreement that would emerge from Camp David. It was American economic aid, investment, and technology that were critical to the reshaping of the Egyptian economy and the stabilization of the Israeli economy.

Analysis of this case suggests that anticipation of synergistic linkages that derive from the fact of rather than the terms of agreement is most likely to occur when security and domestic crises intersect. To the extent that we can generalize from this case, it appears that insofar as threats to security constrain domestic reconfiguration in a deteriorating political economy, agreement which reduces uncertainties about security in a hostile environment will tend to dominate the terms of the agreement.

Examination of the process of agreement at Camp David calls for attention to the impact of a broadly defined set of interactive economic, political, and security variables. Analysis of these variables must include not only their constraining impact on leaders' strategies but also leaders' attempts to reconfigure both the domestic and the security arena and the linkages they identify across the international-domestic divide. It suggests further that when leaders identify synergistic linkages between security and their domestic political economies, issues off the security table will be far more important than those on the table in determining the likelihood of agreements about security.

———————————

I would like to acknowledge the generous support of the United States Institute of Peace, the Peace and Security Competition Fund of the Canadian Institute for International Peace and Security, and the Center for International Studies at the University of Toronto in the research and writing of this chapter. The views expressed are only my own.

NOTES

1. This assumption draws from transformational models in the agent-structure debate in theories of social action. The complexities of the argument are beyond the scope of this chapter, but the fundamental assumption of transformational models is germane: social action is the product of both structural and agential forces. These models view structure as a means to rather than as a constraint on action. See Roy Baskhar, *The Possibility of Naturalism* (Atlantic Highlands, N.J.: Humanities Press, 1979); Anthony Giddens, *Profiles and Critiques in Social Theory* (Berkeley: University of California Press, 1983), esp. chap. 3; Alexander Wendt, "The Agent-Structure Problem in International Relations Theory," *International Organization* 41 (Summer 1987): 335–370; and David Dessler, "What's at Stake in the Agent-Structure Debate?" *International Organization* 43 (Summer 1989): 441–474.

2. For a more detailed examination of the impact of loss aversion in international cooperation, see Janice Gross Stein and Louis W. Pauly, eds., *Choosing to Cooperate: How States Avoid Loss* (Baltimore: Johns Hopkins University Press, 1993).

3. See Shibley Telhami, *Power and Leadership in International Bargaining: The Path to the Camp David Accords* (New York: Columbia University Press, 1990).

4. Telhami, the principal exponent of a structural realist interpretation of Camp David, argues however that this kind of analysis can only explain the tendency toward agreement. The timing and substance of the agreement are explained by bargaining strategies, types of regimes, and leaders' personalities.

5. As Michael Mastanduno, David A. Lake, and G. John Ikenberry note ("Toward a Realist Theory of State Action," *International Studies Quarterly* 33 (December 1989): 457–474, 458), governments may act at home to meet international challenges, and abroad to solve domestic problems. In this case, governments addressed two sets of problems through strategies that operated simultaneously in both arenas. Both at the outset of negotiations and throughout the process, bargaining strategies cannot be explained independently by either the constraints of domestic win-sets or security constraints.

6. See my "Prenegotiation in the Arab-Israel Conflict: The Paradoxes of Suc-

cess and Failure," in Janice Gross Stein, ed., *Getting to the Table: Processes of International Prenegotiation* (Baltimore: Johns Hopkins University Press, 1989), pp. 174–205.

7. There is conceptual controversy over whether the United States should be included as a participant in the process of negotiation, even though it was an outsider to the dispute. I. William Zartman (pers. comm., May 1988) argues that because an agreement between the United States and either of the two parties would not have been sufficient, the United States is best treated as an "interested outsider" in the process. But while the United States was not a direct party to the dispute, throughout much of the process it was the engine of the negotiation, and its side-payments to the two parties were critical to the agreement. Moreover, almost all the negotiation at Camp David took place bilaterally between the United States and each of the two delegations. Consequently, I treat the United States as a direct participant.

8. Janice Gross Stein, "Calculation, Miscalculation, and Conventional Deterrence I: The View from Cairo," in Robert Jervis, Richard Ned Lebow, and Janice Gross Stein, *Psychology and Deterrence* (Baltimore: Johns Hopkins University Press, 1985) pp. 34–59.

9. This document was submitted to a plebiscite and elevated to the level of a "document of the revolution," along with the National Charter of 1962, the March 30 Program of 1968, and the Permanent Constitution and National Action Program of 1971.

10. The fixed platforms were expected to run candidates in elections and form permanent blocks in the People's Assembly. Mark Neal Cooper, *The Transformation of Egypt* (London: Croom Helm, 1982), pp. 126ff., 140, 187.

11. At the end of the two-round process, the center had won 275 seats, the right 12, and the left only 2. In his first speech to the People's Assembly after the elections, President Sadat authorized the conversion of the three platform organizations into political parties. *Al-Ahram*, November 12, 1976.

12. For detailed analysis of the election results, see Cooper, *The Transformation of Egypt*, pp. 204–234.

13. By 1976, Israel's balance-of-payments deficit had reached approximately 4 billion dollars (U.S.), an unprecedented level. See Ann Crittenden, "Israel's Economic Plight," *Foreign Policy* 57 (Summer 1979): 1005–1016.

14. See Janice Gross Stein, "Structures, Strategies, and Tactics of Mediation: Kissinger and Carter in the Middle East," *Negotiation Journal* 1 (October 1985): 331–348.

15. Carter's judgment was widely shared by members of both the old and new administrations. The transition papers prepared by the National Security Council staff and the State Department warned that the status quo in the Middle East was inherently unstable; only progress in negotiation would avoid a slide toward war. Moreover, only sustained diplomatic progress would deny the Soviet Union the opportunity of military and political reentry to the Middle East. Even before his term of office began, the attention of President-elect Carter was captured and sustained by a rare degree of consensus among his principal advisers that a comprehensive settlement of the Arab-Israeli conflict was required if ad-

verse domestic and international consequences were to be avoided. Three relevant documents are "Arab Peace Offensive," January 4, 1977; a paper on the Arab-Israeli dispute dated January 14, 1977; and an undated paper, "Inter-Arab Politics and a Peace Settlement"; see William B. Quandt, *Camp David: Peacemaking and Politics* (Washington, D.C.: Brookings Institution, 1986), p. 36, note 8.

16. An emergency IMF loan of 130 million dollars required that the government reduce its subsidies, which absorbed almost one-sixth of the national income. Dr. Abd al-Moneim al Qaissuni, newly designated Minister of Finance and Economy and former chairman of the Arab National Bank, announced that the government would end or substantially cut subsidy payments for sugar, flour, rice, oil, bottled gas, cigarettes, and beer.

17. In April, he dismissed Mohamed Heikal, the most influential and articulate spokesman of the left, from the editorship of *Al-Ahram*. Shortly thereafter, he released 1,000 members of the Muslim Brotherhood from prison, even though he prohibited the *Ikhwan* from organizing legally as a political group. See John Waterbury, *Egypt: Burdens of the Past/Options for the Future* (Bloomington: University of Indiana Press, 1978), p. 202; Munir K. Nasser, *Press, Politics, and Power: Egypt's Heikal and Al-Ahram* (Ames: Iowa State University Press, 1979), pp. 100–102; Melvin A. Friedlander, *Sadat and Begin: The Domestic Politics of Peacemaking* (Boulder, Col.: Westview Press, 1983); and R. Michael Burrell and Abbas R. Kelidar, *Egypt: The Dilemmas of a Nation, 1970–1977* (Beverly Hills, Calif.: Sage, 1977), p. 38.

18. As he subsequently explained: "The Syrian B'ath party will not go to Geneva; and if it did, the picture would be like this: The Soviet Union has the Syrians in its pocket, and Syria has the Palestinians in its pocket also. In Geneva, we would busy ourselves with all the things we have had enough of—semantic and legalistic arguments, the modalities, and the names of the topical, geographic, and historical committees. All this, in addition to what we know about the nature of the Syrian B'ath party. And the result would be that the Geneva Conference would greatly add to our level of disillusionment." *Oktubar* (Arabic), December 25, 1977, p. 15.

19. Moreover, as Boutrus Ghali, a senior foreign policy adviser to President Sadat, observed: "Arab states have often made some impressive offers of aid, but when it comes down to it, they set unacceptable conditions. I mean, you will have the Saudi government calling and threatening to cut off aid to us, because one of our magazines wrote an unfavorable story about a given prince. . . . That is unacceptable. American aid is stable and predictable." Interview of Boutrus Ghali by Shibley Telhami, Cairo, August 28, 1983, cited in Telhami, *Power and Leadership*, p. 104.

20. The new government was formed on June 20, with 61 of 120 seats in the Knesset. It consisted of the Likud; Shlomzion, led by Ariel Sharon; the National Religious Party, whose dominant Young Guard was committed to retention of the West Bank for religious reasons; and Aguda Yisrael. The Democratic Movement for Change, which emphasized political and economic liberalization in Israel and territorial concessions on the West Bank in exchange for peace, remained outside the government until the end of October.

21. Sadat subsequently told Carter that he had decided to address the Knesset in Jerusalem in part to overcome the powerful lobby groups in the United States and to convince the American public that the Arabs were ready for peace with Israel. He added that he had felt the weight of the Zionist lobby in the United States and wanted to "ease the burdens" on President Carter by some bold action. Quandt, *Camp David*, p. 173.

22. The Egyptian National Security Council met on October 15 for an exploratory discussion. The Egyptian National Security Council consisted of Vice-President Hosni Mubarak; Speaker of the People's Assembly Sayed Marei; Prime Minister Mamduh Selim; General Secretary of the Arab Socialist Union Mustapha Kamil; Minister of War and Deputy Prime Minister Muhammad Abd el-Ghani Gamassy; Director of the General Intelligence Department of the Ministry of the Interior Kamal Hassan Ali; and President Sadat. Other senior advisers were Osman Ahmad Osman, a powerful industrialist; Boutrus Ghali and Usama al-Baz at the Foreign Ministry; and Hasan Kamil from the President's Office.

The civilian technocracy and the military were the most important power centers after the presidency, and the Foreign Office had some weight by virtue of its expertise. The Secretary of the Arab Socialist Union, Mustapha Kamil, represented the industrial and technological sectors. He supported an agreement with Israel brokered through the United States, but worried about a separate peace that would jeopardize subsidies and credit from the oil-producing states. Most of the senior officials in the Egyptian Foreign Office opposed direct bilateral negotiation with Israel, and the Foreign Minister resigned in protest against the President's trip.

There were important divisions among the senior military as well. Vice-President Hosni Mubarak most strongly opposed Sadat's initiative. He generally championed the interests of the Air Force, which was concerned about the supply of highly sophisticated equipment that was expensive and difficult to bring on line quickly. Muhammad Abd el-Ghani Gamassy, the Minister of War, strongly supported closer relations with the United States, in part in the expectation of a supply of American conventional equipment for the ground forces. Sadat included neither Mubarak nor Gamassy in the delegation to Jerusalem: the rivalry between his two senior military advisers increased the autonomy of the President, since neither had the political resources to unify the armed forces in opposition to Sadat. Ehud Ya'ari, "Sadat's Pyramid of Power," *Jerusalem Quarterly* 14 (Winter 1980): 113–114; Friedlander, *Sadat and Begin*; and P. J. Vatikiotis, *The History of Egypt*, 2nd ed. (Baltimore: Johns Hopkins University Press, 1980).

23. For a detailed analysis of the success of this unilateral and self-binding commitment as a negotiating strategy, see my "Deterrence and Reassurance," in Paul Stern, Jo L. Husbands, Robert Axelrod, Robert Jervis, and Charles Tilly, eds., *Behavior, Society, and Nuclear War* (New York: Oxford University Press, 1991), pp. 8–72; and Zeev Maoz and Dan Felsenthal, "Self-Binding Commitments, the Inducement of Trust, Social Choice, and the Theory of International Cooperation," *International Studies Quarterly* 31 (1987): 177–200.

24. Robert Jervis, *The Logic of Images in International Relations* (Princeton, N.J.: Princeton University Press, 1970).

25. Experimental studies suggest that people determine the motives of a donor by how much the gift cost the giver in utility: the greater the relative cost to the donor, the less likely ulterior motives. See Stuart S. Komorita, "Concession-Making and Conflict Resolution," *Journal of Conflict Resolution* 17 (1973): 745–762; and Dean Pruitt, *Negotiation Behavior* (New York: Academic Press, 1981), pp. 124–125.

26. See my "Prenegotiation in the Arab-Israel Conflict" for a discussion of the impact of the process of prenegotiation before Camp David on agenda limitation and problem definition.

27. Israel wanted a bilateral peace treaty and full normalization of relations, complete demilitarization of the Sinai, a limited framework of autonomy for the Palestinians, and no linkage between the two agreements. Egypt wanted only partial demilitarization of the Sinai, a statement of principle on the right of the Palestinians to self-determination, a general framework for resolving the future of the Palestinians, and tight linkage between the two agreements.

28. President Sadat agreed to full normalization of relations with Israel; to substantial demilitarization of the Sinai; to a very general framework on the "resolution of the Palestinian problem in all its aspects," which provided for autonomy and a five-year transition period; and to very loose linkage between the two sets of agreements. Israel agreed to full withdrawal from the Sinai, including the removal of its settlements, and to recognition of the "legitimate rights of the Palestinians." In addition, Israel agreed to a three-month freeze on settlements in the West Bank and Gaza Strip while the framework agreement was being negotiated. See "A Framework for Peace in the Middle East Agreed at Camp David, September 17, 1978," in Telhami, *Power and Leadership*, pp. 225–230.

The duration of the freeze became a subject of intense dispute after the agreement was signed. At Camp David, the length of the freeze was discussed on the twelfth day, one day before the negotiations concluded. The United States understood that Israel had agreed to a freeze during the negotiations for autonomy, which were only expected to last for several months. Nevertheless, the public letter that Carter gave to Begin on the last day stated that the freeze on settlements applied to the *three months* anticipated for the negotiation of a peace treaty between Egypt and Israel. Israel subsequently insisted on this interpretation. The competing expectations were in part the result of sloppy drafting under intense pressure in the last 24 hours of negotiation at Camp David. See Quandt, *Camp David*, pp. 248ff.

29. In December 1977, the Muslim Brotherhood was implicated in a plot to overthrow the regime; and two months later Yusef el-Sabeh, one of Sadat's closest confidants and the editor of *Al-Ahram*, was assassinated, allegedly by Palestinian irregulars. The Ikhwan also won an overwhelming victory in student elections in Egyptian universities. Its success was due only superficially to opposition to direct negotiations with Israel; more important, the Ikhwan was able to organize and recruit among the urban poor who were increasingly disadvantaged. See Israel Altman, "Islamic Movements in Egypt," *Jerusalem Quarterly* 10 (Winter 1979): 87–105, esp. p. 99.

30. The President dismissed Dr. Abd al-Moneim al-Qaissuni, the Deputy Prime Minister for Financial and Economic Affairs, who favored reducing subsidies on basic commodities. At the same time, Sadat ordered the repression of editorial criticism by the left and held a national referendum to approve further action against alleged conspirators. After the referendum on May 21, the president moved immediately and harshly against a wide spectrum of domestic opponents. He recalled journalists from abroad who had written "slanderous" articles, barred Heikal from travel outside the country, arrested and jailed dozens of opponents, and disbanded the Wafd. In the early summer, Sadat broadened the campaign to suppress dissent and, at a meeting of the central committee of the Arab Socialist Union on July 22, announced his intention to create a new political party, the National Democratic Party. R. Michael Burrell and Abbas R. Kelidar, *Egypt*, pp. 17–18.

31. Hosni Mubarak, the Vice-President, was the obvious political leader of those within the military, and those industrialists with close ties to the military establishment, who opposed a bilateral agreement with Israel.

32. Ismail Fahmy, *Negotiating for Peace in the Middle East* (Baltimore: Johns Hopkins University Press, 1983), p. 25.

33. In his memoirs, President Carter emphasizes that Sadat had warned him that if no progress were made by the anniversary of the Sinai Agreement in September 1978, he would consider resigning or perhaps reverting to belligerency. Jimmy Carter, *Keeping Faith: The Memoirs of a President* (New York: Bantam Books, 1982), pp. 315–316.

34. Sadat's anticipation of synergistic linkage between agreement and economic and political benefit was the intervening variable driving the President's reduction of his critical minimum for agreement. These expectations were only partially fulfilled.

American economic and military aid did increase dramatically after the conclusion of the peace treaty between Egypt and Israel. In 1977, U.S. aid commitments to Egypt, both short- and long-term, equalled 816 million dollars. In 1979, after the peace treaty was signed, the United States committed itself to 1.5 billion dollars annually in military aid and a 300 million dollar "peace dividend." Economic and military aid continued to increase in the 1980s to an annual level of 2.3 billion dollars, of which 1.3 billion dollars was military aid. When the contributions of West Germany, Japan, and the World Bank are added to those of the United States, total aid commitments averaged 2.1 billion dollars annually. In the aftermath of the war in the Gulf in 1991, the United States forgave 7 billion dollars, of Egyptian debt. Private foreign investment, however, lagged badly behind government aid. Capital investment from the United States, for example, accounted for only 2.4 percent of the 1.4 billion-dollar investment in all joint projects in 1981–1982.

Even though economic aid increased significantly as expected after the peace treaty was signed, its impact was degraded by a birth rate of one million every nine months, extensive subsidies of basic foodstuffs, a cumbersome bureaucracy, and a decline in oil revenues and remittances from abroad. Although Egypt's economic performance has deteriorated over the last decade, political liberalization has accelerated, and Sadat's successor, Hosni Mubarak, has strengthened the role of the civilian technocracy as the principal counterweight to the growing power of Islamic political movements which challenge the legitimacy of the regime. See *Status of the Open Door Economy in the Arab Republic of Egypt* (Cairo: Central Agency for Public Mobilization and Statistics, February 1982); Marvin G. Weinbaum, *Egypt and the Politics of U.S. Economic Aid* (Boulder, Col.: Westview Press, 1986); and William Burns, *Economic Aid and American Policy Toward Egypt, 1955–1981* (Albany, N.Y.: SUNY University Press, 1985).

35. The money supply grew by 45 percent in 1978. The inflation rate in the first eight months of 1978 passed 50 percent and the balance-of-payments deficit continued to increase. The soaring rate of inflation diverted funds into speculative activity and widened the gap between property-holders and the urban poor. The balance-of-payments deficit in 1978 was 3.25 billion dollars, equal to almost one-quarter of Israel's gross national product. See Crittenden, "Israel's Economic Plight," pp. 1005–1009.

36. After the October War in 1973, American aid jumped from 500 million dollars annually to more than 2.5 billion dollars. Under the Sinai II agreement negotiated in 1975, the United States committed itself to continuing aid of about 2 billion dollars annually. President Carter described Prime Minister Begin's emphasis on the importance of agreement between the United States and Israel: "[Begin] pointed out that there had to be two agreements: . . . the most important was between the United States and Israel; and the other, of secondary importance but obviously also crucial, was between Israel and Egypt. The most important one would have to come first. He wanted the world to know that there were no serious differences between Israel and the United States." Carter, *Keeping Faith*, p. 366.

37. President Carter (ibid., p. 418) recalls: "In my private visits with Sadat, he emphasized again and again that his main concern was about me. . . . It was imperative to him that the United States and Egypt stand together." President Carter astutely noted the tactical implications of the pivotal position of the United States: "I also knew that it was a good negotiating tactic by either Sadat or Begin to reach agreement with me and then to have the two of us confront the third. Sadat had understood this strategy before he arrived at Camp David" (ibid., p. 366).

38. Interview of Tahseen Bashir by Shibley Telhami, Princeton, N.J., March 1984, cited in Telhami, *Power and Leadership*, note 38, p. 250.

39. Zbigniew Brzezinski, *Power and Principle* (New York: Farrar Straus Giroux, 1983), p. 272.

40. Yigal Yadin lost control of an important component of the Democratic Movement for Change, which had joined the government in October 1977 and expanded Begin's majority in the Knesset from one seat to a comfortable majority. Peace Now, a nonpartisan political movement, was organizing publicly to demonstrate support for an agreement with Egypt.

41. At a critical meeting of Carter's advisers on July 6, Brzezinski defined the alternatives as a confrontation with Israel or withdrawal from the process. Hamilton Jordan, the President's political adviser, discussed the forthcoming

Congressional elections explicitly, and argued strongly that Carter could rebuild his ties with the American Jewish community only if he successfully mediated an agreement; only positive results, he insisted, could help the President politically. Quandt, *Camp David*, p. 197; and Brzezinski, *Power and Principle*, pp. 250–251.

42. Sadat offered Gamassy the post of Special Presidential Advisor, and appointed a new Chief of Staff, Major General Ahmad Badawi, the head of military training and a war hero in 1973. The appointment of a popular officer further neutralized opposition within the military. Ehud Ya'ari, "Sadat's Pyramid of Power," pp. 119–120; and Friedlander, *Sadat and Begin*, pp. 238–240.

43. The Liberals, the second-largest party within the governing coalition, supported the agreements. Two smaller groups opposed to the agreement threatened to withdraw from the coalition, but did not have the political resources to survive independently. Efraim Torgovnik, "Accepting Camp David: The Role of Party Factions in Israeli Policy-Making," *Middle East Review* 11 (Winter 1978–79): 18–25.

44. Begin said: "I refuse to convene the Herut Party center. It is unheard of in the history of parliamentary democracy that an issue like this will be decided in party forums." *Ha'aretz*, September 28, 1978.

45. In the aftermath of the publication of a controversial joint Soviet-American communiqué in October 1977, President Carter explained to Dayan that attacks on his policies by American Jews and Congress were of considerable concern to him, and asked Israel's Foreign Minister for help in managing his domestic political problems. Rather than shift in Carter's direction, Dayan exploited his advantage to secure a joint U.S.-Israel statement which further enhanced the image of Carter's political weakness in the Arab world. In September 1977, in a private meeting with Egyptian Foreign Minister Fahmy, the President explained that he could not put any additional pressure on Israel to modify its position; to do so would be "political suicide." On the basis of this conservation, Fahmy concluded that Carter was weak. See Quandt, *Camp David*, p. 115. Indeed, President Sadat aborted this phase of the negotiation in part because of his concern about Carter's weakness, his lack of resolve, and his inability to transcend his political constraints.

46. In 1967, President Nasser changed his estimate of relative Egyptian military capability not in response to any objective change in relative military capabilities, but rather in response to a growing economic crisis at home and challenges to his leadership from the Arab world. See Janice Gross Stein, "The Arab-Israeli War of 1967: Inadvertent War Through Miscalculated Escalation," in Alexander L. George, ed., *Avoiding War: Problems of Crisis Management* (Boulder, Col.: Westview Press, 1991), pp. 126–159.

4

East-West Bargaining Over Germany
The Search for Synergy in a Two-Level Game

Jack Snyder

The pattern of East-West bargaining over Germany between 1945 and 1990 is rife with puzzles and anomalies. Though the period is retrospectively labeled "the long peace," high tensions prevailed throughout much of it.[1] Tensions were often highest when statesmen on both sides were merely trying to consolidate their respective blocs. Attempts at detente sometimes increased tensions, whereas crises reduced them. And the least tense period has coincided with the collapse of Soviet power in this sphere of vital interests, the kind of circumstance that has led many great powers to become recklessly aggressive.

To resolve these paradoxes, it is necessary to understand both the international and domestic levels of the East-West bargaining game. Neither level is sufficient to explain all the puzzles satisfactorily; both levels must be considered simultaneously to unravel most of them. This does not mean, however, that there has been much "synergy" among the various games being played at both levels.[2]

Synergy, the exploitation of the joint gains from cooperative international bargaining to create coalitions favoring cooperation in both countries, is a hallmark of Robert Putnam's concept of the two-level game.[3] Previous works showed how the domestic context affects international bargaining, and vice versa. But they reasoned in the manner of "partial-equilibrium" analysis, first assessing the dynamics in one game and then showing how its outcome constrained choices and outcomes in the other. If Putnam's synergy were strongly at work, this kind of sequential, partial-equilibrium analysis would break down, since outcomes in the international and domestic games would be determined simultaneously and mutually, not sequentially.[4]

In bargaining over Germany, however, synergistic agreements

strengthening the political position of proponents of cooperation in both camps were elusive. Soviet reformers under Khrushchev and Gorbachev hoped for this kind of synergy, expecting a strategy of detente at the international level to hamstring their political opponents both at home and abroad. But both Khrushchev and Gorbachev failed to achieve this. Instead of interacting in a synergistic way, the games at the two levels each had their own logic; each affected the other game primarily by setting some of the parameters within which it operated. Thus, in Putnam's terminology, these cases are best analyzed in terms of separate, though mutually constraining, partial equilibriums in each of the two levels of the game. In the terms used by Andrew Moravcsik in the Introduction to this volume (Chapter 1), the two levels of the Berlin bargaining game have normally been "additive," not "interactive."

This is not surprising, given the nature of the cases. The organization of the state system tends in general to hinder the emergence of political coalitions across state boundaries.[5] Such synergistic linkages are even less likely between states that pose security threats to each other, have limited economic ties, and face sharp social and cultural differences. Especially in such cases, priority must be given to analyzing each game separately as a prerequisite to analyzing the games' mutual effects. While pursuing hypotheses about synergistic interactions in two-level games, it is important not to lose sight of the need for good partial-equilibrium theories at each level.

OUTCOMES IN FOUR PERIODS

In this chapter, I will examine competing explanations for the outcomes of East-West bargaining over Berlin in four periods: under Stalin, especially 1947–49; under Khrushchev, especially 1958–61; under Brezhnev, especially 1970–71; and under Gorbachev. I seek to explain outcomes on the two dimensions that game theory usually addresses: to what extent the outcome was cooperative or conflictual, and to what extent it favored one side or the other. Like other contributions to this volume, this chapter examines whether an international agreement was consummated, and on what terms. Table 1 summarizes the outcomes in the four cases.

TABLE 1.   Bargaining Outcomes in Four Periods

Period	Cooperation or Conflict	Distribution of Benefits
Stalin	Conflict	Stalemate
Khrushchev	Conflict	Stalemate
Brezhnev	Cooperation	Ratified stalemate
Gorbachev	Cooperation	One-sided Soviet concessions

Four kinds of explanations for this pattern of outcomes will be assessed: strictly international explanations; strictly domestic explanations; explanations that examine constraints at each of the two levels, but have no synergistic linkages between them (what Moravcsik calls "additive"); and synergistic explanations, involving the exploitation of cooperative bargaining to create new policy options, and hence new coalition possibilities, in the domestic politics of each side (what Moravcsik calls "interactive"). In particular, I want to use the four cases to assess the explanatory value added by examining synergistic interactions between the two games.

International Explanations

At the international level, I consider two independent variables: the intensity of the security dilemma, and the balance of bargaining power. By the security dilemma, I mean a situation in which steps taken to increase one's own security reduce the security of the other side.[6] The security dilemma should be most intense, for example, when offensive military strategies and technologies have the advantage; when the political status quo is fluid; when offensive political tactics are the best form of self-defense; and when military or political instruments adopted for offensive purposes are indistinguishable from those adopted for defensive purposes. The security dilemma is less intense when defense has the advantage; when the political status quo is clearly defined and stable; and so forth. If the theory of the security dilemma is correct and powerful, these variables should explain outcomes on the dimension of cooperation and conflict.

In the balance of bargaining power, I include both the material resources of the state that can be mobilized to affect the bargaining, and the intensity of the state's motivation to stand firm, to the extent that this is due to the state's position in the international system. A state should be more strongly motivated to stand firm against threats in its own sphere of influence or those that jeopardize its vital security interests. This disproportionate motivation should enhance its bargaining power. If international-level theories are correct, variations in bargaining power should determine who wins conflicts and who gains the greater benefit from cooperation.[7]

Domestic (and Intra-Alliance) Level

At this second level, I consider two independent variables: whether groups having an interest in agreement are relatively strong or weak, and whether each major group enjoys the power to veto ratification. To count as a domestic variable, the strength of groups must be determined by domestic factors, such as the nature of the domestic economy or governmental structure, or the privileged status of a group in light of the prevailing domestic ideology. If this variable is entirely dependent on changes in international structural variables (e.g., factions favoring rollback are weakened when their policies fail abroad), then the international explanation subsumes the domestic one.

The likelihood of ratification of an agreement is also affected by the formal or informal constitutional rules that determine which groups, and how many groups, must accept the agreement for it to be adopted. In a system where many or all key social groups have independent veto power, ratification is less likely, since numerically small minorities can block it. International alliances of sovereign states, like NATO, tend to operate in this fashion, and so do some domestic systems.[8]

In assessing these domestic hypotheses, it is important to beware of spurious causation. Consider, for example, a case where international-level variables create a tight security dilemma, which in turn creates a sense of fear that strengthens hawkish interest groups inside the competing states. In that case, the power of hawkish veto groups might correlate with the outcome, even though the underlying cause might lie largely or even wholly at the international level.[9]

Two Levels Without Synergy: Additive Explanations

A third approach assumes that both the domestic and international games place constraints on the statesman, who occupies the pivot between them. Sometimes the constraints posed by international conditions will be comparatively loose or ambiguous, whereas domestic political constraints are comparatively tight and clear; sometimes the reverse will be the case. In such instances, it will be appropriate to begin by analyzing the level where the constraints are tightest, and then take those findings as given parameters in analyzing the bargaining process at the other level. Though this conception depicts a two-level game, it is not necessarily one in which synergistic issue linkage across the two levels, or transnational coalitions, are salient.

Two Levels With Synergy: Interactive Explanations

"Synergy" means the creation of benefits through cooperation in the international bargaining game that attract new supporters for cooperation in each of the two domestic games. One way to create synergy is to target concessions on "swing voters" who hold the key to gaining domestic ratification of an international agreement. However, the apparent targeting of concessions on swing voters may be a spurious form of synergy, if the concessions they demand are the same as those desired by the broad range of opinion in the target country. Targeting is *not* spurious, however, if *selective* incentives for cooperation are provided to the targeted swing group.[10]

A related concept is that of "positive or negative reverberation," in which concessions or threats from one state affect coalition politics inside another state.[11] It is necessary to beware of spurious claims about reverberation effects in the two-level game. Spurious reverberations would be ones that are completely driven by the structure of the international game. It is clear that hard-line policies and coalitions in the West have sometimes reinforced hard-line policies and coalitions in the East, and vice versa.[12] But this is spurious as a two-level explanation if the policies on both sides are simply a response to underlying incentives posed by the security dilemma.

In short, among the phenomena most distinctive to Putnam's two-level game approach are synergy, reverberation, and targeting. Before Gorbachev, attempts at these strategems in cases of East-West bargaining over Germany either failed or had only a spurious resemblance to the concept in Putnam's theory. And Gorbachev's strategy of synergy also proved to be a failure. The following sections trace this pattern of outcomes in four brief case studies of East-West bargaining over Berlin in 1947–49, 1958–61, 1970–71, and the Gorbachev period.

THE FIRST BERLIN CRISIS

After World War II, the four powers occupying Germany—the United States, the Soviet Union, Britain, and France—were unable to agree on a scheme for regulating the politics and economics of the vanquished foe. Fearing that prolonged uncertainty about Germany's future would play into Soviet hands, the British and Americans moved in 1948 to create a joint currency for their zones in preparation for the formation of a separate West German state. Stalin responded by blockading Western ground traffic to the Western sectors of Berlin, which were surrounded by the Soviet zone. The blockade failed to deter the formation of a separate West German state, and was lifted in March 1949.

Thus, the outcome of bargaining over Germany in the late 1940s was conflictual, not cooperative, and the distribution of gains was a stalemate based on physical control through military occupation. As Stalin put it, "Everyone imposes his own social system as far as his army can reach."[13] An interpretation focusing on the structure of the international game would explain this as the result of a fairly intense security dilemma and a rough balance of power and motivation.

The security dilemma seemed intense above all because the political status quo was fluid. At the end of the war, it was unclear under whose sway Europe's vast economic and military potential would fall. It seemed plausible that the United States might use its great economic resources to wean away the states in the Soviet Union's hard-won security belt in Eastern Europe; it also seemed plausible that Moscow could use Communist fifth columns to take power in the West. Moreover, many of the tactics that each side could use to defend its security in this fluid environment were also tactics that threatened the security of the other. Thus, the Marshall Plan and the formation of the West German state were needed to shore up the internal security of the West, yet they also seemed like a bridgehead for American rollback and a lure to Stalin's satellites. Likewise, Communist strikes in France and the blockade of Berlin were prima facie threats to Western security, but they seemed necessary tactics to derail the consolidation of Western strongpoints that would threaten the East. Since offense and defense were indistinguishable, cooperative bargaining was difficult or impossible.[14]

As it turned out, most of the offensive moves of both sides failed to bear fruit. The strikes and the Berlin blockade simply provoked resistance and unified the Western camp, while Stalin's ruthless consolidation of totalitarian rule in the East gave the West no opening to lure away his clients, except for Yugoslavia. Both sides were strongly motivated to maintain control over vital security interests in their sphere, and each had sufficient economic and military power to deter the other. Thus, a purely international explanation accounts for the general outcome reasonably well.

However, domestic explanations are not completely implausible. Some scholars argue that Stalin's growing militancy was caused not so much by the security dilemma abroad as by his security dilemma at home.[15] In this view, he needed hyper-orthodoxy and the myth of capitalist encirclement to justify a crackdown on pluralistic forces that had been allowed to emerge during the war years. Arguably, Western Cold War policies, including the invitation to Eastern European states to join the Marshall Plan, may have helped militants like Stalin's lieutenant Andrei Zhdanov to prevail over more moderate political elements. If so, this would be an example of negative domestic reverberation, as was the discrediting of Communism in France by Zhdanov's militancy.

For scholars who accept the international explanation, however, talk of such reverberation would be spurious. In their view, Soviet politics was entirely under Stalin's thumb—and even if it was not, outcomes in the domestic game were simply the product of the international-level security dilemma.

THE SECOND BERLIN CRISIS

After the 1953 riots of East Berlin and Lavrentii Beria's ouster from the Soviet Politburo, no significant political figure on either side of the Iron Curtain seriously pursued German reunification as a practical, desirable, immediate policy aim. Each side rated consolidation of its own bloc as a much higher priority than rolling back the opponent's influence in his bloc. Why, then, did it take until the early 1970s to codify a mutual recognition of the European status quo? Why, in particular, was it necessary to transit through a war-threatening Berlin crisis in order to achieve a stable settlement?

The interpretation that I will put forward in this section stresses the perverse dynamic of coalition maintenance within both camps, which forced key actors to pursue more intransigent, offensive strategies than they otherwise would have preferred.[16] Overpromising in the domestic and intrabloc consensus-building process led both sides to adopt strategies of "offensive detente," based on the politically convenient myth that the opponent could be compelled to accept one-sided, peaceful revisions in the status quo. Neither side wanted to run any real risks to unravel the opposing camp, but for leaders on both sides, the myth that this could be accomplished at low cost and risk was an indispensable tool in internal politics.

In November 1958, Khrushchev laid down his ultimatum on Berlin and Germany: either the West would meet a variety of demands, including the acceptance of "free city" status for Berlin, within six months, or else the Soviet Union would sign a separate peace treaty with the German Democratic Republic (GDR). This would give the East Germans the legal status to control Western access to Berlin, and thus permit a Soviet blockade by East German proxy.

For Khrushchev, the ultimatum was intended to serve as a lever to gain a summit meeting with Eisenhower, to resolve German issues like GDR recognition that were hindering the development of U.S.-Soviet detente, and to lay the groundwork for superpower arms control. His urgency to achieve this stemmed from his need to win Politburo support for a reallocation of resources away from defense, in order to redeem the promises on consumer issues he had made in forming his political coalition.[17] For Eisenhower, the decision to string Khrushchev along but make no real concessions stemmed from political imperatives to back Adenauer's policy of nonrecognition, while also avoiding a confrontational, deterrent strategy that would have alienated Britain and played into the hands of domestic proponents of increased spending on conventional defenses.[18] Thus, each side sought to achieve detente, low defense budgets, and the acceptance of the status quo by the other side, while continuing to express its own rollback aims.

This produced a perverse pattern of East-West bargaining, in which false signaling to the opponent and erroneous reading of the opponent's signals helped lure the two sides into staking out incompatible, untenable diplomatic positions.[19] In particular, Western willingness to negotiate led Khrushchev to think his strategy was working, leading him to adopt politically risky unilateral troop cuts. Khrushchev's strategy was exploded when hard-line American speeches just before the 1960 Paris Summit showed that real concessions would not be forthcoming. But by this time, Khrushchev's prestige was too committed to back out easily, so he decided to wreck the summit and try his coercive approach to detente again with a new U.S. President. Only the Berlin Wall crisis put an end to this counterproductive maneuvering, revealing under the threat of an armed clash that both sides cared vastly more about defending the status quo than changing it.

The Second-Level Game in the East

On the Soviet side, a variety of social groups or forces helped shape the political incentives of the top leadership. Some were powerful interest groups, atavisms of the mobilizing, centralizing, militarizing institutions of Stalin's "revolution from above."[20] These included the party apparatus and ideological cadres, with their vested interest in maintaining the historical leading role of the combat party struggling for progressive change against the class enemy, and also the military and heavy-industrial sectors that served them. Broader circles included the cultural and technical intelligentsia, who often favored a relaxation of tensions at home and abroad precisely in order to escape from the oppressive political and economic hand of the party and the military-industrial complex, and also mass consumers, who needed the promise of a better life as an incentive to spur their productive energies.

Whereas some Politburo members tried to gain political support primarily from one of these grass-roots social segments, Khrushchev rose to power by devising a formula that offered something to everyone. The combination of nuclear weapons and a revitalization of Socialist dogma, he argued, would promote detente by sobering the imperialists and encouraging the development of progressive forces within the imperialist camp, which would be attracted to the Soviet peace diplomacy. This would lead simultaneously to Soviet political gains, enhanced Soviet security, lower Soviet defense spending, and a thawing of Stalinist repression within the bloc. Thus, every constituency would be either coopted, or at least decisively rebutted, if this scheme worked.

But the arrival of the ICBM did not lead to the payoffs that Khrushchev had claimed for it. Despite this alleged shift in the "correlation of forces," the United States still resisted arms control, was rapidly moving toward the de facto nuclearization of the Bundeswehr, and kept insisting on free all-German elections as a prerequisite to a summit, and more generally to progress on Khrushchev's detente agenda. After Sputnik, Khrushchev tried to force through a unilateral defense cut in order to make good on his economic promises, but spokesmen for the party apparatus and heavy-industry in the Politburo, Mikhail Suslov and Frol Kozlov, reminded him of his promise that such cuts would come only after there was clear evidence that the imperialists had adopted a more conciliatory line. At the same time, the Chinese and the East Germans were demanding forceful Soviet support for the favorable geopolitical changes that he had implied would follow from the shift in the correlation of forces.

Khrushchev's Berlin ultimatum was designed to square the circle of his contradictory, overcommitted political platform. The six-month deadline for normalization of the status of West Berlin was intended to spur forward movement toward a summit, which would provide some evidence of progress on U.S.-Soviet arms control and detente and perhaps even solve some of the German issues that had been barring such progress. This would allow Khrushchev to claim that the correlation-of-forces theory had worked, that the ICBM had sobered imperialism and made the Socialist bloc secure, and consequently that deep, unilateral defense cuts could safely be made.[21]

By January 1960, this had apparently worked well enough for Khrushchev to announce conventional force cuts, but the speeches by Undersecretary of State Douglas Dillon and Vice President Richard Nixon in advance of the Paris Summit soon made clear that Khrushchev's hopes were illusory. Pressed by Suslov and other representatives of conservative interests on the Politburo, Khrushchev tried to use the U-2 and his antics at the summit to compel Western concessions, but to no avail. Because of the overcommitted logic of the coalition that Khrushchev had put together, the more his diplomatic failures harmed his political position, the more necessary it was for him to gamble on a diplomatic success that would validate the strategic theory that underpinned his coalition.

The Second-Level Game in the West

Internal politics also affected Eisenhower's strategy in responding to the Soviet note on Berlin. On the one hand, Eisenhower rejected Acheson's line-in-the-dust deterrent strategy, because the conventional buildup it implied would play into the hands of those who wanted to raise defense spending. Also, it would alienate the British. On the other hand, recognizing the GDR or making other substantive concessions to defuse the crisis would irritate Adenauer and De Gaulle. Adenauer in particular needed to keep alive the politically useful myth that joining NATO was consistent with reunification, and also to head off charges that a non-atomic German army was just cannon fodder for NATO. Everyone thought Adenauer was just "too good to be true" as a U.S. ally, and consequently must not be undercut in his political struggles with the SPD on one hand, and Strauss on the other.[22]

As a result of these contradictory pressures, Eisenhower and Dulles adopted a strategy of temporizing negotiation with no real intention of making concessions. Summits without substance, unproductive foreign ministers' talks, and acceptance of GDR border officials as "agents" of the Soviet occupation power were reflections of this approach. This strategy kept the Western coalition together on the basis of a least common denominator, but arguably led Khrushchev on in a way that eventually deepened the crisis.

The Structure of the International-Level Game

It might be argued that the structure of the international game provides a more parsimonious explanation for Khrushchev's Berlin diplomacy and for the outcome: a noncooperative stalemate. In this view, Khrushchev, like Stalin and Zhdanov before him, faced a security dilemma, in which offensive threats were needed to achieve defensive goals. West Germany was being remilitarized, and American nuclear weapons were being deployed with Bundeswehr units on a dual key basis. Meanwhile, the West was refusing to recognize the GDR or to accept the idea of peaceful coexistence on terms that would guarantee the integrity and security of the Soviet bloc. Khrushchev happened to hold several offensive cards—the restriction of access to Berlin, the risk of nuclear escalation, support for "progressives" in the Third World—that could be used to pressure the West into accepting a settlement. In this interpretation, an incentive to use offensive means for defensive ends was inherent in the situation. Thus, there was conflict because the security dilemma was tight.[23]

This explanation, however, is not adequate to account for Soviet strategic choices. The European status quo was much more stable and institutionalized in 1958 than it had been in 1947–48. Both military blocs were established, the East-West divide was clearly drawn, and tolerably stable governments were in power in most states. The GDR's problems with rampant emigration accelerated only in 1959, because of foolish, draconian economic policies. Though the Soviets did not yet have modern, survivable strategic nuclear forces, the stability of the military stalemate was assured by Soviet conventional military superiority and numerous

Soviet theater nuclear forces. What the 1961 Berlin confrontation eventually proved—that it was much easier to defend the European status quo than to change it—should have been clear to a reasonable statesman already in 1958. Consequently, the structure of the international-level game is not sufficient to explain Khrushchev's peculiarly belligerent strategy for achieving Soviet security.[24]

Domestic and International Interactions

Most of what I have said above has highlighted the domestic and intrabloc origins of counterproductive interbloc diplomatic strategies. That is, coalition-building and maintaining dynamics led to strategies of "offensive detente," which helped to create the crisis and hindered mutual recognition of the status quo. Conversely, each bloc's external strategy also affected the internal politics of the other side.

Western policies helped give rise to Khrushchev's coalition based on offensive detente, insofar as Western intrasigence helped undercut Malenkov's less offensive detente strategy.[25] Later, West German nuclear deployments and U.S. insistence on linking a summit to a German settlement helped force Khrushchev to try the Berlin gambit. Western moves alone did not necessitate Khrushchev's Berlin diplomacy—but given the Soviet domestic context, they made such a move look necessary to the survival of Khrushchev's domestic political and economic programs. Finally, Dillon's and Nixon's speeches and the U-2 killed Khrushchev's move toward unilateral defense cuts in 1960. Khrushchev's belligerent diplomacy also had effects on American domestic politics, playing into the hands of hawks and those Democrats who wanted to increase military spending.

One reason for these negative reverberations was that the strategies adopted by both sides masked information about their preferences. I have already discussed the allegation that Eisenhower's strategy of temporizing negotiation led Khrushchev on, causing him to deepen his political commitment to a strategy that had no prospect of success. In turn, Khrushchev's strategy also confused the West. To this day, there is no consensus about what Khrushchev was really after in his Berlin deadline gambit. Everyone agrees that the free-city proposal was primarily a lever aimed at gaining progress on one or more issues that he really cared about: GDR recognition, West German denuclearization, a summit, superpower arms control, the atmospherics of detente. But which of these he was really after was obscured by the fact that he had to keep pushing the Berlin issue in order to keep pressure on the United States to have any forward movement at all.

As a consequence, it looked like Khrushchev was not after any one goal in particular, such as recognition or denuclearization, but rather was out for a general humiliation of the United States, and division of the Western alliance. Moreover, it looked like he was pursuing the Bolshevik operational-code strategy of minimum and maximum aims: first engage, then look for weak spots, and exploit all of them to the hilt. In fact, Khrushchev's aims were probably more limited and defensive than this suggests, but his tactics made it hard to know what concessions to offer, and led to the fear that concessions would just be exploited.

The Failure of Synergy

Obviously there was a great deal of interaction between the international and domestic games in this case. Each side's counterproductive negotiating strategy, an outgrowth of the role of veto groups in each side's decision-making process, produced negative reverberations in the politics of the other camp. But true synergy, the exploitation of gains from cooperation to forge new domestic coalitions, was not achieved. A transnational coalition of defense-budget cutters, doves, consumers, arms controllers, and the British, organized and led by Eisenhower and Khrushchev themselves, might in principle have emerged. Khrushchev himself certainly envisioned a tacit coalition of "realists" in both camps against each side's military-industrial complex. Why was he unable to create such a coalition?

On the surface, the answer is obvious: Khrushchev's belligerent tactics undercut the chances of achieving such a transnational coalition. But this explanation begs the question, since Khrushchev's self-defeating tactics derived from the character of his domestic coalition. The question remains: Why did he have to proceed on the basis of his perverse coalition with Suslov and Kozlov, rather than dropping them in favor of a direct approach to a transnational coalition that would have better served his policy goals?

I would offer two general hypotheses in this regard. First, the risk of being exploited in international security cooperation is always a powerful consideration under anarchy. Unless it can be shown that one's vulnerability to such exploitation is low and/or that the risks of spiraling conflict are exceptionally high, the fear of mutual exploitation will make cooperative security coalitions across international borders hard to form.

Second, networks that facilitate the formation of political coalitions are thicker within countries and blocs than between them.[26] In building a coalition, people normally start close to home and then work their way outward. This may be because one is more likely to find allies with common interests closer to home than in the enemy camp. But it may simply be an artifact of proximity, the density of institutional connections, and opportunities for frequent political interaction. Thus, if logrolling starts at home, then by the time a political leader finally sits down with his opposite number abroad he is already locked into a coalition platform that restricts his ability to make new transnational alliances.

The lack of a deep network of East-West political relationships made it much harder to form interbloc than intrabloc coalitions. The detailed international and transnational bargaining needed to arrange such a coalition was utterly inconceivable in an era when simply talking to the other side was a controversial act. By contrast, hawks on the two sides—Adenauer, Ulbricht, the militaries, Mao, Suslov—could form what amounted to a de facto coalition in favor of hostility and arms-racing just by giving belligerent speeches.

THE FOUR-POWER BERLIN AGREEMENT OF 1971

By the early 1970s, statesmen in both East and West had accepted the desirability of a cooperative regime institutionalizing the status quo in Berlin and renouncing the use of force to change borders. They codified this in agreements between the Soviet Union and the Federal Republic of Germany in 1970, and among the four powers occupying Berlin in 1971. Though the negotiation of this collaborative stalemate coincided with shifts in domestic opinion, the changes in the domestic-level game were not causal; rather, they were caused by the clarification of the international situation in the wake of the second Berlin crisis. Thus the outcome could be explained, at least in its general features, without any reference to the domestic level.

The International-Level Game

A systemic explanation for increased cooperation would focus on the solidification of the European status quo between 1958 and 1971. By 1971, power relations were less in flux, offensive means to achieve the consolidation of one's own bloc were less attractive, and in general the security dilemma had become less severe. Thus, cooperation was easier to achieve, based on mutual recognition of the already stabilized status quo.

More specifically, the arrival in the mid-1960s of a stable deterrent standoff between invulnerable nuclear forces made coercive attempts to change the status quo less attractive to attempt and less plausible to fear.[27] In addition, construction of the Berlin Wall increased the security of the GDR, providing a breathing spell for implementing a successful strategy of economic growth and ideological legitimation of the Communist regime.[28] Some authors also argue that the 1968 Soviet intervention in Czechoslovakia further reinforced the stability of the European status quo, by showing conclusively that any improvements in the relations between Western states and East European satellites would have to be negotiated with Moscow. That is, "bridge-building" would not work by means of selective weaning of reformist regimes, but only in the context of a general East-West detente.[29]

One might characterize these developments as systemic changes that mitigated the security dilemma by making conquest, subversion, or alliance-raiding more difficult. Alternatively, one might say that overturning the status quo was already objectively very difficult in 1958. Indeed, that explains why the Berlin crisis turned out as it did in 1961: efforts to defend the status quo succeeded, but moves to change it failed. Thus, the difference between 1958 and 1971 was perhaps not so much a change in objective systemic constraints as a change in the intellectual or political ability to recognize those constraints.

Cognitive Amendments to the International-Level Explanation.   The simplest explanation for the increased willingness to compromise on the basis of the status quo is that statesmen learned as a result of the Berlin confrontation of 1961 (and possibly the Czech events of 1968) that they had no alternative. Under uncertainty in 1958, both sides hoped for favorable changes in the status quo, and feared unfavorable shifts. Likewise, both sides thought that offensive or compellent tactics might be successful. A decade's experience reduced uncertainty about the stability of the status quo, proving these hopes and fears wrong.

Though this is a good explanation for the 1971 agreements, it is important to note that this kind of cognitive explanation cannot fully explain the 1958–61 crisis. It was not just that Khrushchev perceived a fluid political status quo in Central Europe in 1958. Rather, he actively sought to portray the situation as "abnormal" and unstable, as a bargaining ploy in his confrontation with the West.[30] As I argued above, this was because of the domestic political pressures driving him toward a reckless policy.

Domestic or Alliance Politics Explanations.   Some big changes in domestic or alliance politics on both sides may plausibly explain the differing outcomes in 1958–61 and 1971. These may be spurious explanations, however, in the sense that they themselves may be explained by changes in international circumstances, or from learning about them.

The Second-Level Game in the West

The most important change within the Western camp was the changed preferences of the Federal Republic of Germany (FRG). The Willy

Brandt government in 1971 favored trading recognition of the status quo, including GDR statehood, for a normalization of East-West relations, including a Berlin settlement. In contrast, the Adenauer government in 1958–61 had opposed such a trade. This vastly enlarged the "win-set" of the American President in East-West bargaining, facilitating agreement. Therefore, oblique, conflict-engendering bargaining tactics, like those adopted by Eisenhower and Dulles, were not needed in 1971.

What caused this change in West Germany's preferences? One difference is that the West German Social Democratic Party (SPD), always more inclined toward detente with the East, was in power in 1971, whereas the Christian Democrats (CDU) had been in power under Adenauer. But more fundamentally, there had been a change in attitudes, within both the SPD and CDU, which facilitated bargaining on the basis of a recognition of the status quo. By the mid-1960s, the members of the SPD were no longer at all tempted by the notion of a grand accommodation with Moscow in order to achieve German reunification. In part because of this, CDU leaders like Kurt Kiesinger and Rainer Barzel no longer faced Adenauer's problem that the SPD could portray CDU acceptance of the status quo as forsaking the goal of reunification. And in general, the CDU was more relaxed about the irreversibility of the FRG's basic Western orientation. Thus, changing SPD and CDU attitudes increased the size of Brandt's win-set in bargaining with the USSR on Berlin.

Thus, as in Putnam's model, changes in domestic constraints changed both the size of win-sets and the feasibility of international cooperation. At a deeper level, however, these "domestic" changes seem easily explainable in terms of rational learning about the objective constraints and incentives of the international system. The simplest explanation is that SPD and CDU attitudes changed because international events convinced them that their earlier hopes and fears were implausible or obsolete. In this sense, changes in win-sets in the "second-level game" are a spurious cause of increased cooperation.[31]

The Second-Level Game in the East

The domestic game in the Soviet Union under Brezhnev shared some of the key characteristics of the domestic game under Khrushchev: each man adopted a strategy of "offensive detente" as a way of reconciling his self-contradictory logrolled coalition of pro-detente reformers and orthodox interest groups.[32] This rough similarity, in my view, was due to the considerable continuity in the constituencies that the two leaders had to deal with in putting together a ruling coalition. Similar raw materials led to similar winning strategies.

There were two crucial differences, however, between Brezhnev's and

Khrushchev's management of their coalitions. First, Brezhnev learned from Khrushchev's spectacular failures that risky foreign gambits were unlikely to allow an escape from contradictory domestic commitments. It was better, he learned, to keep appeasing the various interest groups and somehow paper over the resulting policy contradictions.

Second, Brezhnev's strategy was to pay off those skeptical of detente (like Suslov) by supporting "progressive change" in the Third World, whereas Khrushchev had tried to address their concerns in Germany.[33] This Third World safety valve allowed bargaining over Berlin to proceed relatively smoothly, without crippling Politburo interference. Overall, Brezhnev's logrolled strategy was still internally incompatible, trying to reconcile expansion and coexistence. But the arena of expansion was different, so Berlin was less affected by the contradictions.[34]

Objective international constraints cannot explain why Khrushchev and Brezhnev were compelled to adopt self-contradictory strategies of offensive detente. But international constraints, and learning about them, *can* probably explain why Brezhnev decided to pay off his hawks, ideologues, and military in the Third World, and in an arms buildup rather than emulating Khrushchev's attempt to outmaneuver his hawks via the Berlin ultimatum. The Berlin solution was risky, flew in the face of firm resistance in defense of the status quo, and therefore did not work. The Third World and arms buildup solution was less risky, and indeed took over a decade to fail.

In short, changes in domestic or alliance politics between 1958 and 1971 neutralized key sources of opposition to a settlement on the basis of recognition of the status quo. Specifically, by 1971 the West German CDU and Soviet conservatives were reconciled to such a settlement. This was accomplished in the former case by changing attitudes and the threat of electoral punishment; in the latter case by side-payments in the Third World. As a result, the size of superpower statesmen's win-sets increased, and agreement was facilitated. However, these developments may be seen as spurious causes of cooperation, since they were probably caused in turn by straightforward learning about the objective constraints of the international situation.

THE GORBACHEV PERIOD

In the wake of the collapse of the Soviet empire in Eastern Europe, East-West bargaining over German unification and conventional arms was cooperative in the sense that the Soviet Union relatively quickly agreed to substantial unilateral concessions. Changes in the international game, especially the decline in relative Soviet power, helped set the context for these developments, but they do not fully explain it. Often, the impending collapse of a great power's strategic position in a region of vital interest simply makes it more belligerent in its determination to prevent falling dominoes. To explain why Soviet new thinkers reacted differently, it is necessary to consider the nature of the domestic coalition that they tried to create.

The new thinkers argued that the old Soviet policies based on enemy images, arms-racing, and autarky were integral to the domestic coalition formed among self-interested bureaucratic groups during the "period of stagnation" under Brezhnev. A new foreign policy, based on increased integration into the world economy and decreased military expenditures, would be required to forge a new progressive coalition based on economic innovation and consumer production. To achieve this, the old approach to detente, based on a tactical stalemate between opposing social systems, would have to be scrapped in favor of a foreign policy aimed at effacing East-West divisions.[35]

In embarking on his new foreign and domestic policies, Gorbachev used glasnost and democratization to curtail the power of the traditional institutions—the Communist Party, autarkic industrial ministries, and the military—whose interests underlay the old logroll supporting the policy of offensive detente. However, it is less clear that the new thinkers succeeded in creating a firm new social base for their own foreign policy. Democratization, even if it were thoroughly carried out, would not automatically create a constituency for internationally oriented market reform, since the Russian populace would (as subsequent events demonstrated) suffer severe costs of adjusting to market conditions. Boris Yeltsin hopes that his populist appeal will convince the Russian people that market reforms are necessary and beneficial. His job of salesmanship would be made easier if cooperation with the West should yield tangible economic benefits, and thus create a constituency for expansion of such cooperation, and for market reform more generally. To the extent that this is what Gorbachev, Yeltsin, and the new thinkers have tried to do, theirs has been a strategy of synergy and positive reverberation.

However, this synergy is operating weakly. Gorbachev's concessions did not cause a decisive influx of capital from new transnational allies, allowing him to pay off domestic supporters of his program of reform. The United States, in particular, argued that decisive market reforms should precede large inflows of Western capital, lest they disappear down the rat-hole of the command economy. Despite Yeltsin's plunge into market shock-therapy in January 1992, transnational economic support was still slow in emerging.

Nonetheless, some synergistic linkages were achieved. The Germans agreed to give the Soviets financial credits to aid their economic reform. Likewise, they paid some of the costs of temporarily stationing Soviet troops in East Germany. In exchange, the Soviets accepted the unification of Germany on Western terms—in particular, Germany's continued membership in NATO. This deal targeted benefits directly on a key swing constituency, the Soviet military, which had been critical of the Soviet retreat from Eastern Europe. By easing the housing and financial problems associated with military redeployment and demobilization, this international linkage was meant to have a synergistic effect on Gorbachev's domestic coalition prospects.[36] The fact that Defense Minister Dmitry Yazov supported the August 1991 coup attempt shows, however, that such international synergies failed to solidify the top military leadership in Gorbachev's camp.

Gorbachev's enlightened foreign policy also won him Western geopolitical self-restraint, not unduly exploiting the Soviets' collapsing position on their western frontiers. For example, in the spring of 1990 President Bush refused to link progress in Soviet-American relations to Soviet acceptance of Baltic independence.

But Gorbachev achieved this Western goodwill and self-restraint at a great price. Instead of targeting small concessions on specific Western groups, he made large, general concessions on most of the issues that had caused tension in East-West relations in the past, and thus favorably affected all sectors of opinion in the West. These across-the-board concessions provided ammunition to Gorbachev's conservative critics, who charged that his whole approach to domestic and foreign policy was undermining the security of the Soviet state.[37]

Putnam's theory may help in analyzing the reasons for the difficulty the new thinkers faced in trying to create synergistic transnational linkages. Putnam argues that such linkages work best when they tap the selective incentives of swing groups, since the payoffs from cooperation can be targeted on groups that count the most politically. Concessions on so-called boundary issues, which did not involve selective incentives, are not focused in this way, and so it is more likely that their political costs will outweigh their benefits. Gorbachev's concessions involved costly retreats on such "boundary" issues and were not directly linked to economic payoffs that might have generated the resources needed to create a stronger constituency for effective reform in Soviet domestic politics.[38]

EVALUATING THE COMPETING EXPLANATIONS

The cases on East-West bargaining over Germany suggest that it is often useful to analyze international negotiation as a two-level game. Sometimes the constraints at the international level were clear and powerful, and drove the outcome at both levels; but sometimes those constraints were weaker and more ambiguous, so domestic constraints played a greater role. Even when politics at both levels played an independent causal role, however, it was usually sufficient to analyze the two-level game in terms of two partial-equilibrium models, each game setting parameters for play in the other. Synergistic interactions, which could only be captured by a general-equilibrium model, were rare.

Realists might try to explain all the outcomes strictly in terms of international-level variables, but this approach would not be satisfactory on its own. This kind of international-level explanation might see the comparatively conflictual outcomes in the first half of the Cold War as due to the fluidity of the political status quo and fluctuations in military power, which heightened security fears on both sides.[39] Once the second Berlin crisis definitively tested the status quo and found it stable, however, security fears were reduced, and a cooperative recognition of the status quo was possible.[40] The collapse of Soviet power explains Gorbachev's one-sided retreats, and the West's disinclination to exploit the collapse explains why the retrenchment has been carried out in a cooperative fashion. In this view, variations in the strength of militant or cooperative domestic factions were largely rational responses to objective changes in international conditions, which were exogenous to the bargaining games (for example, the emergence of secure nuclear second-strike capabilities, which relaxed the security dilemma after the early 1960s).[41]

This tidy account, purely at the level of international system structure, is not implausible. Certainly, if the analyst measures these international variables in terms of the leaders' own *subjective* assessments of them, then the "international level" can explain all the outcomes. But the leaders' assessments of the incentives offered by their international environment were often driven by strategic ideologies, which were shaped in part by domestic or alliance politics, and which sometimes differed markedly from an objective, Martian's-eye-view of international realities. Ideas about the state's vulnerability and the incentives for offensive solutions to security problems were often skewed by domestic-level or alliance-level considerations.[42]

Purely domestic explanations fare better in some periods than others, but overall remain unsatisfactory on their own. Such factors explain the period of the second Berlin crisis reasonably well: strong veto groups on both sides blocked the path to mutually acceptable agreements, and forced groups favoring international cooperation to devise contorted, counterproductive approaches to detente.[43] Domestic explanations for the 1970–71 agreements on Germany and Berlin, however, are for the most part spurious: the weakening of anti-agreement forces on both sides of the Iron Curtain was caused by the objective stability of the geopolitical stalemate in Europe after the arrival of Mutual Assured Destruction and the Berlin Wall. In the Gorbachev period, domestic factors were again important. The attempt to create a new kind of Soviet political coalition based on the empowerment of new political forces required cooperation with the West and rendered the division of Europe undesirable. Strategic concepts discounting the threat from the West helped to justify the continuation of East-West cooperation, despite the collapse of the Soviet security *glacis* in Eastern Europe.

In short, sometimes domestic constraints dominated East-West bargaining over Germany; sometimes international constraints did; and sometimes both were independently important. Thus, one way to think about two-level games is as a contest between constraining forces at each of the two levels. Pressures from one level will push the statesman to exploit whatever ambiguous room for maneuver may exist on the other level, up to the point where the character of the countervailing constraints become clear.

For example, at the outset of Khrushchev's Berlin gambit, international-level constraints during the transition to the new situation of mutual deterrence were unclear and misunderstood, whereas the domestic and intra-allied constraints on both sides were quite tight. But eventually Khrushchev's Berlin diplomacy bumped into clear international constraints that forced a restructuring of Soviet domestic political alignments. In fact, the international-level clarity achieved by the outcome of the Berlin crisis forced players on both sides of the Iron Curtain to take the European stalemate as a given in their domestic coalition-making. Under Gorbachev, international constraints (decreasing Soviet relative power) and domestic constraints (the interests of the Soviet ruling coalition) changed in ways that radically changed the scope of ratifiable cooperative outcomes.

Though bargaining over Germany was often a two-level game, attempts at synergistic issue linkage between the two levels were largely unsuccessful. Domestic coalitions based on synergistic issue linkage in the international-level game were attempted by both Khrushchev and Gorbachev, and both attempts failed. Negative reverberations, in which the hostile policies of one side promoted hostile coalitions in the other, occurred, but their underlying causes are best analyzed by "partial-equilibrium" models operating either at the international level (e.g., the security dilemma) or the domestic level (e.g., veto groups that insisted on belligerent policies). Targeting of swing votes rarely involved selective incentives, since the East-West security questions involved in negotiating the German question have typically involved what Putnam calls boundary disputes.

IMPLICATIONS FOR THEORIZING ABOUT TWO-LEVEL GAMES

The lesson for theorizing about two-level games is not to lose sight of the separate dynamics of the two games while analyzing the interactions between them. Many situations can be described in terms of the language of two-level games: win-sets, reverberations, and targeting abound. But this terminology may mask the underlying reality that the main causal force is coming not from intricate interactions between the two games, but from powerful constraints emanating from one game or the other. If so, the first task of a good analysis of a two-level game should be to construct separate analyses of each game, based on separate theories about political dynamics at each level.

This kind of partial-equilibrium approach is appropriate in analyzing security issues, where the dilemmas of self-help in anarchy make transnational coalitions dangerous. Security bargaining, moreover, is more likely to involve "boundary" issues, and so may offer less scope for synergistic linkages. Partial-equilibrium analysis is especially necessary in the case of relations between states that have limited economic ties or major differences in their social systems and cultural patterns—all factors that hinder transnational linkages. It is a step forward to understand that international politics is often a two-level game, but for many issues and bargaining relationships, there may be few truly synergistic interactions between the two games.

NOTES

1. John Lewis Gaddis, *The Long Peace* (New York: Oxford University Press, 1987). A good, recent survey of the German question during this period can be found in Wolfram Hanrieder, *Germany, America, Europe: Forty Years of German Foreign Policy* (New Haven, Conn.: Yale University Press, 1989).

2. On the two-level game and the role of synergy between the levels, see Robert Putnam, "Diplomacy and Domestic Politics: The Logic of Two-Level Games," *International Organization* 42 (Summer 1988): 427–460 (reprinted as the Appendix in this volume), and Andrew Moravcsik's Introduction (Chapter 1) to this volume.

3. Putnam defines synergy, or synergistic issue linkage, as "issue linkage at Level I that alters the feasible outcome at Level II." "This strategy works not by changing the preferences of any domestic constituents, but rather by creating a policy option . . . that was previously beyond domestic control" ("Diplomacy," Appendix, p. 448). The notion of synergy is in my view the most innovative, though not the only, conceptual development in Putnam's article.

4. Putnam, "Diplomacy" (Appendix, esp. pp. 443–444, 456).

5. Kenneth Waltz, *Theory of International Politics* (Reading, Mass.: Addison-Wesley, 1979), chap. 7.

6. Robert Jervis, "Cooperation Under the Security Dilemma," *World Politics* 30 (January 1978): 167–214.

7. This roughly follows the approach in Glenn Snyder and Paul Diesing, *Conflict Among Nations* (Princeton, N.J.: Princeton University Press, 1977).

8. Note Putnam's similar points in "Diplomacy" (Appendix, p. 439). I discuss the effect of parochial veto groups in Jack Snyder, *Myths of Empire: Domestic Politics and International Ambition* (Ithaca, N.Y.: Cornell University Press, 1991).

9. Throughout this chapter, I use the term "spurious" in a sense that is slightly broader than its normal, technical meaning in the social sciences. A causal relationship between two variables is said to be "spurious" if the two occur together only because a third variable causes them both. I extend this to include not only the case where the third variable directly causes both of the other two, but also where an intervening ("spurious") variable simply transmits the force of the third variable, which is the sufficient cause of the outcome.

10. For example, in order to gain West German ratification of the 1970s treaty renouncing the use of force to change borders, Moscow accepted the demands of Christian Democratic swing voters for linkage to a subsequent Berlin Treaty, but that concession was not a payoff only for swing voters: all Germans were happy to obtain it. See Putnam, "Diplomacy" (Appendix, p. 451), on the concept of targeting; and F. Stephen Larrabee, "The Politics of Reconciliation: Soviet Policy Towards West Germany, 1964–1972" (Ph.D. diss., Columbia University, 1978), pp. 333–336, on the 1970 example.

11. On reverberation, see Putnam, "Diplomacy" (Appendix, pp. 454–456).

12. For some examples, see Jack Snyder, "International Leverage on Soviet Domestic Change," *World Politics* 42 (October 1989): 1–30, esp. 15–21.

13. Milovan Djilas, *Conversations with Stalin* (New York: Harcourt, Brace and World, 1962), p. 114. For historical background on the first Berlin crisis, see Hannes Adomeit, *Soviet Risk-Taking and Crisis Behavior* (London: Allen and Unwin, 1982); and Avi Shlaim, *The United States and the Berlin Blockade* (Berkeley: University of California Press, 1983).

14. Scott Parrish, "Soviet Reactions to the Security Dilemma: The Sources of Soviet Encirclement, 1945–1950" (Harriman Institute certificate essay, Columbia University, 1990), and his Ph.D. diss. (Columbia University, 1992). See also sources cited in Snyder, "International Leverage," pp. 16–17.

15. William McCagg, *Stalin Embattled* (Detroit: Wayne State University Press, 1979); and other works cited in Jack Snyder, "The Gorbachev Revolution: A Waning of Soviet Expansionism?" *International Security* 12 (Winter 1987–88): 93–131.

16. In this section, I draw on James Richter, "Action and Reaction in Soviet Foreign Policy," (Ph.D. diss., University of California, Berkeley, 1989); and Snyder, "The Gorbachev Revolution."

17. In addition to Richter, "Action and Reaction," see Carl Linden, *Khrushchev and the Soviet Leadership* (Baltimore: Johns Hopkins University Press, 1966).

18. See Stephen Ambrose, *Eisenhower*, vol. 2 (New York: Simon and Schuster, 1984).

19. For background on these points, see Richter, "Action and Reaction," and

Jack Schick, *The Berlin Crisis* (Philadelphia: University of Pennsylvania Press, 1971). Glenn Snyder and Paul Diesing, in *Conflict among Nations*, pp. 268–275, put Schick's arguments in a theoretical framework.

20. I argue this, providing citations and some evidence, in "The Gorbachev Revolution."

21. Richter provides a great deal of evidence in support of this interpretation.

22. Marc Trachtenberg, *History and Strategy* (Princeton, N.J.: Princeton University Press, 1991), chap. 5, "The Berlin Crisis."

23. Both Trachtenberg (ibid.) and Schick, *Berlin Crisis*, emphasize the threat of a nuclearized West Germany integrated into NATO, in Khrushchev's calculations.

24. Adomeit, *Soviet Risk-taking*, chaps. 11–13, gives a balanced account of the situation facing the Soviets and East Germans in 1958.

25. Herbert Dinerstein, *War and the Soviet Union* (New York: Praeger, 1959), chap. 4.

26. On policy networks, see Peter Katzenstein, ed., *Between Power and Plenty* (Madison: University of Wisconsin Press, 1978).

27. For the argument that Mutual Assured Destruction (MAD) makes defense of the status quo easier, see Robert Jervis, *The Meaning of the Nuclear Revolution* (Ithaca, N.Y.: Cornell University Press, 1989).

28. A. James McAdams, *East Germany and Detente: Building Authority after the Wall* (Cambridge, Eng.: Cambridge University Press, 1985); Michael Sodaro, "East Germany and the Dilemmas of Detente" (Ph.D. diss., Columbia University, 1978).

29. McAdams, *East Germany and Detente*, p. 95; Larrabee, "Politics of Reconciliation," p. 163.

30. See Hope Harrison, "Was Khrushchev a Student of Thomas Schelling?: Khrushchev's Coercive Diplomacy in the 1958–1961 Berlin Crisis" (unpubl. ms., Harriman Institute, Columbia University, 1987); also Schick, *Berlin Crisis*, p. 102.

31. Some might argue, however, that generational turnover in the West German elite, bringing to power new politicians with different formative experiences, had an independent effect on the outcome.

32. I discuss this in "The Gorbachev Revolution."

33. The most detailed treatment is Richard Anderson, "Competitive Politics and Soviet Global Policy: Authority-Building and Bargaining in the Politburo, 1964–1972" (Ph.D. diss., University of California, Berkeley, 1989). In addition to Suslov, Podgorny also was paid off in this manner; see Anderson, chaps. 9 and 10.

34. Putnam argues that leaders facing domestic opposition to agreement can use the threat of "involuntary defection" to get better terms at the international bargaining table. Thus, Brezhnev should have been able to extract bargaining leverage from the opposition of Suslov and Nikolai Podgorny to linkage between the Soviet-FRG Treaty and the Four-Power Berlin Treaty. But the Soviets, because of the opacity of their political debates and the myth of Communist unanimity, could not openly invoke the threat of involuntary defection. Consequently, they had to argue *on the merits of the issue* that they could not back down.

That is, they had to portray a risk of involuntary defection as a risk of voluntary defection, a tactic that turns Thomas Schelling's thesis on its head. This seriously undercut Soviet bargaining power, especially since the Brandt government's three-vote majority made the German threat of involuntary defection highly credible. See Larrabee, "Politics of Reconciliation," pp. 329, 334–338.

35. In addition to my "Gorbachev Revolution," see Moshe Lewin, *The Gorbachev Phenomenon* (Berkeley: University of California Press, 1988), on domestic developments; and Jerry Hough, *Opening Up the Soviet Economy* (Washington, D.C.: Brookings Institution, 1988), for the international connection.

36. On German financial aid to help Gorbachev's domestic political position, see Ferdinand Protzman, "Bonn to Aid Kremlin Reforms with a $3 Billion Bank Credit," *New York Times*, June 23, 1990, pp. 1 and 4. On the military's political stance, see Michael Dobbs, "Soviet Army's New Battlefield—The Political Front," *Washington Post*, April 15, 1990, pp. A1 and A28.

37. On the conservatives' counterattack against Gorbachev's foreign policy, see for example former Politburo member Yegor Ligachev's remarks on "a new Munich," translated in "Excerpts From Speech by Ligachev to Party," *New York Times*, Feb. 7, 1990.

38. I believe that East-West transnational linkages in support of improved security and economic cooperation are desirable and not completely infeasible, and in "Averting Anarchy in the New Europe," *International Security* 14 (Spring 1990): 5–41, I argue for such a policy. But in an explanatory vein, it would be an exaggeration to claim that such linkages have already succeeded.

39. This view is argued most extensively by Parrish, "Soviet Reactions to the Security Dilemma," and in his 1992 dissertation.

40. This is argued by McGeorge Bundy, *Danger and Survival* (New York: Random House, 1988), chap. 8.

41. Robert Jervis, in *The Meaning of the Nuclear Revolution*, pp. 35–38, notes the connection between the arrival of mutual assured destruction and the declining frequency of crises.

42. For a general discussion on the domestic sources of strategic ideology, see my *Myths of Empire*, chaps. 1 and 2.

43. Snyder, "Gorbachev Revolution," pp. 93–131.

5

Armaments Among Allies
European Weapons Collaboration, 1975–1985

Andrew Moravcsik

For European governments, the arguments in favor of multinational collaboration to produce armaments appear compelling.[1] Politically, arms collaboration cements multilateral bonds among members of the European Community and NATO, as well as bilateral partnerships between countries like France and West Germany. Militarily, collaboration promotes rationalization, standardization, and interoperability (RSI) among military allies, recognized since 1949 by NATO defense planners as a primary Western objective. Economically, collaboration reduces defense expenditures by amortizing the enormous fixed capital and research and development (R&D) investments of high-technology weapons production over longer production runs and by exploiting "learning economies" in the manufacture of complex products. The wastage due to redundant defense-industrial capacity in Europe today totals an estimated 35 billion dollars—27 percent of total European defense spending in 1987.[2]

The world's most intensive efforts at armaments collaboration have taken place between France, Germany, and other European countries. In the decade between 1975 and 1985, Franco-German negotiations included the European Fighter Aircraft (EFA) project, which sought to add France to the Anglo-Italian-German consortium that had produced the Tornado fighter in the 1970s; the Franco-German tank project, which foresaw joint production of a main battle tank; and the Franco-German helicopter project, which envisaged a common family of antitank and air-to-air combat helicopters. Each of these weapons was an expensive, technologically sophisticated system in which the potential for economic gains through collaboration could be measured in hundreds of millions or even billions of dollars. Together, these projects raised the prospect that an entire European generation of the weapons most essential to a modern military force would be developed multinationally.

This prospect was not realized. Negotiations over the EFA collapsed in 1985, with the French opting for independent production of their own fighter plane, the Rafale. The German government quietly withdrew from the tank project in 1982 rather than honor a preliminary agreement with France. Only the helicopter project was launched, leading to the formation of Eurocopter GmbH, a multinational joint venture.

What accounts for these varied negotiating outcomes? More generally, why do so many armaments collaboration projects fail, despite the apparent advantages?

FACTORS IN ARMAMENTS COLLABORATION

The most widespread explanation for the failure of armaments collaboration begins with the assumption that in "high politics," the "national interest," calculated in Realist terms, determines state interests.[3] From this perspective, the source of opposition to collaboration is unambiguously military. "States do not willingly place themselves in situations of increased dependence," writes Kenneth Waltz. "In a self-help system, considerations of security subordinate economic gain to political interest."[4]

In studies of arms collaboration, this argument has been advanced with varying degrees of precision. Some observers simply invoke the allegedly universal instinct to protect "national sovereignty." Others stress distinctive national strategic doctrines, such as France's Gaullist legacy of "national independence." Still others point to divergent military priorities, stemming from different operational specifications and geopolitical positions. Each of these explanations assumes, with Realist theory, that the politico-military leadership controls the state apparatus and responds purposively, even rationally, to an anarchic and potentially hostile international security environment.[5]

The case studies in this essay belie this common perception. Far from being an example of high politics, in which decisions are made by the politico-military leadership alone, arms collaboration generates a great deal of domestic conflict, in which government bureaucracies and private interest groups assume important and unexpected roles. Governments oppose such projects, I will argue, not because collaboration poses a threat to national autonomy or security as classically defined, but because they are unable to negotiate arrangements for apportioning research, development, and production tasks that satisfy powerful domestic economic interests.

To account for national policies, an alternative theoretical explanation for success or failure is thus required, one that takes into account the domestic distributional issues that arise from international interdependence on domestic politics.[6] I argue that in international negotiations over the allotment of industrial tasks in collaborative projects, the economic interest of arms-producing firms are decisive: when domestic arms producers oppose collaboration, they are almost always successful, regardless of the interests of the military or the chief executive. When firms favor a collaborative project, they are equally successful. In turn, these interests for or against collaboration reflect the position of the firm in oligopolistic global export markets. This is true of both France and Germany: despite divergent national-security rhetoric, governments and arms producers of both countries respond almost identically to similar external incentives. Despite the persistence of Gaullist beliefs, for example, the fundamentals of French policy toward European armaments collaboration differs in no essential way from that of its neighbors.

THE ACTORS AND THEIR INCENTIVES

To highlight the decisive determinants of success or failure of negotiations over arms collaboration, it is useful to begin with a schematic model of the key domestic actors and their incentives.

Domestic decision-making over armaments collaboration involves three categories of actors: chief executives (the French President or German Chancellor); top Ministry of Defense officials (the "MoD"); and the main arms producer(s) that contract with the government ("domestic firms"). Chief executives initiate negotiations and intervene intermittently thereafter. High officials plan and execute the negotiations. In the language of the "two-level games" metaphor, domestic producers "ratify" the results. Other domestic actors are rarely involved.

To understand the dynamics of domestic politics, we need to specify the preferences of each group and the external incentives to which they respond. The model developed here assumes that heads of government stress political interests, both international and domestic; MoDs stress the national military interests; and domestic firms stress their own particularistic economic interests in oligopolistic markets.[7] Although the three sets of actors appear to be pursuing qualitatively distinct types of goals, their motivations can be simplified considerably by assuming that the domestic cleavages in negotiations over defense collaboration are not between groups with different diplomatic and strategic priorities, as Realists would have it, but between groups with different economic interests in collaboration. Both the procurement procedures of MoDs and the competitive strategies of domestic industries can be understood as a function of the costs and benefits for each from integration with the global economy—an approach Peter Gourevitch has termed "the second-image-reversed," or "production profile," approach.[8]

The argument here can be summarized as follows: The economic costs and benefits of collaboration can be divided into positive-sum and distributional components. The interest of the military leads them to act as rational consumers for the society as a whole, seeking *positive-sum* gains with their foreign counterparts, while the interests of domestic firms requires the maintenance of their relative position in oligopolistic global markets, leading them to focus on interstate *distributional issues*. The chief executive adjudicates between these competing interests. While chief executives themselves generally accept the military, economic, and diplomatic arguments for collaboration, they are primarily interested in their domestic political position, a situation which grants armaments producers a de facto veto over the ratification of collaboration agreements. Let us now consider the preferences and incentives of each group in more detail.

The Ministry of Defense and Positive-Sum Gains

MoD officials are primarily concerned with the provision of national security.[9] This leads the military to support procurement from the source that can deliver the appropriate weapons on time at the lowest cost ("more bang for the buck"). In contrast to the U.S. Pentagon, which enjoys domestic economies of scale large enough to render autarkic production (and indulgence in interservice rivalry) considerably more affordable, European planners face a steep *trade-off* between autarky and efficiency. European MoDs must pay a much higher price in economic efficiency for policies designed to assure security of supply.[10]

The preference of European MoDs for cost-effective procurement leads them to act, to a first approximation, as rational consumers seeking to exploit the common gains from collaboration.[11] MoDs are primarily interested in the positive-sum gains from collaboration. For military planners, collaboration is a solution to an international collective-action problem, in that it ameliorates the poor efficiency of uncoordinated competition under conditions of surplus capacity. These gains accrue most directly to MoDs, which procure armaments, and thence, one assumes, to taxpayers.[12] Given their preference for cost-effective procurement, MoDs—as distinct from European states and governments as a whole—tend to oppose collaborative ventures only when there is reason to believe that they will not generate the appropriate weapons at lower cost than through domestic production. The greater the economies of scale to be exploited through shared research, development, and production, the greater the incentive to collaborate. High unit cost, small production runs, and high R&D-intensity—hallmarks of the production of tanks, aircraft, and helicopters—signal the possibility of large potential economic gains through collaboration.

Armaments Producers and Distributional Conflict

Domestic armaments producers seek no general social goals; as firms, they engage instead in strategic behavior aimed at maximizing their private gain. Maximizing turnover can be used as a proxy for this interest.[13] For most high-tech armaments, the market is far from perfectly competitive. Firms are nearly always monopolists in their domestic markets and oligopolists in global markets characterized by market imperfections such as increasing returns to scale, learning economies, massive overcapacity, government intervention, and a small number of firms. With fixed costs of R&D and production increasing at double the rate of increases in military spending, many product lines in the armaments industry are approaching conditions of "natural" global oligopoly—in which economic forces would reduce the number of profitable worldwide firms to a handful or, in extreme cases, to a single global monopolist.[14]

Imperfections in domestic and global markets force firms to think strategically. In particular, they must consider the distribution of the costs and benefits from collaboration, which results primarily from the international allocation of future production. Costs and benefits of this sort accrue directly to firms and those in society dependent on them. Firms thus tend to be concerned with their relative position in world markets—and thus with the relative gains, in terms of market position, from collaboration. Collaborative projects are market-sharing cartels, in which shares of research funding, production, and sales are carefully negotiated. If firms gain from a cartel, they will seek to join it; if they lose, they will oppose it. The advantages and disadvantages for firms, and hence their levels of support for collaboration, vary with world market position.

Firms seek to preserve two sorts of competitive assets: technological capabilities, which permit the production of sophisticated products, and export market niches, which permit the amortization of costs over a larger market. To see how global market position, in terms of technology and export shares, translates into corporate strategy, consider two firms, one stronger and one weaker, one "leader" and one "follower." Collaboration can influence the competitive position of leader and follower firms in three ways.

First, *the transfer of knowledge in international collaboration tends to benefit followers at the expense of leaders.* Collaboration forces leaders to share third-country export markets and technical knowledge with followers.

In many civilian areas of the economy, larger, stronger, and more international firms support international cooperation. In an armaments collaboration project—which, in this regard, functions not solely as an agreement to internationalize production, but also as a market-sharing cartel—it is precisely those firms with technological and market assets who have an incentive to block international agreements. Moreover, the more focused a firm's activities are in R&D, the greater the potential conflict with other firms, and the less likely they are to support collaboration.

Second, *the more closely matched firms are technologically, the greater the potential for conflict between them.* The more technologically competent the follower firm, the greater the share of the development work in high value-added core technologies it will demand, and the greater the potential threat it poses to the market position of the stronger firm.[15] Development of such technologies is the source of competitive advantages in these sectors. Very weak followers will be satisfied with a "co-production" project, where they produce components of a product designed by the stronger firm and act as de facto subcontractors. Stronger followers, on the other hand, will demand a "co-development" arrangement, in which major design tasks, as well as production, are shared.

Third, and most important, *the greater the differential between the level of exports of the firms, the less likely is the leader to favor collaboration.* Relative technological position, discussed above, is one determinant of firm preferences toward collaboration, but its explanatory power is limited. Technological capabilities can be exploited economically only if firms can use them to increase turnover, which, in an industry with greater surplus capacity, generally requires an expansion of global market share. In situations where neither of the two countries exports weapons, technological leakage poses relatively little risk to leaders, since governments maintain firm control over domestic markets. With optimal economies of scale in arms production surpassing the domestic market of any single European country, however, export markets have become the key to independent survival. Exports permit firms to amortize fixed costs and increase turnover, as well as in themselves constituting an unregulated, and hence particularly profitable, form of sales.

Exports pose a particularly difficult problem, because any scheme to divide tasks according to levels of domestic procurement effectively transfers a proportion of the export revenues from firms with established export markets (in the previous technological generation) to those without them.[16] Most co-development arrangements are organized according to "*juste retour*" ("just return" or, more colloquially, "you get what you pay for"), a norm whereby development costs, production workshares, and the return from export sales are distributed in proportion to levels of domestic procurement.[17] Firms successful in export markets will thus have a strong incentive to oppose *juste retour* collaboration. While in theory one might negotiate side-payments to counteract the transfer, they are difficult to negotiate, since the uncertainty in predicting future export market position is great. Established exporters tend to overestimate the prospects for future sales. Moreover, in an environment of slack demand, a "fair" split—according to the new market power of the weaker firm—often means a decline in production for the established power.

To summarize: Firms considering collaboration take into account the balance of technological competence and export shares. Firms with the technological competence to produce a weapon on their own, *and* with established export markets to amortize the costs, tend to oppose collaboration, unless they can dominate it through co-production or licensing. Firms that have the technological competence to produce a product, but no established export markets, tend to cautiously support cooperation, if it can be negotiated on a relatively equal basis. Firms that are not capable of self-sufficient production favor collaboration, and negotiate workshare arrangements roughly proportional to their share of total production. There is little conflict in such cases, since the tasks allotted to the weaker firm would often otherwise be subcontracted. These firm-level incentives are summarized in Table 1.

TABLE 1.   Predicted Relationship Between International Market Position and Firm Preference for Collaboration

	Position of Firm One		
Position of Firm Two	Firm with Competence and Exports	Firm with Competence without Exports	Firm without Competence without Exports
Firm with competence and exports	MODERATE TO HIGH CONFLICT: Firms cautious unless they have equal export shares.	HIGH CONFLICT: Firm with exports will oppose cooperation.	LOW CONFLICT: Firm without exports will negotiate a workshare proportional to procurement share.
Firm with competence but no exports		LOW CONFLICT: Workshares divided according to national procurement.	LOW CONFLICT: Workshares divided according to national procurement.
Firm without competence or exports			COLLABORATION TECHNOLOGICALLY IMPOSSIBLE

Chief Executives: Balancing General and Particular Interests

The "two-level games" framework suggests that chief executives are "Janus-faced," uniquely responsible for balancing domestic and international concerns. As Woodrow Wilson observed, and Liberal theories of international relations more generally reiterate, the chief executive has the task of balancing general and special interests.[18] In the case of arms production, chief executives balance the general interest in national security and fiscal responsibility, represented by the military, with the particularistic interest of those who profit directly from armaments production, represented by firms. Individually, chief executives generally accept the economic and military justifications for collaboration, and they see collaboration as an important element in strengthening interstate relations, in this case Franco-German friendship. For this reason, they are likely to be agenda-setters, promoting armaments projects in their early stages. Chief executives tend to be "doves"—their "acceptability-sets" are more conciliatory than those of the ratifying elements in domestic society.

But chief executives are also—and, in this case, primarily—accountable to particularistic domestic constituencies. Their political future depends on their ability to function as *domestic* political actors. As arms collaboration negotiations progress, the details of proposed agreements become more precise and the domestic implications of collaborative agreements become clearer. Domestic groups mobilize, and the conflict between "domestic" and "international" imperatives itself becomes a source of domestic conflict.

In the conflict between general and special interests, theories of collective action suggest that concentrated groups have decisive advantages over diffusely distributed groups.[19] When seeking to implement two-level strategies, chief executives find themselves in a role analogous to what James Q. Wilson, following others, terms a "policy entrepreneur."[20] When the effects of a proposed agreement are certain, concentrated, and heavily biased toward one side of the issue, heads of governments are unlikely to enjoy great leverage, and influence attempts are likely to be costly and difficult. The latter is the situation facing statesmen in arms collaboration negotiations, where, in Wilson's typology, benefits are diffuse and costs concentrated. Wilson concludes that in such situations the side opposed to the policy generally mobilizes and captures regulatory agencies, unless a salient external event allows politicians to mobilize a large percentage of the general public around an issue.

Not only is opposition to collaboration concentrated; it tends to be intense and focused on a short time horizon. The concentration and intensity of opposing interests helps explain why domestic armaments producers, if so inclined, can successfully resist collaboration. Here the comparison with the military is instructive. MoDs are equally concentrated, but they lack equally concentrated, intensely committed political constituencies. The interests of domestic groups involved in armaments procurement, by contrast, are grounded firmly in the domestic political economy. Oligopolistic or monopolistic firms, few in number, encounter little difficulty overcoming the collective action problems of interest-group organization. Even the workforce in most French and German armaments firms can be quickly mobilized to influence collaboration decisions—a fact which helps explain the strong overt support of the French Communist Party for national arms projects, even where they must coordinate their activities with Gaullist businessmen. The knowledge of technological possibilities and true cost estimates held by arms-producing firms can also be an important asset in negotiations. With corporate autonomy or survival potentially at stake in a single decision, corporate preferences are immediate and intensely felt. Since high-technology weapons are large, lumpy goods, often with life-cycles spanning a decade or more, the "shadow of the future" tends to be short, unless the firm involved is a large, diversified company.

Armaments producers thus enjoy decisive advantages over taxpayers on specific procurement issues such as collaboration. Militaries and MoDs, while themselves concentrated, must find support largely among diffuse interest groups, opponents of high defense spending, and supporters of cooperation for purely internationalist reasons. Armaments producers, on the other hand, can draw on direct political influence wielded by concentrated business and labor groups with a strong interest in maintaining domestic production. Businesses and workers disadvantaged by a collaborative project can pressure the government through campaign contributions, elite networks, labor protests, and electoral mobilization against restricting production. At times, they may also exploit a residual sense of nationalism.[21]

Domestic arms-producing firms and their allies in society—including labor unions and parliamentarians—wield more concentrated political power than the MoD, and their views generally prevail. The approval of armaments producers can be viewed as the relevant process of domestic "ratification." It follows that the decisive variable explaining which negotiations succeed and which fail is the global market position of domestic arms-producing firms.

THE CASES: FIGHTERS, TANKS, AND HELICOPTERS

To test this model, we now turn to the three Franco-German negotiations. The fighter plane, tank, and helicopter projects followed a common trajectory. In each case, chief executives launched the negotiations and top MoD officials carried them out—both groups being positively inclined toward collaboration. Major intermilitary disagreements over operational specifications arose early, but were resolved either by the MoDs themselves or at the direct command of heads of government. Discussions then commenced over the quantitative and qualitative distribution of economic production. In each case, this appears to have been the critical point. If the leader firm did not have a strong third-country export position, it was generally willing to consider cooperation—as was Aérospatiale in the case of helicopters—and the negotiation succeeded. If the leader firm enjoyed a strong export position, it tended to oppose the agreement, as did Dassault in the case of fighter planes and Krauss-Maffei in the case of tanks. Such firms were able to spearhead domestic opposition to ratification, and these negotiations failed. The predictions of the model and the empirical findings are summarized in Table 2.

TABLE 2. Domestic Interests and Cooperation: Predictions and Findings

	Predictions and Findings			
	Predicted Firm Preferences	Observed Firm Preferences	Predicted Outcome	Observed Outcome
Cases				
Fighter Aircraft	Dassault opposed; Rolls-Royce and BAe willing to cooperate on an equal basis; MBB, MTU favorable.	As predicted	France opposed; Britain cautious; Germany favorable.	As predicted
Tanks	Krauss-Maffei opposed; GIAT favorable.	As predicted	Germany opposed; France favorable.	As predicted
Helicopters	Aérospatiale cautious; MBB favorable.	As predicted	France cautious; Germany favorable.	As predicted

Now let us examine the cases in more detail.

The European Fighter Aircraft (EFA), 1975–1985

Discussions beginning in 1976 revealed that the MoDs of France, Germany, Britain, and Italy all favored a collaborative project to fill a common fighter-aircraft requirement for the 1990s. (Spain joined the negotiations later.) When detailed discussions commenced in 1981, disagreements emerged over military specifications, such as combat role and capabilities, size, and weight. These were resolved in a compromise agreement on operational requirements reached at a December 1983 meeting of air force chiefs of staff in Köln. The most important compromise concerned weight: the French desire for an extremely light fighter (an empty weight of 7.5 tons) and that of the others for a somewhat heavier design (9.5 tons) resulted in a compromise at 8.5 tons. Each country's needs were estimated—330 aircraft for France, 250 for Britain, 200 for Germany, and 150 for Spain and Italy—with cost and workshare to be divided proportionally.

While the initial agreement at the level of military staffs offered a compromise solution to the conflicts over operational specifications, the struggle over industrial advantages continued between the leading European firms, pitting British Aerospace and Rolls-Royce, the British airframe and engine producers, against their French counterparts, Avions Marcel Dassault and Societé Nationale d'Etude et de Construction de Moteurs d'Aviation (SNECMA). On the surface, the persistence of disputes over the precise weight of the aircraft, which was repeatedly reopened, as well as design leadership and the organization of the project, were still couched in terms of their military significance. In fact, however, these disputes reflected underlying conflicts between national champion firms over leadership and control of the design and production of the airframe and engines. The positions of these firms, as we shall see, were those predicted by the theory of corporate preferences presented above. The disputes proved intractable and ultimately led to the dissolution of the collaborative coalition.

The industrial issues can be divided into two categories: disputes over the airframe and disputes over the engines.

Airframe Design Leadership.   By 1978, Britain, Germany, and Italy had collaborated for ten years on the Tornado multi-role combat aircraft, and had jointly invested in prototypes for the new fighter. Meanwhile, Dassault in France built the ACX/Rafale, its own prototype based on the Mirage 4000—a design developed and abandoned in the early 1980s due to the lack of export opportunities. The British and French designs were to a large extent incompatible. The negotiators were thus divided into two camps from the start, with the Germans trying to mediate between the two, but somewhat closer to the British.

The main obstacle to agreement came from Dassault, a small family firm run by Marcel Dassault, a legendary figure in French industry and politics, and his son Serge. Dassault was the French monopoly producer of fighters. As a technologically competent firm exporting 70 percent of production through the 1970s, Dassault was implacably opposed to collaboration with foreigners. Not only was Dassault a large exporter, but it produced almost exclusively military aircraft, specializing primarily in their design and integration, while subcontracting 75 percent of the actual production to other firms. Because of its dependence on high value-added design tasks in a single sector, any compromise of design leadership by Dassault could not be compensated through subcontracts or civilian-side benefits. As a result, Dassault, unlike any other leading European aerospace firm, had never initiated a collaborative project, although it had inherited a few in the late 1960s through merger with another French producer. Dassault had withstood pressure for collaboration by building small, light, lower-performance fighters (the renowned "Mirage" series), developing successive generations of the Mirage design incrementally, and marketing planes among less-developed countries that could or would not procure from the United States or the Soviet Union. In this way, Dassault had achieved respectable economies of scale.

The decisive concern for Dassault, and thus for the French government, was the effect of collaboration on its export share in third countries, which it calculated as follows: with the exception of Thomson, which had informally been named producer of the radar, French firms expected to gain more from producing 100 percent of the 335 aircraft expected to be procured by the French government, plus 100 percent of French exports, than by producing 25–30 percent of the 800–1,000 European aircraft plus only 25 percent of whatever exports were generated. Unless the EFA generated four times as many exports as Dassault's previous aircraft, or extraordinary side-payments were offered, the French producer would face a substantial loss of turnover. The dismissal of 5,000 workers was predicted and, accordingly, the Communist unions and party (despite ideological disagreements with the Conservative Dassault family) actively joined Dassault in opposing cooperation.[22]

British Aerospace (BAe) and Messerschmidt-Bölkow-Blohm (MBB), by contrast, built more advanced fighters largely for the NATO front, were diversified within and between product lines, were publicly held, and had a history of collaboration. BAe had the technological capability to launch a classic fighter project on its own, but had not done so since the late 1950s. It was a highly diversified firm with extensive civilian interests, and had collaborated with Germany and Italy on the Tornado and with the United States on the Harrier. None of these products had been successful on export markets.[23] MBB had never produced a fighter on its own, and there were doubts whether it had the systems-integration capability to do so. As a result, BAe and MBB proposed institutionalized collaboration on a *juste retour* basis, as had been done through the joint subsidiary Panavia with the Tornado.

As a result of the divergence between the corporate strategies of Dassault and the others, the dispute over the operational specifications of the airframe refused to die, despite the 1983 agreement between MoDs.

British and German industry continued to favor a design with high-performance specifications designed for the military missions in NATO, while their French counterparts preferred a simpler, lighter, and cheaper fighter suitable for export. Technical advisers tended to favor the British design, which used more advanced fly-by-wire technology. Indeed, British industry accused the French of deliberately employing simpler technology in the ACX/Rafale in order to increase its export chances. French officials, on the other hand, mistrusted Britain's pre-existing industrial ties with Germany through the Tornado program. The German government tried to assuage these fears by suspending industrial collaboration with the British for a year and a half. The lack of a comparable response on the part of the French, however, led British officials to suspect that Dassault had no intention of sticking with the project, but simply wanted to stall the negotiations as long as possible before they collapsed, in order to protect sales of the Mirage 2000 and to allow the Rafale to get a jump on the EFA in export markets.[24]

Engine Design Leadership.   Both Rolls-Royce and SNECMA, monopoly producers of engines in Britain and France, respectively, viewed participation in the engine design as a key objective, both in its own terms and as a "technology driver" for civilian activities. Rolls-Royce, the leading engine manufacturer in Europe, saw no reason to grant equal place to the ailing SNECMA, a firm with very weak export and technological performance on the military side.[25] Moreover, Rolls-Royce and SNECMA were export-market competitors on the civilian side, via SNECMA's alliance with General Electric. British negotiators feared that SNECMA would exploit the co-development scheme to accumulate proprietary information on Rolls-Royce's engine designs and then, at its own insistence or under pressure from Dassault, pull out of the project.

Rolls-Royce, a strong leader, was suspicious of collaboration unless it was granted a dominant role; while SNECMA, a weaker firm technologically, but a strong exporter by virtue of its connections with Dassault and GE, opposed collaboration unless granted an equal role. Given its technological weakness, SNECMA was willing to consider collaboration with Rolls-Royce on the engine; as one official put it, "Better 30% of an engine than none at all." SNECMA did not actively oppose the project, nor did it support it. But as long as the French project was alive as an alternative, and as long as Rolls-Royce denied an equal place to SNECMA, it would quietly continue to "drape itself in the tricolor." The German engine firm Motor-Turbinen-Union (MTU), the smallest engine manufacturer in Europe, unable to produce a fighter engine on its own, supported collaboration.[26]

The British government, looking for a way to compensate for slower-than-expected production of the Rolls-Royce motors used in the Tornado, called for the use of engines in the EFA that could also be used to re-engine existing Tornados.[27] This seemingly sensible demand for compatibility exacerbated the conflict of interest, because it excluded SNECMA, which was incapable of designing an engine large enough to power the much heavier Tornado. For this reason, the linkage of the EFA engine to Tornado re-engining was rejected by the French, who preferred the M-88, SNECMA's less powerful engine. Moreover, Rolls was now doubly skeptical, since collaboration would mean sharing the lucrative re-engining contracts for the Tornado with the French, who did not fly the plane. Germany welcomed the compatibility condition, since MTU had established itself as a subcontractor in the design of Rolls-Royce military designs.

The engine design dispute drove renewed disagreements over weight, which, despite their resolution to the satisfaction of the military in 1983, continued to resurface as the most salient issue in the negotiations. The French favored a total weight of 9.25 tons and the British 9.75 tons, but much of this turned on the engine design. Acceptance of the French figure would have prohibited the use of a British engine compatible with the Tornado, while acceptance of the British figure would have prohibited the use of the weaker French M-88 engine.

The Collapse of the Negotiations.   After the 1983 agreement, the negotiations repeatedly stalled over industrial issues, only to be relaunched each time by MoD officials. The French vacillated. When the French MoD reached a compromise, Dassault would raise new demands or reopen old issues. Dassault continued to claim that its experience with delta-winged aircraft with canard foreplanes entitled it to leadership in every area of the project, while the other nations called for equal sharing of responsibility. French officials even complained that Dassault was withholding essential technical information. The British, while of course preferring British leadership, would settle for no less than a multinational consortium along the lines of Panavia. German industry, which had insisted all along that any agreement must make Germany a full partner, including technology transfer from France to Germany, rejected any proposal that would reduce their role to that of a subcontractor, including one proposal that would have given the British and French 33 percent each at the expense of the German share.

German Defense Minister Manfred Wörner, representing the country with the most immediate need for aircraft and the least advanced aeronautics industry, was pressed to defend the stalled project before the Bundestag. In an attempt to break the impasse by restoring Britain and France to a position of equality, he declared that Germany would participate in the project only if the entire aircraft design was new, rather than derived from an existing prototype. French Minister of Defense Charles Hernu immediately responded with the diplomatic dexterity for which the French are celebrated, drafting an open letter to Dassault declaring that the Rafale was not a prototype, but a "technology demonstrator."[28]

In March 1985, the French MoD, which had previously resisted such demands, pressed Dassault's ultimatum that the chief engineer, lead firm, and overall design and management responsibility all be French, that the headquarters be located in France, and that all planned exports be added to the French workshare, thus allowing France 46 percent of the work, Britain 22 percent, Germany 16 percent, and Italy and Spain 16 percent between them. The Germans were alarmed by the French turnaround on issues that they had thought to be settled, as well as by the alarming drop in the German workshare—inspiring a top German procurement officer to call the French "the European Americans."[29]

When the five defense ministers and their military chiefs of staff returned to the negotiating table in May 1985, yet another apparent compromise was reached. France reaffirmed the Anglo-German preference on the weight of the aircraft and its primary air-to-air mission, in return for which the other four governments agreed to include in the calculation of *juste retour* the 85 planes to be procured for the French Navy (in addition to the 220–230 for the French Air Force), thereby raising the French share to 32–35 percent.

Even this was not enough. The breaking point was reached at the meeting of armaments directors on August 1, 1985 in Torino, where the representatives of France and Spain announced that they would not accept the final, "non-negotiable" compromise proposed by the British, Germans, and Italians. The compromise called for an aircraft weighing 9.75 metric tons, powered by an engine with 9.2 tons of thrust, to be produced under the aegis of a multinational organization similar to Panavia. While this was closer to the British position, France was offered a 42 percent workshare—a remarkable concession in a world of *juste retour*. With the engine question unresolved and Dassault still opposed, France refused. French Defense Minister Hernu shuttled to Madrid to coordinate policy, but on September 2 the Spanish government announced that it would join the EFA consortium, which could afford to offer more generous terms. In an October 1985 speech before the National Assembly, Minister of Defense Paul Quilès launched an all-French Rafale project.

The Aftermath. The French Rafale and, to a lesser extent, the EFA have both been in crisis since their launching. Rising cost estimates for both aircraft have been the source of constant political controversy. A

French parliamentary report analyzed the cost structure of the Rafale and pronounced it "unfinanceable" without international collaboration. Yet repeated attempts to find foreign partners have failed. The French Navy launched an unprecedented campaign to avoid procurement of a French aircraft, publicly advocating off-the-shelf procurement of American F-18s instead. A scandal, quickly dubbed "l'affaire Rafale," broke out when the government suppressed unfavorable cost estimates, during which Prime Minister Michel Rocard openly dubbed the project "a disaster." When the French government moved to consider canceling it, however, business and labor moved in unison: while the representatives of Dassault were meeting with the Prime Minister's staff, hundreds of workers picketed the courtyard of the Hôtel Matignon. The project was saved, yet remained financially troubled.[30]

Exports promised no relief. A few weeks after the French withdrawal, Saudi Arabia surprised European producers with the announcement that it would purchase hundreds of Tornados instead of the Mirage 2000s—a sale called by some the "deal of the century." The sale would tide British producers over from production runs of the Tornado for European deployment to the first production runs of the EFA. This was a major blow to Dassault, whose new-order books have remained nearly empty ever since. Some analysts believe this deal signaled the beginning of a permanent decline in Dassault's export performance, due to stiffer European competition, greater indigenous production in the Third World, and the reentry of the United States onto world markets.

The EFA limps along with less fanfare. The costs, shared among four countries, are more manageable, but in an era of declining defense budgets, rising budgetary estimates have nonetheless forced the German government to cancel or delay more than one hundred other programs. By late 1992, in the face of severe fiscal constraints, Defense Minister Volker Rühe appeared to have convinced his government to try to scale back the EFA project significantly. The Germans have repeatedly threatened to withdraw from the project and seek a more cost-effective aircraft in collaboration with the United States. Yet, as the economic incentives would predict, it has failed to do so.[31] Nevertheless, the EFA, which already appears too expensive to challenge the American competition, will probably not be the beneficiary. Without collaboration, all European countries lose in the long term.

The Franco-German Tank, 1977–1983

Among arms-collaboration projects, a common tank is perhaps the oldest dream of European military planners. In 1956, the Finabel committee, comprising the army chiefs of staff from France, Germany, Italy, Belgium, Holland, and Luxembourg, met to set standards for a common

NATO tank. A bilateral accord on a common tank signed in 1957 between French and German MoDs reiterated the NATO specifications. The following year, NATO authorized the construction of two national prototypes.

By 1960, it had become clear that the two prototypes could not be integrated, whereupon the respective MoDs agreed to form a tripartite committee, with an Italian as chairman, to choose between them. However, two months before the competition, scheduled for September 1963, Germany and then France each announced their intention to build their own tanks—the Leopard I and the AMX-30, respectively—regardless of the outcome. A major reason for the split was the commercial rivalry, with each side hoping for export sales that would justify their decision to support an autarkic program.[32]

The German hopes were vindicated. Over the following fifteen years, the German Leopard I became a worldwide success and netted large profits for two German firms: Krauss-Maffei, the main contractor, and Krupp MaK, its leading competitor and major subcontractor. The Leopard I was considered by many to be the world's best tank in its class, with nearly half of production exported to seven NATO countries.[33] As with the French firm Dassault in aerospace, the dependence on military production, on design tasks, and on exports was clearly reflected in Krauss-Maffei's bottom line. By the late 1970s, Krauss-Maffei had become dependent on military products for nearly 95 percent of sales, of which the Leopard tanks constituted over 75 percent. The Leopard II contract in the early 1980s, which had been heavily supported by industry as a "follow-on" to avoid idle capacity after the Leopard I, transformed several years of losses into consistent profits.[34] Krauss-Maffei focused primarily on design, subcontracting more than half of production to other firms, including Krupp MaK. Krauss-Maffei's corporate structure resembled that of Dassault in aerospace. Like Dassault, Krauss-Maffei is essentially a design firm, employing seven engineers for every skilled assembly worker.[35] It is also a family firm, with 95 percent of the stock held by the influential Flick family, which had gained considerable notoriety through a campaign-financing scandal. As with Dassault, Krauss-Maffei's close informal ties with the German government helped it to resist efforts to merge its operations or divide its role as main contractor with Krupp MaK.[36]

The French tank program was far less successful. The French tank, the AMX-30, was designed and assembled by Groupe Industriel des Armaments Terrestres (GIAT), a state-owned armory that was successfully resisting, with strong support from Communist unions, the general trend toward privatization of defense production. (Many of the subcontractors, however, were important private firms.) By the late 1970s, no country could sustain an economic level of tank production without exports, and only the Germans and the Americans had made consistent inroads into important third-country export markets.[37] The AMX-30, militarily far less impressive than the Leopard, was exported to only one client: starting in 1977, 900 tanks had been delivered to Saudi Arabia.[38] By the 1980s, the French tank industry, according to the estimates of the French General Philippe Arnold, lagged two technological generations behind that of the Germans.[39] GIAT was committed to exports, but had been relatively unsuccessful at promoting them. It supported cooperation on an equal basis, with the clear intention of employing German technology to construct a tank that could be exported more profitably to the Third World, particularly to turbulent areas to which the German government banned official exports.

The Negotiations.   In 1976, the French government began to consider options for replacing the AMX-30. The MoD strongly supported a joint Franco-German program. Tanks and helicopters were the key equipment priorities for the French Army. With tight budgets, particularly after the Socialists came to power, a joint program seemed to promise a state-of-the-art tank while economizing on R&D and obtaining some development work for domestic producers.[40] At a tripartite ministerial meeting on November 3 and 4, 1977, the three governments launched formal negotiations on a joint project to develop a successor tank to the German Leopard I, the French AMX-30, and the British Chieftain, for deployment in the 1990s.[41]

The British, who had only recently ended unsuccessful negotiations with the Germans and had no immediate requirement for a tank, quickly dropped out.[42] Helmut Schmidt and Valery Giscard d'Estaing, however, remained positively inclined toward a joint project, as much for symbolic as for economic reasons. With the exception of a few Franco-German summit meetings, however, the talks were carried out by the MoDs, represented by their national armaments directors. Initially, the German MoD, led by Armaments Director Hans-Ludwig Eberhard, cautiously supported the project. The decision to replace half the force with Leopard II and half with the Franco-German tank made sense, since the latter was seen in German eyes as an improved and modified version of the former. An impasse in the negotiations between MoDs over the detailed operational concept for the tank was broken in 1979 when Schmidt and Giscard simply ordered their respective military officials to reach an agreement. This display of political will at the highest levels resulted in the signing by the respective national armaments directors, Hans-Ludwig Eberhard and Henri Martre, on January 31, 1979, of a statement of intention to reach agreement on a common tank concept.

In February 1980, at the Franco-German summit in Paris, the negotiations were given another high-level impetus by an agreement between Schmidt and Giscard to promote the tank project as a symbol of bilateral solidarity. Various points of disagreement were addressed at the summit, most importantly the question of exports. The most visible problem with exports concerned the sensitivity of the German government, particularly in the SPD, to arms exports. German arms-export control legislation is strict and had been applied with particular stringency to the export of tanks—a notorious symbol of German technical expertise.[43] Nonetheless, the heads of government resolved the issue in the same way that it had been dealt with in previous projects, namely by Germany deferring to the French demand that each country be permitted to export its production according to its own laws. Because of the sensitivity of tank exports, a special provision was added allowing either side to call for bilateral consultations to discuss individual cases.[44] The compromise was codified in an agreement between the respective defense ministers, signed on February 5, 1980. German Defense Minister Hans Apel opposed the project, but was kept uninformed until a few days before the summit and then obeyed a direct order from Schmidt to sign.[45]

Industrial Interests. With the disputes over military specifications enroute to resolution, industrial issues rose to prominence. For Krauss-Maffei, the Franco-German project posed two concerns. First, a Franco-German project would cede half of the gains from supplying the NATO market, where the Leopard was dominant, to the French partner. Krauss-Maffei feared that France would export at subsidized prices to the Third World (where German export restrictions blocked direct exports) and then, perhaps, challenge German exports to their traditional NATO "club." At the very least, the Franco-German tank might compete directly against the Leopard II, undermining hopes that it, like the Leopard I, would become the standard tank for continental Europe. These fears appeared to be confirmed when shortly after the announcement of the Franco-German project, the Belgian government—Belgium being a nation where much of the defense industry is dominated by links to French firms—declared that it planned to switch from the Leopard to the new product. The importance of exports and industrial development to the French was also demonstrated by their insistence that no American parts can be used, so as to circumvent any U.S. export-control problems, while the Germans favored procurement of the most economical components. A 1980 internal French memorandum concluded that greater exports and turnover were possible with a jointly produced tank than with a follow-on to the AMX-30.[46]

German industry also worried that the exchange of technology would favor the French—a view shared by many French experts. French industry sought to acquire German technological know-how in areas such as diesel-engine technology, chassis development, and armaments, and the long-term effect might have been to bring the French up to world standards in tank production. Although the market position of the Leopard series, and the acknowledged superiority of German armor, suggested German leadership in the project, French industry lobbied heavily for an equal share in a wholly new, co-developed tank, rather than a role as licensee for a modified Leopard II. French firms had done a considerable amount of R&D, some of it utilizing spin-offs from aerospace, which they felt entitled them to an equal share in the project. In a series of articles in the French press concerning the engine, turret, hydraulic suspension, and particularly electronics, French industry stressed its ability to contribute equally to the project. There was widespread (and, in retrospect, justified) skepticism from German industry about these claims, because the promising, but piecemeal French R&D on tanks had never been integrated into a workable, let alone marketable, product.[47]

Krauss-Maffei's major interest was to preserve its global market position by opposing any cooperative venture involving an equal division of design tasks. Nonetheless, Krauss-Maffei initially gave its cautious support to plans for collaboration, since the proposed venture seemed to resemble a co-production rather than co-development scheme, not unlike those which Germany had arranged with other NATO countries, in which the end-product would be an improved version of the Leopard II—a Leopard "II½," as it came to be called. Such a project would grant German firms access to the large French market and secure development funding, estimated to total 1.5 billion deutschmarks, to further improve the Leopard II.[48]

The Collapse. As negotiations between MoDs continued, contentious issues, ostensibly concerning technical specifications, were focused increasingly on the underlying industrial conflict. In late 1980, it became clear that the German government was standing by its producers' preference for co-production of a modified Leopard II over co-development of a new tank. The Germans favored retaining and improving the chassis of the Leopard II, with common work proceeding on the turret, while the French wanted a wholly new design.[49] Another disagreement emerged over weight. With the budget constraints of the Third World export market in mind, the French favored a light tank chassis (less than 50 tons), while the Germans who employ a large number of their tanks themselves on the European central front and exported only to NATO countries, favored a heavy one (closer to 60 tons).

By the second half of 1980, disagreements over the nature of the final product, as well as project leadership, had dissipated the initial interest of German industry. Wolfgang Raether, the Krauss-Maffei board member responsible for armaments technology, publicly conceded that the respective militaries were overcoming their differences, and that a European solution would permit the exploitation of greater economies of scale. But the French solution of "starting over from Adam and Eve" with a new design, he argued, would be far less economical than building an improved Leopard II. German manufacturers would also have to give up the production of certain components, which Krauss-Maffei firmly opposed. The French proposal to take over electronics, an increasingly important part of tank production, Raether argued, did not reflect "German technical ability." In vain, French diplomats argued that exports via France to Third World countries where direct German exports were restricted might actually increase the turnover of German firms. One French lobbyist in Bonn enthused that "a combination of French genius and German perfectionism would be unbeatable on world markets." But German firms considered the political and industrial risks too high.[50]

Despite the increasingly skeptical posture of German industry, the two MoDs, with support from both heads of government, pressed ahead. In February 1981, an agreement was signed on the definition phase, which called for a common turret to be mounted on two separate chassis. The French also agreed to produce a heavier tank, with independent work to continue on a lighter chassis. This in turn sparked further disagreements on whether the new turret would be optimized for the Leopard II or for both designs. An initial production run of 4,500 was foreseen, with 2,500 for Germany, 1,500 for France, and 450 for the Netherlands. The costs were estimated at a minimum of 22.5 billion French francs, or about 5 million FF per tank. R&D costs and project leadership were to be split evenly.[51]

The French, who had no intermediate-generation tank analogous to the Leopard II, continued to favor the date of 1991.[52] Outside of the Communist unions, who had always supported autarkic production in state-owned armories, and the nationalist right, French support for the agreement continued to be broadly based. As the negotiations dragged on, Mitterrand pressed Schmidt for a definite decision, which had to pass through the German Bundestag.

In November 1981, the Germans began to question the calendar for procurement. This concern, though ostensibly military, resulted primarily from the underlying industrial conflict. If the tank was to be a new design and not an improved Leopard II, the German government favored a later date for bringing it into service, around 1995 or 1996. The German military worried that a tank designed for the 1991 date would be outmoded by the time the German procurement began. A number of issues finally combined to sink the tank in the Bundestag. Among German parliamentarians, support for the project was waning, with all three major parties—the CDU, SPD and FDP—eventually officially opposing the project. The Defense Committee resented not having been consulted by Schmidt throughout the negotiations. This opposition resulted in a series of negative reports by the Bundestag in late 1981 and early 1982. Cost constraints and scheduling issues were important to the Budget Committee. Given the military budget crisis, the German government was hesitant to fund a new tank project when the Leopard II has just entered into service. On balance, the military felt that if the project were more than an improved Leopard II, they would prefer to postpone the development in order to assure a more technologically sophisticated tank. Moreover, the FDP and SPD were traditionally suspicious of arms exports, which might increase via French factories. The most decisive issues, however, appear to have been industrial. Leading defense experts from the CDU and SPD on the Defense Committee of the Bundestag stressed the risk of surrendering Germany's clear technological lead to France, only to have it exploited on export markets, as the most serious reason for their skepticism. Germany, a leading SPD defense analyst declared, must fight for its "rightful interests."[53]

Schmidt failed to gain the support of his own party in the Bundestag, let alone the opposition, and upon his departure from office in September 1982 the project seemed dead. On November 30, 1982, French Prime Minister Mauroy announced before the Senate that France would go ahead alone with its tank, named the "Leclerc," but the French government still hoped that collaboration could be arranged. The MoD stalled for time by announcing a modernization of the AMX-30, while continuing to look for European collaborative partners with whom to pursue the new tank project. Mitterrand raised the issue again with the new Chancellor Kohl and his Defense Minister Manfred Wörner, but the negotiations lapsed for good in 1983.[54]

The Aftermath. The launching of the Leclerc tank failed to silence domestic critics who argued that the French Armée de Terre is falling still further behind in armored technology. In an unusual breach of the strict *"devoir de réserve"* imposed on the French officer corps, General Philippe Arnold, former Aide-de-Camp to Giscard and Commander of the 1st French Armored Division, publicly deplored the failure of the Franco-German tank project and criticized the French government for fielding armored forces inferior to those of Germany and the United States. Although General Arnold was suspended from his duties for speaking out, his comments were widely considered representative of majority opinion in the French military.[55] In 1987, GIAT unveiled its prototype of the Leclerc, scheduled for 1991 production. Experts consider it substantially inferior to the improved Leopard II or the American

Abrams M-1. The continuing weakness of the French tank production was demonstrated on export markets. When the Saudi government announced its intention to procure a new generation of tanks, the French did not even make the short list, despite the fact that Saudi military was already using the AMX-30. With the Germans refusing to enter the competition, the finalists were the American M-1 and the Brazilian Osorio.[56]

The Franco-German Helicopter, 1985–1990

France, Italy, Germany, and Britain held exploratory discussions in 1975 about co-development of a day/night all-weather attack helicopter. In November 1976, France and Germany signed a Memorandum of Understanding to begin conceptual studies.[57] As in the other two cases, heads of government and MoD officials in both countries favored the project, and they were to intervene twice more, once in 1982 and once in 1986, to revive it.

Differences between the French and German military over the operational specifications of the helicopter were, as in the other two cases, the first issues to be raised. French tactical doctrine called for teams of two light helicopters, one to perform anti-tank missions and the other to defend the mission against attacking helicopters; German doctrine called for a single heavy helicopter to perform both tasks. Accordingly, the French favored a lighter helicopter with a single engine and the Germans a heavier helicopter with two engines. Also, the French military favored a configuration with the two-man crew sitting side-by-side, while the German military favored a configuration with one crew member sitting behind the other. Finally, as in the tank case, there were differences over replacement schedules, with the Germans requiring the helicopter before the French. Indeed, in the early stages of the discussions, the German military favored licensed production of the U.S. Hughes AH-64 Apache.

These differences between the MoDs over military specifications and scheduling were as great or greater than in the cases of tanks and fighters. Despite their seriousness, however, they were overcome, like previous disagreements, through compromise, often backed by direct pressure from heads of government. It was agreed to pursue the German conception of a heavier helicopter with the two crew members sitting one behind the other. The case of helicopters differs strikingly from those of tanks and fighters, however, in that producer interests converged. From the moment the German military issued its requirement, Aérospatiale in France and MBB in Germany were interested in collaborating on the project. At three key points in the negotiations—during the years 1982,

1985, and 1986—industry kept the momentum going when officials seemed unable to come to an agreement.

Industrial Interests. These convergent corporate strategies are grounded in the global market position of the two firms. Most important, neither national champion was established in global markets for military helicopters. Aérospatiale was somewhat more technologically advanced than MBB and had exported some military helicopters, but the product line was not a priority for the firm. Moreover, its history of collaboration with Westland (UK) in the previous generation meant that the collaborative venture would involve no reduction in market share over prevailing levels.[58] Both firms, moreover, were highly diversified across product lines. Aérospatiale's diversified production base permitted it to use the technological and financial gains from collaboration to bolster its preeminent position in the production of civilian helicopters, in which it was a world leader and MBB was not a significant player. Hence Aérospatiale (unlike Dassault or Krauss-Maffei) tended to think long-term, taking into account the possibility of iteration and linkages between product lines. Aérospatiale's corporate commitment to international collaboration was broad-based; 60–75 percent of its business, including the Airbus family of commercial jetliners, already came from collaboratively produced products. The two firms were already working together on a range of projects, including some helicopter subsystems, joint missiles, and civilian airliners. As the theory of corporate preferences outlined above would predict neither Aérospatiale nor MBB pushed for a national project.

Discussion over industrial issues still provoked conflict. French industry and government saw the project as a source of technology and exports. As in the case of fighter planes, France seemed more willing than Germany to sacrifice performance to keep costs down, and to guarantee domestic production and exports by avoiding American components. The most important industrial conflict involved electronic systems, particularly the optronic systems—night vision, target acquisition, and fire-control technology—to be employed in the helicopter. While the German government favored procurement of an American-made system that had already been tested, so as to reduce the cost, risk, and duration of development, French government and industry insisted on a system developed and produced entirely in Europe and employing infrared technology. French industry, led by Aérospatiale and Thomson, argued that an independent technological base was needed to be competitive on global export markets. This industrial dispute also helps explain the tenacity with which each country defended certain operational specifications, such as the seating configuration, which were related in a complex way to the radar dispute. German industry had no strong interest one way or the other.[59]

The Negotiations. In October 1979, a Memorandum of Understanding specifying an 18-month period to define the project was signed. No further agreement was reached, however, and in late 1981 the two national armaments directors turned the project over to industry. Aérospatiale and MBB presented two proposals, one resembling the French plan, the other the German. Both were rejected by the opposing government. The project appeared dead. Industry explored other options, but continued to press for a multinational project.

In early 1982, with Bundestag opposition to the tank project becoming insurmountable, the German government searched for a symbolic security project with which to smooth political relations with Paris. At the suggestion of the German Armaments Director, who sought above all to avert yet another attempt to revive the ill-fated battle tank, the German government proposed to resuscitate the helicopter project. At the Franco-German Summit in October 1982, Kohl and Mitterrand sought a collaborative project to symbolize renewed Franco-German military cooperation, and the joint project was announced shortly thereafter.[60]

A year later, in November 1983, the respective ministers of defense, Wörner and Hernu, signed an agreement announcing their governments' intention to launch the development phase. Negotiations over military specifications continued until May 1984, when an accord was signed on joint development and production. The agreement, which reflected compromises reached during the preceding year, called for three versions of the helicopter to be produced from a single airframe. A family of three helicopters—the HAP (Hélicoptère d'appui et de protection), the PAH-2 (Panzerabwehrhubschrauber, zweite Generation), and the HAC-3G (Hélicoptère anti-char, troisième generation)—were planned. The agreement also called for the construction of seven prototypes.

Disagreements over the electronic systems remained. The May 1984 agreement permitted each country to choose its own electronic subsystems, but continuing complications over the seating appeared to render this solution unworkable. In November 1987, the German military, under pressure from Chancellor Kohl, finally acquiesced in outfitting the helicopter with a Franco-German, rather than an American, radar.[61] The May 1984 agreement also gave program leadership to MBB, despite the technological superiority of Aérospatiale, on the grounds that the French had been granted project leadership on the Alpha Jet project and that a 1978 agreement between France, Britain, Germany, and Italy had designated Germany as the European leader for anti-tank helicopters. Oddly enough, this arrangement was not supported by its main beneficiary, MBB, which feared that Aérospatiale, a more technologically advanced firm, would withdraw from the agreement, and hesitated in any case to accept legal responsibility for the entire project. MBB and Aérospatiale circumvented these problems on their own by turning the entire project over to a common jointly held subsidiary, Eurocopter GmbH, under whose supervision the project has advanced steadily. In mid-1990, joint participation through Eurocopter in another helicopter project, the NH-90, was announced. The integration of French and German military helicopter production in Eurocopter GmbH appears to mark a decisive transformation of industrial structure.[62] Thus, although the initial military objections were strongest in this case, the doubts about the financial soundness of the project remain, the helicopter collaboration must be judged a success.

The Future: A Two-Level Strategy for the European Armaments Industry?

By the late 1980s, in the wake of the negotiations on the three projects examined above, European statesmen stood at an impasse. Efforts to entice unwilling national champion producers into collaborative armaments projects had proven difficult, and the results varied greatly across sectors. In some sectors, such as helicopters, bilateral consortia (Franco-German and Anglo-Italian) compete against one another; in others, such as fighter planes, the continent's leading producer continues to battle a growing consortium of competitors; in still others, such as tanks, there is almost no collaboration. Armaments producers have often thwarted attempts to use domestic policies such as nationalization or concentration to undermine their opposition to collaboration.

In light of the failure of many attempts at collaboration—as well as the budget crisis and, more recently, the decline of the Soviet threat—European procurement officials are coming to accept the need to treat armaments collaboration as something akin to a two-level game. Initially, such efforts took the form of attempts to undermine domestic opposition to collaboration through greater government control over, and in France, nationalization of, national champions. This strategy was ineffective, particularly in France, since the same underlying industrial interests remained. As a result, governments turned in the late 1980s to strategies that use international arrangements to undermine domestic constituencies. Such efforts have centered on proposals developed by two organizations: the Independent European Programme Group (IEPG), a group consisting of all European NATO members, and the European Community (EC).

In November 1988, after a decade of inactivity, the IEPG approved an "Action Plan" aimed at creating a "common European arms market."[63] The IEPG reform package can be seen as an effort by defense ministers and national armaments directors, working in concert, to alter the incentives facing European defense producers. The IEPG plan comprises a number of reforms, including open competitions for smaller contracts, subject to the proviso that the gains from all projects should balance one another out over an "appropriate period of time." This proposal builds on the experience of France and Britain, who have implemented a similar bilateral program of monitored "cross-purchasing" over the past few years.

The French government has proposed, and the IEPG has authorized, a common European military research program modeled on the civilian EUREKA program. This program, called EUCLID, will offer financial incentives to multinational research consortia working on areas such as advanced micro-electronics, artificial intelligence, and composite materials. One purpose of the program is to accustom European firms to collaboration and "prime the pump" for future projects. MoD officials hope that collaboration in early stages of a project will foster cooperation in later stages of weapons development.[64]

The IEPG reforms have taken place in an economic environment influenced by "European 1992"—the attempt to complete the liberalization of the Common Market, which includes a proposal to open public procurement.[65] The push to rationalize civilian industries, particularly electronics, has had the side-effect of changing the incentives facing domestic armaments producers. In sectors with considerable spillover from civilian to military technologies, international mergers and diversification on the civilian side create incentives for similar cooperation on the military side. This process has dovetailed with a more permissive attitude on the part of MoD officials toward foreign participation in domestic firms. A rash of international mergers, acquisitions, and investment has followed (e.g., Siemens-GEC-Plessey, Thomson-British Aerospace). Armaments producers increasingly face market incentives to increase efficiency. Private firms, like the French missile producer MATRA, have aggressively pursued multinational mergers and collaborative ventures.

The prospects for IEPG and EC efforts to promote international cooperation remain unclear, but their intent is unequivocal. In the blunt language of a high French MoD official, they constitute "an attempt to regain control of our own industry."[66] Liberalization of procurement for smaller goods, common R&D programs, and the possibility for cross-national investment and takeovers are all deliberately designed to undermine the opposition of domestic armaments producers to their own governments by creating common institutions and a competitive international environment. Such strategies are promising because, while a frontal assault by governments on domestic monopolies may fail, firms can be enticed, through positive incentives, to embark on policies that alter their long-term corporate strategy. It is too early to know whether such efforts will succeed.

TWO-LEVEL GAMES AND ARMS COLLABORATION

Support for the Proposed Model of Collaboration

Both the process and the outcomes of the three negotiations examined in this chapter confirm the theory of collaboration outlined in the initial section. Chief executives and MoDs are inclined to support armaments collaboration. MoDs often have technical disagreements, but they inevitably resolve them on their own or at the direct order of the head of government. Chief executives act as agenda-setters, but their influence declines as ratification nears and agreements become more concrete. In each of the three cases, the "acceptability-sets" of heads of government were consistently closer to one another than the two domestic win-sets, which are determined by the dominant social actors who "ratify" agreements, namely, defense producers and their allies. The interests of producers reflect their position in global export markets.

The three cases discussed here suggest that armaments collaboration is possible only when the leading industrial firm in Europe does not need to defend export interests, and therefore chooses not to oppose the agreement. In the aircraft and tank cases, strong leader firms (Dassault and Krauss-Maffei) blocked collaboration with weak leaders for fear of surrendering technological and market pre-eminence. In the case of helicopters, Aérospatiale enjoyed a stronger world market position than MBB, but its weak overall export position in military helicopters, as well as its previous experience with collaboration and its fortuitous pattern of diversification into civilian sectors, led it to support collaboration. MBB, with no plans for independent export expansion, was accommodating. In short, the public gains from collaboration cannot be achieved unless firms anticipate private gains. The importance of firm preferences holds cross-nationally: France and Germany, however different their foreign policy priorities and military doctrines, react similarly to similar situations.

In the process of interest formation, domestic conflict was important and, in this descriptive sense, the state is a non-unitary actor. Yet it is essential to distinguish between the *existence* of domestic divisions and their *importance as explanatory factors*. The nature and outcome of the domestic conflict, while important as a "transmission belt" between international incentives and political outcomes, can be predicted by employing a unitary-actor assumption, namely, that the state will eventually pursue a policy that reflects industry preferences. Since industry preferences are based on the global market position in that sector, and industry tends to get its way, there is little need to invoke an independent theory of domestic politics. A pure "second-image-reversed" approach, in which domestic conflicts mirror global market position, provides an adequate explanation.[67]

To be sure, this situation is unsatisfactory for governments. In recent years, governments have thus turned to two-level strategies, such as the nationalization of recalcitrant domestic firms. These policies not being entirely successful, governments are now working together to restructure the international incentives facing firms. Policies to promote transnational corporate restructuring, diversification, and collaborative R&D are the result. By offering short-run incentives to domestic firms, governments can induce them to change in such a way as to alter their long-run behavior. Once domestic opposition has been quelled, governments hope to achieve their international goals.[68]

Five Hypotheses About Two-Level Strategies

Why did two-level strategies play a marginal role in the case of armaments collaboration? And insofar as they were attempted, why were they relatively ineffective? The evidence presented here permits us to decisively reject one obvious answer, namely, that this was a case of security cooperation, in which there were few important domestic conflicts. The MoDs favored collaboration, but industry often opposed it. The symbolic importance of armaments production for national security, the legal power and access to high-quality information enjoyed by national executives, and the monopsony position of governments would seem to permit them to mobilize domestic society more or less as they wish. Policies of targeting side-payments to particular subcontractors, suasive linkage between collaboration and Franco-German relations, and/or collusion between statesmen could be predicted. Although some of this took place, it was ineffective at promoting cooperation.

The following five hypotheses are drawn inductively from this case, but appear to be of sufficient theoretical interest to warrant further consideration in other, similar cases. In general, they suggest some of the limitations of two-level strategies in cases such as armaments collaboration.

1. *The existence of strong, concentrated opposition does not expedite successful two-level strategies to reshape "win-sets."* The efficacy of the instruments at the disposal of a "policy entrepreneur" to shift win-sets and create coalitions is related to the nature and distribution of domestic and foreign interests. Specifically, the prospects for successfully employing the strategies outlined in the introduction—suasion, targeting, tying hands, cutting slack—rest on the existence of malleable domestic actors. In each case, new actors must be mobilized or existing actors must be confronted with incentives to act differently than they otherwise would. Attempts to manipulate domestic actors in this way will be most effective when their

interests are uncertain or weak, their knowledge is incomplete, their power is marginal, or their interests are balanced. Targeting and linkage, for example, are more effective strategies when they can be focused on swing groups.[69]

There were similar limitations on two-level effects such as "targeting" and "tying one's hands." Such efforts remained relatively rare and enjoyed little success. In the fighter-plane negotiations, for example, the Germans and British hoped to gain support for the project from the powerful French firm Thomson by pre-committing themselves to procurement of a French radar. But Thomson was in a weak domestic position, since its potential main contractor in a national project, Dassault, was threatening to turn to a subsidiary, Electronique Serge Dassault, for electronic components. Thomson refused to step out of line. Negotiators also attempted to convince others, in both domestic and international fora, that win-sets were linked. The future of Franco-German relations, it was argued, rested on projects like these three. Such claims—while given wide circulation in the *Economist, Le Monde*, and *Frankfurter Allgemeine Zeitung*—appear not to have impressed influential domestic groups.

2. *In cases of concentrated opposition by economic interest groups, fundamental social restructuring may be the only way to create the political preconditions for collaboration.* As we have seen, it is difficult for statesmen to "reshape the win-set" when the interests of social groups are concentrated and well organized, as in the case of armaments collaboration. A tenacious statesman may be forced to adopt a strategy of socioeconomic reform. In the case of arms collaboration, chief executives have recently attempted to design policies to eliminate or dilute the power of concentrated arms-exporting firms. The French governments of Giscard and Mitterrand both attempted to nationalize Dassault or to merge it with the more collaboratively inclined Aérospatiale. In France, such frontal attacks were blocked, although the expansion of British Aerospace and the creation of Deutsche Aerospace suggest that it may have been more successful elsewhere. More recent attempts to coordinate cross-purchasing and cross-investment agreements on a Continental scale demonstrate that in an interdependent world, statesmen will turn to two-level strategies where domestic policies fail. Only changes in industrial structure, whether through corporate collaboration in Eurocopter or as a byproduct of Europe 1992, promises to undermine industrial opposition.

3. *When negotiations involve public or widely dispersed benefits, suasive strategies will be used; when they involve privatizable and more concentrated benefits, targeting will be used.* Firms mobilize for or against collaboration in response to the desire to capture specific private goods, while the public and its representatives mobilize for or against collaboration in

response to the potential public good of more efficient procurement, a stronger national defense, or more responsible fiscal management. To implement a targeting strategy, statesmen must be able to identify specific private goods characterized by excludability and rivalry. A suasive strategy is generally more appropriate where there is a broad, diffuse commitment to a certain end, often a public good. The evidence presented here suggests that when statesmen attempt to undermine a private interest, such as corporate opposition to an arms project, by tying it to broader issues, such as the future of Franco-German relations, they are likely to fail.

4. *Cross-national discrepancies in information about ratifiability are nonexistent, at least among democracies, and hence cannot be exploited to gain diplomatic leverage.* The two-level games model suggests that a statesman might gain a more advantageous agreement by exploiting—or, more subtly, by feigning—a small win-set. The former strategy is recognized, and the evidence in this study, particularly the generosity of the final offer to France in the EFA negotiations, suggests that these predictions are correct. The latter strategy, one of duplicity, rests on the existence of "informational discrepancies" (or "asymmetries") regarding domestic ratifiability between chief executives. Statesmen must be better able to assess their domestic constraints than their counterparts abroad. The evidence here suggests that interstate informational discrepancies regarding the ratifiability of agreements hardly exist among European democracies, even in the relatively secretive matter of armaments. This is the only way to account for the otherwise paradoxical empirical finding that statesmen were not always the best judges of their own domestic situation. The estimates of skeptical foreign firms like BAe about the size of the French win-set, while perhaps based on less hard information, appear to have been more accurate than those of the French government. Statesmen appear to misjudge their own domestic constraints as often as do foreigners.

In the case of fighter planes, the French government did attempt to exploit Dassault's intransigence (i.e., the small French domestic win-set) to extract a larger workshare for French firms—a tactic that appears to have succeeded insofar as the final offer to France gave Dassault a disproportionate share of the contracts. But this result is explicable largely by the fact that the threat of French defection was real. Insofar as the French negotiators attempted to extract more concessions from the Germans and British by exaggerating the extent of Dassault's intransigence, the strategy backfired, for such tactics can be exploited by domestic actors against their own government. After the negotiations broke down, French negotiators felt that they had tried to extract too much compensation in exchange for Dassault's participation, and had exhausted foreign goodwill and empowered their own firm in the process.[70] Dassault and, to a lesser extent, BAe also attempted to undermine their governments' will to collaborate by pre-committing the government to autarkic policies. The two firms rushed the testing of high-visibility prototypes, seeking to accumulate sunk development costs, create nationalist sentiment, and demonstrate their ability to lead the project alone.

These cases suggest that, among modern information-rich democracies, it is extremely difficult for negotiators to mask their true domestic win-set, even in a sensitive area of national security like weapons procurement. Situations in which vital information about ratifiability is in the hands of only one party are rare. Statesmen have numerous independent means of assessing the domestic constraints faced by their counterparts, including diplomatic information-gathering, reading the commercial press, or hiring consultants, all of which are employed by European governments. Unless one or both statesmen are actually in a position to decisively reshape their domestic win-set through sudden, unforeseen action—a rare state of affairs in a democracy—attempts to dissemble will be detected.

5. *Statesmen are less aware of and less constrained by their domestic constituencies during early stages of negotiations, which may lead them to misjudge domestic constraints.* As negotiations progress, societal actors reveal their preferences and domestic constraints become more apparent. In the cases of armaments collaboration, domestic actors appear to have understood more clearly than their governments whether agreements were ratifiable. The ability of domestic groups to disguise their preferences and provide selective information affords them some influence over the way governments conduct negotiations. In the fighter case, for example, British observers claimed that Dassault cynically encouraged pro-collaborative forces in the French government simply in order to delay the launching of a collaborative project they had no intention of joining. While Dassault may have deliberately manipulated the French government, Krauss-Maffei appears simply to have withheld judgment until the precise details of the agreement became clear, at which point the firm voiced its opposition. Schmidt had already invested considerable political capital in a project that his government was then unable to ratify, just as French negotiators invested a great deal in the fighter negotiations, only to see them fail. These misjudgments confirm that there may be high uncertainty inherent in judging domestic constraints early in the negotiating process, but that interest alignments become clearer during the course of a negotiation.[71]

CONCLUSIONS

The three cases examined in this chapter demonstrate both the importance of two-level-games strategies and the difficulty of employing them.

While national chief executives occupy the critical position of gate-keepers, adjudicating disputes between international and domestic imperatives, their autonomy is nonetheless constrained. Many of the limitations of two-level strategies *as policy* permit us to better understand the two-level-games approach *as theory*. For example, among information-rich democracies, it appears to be nearly impossible to disguise the size of the win-set. Also, as the two-level-games approach predicts, statesmen can act autonomously to set the agenda for international negotiations, but their autonomy shrinks as ratification nears and the terms of the agreement become clearer.

The specific key to cooperation or conflict in the armaments sector is the primacy of concentrated domestic interests over a diffuse national security interest. This theoretical approach—which contrasts the domestic organizational capabilities of different groups—is normally associated with Liberal theories of trade disputes and other manifestations of "low politics."[72] Since the approach illuminates a "high politics" case of considerable military and economic importance, there is reason to believe it is also widely applicable in cases—such as civilian high-technology production—where we would expect international imperatives to be less compelling.

NOTES

1. The theoretical analysis and empirical research contained in this chapter is drawn from work in progress on the political economy of international cooperation in strategic industries. See also my articles, Moravcsik, "The European Armaments Industry at the Crossroads," *Survival* 32 (January–February 1990): 65–85, and "Arms and Autarky in Modern European History," *Daedalus* 120 (Winter 1991). For comments and suggestions on various parts of this project, I am grateful to Anne-Marie Burley, William Jarosz, Robert Keohane, Fareed Zakaria, and members of the project. For logistical assistance, I thank the Program on International Politics, Economics, and Security (PIPES) at the University of Chicago.

2. Western European Union, Document 1119, par. 7, 11 May 1987. See also C. Julien, "Les armes de l'Europe," *Le monde diplomatique*, January 1988: 22, cited in Jonathan Story, "La communauté européenne et la défense de l'Europe," *Studia Diplomatica*, March 1988: 274. Classified estimates by the French National Assembly suggest that the unit price of the Rafale would be some 25 percent cheaper if produced on a European collaborative basis; Michael Bernard, "Projet de Rapport d'Information sur L'Avion de Combat Tactique" (Mimeo., Paris: Assemblée Nationale, February 1988). A recent European Community study suggests that the savings would be 40 percent or more: Aviation Week and Space Technology, 3 September 1990, 69. For a rebuttal of counterclaims that the inherent inefficiency of collaborative projects soaks up the potential gains, see Moravcsik, "European Armaments Industry," pp. 74–76.

3. See, for example, David Garnham, *The Politics of European Defense Coopera-tion: Germany, France, Britain, and America* (Cambridge, Mass.: Ballinger, 1988), pp. 67–68, 70; Jérôme Paulini, "Politique spatiale militaire française et coopéra-tion européenne," *Politique étrangère* 52 (Summer 1987): 443. On the wartime importance of domestic modification capabilities, see Trevor Taylor and Keith Hayward, *The UK Defence Industrial Base: Developments and Future Policy Options* (London: Brassey's, 1989), pp. 102–103. In his classic work, Henry R. Nau, *National Politics and International Technology: Nuclear Reactor Development in Western Europe* (Baltimore: Johns Hopkins University Press, 1974), generalizes this line of argument in his analysis of variations in cooperation on high technology, which he attributes, at least in larger countries, to political interests.

4. Kenneth Waltz, *Theory of International Politics* (Reading, Mass.: Addison-Wesley, 1979), p. 107.

5. For further implications, see Joseph M. Grieco, "Anarchy and the Limits of Cooperation: A Realist Critique of the Newest Liberal Institutionalism," *Inter-national Organization* 42 (Summer 1988): 485–508.

6. Elsewhere I have argued that this is characteristic of the "Liberal" ap-proaches to international politics. See Andrew Moravcsik, "Liberalism and Inter-national Relations Theory" (Cambridge, Mass.: CFIA Working Paper 92–6), 1992.

7. For analyses that relate conflicting priorities to conflicting interest groups, see Christian Schmidt, "A la recherche d'une economie politique des programmes d'armament," *Chroniques d'actualité de la SEDEIS*, 15 June 1987, pp. 226–233; Mi-chael Brzoska, "Economic Problems of Arms Production in Western Europe—Di-agnoses and Alternatives," in Helena Tuomi and Raimo Väyrynen, eds., *Militariza-tion and Arms Production* (London: Croom Helm, 1983), pp. 59–92; Edward A. Kolodziej and Frederic C. Pearson, "The Political Economy of Making and Mar-keting Arms: A Test for the Systemic Imperatives of Order and Welfare" (paper presented at the International Studies Association convention, London, 1989).

8. Peter Gourevitch, *Politics in Hard Times: Comparative Responses to Interna-tional Economic Crises* (Ithaca, N.Y.: Cornell University Press, 1986).

9. Herbert Wulf, "Europäische Zusammenarbeit in der Rüstungsproduktion: Ziele, Probleme und Perspektiven," in Luther Brock and Mathias Jopp, eds., *Sicherheitspolitische Zusammenarbeit und Kooperation der Rüstungswirtschaft in Westeu-ropa* (Baden-Baden: Nomos Verlag, 1986), pp. 107–128. This assumption may seem strange to the American reader. In the United States, the interests of indi-vidual services play a more important role, in part because of the lack of a civilian procurement agency such as the French Delegation Général pour l'Armament, and in part because of the greater economic means at the disposal of the military. Moreover, given the extreme resource constraints under which European coun-tries function, efforts to strengthen the equipment base of their particular service often lead to the same outcome.

10. For a more detailed derivation and an evaluation of the concept as a source of insight across modern European history, see my article, "Arms and Autarky."

11. Some may view this as a reckless assumption, but the negotiating history

of these projects bears it out. I present additional evidence, drawn from national defense plans, procurement policies, and negotiating histories, in the final section of "Arms and Autarky" and in "European Armaments Industry," pp. 66–67, 76.

12. It is also possible that the reduction in cost will increase exports enough to offset the loss of domestic market share. But the elasticity of third-country demand for weapons is not so steep as to facilitate this trade-off.

13. Cost-plus pricing, widely used in Europe, means that increases in turn-over generate increases in profits. Under fixed-price contracting, however, the same rule of thumb applies.

14. Timm Meyer, "Collaboration in Arms Production: A German View," in Karl Kaiser and John Roper, eds., *British-German Defense Cooperation: Partners Within the Alliance* (London: Royal Institute of International Affairs, 1988), p. 246. On the pressures facing the industry, see Moravcsik, "European Armaments Industry," pp. 67–69; and Michael Moodie, *Defense Implications of Europe 92* (Washington, D.C.: Center for Strategic and International Studies, 1990), pp. 7–12.

15. Cf. Jonathan B. Tucker, "Partners and Rivals: A Model of International Collaboration in Advanced Technology," *International Organization* 45 (Winter 1991): 83–120. This incisive and rigorous analysis, which appeared after I had completed several drafts of this chapter, uses a comparison of the Alpha Jet and European Fighter Aircraft projects to support the hypotheses that relative advantages in technological competence are both the primary objective and the primary cause of international conflicts in this area. Tucker focuses on technolog-ical leakage, not conflict over high value-added production. We also differ on specification. Tucker's model does not distinguish theoretically between the in-terests of domestic actors, nor does it incorporate export shares, which I believe to be the central distributive concern of these firms, even more important than technology.

16. Side-payments are, of course, a possible solution to this problem. But there are three reasons why they rarely permit governments to overcome the problem: (1) exports are unpredictable, and it is difficult to calibrate such side-payments precisely; (2) high levels of exports amortize the fixed costs of produc-tion and development, thus creating less economic pressure to collaborate; and, most important, (3) the technological levels of weaker firms are generally rising of their own accord, due to the diffusion of technology, creating surplus capacity and a vested interest in defending sunk costs and existing market shares. For the latter reason, market leaders are almost always declining, which makes it difficult for them to accept a realistic side-payment.

17. Jonathan Tucker argues, in "Partners and Rivals," that if technology lev-els differ greatly, then the weaker country will sometimes pay a premium for cooperation. But this is by no means generally the case. A small country willing to produce low-technology portions of the plane is often an asset, helping to finance high-technology production in other areas.

18. Moravcsik, "Liberalism and International Relations Theory."

19. Mancur Olson, *The Logic of Collective Action: Public Goods and the Theory of Groups* (Cambridge, Mass.: Harvard University Press, 1965).

20. James Q. Wilson, *Political Organizations* (New York: Basic Books, 1973), p. 196.

21. Charles E. Lindblom, *Politics and Markets: The World's Political-Economic Systems* (New York: Basic Books, 1977), pp. 170–188. It is also true that the higher the exports, the less costly is autarky. But it would seem implausible to attribute the view that cooperation is not worthwhile to statesmen who have elected to invest in lengthy negotiations.

22. Interview with Ingenieur-Général de l'Armament Henri Conze, Paris, 15 December 1988.

23. BAe had produced the vertical take-off Harrier, the second generation of which was co-developed with McDonnell-Douglas, as well as trainers.

24. Fly-by-wire technology links mechanical parts of the plane electronically, thereby permitting more sophisticated aerodynamic design. British industry believed that it was technologically infeasible to meet the common performance targets with an aircraft of the weight proposed by France. Interview with Martyn Bittleston, British procurement official, International Institute for Strategic Studies, London, May 1989; also Keith Hayward, *The British Aircraft Industry* (Manchester, Eng.: Manchester University Press, 1989), p. 182.

25. SNECMA was involved as a financially equal partner in an immensely successful civil engine consortium with General Electric, while Rolls-Royce produced its own engines, as well as participating in a corporate alliance with Pratt and Whitney on the civilian side, and with the other Tornado countries on the military side.

26. Guy Doly, "De l'avion de combat Européen à l'avion de combat tactique" (unpubl. paper, Paris: Institut Français de Relations Internationales, n.d., probably 1985–86), p. 1, bases this analysis on interviews. This interpretation is supported by Conze, the French chief negotiator.

27. While BAe and Rolls-Royce preferred to develop a wholly new engine (the "X-40") for the plane, they viewed a derivative of the RB-199 originally developed for the Tornado (the "XG-20") as a second-best alternative. The push to include a clause on compatibility with the Tornado in the agreement was spearheaded by Michael Heseltine who, despite his later pro-European sentiments, drove a hard bargain.

28. He also threatened to move forward with McDonnell-Douglas and General Electric to develop a German-American fighter plane.

29. Doly, "De l'avion," p. 4.

30. Interview with Marisol Touraine, aide to Prime Minister Rocard, Paris, 1989.

31. On the potential consequences for German industry, see *Aviation Week and Space Technology*, 3 September 1990, 69. On delays, see Moodie, *Defense Implications*, p. 17.

32. *Le Monde*, 24 March and 25 July 1963; *Le Journal de Genève*, 10 October 1962 and 5 August 1963; *L'Express*, 23 October 1967.

33. *Handelsblatt*, 22 June 1977. Krauss-Maffei gains a greater share of production on exported tanks than on domestically procured ones.

34. Exports rose from 13 to 26 percent of turnover. While Krauss-Maffei itself provides only 10–20 percent of the value-added, its profits from that proportion are thought to be disproportionately large. Krauss-Maffei produces the chassis of the tank, as well as performing the integration and part of the final assembly. Interestingly, the number of workers at Krauss-Maffei actually decreased as its turnover and exports increased. *Handelsblatt*, 10 February 1983; *Rheinische Post*, 19 March 1977; *Unsere Zeit*, 27 August 1981; *Die Zeit*, 30 September 1977.

35. This means, as in the case of Dassault, that sharing of design tasks cannot be compensated by an allocation of production tasks: *Blick durch die Wirtschaft*, 6 December, 1977. Krupp's subsidiary, MaK, is dependent on military sales for about 50 percent of turnover: *Die Zeit*, 30 September 1977.

36. Krauss-Maffei is a subsidiary of the conglomerate managed by Friedrich Flick. Moreover, the firm is based in Bavaria, and thus profited from the support of Franz-Josef Strauss: *Die Zeit*, 30 September 1977. Because of the importance of electronics in the Leopard II, a plurality of the production takes place in Nordrhein-Westfalen.

37. Independent French and German tank production, alongside the British, American, Swedish, and Swiss programs, contributed to massive overcapacity worldwide. The United States deploys 7,000 tanks, as opposed to 1,500 French, 3,000 German, and about 1,000 or more by other Europeans. See Gilles Marcoin, "L'echec du projet franco-allemand sur le char des années 90" (mimeo., Paris: Institut Français de Relations Internationales, 1986).

38. *Le Figaro*, 8 January 1982. France exported AMX-13s to Greece, Spain, Saudi Arabia, and some South American and South Asian countries.

39. See Christian Muguet, "Rüstungsindustrie und Kooperationspolitik: Erfahrung und Reichweite der deutsch-französischen Zusammenarbeit," in Brock and Jopp, eds., *Sicherheitspolitische Zusammenarbeit und Kooperation der Rüstungswirtschaft in Westeuropa*, p. 135.

40. *L'Express*, 8 October 1982. On the focus on tanks and helicopters, see the statements of Charles Hernu in *Le Figaro*, 29 November 1982.

41. This account draws on Marcoin, "L'echec du projet"; Cathleen Fisher, "Franco-German Armaments Cooperation," in Robbin Laird, ed., *Strangers and Friends: The Franco-German Security Relationship* (London: Pinter, 1989), pp. 72–85; Stephen Kocs, "France, Germany, and the Politics of Military Alliance, 1955–1987" (Ph.D. dissertation, Dept. of Government, Harvard University, 1988), pp. 306–313.

42. Mark Metcalf and Martin Edmonds, "RSI and the Main Battle Tank, 1970–1980," in Martin Edmonds, ed., *International Arms Procurement: New Directions* (New York: Pergamon, 1981), pp. 148–152.

43. Stephen Kocs points out that the German arms-export policy was particularly restrictive for armored vehicles. In "France, Germany," p. 308, Kocs cites Eckhart Ehrenberg, *Der deutsche Rüstungsexport: Beurteilungen und Perspektiven* (Munich: Bernard and Graefe, 1981), pp. 100–101.

44. Kocs, "France, Germany," p. 310; *L'expansion*, 18 November 1983, cited in Muguet, "Rüstungsindustrie," p. 135. A 1972 agreement between France and

Germany permits each nation to export jointly produced arms according to its own laws. Had the export question remained a serious issue, further disagreements might have been addressed through clauses in the agreement limiting exports to specific countries. This had frequently been done before, as in the limitations of sales of Alpha-Jets to Finland.

45. Kocs, "France, Germany," p. 310. Apel opposed the tank not because he opposed collaboration, but because he faced unexpected budget constraints and also because he felt that in future combat, tanks, like tactical aircraft, would be supplanted by rockets and wheeled vehicles: *Berliner Morgenpost*, 12 February 1981.

46. Marcoin, "L'echec du projet," p. 5; *Der Spiegel*, 23 April 1979; cf. *Le Figaro*, 10 March 1981.

47. See, for example, *Le Figaro*, 21 December 1981 and 8 January 1982. Krupp MaK had developed plans for revolutionary new technology to replace the classical tank turret, which also would have stripped the French of their only area of apparent comparative advantage: *Libération*, 9 September 1980.

48. *Süddeutsche Zeitung*, 26 January 1961; *Der Spiegel*, 11 February 1980.

49. Marcoin, "L'echec du projet," p. 4. The chassis is the one major subsystem actually produced by Krauss-Maffei.

50. "... und das ist schlecht," Raether concludes in no uncertain terms: *Die Zeit*, 25 July 1980. The first hint came when the heads of state also agreed to place political and industrial coordinating committees, based in Hamburg, under the control of a Paris-based steering committee. Cf. *Süddeutsche Zeitung*, 9 February 1980; *Frankfurter Allgemeine Zeitung*, 8 February 1980; *Liberation*, 9 September 1980. I also draw on an interview with François Heisbourg, Devon, England, October 1988.

51. The turret compromise was suggested by West German representatives, and agreed to by both sides in December 1980. See Fisher, "Franco-German Armaments Cooperation," p. 96; Kocs, "France, Germany," p. 309; *Quotidien de Paris*, 2 November 1985.

52. Marcoin, "L'echec du projet," pp. 3–4; *Quotidien de Paris*, 2 November 1985; Muguet, "Rüstungsindustrie," p. 136; *Süddeutsche Zeitung*, 29 November 1982.

53. See the statement by Carl Damm, CDU, and Herman Schmidt, SPD, members of the Bundestag's defense committee, in *Die Zeit*, 25 July 1980. Apel opposed the funding and tried to cut it out of the defense budget in March 1981: Marcoin, "L'echec du projet," p. 7. Wörner opposed it as well: *Süddeutsche Zeitung*, 29 November 1982. The German armaments director told his French counterpart that the Bundestag opposed a new tank because the Leopard II had just entered into service: Marcoin, "L'echec du projet," pp. 3–4.

54. *Le Figaro*, 30 November 1982; Kocs, "France, Germany," pp. 312–313; *Le Monde*, 19 March 1983.

55. On "l'affaire Arnold," see *Le Monde*, 2, 4, and 20 November 1985; *Le Figaro*, 4 November 1985. When General Dalaunay, the previous Chief of Staff of the Army, termed Arnaud's criticisms "things everyone already knows," no one in the French government offered more than a pro forma response.

56. *Libération*, 18 February 1988.

57. Discussion of the Franco-German helicopter is based on Henri Louet, *Rapport d'information par la Commission de la défense nationale et des forces armées sur la coopération industrielle franco-allemand en matière d'hélicoptères de combat* (Paris: Assemblée Nationale, troisième session extraordinaire de 1985–1986, no. 249); Fisher, "Franco-German Armaments Cooperation," pp. 98–100; Kocs, "France, Germany," pp. 320–327; Gustav A. Bittner, "Deutsch-Französische Rüstungsproduktion: Eine positive Bilanz," in Karl Kaiser and Pierre Lellouche, eds., *Deutsche-Französiche Sicherheitspolitik* (Bonn: Europa Union Verlag, 1986).

58. This suggests that once European firms have developed products collaboratively, they are more likely to collaborate in future generations of that product line. The reason is not because institutions have their own independent power to shape incentives, as "modified Structural Realists" would argue, but because firms alter their corporate strategies and productive investment in light of existing possibilities.

59. Fisher, "Franco-German," p. 98. The French system of a mast-mounted system permitted a seating configuration side-by-side, while the Martin Marietta system favored by the Germans, which would have to be mounted in the nose, required that the two crew members sit in a tandem configuration, one in front of the other.

60. Kocs, "France, Germany," p. 323; interview with Hans Rühle, former German National Armaments Director, Washington, D.C., 2 May 1990. The European Fighter Aircraft project was not far enough along to be relied upon, and lacked the symbolic value of a bilateral program.

61. The financial protection afforded by a joint company was particularly important to MBB, because for the first time it was being held to fixed-price contracts on a large international collaborative project.

62. *Armed Forces Journal International*, May 1990: 37; *Interavia* 45 (July 1990): 544–548; Kocs, "France, Germany," p. 325. The responses of Aérospatiale and MBB to this situation of technological asymmetry are difficult to explain without understanding the lack of interest by both firms in third-country export markets.

63. On this plan, see Moravcsik, "European Armaments Industry," pp. 69–71.

64. Moodie, *Defense Implications*, p. 27–28.

65. Moodie, *Defense Implications*. On the negotiation of the European Single Act, see Andrew Moravcsik, "Negotiating the European Single Act: National Interests and Conventional Statecraft in the European Community," *International Organization* 45 (Winter 1991): 19–56.

66. Interview with Philippe Roger, Sous-Directeur Alliance Atlantique, Délégation aux Relations Internationales, Ministry of Defense, Paris, 16 February 1989.

67. On transmission-belt theories, see the Introduction to this volume.

68. This new strategy, one might argue, is also explicable in terms of the international level alone, since it involves the use of one international strategy to undermine domestic opposition to another. The new reforms do not directly alter the nature of domestic politics (i.e., the fact that firms get their way), only

the international environment in which domestic politics occurs. While I am sympathetic to this argument, it is important to remember that one must use a theory of domestic politics to explain why the state, while unable to directly force firms to collaborate, can employ instruments to slowly alter the incentives facing firms. The answer appears to lie in the different incentives to firms (positive inducements in the R&D programs vs. negative inducements in collaboration) and the divergent time-horizons of governments and firms.

69. This line of argument follows from studies of interest-group activity based on theories of collective action. See Olson, *Logic of Collective Action.* For a more recent application to trade policy, see Joanne Gowa, "Public Goods and Political Institutions: Trade and Monetary Policy Processes in the United States," *International Organization* 42 (Winter 1988): 15–32.

70. Interview with François Heisbourg, Director, International Institute of Strategic Studies, London, October 1988.

71. This finding may also reflect a number of other possible causes, or simple case-selection bias; see Introduction to this volume.

72. See my "Liberalism and International Relations Theory."

PART 3

Economic Disputes

6

The 1933 World Economic Conference as an Instance of Failed International Cooperation

Barry Eichengreen and Marc Uzan

The 1933 World Economic Conference is a classic example of failure to achieve international agreement. In June of that year representatives of the nations of the world assembled in London to negotiate a coordinated response to the economic crisis of the 1930s. They achieved nothing. The issues that led them to convene the conference included exchange-rate instability, deflation, tariffs, and external debts. They made no significant progress on any of these fronts. Following the conference, the already fragmented international monetary system splintered into yet additional currency blocs. Deflationary pressure on the gold-standard countries intensified accordingly. International trade was stagnant. The problem of intergovernmental debts remained a bone of contention among the Allies, while the overhang of defaulted commercial debts impeded the recovery of international capital markets. The economic crisis lingered, doing nothing to nurture political moderation at home or to encourage collaboration in the diplomatic sphere.

No existing explanation for the failure of the conference is entirely satisfactory. One thesis is that U.S. insistence that certain issues (war debts, tariff rates) be declared off limits doomed the conference to failure. Unfortunately, it is not clear why this should have made agreement on issues such as exchange rates and monetary reflation more difficult. A second popular thesis is that Roosevelt's decision to take the dollar off gold torpedoed the conference. Again, it is not clear why, if it was possible to envisage an agreement prior to dollar devaluation, Roosevelt's action should have so dramatically transformed matters. Nor is there in the literature an adequate explanation for Roosevelt's decision.[1]

In this chapter we reassess the failure of the 1933 World Economic Conference, adding what are, relative to the existing literature, two novel elements. The first is domestic politics. In 1933, we argue, domestic politics severely restricted the scope for agreement. Those who, prior to the conference, thought that they envisaged the outlines of an agreement neglected this critical influence.

The second element is the conceptual framework that negotiators brought to the table. Policy-makers were unable to agree on a concerted response to the economic crisis because they perceived it in very different ways. Lacking a shared diagnosis of the problem, they were unable to prescribe a cooperative response. Actions that are commonly portrayed as perverse appear logical once the absence of a common conceptual framework is recognized.

Both elements are necessary to understand the failure of the conference. Had negotiators possessed compatible conceptual frameworks, it might have been possible to strike a purely monetary deal. France, Britain, and the United States could have agreed to simultaneous changes in domestic monetary cum exchange-rate policies, none of which were desirable in isolation but, when undertaken simultaneously, would have left all three nations better off. That national delegations conceived the role of monetary policy in very different ways prevented them from negotiating a mutually acceptable monetary response.

Even with a purely monetary agreement ruled out, conceptual differences did not in principle preclude a cross-issue deal involving monetary concessions by Britain, tariff concessions by France, and war-debt concessions by the United States. But such cross-issue agreement foundered on domestic politics (primarily the opposition of French agriculture to trade liberalization). Domestic political obstacles proved insurmountable because the structure of domestic political institutions, particularly in France, vested special-interest groups with considerable leverage.

Our analysis has implications for several separate literatures in economics and political science. It illustrates some of the uses of the literature on issue linkage[2] and of that relating domestic and international policies.[3] Its emphasis on the importance of negotiators' conceptual frameworks bears on the role of ideas in policy-making.[4] It provides an application of the literature in economics concerned with the scope for cooperation when national policy-makers subscribe to different models.[5] But it transcends that literature by endogenizing policy-makers' choice of model.

The first section of this chapter sketches the background to the period and provides a narrative of events. In light of this account, the next section indicates the limitations of existing explanations for the failure of the conference. The third section introduces the role of competing conceptual frameworks, and the next adds domestic politics. The conclusion attempts to relate these strands to the recent literature on diplomacy and domestic politics.

THE 1933 WORLD ECONOMIC CONFERENCE

This section provides an account of the 1933 World Economic Conference to familiarize the reader with the principal events that we seek to explain.[6] It documents the ways in which those events have been analyzed by previous scholars and allows us to identify some limitations of the interpretations that dominate the literature.

Background

The year 1932 marked the trough of the business-cycle downturn that began in 1929. By 1932 the volume of global manufacturing production had fallen to less than 60 percent of 1929 levels. Primary production fell less dramatically, but it too reached its trough in 1932.[7]

The collapse of foreign trade and finance encouraged the belief that the crux of the problem lay in the international sphere. By 1932 the value of trade had fallen to less than half of its 1929 value. Following the imposition of the U.S. Smoot-Hawley Tariff in 1930, trade barriers around the world reached new heights. International lending, which had peaked in 1928, evaporated with the outbreak of sovereign default in Latin America in 1931 and its spread to Central and Eastern Europe in 1932. Debtor countries such as Argentina, Australia, Brazil, New Zealand, and Venezuela had been forced off the gold standard soon after the Great Depression struck. With Britain's devaluation in September 1931, international monetary instability spread to the core of the gold-standard system. By the end of 1931, more than two dozen countries were off the gold standard. What had once been a unified international monetary system was, like Gaul, divided into three parts: countries with devalued currencies, those under exchange control, and a residual bloc still on the gold standard.

These problems pointed to the issues that would form the agenda for a prospective conference: deflation, trade barriers, external debts, and exchange-rate instability. Discussions of deflation emphasized not only the collapse of price levels; the decline in output and the rise in unemployment also fell under this heading. There was a tendency to impute a causal connection to the simultaneous collapse of prices and production. Action to stabilize prices, and ultimately to raise them, was viewed in some circles as necessary and sufficient to bring the Depression to an end.

The problem of trade barriers encompassed both tariffs and quotas.

The United States had imposed the Smoot-Hawley Tariff in the summer of 1930. Within months of sterling's devaluation, Britain had imposed a general tariff and negotiated tariff preferences with the members of its Commonwealth. France, Belgium, and the Netherlands responded with increasingly comprehensive import quotas. Particularly troubling to contemporaries was the growing prevalence of clearing arrangements. Starting in 1932, Germany negotiated clearing arrangements designed to maximize its market power internationally and balance its trade bilaterally. Central and Eastern European nations in Germany's orbit followed suit.

Under the heading "external debts" fell a potpourri of financial obligations. The most controversial item remained German reparations and Allied war debts to the United States. Germany's obligation, established originally at another London conference in 1921, had been scaled back under the Dawes Plan in 1924, under the Young Plan in 1930, and at the Lausanne Conference in 1932. Controversy arose from the fact that war debts had not been reduced commensurately. To gain access to the U.S. capital market, the European Allies had negotiated war-debt settlements with the United States, generally between 1923 and 1926. These agreements remained in place until in June 1931 the Hoover Moratorium suspended war-debt and reparations payments for a year. At Lausanne in the spring of 1932, Germany's obligation was extinguished in return for its promise to deliver 3 billion reichsmarks of bonds. But the French and British publics objected to an agreement eliminating German reparations without also writing down Allied war debts to the United States. The representatives of the European Allies therefore signed a gentleman's agreement not to ratify the Lausanne Convention until a settlement had been reached with the U.S.

The exchange-rate problem was the most contentious of all. Sterling fell from U.S. $4.86 on September 19, 1931, to $3.25 by the beginning of December. It fluctuated between $3.15 and $3.70 over the course of 1932. In the absence of significant inflation in Britain, this was a dramatic shift in relative prices to be accommodated by the remaining gold-standard countries. In addition to the Commonwealth, most of Britain's foreign trading partners depreciated their currencies along with sterling.

The 1933 World Economic Conference was not the first international meeting at which such problems were discussed. Previous economic conferences at Brussels in 1920 and Genoa in 1922 had been less than totally successful, however. Neither led to reconstruction of the international economic system along the lines envisaged in the delegates' resolutions. It was some years, therefore, before another such meeting was convened. Finally in 1930, Germany, dissatisfied that the Young Plan negotiations had been limited to a subset of economic issues, proposed a world economic conference. The possibility was raised again in 1931 during the Franco-American dispute over the Hoover Moratorium and in 1932 during Anglo-American discussions. The Lausanne Conference set the stage. The delegates at Lausanne, in addition to annulling Germany's reparations schedule, called upon the League of Nations to convoke an "International Monetary and Economic Conference" to address economic problems on a global scale.

Objectives of the Participants

The central participants at the London Conference were the United States, the United Kingdom, and France. Dozens of other nations attended, and some, such as Germany, were prominent in the proceedings. But the United States, Britain, and France were the central players. Any cooperative response to the economic crisis hinged upon their agreement.[8]

France attached priority to the restoration of international monetary stability, by which was meant a return to the gold standard by Britain and its trading partners and the removal of exchange control by Germany and other Central European countries.[9] Monetary stabilization along orthodox lines was, in the French view, the only means of reviving investor confidence and laying the basis for sustainable growth. The French regarded tampering with the gold standard as inconsistent with this end. Hence they opposed schemes to redistribute the Bank of France's excess gold reserves to other countries, to reduce gold cover ratios, to encourage central banks to hold foreign-exchange reserves, and to moderate the independence of central banks. The Bank of France and its governor, Clement Moret, were even more hostile to these expedients than was the French Treasury under Georges Bonnet. The French also wished to preserve their freedom to use instruments such as tariffs and quotas which insulated them from financial and economic disturbances abroad.

Britain's priority was reflation, which meant freedom from external constraints on the policy of cheap money.[10] By 1932 the British Treasury, which took the lead in international negotiations, had been converted to the advantages of low interest rates and rising prices. Unless Britain received a guarantee that other countries would adopt a similar posture, it was unwilling to return to gold. To insure that the stabilization of sterling would not prevent Britain from pursuing reflationary policies, the British asked for four specific concessions: a war-debt settlement, which would stem the drain of gold to the United States; a commitment by foreign central banks to initiate expansionary open-market operations, which required changes in the statutes preventing the Bank of

France from engaging in such actions; a redistribution of existing gold to countries with insufficient reserves, enabling them to relax their exchange controls and stabilize their currencies; and finally, commercial policy concessions by the United States and France, which would prevent their trade balances from moving into strong surplus and keep them from draining gold from other countries pursuing reflationary policies.

Both Britain and France hoped that a war-debt settlement might be negotiated in London. Though war debts were formally outside the terms of reference of the conference, they nonetheless figured in the calculations of British and French negotiators. For their part, some U.S. officials recommended offering war-debt concessions if the Europeans acceded to other American demands.[11]

U.S. demands were difficult to anticipate. The Hoover Administration was thought to support the French campaign for a generalized return to gold. Hoover's 1931–32 moratorium had demonstrated a new flexibility on the issue of intergovernmental debts. The position of the incoming Roosevelt Administration was less clear. Roosevelt had avoided addressing the merits of the gold standard and devaluation during the election campaign. But by delegating such discussion to hard-money Democrats, he left the impression that he too was sympathetic to the French position. Unlike the Republicans, the traditional party of protection, a Democratic administration was seen as more likely to press for tariff reductions.

No international conference could succeed without U.S. participation. American isolationists having thwarted efforts to include the United States in previous international economic conferences, by 1932 the U.S. had acquired a reputation for boycotting such assemblies. Knowing this, the U.S. could demand a price for its participation. With the dollar still on gold, it was likely to be asked for concessions on war debts and import tariffs. It therefore demanded that war debts be excluded from the agenda and that there be no discussion of specific tariff rates. Neither sanction was binding, however. Tariffs and war debts featured in the informal discussions of treasury and central-bank officials and were alluded to in conference proceedings, starting with British Chancellor Neville Chamberlain's opening address.

Preliminary Discussions

At Lausanne it had been agreed to appoint a Committee of Experts to set the agenda for the London Conference. The British and French experts were closely affiliated with their countries' respective treasuries. On the British side, they were Sir Frederick Leith-Ross, long-time high Treasury official, and Sir Frederick Phillips, head of domestic financial affairs at the Treasury. On the French side they were Charles Rist, long-time government adviser, and Jean Parmentier, honorary director of the Treasury. The American experts were less intimately associated with the U.S. State and Treasury departments: they were John H. Williams, professor of economics at Harvard University, and Edmund E. Day, a former Harvard professor currently director for social sciences at the Rockefeller Foundation.

The Committee of Experts convened in Geneva at the end of October 1932. Deep divisions immediately surfaced between countries on and off gold. The French and American experts demanded that Britain restore gold convertibility as a precondition for further talks. Leith-Ross and Phillips countered with a demand for international action to raise the level of prices in gold-standard countries as a precondition for currency stabilization. The French dismissed reflationary initiatives, especially when undertaken by countries off the gold standard, as not merely ineffectual but counterproductive. Only currency stabilization on a gold basis, they argued, would succeed in restoring confidence and encouraging investment.

At this stage, the U.S. position had more in common with France's than with Britain's, although the experts' statements remained vague pending the outcome of the November presidential election. That outcome was known when the experts reconvened in the second and third weeks of January, but not the intentions of the president-elect. With the United States and France preoccupied by domestic affairs (the interregnum between administrations in the U.S., a budgetary crisis in France), the British experts assumed responsibility for drafting the annotated agenda. Their document, when it emerged, recommended establishing a common international monetary standard, increasing the level of prices, abolishing exchange controls, and removing trade restrictions. Jockeying took place over the order of the list, but the final version of the agenda made clear that these four objectives were linked.

To achieve them, governments were encouraged to take a mixture of steps, some reflecting French gold-standard orthodoxy, others British insistence on cheap money. The former included balancing budgets, removing exchange controls, and enhancing central-bank independence. The latter included liberal money and credit policies and steps such as debt settlement to encourage international lending. The question was whether what were in effect two distinct strategies could be successfully reconciled.

The Conference and Its Breakdown

Roosevelt's decision on April 19 to accept the Thomas Amendment and take the United States off gold threw a wrench into conference preparations. It seemed likely that the dollar would fall significantly against gold and that, to keep pace, the Bank of England would depreciate sterling. Exchange-rate fluctuations might be considerable. It seemed doubtful that countries would be able to agree to a general currency stabilization or to negotiate a package of bilateral parities and tariff reductions with currencies fluctuating violently against one another.

Hence, the Washington Conversations, of late April and early June, in which Roosevelt and his advisors met with representatives of 11 nations, came to be seen as a critical opportunity to negotiate a tariff truce and an exchange stabilization agreement. The truce was successfully concluded: the United States, the United Kingdom, France, Germany, Italy, Japan, Belgium, and Norway agreed not to increase tariffs or tighten quotas for the duration of the conference. Exchange-rate stabilization proved a more difficult nut to crack. Starting on April 25, Leith-Ross, now the British government's Chief Economic Adviser, met with James Warburg, Roosevelt's confidant on monetary matters, to discuss stabilization. The views Warburg conveyed to Leith-Ross were personal; they had not yet been endorsed by the President.[12] Warburg suggested that the franc and the dollar be stabilized at par and that sterling be stabilized in the neighborhood of $3.50. This $3.50 was acceptable to the British, who also found congenial Warburg's proposal that countries reduce gold cover ratios to 25 or 30 percent, remove exchange controls, and readjust war debts.[13]

Unfortunately, neither Roosevelt nor the financial markets were of the same mind as Warburg. Within a fortnight of the Warburg–Leith-Ross conversations, the dollar had fallen to $4 against the pound. Warburg modified his plan to incorporate a 15 percent discount of the dollar against gold.[14] The French, invited to contribute their opinion, rejected anything less than dollar stabilization at the old gold parity. By mid-May, however, they were forced to acknowledge the unrealism of this demand. They then pressed for stabilization at current levels. Warburg offered a plan under which the three governments would each contribute 500 million dollars to a joint stabilization fund, without saying anything about the level at which exchange rates would be stabilized. The British refused to peg sterling to the dollar without further information about the new U.S. administration's monetary intentions. The French feared that if Roosevelt utilized the inflationary powers granted him under the Thomas Amendment, France's 500 million dollar contribution would be expended immediately in support of the dollar and the President's reckless monetary experiment. And Roosevelt was not yet prepared to commit himself. Each government held its breath, hoping that the others would give in first.

As May turned to June, still no agreement to stabilize exchange rates had been reached. Responding to French requests, the three countries convened exchange-rate stabilization talks at the British Treasury on June 10, two days before the conference was scheduled to open. Representatives of the three treasuries met in one room, and Clement Moret of the Bank of France, Montagu Norman of the Bank of England, and George Harrison of the Federal Reserve Bank of New York met in another.

The French opened with a demand for immediate stabilization of sterling and the dollar within 1 percent bands, offering no quid pro quo. Stabilization would be feasible, argued the Bank of France's representatives, only if each government issued a detailed statement of intentions. The French Treasury representatives, Jacques Rueff (financial attaché to the French Embassy in London) and Jean-Jacques Bizot, more cognizant of British and American resistance, accepted a counterproposal that the three nations jointly issue only a general statement of their desire for exchange-rate stability. The British and Americans agreed on the desirability of 5 percent bands, but disagreed on the appropriate level for the sterling-dollar rate, the Americans preferring more than $4, the British preferring less.

Within five days negotiators agreed to compromise. The British and American governments would limit currency fluctuations for the duration of the conference. The pound would be held at $4 plus or minus 3 percent. Only in the event of "exceptional and unforeseen circumstances" would currencies be allowed to deviate from this band.

Rumors surfaced that there existed an agreement, but without confirmation of the rate. On June 16 the dollar gained 4 percent against gold, and U.S. stock and commodity prices tumbled, anticipating that the Federal Reserve would be forced to adopt a more restrictive stance. If Roosevelt retained doubts about the connection between currency depreciation and commodity prices, they were vanquished by these events. On June 17 he instructed his representatives to disown the agreement, rejecting stabilization of the sterling-dollar rate at current levels but leaving open the possibility of future action at a more favorable level. The impression gained by their foreign counterparts was that prospects were bleak for dollar stabilization at any level.

France's fall-back position was a currency stabilization agreement which excluded the United States. The British agreed to consider yet another joint declaration if the French would draft it and secure the support of the other gold countries. The document resembled nothing so much as the general statement of principles that had been suggested by British and U.S. treasury representatives at the outset of talks. Specific exchange rates and techniques for achieving them were conspicuous by their absence.

French hopes that Britain would accept even a weak stabilization agreement without U.S. concurrence proved mistaken. The British forwarded the document to the Americans, making clear that their participation was contingent upon that of the United States. Roosevelt's closest advisor, Raymond Moley, recently arrived in London, was favorably inclined. In New York, Treasury Secretary Woodin and Bernard Baruch concurred. Once again, however, Roosevelt ignored his advisors' recommendations. On July 1, he informed London of his decision. The next day his famous "bombshell" message to the conference, in which he denounced the argument in favor of stable exchange rates as a "specious fallacy" and derided "old fetishes of so-called international bankers," put an end to tripartite talks.[15]

In despair, the French suggested immediate adjournment. The British were inclined to agree. To save face, it was decided to soldier on. The subcommission on financial reconstruction issued a vague statement that debtors should pay their debts, but that creditors should be understanding if they did not. The subcommission on monetary problems affirmed the superiority of the gold standard over alternative monetary arrangements, but offered no useful suggestions of how it might be re-established. The conference adjourned at the end of July with negligible accomplishments to its credit.

LIMITATIONS OF EXISTING EXPLANATIONS

The two leading explanations for the failure of the conference both blame the United States. One emphasizes U.S. insistence that war debts and specific tariff rates be excluded from the agenda, the other Roosevelt's bombshell rejecting stabilization. Neither is wholly satisfactory.

The first explanation has two limitations. First, it is not obvious why the exclusion of war debts and tariff rates rendered agreement on exchange rate and monetary questions impossible. Excluding war debts and tariff rates from the agenda did not prevent the three countries from agreeing to stabilize their currencies, reduce their gold cover ratios, and expand their money supplies. France would have obtained the exchange-rate stability it desired, the United States and Britain the reflationary initiatives to which they attached priority. The U.S. would not have granted war-debt concessions, nor would it have been forced to reduce tariffs. Thus one can plausibly argue that the U.S. could have emerged from the conference as well off as in the hypothetical situation in which both war debt and tariff revision had been negotiated. Other countries would have obtained neither debt relief nor improved access to the U.S. export market. Hence their enthusiasm for a prospective agreement surely was dimmed by the U.S. strategy. But it was the U.S., not other countries, that refused to stabilize. The problem was not that the U.S. had too little to offer; rather, it was that Roosevelt regarded France and Britain's counteroffer as inadequate.

The second limitation of this explanation is that, in the case of war debts at least, it is not clear that the exclusion rule was binding. The United States wished to separate the discussion of war debts from other issues, but not to prevent such discussion entirely. This was the same approach taken to tripartite exchange-rate stabilization talks, namely, to segregate them from the proceedings of the World Economic Conference on the grounds that they directly involved only a subset of countries. During the Washington Conversations, extensive discussion of war debts had ensued, covering reduction of capital, elimination of interest, and other options. Formal cancellation may have been impossible, but this did not necessarily exclude close substitutes. When the June 15 payment came due, in the midst of the conference, the U.S. agreed to accept token payment of 10 million dollars. The U.S. strategy prevented a war-debt settlement from being negotiated at the conference itself, but it did not prevent the negotiation of debt revision as part of a broader agreement.

The other explanation, emphasizing Roosevelt's refusal to stabilize, is not so much flawed but incomplete. That the President's bombshell halted negotiations is indisputable; the question is what led him to take that step. The literature tends to portray Roosevelt's action as idiosyncratic. In the remainder of this chapter we suggest that two more systematic factors were at work: the incompatibility of the conceptual frameworks that informed national negotiating positions, and domestic politics.

THE ROLE OF COMPETING CONCEPTUAL FRAMEWORKS

The Nature of the Frameworks

One reason that French, British, and U.S. representatives found it difficult to agree was that their negotiating positions were informed by different conceptual frameworks.[16] By 1933 the interpretation of the slump presented by Keynes to the Macmillan Committee three years earlier had been accepted by the British Treasury and, with reservations, by the Bank of England. In this view, Britain's Depression had resulted from a deflationary shock imported from abroad. World prices had collapsed starting in 1929. The decline of international prices had not reduced domestic prices commensurately; instead, rigidities in the domestic wage-price structure had produced the macroeconomic slump. Financial contracts were nominally denominated and ran many years to maturity. Hence the fall in prices had raised the real burden of debts, eroding the creditworthiness of borrowers and discouraging investment. The failure of money wages to fall proportionately had inflated real labor costs, discouraging production and employment. The growing market power of unions had reinforced labor's traditional desire for a wage structure that was stable across workers and over time; this had contributed to the failure of money wages to adjust. Trade Boards, established just prior to World War I, set minimum rates of pay for unskilled workers, effectively placing a floor below the entire structure of labor costs. The authorities' failure to reduce unemployment benefits along with wages further exacerbated the problem.[17]

This interpretation of the crisis pointed to an obvious policy response. Monetary policy should be used to stabilize prices and eventually to restore them to 1929 levels. Starting in 1932, the Bank of England had begun to take the necessary action. Bank rate had been reduced to 2 percent. Credit had been provided in quantities sufficient to halt the decline of prices.

Central to the British view was a preoccupation with the external constraint. If the exchange rate was fixed, it was impossible for any one central bank to pursue reflationary initiatives. Measures to raise the domestic price level would erode international competitiveness, undermining the balance of payments. If the central bank reduced domestic interest rates, capital would flow out, worsening the capital account of the balance of payments. If it stimulated domestic demand, imports would flow in, worsening the current account. In effect, a central bank committed to defending a fixed exchange rate lacked the capacity to run independent reflationary policies. Unless reflationary initiatives were coordinated internationally, currency depreciation was a necessary concomitant of cheap money.

French policy-makers attributed the crisis neither to deflation nor to the passivity of policy-makers, but to monetary instability. Unlike the British, who argued that under the gold standard monetary authorities possessed inadequate discretion, in the prevailing French view the opposite was true. Growing reliance on foreign-exchange reserves had relaxed the gold-standard constraints. Central banks had willingly accumulated sterling and dollar balances over the second half of the 1920s, allowing the Bank of England and the Federal Reserve System to indulge in excessively expansionary monetary policies. In this view, productive capacity worldwide had expanded more rapidly since 1913 than the supply of monetary gold. Since the demand for money rose with the level of activity, lower prices were necessary to provide a matching increase in the supply of real balances. Under the gold standard, a smooth deflation like that of 1873–93 was the normal response. But in the 1920s central banks had used their discretionary power to block the downward adjustment of prices. They recklessly pyramided domestic credit on foreign-exchange reserves. Liberal supplies of credit had fueled speculation, raising asset prices to unsustainable heights and setting the stage for the stock-market crash. Following this shock, central banks rushed to liquidate exchange reserves, and prices fell abruptly. One point on which French and British experts agreed was that this sudden deflation was far from smooth: it produced bankruptcies among debtors, discouraged investment, and disrupted activity. The insufficiency of investment that resulted was the proximate source of the slump.[18]

In France, then, the Depression was seen as an inevitable consequence of the unrealistic policies pursued by central banks in preceding years. To now prevent deflation from running its course threatened to inaugurate another era of speculative excess and, ultimately, another depression. It was better to allow excess liquidity to be purged and prices to fall to sustainable levels. Only then would the confidence of investors be restored. Only then could sustainable recovery commence.[19]

Nothing more dramatically symbolized this problem of financial instability than disarray in the international monetary sphere. Exchange-rate instability discouraged domestic investment and international trade. Restoring the international gold standard was the single most important step policy-makers might take to promote investor confidence.

In contrast to France and Britain, there existed no dominant economic model in the United States.[20] In part this reflected the ongoing transition from the Hoover to the Roosevelt administration. In part it reflected Hoover's eclecticism and Roosevelt's taste for experimentation. In part it was symptomatic of deep disagreement in academic and official circles. The American model, insofar as the label has content, incorporated elements of both its French and British counterparts, taking on a more British flavor with the passage of time. In addition, however, the American framework had distinctive elements of its own.

Hoover shared the French explanation for the slump that emphasized the abuse of credit.[21] He blamed excessively accommodating Federal Reserve policy between 1925 and 1927 for provoking the stock-market boom and the crash to whose effects the economy was still striving to adjust. But Hoover and his colleagues supplemented the French explanation with one akin to the British, holding that the unregulated economy was inherently unstable. Economic activity, they held, was given to periodic slumps that should be offset by measures to stimulate demand. Demand could be sustained during cyclical downturns by accelerating the rate of public-works spending, by reducing interest rates, and by preventing management from cutting wages. The appropriate policy response to the slump was to cut interest rates and stabilize prices in order to stimulate capital investment, to persuade employers to pay stable wages in order to stimulate consumer demand, and to increase government spending to stimulate employment directly.[22]

When the Hooverites contemplated the external constraint, the inconsistencies in their conceptual framework became apparent. Adopting the French explanation of the slump as a result of a massive abuse of credit, they attached priority to maintenance of the gold standard. Gold convertibility was essential for the maintenance of investor confidence and to prevent renewed speculative excesses. During the 1932 electoral campaign, Hoover continued to tie his political fortunes to the gold standard. An absence of speculative excesses was not sufficient, however, to stabilize an unstable economy. Demand stimulus was also required. But each of the demand-side measures the Hooverites proposed threatened gold convertibility. Increased public spending promised to suck in imports. Low interest rates threatened to provoke a capital outflow. High wages eroded the competitiveness of U.S. exports. The two strands of thought proved incompatible.

Previous authors have noted that the Hoover Administration had in its portfolio all the policy instruments needed to counter the Depression, but was strangely hesitant to utilize them on the requisite scale.[23] Public works spending remained tentative. Aside from the spring of 1932, the Federal Reserve engaged in few expansionary open-market operations. The administration's high-wage policy was abandoned in 1931. The explanation is simple enough. Deficit spending, monetary expansion, and high wages threatened the gold standard. Absent a willingness to abandon gold, demand-side policies could be used only with moderation.

The relationship of Hoover's model to Roosevelt's is a contested issue among historians. Most writers have portrayed the Roosevelt Administration's model circa June 1933 as a revolutionary break with its predecessor. In fact, Roosevelt's model can be seen as essentially the same as Hoover's in its emphases on high wages (New Deal Labor codes), farm purchasing power (agricultural set asides), slowly rising prices (the gold-buying program and industrial price-maintenance schemes), public spending (the Tennessee Valley Authority and other New Deal programs), and the need for financial stability (to be obtained through banking reform). Roosevelt, like Hoover, apparently shared the diagnosis of the Depression as a reflection of insufficient demand.[24] Roosevelt simply reversed the priority Hoover had attached to exchange-rate stability over demand stimulus.

Origins of the Frameworks

It seems extraordinary that policy-makers in these three countries could have perceived the causes of the slump in such radically different ways.

In fact, their divergent conceptual frameworks directly reflected their nations' different historical experiences. Britain had endured deflation throughout the 1920s. The Bank of England had first pursued restrictive policies in order to restore the pre-war sterling parity in 1925. Prices had continued to fall, albeit at a slower pace, over the second half of the 1920s. Recorded unemployment had hovered in double digits, suggesting an association between deflation and joblessness. Britain had experienced a series of exchange-rate crises, in 1927, in 1929, and most seriously in 1931, each of which had forced the Bank of England to tighten the monetary screws.

A decade of high unemployment and labor disputes had focused attention on nominal wage inertia as a central factor in the propagation of the deflationary impulse. The downward inflexibility of money wages, it was widely believed, reflected the spread of unionism and the growth of labor militancy. Union density declined in the 1920s from its immediate postwar peak, but labor organization continued to exceed the levels reached before the war.

Just as the 1920s had sensitized the British to the dangers of deflation and fixed exchange rates, the abandonment of gold in September 1931, and its aftermath, had impressed them with the advantages of the alternative. At last the Bank of England had been able to relax its monetary stance. Following a short period of adjustment, industrial production had begun to rise. The efficacy of monetary reflation and of a floating pound sterling was readily evident to British observers.

British insistence that an international commitment to reflationary measures precede the restoration of fixed parities similarly reflected the experience of preceding years. At the Genoa Conference in 1922, British Treasury experts had warned that restoration of the international gold standard might give rise to deflationary pressure. They had proposed a convention to supplement gold reserves with convertible foreign exchange. But the resolutions adopted at Genoa had not been systematically implemented, and consequently, the British believed, the disaster of which they had warned had come to pass. Starting in 1929, the British Treasury and the Bank of England had urged the U.S. Federal Reserve System and the Bank of France to expand, and thereby to relax the external constraint on British monetary policy. Neither foreign central bank had cooperated. This experience led British policy-makers to demand an explicit commitment to internationally coordinated reflationary initiatives before agreeing to return to gold.

Financial instability was the dominant characteristic of French experience in the postwar decade. During the period when gold convertibility was suspended, France had experienced persistent inflation accompanied by financial and political chaos. The Bank of France had used its discretion not to stabilize the economy but to finance government budget deficits through domestic credit creation. French observers consequently associated monetary discretion with financial instability. Only following the re-establishment of constraints on monetary policy, in the form of gold convertibility and statutes prohibiting the Bank of France from undertaking most open-market operations, had inflation been halted and a basis for sustainable growth been laid. It is not surprising, then, that discretionary monetary policy was associated with financial instability in general, and exchange-rate instability in particular, and that the French sought an explanation for the slump in the breakdown of the international monetary system.

French observers did not share the worries of labor-market inflexibility characteristic of the British. Recorded unemployment had been low throughout the 1920s.[25] Mobility between the urban and rural sectors remained higher than in Britain. Nor did France possess an unemployment insurance system comparable to Britain's. Unemployment benefits were strictly limited, and public relief was provided locally. French experts such as Jacques Rueff ascribed British unemployment to the excessive generosity of its unemployment insurance system and attributed the smoother operation of the French labor market largely to the absence of such a system.[26]

The recent historical experience of the United States similarly helps to explain the Hoover Administration's failure to appreciate the conflict between the gold standard and demand stimulus. Ever since 1914, the U.S. gold standard had been secure. The U.S. was the one belligerent that had not been forced to suspend the gold standard during World War I. It had enjoyed persistent balance-of-payments surpluses throughout the 1920s. Gold reserves continued to flow toward the U.S. during the first two years of the slump. By 1931, there existed an entire generation of American policy-makers without firsthand experience with threats to gold convertibility. The situation changed following sterling's devaluation in September 1931, but policy-makers were slow to incorporate this new information.

Effects of the Frameworks

For competing conceptual frameworks to influence negotiations, they had to be embraced by government ministries. Officials from those ministries had to be vested with responsibility for negotiations.

The leading proponents of the French model were Charles Rist and Jacques Rueff. Rist was the preeminent French academic economist of his generation. He had been assistant governor of the Bank of France from 1926 through 1929 and advised a succession of governments. He had provided a fully articulated statement of the French model of the Depression as early as 1931.[27] The authority of Rist, combined with his connections to government, facilitated the acceptance of his views. Jacques Rueff, also a professional economist and long-time financial attaché to the French Embassy in London, played an important role in disseminating Rist's views within the French Treasury. Rueff authored a series of memoranda analyzing the international economic situation that circulated widely within the government.

Rist was appointed to the Committee of Experts and conferred with Ministry of Finance officials in the interval between successive meetings of the preparatory committee. At the critical stabilization negotiations, Rist's views were ably represented by Rueff.

Evolution of the British model was more complex. As mentioned above, Keynes had offered a statement of the model in private evidence to the Macmillan Committee. The Economic Advisory Committee, established by the second Labour Government in 1929, provided a vehicle through which Keynes and his followers within government were able to disseminate his views.[28] The Bank of England, and to a lesser extent the Treasury, resisted aspects of his analysis. The Bank continued to evince a strong preference for currency stabilization, but once establishment of the Exchange Equalisation Account transferred much responsibility for exchange-rate management from the Bank to the Treasury, its views carried less weight. The Treasury prepared the memoranda that informed the British negotiating position. Treasury officials represented Britain on the Committee of Experts and at the London Conference.

The absence of a dominant U.S. model was reflected in American representation at the London Conference. John H. Williams, though a leading academic authority, was not a member of Hoover or Roosevelt's inner circle or an intimate of the U.S. Treasury or the Federal Reserve Board. He was a strong proponent of fixed exchange rates, a fact indicative of his distance from Roosevelt. Oliver Sprague, a Harvard professor who previously advised the Bank of England on exchange-rate questions, had recently taken a similar position in the U.S. Treasury, but his influence over Roosevelt's opinions was not great. James P. Warburg, son of Paul Warburg and vice-president of the Bank of Manhattan, was the source of a series of creative proposals, but these were resisted by Roosevelt's other advisers and rejected by the President. Raymond Moley, Roosevelt's closest advisor, had been "a professor of Criminology at a girls' college" and was "almost completely lacking in detailed [financial] knowledge," as Leith-Ross disparagingly put it.[29] The composition of American representation seemed designed to maximize the distance between London and Washington.

The adherence of national representatives to these different models led to both general disagreements and specific misunderstandings. General disagreement made it impossible for the three national delegations to adjust exchange-rate and monetary policies in ways they all preferred. Had the representatives of the three governments all subscribed to the British model, it would have been straightforward to trade a French commitment to reflate for British and American commitments to stabilize their exchange rates. All three countries would have been able to expand supplies of money and credit, at the same time avoiding the disruptive effects of exchange-rate instability. All three, according to the British model, would have been better off.

Alternatively, had the representatives of all three governments subscribed to the French model, it would have been straightforward to agree to stabilize exchange rates and restore gold convertibility. Having eliminated the debilitating effects of exchange-rate instability, they all would have been better off. But lacking a common model, it was impossible for the three parties to agree on a package of exchange-rate cum monetary policies.

The predominance of different models also led to specific misunderstandings that disrupted communication and impeded negotiation. When, for instance, following Roosevelt's bombshell, the French attempted to negotiate a separate stabilization agreement with the British, French officials—Georges Bonnet in particular—assumed that their British counterparts shared their belief that exchange-rate variability handicapped recovery efforts. Bonnet had discussed financial issues with the British Chancellor, Neville Chamberlain, during a preconference visit to London. Chamberlain, in the British view, had agreed only on the desirability of limiting international financial instability. He had avoided the issue of what Britain would do in the event of dollar devaluation.[30]

In the French view, however, Chamberlain and the British shared the priority France attached to minimizing financial instability. Bonnet's impression was that he and the British Chancellor agreed completely on the need to restore exchange-rate stability. Bonnet came away convinced that the British would soon return to gold, presumably in the summer of 1933. The question was merely whether, before returning to gold, they would require an international convention on the operation of the monetary system, or whether British officials would settle for an informal understanding. The French misinterpreted British concern that dollar devaluation would transfer Britain's competitive advantage to the United States for an aversion to exchange-rate flexibility in general. Hence they were misled into believing that the British might agree to exchange-rate stabilization without U.S. participation.[31]

Similar factors appear to have influenced the perceptions of the American members of the Committee of Experts. Their cables to Washington did not provide a sense of British skepticism regarding stabilization or of the priority British negotiators attached to monetary reflation. They implied that their British counterparts shared their own desire for exchange-rate stabilization. Some of these cables mentioned in passing war-debt forgiveness and tariff concessions as the price that the British might demand for agreeing to stabilize sterling. When the American experts returned to Washington, even these caveats receded from view.[32]

Thus, the prevalence of different conceptual frameworks in different countries precluded the negotiation of a purely monetary deal. In principle, one can imagine that things could have turned out otherwise. One can imagine that representatives of the three nations could have agreed on a common set of actions for entirely different reasons. Frankel and Rockett show that there exist cases where policy-makers, despite subscribing to different models of the economy, can all be rendered better off by an agreement to cooperate.[33] But they also show that such cases are relatively rare, and the 1933 World Economic Conference does not appear to have been one of them. In 1933 the competing conceptual frameworks strongly pointed to the desirability of incompatible policies, causing negotiations to break down.

THE ROLE OF DOMESTIC POLITICS

Incompatible conceptual frameworks prevented the negotiation of a mutually acceptable package of exchange-rate and monetary reforms. In return for agreement to stabilize sterling, the British demanded structural reforms that guaranteed monetary reflation by France and dollar stabilization by the United States. The French viewed monetary reflation as counterproductive and therefore an unacceptable price to pay. The U.S. refused to stabilize the dollar because it did not see what it would get in return.

Yet exchange-rate and monetary policies were not the only variables that might have been bartered in London. In return for British and American agreement to stabilize their exchange rates, France might have agreed to relax its tariffs and quotas. Additional French imports from the United States and Britain would have permitted the Bank of England and the Federal Reserve System to expand domestic credit and stimulate demand without driving the British and American balances of payments into deficit and renewing the conflict between internal and external balance. France would have gained the exchange-rate stability she desired. The U.S. and Britain would have been able to engage in the monetary reflation to which they attached priority. French gold would have been redistributed to other countries without infringing on the autonomy of the Bank of France.

This chain of quid pro quos remained no less feasible after the United States abandoned gold. Before April 1933, a mutually acceptable package would have entailed British agreement to stabilize, French agreement to liberalize, and U.S. agreement to forgive war debts or reduce tariffs. After April 1933, it would have required Britain to stabilize, France to liberalize, and the U.S. to stabilize the dollar and perhaps grant war-debt or tariff concessions. Roosevelt's pre-emptive strike may have increased the tariff reductions that France (and perhaps also Britain) would have to offer, but it did not obviously alter the nature of the package.

The terms of this deal had been foreseen by Treasury Secretary Ogden Mills in the final months of the Hoover Administration.[34] The exchange of tariff concessions for exchange-rate stabilization had been implicit in the Draft Annotated Agenda of the Committee of Experts. Officials within the French Finance Ministry anticipated that the government would be asked to barter trade liberalization for monetary stabilization by countries that blamed French import quotas for the instability of currencies.[35] French officials envisaged the outlines of a trade in which Britain stabilized sterling, the United States forgave war debts, and France reduced its trade barriers and perhaps also adopted measures to redistribute its excess gold reserves.[36] Here, however, was where domestic politics entered the story. Domestic pressures made it impossible for France to offer tariff concessions. Pressures for reflation and silver monetization in the United States made Roosevelt hesitate to stabilize the dollar. Though there may have existed a policy trade acceptable to negotiators, it was not acceptable to those on whose support they relied.

French Politics

The Daladier government was in an extremely tenuous political position. It was one in a series of 11 ministries to hold power in the period of political instability from May 1932 to May 1936. Throughout the period, the Radical Party occupied the center of the political spectrum.[37] Though it gained 200,000 votes from the moderates and lost none to the Socialists in 1932, the party was still a minority in the Chamber of Deputies. To govern, a Radical premier had to satisfy the demands of his own constituency and at the same time retain the support of the Socialists and Rightists whose votes were needed to sustain the government.

The dominant characteristic of this polity was its fragmentation. The Right was split into two major parties, the Alliance Démocratique (representatives of big business who embraced the rhetoric of economic mod-

ernization) and the Fédération Républicaine (large land-owners and no-
tables from predominantly Catholic regions). The Socialists were split
between the more moderate Vie Socialiste, which favored cooperation
with the Radicals, and the Bataille Socialiste, whose members advocated
collective action and collaboration with the Communists.[38]

The Radical Party is itself best thought of as a loose coalition of moderate politicians representing rural, provincial regions. It was the party of
the independent peasants and lower middle classes (independent propri-
etors, farmers, artisans, and civil servants).[39] Perhaps reflecting this diversity, the Radicals lacked a consistent economic program. The one
economic goal that united them was the priority they attached to the
maintenance of financial stability. A Radical government had presided
over the inflation of the 1920s and had been brought down by the franc's
collapse, opening the door to six years of conservative rule. At each party
congress, the one issue on which there existed consensus was the need
to prevent this from happening again.

The composition of the cabinet was critical to the formulation of economic policy. Until Leon Blum created a Ministry of National Economy
in 1936, there was no office responsible for economics. The office of
Undersecretary of State for Economic Affairs created by André Tardieu
in 1930 possessed little influence. The economic policy of the Herriot
and Daladier governments emerged from bargains between ministries
representing different interest groups.[40]

From Poincaré's return to power in 1926 until the 1932 elections,
France had been led by governments of the Right. The 1932 elections
then returned a Left-wing majority. A coalition government of Radicals
and Socialists would have possessed a comfortable majority. But the massive reduction of defense spending, tax increases, and national wheat
and fertilizer boards demanded by the SFIO (Socialists) as their price for
participation in a Cartel des Gauches were unacceptable to the executive
committee of the Radical Party. Instead, Edouard Herriot formed a Radical government to pursue a more orthodox economic program in which
the SFIO refused to participate, but to which it lent support. Herriot's
government was continually harassed from the Left for its failure to
raise taxes and reorganize the economy, and from the Right (including
conservative Radicals) for its inability to cut public spending. Its downfall
began in June 1932, when a bill to balance the budget which included a
5 percent reduction in the salaries of public servants was demolished
by Left-wing Radicals and Socialists on the Finance Committee of the
Chamber. Herriot fell in December 1932, ostensibly over his willingness
to make another war-debt payment to the United States, in reality over
his inability to break the budgetary deadlock.

Though Daladier was to the left of Herriot, the composition of his government was little different. Daladier was forced to make repeated concessions to both the Socialists and the moderate Right to retain their support.

For its survival, the Daladier government depended in particular on the support of deputies from predominantly agricultural *départements,* who returned Radical, Fédération Française, or Vie Socialiste deputies to the Chamber. This particular constituency was in dire straits. The crisis of French agriculture intensified as the London Conference approached. Since 1931, agricultural prices had been supported through the application of import quotas.[41] In 1932, an abundant harvest put further downward pressure on domestic prices. French wheat prices fell by 40 percent in the year ending in April 1933. A variety of measures had already been taken by previous governments to support the domestic wheat market. But in the spring of 1933 Daladier came under intense pressure from Socialists and Radicals in the Chamber of Deputies to introduce more comprehensive measures establishing a minimum wheat price. Though the bill was passed quickly, it was not clear that the government would in fact intervene to set a binding floor on domestic wheat prices, since it lacked financial resources. What was clear was that any attempt to support domestic wheat prices would be futile if import restrictions were relaxed.[42]

The French were perfectly aware that they would be asked at the London Conference to offer commercial concessions.[43] Georges Bonnet had in fact implied a willingness to consider relaxing French quotas in his preconference meeting with Chamberlain in London in March.[44] Agricultural interests were vigilant to this possibility, and made their objections known.[45] Each *département* had a Chamber of Agriculture which met regularly and lobbied elected representatives and ministerial officials. Following the example of the Confederations Générale de Planteurs de Betteraves (1921) and the Association Générale des Producteurs de Blé (1924), special associations were formed to represent the interests of producers of particular products. By the 1930s, half of the farmers belonged to such agricultural unions. These organizations have been called the "first really effective farm pressure groups France had ever known."[46]

Despite the inability of the farmers to unite behind a single political party, their interests were ably represented in the Chamber of Deputies. Though they made up only a third of the national electorate, rural voters accounted for the electoral majority in more than half of all districts. According to Gordon Wright, only one in four deputies could safely ignore rural interests if he hoped to be re-elected. The electorate for the Senate was if anything even more disproportionately rural.[47]

The effectiveness of the agricultural lobby is illustrated by an incident in early 1933. On February 27, Jacques Rueff had spoken to a conference at the Sorbonne presided over by Charles Rist. Rueff had emphasized the merits of trade liberalization. The speech provoked "acerbic" and "emotional" responses in the agricultural press, according to the Minister of Agriculture, Henri Queuille, who on March 11 sent a letter denouncing Rueff for his "total ignorance and lack of comprehension" of the question to various members of the government, and specifically to Rueff's superior, Georges Bonnet.[48]

Along with Queuille, the leading cabinet spokesman for the protectionists was Louis Serre, the Minister of Commerce. In early April, at an interministerial conference to determine the French position for the London Conference, Serre noted that other countries would demand the suppression of quotas and the reduction of tariffs. He proposed raising tariffs immediately to provide scope for reducing them later without undercutting the protection afforded agriculture and industry. Those present unanimously agreed that the French government could not adopt an entirely negative attitude on trade liberalization which would isolate it at the conference. At the same time, it was regarded as unacceptable to renounce the policy of tariffs and quotas.[49]

The National Confederation of Agricultural Associations petitioned the government in April, protesting against the adoption of measures of trade liberalization proposed by the Preparatory Commission of Experts.[50] Departmental chambers of Agriculture and Commerce bombarded the Finance Commission of the Chamber of Deputies with letters denouncing commercial concessions. The Finance Commission forwarded these letters to the Ministry of Finance.[51] Most of the letters are dated late May and early June, as if the local chambers had the London Conference in mind. The text of each letter contained the resolution adopted (often unanimously) by members of the chamber. Many of these resolutions were virtually identical, suggesting a coordinated, concerted campaign.

These pressures clearly affected the negotiating position of the French delegation to the conference. In his opening statement, Daladier stressed the importance of currency stabilization, but made no mention of trade restrictions. He linked the plight of the farmers to the Depression in other sectors, asking, "How could the hundreds of millions of farmers, who had been suddenly deprived of their purchasing power and their ability to consume, continue as customers of industry, banking, and finance?"[52]

The tenuous political position of the Daladier government also reinforced its commitment to the gold standard. The year 1933 saw the first glimmerings of resistance on the Left to gold convertibility and monetary deflation.[53] Though it could not afford to antagonize the Socialists, the

Daladier government did not budge. Its allegiance to the gold standard reflected the government's failure to contain the fiscal crisis and the price extracted by the Bank of France for continued assistance. Persistent budget deficits burdened the Herriot and Daladier ministries alike. The Right successfully resisted tax increases, while the Left rejected cuts in public services and veterans' pensions. There existed no viable parliamentary coalition to restore fiscal balance. Given the narrow French money market, it was difficult to finance deficits through sales of bonds to the public. Banks were willing to absorb treasury bills only if they were assured of Bank of France rediscounts in the event they needed additional cash. Successive governments were forced to rely on the central bank's willingness to discount treasury bills. Since the Bank of France could refuse to discount government paper, Daladier was forced to negotiate. The bank's governor, Clement Moret, attached the central banker's traditional priority to monetary orthodoxy, and specifically to maintenance of the gold standard. Moret and his colleagues demanded that Daladier reaffirm his commitment to gold convertibility. Unless it managed to construct a viable fiscal coalition, the government had no choice but to accept the bank's terms.[54]

U.S. Politics

Where Daladier's support was narrow, Roosevelt's was broad. Winning 472 electoral votes, he was supported by every region of the country. Urban workers, reacting against unemployment, voted for Roosevelt in large numbers. So did large numbers of midwestern farmers reacting against the slump in agricultural prices.

Nonetheless, two levels of politics impinged upon decision-making by the American chief executive: congressional politics and politics within the executive branch. Roosevelt's advisors had diverse views on international economic policy.[55] Cordell Hull, Roosevelt's Secretary of State, was the personification of internationalism; his Assistant Secretary, Raymond Moley, was a strong nationalist. Hull believed passionately in the need for tariff reductions; Moley worked to prevent them. The same tug-of-war occurred in other departments. Contemporaries viewed Roosevelt's appointments as indicative of indecisiveness or confusion; historians have come to view them as his systematic attempt to minimize dependence on particular ideological perspectives.[56] Whatever the case, the policy promoted rivalry and maneuvering within the administration, with leaders of each faction attempting unsuccessfully to control access to the President.

Turning to congressional politics, Roosevelt, like Daladier, was under pressure to do something for the farmers. Western and southern congressmen united in the campaign to secure agrarian relief. Even Republican progressives from rural districts joined what was traditionally a Democratic campaign. Demands for higher prices by this agrarian bloc complemented those of silver-mining interests urging reflation through silver monetization. A series of bills demanding silver coinage or reflationary open-market operations were introduced in 1932.

But it was only in 1933 that the agricultural bloc and the silverites formed an effective alliance.[57] In debate over Senator Burton Wheeler's amendment to the farm bill, senators from silver-mining states repeatedly invoked the plight of the farmers, prescribing monetary measures designed to raise prices. Senators from agricultural states stressed that their constituents' difficulties were shared by the residents of industrial regions as well. On April 17 the Senate, by 33 to 43, defeated the Wheeler Amendment, which would have permitted unlimited coinage of silver at a ratio to gold of 16 to 1. All 14 senators from the seven silver-mining states of the west voted for the amendment; they were joined by 19 others from the midwest and the south. The Administration was aware that at least 10 senators had withheld their support only because of the extremity of the measure.[58]

Roosevelt sought to channel these pressures by endorsing the more moderate Thomas Amendment. According to Raymond Moley, Roosevelt still had no specific economic program in mind and agreed to the Thomas Amendment only to contain the rebellion of the Senate inflationists. "The cold fact," wrote Moley, "is that the inflationary movement attained such formidable strength by April 18th that Roosevelt realized that he could not block it, that he could, at most, try to direct it."[59] The Thomas Amendment and the gold embargo were the most conservative steps that Roosevelt could take in response to inflationist pressure.[60]

The Thomas Amendment authorized but did not require the President to stimulate inflation in various ways. He could instruct the Federal Reserve System to purchase up to 3 billion dollars of government securities. If it refused, he could authorize the issue of 3 billion dollars of greenbacks. He could reduce the gold content of the dollar. He could authorize the coinage of silver. Roosevelt had been forced to accommodate mounting inflationist pressure in Congress, but he may have been happy to do so, both because the step was consistent with his own inflationist inclinations and because it permitted him to do so in a way that derailed more radical options.

If domestic politics mandated dollar devaluation, did they also preclude stabilization at a lower level? Three billion dollars of open-market purchases need not have depressed the dollar by more than 15 percent, a level at which the French and British were willing to contemplate stabilization. Had Roosevelt opted for additional silver monetization, however, he might have found himself unable to peg the dollar. Thus, silverites in Congress were certain to resist any stabilization plan, as Cordell Hull warned Ramsay MacDonald on June 19.[61]

It is not necessary to argue that domestic political pressures were wholly responsible for Roosevelt's decision. One must also consider the President's model of the economy and the failure of other countries to offer him something attractive in return. Roosevelt was gravitating toward the gold-buying program of the autumn, which was incompatible with a stabilization agreement. Such is the implication of his statement, on June 28, that it would not be a disaster if France was forced from the gold standard, since this would not interfere with his policy of raising domestic prices.[62] And France and Britain were unable to offer either commercial policy concessions or a credible commitment to reflate that might permit him to finesse this conflict.

Domestic political pressures also impeded efforts to extract commercial concessions from the United States. The Smoot-Hawley Tariff had been passed in 1930 by an alliance of agriculture (mainly representatives of the grain producers of the midwest) and light industry (such as New England textile, shoe, and glove manufacturers).[63] The traditionally protectionist Republicans had lost ground in Congress as a result of the 1932 elections, but pressure for protection emanating from agriculture and light industry had intensified as the slump deepened. The Americans on the Preparatory Committee of Experts, themselves sympathetic to tariff reduction, were instructed to veto statements to this effect because they were unacceptable to the U.S. Congress.[64] Tariff reduction was likely to antagonize the same agricultural interests pressing for silver inflation. Congressional leaders warned Roosevelt that significant changes in U.S. tariffs were impossible. On the eve of the conference, Roosevelt informed a disappointed Cordell Hull that the introduction of a bill that would have permitted the President to conclude trade agreements without Senate ratification was "highly inadvisable."[65]

British Politics

The National government that came to power in the summer of 1931 was a peculiar coalition led by a Labour Prime Minister, Ramsay MacDonald, but featuring Liberal and Conservative ministers. Following sterling's embarrassing devaluation in September, the Conservatives, campaigning on the need for sound finance and tariff protection, scored a resounding victory. In the new House of Commons, Conservatives occupied 473 of 615 seats. Thus, in contrast to the situation in France and the United States, the National Government did not have to worry about Parliamentary resistance to its policies so long as these remained consistent with the Conservative Party's election manifesto.

But Stanley Baldwin, the Conservative leader, could not force Mac-Donald's resignation, since the Conservative supporters of the National government had campaigned on the need for collaboration in time of crisis. Hence the Cabinet, not Parliament, was the principal battleground on which policy decisions were fought. On one side was MacDonald, an internationalist inclined toward collaboration with the United States and France. On the other was the new Chancellor of the Exchequer, Neville Chamberlain, heir to the fair-trade campaign initiated by his father, Joseph Chamberlain, and an advocate of tariffs and imperial preference. The Foreign Office and the Bank of England supported the Prime Minister. The Treasury and the Board of Trade fell in behind the Chancellor.

The nationalist position and its advocates were on the ascendant throughout 1932. Over Liberal opposition and Labour qualms, a general tariff was introduced in the early months of 1932.[66] The tariff bill passed its second reading by 454 votes to 78. Sterling was allowed to decline dramatically against the gold currencies. The locus of control over monetary policy shifted from the Bank of England to the Treasury, Chamberlain's bailiwick, following establishment of the Exchange Equalisation Account in the summer of 1932.[67]

The depth of support for tariff protection, which most Conservatives regarded as a matter of principle, would have made the extension of dramatic commercial concessions difficult. Neither Chamberlain nor his followers ruled out modest trade reforms, however. Chamberlain spoke of the need for tariff reductions and the abolition of quotas in his opening address to the conference.[68] No matter of principle stood in the way of agreement to stabilize currencies, which Chamberlain appears to have been willing to commit to in May and June of 1933. The problem was that the concessions offered by other governments were regarded as inadequate to justify this sacrifice.

IMPLICATIONS

The puzzle is that there existed one or more potential agreements that dominated the actual outcome in the sense that they would have enhanced the welfare of all three nations involved, and yet negotiations failed. We have argued that this failure can only be understood in terms of the importance of competing conceptual frameworks and domestic political constraints. In concluding, we explore the extent to which the factors highlighted by our account can be related to Putnam's concerns.[69]

The existence of competing conceptual frameworks can be thought of as limiting negotiators' "acceptability-set" (the set of policy trades that all negotiators regard as an improvement over the status quo). Trades that involved only exchange-rate stabilization by Britain and the U.S., and reductions in cover ratios and authorization to conduct open-market operations for the Bank of France, were unacceptable because of the different conceptual frameworks that informed national negotiating positions. An agreement that involved only exchange-rate and monetary policy would have been acceptable to all three countries had they embraced a common conceptual framework, whichever of the three frameworks they chose. But lacking a common framework, compromise on exchange-rate cum monetary disputes required at least one country to accept a position that was worse than the status quo. For such a compromise to lie in its "acceptability-set," that country required compensation, generally in the form of foreign commercial concessions.

The domestic political constraints confronting negotiators can be thought of as limiting their "win-set" (the subset of policy trades acceptable to negotiators that is also "ratifiable"). The opposition of the Bank of France, which exerted considerable leverage over government policy, in conjunction with the strong preferences of the government's own electoral constituency, prevented France from being the one to adopt an exchange-rate cum monetary position regarded as worse than the status quo. At the same time, the pivotal political position of farmers and other groups with protectionist inclinations prevented French negotiators, who would otherwise have been willing to do so, from offering the commercial concessions required if other countries were to adopt otherwise unacceptable exchange-rate and monetary policies. Domestic political constraints were also operative in the United States. Opposition of the silverites to exchange-rate stabilization, and of midwestern agriculture and light industry to trade liberalization, raised the costs to Roosevelt of stabilizing the dollar and of reducing U.S. tariffs, at least one of which would have been required by foreign countries.

Relative to other case studies collected in this volume, the role played by interest-group politics has two striking characteristics. First, transnational links among interest groups were relatively unimportant. Such alliances were not unknown, but in 1933 they had relatively little impact on negotiations. We conjecture that their relative insignificance reflects the fact that market structures likely to facilitate transnational alliances, such as multinational corporations and foreign branches of domestic banks, were not yet as pervasive as they became subsequently. In addition, in 1933 effective alliances would have had to cut across conventional lines. French free-traders would have had to ally not with American free-traders but with American advocates of debt forgiveness and the gold standard. These individuals were occasionally but not uniformly the same. Hence previous international contacts between special-interest groups did not provide a convenient basis for transnational alliances in 1933.

Domestic politics would not have posed an obstacle to agreement if side-payments could have been arranged for interest groups who would have been adversely affected. Why were additional agricultural subsidies not offered French farmers who resisted trade policy concessions, for example? Here the broader economic and political context in which negotiations took place was critically important. France was suffering through a series of severe budgetary crises that posed a threat to the stability of the franc. Deficit finance of additional agricultural subsidies threatened to drive her off the gold standard. Hence additional agricultural subsidies could be extended only if taxes could be raised. Once again, the fragility of parliamentary support for Daladier, and the ability of each member of the coalition to bring down the government through its defection, prevented the Chamber from raising the taxes of any interest group.

This study speaks to the question of how to conceptualize the role of chief executive. Is the head of government merely a cipher interested in staying in power? Does he simply mirror the preferences of the majority of interest groups? Or does the chief executive have independent capacity to shape opinion in ways that transform the scope for agreement? This case suggests that there exists no single answer to this question. In the United States the chief executive enjoyed considerable latitude. Possessing a comfortable Congressional majority, and with four years until the next presidential election, he could afford to adopt a policy that, in the short run, antagonized a portion of his constituency. In France the Prime Minister had little independence. A policy which alienated even a small fraction of his supporters promised to bring down the government.

This suggests that the latitude enjoyed by the chief executive in international negotiations depends on the structure of the institutions linking the head of government to his constituency.[70] Among the relevant institutional arrangements is the ratification process. In 1933, an agreement to reduce U.S. tariffs would have had to be ratified by a Congress in which protectionist interests possessed disproportionate influence.[71] This was regarded as infeasible, and tariff reductions were not seriously discussed at the London Conference. In 1934, with passage of the Reciprocal Trade Agreements Act, ratification was taken out of the hands of Congress, providing additional flexibility for a chief executive wishing to make trade liberalization part of a package deal. The institutions that structure the ratification process are bequeathed by history, but scope for altering them depends as well on domestic political constraints, as Roosevelt observed in 1933.

But to focus on institutional determinants of "ratifiability," narrowly defined, is to overlook other institutional arrangements that critically regulate the independence of the head of state. Chief among these is the structure of the electoral system. In France, a major part of the explanation for the government's fragility was the modified proportional representation system under which deputies were elected. This led to a proliferation of political parties and to the election of deputies who represented highly specialized interest groups. Assembling a viable coalition was difficult. Policies which alienated even a small number of deputies on the fringes of the governing coalition were infeasible. In the United States, in contrast, a majority-representation electoral system suppressed significant third parties even in the turbulent circumstances of the 1930s. Disaffected voters simply shifted parties, in this case from the Republicans to the Democrats, endowing Roosevelt with a comfortable majority and considerable latitude.

Ultimately, Roosevelt used the latitude he enjoyed not to engineer an agreement but to block one. The U.S. chief executive seems to have been personally uncertain about the comparative merits of dollar stabilization, expansionary open-market operations, and gold purchases. This uncertainty heightened his desire to keep all options open, which posed an obstacle to international agreement.

Rather than attributing the failure of the World Economic Conference to Roosevelt's personal characteristics, however, it is more useful to focus on systemic factors that impeded the successful conclusion of negotiations. In this chapter we have argued that competing conceptual frameworks and domestic politics were the most important such factors. The former precluded the negotiation of a purely monetary agreement, while the latter prevented the conclusion of a cross-issue deal involving monetary policy, tariffs, and war debts. Both factors are therefore necessary to explain the breakdown of the conference. The implication is that, even if the outcome of the 1932 elections in the United States had been different, the outcome in London might have been the same.

Much of the work on this paper was undertaken during visits by Eichengreen to the Ecole des Hautes Etudes en Sciences Sociales in Paris and by Uzan to the University of California at Berkeley. Eichengreen's research was supported in part by grants from the EHESS, the German Marshall Fund of the United States, and the National Science Foundation, Uzan's by the Caisse des Depots. We acknowledge the permission of the French Ministry of Finance, the Bank of France, and the British Public Record Office to cite documents in their possession. We thank Kenneth Mouré, Robert Putnam, Harold Jacobson, Peter Evans, and participants in the Stanford and Cape Cod meetings of the study group for comments on prior drafts.

NOTES

1. The first thesis is propounded by Sir Frederick Leith-Ross in *Money Talks: Fifty Years of International Finance* (London: Hutchinson, 1968), p. 125, for example; the second by Charles Kindleberger, *The World in Depression, 1929–1939* (Berkeley: University of California Press, 1973). We point to some limitations of these arguments below.

2. Ernst Haas, "Why Collaborate? Issue Linkage and International Regimes," *World Politics* 32 (1980): 357–405.

3. Robert Putnam, "Diplomacy and Domestic Politics: The Logic of Two-Level Games," *International Organization* 42 (1988): 287–316 (see Appendix to this volume); James Alt and Barry Eichengreen, "Parallel and Overlapping Games: Theory and an Application to the European Natural Gas Trade," *Economics and Politics* 1 (1989): 119–144.

4. Peter Hall, *The Political Power of Economic Ideas* (Princeton, N.J.: Princeton University Press, 1989); Judith Goldstein and Robert Keohane, "Ideas and Foreign Policy," unpub. ms., 1990.

5. Jeffrey Frankel, "Obstacles to International Economic Policy Coordination," *Essays in International Finance* no. 64 (Princeton, N.J.: Princeton University Press, 1988); Jeffrey Frankel and Katherine Rockett, "International Macroeconomic Policy Coordination When Policymakers Do Not Agree on the True Model," *American Economic Review* 78 (1988): 318–340.

6. Secondary sources upon which this account draws are H. V. Hodson, *Slump and Recovery, 1929–1937* (London: Oxford University Press, 1938); Abdul Hasib, *Monetary Negotiations in the World Economic Conference, 1933* (Allahabad, India: Muslim University, 1958); S. V. O. Clarke, "The Reconstruction of the International Monetary System: The Attempts of 1922 and 1933," *Essays in International Finance* no. 33 (Princeton, N.J.: Princeton University Press, 1973); Kindleberger, *World In Depression;* Ian Drummond, *The Floating Pound and the Sterling Area, 1931–1939* (Cambridge, Eng.: Cambridge University Press, 1981).

7. See League of Nations, *World Production and Prices, 1937/38* (Geneva: League of Nations, 1938).

8. A limitation of this discussion is its focus on the United States, France, and Britain. A comprehensive account would analyze also the role played by other countries. Our emphasis on exchange rate stabilization negotiations, in which these three were involved to the exclusion of other countries, provides some justification for the disproportionate attention they receive here.

9. A clear statement of French priorities is in French Ministry of Finance Archives (FMFA) B32319, "Position Française à la Conférence de Londres," June 8, 1933.

10. What follows is based largely on British Public Record Office (PRO) Cab 29/140, Committee on the Economic Conference, "Policy of United Kingdom on main questions raised on agenda," May 1933; and PRO T177/12, "Leith-Ross memorandum," Dec. 20, 1932.

11. U.S. Department of State, *Foreign Relations of the United States* (Washington, D.C.: GPO, 1933), 1:597–600.

12. Roosevelt had, however, publicly avowed his support for the principle of currency stabilization. A U.S. State Department press release, dated May 16, 1933, quoted him as stating that "The conference must establish order in place of the present chaos by a stabilization of currencies"; cited in Dean Traynor, *International Monetary and Financial Conferences in the Interwar Period* (Washington, D.C.: Catholic University Press, 1949), p. 114.

13. Details of Warburg's initial proposal are described in Daniel Bennett Smith, "Toward Internationalism: New Deal Foreign Economic Policy, 1933–39" (Ph.D. diss., Stanford University, 1983), p. 47.

14. These incarnations of the Warburg Plan are reviewed in Richard Sayers, *The Bank of England, 1891–1944* (Cambridge, Eng.: Cambridge University Press, 1976), app. 27. See also Susan Howson, "Sterling's Managed Float: The Operations of the Exchange Equalization Account, 1932–39," *Essays in International Finance* no. 46 (Princeton, N.J.: Princeton University Press, 1981). British and French objections are described in PRO T175/83, "Declarations by the Bank of England and the Bank of France," May 23, 1933.

15. France made one final attempt to secure separate British agreement, which the latter rebuffed. PRO Cab 29/142, part 2, "Note of a conversation in the Treasury Board Room on Sunday, 2nd July 1933, at 5.45 p.m." As Neville Chamberlain explained to Charles Rist, "Now that there had been a public refusal on the part of the United States, the government of the United Kingdom could not associate itself with a European bloc, since this would be taken to mean that in the differences between the gold-standard countries and the United States, the United Kingdom joined with the former, whereas in credit policy we were more in sympathy with the United States."

16. Two previous studies of the period which make this same point are John S. O'Dell, "From London to Bretton Woods: Roots of Economic Diplomacy," *Journal of Public Policy* 8 (1989): 287–316; and Barry Eichengreen, *Golden Fetters: The Gold Standard and the Great Depression, 1919–1939* (New York: Oxford University Press, 1992).

17. Frederick Phillips provided an explicit statement of this view as early as September 1931: Susan Howson, *Domestic Monetary Management in Britain, 1919–38* (Cambridge, Eng.: Cambridge University Press, 1975), p. 83. In October 1932, he composed a memo emphasizing the relevance of the relationship between prices and costs and of impediments to cost adjustment to proposals that Britain return to gold: PRO Cab 58/183, "The foreign demand for the return of the United Kingdom to gold." Additional references to Treasury arguments along these lines are provided by Alan Booth, "Britain in the 1930s: A Managed Economy?" *Economic History Review* 40 (1987): 499–522.

18. See, for example, Charles Rist, "Caractère et origine de la crise de 1929," *Essais sur quelques problèmes économiques et monétaires* (Paris: Recueil Sirey, 1933), pp. 325–343. That the same model was prevalent in official circles is evident, for example, in the minutes of the proceedings of the Regents of the Bank of France: Bank of France Archives, "Procès verbaux," March 9, 1933.

19. Rist, "Caractère et origine," pp. 341–342, noted that monetary reflation was the alternative to further price declines. But, he observed, "qui, [après les

expériences des quinze dernières années,] voudrait s'engager dans une voie aussi dangereuse?"

20. William J. Barber, *From New Era to New Deal* (Cambridge, Eng.: Cambridge University Press, 1985), and Daniel R. Fusfield, *The Economic Thought of Franklin D. Roosevelt and the Origins of the New Deal* (New York: Columbia University Press, 1955), are basic sources on the evolution of academic and official analyses of the macroeconomy in the United States.

21. See Herbert Hoover, *The Memoirs of Herbert Hoover: The Great Depression, 1929–1941* (New York: Macmillan, 1952), chaps. 1–2, for what is admittedly a retrospective view.

22. The demand-oriented aspects of this model were not widely embraced within either the Treasury or the Federal Reserve System. For details, see Barber, *From New Era.*

23. Barber, *From New Era,* is a good example of the genre.

24. Fusfield, *Economic Thought,* pp. 254–255.

25. The low level of recorded unemployment reflected the limited data gathered on the subject as much as the state of the French economy, but this did not modify the outlook of officials. See Robert Salais, "Why Was Unemployment So Low in France During the 1930s?" in Barry Eichengreen and Timothy J. Hatton, eds., *Interwar Unemployment in International Perspective* (Dordrecht, Neth.: Kluwer, 1988), pp. 247–288.

26. His analysis of British unemployment may be found in Jacques Rueff, "L'assurance chômage cause du chômage permanent," *Revue d'économie politique* 45 (1931): 211–242.

27. Rist's "Caractère et origine" was prepared for and published by the League of Nations in June 1931.

28. Susan Howson and Donald Winch, *The Economic Advisory Council* (Cambridge, Eng.: Cambridge University Press, 1977), describe the activities of the Economic Advisory Council.

29. Leith-Ross, *Money Talks,* p. 165.

30. The British account of the Bonnet-Chamberlain talks is PRO 371/17304, "Notes of meetings held in the board room, Treasury, on Friday, 17 March 1933."

31. George Bonnet, *Vingt ans de la vie politique, 1918–1938* (Paris: Fayard, 1969), pp. 161–162. Secretary of State Cordell Hull's European contacts verified that Bonnet took away the impression that Britain was about to return to gold: *Foreign Relations* 1:471–472. The French record of the Bonnet-Chamberlain discussions, *Documents Diplomatiques Francais,* "Competes rendus: entretiens franco-britanniques du vendredi 17 mars 1933" (Paris: Imprimerie Nationale, 1st series, vol. 3, 1977), pp. 1–15, touches on this point on p. 10. Similarly, on the eve of the conference the French financial attaché in Britain erroneously reported that "British opinion has become almost unanimous in recognizing the necessity of returning to an international standard of values as soon as possible, and the Treasury as well as the Bank of England declares that this standard can only be the gold standard": FMFA B32321, "From the Financial Attaché to the French Embassy in London," May 31, 1933.

32. *Foreign Relations* 1: 839–840 and 453–457, 463.

33. Frankel and Rockett, "International Macroeconomic Policy Coordination."

34. James Ray Moore, "A History of World Economic Conference, London 1933" (Ph.D. diss., State University of New York at Stony Brook, 1972), pp. 86–87.

35. Herbert Feis, *1933: Characters in Crisis* (Boston: Little, Brown, 1966), pp. 33, 116; Moore, "History," p. 74; FMFA B32317, "Note sur la 2nd réunion de la Commission préparatoire de la Conférence de Londres," Dec. 29, 1932; FMFA B32317, "Note au sujet de la Conference Mondiale, Nov. 15, 1932."

36. FMFA B32319, "Note sur la situation de la France à la Conférence Économique Mondiale," March 1, 1933.

37. Useful surveys of French politics in this period include Edward Mead Earle, *Modern France: Problems of the Third Republic and Fourth Republic* (Princeton, N.J.: Princeton University Press, 1951), and Edouard Dubief, *Le déclin de la Troisième République* (Paris: Seuil, 1984).

38. An explanation for this proliferation of parties is the modified form of proportional representation under which deputies were elected: see Peter Campbell, *French Electoral Systems and Elections, 1789–1957* (New York: Frederick A. Praeger, 1958). We return to this point in our concluding section.

39. Peter Larmour, *The French Radical Party in the 1930s* (Stanford, Calif: Stanford University Press, 1964), p. 31.

40. Julian Jackson, *The Politics of Depression in France, 1932–1936* (Cambridge, Eng.: Cambridge University Press, 1985), p. 20.

41. See Ethel B. Dietrich, "French Import Quotas," *American Economic Review* 23 (1933): 661–674; and Frank Arnold Haight, *A History of French Commercial Policies* (New York: Macmillan, 1941), pp. 163–165.

42. Jackson, *Politics of Depression*, pp. 63, 69.

43. FMFA B32319, untitled memorandum, Feb. 27, 1933.

44. Drummond, *The Floating Pound*, p. 142.

45. The 1920s had witnessed the emergence of a vocal, organized French peasantry. See Gordon Wright, "Peasant Politics in the Third French Republic," *Political Science Quarterly* 70 (1955): 75–86, and *Rural Revolution in France* (Stanford, Calif.: Stanford University Press, 1964).

46. Wright, "Peasant Politics," p. 79. Only in Brittany did agricultural unions fail to take root: see Annie Moulin, *Les paysans dans la société française* (Paris: Seuil, 1988), chap. 4.

47. Wright, *Rural Revolution*, p. 14.

48. The quotes are Rueff's characterization of the Queuille letter, which appears in Rueff's autobiography, *Oeuvres complètes: I. De l'aube au crépuscule* (Paris: Plon, 1977), pp. 114–115; the conference presentation is given on pp. 321–332. Queuille was a long-time supporter of French import quotas, which he viewed as indispensable for the survival of French agriculture in the Depression: Frank Arnold Haight, *French Import Quotas* (London: P. S. King, 1935), p. 100.

49. FMFA B32317, "Compte-rendu de la 2ème séance de la commission interministérielle," April 8, 1933.

50. FMFA B32317, "Observations présentées au nom de l'agriculture française au gouvernement et à M. le Président Herriot," April 12, 1933.

51. The letters are collected in the French Ministry of Finance archives, FMFA B32321.

52. League of Nations, *Journal of the Monetary and Economic Conference* no. 4 (London, June 14, 1933), p. 12.

53. Kenneth Mouré, "As Good As Gold: French Monetary Management, 1928–1936" (Ph.D. diss., University of Toronto, 1988), pp. 274–277.

54. Moore, "History," pp. 117–119. Another option was to limit the bank's independence, as subsequent governments succeeded in doing. But in 1933, memories of inflation a decade earlier remained too vivid to allow Daladier to appoint a replacement for Moret or tamper with the composition of the Council of Regents.

55. A good source on internal politics in the Roosevelt Administration and their relationship to the World Economic Conference is Smith, "Toward Internationalism."

56. See, for example, Frank Freidel, *Franklin Roosevelt: Launching of the New Deal* (Boston: Little, Brown, 1973).

57. See Jeanette Nichols, "Silver Inflation and the Senate in 1933," *Social Studies* 25 (1934): 12–18; and John A. Brennen, "The Senate Silver Bloc and the First New Deal" (Ph.D. diss., University of Colorado, 1968).

58. Raymond Moley, *After Seven Years* (New York: Harper, 1939), p. 158.

59. Ibid., p. 157.

60. James Byrnes, *All in One Lifetime* (New York: Harper, 1958), p. 77. Some historians question whether Roosevelt was in fact forced by domestic political considerations to accept the Thomas Amendment. See Freidel, *Franklin Roosevelt*, pp. 331, 333. For present purposes it is necessary only to observe that domestic politics influenced the decision.

61. See Nichols, "Silver Inflation." Cordell Hull alluded to such considerations in international discussions. "After some preliminary discussion Mr. Hull raised the question of stabilisation. He had during the last 24 hours become very doubtful as to whether any measure of temporary stabilisation could be achieved. He described the internal situation in the United States which made this doubtful. Speaking in great confidence, he said that the forces of inflation were at the moment rather powerful and had succeeded in preventing an agreement being approved. He thought that the best chance was for this conference to get some broad programme covering both the monetary and economic branches of the work which would be interdependent and coordinated." PRO Cab 29/142, "Note of a conversation between the Prime Minister and Mr. Hull on Monday, 19 June 1933, at 11.30 a.m."

62. *Foreign Relations* 1: 660–661. The fact that U.S. prices had risen in the first month following the gold embargo should have worked to strengthen Roosevelt's belief in the efficacy of further depreciation.

63. The composition of support for Smoot-Hawley is analyzed in Barry Eichengreen, "The Political Economy of the Smoot-Hawley Tariff," *Research in Economic History* 12 (1989): 1–44. A different perspective, emphasizing the proce-

dures by which tariff policy was made, is E. E. Schattschneider, *Politics, Pressures, and the Tariff* (New York: Prentice Hall, 1935).

64. Leith-Ross, *Money Talks,* p. 153.

65. Cordell Hull, *The Memoirs of Cordell Hull* (New York: Macmillan, 1948), vol. 1, p. 251; Moore, "History," p. 170. Thus, the Reciprocal Trade Agreements Act would have to wait until 1934: see Stephan Haggard, "The Institutional Foundations of Hegemony: Explaining the Reciprocal Trade Agreements Act of 1934," *International Organization* 42 (1988): 91–120.

66. The British debate over tariff protection in 1932 is analyzed in Barry Eichengreen, "Sterling and the Tariff, 1929–32," *Princeton Studies in International Finance* no. 48 (Princeton, N.J.: Princeton University Press, 1981).

67. French observers, noting "serious differences" between the Treasury and the Bank of England, concluded that it was "the position of the Treasury which is actually the one of the British government": FMFA B32319, "Position du Gouvernement Britannique." According to the French, the Bank of England was skeptical that prices could be raised and prosperity restored simply through the application of a liberal credit policy. While cheap money was necessary for recovery, it was not sufficient. Also required were secure political conditions and a modicum of free international trade.

68. League of Nations, *Journal of the Monetary and Economic Conference,* 4 (June 14, 1933): 24–25.

69. From this point, all phrases in quotation marks are taken from Putnam's article.

70. Readers in international relations will recognize echoes of the strong state/weak state distinction—Peter Katzenstein, ed., *Between Power and Plenty* (Madison: University of Wisconsin Press, 1978)—although we qualify this view below.

71. This is the argument of Schattschneider, *Politics, Pressures.*

7

The Interaction of Domestic and International Politics
The Anglo-American Oil Negotiations and the International Civil Aviation Negotiations, 1943–1947

Helen Milner

INTRODUCTION

Toward the end of World War II, British and American policy-makers realized that the profound changes wrought by the war and other economic developments necessitated collaborative attempts to manage the new postwar international political economy. The negotiations between the United States and Great Britain for managing the world petroleum market and the international civil aviation system played an important role in constructing this new postwar system. These negotiations took place roughly between 1943 and 1947. Their outcomes established the practices and norms for these industries for much of the postwar period. Today, the Chicago Convention and Bermuda Principles, set in the mid-1940s, still guide international civil aviation, while up to the early 1970s the arrangements made in the late 1940s guided the world oil market.

These negotiations are interesting to compare, because one was a failure and one a success. The Anglo-American oil agreement died in the late 1940s, as a result of "involuntary defection" by the United States. It was never ratified by the United States, and in its wake the major international oil firms organized their own system for controlling oil. In contrast, the negotiations over civil aviation set the terms for the system over the postwar period. The first negotiations in 1944 led to the Chicago Convention, which laid down the basic framework for the international civil aviation system. This conference, however, failed to settle many specific issues about the system. Later negotiations between the United States and Britain, in 1946, settled many of these issues and became a model for future bilateral arrangements.

This chapter addresses the puzzle of why the two negotiations had such different outcomes. Why did the negotiations on oil fail and the ones about aviation succeed? Why were the same two countries in the same period of time unable to find agreement on the oil issue and able to find it in aviation? Differences in the ability to cooperate are often attributed to differences in the prevailing international conditions. But the international environment of these two negotiations was very similar. They occurred almost simultaneously, involved the same countries and often the same decision-makers, and were affected by the same changes in the global balance of power. In both cases, the United States was replacing British control and held the ascendant position. Its "hegemony" then does not seem to be the key variable explaining its capacity to devise cooperative agreements with other countries. The difference in outcomes is even more puzzling because the conflicts separating the two countries in the aviation case were greater than those surrounding the oil one. In both cases, the primary issues at stake were similar. They centered on the amount of international regulation of each industry desired by the two countries. The overlap in British and American answers to this question was greater in oil than in aviation, but cooperation on oil proved more elusive.

The answer to this puzzle lies in domestic politics. Different domestic political alignments promoted cooperation in aviation and hindered it in oil. The two countries' international positions had less to do with their ability to negotiate successful and favorable international agreements than did their domestic political environments. Indeed, three domestic factors played a key role: the structure of domestic preferences, the ratification process, and the strategies used by the government to secure internal support. The two cases show the critical importance of these domestic factors, as well as of the influence of certain international elements, on the ability of nations to cooperate.

THE ANGLO-AMERICAN OIL CASE

The U.S. oil industry was divided into two groups. It consisted first of five large international firms (the majors), who after World War I developed extensive foreign operations.[1] After 1919, they expanded into the Middle East, which was controlled by the British and their oil firms. After much U.S. pressure, several U.S. majors—Standard Oil of New Jersey (SONJ) and Socony-Vacuum—negotiated access to the area under the 1928 Red Line agreement.[2] While enabling the two U.S. firms to enter the area, this agreement denied them access to other parts of the Mideast. In contrast, not being limited by this agreement, the other three majors developed other fields in the Middle East, most importantly a large concession in Saudi Arabia.[3] These moves gave the American companies a foothold in the otherwise British-dominated Middle East. As more oil was discovered there, the American majors sought to increase their capacity, pushing for "equal access" to Middle Eastern concessions and for the revision of the Red Line and other restrictive agreements favoring the British.[4]

The second component of the U.S. oil industry was the domestic producers (the independents), which tended to be small and numerous. Moreover, unlike the majors, they derived their profits from domestic production and were unable to control oil production and prices without government help. After more domestic discoveries in the 1930s, fears of an oil glut led the independents to rely upon the Texas Railroad Commission to regulate oil production in order to keep prices up.[5] The domestic firms' interests were intrinsically opposed to those of the majors: they opposed the importation of large quantities of cheap foreign oil, since this would drive oil prices down and put domestic producers out of business. The international firms, in contrast, made vast profits from their cheaply produced foreign oil; and, while not wanting to undermine high oil prices, they did lead the movement to "conserve" domestic oil by replacing it with foreign oil.[6]

The interests of these two groups were mixed; cooperation was necessary to maintain high prices, but conflict over how much of whose oil—foreign or domestic—would be sold was endemic. In addition, the two groups had different channels of access to the U.S. government. The international majors had access to the executive branch, especially the departments of State and Interior and later the Petroleum Administration for War (PAW). The independents, in contrast, had close friends in Congress. In particular, the members from Texas and Oklahoma—big oil-producing states—listened carefully to the problems of the small domestic producers. This division within the U.S. industry had critical consequences for the Anglo-American oil agreement.

Prior to World War I, the U.S. government was not much interested in the oil industry. The war changed this by causing oil shortages which raised fears of such shortfalls in the future. This concern was heightened because U.S. firms were shut out of many foreign oil markets by the British cartel. After World War I, the U.S. government decided to aid its international firms. It helped them to gain access to Middle Eastern fields in Iraq and Kuwait and later to negotiate the Red Line Agreement.[7]

During World War II, the U.S. government realized that petroleum was a vital, strategic resource; control over oil became "an instrument of national survival."[8] In addition, interest in access to foreign oil—especially the vast resources of the Middle East—heightened. While U.S. domestic production had grown dramatically, fear of oil shortages became foremost in many policy-makers' minds. The promotion of foreign oil production, in particular that of the Middle East, became a central goal for U.S. policy-makers in the early 1940s. The departments of State and Interior, the Joint Chiefs of Staff (JCS), and PAW all saw the need to increase the exploitation of Middle Eastern oil and favored attempts to "conserve" U.S. domestic supplies.[9] These goals were similar to the interests of the majors and conflicted with those of the small independents. A key issue for the government, however, was how best to achieve these ends, and in this choice of approaches lay the potential for conflict with the majors.

The United States pursued three different approaches: direct government control of the industry, intergovernmental cooperation, and a private global cartel. The first, involving direct government participation in the oil industry, was favored by Harold Ickes, Secretary of the Interior and head of PAW, and the JCS. It was modeled after the British approach, which involved having a majority position in the Anglo-Iranian Oil Company (AIOC). Ickes and the Navy argued that the U.S. government should protect its oil interests abroad by owning a direct stake in them; it should have a "chosen instrument" to pursue its goals. With a government-owned firm, they reasoned, the British would not be able to restrict or take over U.S. oil concessions in the Middle East. Ickes thus developed a plan in 1943 for a government-owned Petroleum Reserves Corporation (PRC). The corporation was to buy 100 percent ownership of the interests of Standard Oil of California (SOCAL) and Texaco in Saudi Arabia and build an oil pipeline stretching from the Persian Gulf to the Mediterranean, to establish a U.S. presence in and control over the area.[10]

These two plans for government control of the industry generated widespread opposition. While Ickes was able to get Roosevelt's support, the domestic firms, some of the majors, Congress, the British, and the Department of State all opposed these ideas. The domestic independents felt the PRC was government intervention at its worst. Not only did they oppose federal intervention that might challenge their system of regulation—i.e., the Texas Railroad Commission and other state-run efforts to set oil prices—but they also saw this intervention as favoring the majors. The PRC would, in their opinion, flood the market with cheap imported oil that had been produced or subsidized by the U.S. government. Conservation by promoting cheap Middle Eastern oil was not in their financial interest.[11] Many in Congress also opposed the PRC. Some were just against government intervention in principle; others opposed any efforts to extend executive branch privileges (anti-New Deal); and others responded to the complaints of their oil producers about the damage the PRC would do to their states' interests. In response, Congress set up a special committee to investigate the PRC.

The State Department opposed the PRC less directly and for a number of different reasons. The initial idea for a PRC had come from State, but Ickes had taken charge of the plan and changed it. The State Department agreed with Ickes that the United States should do more in the Middle East to promote oil production there and conservation at home. But Secretary of State Cordell Hull and his economic advisor Herbert Feis feared the PRC would backfire and endanger U.S. interests in the Middle East. The State Department, however, favored the idea of negotiations with the British. Hull and Feis felt that the international oil market could be securely controlled only if the British and Americans cooperated. Unilateral actions, like the PRC, threatened a conflict between the two countries, which would damage both their interests. A cooperative diplomatic solution had the added benefit that it would give control over oil policy back to the State Department.[12] Bureaucratic infighting thus had a hand in the initiation of the Anglo-American oil agreement.

Finally, the majors were not happy with the PRC and pipeline plans. The firms that would not directly benefit from them—SONJ and Socony-Vacuum—opposed the plans as giving unfair advantages to SOCAL and Texaco. They sided here with the domestic independents. SOCAL and Texaco, however, did not want to lose their very profitable interest in Saudi Arabia to the U.S. government, and they thus negotiated long and hard with Ickes over the deal. This gave the PRC's opponents time to mobilize. Hence, by the time SOCAL and Texaco reluctantly agreed to sell a third of their interest in Saudi Arabia to the PRC, Ickes faced so much opposition, especially within the PAW from Socony and SONJ, that he ended negotiations.[13] Thus died the PRC, and the government's first option for promoting its goals via direct federal intervention. The other two options—intergovernmental cooperation with the British and a private cartel run by British and American international firms—remained to be explored.

On the eve of the negotiations, then, the structure of domestic preferences on three issues conditioned the "acceptability-sets" of the major American actors. First arose the question of how the industry should be structured internationally and its relationship to the government. Should the international segment of the industry be controlled by some government-controlled entity (a "chosen instrument"), as in the United Kingdom, or should one or a number of private firms compete for oil markets? In pushing the PRC, Ickes and the Navy favored the chosen-instrument approach, while all other key actors opposed it. The second issue was whether the industry should be "regulated" internationally or allowed to operate as a free market. Ickes, the Navy, the State Department (Hull), and the majors saw merit in regulating the market to prevent shortfalls and secure U.S. interests abroad. The independents and their friends in Congress feared that regulation would upset their own domestic regulatory schemes; through regulation at the international level, they realized, the majors and no longer the independents would set prices in the United States. A third and related issue was whether this international regulation should be conducted by the private firms or through an intergovernmental agreement. Ickes, the Navy, and the State Department favored the latter course; the majors preferred an intergovernmental accord under two conditions: that it allow cooperation among the U.S. firms, and that it end British discrimination and domination of the international oil market. Without these two conditions, they preferred a private approach. The initial U.S. "win-set" then did not include the chosen-instrument approach (i.e., the PRC), but did include certain forms of intergovernmental agreement to regulate the oil market. Much depended on the ratification process, though. If the agreement were treated as an executive agreement, then the independents and Congress would have less voice in its ratification. If it were a treaty, then the opponents of international cooperation would have greater veto power through their influence in Congress.

The British Actors

British preferences were simpler and less divided than those in the United States. The British had two oil firms: one, half Dutch, was the giant international firm Royal-Dutch-Shell; the other was created by the British government to develop the oil fields of Iran (Persia) in 1909—the Anglo-Iranian Oil Company (AIOC).[14] These two companies had common interests, namely, controlling the international supply of oil to keep prices high and to prevent other firms, especially the Americans, from getting access to international oil fields. Like the American majors, these two counted on the support of their government. But the relationship between the British government and these firms—especially the AIOC, which was 51 percent government owned—was very close.[15] The government saw the firms as the means of promoting its national interest in having a large, secure supply of oil, since Britain had no domestic reserves at the time. Thus, unlike the U.S. industry, the British one was well-established worldwide, was internally unified with the experience of a long-running cartel, and had close relations with the government.

The British government had long been concerned with both oil and the Middle East. The government began even before World War I to promote the development of a secure oil supply in the Middle East.[16] It founded the AIOC—its chosen instrument—to control a monopoly interest in Iran, and it helped both the AIOC and Shell to develop production in other areas, such as Iraq and Kuwait. The British also saw the Americans as threatening. They believed their imperial ties, vulnerability in oil, and earlier commitment should make the Americans respect their oil interests in the Middle East. But the British also realized that the balance of power globally was changing, that the Americans were growing stronger daily, and that in time they would have to make concessions to the Americans.

The British government by 1943 preferred a cooperative solution to managing the world oil situation. The government did not want the United States to take unilateral action, like the PRC plan, since they knew the U.S. would prevail in the end. It also could not afford overt conflict with the U.S. for three reasons. First, the British depended on the U.S. to carry on the war. Second, such conflict would be exploited by Middle Eastern governments to increase their aid or oil royalties, an outcome that damaged both U.S. and U.K. interests. Third, such conflict could undermine postwar Anglo-American cooperation, which would be crucial for dealing with the Soviet Union, which the British saw as a threat, especially in the Middle East. For these reasons, the British favored a negotiated settlement with the U.S. over the management of international oil markets.[17]

The "acceptability-sets" of the British on the eve of negotiations involved the same three issues as in the United States. The first issue, the development of a chosen instrument, had already been decided. No one in the government or industry opposed the AIOC. As for international regulation, the government and the companies favored it, since the controls could help prevent overproduction and check the rising dominance of the United States. Because the U.S. oil firms for antitrust reasons could not negotiate as a group, the British realized that only an intergovernmental agreement would suit their purposes. The British "win-set" included a bilateral agreement regulating oil markets and fixing the status quo in Middle Eastern oil concessions. Given the U.K.'s parliamentary system and the wartime coalition government, the ratification process mattered less. Only a change in government might alter the win-set.

The Anglo-American Oil Negotiations

Ickes' plans for the PRC and pipeline led to the convergence of a number of different groups' interests in a bilateral, intergovernmental agreement over oil. But the idea for a negotiated settlement was evident even before Ickes' PRC plan surfaced. The idea of a bilateral agreement was broached by the British and pushed by a tacit transnational coalition.

While the Americans worried about petroleum shortages in the future, the British feared an oil glut. Leaders of the AIOC believed the companies would be unable after World War II to resist ruinous price wars, since antitrust laws in the United States would prevent cooperation

among the firms. Thus the U.S. and U.K. governments had to get involved. During 1943, then, the AIOC proposed that the United Kingdom
seek a bilateral agreement with the United States. The Foreign Office
liked the idea, but Churchill felt that the Americans had to initiate it.[18]

The Anglo-American oil negotiations were initiated by a tacit transnational coalition. The British oil company, AIOC, stimulated interest in
the idea after talking to the British Foreign Office, American majors,
and the American government (PAW). AIOC's discussions raised the
issue on both sides of the Atlantic and helped the different groups realize
the convergence of their interests. All four groups—the British and
American oil majors and governments—had a common interest in some
sort of cartel that regulated supplies and promoted the "orderly" marketing of Middle Eastern oil worldwide. From there, their interests diverged, with the Americans hoping to alter the existing "property rights"
set by the British during their period of hegemony. The British wanted
to check the rising tide of American influence and retain their position
in the Middle East. AIOC agreed with the British government, while the
American majors envisioned cooperation with their government only if
they could obtain antitrust exemptions and promote their position in the
Middle East. A mixed set of common and conflicting interests, then,
pushed this transnational coalition to start negotiations.

By the fall of 1943, both PAW and the State Department were developing the idea of bilateral negotiations. Several months of bureaucratic
infighting between Hull and Ickes followed. Finally, in December 1943,
without Roosevelt's approval, Hull formally proposed talks to the British
Ambassador in order to preempt Ickes. Soon after, Hull received consent
from the President to open negotiations. Ickes, feeling outmaneuvered,
tried to regain control of oil policy-making. He thus proposed to Roosevelt that the negotiations be held at the cabinet level—not at the technical
level, as Hull proposed—and that he lead the U.S. negotiation team.[19]
Hull objected; and Roosevelt compromised, keeping the negotiations at
the cabinet level but putting Hull in charge and Ickes second in
command.

This bureaucratic infighting between Ickes and Hull had two delete-
rious consequences. First, discord within the U.S. government meant
that little attention was paid to the views of the U.S. oil industry. No
formal consultations were held with the industry in this initial period.[20]
While the majors had raised the idea of negotiations, they had not been
consulted about their substance. The domestic independents had been
left out of any consultations. This would have grave consequences for
the agreement's ratification.

Second, this bureaucratic infighting annoyed the British. While AIOC,
backed by the Foreign Office and the British JCS, had raised the idea of

negotiations, the British wanted to retain tight control over them. They did not want to change their restrictive policies or relinquish their oil concessions in the Middle East. When Hull offered to conduct negotiations at the technical level, the British agreed, feeling they could withstand any U.S. pressure at this level. Hence, when Ickes prompted Roosevelt to alter the level of negotiations, the British became angry. Unilateral moves by the United States, such as the PRC and this change in the negotiations, convinced parts of the British government that "the American intent was competitive and hostile."[21]

Debate within the British government over how to respond to the U.S. negotiation offer followed. Only an exchange of cables between Roosevelt and Churchill induced the British to conduct the talks on American terms. Roosevelt, feeling pressure to act on the oil issue because of the congressional uproar about the PRC and the upcoming elections, used threats and promises to induce the British to negotiate. He indicated his impatience with the British, but he also promised that "we are not making sheep's eyes at [British] oil fields in Iraq or Iran," thus relieving British fears of a change in the status quo.[22] This action brought the British to the negotiation table, but it undermined support for the agreement among the U.S. majors.

It is unclear to what extent the U.S. government shared the international firms' desire to alter British restrictions and concessions in the Middle East. The government's philosophy opposing discrimination against U.S. firms abroad and pushing for an "Open Door" policy suggest that this goal may have been part of the government's position initially. This goal was the core of the U.S. oil majors' position. They sought two principal objectives: (1) an end to British restrictions in the Middle East and renegotiation of the concessions in Kuwait and Iraq; and (2) the development of an "orderly" system for managing the production and sale of oil internationally.[23] An intergovernmental accord which did not forward these aims was not in their "acceptability-sets."

The British government and companies opposed the former but approved of the latter objective. Desiring bilateral cooperation to regulate oil prices and supplies to avoid price wars, both the companies and the government were intent upon preventing any changes in the existing pattern of Middle Eastern oil concessions, which favored the British. An agreement that altered the status quo was not in the British "win-set." Thus, the British refused to negotiate until the Americans assured them that Britain's position in the Middle East would be respected. When the United States did so, however, the U.S. majors lost interest in the agreement.

The first round of negotiations from April to May 1944 went smoothly. The United States proposed the creation of a joint petroleum commission to regulate the development, supply, and availability of oil worldwide. The British succeeded in having the Americans make the commission advisory rather than regulatory. They got the Americans to agree not to disturb existing concessions, although conceding that in the future oil development should not be impeded by government restrictions. Finally, the British made the agreement very general and vague. They prevented the Americans from mentioning the Middle East, so that the agreement seemed to refer to oil production globally. The British succeeded in making no specific commitments, giving nothing away, and framing a very vague set of principles for a bilateral commission to guide petroleum development.[24] They did make one concession. They wanted to insert a clause to enable them to restrict British oil imports to those paid in sterling rather than dollars in a time of balance-of-payment difficulties. The United States objected, seeing it as a discriminatory device. The U.S. team convinced the British to drop this proposal by pointing out that the U.S. majors would oppose any such clause and veto the entire agreement if this restriction was included.[25] On this, the British backed off, but they generally prevailed in the initial negotiations.

In May 1944 the initial negotiations resulted in a "memo of understanding." While the British and American governments reacted favorably to the memo, opposition within each country arose. Within the British cabinet, the memo created dissension. Lord Privy Seal Beaverbrook was its most bitter opponent; he objected to the overall memo and specifically to the failure to include a balance-of-payments exception for "sterling oil."[26] The U.S. executive branch was pleased with the memo, but annoyed by the slow British response. Ickes and Roosevelt wanted the agreement signed before the presidential election in November. Not knowing of the divisions within the British cabinet, the U.S. negotiators felt the British were stalling to gain advantage. In addition, the delay allowed the terms of the memo to become public and gave time for opposition to form. Two points of contention appeared. First, support from the international oil firms hinged on the inclusion of an antitrust waiver in the agreement. The operation of a binational oil cartel would receive the cooperation of the majors if and only if they were protected from the government's own laws designed to prevent such collusion.[27] For the independents, the agreement was one more attempt at federal government intervention in the industry; they opposed it on the same grounds as they opposed the PRC and pipeline plans.[28] Worse, they feared the joint commission might take over the role of the various state commissions—like the Texas Railroad Commission—that regulated supply domestically. For these reasons, the independents urged their friends in Congress to derail the agreement.

Despite opposition in both countries, the negotiations resumed in late

July 1944 and proceeded smoothly. The British raised three objections, dropping two of them at American insistence. But the final point was the old issue of "sterling oil." After U.S. negotiators resisted this clause, the British dropped the issue but added a letter containing their position on it. On August 8, 1944, the agreement was signed by the two nations.

The Anglo-American oil agreement ran into intense, immediate opposition in the United States. Four groups within the U.S. opposed the agreement, while its initial supporters grew lukewarm and finally opposed. The domestic independents railed against it as they had against the PRC and the pipeline. They hated Ickes and his governmental activism; they felt the language was so vague that the joint commission could challenge state control of domestic oil; they felt it favored the majors; and they believed it would lead to flooding the U.S. market with cheap foreign oil and thus the erosion of their profits.[29] The independents used Congress to undo the agreement, as they had successfully done in the PRC and pipeline cases. They had an ace up their sleeve in this case, for the head of the Foreign Relations Committee was none other than a Texan, Tom Connally. Connally fought for the independents. His first step was to force the State Department to alter the status of the accord from an executive agreement to a treaty, requiring Senate ratification.[30] This proved the kiss of death for the agreement, which not only annoyed Senators from oil states but also smacked of further federal intervention and was thus opposed by anti-New Deal members as well. Change in the ratification procedures then enlarged the veto power of the independents.

Other domestic groups also found the agreement objectionable. Within the executive branch, opposition mounted. The Justice Department thought the antitrust clause inserted at the majors' request was too general and intervened to write a narrow exemption. At this point, the agreement lost its only U.S. domestic supporters, the majors. While never enthusiastic about it, since it did not end or alter British restrictions on Middle Eastern oil production, the majors supported it as a means of forming a government-sanctioned cartel—their second objective. Once antitrust immunity was questionable, the majors lost any interest in fighting the domestic independents over this agreement.[31] Had the executive branch offered the majors broad antitrust immunity, the firms might have fought for the agreement in Congress. The failure of the executive to adopt such a strategy to gain domestic support doomed the accord.

The structure of domestic preferences, the ratification process, and the domestic strategy of the executive branch thus proved crucial. Agreement with the British became impossible, despite British enthusiasm for the bilateral accord achieved. After a cold reception in the Senate, the State Department withdrew the treaty for revision in January 1945. In consultation with the oil industry and senators, Ickes revised the agreement. But conditions had changed by the time it was ready for ratification. Roosevelt's death and the departure of Ickes and Hull left the agreement without support in the United States.[32]

The costs of this agreement for key U.S. groups became so high that no intergovernmental agreement seemed better in the end. Another arrangement was worked out by the firms soon after. The British and American oil majors negotiated their own private cartel for controlling oil supplies and prices by 1946.[33] With the demise of this intergovernmental agreement, the third option of a private industry-run cartel emerged as the solution to the postwar problem of managing the world oil market.

THE CIVIL AVIATION CASE

The major actors in these negotiations were the United States and its firms; Britain and its firm, the British Overseas Airways Corporation (BOAC), and the British Dominions. Prior to the 1940s, national sovereignty over the air was the norm. Each country controlled who had access to its air space and landing rights, and each was free to negotiate away these privileges.[34] In contrast to ocean commerce, where "freedom of the seas" prevailed, in international air commerce restrictions on travel were the norm.

The U.S. Actors

The U.S. civil aviation industry was also divided into two groups. On the one side was Pan American Airways (PAA), the only U.S. airline with international routes before World War II. PAA developed its world routes first in Latin America during the interwar period at the prodding of the U.S. government.[35] At this time the airline negotiated its own unilateral agreements for access to foreign nations' air space; lacking their own airlines, other countries gave PAA access in return for service. By the early 1940s, PAA had monopolized international air routes in Latin America and Asia and had become the U.S. government's "chosen instrument."[36] When, however, PAA attempted to open an air route across the Atlantic it ran into trouble. Because European nations had their own airlines, PAA could no longer negotiate its own unilateral agreements for access to these markets. The Europeans wanted reciprocal access to U.S. air space and fields, which could only be given by the U.S. government. PAA had then to depend on the U.S. government to negotiate the Atlantic air routes. This raised the issue of whether the government was going to continue to allow PAA to exert monopoly control as its "chosen instrument," or would encourage competition for international air travel.

During the Hoover Administration and the first years of the Roosevelt one, PAA had close relations with the government. The U.S. government used PAA as a means to forward its foreign policy in Latin America. Over time, this relationship grew strained, and the government accused PAA of abusing its monopoly position and criticized its subsidy payments, which equaled the amount paid to all the other domestic airlines combined.[37] By 1940, the Civil Aeronautics Board (CAB) and other elements within the executive branch decided it was time to promote competition for international transport.[38] They wanted to break PAA's monopoly and move toward a system of regulated competition. Thus when a new company, American Export Airlines (AMEX), sought approval and funding for routes across the Atlantic, the CAB agreed. PAA objected and used its influence in Congress to block this move by having Congress refuse to appropriate funds for AMEX. PAA had important allies in the Senate: Senators McCarran and Brewster—both on the Aviation Subcommittee of the Commerce Committee, which formed airline policy—were in favor of a "single all-American flag line" to represent the United States in international travel.[39] With Congress opposed, the administration lost this battle. Its relationship with PAA turned hostile, prompting the executive to seek new ways to break PAA's monopoly.[40]

The second part of the U.S. airline industry included the 18 domestic airline companies. Before World War II these firms did not operate abroad, but many were eager to do so, since the international market looked lucrative. These firms opposed PAA's attempt to retain its monopoly, and they urged the government to allow competition in world travel. Seventeen of these airlines formed a political association, the Airlines Committee for U.S. Air Policy, to influence U.S. policy and counterbalance PAA.[41] This group's preference for regulated competition aligned them with the executive branch in opposition to PAA and its Congressional allies.

The executive branch had changed sides by 1940. While initially promoting PAA as its "chosen instrument," the administration later adopted competition as its preferred course. To fight Pan Am, the "administration went so far as to form a new alliance with the domestic airlines to break PAA's seeming monopoly in the international field, even if the action was delayed by the war."[42] During World War II, the Roosevelt Administration used its wartime policy instruments to overturn PAA's monopoly by awarding foreign air routes to U.S. military bases to other domestic carriers.[43] PAA had strong ties in Congress, which it used to resist this. PAA lobbied for a single international airline and got the Senate Commerce Committee to develop a bill, the McCarran bill, to force the administration to follow such a plan. Because of strong opposition by the domestic airlines and the administration, the bill failed to become law, and PAA's monopoly was broken.[44] The result was to foster competition among U.S. airlines in international routes, but also to throw U.S. regulation of these routes into chaos. Because of the emergence of foreign airlines and the breaking of PAA's monopoly, nations had to negotiate agreements about the international use of national airspace if air travel was to grow. The U.S. airline industry and government both realized this by the middle of the war and began planning for the postwar system.

The U.S. government's international negotiating position grew in part out of this domestic battle with PAA and its Congressional allies. U.S. policy-makers recognized the need for international agreement to organize the world's air routes, but they preferred a competitive approach to air travel. They sought to extend the "Open Door" principle to this issue-area. Opening all other countries' air space was in the interest of the United States, since American planes dominated world travel by the 1940s. Such an "Open Door" policy would guarantee that American companies remained dominant. The government opposed discrimination against U.S. carriers and wanted to help them obtain access globally. The administration thus advocated the "Five Freedoms": (1) the right to fly across another country without landing; (2) the right to land in another country for refueling or repairs, but not to take on or let off passengers; (3) the right to carry passengers from its own country to another; (4) the right to carry traffic from a foreign country home; and (5) the right to carry passengers from one foreign country to another. Without the adoption of these freedoms, the U.S. industry would be in a disadvantaged position. "The Five Freedoms became part of U.S. civil aviation policy because it was believed that unrestricted traffic was the only means by which Americans could take advantage of their special aviation assets to build up a truly worldwide service."[45]

The "acceptability-sets" of the U.S. actors on the verge of the negotiations can be described in terms of the same three sets of issues used for the oil case. On the problem of the "chosen instrument," PAA preferred having a government-supported monopoly, as did its supporters in Congress. The executive branch opposed this, arguing for competition. It garnered support for this position from the alliance of domestic airlines. On the question of international regulation of air travel, the executive branch opposed any regulation of routes, prices, or frequency of flights, pushing for an "Open Skies" approach based on the Five Freedoms. The domestic airlines approved of the Five Freedoms approach, but wanted to combine this with regulation of prices. PAA, on the other hand, wanted exclusive access to foreign airspace and international regulation to continue its monopolistic practices. The third problem involved who was to do the regulating. Was it to be done by some intergovernmental agreement or by a cartel run by the industry itself? The executive branch preferred an intergovernmental approach, while the domestic airlines and PAA preferred an industry-run cartel. All the major U.S. actors supported the opening of international airspace according to the Five Freedoms; they disagreed on the extent and nature of international regulation of air travel.[46]

The British Actors

The British air transport industry was weak after World War II. While a leader in air transport before the 1940s, Britain agreed to build only jet fighters during the war and to let the United States deal with air transport.[47] Hence, at the end of the war, the British faced an American aircraft industry that had superiority in transport development and global airlines already operating. Indeed, by 1943 the U.S. controlled 72 percent of world air travel; the British held only 12 percent.[48] The British industry consisted of one government-owned corporation, BOAC, born in 1939 out of the remains of the ailing Imperial Airways Company. BOAC was the British government's "chosen instrument," as PAA had been for the U.S. in the 1930s. It was "the weapon of the British in their fight for a share of postwar air commerce."[49]

For the British government, promotion of international aviation was essential for its foreign policy and economic goals. International air connections could serve as a means to keep control over Britain's far-flung colonies and to exercise influence abroad generally.[50] The maintenance of an aviation industry could also promote British trade and help the country's balance of payments. For these reasons, the government sought to promote British aviation. Domestically, it subsidized the industry, and internationally it fought for global regulation of the industry to contain American competition. The British felt that only in a regulated system could their industry hold its own against the Americans. Their goal was an international regulatory scheme—something like the American CAB for the international market.[51] BOAC and its government seemed unified in this position. The British thus opposed the Americans' Five Freedoms plan. In particular, they objected to the fifth freedom, which they saw the Americans using as a means to "snatch all of their traffic."[52] The British wanted their "fair share" of international aviation, but they realized this could only be accomplished with U.S. agreement. As the world's two main rivals in air transport, the U.S. and Britain saw that if they did not cooperate third countries would play them against one another and they would both have to pay more for access to foreign markets.

BOAC and the British government agreed on the need for monopoly in air transport and the use of a "chosen instrument." They both opposed any multilateral extension of the Five Freedoms, preferring to negotiate bilateral agreements including the first four freedoms. The government and industry also agreed on the need for international regulation of air routes, prices, and frequency, to ensure that their industry had an equitable share of air traffic and to halt the Americans' advance. The government initially pushed for multilateral negotiations. In such a forum, the British could ally with their colonies and Commonwealth countries in stronger opposition of the United States. Multilateralism was favored only if this alliance was possible. On the issue of intergovernmental regulation versus a private cartel, the government desired the former, while BOAC preferred a cartel as long as the U.S. industry consisted of one firm. With more than one U.S. firm, a cartel would be difficult to run without government help. The British win-set then consisted of a negotiated settlement involving an international regulatory mechanism and the reciprocal exchange of air rights.

International Civil Aviation Negotiations

Prior to World War II, international air transport was disorganized. National sovereignty over landing rights prevailed, and access to foreign airspace and airports had to be negotiated bilaterally. During the war, many countries acknowledged the need for a better system for organizing the world's airspace.

In 1943 the British and their dominions called for an international authority to guarantee the first four freedoms advocated by the United States and to regulate routes, rates, and frequencies of flights. They wanted the fifth freedom to be negotiable bilaterally. The U.S. position called for complete freedom of the skies. It advocated acceptance of the Five Freedoms and creation of an international organization with limited and noncompulsory powers. The U.S. government opposed any attempt to regulate the skies; unlike its domestic system, it wanted no regulation of rates, frequencies, or routes.[53] U.S. airlines were less opposed to international regulation, but were divided on whether a single line ("chosen instrument") or all domestic lines should be allowed to compete internationally. The U.S. industry and government both wanted an international conference to discuss these proposals.

Prior to this conference, BOAC and PAA tried to organize their own air cartel. Secretly, the two chief executives of the firms agreed to divide up the world's airspace.[54] When news of this private cartel leaked, both governments denounced it. The U.S. administration did not want PAA to have a monopoly on international air routes; it preferred competition.

The British government was also embarrassed by the cartel, less for its substance than for its concealment from the government, which owned the firm. Transnational links existed in the aviation case, but they were a hindrance to intergovernmental agreement. PAA and BOAC had overlapping interests, but these were outside the acceptability-set of at least the U.S., if not also the British, government.

In November 1944, a conference to discuss these proposals, involving 54 nations, began in Chicago. Negotiations quickly turned to narrowing the differences between the U.S. and British proposals. All countries agreed on the need for technical and safety cooperation and on the first two freedoms of the skies. To cover these points of agreement, the conference drew up two agreements. The first, the Convention on International Civil Aviation, embodied a general set of rules and created the International Civil Aviation Organization (ICAO) to monitor the system and enforce technical and safety regulations. The second, the International Air Transit Agreement, enshrined the first two freedoms and thus ensured free navigation around the globe. It involved a significant relaxation of previous restrictions on air transit and was a multilateral accord.[55]

The conference had more difficulty with the other three freedoms and the issue of regulation. After much argument, a statement providing for the recognition of the third, fourth, and fifth freedoms—the International Air Transport Agreement—was drawn up. But few countries—the United States, Sweden, and the Netherlands only—signed this; most important, Britain refused. Hence, the conference ended with no agreement on these last freedoms. The major point of contention was the fifth freedom, which allowed a carrier from country A to transport passengers from country B to country C. This "freedom" put foreign international carriers into direct competition with national ones. The British and others opposed it then because they feared that the U.S., given its substantial lead in civil aviation, would use this "freedom" to drive other countries' airlines out of business. This "freedom" had direct commercial advantages for the U.S. with its superior civil aviation system. The British and others wanted to restrict this freedom to ensure that their airlines survived. The British desired to regulate rates and frequencies for the same reason. They feared that without such regulation, especially of rates, the U.S. companies could drive their firms out of the market through price wars.[56] With no agreement over the fifth "freedom" or on the issue of regulation, the conference ended. Some cooperation was established at Chicago, but key issues were left undecided.

In the wake of this conference, the United States decided that organization of the air routes was crucial and must proceed even without a multilateral agreement. During and after the conference, Churchill and

Roosevelt corresponded and urged agreement. But air relations between the two deteriorated. The two countries vied for rights to airspace globally, causing friction in their general relations. Out of concern for their alliance relations, and because of pressure exerted by the United States through its creditor position, the two countries finally agreed to new negotiations. The British, facing a balance-of-payments crisis, were negotiating for a 3.75 billion dollar loan from the United States in 1946. Evidently there were links between receipt of the loan and progress in the air negotiations.[57] As one U.S. official said, "It had been subtly pointed out the bad effect it would have on the British loan negotiations if a strong effort to reach some agreement were not made before the loan came up for debate in the Senate. It was no secret that the airlines lobby would work against the British loan if [U.S.] aviation interests continued to be ignored."[58]

The United States thus initiated bilateral negotiations with its most important competitor and ally, the United Kingdom, in Bermuda in February 1946. These negotiations covered the same issues as the Chicago Conference, and the two countries took the same opposing positions initially. The key issues were the regulation of rates and frequencies and the fifth freedom. After much haggling, the Americans agreed to allow rates to be regulated, but only by an association run by the international airlines, the International Air Transport Association (IATA). In exchange, the British agreed that frequencies would be left to each country to decide. On the last issue, both compromised. Britain accepted the fifth freedom in principle, but both agreed it could only be used "reasonably." "Fair play" came to be the guiding principle for its use; the U.S. government's quest for an unregulated system was denied.[59]

This bilateral negotiation settled the key issues on civil aviation for the two countries.[60] This agreement, as most assessments concur, contained terms closer to the British preferences than the Americans'.[61] Despite the threat of the loan, the United States compromised its central principle; it acquiesced to the idea of a regulated system. The British, while compromising, severely hedged in use of the fifth freedom and prevented a competitive system from emerging.

The aviation agreements, however, almost suffered the same fate as the Anglo-American oil agreement. Opposition to the Chicago and Bermuda agreements arose at their conclusion. Some in Congress felt the British had gained the upper hand in the negotiated settlement. PAA and its congressional allies also objected to certain terms of both the Air Transport Agreement of Chicago and the Bermuda Agreement. The airline wanted to retain its status as a monopoly, as the chosen instrument of the United States. Many senators shared PAA's view and felt the agreement should be ratified as a treaty, not as an executive accord. Unlike the oil case, the agreements regulating air traffic fell within the acceptability-sets of the domestic airlines and important parts of the executive branch.

The agreements had strong domestic support, gained in part through the use of side-payments by the executive branch. By allocating international routes to the domestic lines, the executive branch ensured that they would have an interest in an Open Skies system. With gains available through these new routes, the domestic airlines were willing to lobby Congress and battle Pan Am for the agreements. Ratification of the International Convention of Chicago and the Bermuda Accord, however, hinged on gaining support from the key senators involved in aviation. Pressure from the domestic airlines, plus an adroit strategy by the executive branch, gained this senatorial support. Many in the Senate, because of Pan Am's pressure, intended to veto the International Convention of Chicago, establishing the ICAO, which required Senate ratification as a treaty. In order to forestall this, the administration agreed to renounce the Air Transport Agreement—which was a dead letter in any case, since few countries ever signed it—if Congress would pass the Convention. The Convention passed, and the Bermuda agreements were kept as executive accords.[62] Successful cooperation in this issue evolved out of these two negotiations.

CONCLUSIONS

This chapter has explored a case of failed international cooperation and one of successful cooperation. In conclusion, it addresses the puzzle of why intergovernmental cooperation in oil failed to result, while it did in aviation. The emergence of cooperation is often explained by international conditions. Since external conditions were the same during the two negotiations (i.e., the end of the war, U.S. economic hegemony, and growth of the Soviet threat), it is difficult to use them to explain the two cases' divergent outcomes. Indeed, international conditions were highly favorable to the emergence of cooperation in both cases. In terms of three commonly cited conditions for cooperation, the oil and aviation cases were highly propitious.[63] The structure of the game for the two states in each issue was one of mixed motives, both common and competing interests. Moreover, the games were also iterated, since the two countries would have to deal with each other on many other issues in the postwar world. And the number of players was small: two countries. Some external conditions for successful cooperative agreement were evident in both cases.

Why did the aviation negotiations succeed and the oil negotiations fail? Three domestic factors and two international ones help explain this puzzle.

1. The structure of domestic preferences was critically important. It largely determined the nature of the countries' win-sets and influenced other explanatory variables. The preferences and influence of domestic actors differed in the two cases. The oil agreement failed because of involuntary defection by the United States. The executive branch could *not* get Congress or key domestic actors to ratify it. Early on, a coalition of the international firms and the executive branch dominated the issue area. They preferred an international settlement to regulate oil production and allow greater U.S. participation in Middle Eastern oil. As the chief negotiators compromised with the British, and as the shape of the agreement clarified, opposition grew in the United States. The independents and their allies in Congress denounced the agreement, and the international firms lost interest, since their minimum conditions were not met. The loss of the international firms' support may have been the key to undermining the agreement. By 1946, they preferred negotiating a private cartel more than attempting to get the binational accord ratified. Had the accord done more to alter the status quo in the Middle East and had it given them antitrust immunity, it might have prompted their support and been ratified. The independents' strong influence in Congress was also important. Perhaps even with the support of the majors the agreement might have failed, because of the independents' opposition. But it is clear that without backing from either segment of the industry, the intergovernmental agreement was doomed.

In the aviation case, the structure of domestic preferences differed. All domestic groups favored an international agreement. This resulted from the structure of the aviation issue. Intergovernmental cooperation was essential in the aviation case, while less so in the oil one. Rights to foreign airspace had to be decided through intergovernmental negotiation; without a mechanism for exchanging these rights, no airline could fly beyond its national borders. In contrast, the control of global oil production and the rights to foreign oil concessions could be arranged without government intervention by the firms themselves. For both sides, the costs of no-agreement were higher in the aviation case than in the oil one, which helps to explain the differential outcomes. Furthermore, in the aviation case the costs of no-agreement were higher for the United States than for the United Kingdom since the U.S. did not have access to colonies or Commonwealth connections.

While internal consensus on international cooperation existed, domestic divisions in the United States on other aspects of aviation were evident. The extent of international regulation and the issue of the "chosen instrument" divided the executive branch, the domestic airlines, and Pan

Am. Unlike the oil case, all of the industry—the domestic airlines and even Pan Am—desired a regulated system, especially an industry-run organization like IATA. Such regulation of prices and routes would enable them to expand into international markets and to run an oligopoly globally. This solution was not preferred by the U.S. executive branch, which believed in a more competitive, Open Skies arrangement. On the "chosen instrument" issue, however, Pan Am differed from its domestic competitors, since it wanted to keep them out of international travel and retain its monopoly. This was opposed by both the executive branch and the domestic airlines, who preferred competition within the United States for international routes. Pan Am only objected to the international agreements when it realized that they meant the loss of its monopoly status in the United States. Broad agreement on the need for intergovernmental cooperation thus existed among all of the important domestic groups, although controversy surrounded the exact terms of this cooperation.

The Chicago and Bermuda agreements satisfied to some extent both the U.S. government's and the industry's minimum position for more "Open Skies." The U.S. compromise of agreeing to regulate rates and moderate use of the fifth freedom allowed agreement with the U.K. to open international routes and did not undermine support at home, since the domestic airlines and even PAA favored international regulation. The terms of the agreements were closest to those of the U.S. domestic firms. This induced their keen support for the agreements and ensured their determined opposition to PAA's attempts to scuttle them. Allied with the executive branch, then, these domestic firms used their influence in Congress to make ratification possible.

In both cases, international compromise by negotiators affected the ratifiability of the agreements. The usual dilemma is that compromise with the other country, necessary for international agreement, reduces support at home, often making the agreement unratifiable. The compromise made by the United States in the oil negotiations did just this: it eroded domestic support and fanned opposition. In the airline case, the compromises remained within the industry's acceptability-set, although outside the initial one of the U.S. executive branch. An agreement without support from any part of the key domestic groups involved is unlikely to be ratifiable. But one with the support of even a minority of these groups may well be acceptable. Domestic divisions may then allow policymakers to ally with certain domestic groups against opponents of international cooperation, and prevail. The worst situation for ratification is when the executive faces a unified industry which both opposes the agreement and has allies in the legislature. This is likely to be valid in the British case as well.

2. The ratification process is important. How an agreement must be ratified shapes which domestic interests will be involved, and thus the nature of the win-set. As an executive agreement, the Anglo-American oil accord might have been ratified because the independents would not have been able to stop it. But as a treaty, the accord was subject to a senatorial vote, which meant the independents could exert their influence to derail it. PAA's attempts to push Congress to declare the Chicago and Bermuda agreements to be treaties served a similar purpose. The airline's allies in the Senate could then fan opposition to the treaties. But the active lobbying of the domestic airlines against PAA, and for the agreements, dissipated PAA's influence in Congress. The effects of different ratification processes are linked to the structure of domestic interests.

Differences in the British and American political systems made the ratification process a more important variable in the United States. In the British parliamentary system, ratification relies on the majority party and its leadership. Domestic groups that are important constituents for this majority may be able to derail agreements they oppose, but groups outside the majority can exert little influence. The U.S. system of executive-legislative checks and balances makes the ratification process more variable and involves a larger number of domestic actors. If important groups are unified in opposing an agreement preferred by the executive, the best chance for ratification is through an executive agreement. This situation is likely, however, to trigger Congressional pressure for its consideration as a treaty. In the U.S. case, the executive can best overcome the political system's high ratification hurdles by employing various strategies to divide and coopt domestic groups.

3. The strategies used by the executive to construct support for an international agreement are the third important factor. In the oil case, the executive's failure to adopt two strategies can help explain its failure. First, it never included the oil industry and its Congressional allies in preparation for or in the negotiations themselves. This made even the more sympathetic parts of the industry, the majors, detached from and suspicious of the agreement. The British did include their firms and had no trouble with ratification. As Gilbert Winham has pointed out, procedures that draw into the negotiation process societal actors who could become opponents can turn them into supporters.[64] The American negotiators in the airline case employed this strategy. Representatives from the airlines and Congress were consulted regularly and included in the negotiations. Even early opponents, such as Senator Brewster, were involved, and later supported the agreements.

Second, the American executive branch never used side-payments to increase internal support for the oil accord. In fact, its biggest mistake was to reduce antitrust immunity for the majors. This meant that no domestic group was willing to oppose the independents in Congress. In contrast, in the airline case the executive increased support from the domestic airlines by giving them stakes in international air routes they desired. The strategies pursued domestically by negotiators may make an important difference to the ratifiability of an agreement.

4. An international factor important to the success of the negotiations was the possibility for transnational coalitions. As one scholar has argued, "The existence of transnational networks is of crucial importance in such multiple-level bargaining. Networks facilitate the distribution of information . . . and are instrumental in building coalitions and mediating divergent interests."[65] Given the structure of domestic preferences, the possibility for transnational coalitions existed in both cases. In the oil case, the transnational alliance among the U.S. majors, AIOC, and the British Foreign Office helped initiate the negotiations. Without it, knowledge of the overlapping national interests in controlling the oil market might not have surfaced. However, the tacit re-emergence of this coalition in 1946 further undermined interest in the agreement, since these actors felt the market could be managed without government interference. Transnational alliances involving nongovernmental actors may result in private international cartels rather than intergovernmental cooperation.

In the aviation case, the coalition between Pan Am and BOAC threatened to undermine an intergovernmental settlement. But the transnational coalition that arose to halt the airlines' planned cartel made such an agreement more possible. The tacit alliance of the U.S. executive branch, the British government, and the U.S. domestic airlines propelled the negotiations forward. Transnational coalitions may be a prerequisite to success in building international cooperation, either privately or intergovernmentally.

5. Finally, issue linkages by the countries may play a role in securing cooperation. Often these linkages do not need to be manipulated consciously; one or both sides may recognize their salience without the other evoking it. In both cases, the United States and United Kingdom were more willing to cooperate because of their wartime relations, their need to get along on other issues, and their concerns over the stability of the postwar system. Willingness to compromise may have been engendered by these tacit linkages. It is difficult to find direct evidence of their impact. Some have suggested that issue linkage was crucial to the success of the aviation negotiations. They claim that a tacit link between the negotiations and the U.S. loan to the U.K. in 1946 may have induced the British to negotiate in Bermuda. It is curious, however, that the loan was not used in the oil negotiations, which also continued into 1946. In any case,

because of this linkage, the benefits of intergovernmental agreement in aviation may have been increased further for both countries.

In general, differences in the net costs of agreement and no-agreement help explain the differential success of these two cases. These costs depended fundamentally on the structure of domestic interests and the ratification process. The costs of no-agreement were higher for both countries in the aviation case, since no-agreement meant in effect no international commercial aviation. In the oil case, the costs of agreement for the entire industry came to outweigh the costs of no-agreement; hence the accord failed to win legislative support. Increasing the costs of agreement for one side by pushing it to compromise will at some point make the costs of no-agreement palatable. In the aviation case, the costs of agreement never rose that high, since U.S. compromises did not alienate key domestic support. Differences in the relative costs for each side of agreement or no-agreement thus can be seen as the proximate factor accounting for successful international cooperation.

Overall, the two cases suggest that no single factor can explain international agreement. The most powerful influence seems to be the structure of domestic preferences. Other factors—such as the ratification process or transnational coalitions—while they at times depend on the nature of domestic preferences, can also exert independent influences. Agreement among nations is thus best seen as a complex process, emerging out of the internal and external environments of the states involved.

NOTES

1. Irvine Anderson, *ARAMCO, the U.S., and Saudi Arabia* (Princeton, N.J.: Princeton University Press, 1981), p. 14.

2. Louis Turner, *Oil Companies in the International System* (London: Allen-Unwin, 1978), pp. 26–27; John Blair, *The Control of Oil* (New York: Vintage, 1976), pp. 29–31; Anderson, *ARAMCO*, pp. 18–21.

3. Anthony Sampson, *The Seven Sisters* (New York: Viking, 1975), pp. 108–110; Anderson, *ARAMCO*, pp. 24–26.

4. Anderson, *ARAMCO*, pp. 46–49; Michael Stoff, *Oil, War and American Security* (New Haven, Conn.: Yale University Press, 1980), pp. 43–61.

5. Sampson, *Seven Sisters*, pp. 89–90.

6. Blair, *Control of Oil*, pp. 156–165; Anderson, *ARAMCO*, pp. 10–13.

7. Sampson, *Seven Sisters*, pp. 78–81; Blair, *Control of Oil*, pp. 33–34.

8. Aaron Miller, *Search for Security* (Chapel Hill: University of North Carolina Press, 1980), p. 62.

9. Ibid., pp. 63–64; David Painter, *Oil and the American Century* (Baltimore: Johns Hopkins University Press, 1986), p. 47.

10. Miller, *Search For Security*, pp. 73–78, 96; Anderson, *ARAMCO*, pp. 50–55, 80–82; Painter, *Oil*, pp. 52–59.

11. Miller, *Search for Security,* pp. 97–98.

12. Ibid., p. 83; Anderson, *ARAMCO,* pp. 68–70; Stoff, *Oil, War,* pp. 109–110.

13. Anderson, *ARAMCO,* pp. 62–63.

14. Sampson, *Seven Sisters,* pp. 65–67, 74.

15. Ibid., p. 67.

16. Ibid., pp. 52, 61–67.

17. Miller, *Search For Security,* pp. 85–89; Stoff, *Oil, War,* pp. 104–107.

18. Anderson, *ARAMCO,* pp. 71–72.

19. Ibid., p. 83.

20. Ibid., p. 77.

21. Ibid., p. 85.

22. Stoff, *Oil, War,* p. 148.

23. Ibid., pp. 91–93, 119; Painter, *Oil,* p. 48.

24. Miller, *Search For Security,* pp. 102–104; Stoff, *Oil, War,* pp. 155–156.

25. Anderson, *ARAMCO,* pp. 90–91; Stoff, *Oil, War,* pp. 165–166.

26. Anderson, *ARAMCO,* p. 92.

27. Ibid., p. 91.

28. Painter, *Oil,* p. 62; Anderson, *ARAMCO,* pp. 96–99.

29. Anderson, *ARAMCO,* pp. 96–99, 104; Stoff, *Oil, War,* p. 181.

30. Anderson, *ARAMCO,* p. 103; Stoff, *Oil, War,* pp. 180–181.

31. Anderson, *ARAMCO,* p. 105.

32. Stoff, *Oil, War,* pp. 185–192.

33. Ibid., p. 194.

34. Christer Jonsson, *International Aviation and the Politics of Regime Change* (New York: St. Martin's Press, 1987), pp. 26–31.

35. See Henry Ladd Smith, *Airways Abroad* (Madison: University of Wisconsin Press, 1950), pp. 4–36, for the story of PAA's rise.

36. Frederick Thayer, *Air Transport Policy and National Security* (Chapel Hill: University of North Carolina Press, 1965), pp. 33–34; Smith, *Airways Abroad,* pp. 13, 69.

37. Thayer, *Air Transport Policy,* pp. 34–35.

38. Smith, *Airways Abroad,* pp. 46, 49–52.

39. Ibid., pp. 59–60, 205–206, 219.

40. Thayer, *Air Transport Policy,* p. 37.

41. Smith, *Airways Abroad,* pp. 207–210.

42. Thayer, *Air Transport Policy,* p. 37.

43. Smith, *Airways Abroad,* pp. 269–277.

44. Thayer, *Air Transport Policy,* pp. 68–72.

45. Smith, *Airways Abroad,* p. 117.

46. For a good summary of the different positions, see Smith, *Airways Abroad,* pp. 129–148.

47. Ibid., pp. 70–71; Thayer, *Air Transport Policy,* pp. 75–76.

48. Smith, *Airways Abroad,* p. 109.

49. Ibid., pp. 101, 107.

50. Robert Thornton, "Governments, International Airlines, and Change" (Ph.D. diss., University of Michigan, Ann Arbor, 1969), pp. 21–22.

51. Smith, *Airways Abroad,* p. 110; Thayer, *Air Transport Policy,* pp. 75–76; William O'Connor, *Economic Regulation of the World's Airlines* (New York: Praeger, 1971), pp. 27–29; Virginia Little, "Control of International Air Transport," *International Organization* (February 1949): 31–33.

52. Smith, *Airways Abroad,* p. 117.

53. R. Hackford, "Our International Aviation Policy," *Harvard Business Review* 25 (Summer 1947): 492–493; O'Connor, *Economic Regulation,* pp. 20–23; Thayer, *Air Transport Policy,* p. 75; Lloyd Gardner, *The Economic Aspects of New Deal Diplomacy* (Boston: Beacon Press, 1964), pp. 270–275.

54. Smith, *Airways Abroad,* pp. 177–178; Jonsson, *International Aviation,* pp. 109–110.

55. See Smith, *Airways Abroad,* pp. 163–204, for the story of the conference in detail; John Cooper, *The Right to Fly* (New York: Henry Holt and Co., 1947), pp. 157–196; Hackford, "Our International Aviation Policy," pp. 493–495; O'Connor, *Economic Regulation,* pp. 41–45.

56. Hackford, "Our International Aviation Policy," pp. 494–495; O'Connor, *Economic Regulation,* pp. 30–36, 41–45.

57. Smith, *Airways Abroad,* pp. 256–258; Thornton, "Governments," pp. 53–57; Jonsson, *International Aviation,* pp. 114–118.

58. Smith, *Airways Abroad,* p. 258.

59. Hackford, "Our International Aviation Policy," pp. 496–499; O'Connor, *Economic Regulation,* pp. 45–49; Smith, *Airways Abroad,* pp. 257–260; Little, "Control," p. 34.

60. A multilateral accord was not initially achieved. But over time, as more and more countries negotiated cooperative arrangements exchanging landing rights, a multilateral-like system emerged. Since many countries choose to use the Bermuda Agreement as the formula for their bilateral accords, the regime that emerged has had standardized terms which make it similar to a multilateral system. Little, "Control," pp. 39–40.

61. Smith, *Airways Abroad,* pp. 257–263; Thornton, "Governments," pp. 154–157; Jonsson, *International Aviation,* pp. 46, 48.

62. Smith, *Airways Abroad,* pp. 196–202, 262–268, 311–323; Hackford, "Our International Aviation Policy," pp. 499–500.

63. Kenneth Oye, ed., "Cooperation Under Anarchy," special issue, *World Politics* 38 (October 1985).

64. Gilbert Winham, *International Trade and the Tokyo Round Negotiations,* Princeton, N.J.: Princeton University Press, 1986), chap. 8.

65. Jonsson, *International Aviation,* pp. 74, 76.

International Threats and Internal Politics

Brazil, the European Community, and the United States, 1985–1987

John S. Odell

"Cooperation" normally suggests a process intended to make both or all parties better off. An explicit search for joint gains is a prominent feature of many of the negotiations analyzed in this volume. Virtually all bargaining, however, even that dominated by a search for common value, also involves issues on which the parties' interests conflict. Many other interstate negotiations, in fact, are largely or wholly distributive or zero-sum. In those cases, one state seeks actions by another without giving up anything in return, the other either maneuvers to minimize its concessions or counterattacks, and neither makes much effort to formulate new joint-gain arrangements. Nevertheless, when the parties end such a dispute with an agreement embodying an unequal exchange of concessions, this outcome too is fairly considered an instance of limited cooperation, at least in contrast to a breakdown of the relationship, resort to economic sanctions, or war. Often, even the party accepting a loss relative to its status quo point remains better off than it would have been by refusing the last offer on the table.

This chapter concentrates on the distributive dimension of international negotiation. It shares this feature with other essays in this volume concerned with Soviet-American crises, Japan-U.S. trade negotiations, and human rights disputes. More specifically, this chapter investigates the use of overt threats as a strategy in international economic bargaining, and the conditions that shape the outcomes of such encounters. One central analytical question is whether agreement will be reached or not. A second is the terms of the outcome, whether explicit or tacit; if the demands cause a shift in value from one party to the other, how far will the movement go? A third dimension is the cost of the process of reaching the outcome. A costly process can consume value greater than the gains eventually achieved.

233

Practitioners of international relations have long been divided over the role of coercion. One perspective assumes that world politics is essentially a jungle where only the fittest prosper, and that failure to use the power available to a state simply opens it to exploitation by others. For this "realistic" school of thought, whether threats are explicit or implicit, and whether we like them or not, coercion often pays. To a second school of thought, coercion rarely pays, at least not in the long run. A more Grotian outlook sees not a world of anarchy but a world laced with institutionalized relationships built on mutual benefit and histories of cooperation, overlying the conflicts of interest and power rivalries. Introducing explicit threats and sanctions into such a world damages that valuable network, often costing more than it gains in the long run. Each of these perspectives can be misleading, however, if left at the level of high abstraction. The effects of coercion attempts vary, and one thing they depend upon is internal politics.[1]

One possible impediment to compliance, even by a clearly weaker power, will be found, ironically, inside the threatening nation itself. If constituents of a threatening government—call it A—oppose implementing the threat, they may persuade their government not to implement it, or may impose internal political costs on that government if it goes ahead. The greater the net opposition or the likely net political cost of implementing the threat in state A, and the more target B is aware of it, the less the threat's credibility, and the less likely government B will be to comply, other things being equal. In this view, some fairly high degree of internal consensus is necessary in order to realize benefits of international power via coercion.[2]

A second impediment may be found within the target nation. Assuming a credible threat—that is, even when a plausible reading of B's national interests dictates agreeing—and even when B's chief executive personally would prefer to do so, B will not do so to the extent that its executive faces greater net internal political penalties from complying than from accepting the consequences of no-agreement. A second proposition holds that the greater the likely net internal political loss to the executive from agreeing, relative to the net internal loss from standing firm, the lower the probability of agreement on the terms demanded, other things being equal. In principle, threats can generate hostility to agreement in the target country as well as fear of the cost of refusing. A hard-line stand could be highly popular and international accommodation quite risky at home, on balance; or the two could be reversed; or either could yield a net zero in domestic politics. In other words, what matters is whether either alternative falls within the country's Level II win-set, and which alternative would "win" by the largest "vote." This second hypothesis disregards external interests as such, in order to concentrate attention purely on the domestic political calculus.

This chapter attempts to substantiate these two simple propositions in a preliminary way and hence to suggest that they merit further study. It presents a focused contrast of two economic-policy cases that differ in theoretically relevant ways and yet are similar in other important respects. One of the two episodes has the further analytical value that it presents change in both independent variables over time. The purpose here is neither to report a full-dress test of these hypotheses nor to provide a comprehensive history of either dispute. Of course factors other than these can also be expected to affect credibility and compliance in general and in these cases, but this essay abstracts from many considerations in order to focus attention clearly. In concluding, however, I shall raise additional theoretical issues emphasized elsewhere in this volume.

During the 1970s, and especially the 1980s, the United States turned to explicit threats as a means for achieving economic concessions from friends and allies more often than in earlier decades.[3] Washington issued ultimatums and threats of economic retaliation as responses to economic distress and practices of other societies that were regarded as unfair. Some of these U.S. actions were results of institutionalized anti-dumping mechanisms. Beyond those mechanisms, however, Washington also used ad hoc threats to deal with problems in particular industries and countries. The most notable sign of this shift appeared in September 1985, when the Reagan Administration relaxed the traditional restriction against executive initiation of trade negotiations conducted under threats of retaliation, and began several of them. Washington also pressed other countries for currency adjustments and changes in national economic policies.

The outcomes have varied. Consider, for example, two similar attempts by the same President and Administration during the same time period. In September 1985 President Reagan threatened Brazil with economic retaliation if it did not change its program designed to promote a national computer industry and displace U.S. and other foreign firms. In March 1986 Reagan also threatened the European Community (EC) with trade sanctions if it did not remove new barriers to U.S. feedgrain exports to Spain and Portugal. These restrictions had just been imposed pursuant to the treaty whereby the two Iberian states had become new members of the Common Market. Both Brasília and Brussels promptly and angrily threatened counter-retaliation.

In the end, the Brazil-U.S. dispute dragged on for some 36 months and yielded only a fragile, tacit agreement which collapsed dramatically at one point, and which in the end provided little commercial value to the United States beyond the status quo ante. Meanwhile, the EC-U.S.

negotiation ended after ten months with a formal agreement breaching the enlargement treaty and making substantial EC commercial concessions to the United States. Because these two cases occurred during the same period, shifts in U.S. global hegemony or different macroeconomic conditions cannot help us explain these puzzling differences. Why, then, did the coercive strategy yield less from the weaker country and more from the largest trading unit in the world?

ANALYSIS WITH UNITARY ACTORS

Much international bargaining theory and international law assume that states are unitary actors. While this assumption is quite valuable for some purposes, it can also be insufficient or misleading. Here a conventional international power analysis based on this unitary assumption is not adequate to explain this difference in bargaining outcomes. Of course the EC is a much more powerful player than Brazil, with the wherewithal to do far greater harm to the U.S. economy in a serious trade war. In 1986, the United States relied on the EC to purchase 24 percent of American exports, while only 2 percent of its exports were going to Brazil.

A more refined measure of dependence would consider exports as a share of the economies' total production, since some economies rely on trade much more than others, and would also examine dependence in both directions. Thus in 1986 EC exports to the United States were equivalent to 2.3 percent of combined EC gross domestic product, while the U.S. was exporting 1.3 percent of its GDP to the EC. Meanwhile, Brazil's exports to the U.S. also came to 2.3 percent of Brazilian GDP, while U.S. exports to Brazil were only 0.09 percent of the vast U.S. economy. That is, by this broad trade measure, while the EC was almost twice as dependent on the U.S. as the U.S. was on the EC, Brazil was 26 times as dependent on the U.S. as vice versa.[4] Moreover, in the mid-1980s the developing country was struggling with a serious debt crisis.

Furthermore, the EC had established its own reputation for a willingness to call Washington's bluff and to counter-sanction, going back to the infamous "chicken war" of the 1960s. In that early challenge to the EC Common Agricultural Policy (CAP), the U.S. had threatened and then implemented modest economic sanctions against the EC, which nevertheless had simply refused to budge, despite a GATT panel ruling in favor of the U.S. interpretation. In 1982 and again in 1984 Brussels had explicitly threatened retaliation if the U.S. imposed unilateral restrictions on European steel. The year before the enlargement dispute, the EC had matched U.S. sanctions on European pasta by implementing counter-sanctions against American citrus products. Brazil had very little reputation for retaliation that might have bolstered the credibility of counter-threats.[5]

In short, from this standpoint it would be reasonable to expect the United States to have greater success with Brazil. Why, then, did the giant European Community soon "blink" while Brazil held out with considerable success?

U.S. THREAT CREDIBILITY AND U.S. POLITICS

A central part of the answer is that the American threat against Europe was more credible than that directed at Brazil, partly because of the respective negotiating tactics chosen, and fundamentally because of differing Level II conditions in the United States. In each case, the other negotiators implicitly read American credibility, including especially information on Level II, and acted accordingly. Lower credibility in the Brazilian case encouraged greater resistance.

One tactical difference between these two cases was that the threat toward Brazil was less specific. The Administration did not publicize an estimate of the value of the harm Brazil was alleged to have done to U.S. interests, and at the outset Washington did not identify the Brazilian industries that would become targets if the sanctions were carried out. There was also no specific action by Congress urging the President to carry out this threat in particular.

President Ronald Reagan made the announcement in his regular radio address to the nation on Saturday, September 7, 1985. He said his Administration was concerned about unfair foreign trade practices and had ordered three investigations under the authority of section 301 of the U.S. Trade Act of 1974. Targeted were Japanese restrictions on tobacco imports, a South Korean law preventing U.S. insurance companies from competing equally, and the informatics law Brazil had adopted in 1984 to codify its decade-old *reserva de mercado* (market reserve) program. This was the first time a president had initiated such cases; until then, investigations had begun only at the request of U.S. industries. Section 301 permitted the President to impose retaliatory penalties on Brazilian exports to the United States if his investigation determined that Brazil had maintained "unjustifiable or unreasonable" import restrictions or other policies damaging U.S. commerce. The U.S. set itself a decision deadline of one year later. In his speech, Reagan said that "we will take trade counter-measures only as a last resort." U.S. Trade Representative Clayton Yeutter told reporters that under the law, "for all practical purposes the President can do essentially what he wishes by way of retaliation" if foreign governments do not cooperate.[6]

In contrast, Washington moved more concretely and brutally against the EC from the outset, detailing target industries and setting extremely tight deadlines. On March 31, 1986, President Reagan announced that the United States would impose huge trade sanctions almost immediately unless the EC rescinded the quotas on oilseeds and grains in Portugal and provided adequate compensation for the higher tariffs in Spain. "We cannot allow the American farmer, once again, to pay the price for the European Community's enlargement," he declared.[7] The Office of the U.S. Trade Representative (USTR) promptly issued a "hit" list of EC products that would be the victims.[8] The magnitude of EC export loss was designed to total an unprecedented 1 billion dollars, which would make this easily the most severe trade war the two had ever fought. Penalties were designed separately for the Portuguese and Spanish issues.

Moreover, Washington did not merely start an investigation but immediately lit the retaliation fuse. The *Federal Register* announced that penalties would be applied automatically, beginning on May 1 for the Portugal issues and July 1 for the Spain complaints, unless the EC backed down.[9] The cannons would fire without further action unless steps were taken to disarm them. Agriculture Secretary Richard Lyng reported drily that "our intention is to bring the EC to the negotiating table as soon as possible."[10]

Underlying the difference in American tactics was a basic difference in the relevant U.S. markets and domestic politics. U.S. constituents' preferences regarding strategy toward Brazil—even those of the computer firms themselves—were divided at best, or even largely opposed to Reagan's open coercion, while the EC measures unified U.S. feedgrain producers and other constituents behind a coercive strategy with a vengeance.

Opposition on Computers

In 1984, U.S. computer companies had mixed feelings about the new Brazilian law. All regarded the country as a great potential market, and some hoped for a policy turnaround eventually. Despite obstacles and costs, some had learned how to operate profitably in segments lacking local competition, while others were suffering. The giant IBM had been producing office machines in Brazil for decades, and its subsidiary there was reported to be highly profitable at this time. Located on the inside, IBM do Brasil actually benefited from the market reserve, which kept Digital Equipment and other minicomputer makers from setting up local manufacturing subsidiaries and made it more difficult for Japanese mainframe producers to export into Brazil. Most U.S. firms did not see the new law itself as a major change, but more a codification of existing practice, which for many meant a long story of irritations. One summed it up: "If a company is in Brazil it will tend to stick it out; but if a company is not now operating there, it is a place to avoid."[11] The industry as a whole was not lobbying for a shift to a more aggressive bargaining strategy in 1985, before Reagan's speech.

At the end of the summer, however, the Reagan Administration decided to make major changes in its approaches to exchange rates and international trade in general, as it saw a gargantuan trade deficit stimulating intense internal pressure for protection and aggressive action against other countries. By then, indignation about trade had spread well beyond the Democratic opposition to Republican members of Congress, corporate executives, and even farmers dependent on exports.

As part of this policy reappraisal, an interagency committee, headed by the USTR, prepared a list of cases that might be investigated under Section 301. After having identified Japan and Korea, according to one well-informed participant,

> we needed a non-Asian LDC [less developed country], we needed a "new issue," and we needed one where you could avoid going to the GATT. . . . With these [section] 301 cases we were putting these issues on the international trade agenda. And to that degree, I would say that this 301 case was a success. The intellectual property rights issue was agreed to at Punta del Este [where GATT opened a new multilateral round in 1986], and if we hadn't been attacking the Brazilians on this, I don't think we would have had as much support from the Europeans and the Japanese to do that.[12]

According to this official, Brazil was chosen early and by unanimous agreement. "The view was that Brazil was an outlaw country, never following the rules on anything." Not all were enthusiastic about picking the informatics sector in Brazil, however. At least one policy-maker preferred a different current bilateral trade issue because it seemed more "winnable." But a key participant said of the informatics case:

> I thought we had broad industry support. I was convinced it was the right issue. Now, whether we would win or lose was not so clear. And what we would do if they didn't make concessions, we didn't quite figure out at that time.

Reportedly, an emergency meeting was held with U.S. industry representatives only a day before Reagan's speech, more in order to notify them than to learn from them. A well-informed industry representative recalled, "The companies were shocked. I'm not sure, but I would guess the companies told them not to do it. I doubt any lobbied them to do it." Another grumbled, "There was *never* any enthusiasm for the case from those who knew Brazil."[13]

Immediately Brazil discovered that supposed major beneficiaries of the pressure were not pressing for this coercion, and might well oppose actually carrying out the threat. A few days after the speech, IBM and Burroughs officials, attending a private symposium with Brazilians in Washington, said they thought Reagan's action was inopportune, according to a Brazilian present. A Brazilian government negotiator later recalled:

> The U.S. companies were divided. IBM was neutral. They passed the word that they had not asked for the 301; it was really government inspired. The companies knew better than the U.S. government how difficult it would be in Brazil.[14]

IBM made a point of staying away from meetings with U.S. negotiators for many months. If the President were to have carried out the threat, and his Democratic rivals in Congress had then called these firms to testify in public hearings, the results could have been embarrassing, which implied that USTR would have had a difficult time convincing the White House to approve actual sanctions in the first place. Brazilian clients retained former U.S. policy-makers as advisers, who explained all this to them. Reagan's and Yeutter's credibility was seriously undermined as soon as they had issued their threat.

The U.S. computer and electronics industries were represented politically by two major organizations. A few large multinational firms dominated the Computer and Business Equipment Manufacturers Association (CBEMA). IBM and Burroughs (later Unisys) each had a major investment stake exposed inside the country, and Hewlett-Packard had established a small foothold in the 1960s. IBM was highly dependent on world markets, especially considering earnings from its overseas subsidiaries as well as exports from U.S. territory. The large firms had the capital to weather storms and hold out for long-term gains. CBEMA testified on their behalf at Washington hearings on the Brazil case in October 1985, and strongly advised against trying to change the Brazilian law itself. Instead, CBEMA wanted negotiations to prevent the market reserve from being extended to products not yet restricted, to improve the way the law was implemented, and to assure that the program would be phased out eventually.[15] Otherwise this group sought, if anything, to restrain the Reagan Administration, not to whip it into fiercer attacks. CBEMA avoided contact with the press on this issue.

Some companies other than the largest were in different positions with respect to Brazil. Some were not inside but wanted to get in. Others, like Tektronix, had been in Brazil and then had been shut out. Still others, such as many in the much larger American Electronics Association (AEA), had no stake there, did not expect to have one, and did not know Brazil. Some of these paid no attention, while others wanted to set a global example. The AEA, representing some 2,800 companies in electronics defined more broadly, had been somewhat more aggressive than CBEMA. For instance, in August 1985 the AEA had urged the Administration to strip ten countries, including Brazil, of their zero-duty treatment under the Generalized System of Preferences unless they indicated a willingness to halt violations of intellectual property rights at home. After Reagan launched his 301 initiative, however, the AEA, like CBEMA, called for mutually beneficial negotiations to improve Brazilian informatics policies, at the industry-to-industry level as well as between the governments.

Unity on Feedgrains

In early 1986, in contrast, EC enlargement and its context unified American feedgrain producers in furious protest. Corn (maize) farmers, the primary affected group, are not a multinational industry with overseas investments that could become hostages, nor did they depend on exports to the same extent as some commodity sectors. While about two-thirds of U.S. wheat and cotton was exported, between 60 and 70 percent of the corn crop was sold at home. Feedgrains too would suffer in a major international political conflict, but not quite to the same potential extent as the more extended multinationals. U.S. farmers were already suffering through a painful period of declining exports and declining income. Corn exports from the U.S. to the EC-12 had already plummeted from 14.2 million tons in 1982 to 6.0 million tons in 1985, before Spanish and Portuguese accession and the new barriers. The Iberian countries nevertheless remained the third-largest export market in the world. To U.S. grain farmers, this was yet another blow in a long history of unfair European agricultural policies.

Three weeks after the enlargement treaty took effect, major elements of the broad U.S. farm lobby joined forces with the feedgrains group to urge President Reagan to take immediate action, "to respond promptly and forcefully . . . to gain full compensation; . . . lack of firmness now would encourage a greater surplus of EC grain production and might well lead to more sweeping trade restrictions of this type in the future."[16] On April 17 the U.S. Senate passed a concurrent resolution urging the President to retaliate in the absence of prompt and complete compensation, notwithstanding the EC threat of counter-retaliation.

No constituents, least of all beneficiaries of the U.S. threat, took any known actions to undercut Reagan's credibility in this case, to put it mildly. The four associations representing all the affected producers of corn, barley, and grain sorghum unified their lobbying positions throughout this negotiation by speaking through a trade policy coordinating committee. Far from restraining the Administration, they pressed it repeatedly to raise its price for peace. The producers wanted Washington to demand that the EC agree to eliminate its own subsidies on exports, which it used to move its surpluses into third markets, where they could displace other U.S. exports.[17] This demand would have been far more difficult for the EC to accept than even breaching the new treaty by importing a guaranteed quota of corn corresponding to Spanish and Portuguese imports before accession, which is what Washington did demand. The U.S. growers feared that any recovery they achieved through such a quota would be offset immediately by increased EC subsidized competition in third markets (which did occur later, to some extent). A delegation of American farm leaders traveled to Europe during the summer to deliver their message in person to farm and government leaders there, further demonstrating American unity and firmness.

They maintained fierce pressure on the Administration right down to the wire, attempting to convince officials that compromise did not fall in the win-set. In early July, Brussels and Washington reached a temporary "truce" extending the time for negotiation until December 31. In return, Yeutter achieved special EC agreement to import U.S. feedgrains for six months, though at levels well below the compensation he had been demanding. For his American constituents, this truce was "a bitter pill to swallow."[18] In the fall the growers increased their demands, calling on Washington to hold hostage the possibility of a GATT agreement covering all agriculture in the Uruguay Round until the EC paid corn compensation.[19] In December the Feed Grains Council lectured American negotiators again quite explicitly:

> Our membership has clearly indicated that the feedgrains sector is willing to face the possible consequence of EC counter-retaliation. What they are not willing to face is anything less than full compensation for the Spanish market, or a lack of resolve by our government if such compensation cannot be achieved. . . . The time has come to draw the line and take a strong stand against the unfair trading practices of the European Community. Any further delay in the settlement of this dispute is totally unacceptable.[20]

When asked whether other U.S. interests, especially those facing possible counter-retaliation, pressed for accommodation, one American negotiator replied:

> Sure, we heard from them. We got a few letters saying they were concerned about it, but they were not beating our door down. It was not heavy-duty political pressure. The corn gluten feed people [targeted by Brussels] have their own zero [duty] binding in the EC. They know that if they want us to go to bat for them, they have to play along sometimes when we're working for somebody else. We did hear a lot from the import interests—representing the French products, Belgian endive, and so forth.

These relatively quiet, routine efforts were no match for the corn grow-ers, and not comparable to the computer multinationals in the Brazil case, who were themselves to be beneficiaries of the threat.

Subsequent interviews with Brazilian and European negotiators reveal a significant difference in American threat credibility. One official in Brasília, for example, asked whether retaliation had been expected actu-ally to occur, replied:

> We had mixed expectations in Brazil; some people said they did, others that they didn't. Those who were opposed to having negotiations in the first place said they did not expect retaliation, and so forth.[21]

No mix was found in Europe. No European official consulted in Brus-sels, Paris, London, or Washington reported thinking that the U.S. threat against the EC had been a bluff; all said they had taken it quite seriously indeed. A participating EC Commission official replied: "I think every-one was pretty much convinced that they would do it." Two emphasized that the U.S. had done it before, referring to sanctions the previous year in the citrus/pasta dispute. A French official, when asked what had convinced him that the U.S. would carry through, replied that he had visited several different agencies in Washington, which often express different views on the same issue. This time he had heard the same complaint about Spanish accession in the same terms, even from the Department of Commerce. "It was very clear that a very powerful lobby was working the agencies on this issue."[22]

In sum, the U.S. threat was less credible in Brazil than in Brussels. The difference was partly due to the tactics employed, and these in turn reflected different Level II conditions in the threatening country. In the informatics case, no constituents had been pressing for a shift to open coercion, the putative beneficiaries' preferences were divided, and major firms took steps that undermined Reagan's credibility. In the feedgrains case, the most directly affected groups demanded an even tougher line than their government would accept, and domestic opposition to imple-menting the threat was weak. Even though the U.S. capacity to hurt Brazil was far greater, the likelihood that this capacity would be used seemed lower on balance, undermining compliance.

THE STRUCTURE OF INTERESTS AND REVERBERATION IN BRAZIL AND EUROPE

A second major reason for the contrast in negotiating processes and outcomes is found at Level II in the targets. Initially, the overt American threats evoked political pressures hostile to the U.S. position inside both Brazil and the EC: Washington created negative reverberation abroad.

This may have initially reduced the win-set in each case by undermining support for any agreement with the Americans on this issue. Almost immediately in Europe, however, a constituency for concessions also began to express itself, cautiously at first, but eventually overpowering the European hard-liners and contributing to the earlier settlement and an outcome with greater gain for the U.S. side. The U.S. threat convinced major actors that their alternative to agreement with the United States was much worse than they had thought at the beginning of 1986. Positive reverberation for the U.S. position was longer in coming and relatively weaker inside Brazilian politics, though it probably did have some effect there as well.

Stronger Forces for Concessions in Europe

In the EC, internal pressures for concessions eventually proved to be greater than those for standing fast. The entire EC did consistently defend the enlargement decision as proper under the GATT, and all, including Thatcher's Britain, denounced Washington's "Ramboism." Once Washington had convincingly demonstrated a willingness to go to trade war over the issue, however, France became largely isolated in the hardline position. Though Bonn and London felt Washington was in the wrong, and sympathized with the French farmers, they were far from prepared to suffer a trade war with America over the issue.

The initial reaction to Reagan's harsh ultimatum was equally negative. On April 9 the EC Commission approved a list of U.S. farm products for counter-retaliation. Commissioner for External Affairs Willy de Clerq told U.S. journalists in Brussels, "We do not like Rambo-style diplomacy. There is no reason to confront us with deadlines, with ultimatums." Professing a desire to settle the issue amicably under GATT rules, he cautioned: "But I must underline our firm determination to defend the legitimate interests of the EC." Counter-retaliation would follow any U.S. measures "in complete symmetry."[23] In response to U.S. measures concerning Spain, the EC wheeled out three of the biggest cannons it had: counter-threats to restrict U.S. exports of corn-gluten feed, wheat, and rice.

Already in the first two weeks, however, differences among the most powerful EC member states became visible. French Minister for Agriculture Francois Guillaume described the American demands as "completely unacceptable,"[24] and demanded that Brussels not cave in. West German Economics Minister Martin Bangemann warned, however, that "an escalation of trade restrictions" could "spill over into the industrial area with unforeseeable consequences for growth and employment. . . . The Community should not take part in verbal muscle-flexing, but should rather make unmistakably clear its readiness to negotiate and its interest in a settlement."[25] When the EC Council met on April 21 to approve the Commission proposals, the French and Portuguese governments supported the Commission's approach without reservation, but they were the only states to be so enthusiastic. West Germany, Denmark, and the Netherlands were noticeably reticent about counterthreats.[26]

Understanding the European responses requires a brief investigation of the structure of economic and political interests there. The sector with the most to lose from compliance with Reagan's demand was French maize growers. France was the largest EC maize-producing country—growing nearly half the EC-12 crop in 1984–85—and the only one producing a surplus relative to domestic consumption.

During the mid-1980s European farmers, like their American counterparts, were suffering a painful decline in real income, despite the CAP. In 1985 agricultural real income dropped to its lowest point in fifteen years. French cereals growers suffered a 20 percent shrinkage in net revenue that year, as costs rose while output prices in fact slid.[27] Urgent pleas for help were mounting on the desks of national parliamentarians and EC officials in Brussels, just as in Washington. French farmers had a particular interest in the Spanish maize market. Enlargement would bring increased competition in other products such as fruits and vegetables, and gains for maize exports had been a crucial offset in earning their political support for enlargement itself.

On the other hand, while only one of the Community's three most powerful states was a maize exporter, West Germany and the U.K. were both maize importers. They stood to lose virtually nothing—in economic terms—from compliance. At the same time, the sudden, huge Reagan threat raised the cost of standing firm for them as well as for France. The USTR carefully selected retaliation items that would hit most EC member states, while concentrating roughly half the total burden on France. White wine, one of the EC's leading exports to the U.S., with sales valued at 204 million dollars in 1985, came from France, Germany, and Italy. Brandy and cognac were major French exports, and their producers and distributors were known to be well organized politically. Cheese was for France and the Netherlands, gin and whiskey for Britain and Ireland; olives would cover all the Mediterranean countries. This product list soon led wags to dub the dispute "the yuppie war."

It is true that while London and Bonn faced little national economic cost from accepting the U.S. demand, they did face broader costs. The enlargement treaty had been ratified by all twelve parliaments and was in effect. Furthermore, the American threat directly challenged the fundamental EC legal and negotiating position on enlargements. The EC had long interpreted the GATT as requiring parties forming a customs union to compensate third parties only if those nations' interests are damaged on the whole, not on a product-by-product basis. EC "debits" on cereals are offset by "credits earned" by third countries on other products. Spanish and Portuguese industrial protection was quite high, and Brussels showed that, after accession was completed, the average level of protection—combining industrial and agricultural sectors—would clearly be lower in both countries, not higher. London and Bonn agreed that the U.S. was already receiving enough compensation for feedgrains via other products. Their joint bargaining reputation for firmness would suffer if they yielded in this instance, perhaps encouraging challenges in others. These governments shared their general commitment to EC institutions and mutual support, for broad political reasons. Still, the heavy and credible U.S. threat soon placed great strain on these common political interests.

Later asked why trade war had not broken out in July, one Commission negotiator replied:

> From the U.S. side, the EC was beginning to give up on its principle that we did not owe any compensation. For the European side, once we realized that there was a risk of a major trade war and possible strains on cohesion in the Community—our tendencies were far from unanimous—we saw that probably we would not have successfully resisted a trade war. It was decided that it would be better to drop something on the table, something limited, that would not prejudge our position later, but would allow time for people to realize that such a thing was a possibility. . . .
>
> The problem of cohesion would arise because decisions have to be ratified by the member states in the 113 Committee. That committee makes decisions by a qualified majority. On a serious issue like 24:6 [this issue], we realized that we might not get one. There would be nothing more serious for Community cohesion than having the member states refuse to ratify an agreement the Commission had negotiated.

These negotiations continued to be tense and difficult, with grain producers on both sides of the Atlantic maintaining unrelenting pressure. While both negotiating teams hailed the July interim settlement, farmers on each side angrily blasted their representatives for weakness. On the Fourth of July, the French Association of Maize Producers (AGPM), joined by other French farm groups, mounted vocal demonstrations in Paris and dumped two tons of maize onto the streets in protest. They demanded to know why they should be the only Europeans to pay for enlargement. They called the settlement "a veritable Munich."[28] The EC-wide farm lobby supported them with its own denunciations. Rumors had it that the French government yielded to this setback only after the EC had agreed to side-payments in the form of restitutions to finance exports of French maize that otherwise would have been sold in Spain.[29]

Meanwhile, other European special interests likely to be hurt by a trade war also made their voices heard, though usually behind closed doors. In France,when cognac producers made their quiet contacts, the government assured them that in the end the Americans would not go through with their threats.[30] A Washington policy-maker saw signs of greater concern. "The British, the gin people and so forth, were working frantically to try to head off U.S. retaliation."[31] According to a Brussels participant, "some of the biggest pressures on the Commission to reach a settlement came from the industrial people, people like Volkswagen and whiskey, who were very afraid of a trade war." Automobiles were not on the American retaliation list, but a large EC-U.S. trade war could have had serious long-term consequences for the world trading system. Industrialists might also have been anticipating and countering pressure on Brussels from French farmers to offer to take more industrial imports as substitutes for maize.

Direct lobbying by industry groups is not as common in Brussels as in Washington; national governments are the key actors. In this case, the German government pressed hard for a settlement. A well-placed participant reports that the French government's hard-line position against any permanent concessions softened significantly in October 1986. They "wanted to avoid a major break with Germany." The Germans had worked quite closely with the French at Punta del Este, supporting French demands concerning the agenda of the new Uruguay Round. The French were grateful, and "a trade war with the United States would have upset the Germans very much." The Chirac government had made close ties with West Germany a central policy plank. On this analysis, Paris eventually accepted a maize setback in recognition of Bonn's compensation in the broader GATT negotiations, and in order to protect that support for the future.

As the December deadline approached, the two sides' moves began hinting at a serious search for agreement, but they failed to bridge the wide gap between them. The U.S. reduced its claim for losses in Spain from an estimated 600 to 400 million dollars. The EC offered a proposal guaranteeing that Spain would import 1.6 million tons of maize and sorghum per year for four years, but the U.S. would not accept less than 4.4 million tons for an indefinite period.

On December 30, President Reagan ordered retaliatory 200 percent duties on about 400 million dollars' worth of European brandy, white wine, gin, cheeses, olives, and other goods. French brandy and wine would account for 250 million dollars of the total. At the same time, it was noted that hearings would be held on the final product list, and that the penalties would not take effect until the end of January, thus actually providing still more time for bargaining. The EC repeated that it would impose counter-measures if the U.S. struck.[32]

The two sides reached a final settlement on January 29, 1987, after a classic all-night haggle, and after Washington agreed for the first time to accept a small amount of its compensation in industrial sectors. The outcome, while falling short of initial American goals, was a major setback from the EC's status quo and its legal principle. The EC agreed to cancel its new quota reserving 15 percent of Portugal's market for EC suppliers. More important, the EC guaranteed that Spain would import at least 2 million metric tons of maize and 300,000 tons of sorghum from third parties each year for the next four years. U.S. negotiators valued the European concessions at about 400 million dollars per year, and suspended their retaliatory measures. French maize growers received export-subsidy side-payments, and (for several reasons) European maize exports subsequently increased.

One European participant analyzed this outcome as follows:

> Once the EC realized that they had to pay a price for enlargement, then it came down to an internal struggle over who was going to pay. This is always the way it is in the EC. At the outset, the government of France took the position, "to hell with the United States." But this was not realistic. France was the only country that had a problem. The British and the Germans were not going to be willing to go to a trade war with the United States on behalf of French maize. Politically, it was not possible to build up a big enough coalition in Europe to support this hard-line view.[33]

Weaker Forces for Concessions in Brazil

In Brazil, in contrast, the American threat evoked Level II political pressures for standing fast that clearly exceeded those for making concessions. This extreme imbalance held for many months until Washington changed its signals, and even then the imbalance was not reversed.

As it happened, President Reagan chose Brazil's Independence Day for his slap, and the immediate reverberations ranged from cold outrage to hot fury. Arthur Virgilio, majority whip in the Brazilian Chamber of Deputies, demanded indignantly, "Who does Reagan think he is, threatening us?" He declared, "The fight for the market reserve is as important today as was the struggle for state control over oil some years ago." Senator Severo Gomes, a former Minister of Commerce and Industry, denounced Reagan's statements, saying "They are not typical of any president, unless he [Reagan] considers us his lackeys." Brazilians felt the message was, "It's okay for us to produce shoes, but high-tech is for grown-ups."[34]

The executive secretary of the Brazilian computer industry association

ABICOMP, noting that Brazil accounted for only 1 percent of the world computer market, declared, "It is ridiculous to suggest that the American industry is harmed because it is not exporting computers to Brazil." The United States had a huge surplus, not a deficit, in its informatics trade with Brazil. Foreign firms' sales in Brazil had been rising smartly despite the market-reserve policy, which did not restrict sales of mainframes and their software, only lesser technologies. One minister threatened that if the United States struck, Brazil could respond by opening its market to Japanese automobiles.[35] The informatics dispute became front-page news in Brazil for months, the biggest problem in relations with the United States in a decade. At the outset, virtually no voices calling for concessions were heard publicly.

Facing this severe imbalance in the internal political costs of making concessions and holding firm, it is not surprising that Brazilian President Sarney studiously avoided any step that could be seen as bending to foreign pressure.[36] In fact, Brasília essentially refused to negotiate with Washington bilaterally over this issue for eight months. Its basic position was that its market reserve was a typical domestic measure to promote an infant industry, and as such was not inconsistent with the GATT.

Even prior to the American demarche, the informatics program had enjoyed unusually broad political support in Brazil, at least on the surface. The economic constituency benefiting most directly from the status quo consisted of the computer hardware and software producing firms that had started their businesses under the umbrella of the *reserva de mercado*. The government had launched the program in the early 1970s with the goal of developing a national informatics capability independent of foreign firms. During the 1960s virtually all Brazil's informatics technology came from abroad, in the form of small and medium-sized mainframe computers, 80 percent of them from IBM.

The market-reserve plan called for national production of the more modest technologies, learning by doing, and expansion up the technical scale to displace foreign firms from more advanced products as Brazil developed the capacity to do so. This implied reliance on foreign firms for the higher end of the scale, blocking them out of the lower end, and maintaining the flexibility to move the dividing point upward. Thus the tools of the program included state investment in a joint venture to produce the country's first minicomputer in the early 1970s, bans on imports of mini- and microcomputers in the mid-1970s, and other measures.

Some of the nation's largest bank conglomerates invested in informatics production, establishing a half-dozen large firms to produce equipment for automating banks and supermarkets as well as a wide range of other computer components and end-products. Meanwhile, the invention of the personal computer spawned many smaller firms as well.

By 1983, 118 new companies were producing clones of the IBM and Apple personal computers. Overall, foreign firms' market share eroded during the 1979 to 1986 period from 77 percent to 49 percent. Their own sales increased 130 percent over the seven years—but in the protected sphere, national firms' revenues were multiplying by 700 percent.[37] Thus by 1985 producers in Brazil were structured in three wings: the multinational subsidiaries, who generally chafed against the program's restraints and intrusions; relatively large Brazilian firms benefiting from but probably having less, or less permanent, need for the program; and the small firms, many of which would not have survived without it. The Brazilian computer market was rated eighth largest in the world, and was growing rapidly.

The status quo in Brazil was also supported by significant political constituencies, political actors who had identified their interests with it. The military services, especially the Navy, had led initiation of the program, seeking to free themselves from dependence on foreign countries for intelligence and weapon-system controls. They created a special bureaucracy, the *Secretaria Especial de Informática* (SEI), or Special Informatics Agency, under the authority of the National Security Council, to make the regulatory decision affecting foreign and national producers.

In 1984, as the nation was preparing to return to democratic institutions, the outgoing military government sought to make the program permanent and more legitimate by having the Congress approve it by statute. During this process, some sectors of Brazilian business did criticize SEI and its program for excessive regulation. In April the political right introduced its own bill—to abrogate the market reserve, dismantle SEI, and replace both with a system of tariffs and joint ventures with foreign firms.

The largest opposition political party, however, the Brazilian Democratic Movement Party (PMDB), introduced several bills of its own to strengthen the market reserve. During the elections, the victorious PMDB presidential candidate, Tancredo Neves, and his running mate José Sarney, strongly endorsed it. The Chamber of Deputies passed a compromise bill extending the program until 1992 by a near-unanimous vote of 378 to 1. In short, the program Reagan chose to attack enjoyed broad political support spanning elements of both the military and the left.

Despite this Level II imbalance, the tone of the bilateral dispute changed somewhat after May 1986, when the superpower, not the developing country, pulled back. The U.S. State Department used an official visit to Brasília to "cool things off," as one diplomat put it. Deputy Secretary of State John Whitehead signaled that Washington would not attempt to change the informatics law; its objection was with the arbitrary way in which SEI interpreted it. He also said the United States was no longer threatening sanctions or imposing deadlines. Brazilian leaders regarded these statements as providing some room for maneuver, and the government agreed to begin negotiations.[38]

By this time, a few Level II constituents in Brazil were again beginning to voice preferences for change in the same direction sought by Washington. Most major industries not involved in computer production were potential customers whose self-interest, at least viewed over the short term, presumably meant paying the lowest possible price for the best technology available worldwide. In addition, SEI had such broad regulatory discretion that its restrictions and delays impeded any producer who sought to import any machine or part containing a digital component, as well as others seeking to form joint ventures with foreign firms. For many industries, however, informatics costs may not have amounted to a large share of total costs.

Economic interests in informatics liberalization were still represented by political actors, including the more conservative national political party, but this party had declined badly after 1984. The Federation of Industry of the State of São Paulo, however, remained a large and influential standing organization available to help crystallize and articulate their policy preferences.

The week Whitehead was in Brasília, the independent magazine *Veja,* comparable to *Time,* charged that SEI was multiplying its powers beyond the law and invading areas that did not belong to it. Every manufacturing project in this country touching electronics in any way was forced to pass through the hands of only 70 persons to get approval, the journal said. One industrialist complained that he had had to travel to Brasília at least twelve times to get permission to import a machine for frying potatoes; it incorporated a microprocessor to regulate oil temperature. Eugenio Staub—the leading Brazilian producer of audio components, a maker of microcomputers, and a member of CONIN, a new official council established to supervise the informatics program—said he did not see problems with letting foreign firms play a larger role within the reserved market: "Competition is also part of the market system." The magazine also questioned the Foreign Minister's initial stand that "there is nothing to negotiate." "This denies the very essence of diplomacy," contended *Veja.* The article's title described Brasília's decision to talk to Washington as a "return to the real world."

The threat of sanctions had also implicated export industries. The computer industry itself did not export to the United States and thus was not subject to American import barriers. It did rely heavily, however, on imports of U.S. components, the flow of which could in principle be interrupted. The largest Brazilian export products destined for the U.S.

market were shoes, coffee, orange juice, motor fuel, vehicle engines and other automobile components, sugar, tin, ethyl alcohol, shellfish, and steel products. Any of those producers, and perhaps others, could in principle suffer under a no-agreement outcome, but uncertainty due to Washington's ambiguity may have reduced pressure for accommodation from them. Some export interests did begin calling on the government to soften its position. During the Brazilian winter, Ozires Silva, the president of Petrobras and former chairman of Embraer, the state enterprise exporting small aircraft to the U.S., spoke publicly in favor of a negotiated settlement. Silva reportedly met in private with President Sarney several times to express these concerns.

During this period, elements within the Brazilian government also began to question the status quo. The Foreign Minister publicly criticized SEI, whose most vociferous official opponents were the ministers of Commerce and of Communications. They too advocated a more flexible negotiating posture. The Ministry of Commerce and Industry was concerned about damage to export industries from retaliation, and about long-term costs to informatics-user industries. Large companies in the telecommunications sector were having difficulties with SEI regulators. Thus counter-pressures had begun to appear, but they remained far weaker than those of informatics defenders.

When the Reagan Administration had nearly reached its deadline of September 1986, the provisional outcome was virtually no different from the status quo. During a meeting in August, the Brazilian delegation indicated a willingness to undertake some measures consistent with the law which were sought by Brazilian constituents, and which Washington could describe as concessions back home. These included trimming SEI's wings to the extent of issuing a list of products that were outside its authority at that time. They promised to set up a committee to investigate complaints from foreign investors, and reported that the Brazilian government was preparing a bill that would provide copyright protection to software. None of these measures was yet in place, however, and none guaranteed measurable commercial gain to U.S. firms. President Reagan decided to move the deadline for decision to December 31, 1986. At the end of twelve months, superpower coercion had changed very little in Brazil, in sharp contrast to the EC case.

U.S. THREAT CREDIBILITY AND INFORMATICS, ROUND TWO

The subsequent phase of this informatics case provides an interesting theoretical variation that further confirms the first proposition. During the second year of the dispute, the U.S. electronics and software industry came together in favor of retaliation for the first time. As a result, the

U.S. government's credibility increased, and Brasília made its only substantial concession.

In late 1986, Brazilian nationalists prevailed over their more internationalist rivals in the drafting of key provisions in the government's new software bill. The bill would not have extended the existing copyright law for literary works to software, but instead would have created a sui generis software protection regime. Protection against piracy would have been guaranteed for a 25-year period, to foreign as well as Brazilian software. However, the bill also codified several restrictions that would have prevented many foreign programs from entering Brazil legally in the first place. It authorized SEI to deny a license whenever a "functionally equivalent" Brazilian program could be found. That is, the bill codified the market reserve for software as well as hardware, which had always been the intention of Brazilian nationalists and a red flag for U.S. negotiators. The growing market for personal computer software could be completely closed to foreign inventors. In some cases, foreign authors would be required to divulge the program's secret "source code" when they transferred technology into Brazil.

Ironically, this internal victory by the Brazilian nationalists subsequently backfired against them, indirectly via U.S. internal politics. The bill alarmed American firms, including IBM, and it unified them politically. As they were studying the bill, the December Reagan deadline approached. The Administration decided to postpone retaliation again and continue the negotiation. Victory was declared with respect to two major issues, but regarding software protection and foreign investment regulation the President directed a further "final effort," and set July 1, 1987, as yet another deadline for a retaliation decision.

CBEMA testified in March 1987 that the results overall were "disappointing," saying there had been no acceptable movement on software protection or investment regulation. Regarding software, the United States had managed to push other countries into joining a worldwide trend toward a standardized approach under international copyright norms. Brazil was a major holdout, planning on a sui generis approach that fell short of international norms. In fact, CBEMA's president observed:

> If the proposed software legislation goes through as currently drafted, we would be worse off than we were at the opening of the 301 investigation, because there is a judicial basis for the interpretation of existing law such that computer software is protected under the copyright law. Failure to satisfactorily resolve this issue would, I fear, send a signal to the rest of the world that we are not really serious either about protecting such intellectual property as copyright software under the international copyright regime, or about taking action against unfair trade practices.[39]

The position of the American Electronics Association also hardened. The AEA now laid down four minimum objectives for the last three months of negotiations. If sufficient progress were not made on these points before July, "we believe it would then be appropriate for the Administration to take the next step in the process of implementing the President's October decision."[40]

In May the AEA, CBEMA, and two other industry associations met with the Brazilian Ambassador in Washington to communicate their vigorous opposition openly and directly, something they had been quite reluctant to do. This was the first time in this dispute that U.S. computer and software companies had mounted a joint policy protest to the Brazilian government. They gave the Ambassador a three-page memorandum listing amendments to the software bill that would meet their minimum concerns and "avert escalation." They made it clear that U.S. companies, including those firms with investment stakes in Brazil, were all agreed for the first time to support retaliation if these terms were not met. The Ambassador scheduled an immediate personal meeting with President Sarney to convey what he had heard.[41]

At the end of May, the Secretary General of SEI, a Foreign Ministry diplomat, a U.S. Embassy officer, and the U.S. Commerce Department's specialist on copyright met in absolute secrecy in Brasília to discuss foreign suggestions for changing the bill under consideration in the Congress. The Brazilians agreed to a significant concession, changing Articles II and IV on copyright. Rather than a sui generis regime, the modified bill would extend the prevailing intellectual property law to software. Brazil continued, however, to reject compromise on the marketing regulations that would discriminate against imports. The Brazilians regarded this bill as implementing the 1984 law with respect to software, and insisted the market reserve principle was untouchable. Also, the bill would still require that owners divulge their source codes in any cases of technology transfer. The Brazilian officials then presented what were described as mere technical adjustments to the PMDB majority leader in Congress for inclusion in the final bill. In fact, this was an international concession, a change in policy that would not have been undertaken without U.S. pressure.

In Washington, the cabinet's Economic Policy Council was united in a decision to retaliate at last, if at least one house of Brazil's Congress did not pass even this modified software bill.[42] This consensus included the secretaries of State and Treasury—notwithstanding pending talks on debt problems. Brazilian counter-threats, and concerns over the negative reverberations in Brazilian politics.

The lower house of the Brazilian Congress passed the bill on June 24. It would still need approval in the Senate in order to take effect. In

June, SEI also announced several decisions on investment modernization projects and piracy complaints that were favorable to U.S. firms. The U.S. companies told the Reagan Administration that they were not in favor of retaliation, in these circumstances, but also not satisfied with this partial action. On June 30 President Reagan announced that he was suspending the part of the investigation concerned with intellectual property protection. The three parts suspended so far would remain suspended until terminated or reopened. He directed Yeutter to continue the investigation of investment problems, but did not set any new deadline. Meanwhile, Yeutter's staff were raising glasses of champagne to celebrate what they hoped had been the last act of their long-running drama.

During Brazilian Round Two, the second independent variable—the distribution of internal costs within the target nation—may also have shifted somewhat at the expense of the hard-liners. While Brazilian interest groups that bore costs of SEI regulations had expressed some criticism of the informatics program prior to September 1985, the highly charged political atmosphere of Round One seemed to intimidate them for some months. The May 1986 article in *Veja,* however, testified to a spreading public awareness of problems with the status quo at home. During Round Two, representatives of the U.S. and Brazilian electronics industries met together in private at Harvard University, and these meetings might have increased the Brazilians' sensitivity to the benefits they themselves would reap from reducing SEI's regulations. In late 1986, the São Paulo Federation of Industries presented a paper to the government proposing changes in the program. Export industries began to lobby in favor of flexibility with the Americans in order to avert a trade war. The Brazilian Exporters Association had formed a "Group of Thirty," representing the country's largest exporting firms, in response to the widening range of political problems facing Brazil's exports. These leading executives also traveled to Washington more than once during this extended dispute.

Nevertheless, any shift in President Sarney's internal political costs was only a matter of degree. Informatics producers and sympathetic bureaucrats did not relax their public campaign to stiffen the government's back. Accordingly, the Brazilian concession of mid-1987 was only a partial move, and was not acknowledged publicly as a concession to the United States at all.

In summary, the contrasts between the European and Brazilian disputes and between the two Brazil phases illustrate the two hypotheses. The greater the internal opposition to carrying out a threat within the threatening nation itself, the lower the credibility, and the less likely the target capital will be to comply. Within the target nation, the greater the net internal political cost of compliance for the executive, relative to net internal political cost of no-agreement, the less likely the target government will be to accept agreement on the terms demanded.

OTHER VARIABLES IN TWO-LEVEL NEGOTIATIONS

Transnational Links or Alignments

Several other analytical questions and ideas discussed in this volume are also raised here, but several seem to shed less light on these cases than others. First, for example, it might be supposed that transnational investment by interested parties is a restraining condition on intergovernmental conflict and a force favorable to accommodation in general. We have seen that a major difference between the informatics and enlargement cases is that, in the first, putative beneficiaries of the coercion were transnational enterprises having major investments in the target country, while the beneficiaries in the enlargement case were not exposed to counter-retaliation in this way. But in 1987 the same computer firms united behind a coercive threat, which produced the only significant Brazilian concession in this negotiation. We also know of other cases in which multinationals have sought the intervention of their home governments to fight local authorities. Whether multinationals' behavior is united or divided is important for outcomes, and this case illustrates that their unity and division are subject to political influence.

In the informatics case, some of the American multinationals and some large Brazilian firms were represented on a standing private-sector Brazil-U.S. Business Council. Members of this transnational association favored some changes in the Brazilian program, and attempted to act as a back channel of communication between the two governments during the dispute. President Sarney, for example, used this channel at one point to communicate unofficially that his administration would not seek to extend the market reserve beyond 1992. This position was, however, made official in 1986, and in any case it did not amount to a major concession, since it required no change from current policy and also would not constrain the Brazilian Congress in the future. American executives might have used this Business Council channel to increase sympathy for the U.S. government position in Brazil, but it is difficult to show that official moves would have been different without this effort. Little evidence has been found of U.S. multinational enterprises weighing into the enlargement dispute.

More generally, transnational links between societies transmit information directly in each direction, providing alternatives to official channels. Thus such links should reduce the chance that states will succeed with bluffs, with threats that could not win ratification in the threatening country. In both these episodes, firms and organizations on one side monitored developments on the other side, including evidence bearing on threat credibility. Thus, for example, not only did the Brazilian Embassy and visiting government delegations report on internal conditions in Washington, but the private Brazilian computer lobby retained its own representation there, a firm including a former USTR leader and a former U.S. Ambassador to Brazil. With such well-connected transnational allies, the targets of coercion were even better positioned to assess the likelihood that the threat would be carried out. In the absence of transnational links, the parties would have relied only on their embassies—which however, in these cases, were well informed themselves.

Issue Linkage

All sides were careful to isolate both these disputes from other issue areas. In neither conflict did either official negotiator link his demands or proposals to developments in the Uruguay Round of trade negotiations or to security arrangements. Neither the American nor the Brazilian government explicitly linked its position on informatics with concurrent debt negotiations.

Clearly, the American threats did link the computer issues with Brazilian export trade, and feedgrains with European exports, in an effort to stimulate internal pressures abroad for concessions. This tactical linkage did elicit such pressures strongly in Europe, where intended target industries were named, and to a lesser extent in Brazil, where they were not identified explicitly. It is also clear that U.S. open coercion simultaneously fueled political opposition to any change in both cases.

In Brazil (but not in Europe), there were constituents who sought policy change (at least tighter constraints on SEI) for their own reasons, and it might be supposed that this international linkage was synergistic, in the sense of helping Brazilian informatics users and internationalists achieve changes they could not have accomplished otherwise. But the program did not change much, and several Brazilian officials insist that internal pressures alone would probably have led to somewhat tighter constraints on SEI, perhaps a year or so later than was the case.

With commercial sanctions, a further sense of product or issue linkage is entailed. If the threat had been implemented and European or Brazilian exports to the United States had been curtailed, then the U.S. industries relying on this trade would have been inconvenienced, or worse. How much these prospective or actual losses would affect negotiators' behavior depends on the relative importance of these losses to the user industries or consumers, and on how well organized these groups are for influencing international negotiations. In the United States, there was some mild pressure for caution in the feedgrains case. This "boomerang" effect was potentially greater in the Brazil case; USTR was concerned enough about users of some of the largest Brazilian exports to avoid those items in the target planning.

In cooperative bargaining, such as at the 1978 Bonn Summit, positive issue linkage—that is, offering a contingent exchange of value—often facilitates agreement that benefits both sides, in some cases by means of synergy, as in that 1978 case. It was the absence of such tactics that led to the selection of these two episodes of coercive bargaining—but if such tactics had been used here as well, agreement might have been reached with less friction and cost, though perhaps with less U.S. export gain in the EC case.

Ratification Rules and Win-Sets

Rules regulating whether and how a Level I agreement must be ratified at Level II may shape the country's win-set, and hence the outcome at Level I. Each of these international deals did have to be ratified, formally in Europe and informally in Brazil, but neither case presents a ratification failure, as with many IMF stabilization agreements, for example.

The relevant institutions might also shape the content of ratified agreements, however. The most prominent institutional difference here is that target B was a nation-state in one case and the supranational European Community in the other. If one assumed that Brussels leaders have less autonomy from member governments than Brazil's President has from his constituency, then one might expect the EC negotiator to be in a stronger position vis-à-vis the United States, improving its international bargaining outcome relative to Brazil's.[43] In fact, however, it appears that Brazil's President and negotiator in this case were entangled by domestic political constraints as significant as those of the EC's leaders.

It is true that Brussels' autonomy is constrained. EC rules designate the Commission as the Community's agent dealing with third parties on matters relating to the Common Commercial Policy, as well as on certain other issues. Under the Treaty of Rome's Article 113, the Commission makes recommendations to the European Council, consisting of member-state delegates from Level II. The Council authorizes the Commission to open negotiations with third countries, and under Articles 114 and 228 the Council is empowered to conclude such agreements on behalf of the EC, acting by qualified majority. At the end of the Tokyo Round, the Council in fact twice rejected final deals presented to it by the Commission, forcing further external negotiations.[44] The Commission is also required to consult during the trade-negotiation process with a special advisory committee appointed by the Council, known as the 113

Committee. Thus EC institutions did give Level II players continual access to the process, as well as a veto over the outcome. The Council ratified and made binding the January 1987 settlement.[45]

In Brazil, any formal agreement with the United States to change the informatics law would have required analogous ratification by Brazil's Congress. Lesser but significant changes could have been accomplished without formal Congressional action, but such moves by President Sarney could have been overturned promptly by the Congress if he had failed to achieve substantial informal support. Moreover, this new President was in a particularly weak political position during this period. José Sarney had been elected Vice President on the coattails of the popular opposition leader Tancredo Neves, and Sarney had taken office as President only because Neves had died suddenly after the election but before assuming office. Sarney had only a narrow political base of his own and could not control Congress easily. Thus he and his negotiators had to keep a close eye on the effective political actors at Level II, in much the same way the EC Commission negotiators responded to the French, Germans, and Spaniards. President Sarney also maintained direct communication with Brazil's chief negotiator throughout the informatics dispute, and his comments reflected keen sensitivity to Brazilian political reactions to the negotiations.[46] In short, a significant difference between the two cases on this score is difficult to document, despite the institutional differences, and hence we are not able to conclude much with respect to this proposition.

Both the EC and the U.S. implemented their formal settlement as agreed. The informatics outcome is more ambiguous: no formal agreement was reached, but the events of June 1987 are best interpreted as a tacit agreement with modest scope and fragile foundations. Brazil narrowed SEI authority to some degree and agreed to change its software bill, and in return the U.S. suspended the software and other dimensions of its 301 investigation.

Subsequent events revealed the fragility. In September, SEI rejected a pending appeal by Microsoft Corporation to license its popular MS-DOS program for sale in Brazil through Brazilian companies. This was the U.S. firm's effort to displace the use of pirated copies with legal arrangements that would earn income. SEI's rationales for excluding MS-DOS were that a Brazilian firm was offering an equally good program and that prevailing law encouraged this sort of import barrier. North Americans, including the more cautious CBEMA, were uniformly outraged, since they had suspended the software investigation on the understanding that Brazil would now take or permit legal efforts to suppress piracy and that American firms would profit.

In fact, however, the June tacit agreement was too ambiguous to sustain a claim that this SEI rejection contradicted it. There is no evidence that the Brazilian government made any official promise, even secretly, to do more than enact the new software bill, which it did do later. SEI correctly pointed out that the new bill did not yet have legal force. This new uproar led to a fall 1987 decision by President Reagan to order retaliation against Brazil—which itself was not implemented, however, after Brazil made a fractional concession on the MS-DOS issue. Eventually the U.S. formally closed its 301 investigation.

Finally, one aspect of U.S. ratification rules had a direct bearing on threat credibility. When the President orders trade retaliation, hearings are held first to allow U.S. industries to object to the selection of particular products for the "hit list." Regularly, industries relying on those products do attempt to remove them from the list. The effect is to constrain the executive's ability to carry out effective sanctions or to threaten credibly, and over time to undermine a reputation for toughness. A different set of institutions, giving the executive authority to impose trade sanctions without consultations, would have heightened credibility in each of these disputes.

CONCLUSION

Why, then, did U.S. coercive attempts yield varying outcomes in these two cases—costly frustration on all sides in informatics, and more substantial concessions regarding feedgrains in Spain? From one angle, the U.S. negotiator's choice of strategy was clearly less adept in the former case. Washington chose to use overt threats at Level I in the absence of Level II conditions at home and abroad that are probably necessary for an openly coercive international strategy. The EC case matched the same strategy with the presence of those conditions, and the result was a shorter process and substantial commercial concessions, at least in the short run. In both cases, Reagan and Yeutter angered friends abroad, but with Brazil the Administration seemed to achieve the worst of both worlds. It announced an investigation of a politically popular program, suggesting hostility toward Brazil; issued an ultimatum on a national independence day; and yet did not go far enough to make its threat credible. If this study has any practical implications, at least one, certainly, is that inept coercion is to be avoided. Another implication is the importance of U.S. domestic solutions to U.S. international trade problems.

Did Washington blunder into this particular morass? Was it simply imperfect information, a failure to consult accurately with the interested industry before going ahead? Ignorance may have played a role in the case of some U.S. officials, but at least one participating Latin America specialist specifically advised against choosing the computer industry, precisely on the grounds that it was not as "winnable" as other issues on the agenda at the time.

Another part of the answer may come from the simultaneous Washington effort to influence the agenda of the coming multilateral Uruguay Round negotiations. The same officials who picked Brazilian informatics were also responsible for the latter. As one of them suggested, even failing in Brazil might have produced a gain in Geneva. By engaging in a bilateral conflict over the "new issues" Washington sought to add to the agenda—protection of intellectual property rights and high-technology industry—the United States communicated its seriousness outside the bilateral relationship. The 301 cases may have been seen as a way to give the rest of GATT a (negative) incentive to create new multilateral rules governing these issues; otherwise, the Americans will take matters into their own hands. If so, this case raises a question about the common theoretical argument that the presence of multilateral trade negotiations will act as a constraint on aggressive national policies, for fear of disrupting the regime.

Finally, this study suggests the value of broader investigation of its two main theoretical claims. In coercive distributive bargaining, if a substantial share of the constituents of threatening government A who stand to benefit from B's compliance nevertheless oppose implementing the threat, and if state B is aware of this internal opposition, the credibility of A's threat will be undermined, other things being equal, even when A has much greater power resources and B is highly vulnerable to them. Second, even when one reading of B's interests dictates complying, and even when the government executive prefers to do so, B will not do so if the executive faces greater internal political penalties from complying than from accepting no-agreement.

The author is grateful to the Ford Foundation, the Social Science Research Council, and the Pew Charitable Trusts for supporting work that contributed to this study. Discussions of previous drafts at the University of Southern California and at meetings of the Ford Foundation Project on Domestic-International Interactions contributed material improvements. In particular, David Baldwin, Peter Evans, Joanne Gowa, Harold Jacobson, Robert Jervis, Stephen Marks, Benjamin Moore, Robert Putnam, Ricardo Saur, and Richard Smoke read the paper and made helpful suggestions. Anne Dibble and Margit Matzinger-Tchakerian, co-authors of related works, have given permission to draw on those studies here. The author alone is responsible for any remaining weaknesses.

NOTES

1. A fuller discussion of coercion in international-relations theory would develop many other points and qualifications as well. For instance, some "realists," like Hans Morgenthau, caution against imprudent coercion.

2. Although bargaining theorists have discussed threat credibility for years, there seems to have been little systematic investigation of internal political conditions that affect it, especially on international economic issues, where internal divisions are particularly likely. See brief references in Thomas Schelling, *The Strategy of Conflict* (Cambridge, Mass.: Harvard University Press, 1960), pp. 22 and 28, and *Arms and Influence* (New Haven, Conn.: Yale University Press, 1966), p. 50, note 9. Of course many empirical studies cited in this book have included concern with some connection between international bargaining in general and domestic politics. Additionally, mention might be made of James Alt and Barry Eichengreen, "Parallel and Overlapping Games: Theory and an Application to the European Gas Trade," in John S. Odell and Thomas D. Willett, eds., *International Trade Policies: Gains from Exchange Between Economics and Political Science* (Ann Arbor: University of Michigan Press, 1990), pp. 75–104; John A. C. Conybeare, *Trade Wars* (New York: Columbia University Press, 1987); John S. Odell, "The Politics of Debt Relief: Official Creditors and Brazil, Ghana, and Chile," in Jonathan D. Aronson, ed., *Debt and the Less Developed Countries* (Denver: Westview Press, 1979), pp. 253–281; and Odell, "The Outcomes of International Trade Conflicts: The U.S. and South Korea, 1960–1981," *International Studies Quarterly* 28 (1985): 263–286. Barry Eichengreen suggests, in *Golden Fetters: The Gold Standard and the Great Depression, 1919–1939* (Oxford, Eng.: Oxford University Press, 1992), that the credibility of a promise, the government commitment to defend an exchange rate with monetary reserves, also depends on domestic political conditions.

3. This might be partly because implicit threats and anticipated consequences had been sufficient more often in the past.

4. Trade data from International Monetary Fund, *Direction of Trade Statistics Yearbook 1989*, and GDP data from United Nations, *Statistical Yearbook 1987*. Naturally, these are only broad measures of power potential, and thus convey only the general relationships that would underlie decisions.

5. Many other power dimensions might be explored as well. For instance, it might be supposed that the EC faced a greater external security threat than Brazil, and hence needed U.S. military protection to a greater extent, which should reduce the apparent power advantage by some degree. At the same time, however, the United States also needed NATO for its own security more than it needed Brazil, partly offsetting this apparent reduction.

6. For a full account of this episode and its background, see John Odell and Anne Dibble, *Brazilian Informatics and the United States: Defending Infant Industry Versus Opening Foreign Markets* (Los Angeles: University of Southern California Center for International Studies, 1988, distributed by Institute for the Study of Diplomacy, Georgetown University); Peter Evans, "State, Capital, and the Transformation of Dependence: The Brazilian Computer Case," *World Development* 14 (1986): 791–808, and "Declining Hegemony and Assertive Industrializa-

tion: U.S.-Brazil Conflicts in the Computer Industry," *International Organization* 43 (Spring 1989): 207–238; and Emanuel Adler, "Ideological Guerrillas and the Quest for Technological Autonomy: Brazil's Domestic Computer Industry," *International Organization* 40 (Summer 1986): 673–706.

7. *Agra Europe,* April 11, 1986.

8. *Agra Europe,* April 4, 1986.

9. *U.S. Federal Register* 51 (April 3, 1986): 11532–11533.

10. Letter to U.S. Feed Grains Council, April 15, 1986. For a full account of this episode, see John Odell and Margaret Matzinger-Tchakerian, *European Community Enlargement and the United States* (Los Angeles: University of Southern California Center for International Studies, 1988, distributed by the Institute for the Study of Diplomacy, Georgetown University).

11. This section is based on an interview with a U.S. industry representative, 1987. All interviewees spoke on condition of anonymity.

12. Personal interview in Washington, D.C., 1987.

13. Personal interviews in Washington, D.C., 1987.

14. Confidential interview, 1987.

15. Letter from Vico E. Henriques, President, CBEMA, to USTR, Oct. 11, 1985.

16. Letter to the President from National Grange, U.S. Feed Grains Council, American Soybean Association, National Association of Wheat Growers, and 11 other organizations, March 21, 1986.

17. Letters from U.S. Feed Grains Council to U.S. Secretary of Agriculture, May 5, 1986, and to USTR, May 14, 1986; letter from Acting Secretary of Agriculture to U.S. Feed Grains Council, May 29, 1986.

18. Letter from National Corn Growers Association to USTR, July 11, 1986.

19. Letter from U.S. Feed Grains Council to USTR, Oct. 8, 1986.

20. Letters to USTR, Dec. 2 and Dec. 17, 1986.

21. Interview in Brasília, 1987. A different official, evidently belonging to the first group, recalled that in the early months of the dispute he had feared the U.S. government would retaliate even without strong U.S. industry support, but that events in 1986, discussed below, seemed to ease this risk.

22. Interview in Paris, 1988.

23. *International Trade Reporter,* April 16, 1986.

24. *Agra Europe,* April 4, 1986.

25. *International Trade Reporter,* April 16, 1986.

26. G. N. Yannopoulos, *Customs Unions and Trade Conflicts: The Enlargement of the European Community* (London: Routledge, 1988), p. 122.

27. Association General des Producteurs de Mais, *Rapport d'Orientation 1986,* p. 5.

28. *Le Monde,* July 5, 1986.

29. *Agra Europe,* July 4, 1986.

30. Personal interview with a French official, 1988.

31. Personal interview, 1988.

32. *New York Times* and *Wall Street Journal,* Dec. 31, 1986.

33. Personal interview, 1988.

34. *New York Times,* Sept. 16, 1985; *Veja,* Sept. 18, 1985; and *Wall Street Journal,* June 5, 1986.

35. *New York Times,* Sept. 16, and *O Estado de São Paulo,* Sept. 21, 1985.

36. Later evidence suggested that President Sarney personally disliked the informatics program and preferred to dismantle it. See Odell and Dibble, *Brazilian Informatics.*

37. ABICOMP report, 1987.

38. Parenthetically, these new U.S. signals did not result from a coordinated, unitary decision in Washington to change course. Reportedly, Whitehead had signaled a relaxation of pressure without prior approval, and some Washington officials were furious. (Brazilian Foreign Ministry statement published in *O Globo,* May 28, 1986, and interviews in Brasília and Washington.)

39. Statement of Vico E. Henriques, President, CBEMA, before USTR, March 12, 1987.

40. William K. Krist, Vice President, International Trade Affairs, AEA, before USTR, March 12, 1987.

41. A copy of the memorandum supplied by, and an interview with, a participating business representative in Washington.

42. Interview with a participating American official.

43. Putnam, "Diplomacy and Domestic Politics," proposes that "the greater the autonomy of central decision-makers from their Level II constituents, the larger their win-set, and thus the greater the likelihood of achieving international agreement. . . . However, two-level analysis also implies that, ceteris paribus, the stronger a state is in terms of autonomy from domestic pressures, the weaker its relative bargaining position internationally."

44. Paul Taylor, *The Limits of European Integration* (New York: Columbia University Press, 1983), pp. 132–135.

45. *Official Journal of the European Communities* 30 (April 10, 1987), L98, pp. 1–6. Actually, EC negotiations might be understood even better through an explicit three-level model. Level II in this case consists of the national governments, while firms and domestic groups (Level III) naturally attempt to influence their capitals, and vice versa. Moreover, national farm groups have created direct lobbying federations in Brussels as well. Unfortunately, however, an analysis encompassing the interactions of three levels in full complexity is beyond the scope of this study. The logical and empirical implications of combining three levels would be interesting lines for further inquiry.

46. Personal interviews at Itamaraty, Brazil's Foreign Ministry, 1987.

U.S.-Japan Negotiations on Construction and Semiconductors, 1985–1988
Building Friction and Relation-Chips

Ellis S. Krauss

INTRODUCTION

Since 1985 the United States and Japan have engaged in intense negotiations to resolve major conflicts over several trade issues. Two of the most severe disputes (both in 1985–1988) involved American firms' access to Japanese construction markets and charges of Japanese dumping of semiconductor chips in American and other foreign markets, combined with barriers to American sales of chips to Japan.[1] This chapter will compare these two negotiations, concluding that only the interrelationship of domestic and international variables can explain the outcomes.

In the construction case, after two years of intense and often acrimonious negotiations, a lasting agreement was reached in March 1988 without the application of American sanctions, despite complaints from the American construction industry and further investigations. In the semiconductor case, over a year of negotiations produced an agreement in August of 1986. But it quickly unraveled, because of Japanese chip firms' alleged violations of the accord and government failure to move quickly on other promises. This led to U.S. retaliation by 300 million dollars in sanctions against Japan, imposed by the President in March 1987. During the tenure of the original agreement only part of those sanctions was lifted, and disagreement continued over interpretation of some parts of the pact. In short, the perceived "defection" of the Japanese from the accord led to American retaliation.

Both these cases involved the same nation-states, two advanced industrialized "Western" nations, in roughly the same time period, in a political conflict over economic issues concerned with market competition and access. Yet the process by which these two conflicts were negotiated had both different and similar elements. More important, there were different agreement outcomes in the two cases—one agreement did not "hold" and resulted in the imposition of American sanctions, and the other held without sanctions—but the outcomes were similar in substance. What accounts for these complex results? Can these differences (and similarities) be explained solely by domestic (Level II) politics? By variations (or equivalences) in the national interests, binational relationship, and negotiating process (Level I) across the two issues? Or, as I will argue, by the particular patterns of "two-level games": by the interaction of domestic and international variables?

THE CONTEXT: U.S.-JAPAN TRADE FRICTION

In the early 1980s, the U.S. government sought to deal with increased competition from Japanese industry in the American market, and calls for government action to protect U.S. industries, by inducing Japan to limit their exports to the United States, as in the voluntary export agreements on steel and autos.[2] Increasingly, however, the Americans sought also to open specific Japanese markets to American goods where these were perceived as closed. Frustration in Congress over continuing trade deficits, largely directed toward Japan, heightened—in the midst of the semiconductor negotiations and at the beginning of the construction issue. It appeared that the trade threat from Japan might be an effective issue for the Democrats, so the Reagan Administration, ideologically dedicated to "free" and "fair" trade, also began to use more forceful means to apply pressure to the Japanese.

As such pressure and charges mounted, the Japanese became irritated but also increasingly concerned about American protectionist sentiments that might affect their access to the lucrative American market. They also wanted to avoid the embarrassing political stigma of being branded internationally as an "unfair trader." The skill with which a Japanese prime minister managed these tensions and avoided retaliation from the United States increasingly became a factor by which the Japanese chief of government (hereafter COG) was evaluated.

It is against this background that both disputes unfolded.

SEMICONDUCTORS: DOMESTIC VARIABLES

The Issue

By the mid-1980s, the Japanese share of the U.S. semiconductor market had surpassed the relatively constant U.S. share of the Japanese market, and Japanese suppliers' worldwide market share was in the process of

TABLE 1.   U.S. and Japanese Semiconductor Manufacturers'
Percentage Share of Each Other's and Worldwide Market, 1984–1989

	1984	*1985*	*1986*	*1987*	*1988*	*1989*
U.S. share in Japan	11.2	8.5	8.6	9.6	10.2	11.0
Japan share in U.S.	14.3	11.8	13.9	16.6	24.3	26.6
U.S. share worldwide	53.6	48.9	42.4	40.9	37.4	37.3
Japan (Japan-based) share worldwide	36.9	41.2	46.0	47.7	51.2	50.4

SOURCE: Semiconductor Industry Association.

surpassing that of American companies (see Table 1). The semiconductor conflict thus involved two separate but linked issues: American charges that the Japanese chip-makers were dumping semiconductors in the U.S. market below fair market value, and charges that Japan was not providing access to its domestic market for foreign chip-makers. There were important connections between the issues. First, access was seen by U.S. industry as a key to competitiveness in the American market: the protected home market enabled Japanese chip-producers to keep production costs down and undercut American manufacturers. Second, several anti-dumping cases, in addition to possible retaliation under Section 301, provided the U.S. leverage for negotiating market access.

For the Japanese, the main issues were preventing the United States from branding Japan as an unfair trader and imposing sanctions and anti-dumping tariffs, while protecting the competitiveness of this industry that was central to future economic growth.

The United States

Actors, Institutions, and Coalitions.   The Department of Commerce and the U.S. Trade Representative (USTR) were leading actors. There was a partial division of labor between the two, with USTR primarily responsible for the Japanese-market access dimension of the dispute, and Commerce with the dumping in U.S. markets. The Department of State was involved in the negotiations, but despite some internal resistance, and dislike in some quarters for the type of agreement being negotiated, State generally wound up supporting Commerce and USTR.

One key to State's ultimate support was that the industry early on convinced Secretary of State George Shultz of Japan's anomaly as a small market for U.S. chips compared to the rest of the world. Another factor was the particular negotiator for State, who knew and worked well with the negotiators from the other departments and the industry lobbyists.[3] There were also political pressures on Shultz and the State personnel involved in negotiations: they perceived that State needed to shore up its credibility in Congress and the executive branch by defining American interests more broadly to include economic as well as political and security concerns.[4]

The White House tended to be more concerned with the ramifications of the dispute for U.S.-Japanese relations, but this was counterbalanced by the importance of the industry to the U.S. national interest. The White House at one or two points did tend to oppose Commerce or the USTR, but eventually deferred to the two departments' views.[5] Thus on this issue, whatever the internal strains and differences between them, the actors involved tended to arrive at a consensus on the American position vis-à-vis Japan.

A major cause of the relative unity of action on the American side was the influence of the industry. The Semiconductor Industry Association (SIA)—composed of more than 50 of the major chip manufacturers—was established in the late 1970s explicitly to respond to the Japanese challenge.[6] In 1985 the SIA had filed a case under Section 301 of the U.S. Trade Act of 1974 charging the Japanese with protecting their domestic industry and violating a previous (1983) agreement.[7] SIA and individual chip manufacturers were the chief initiators and catalysts of the dispute (both in lobbying government and in initiating formal dumping and unfair trade charges against the Japanese) and provided much of the energy behind it.

Neither the semiconductor industry nor the more general microelectronics industry, however, was a homogeneous entity. The SIA included firms that specialized in different types of chips: e.g., Dynamic Random Access Memory chips (DRAMs) of different sizes, or Erasable Programmable Read-Only Memories (EPROMs); different types of companies: merchant companies that primarily produced and sold chips, vs. captive companies like IBM that both produced and used its own chips; and different philosophies concerning government action against Japan.[8] Additionally, there was the problem of the end-users: the American computer industry itself was divided, with some firms not enthusiastic about any trade action that would raise the prices of chips they bought, including many Japanese-made chips.

The SIA moved early and well to mend these divisions within industry. It mobilized its members to work toward a common goal that would benefit all: greater access to the Japanese market. After individual companies filed anti-dumping suits against Japanese firms on 256K DRAMs and EPROMs, both types of American market-penetration concerns were added to its goals. Further, the anti-dumping position that SIA forged provided trade-offs to *both* manufacturers and end-users, and thus enhanced the prospects for alliance. Thus, while U.S. users might face higher prices if the suppliers succeeded in stopping dumping, U.S. suppliers agreed not to push for quotas or floor prices, i.e., Japanese suppliers could sell as much as they wanted at whatever price they wanted (even below U.S. suppliers' prices) as long as it was above the individual firm's cost of production (not "dumped," by this definition).[9]

Captive firms such as IBM, previously unenthusiastic about trade action, agreed to stand aside and let SIA proceed. The American Electronics Association (AEA), representative of the users, was briefed as early as 1985 and consulted more intensively thereafter when necessary.[10] Users, in any case, had far less consensus among themselves and were less capable of influence in Washington than the SIA, "the slickest lobby in town," according to observers of the industry.[11] With internal agreement within the industry on its goals, SIA began intensive lobbying in both the legislative and executive branches, using the formidable expertise and experience of its officers and lobbyists.

The dumping suits played a major role in U.S. politics on the semiconductor negotiations, performing both domestic and international functions. Domestically, once the dumping suits were filed, the issue of Japanese unfair penetration of U.S. markets became formally linked to the issue of American access to the Japanese market. Further, the suits gave legal authority and mandates to those who wished to stand tough against Japan. The White House's backing down at points at the insistence of Commerce, referred to above, was in part a function of the legal authority given to the latter by the dumping suits.[12]

Finally, the suits imposed deadlines and raised the stakes of the negotiations on *both* sides in the dispute. Whereas trade retaliation under Section 301 of the Trade Act was primarily a political decision giving great flexibility to both the USTR and the COG in whether and how to respond, anti-dumping cases involved legal proceedings and judgments, required responses, and imposed deadlines.[13] This certainly increased the bargaining power of the American side, which was one intent of the companies that filed the suits;[14] but it may also have helped structure the domestic relationships by increasing the credibility of the industry's claims and pressures and by inducing cooperation on strategy from any reluctant members of the American side (sanctions might be applied against Japan, in any event; getting a trade agreement might actually help prevent likely retaliation).

Alternatively, if no agreement was negotiated but the dumping suits succeeded, U.S. chip prices would rise, making them uncompetitive with markets elsewhere.[15] The U.S. side thus had the incentive to negotiate an agreement rather than merely settle for dumping penalties. Thus the dumping suits provided the U.S. side with greater bargaining leverage, structured the negotiations, and helped create consensus both on strategy and on the value of accomplishing an agreement.

In Congress, a bipartisan core group from both houses had been mobilized by SIA to pressure the executive branch.[16] Such Congressional concern, intensifying with burgeoning trade deficits after 1985, particularly created pressure on agencies like State[17] that were more ambivalent about the issue, but whose credibility was at stake. Various bills and resolutions were introduced in Congress during the conflict, pressuring the Japanese with threats of retaliation. Congress, however, never actually passed retaliatory legislation, thus playing a somewhat lesser role than in the construction dispute, as we shall see.

The American Win-Set.   Thanks to SIA's early and effective internal and external consensus-building and the role of the dumping suits, the "acceptability-sets" of the major U.S. actors proved to be very similar. This consensus, especially its inextricable linking of Japanese market access with U.S. market-protection goals, and the broad coalition of interests it represented, was to fundamentally shape the American "win-set" and the strategies and dynamics of the international negotiations.

To obtain ratification by a majority of the major players on the U.S. side enfranchised in this dispute, the following would be required:

1. Japan's government would have to make efforts to remove the obstacles to a substantial increase in the U.S. market share of semiconductor sales in Japan. The expectation was that the American firms' share should at least double in the near future. U.S. firms had held a consistent 8–10 percent of the Japanese market for years (see Table 1). A previous study had shown that if barriers had not existed in Japan, the U.S. would have had over 30 percent of the market.[18] This was a starting figure for negotiation, however; ratification could have been obtained with less—generally the bottom line of acceptability for ratification was an expectation of improvement to at least 20 percent.[19]

2. The dumping of chips in the U.S. by *all* Japanese firms selling in the American market would have to end, and a monitoring device established to implement this. All Japanese firms would have to stop selling chips in the U.S. market at prices lower than production costs or "fair market value." The key term here is "*all*" companies. The major actors agreed that a settlement that allowed any Japanese firms to continue dumping would not protect U.S. firms sufficiently. Thus, the use of average pricing in monitoring dumping was unacceptable because it would enable some individual Japanese firms to continue dumping as long as others sold at higher than the average.[20] Equally important, average pricing would have split the U.S. domestic coalition by allowing inefficient Japanese producers to cut their prices down to the average (anger-

ing U.S. suppliers), and efficient Japanese suppliers to price up to the average (angering U.S. end-users).[21] Therefore, the monitoring data used had to be *firm-specific.*

3. The dumping of chips by Japanese firms in Japan and third countries would have to be prevented, and a monitoring device established to implement this. Major U.S. government and industry actors agreed that any pact had to deal with sales of chips in other countries, lest any agreement forbidding Japanese companies to dump in the U.S. be undermined by Japanese companies selling underpriced chips in Japan and abroad, and end-users going there for their chips. Thus third-country markets would have to be monitored.[22]

4. Existing dumping suits would have to be suspended, not terminated. Termination would undermine U.S. leverage to prevent violations; mere suspension (in exchange for an agreement along the lines above) would expedite reinstituting them if necessary.

The fact that both market access and U.S. market penetration solutions were linked by the industry gave the U.S. win-set a very specific shape and narrow range: no agreement would be ratified by the key actors without these—and all these—requirements included.

Japan

Actors, Institutions, and Coalitions. The powerful Ministry of International Trade and Industry (MITI) was the chief bureaucratic actor.[23] MITI was known for its management of industrial and trade policy and its "administrative guidance" of industry. For example, it had successfully implemented the Voluntary Export Restraint (VER) in automobiles in the early 1980s, despite the objections of some Japanese auto companies.[24] As Japanese industries gained in strength and became more internationalized, however, MITI's coercive role in some industries—semiconductors being one major example—had declined.

An agreement with the United States would give MITI new power and mechanisms to monitor chip producers, and thus reestablish its influence in the industry. I do not know whether this objective explicitly motivated MITI's initial goals and strategy, but its subsequent establishment of monitoring mechanisms went even further than the agreement necessitated, suggesting that MITI hoped to use the negotiations to enhance its domestic power.[25]

The semiconductor industry in Japan, like many Japanese industries, was basically oligopolistic, with a limited number (about ten in chip production) of large companies, many of them the larger, diversified electrical firms (Hitachi, Toshiba, NEC, and so on). In contrast to the more diverse U.S. industry, these firms were relatively vertically integrated, serving as end-user computer manufacturers as well as chip producers. The industry was concerned about anti-dumping and other retaliation by the United States in the event agreement failed. But many companies preferred no-agreement, and adjusting to American tariffs, to an agreement that involved MITI control over prices at home and abroad and required them to divulge proprietary manufacturing-cost information to the U.S. government (for fear it would leak to their American competitors).

The industry was split to some extent, since not all the major companies were named in the dumping cases and thus subject to the brunt of penalties for no-agreement. Further, some had a higher stake in an agreement because they produced many other electrical consumer-goods that could be targeted by U.S. retaliation.

As in every trade dispute with the United States, the Prime Minister's prestige was closely tied to his ability to resolve it. In the semiconductor case, this meant that the Prime Minister and Liberal Democratic Party (LDP) leaders were allied with the bureaucratic agency, MITI, to try to settle the dispute without American retaliation. The conflict was between government and industry. Because MITI's aims in the dispute coincided with the COG's, and MITI was relatively influential within the government, the COG left much of the dispute in MITI's hands.

The Japanese Win-Set.   Because of the fundamental divergence between government and the industry, and the divergence of stakes within the industry, the Japanese win-set was closely constrained and far from the American win-set in key ways. An acceptable agreement would have to:

1. Terminate, or at least suspend, the dumping cases and the pending Section 301 case.

2. Avoid American retaliation.

3. Keep expansion of American market share to the minimum necessary to avoid retaliation. It is unlikely that a 20-percent or more share would have received ratification by industry. Expanding U.S. market share by a few percentage points—into the teen range—probably could have been ratified.

4. Avoid monitoring systems that would involve third countries or force Japanese firms to give proprietary information to the U.S. government.

Here MITI and industry's acceptability-sets diverged: MITI could live with strict monitoring systems involving third countries or providing information to the U.S. government (with proper safeguards to avoid divulgence to American firms), but many of the firms in the industry were very unlikely to ratify an agreement with these provisions. The question for industry was at what point attaining goals 1 and 2 above was worth acceding to the controls and information provision it wanted to avoid.

Key industry players' problems with both strict monitoring and a sudden, large expansion of the American market share restricted the Japanese win-set to the items above, and on these items the U.S. and Japanese win-sets were far apart.

SEMICONDUCTORS: THE PROCESS OF INTERNATIONAL NEGOTIATIONS

Initiation

The 1985–1987 semiconductor negotiations were actually the third in a series. Agreements in 1982 and 1983 had covered both the dumping and market-share issues, but had been confined to vague promises and insufficient implementation mechanisms. Overcapacity and declining prices in the international market in 1984–85, leading to severe difficulties for U.S. firms, made the American industry determined to find more effective means.[26]

In mid-1985 the SIA filed a petition under Section 301 stressing the policies, barriers, and market structure in Japan that impeded U.S. firms' access and created incentives for dumping. It asked the President, who has the power under the 1974 Trade Act to take any actions necessary to respond to findings of unfair trade practices, to negotiate greater market access and an end to dumping.[27]

Meanwhile, Intel and two other firms filed a suit claiming Japanese firms were dumping EPROMs. In November 1985 the International Trade Commission issued a preliminary finding that Japanese firms had indeed harmed U.S. industry, a prelude to a Commerce decision on whether dumping had actually taken place.[28] Almost simultaneously, a "strike force" set up by Reagan and headed by Commerce Secretary Baldrige recommended the initiation of unfair-trade complaints against Japan on chips, and a month later Commerce initiated an anti-dumping case charging Japanese firms with dumping 256K DRAMs.[29] Such self-initiation without an industry petition was almost unprecedented, and a former Commerce official[30] instrumental in this action has affirmed that its purpose was strategic: 256K DRAMs were one market niche where the Japanese dominated (few American firms manufactured them) and thus the threat of retaliation would hurt them more than in EPROMs, where U.S. firms had the lead. The White House made an effort to undermine this attempt, but backed down when Baldrige stood his ground and cited his legal authority to proceed.[31]

Negotiations

The Japanese attempted to head off the filing of the dumping charges.[32] When the United States in December for the first time formally linked the dumping problem with the market-access issue, however, Japan proposed to "encourage" its major producers to purchase more U.S. chips, leading to small but progressive market-share increases, and to establish an export floor price for all types of chips, based on a formula for a "typical" firm of various types. In exchange, the Japanese wanted the Section 301 investigation discontinued, and the anti-dumping cases suspended or terminated, with no new ones to be opened.[33] The offer was unacceptable to the United States, because the floor-pricing system was not based on firm-specific data and the deal did not apply to the Japanese home market[34] or third-country sales.

Negotiations continued during the winter, with the Japanese eager to forestall the inexorable progress of anti-dumping cases,[35] but firmly rejecting any guarantees of a specific domestic-market share to the Americans.[36] In March 1986, however, USTR Clayton Yeutter strongly pushed the market-access problem in discussions with MITI Minister Watanabe. U.S. negotiators claim he specified that the United States wanted at least a 20-percent market share within the next five years, and that his Japanese counterpart indicated his understanding. The later side-letter on market access was supposedly based on these talks.[37]

The talks continued on this and other issues, but broke down in late March,[38] with third-country dumping still a major stumbling-block. By late May a general "framework" for agreement had been developed, but many major details needed to be worked out.[39]

The United States intensified pressure on Japan in numerous ways. Various anti-dumping rulings, all against the Japanese, had increased the prospect that the cases would result in penalties.[40] The sub-cabinet-level Trade Policy Review Group (TPRG) and the cabinet-level Economic Policy Council (EPC) met to discuss the market-access issue, and the EPC unofficially decided that unless it got an agreement soon, the United States would apply Section 301 retaliation. This decision was informally communicated to the Japanese, and, according to one former U.S. trade official, it really "drove them wild."[41]

Agreement

The pressure by the United States produced enough progress that in early July 1986 the U.S. Commerce Department and Japanese firms signed suspension agreements in both the EPROM and 256K DRAM dumping cases. The United States warned that it would reinstitute the cases if no agreement were reached on the remaining issues. It also pushed back the deadline for a settlement to late July.[42] Setting and pushing back deadlines represented a conscious carrot/stick strategy on the part of the U.S. negotiators.[43] Congress, which had been continually "worked" by the SIA during the negotiations, also began threatening moves.[44] As the final deadline approached, the major issues remaining were Japanese reluctance to accede to American demands for third-country controls and for proprietary information on manufacturing costs.

MITI and the Japanese government were divided on whether to concede to the Americans. As one of the main Japanese negotiators said, referring to his American counterpart: "Mike Smith and I were in the same position. . . . We had to persuade constituents this is the best we could get."[45]

Industry also was not happy. According to industry and analyst sources, many Japanese producers thought that Japan had already made too many concessions. The producers reportedly preferred to accept anti-dumping duties than to agree to these provisions. An American industry analyst in Japan said:

> They were hoping just to pay dumping duties. They expected that MITI would take care of them better, but the agency buckled under to political pressure.[46]

Japanese companies were clearly dissatisfied about the shape of the emerging agreement. Yet at literally a few minutes before the midnight (July 31) final deadline for settlement set by the United States, an agreement was reached. It gave the U.S. everything it had demanded, including Japanese government monitoring of export prices and third-country markets, and provision of firm-specific manufacturing data to the U.S. Commerce Department to determine whether dumping, as defined by the Americans (selling below production cost or market value), was occurring.[47]

In the agreement itself, the Japanese government pledged only to make aggressive efforts to get its firms to increase American sales in Japan; in a secret side-letter to the accord, however, the Japanese government more specifically recognized the American expectation of an increase in foreign sales to 20 percent of the market within the five-year term of the agreement.[48]

In the U.S., SIA and government officials hailed the agreement. It was attacked, however, by critics and computer manufacturers for violating free trade and raising the price of chips for U.S. computer and other manufacturers.[49]

Defection and Retaliation

Less than two months after the agreement was signed, SIA began complaining to U.S. officials about possible dumping violations.[50] These complaints intensified in October, as reports indicated that chips were being sold outside the United States well below the fair-market prices set by the Commerce Department, and computer-makers began threatening to assemble their products abroad rather than buy the much higher-priced U.S. chips.[51] Part of the problem was that Commerce had set the U.S. fair-market price very high after the agreement, because at first it had received only partial data from Japanese firms about manufacturing costs.[52] The SIA had to make strenuous efforts with the AEA and other manufacturers to maintain support.[53] With improved data from more Japanese firms cooperating, official prices began to come down substantially, and much of the U.S. domestic resistance to the agreement subsided.[54]

Meanwhile, dumping by Japanese companies appeared to U.S. officials and firms to have continued in third-country markets in East Asia, and no improvement at all had occurred in U.S. sales in Japan since the agreement. Through the fall the United States had several meetings with MITI about these problems. Finally, in January 1987, the U.S. negotiators gave MITI an ultimatum: stop third-country dumping and improve market access by April 1, or the U.S. would have to retaliate.[55] At least some Japanese officials believe that it was not the dumping issue that provoked retaliatory possibilities, but failure of U.S. market share to improve in the months after the agreement was signed.[56] When the Japanese equivocated on third-country dumping, the negotiators returned to Washington to "sell it [retaliation] to our government."[57]

It sold, despite reticence in the White House and State, in large part because those urging sanctions presented it as a case of the Japanese breaking a signed agreement. The evidence of violations was there, and the credibility of the U.S. government was said to be at stake.[58] Moreover, Congress had become increasingly angry over the evidence of violations, as well as over statements made by a MITI official in another dispute over supercomputers.

Although MITI tried desperately to stop third-country dumping by curbing excess capacity in Japan and tightening export controls,[59] further cases occurred.[60] Meanwhile, both the U.S. Senate and House passed unanimous resolutions urging retaliation. The SIA, concerned about a forthcoming summit meeting between President Reagan and Prime Minister Nakasone, quickly urged the President to retaliate.[61]

Toward the end of March the EPC concluded that Japan violated the agreement, and the next day the President decided to impose

100-percent retaliatory tariffs on electrical devices worth 300 million dollars, approximately half for the dumping violations and half for the lack of improvement in market access.[62] The list of retaliatory items eventually approved was itself a work of political craftsmanship designed to maintain the coalition supporting the agreement and retaliation. The sanctions list did not include semiconductors, because that would only exacerbate the problem of high prices for U.S. end-users; products were picked that did not hurt U.S. industry and for which there was an American producer who would benefit from the higher prices its Japanese competitor would now be charging; and some products were picked to injure the specific Japanese companies still dumping.[63]

At the June 1987 Venice summit of the leading industrialized countries, Reagan announced a partial reduction of tariffs, with a further reduction announced by Commerce before the end of 1987. Third-country dumping had by and large stopped, but the American share of the Japanese chip market had not improved as much as expected.[64] The remainder of the tariffs—about half the original level imposed—remained.

CONSTRUCTION: DOMESTIC VARIABLES[65]

The Issue

The United States wanted more contracts, especially for high-tech services, in Japanese construction markets, from which it felt unfairly excluded by both official and informal practices. Progress would require penetrating the dense private industry, and government-industry, relationships involved in contracting for public and semi-public works.[66] The dispute was initiated over one airport construction case—Kansai International Airport (hereafter KIA)—but widened beyond it; the United States threatened to apply Section 301 sanctions against Japan if its demands were not met.

For Japan, the main issue was the American threat to its public-works bidding system—in which there were major domestic political and economic stakes. Another issue was to avoid retaliation by the United States.

The United States

Actors, Institutions, and Coalitions.   Three bureaucratic actors, the Commerce Department, USTR, and State Department, played major roles in the negotiations. Commerce, the leading U.S. agency in talks, was split. Some officials, fearing that the U.S. construction industry would not be able to take advantage of any access negotiated, would not have minded if the talks failed and the United States retaliated under Section 301.

Others wanted the negotiations to succeed, to keep the issue under Commerce leadership, for once Section 301 was applied the initiative would move to USTR. USTR wanted the Japanese construction markets opened as part of its general mandate to negotiate wider access for American products with trading partners. Commerce was closer to the U.S. construction industry, while USTR was sensitive to congressional pressures. These factors generally led both Commerce and USTR to push strongly for a tough negotiating stance against the Japanese.

The State Department (including its Tokyo Embassy) was concerned with the negative implications of the construction friction on broader U.S.-Japanese relations—it just wanted the issue resolved as quickly and amicably as possible. In addition, State's earlier acquiescence on retaliation in the semiconductor dispute, and the subsequent damage to U.S.-Japan relations, may have convinced it to resist such retaliation in the construction case.[67] State was not a major actor in the working-level negotiations, but in later stages would play an independent role in trying to prevent U.S. retaliation. Commerce and USTR wanted the option to apply Section 301 to pressure Japan; State (sometimes with sympathy from some White House officials) wanted to avoid sanctions.

Congress had become increasingly irritated with Japan over trade, and Democrats threatened protectionist legislation. Republicans, while wanting to support Reagan's free-trade philosophy, saw the opening of Japanese markets as a way to diffuse both the political and protectionist threats of Democratic initiatives. Sen. Frank Murkowski (R-Alaska), interested in equity of access in service markets, played the most active role.

The U.S. construction industry was split between a few larger international firms who wanted to get into the Japanese market and were willing to accept reasonable opportunities to do so, and others, represented by the International Engineering and Construction Industry Council (IECIC), who were alarmed by the increasing Japanese success in the American construction market. The latter group would not have minded if negotiations failed and sanctions were used against Japan, especially shutting the Japanese out of the U.S. building market.[68]

The White House was cross-pressured, wanting to maintain the stability of U.S.-Japanese relations and the free-trading system, and to avoid retaliatory measures against Japan—but, also under tremendous pressure from Congress and part of its own administration (especially Commerce and USTR) to do something to open Japanese construction markets.

The U.S. presidential/congressional system was an important factor at the domestic level. One of the major underlying themes of the dispute was the Administration's attempt to keep the initiative for trade policy in the executive branch and forestall congressional retaliation, both in general and in this case in particular. When the executive branch was stymied in retaliating against the Japanese by its own internal divisions, Congress could, and did, do so instead.

The American Win-Set. The basic elements of the American win-set involved:

1. Fundamental reform of Japanese bidding procedures in the KIA construction sufficient for the Japanese government to guarantee that American firms would not be discriminated against.

2. Procedures that would make it very likely that American firms would win lucrative contracts, especially in high-tech aspects of the airport construction such as terminal design and baggage handling.

3. Assurances that the KIA settlement would also be applied to a fair number of other public and semi-public works.

That the American win-set involved the above features was not clear at the beginning of the dispute. At first, the negotiating position of the U.S. side was very different from this win-set, in part because of uncertainties and ignorance about the Japanese system. Initially, the U.S. made strong demands for complete revision of the Japanese bidding system to make it like the American system, and for participation of American firms even in the first (landfill) stage of the KIA project. Second, conflict among U.S. key actors initially obscured the fact that the issue was less over the nature of the settlement than over the strategy used to influence the Japanese. State and the COG would probably have accepted any solution as long as it did not involve retaliation against Japan. Finally, IECIC's probable preference for no-agreement as a justification for shutting Japanese firms out of the U.S. market turned out not to constrain the win-set, because IECIC was not a strong player in this dispute: as long as major international firms would ratify an agreement along the lines above, the rest of the industry had to go along.

Japan

Actors, Institutions, and Coalitions. Three ministries were the major participants in negotiations on the Japanese side: Construction (MOC), Transportation (MOT), and Foreign Affairs (MOFA). The former two had jurisdiction over the public and semi-public works involved and, because of close ties to the domestic construction industry and a vested interest in the established system of bidding, were strongly resistant to American demands for changing procedures and relationships. MOFA though, like the U.S. State Department, was more interested in preserving the stability of the overall U.S.-Japanese relationship. All three agencies were always collectively involved in the working-level negotiations. MITI was mostly on the sidelines in this dispute, but it did become involved at later stages when American trade retaliation threatened to impinge on its jurisdiction. MITI wanted the issue resolved so as not to exacerbate general trade relations.

The Japanese construction industry, well organized into trade associations, had a vested interest in the status quo. When the issue extended to all public works and threatened to undermine long-standing relationships within industry and between it and government, the industry became concerned. Most major firms stood to lose by too much change in the system and hence opposed too many concessions. Because the industry was one of the major financial contributors to the LDP and employed directly or indirectly about 10 percent of the work force in Japan, it also wielded substantial political influence on the government. However, because of the industry's dependence on public-works contracts and its established ties to particular politicians, including the COGs during the dispute, government also had a great deal of leverage with the industry.[69]

The Japanese Prime Minister (first Nakasone and later Takeshita) and a chief aide (especially Ozawa Ichirō, the Deputy Chief Cabinet Secretary) were under tremendous cross-pressures. All three had close political ties to the construction industry and well understood the political stakes involved in the Japanese public-works and bidding systems. Yet the overall national interest of Japan demanded a settlement that avoided U.S. retaliation, particularly because Japan was simultaneously involved in other difficult disputes (e.g., semiconductors and agriculture) that further trade friction could exacerbate. Moreover, the personal and political prestige of the COG was heavily at stake. Nakasone's domestic political popularity and clout with his party had come to rest heavily on his skill in mitigating U.S. trade retaliation. When Takeshita succeeded him, he was being explicitly measured against Nakasone in the same way.

The Diet as a whole played no role in the conflict, but members of the ruling LDP did. The party and many individual LDP Diet members receive major financial contributions from the construction industry, giving it major political clout with the party and its leadership. Further, the construction "policy tribe" (*zoku*)—one of the groups of senior LDP Diet members with close ties to particular interest groups, who push for those interests and mediate between the interest groups and the bureaucracy—is particularly powerful in the LDP.[70] The LDP, on the other hand, also understood the need to pacify the U.S. and avoid both the material and symbolic costs of U.S. retaliation to the Prime Minister and the party.

The divisions and coalitions on the Japanese side resembled the American ones. The MOC and MOT were firmly against too many concessions, especially on the bidding system, while MOFA and MITI were more interested in settling the conflict without retaliation by the U.S. The PM's Office tended toward the latter approach, while recognizing the political limits on any drastic change in the system.

Institutional and jurisdictional factors on the Japanese side made for somewhat different patterns than on the American side, despite the similarity of coalitions. The perpetual dominance of the ruling LDP in a parliamentary system meant that COG-legislative relations were not salient; rather COG-bureaucracy, COG-party, and bureaucracy-bureaucracy relations were crucial, as is fairly typical of Japanese policy-making. The main conflict domestically pit the COG against MOC and MOT, which with their construction *zoku* within the party resisted concessions and sought to control the negotiations themselves. Nonetheless, the close ties of the COG (especially Takeshita) and Ozawa to the construction *zoku* of the party also influenced the negotiations.

There were also conflicts between the MOC and MOT versus MOFA. Because MOFA was part of the negotiating team, however, it had to coordinate its views with the hard-line views of the other two ministries. Thus, although there was a tacit cross-national "alliance" between MOFA and State at various stages of the negotiations to try to bring about a settlement, MOFA was much more constrained by its leadership role in the collective Japanese negotiating team. MITI, however, was more like State—limited in its ability to influence events directly, but desirous of a settlement, with some autonomy to maneuver indirectly to influence negotiations toward concession and settlement at certain stages.

The Japanese Win-Set. 1. Preserve the "designated bidder" system. No agreement could have been ratified on the Japanese side that involved a total change in the Japanese public-works bidding system—the political and economic stakes for all major actors were too high for that.

2. Confine any procedural changes to later stages of KIA construction. The PM's office and MOFA (and even the construction industry) were willing to allow American firms to participate in the second stage of the KIA project, but the Japanese deemed the first stage, mostly landfill work, to be too far along to incorporate foreign firms without causing considerable delay in the project.

3. Limit the agreement to KIA, without any application to other public or semi-public works projects. Many key actors, even those most resistant to concessions, were probably resigned to some procedural concessions on KIA; a wider agreement that guaranteed American participation in the entire public and semi-public works system, however, would probably not have been ratified initially by MOC and the construction industry.

Note that the American and Japanese win-sets were generally compatible, except on the application of a KIA settlement to other construction projects. On this latter point, fundamental movement would have to take place on one side or the other to reach a ratifiable agreement.

CONSTRUCTION:
THE PROCESS OF INTERNATIONAL NEGOTIATIONS

Initiation and Early Stages

U.S. Commerce Department personnel initiated the dispute, with efforts to mobilize American business to penetrate the Japanese construction market, especially to bid on the new KIA project. Commerce and USTR then demanded American access to this project, including its initial stages, through modification of the Japanese public-works bidding procedures to make them more like the U.S. system. The Japanese responded by holding out the possibility of American firms' participation in the second stage of KIA, but within the current Japanese system.

At the October 1986 Kansai International Seminar, the Commerce official who led the delegation seemed to accept the Japanese position on maintaining the current system, with American participation in the second stage of the project, as long as U.S. firms receive nondiscriminatory treatment. This "podium policy" differed from the official American position and the preferences of key actors in Congress and industry, and seemed to have a "reverberation" effect. Although the original American demands were to be sporadically revived in subsequent negotiations, from this point on the focus of the American demands shifted to modifications in the existing Japanese system to incorporate American concerns, and primarily to participation in the later stages of construction.[71]

Throughout the talks, two major weapons of domestic politics were used by American negotiators. One was congressional hearings and threats of independent congressional action. Beginning with a hearing in the spring of 1986 that helped stimulate political interest in this issue in Congress, hearings allowed industry representatives and Congressional critics to communicate their expectations publicly, and pressure the administration to maintain heat on the Japanese. They also provided leverage for U.S. negotiators to gain further concessions. American negotiators visiting Tokyo would frequently tell the Japanese of Congress' dissatisfaction and point to a recent congressional hearing to underline the need for further concessions if there was to be American ratification.[72]

The U.S. negotiators also constantly told the Japanese that if they did not accede further to American demands, Congress might respond with retaliatory or protectionist legislation. This may be seen as a variation of the "good cop, bad cop" ploy. It also indicates a tacit Level II alliance between the executive and legislative branches, even as they seemed to disagree on other aspects of handling the conflict: representatives of the administration, even while trying to avoid independent Congressional retaliation, used Congressional pressure in their persuasion of the Japanese. As I. M. Destler notes, "hyping the 'protectionist threat' from Congress so as to create pressure on foreign governments to come to terms and to render legislative action unnecessary" is a "game familiar to trade practitioners."[73]

The Americans' other major weapon was the constantly reiterated threat of Section 301 trade sanctions. One aim of both the congressional and the Section 301 threats was to widen the coalition of Japanese actors favoring concessions to the Americans (the PM, MOFA, and MITI) and to provide more credibility to these actors.[74] Section 301 threats, therefore, were intended to influence the opponent's domestic politics. As we shall see below, however, they also unintentionally created domestic American opposition and cross-national alliances to block such sanctions. If the major U.S. weapon during the semiconductor negotiations was the legal threat of anti-dumping cases, in construction the Americans used the more political—and double-edged—threats of congressional action and Section 301 sanctions.

By November 1987, American pressures and threats and extensive negotiations had won Japanese agreement on the KIA project that acceded to the basic American demands; the fundamental division remaining between the two sides' win-sets and negotiating positions was the issue of applying the KIA solution to other public and semi-public works projects.

Summit Meetings and Leadership Change

During the 1987–88 negotiations, there were three U.S.-Japan summit meetings (April and September 1987 and January 1988) and one major leadership change—the retirement of Prime Minister Nakasone, and his replacement by Takeshita, in November 1987. These events affected both the negotiations and domestic politics.

On the one hand, summit meetings sometimes produced misunderstandings that undermined movement toward agreement and unintentionally produced "negative reverberation." In the September 1987 Nakasone-Reagan summit, the Japanese Prime Minister pledged to apply the newly agreed-upon KIA procedures to other construction projects. The Japanese interpreted the pledge as applying only to projects other than public works, but the Americans viewed it as applying to public works as well, and saw the Japanese interpretation as reneging on Nakasone's pledge.[75]

On the other hand, as summits approached, the U.S. negotiators turned up the pressure and the Japanese government tried to satisfy the Americans in order to settle or de-escalate the issue. These efforts sometimes also intensified conflicts among the Japanese actors.[76] The transition from Nakasone to Takeshita in November 1987 had a similar effect, as both sides worked feverishly but unsuccessfully to gain an agreement prior to the leadership change.[77]

Often, the summit meetings and the leadership change were used by some on the American side to justify postponing retaliation.[78] For example, Secretary of State Shultz convinced the Reagan Administration to defer action against Japan until after the first Reagan-Takeshita summit in January 1988, despite pressures to apply Section 301. "Shultz feels it would be too much of a slap at Japan to do anything during Takeshita's honeymoon period, and he's gotten the cabinet to go along," explained one official.[79] This incident illustrates Putnam's argument that each negotiator has a strong interest in maintaining the popularity of his opponent,[80] as the Reagan Administration obviously did not want to undercut support for the leader who would have to arrange a new win-set to gain agreement.

It also illustrates the tacit cross-national alliance between State and the Japanese government to avoid exacerbating tensions in the overall relationship. State's action, however, was to produce a backlash in Congress that fundamentally affected the negotiations.

Congressional Retaliation: Changing the Japanese Win-Set

The decision of the Reagan Cabinet to postpone the application of Section 301 triggered congressional anger. On December 22, 1987, the U.S. Congress passed a funding bill with the "Murkowski-Brooks Amendment" attached that would bar Japanese firms from federally funded construction projects for one year.[81]

Although the Murkowski-Brooks Amendment had only minor practical economic effect on the Japanese, it changed the calculus of Level I negotiations. First, it damaged Prime Minister Takeshita's political credibility in the crucial early stages of his administration, increasing the urgency for him to get an agreement. Second, now that the U.S. public-works ban was in effect, stalemate and the status quo no longer favored the Japanese but rather favored the Americans (especially since this is what some in the American domestic industry really wanted, anyway).

Most important, this congressional retaliation raised the economic stakes of continued stalemate for the Japanese. If the ban on Japanese firms in the U.S. had already been accomplished by congressional action, then any future executive Section 301 retaliation would probably go beyond a mere ban on Japanese bidding in U.S. public works (e.g., not only tariffs or bans on exports related to construction, such as machinery, but also items unrelated to construction). This brought into the picture new actors and domestic pressures: MITI and other industries now had a vital stake in an agreement, because any trade retaliation would affect MITI's jurisdiction and injure other industries.[82] These factors seem to have expanded the Japanese win-set to include U.S. access to projects other than KIA.

Congressional retaliation spurred new efforts by the U.S. Embassy in Tokyo and the Prime Minister's Office to facilitate an agreement. Informal contacts led to secret meetings between embassy officials and Deputy Chief Cabinet Secretary Ozawa Ichirō, also a leader of the "construction tribe" in the LDP with very close ties to the industry and the MOC. In effect, the tacit alliance between State and segments of the Japanese government which wanted the issue settled now evolved into direct contacts.[83]

These unofficial talks produced a "framework" for a settlement that revolved around American acceptance of the Japanese public-works system as "fair," in return for opening further specific public-works projects to American participation.[84] Details of how many and which projects were to be opened to the Americans remained to be negotiated. Although IECIC maintained some skepticism about the new offer's practical results, two larger American construction firms announced plans to link up with major Japanese companies in joint ventures.[85]

The American domestic politics leading to congressional retaliation had produced a more direct transnational alliance between parts of the Japanese and American governments, producing a new arena of Level I negotiations, and movement of the Japanese win-set closer to the American win-set on the major remaining issue of extending the KIA formula to other public and semi-public works projects.

Agreement

The modified Japanese win-set and the new "framework," however, did not immediately produce an agreement. The Japanese offered 6 projects to American participation, whereas the Americans wanted 14. More important, it was revealed that in the two airports on the Japanese list the terminal buildings were excluded, as the Japanese considered these private construction because they were being built by private firms (and thus not subject to governmental agreement).[86] The Japanese negotiating position still aimed at minimizing the consequences of agreement.

In response, following the recommendation of a subcabinet committee that Section 301 sanctions be invoked, the cabinet-level EPC authorized

Commerce to resume negotiations with Japan, but with a two-week deadline to resolve the conflict.

This time State concurred, in contrast to its previous resistance against sanctions at both the sub-cabinet and cabinet levels, and there were no reports of White House resistance, either. Indeed, the White House was rumored to have sent down word that the dispute was to be resolved one way or the other soon, to avoid further exacerbating U.S.-Japanese relations. One explanation for the changed negotiating stance of State and the COG on strategy may lie in domestic political developments during the same period.

In response to the Japanese offer in January, a State Department official indicated in a public briefing that the new proposal met American demands. His action was immediately denounced by other government and industry sources, however. Mark Chapin, an executive of the National Constructors Association, even said, "Why should State consult us? They represent the Japanese. . . . They're the enemy for us, just as the Japanese are."[87]

In February, public controversy had also embroiled the White House. Commerce Undersecretary Bruce Smart, who had headed the negotiating team, resigned in late February, and the name of his deputy, J. Michael Farren, who had also been intimately involved in the negotiations, was submitted as his replacement. It was reported, however, to have been rejected by the White House, amid charges of Japanese influence on the decision.[88]

Japanese intransigence on the terminal-building investigation, combined with the domestic political controversies that had subjected both White House and State to public criticism, seemed to produce for the first time a unanimous willingness to apply Section 301 sanctions if the Japanese did not accede.

Faced with an ultimatum, the Japanese sent Deputy Cabinet Secretary Ozawa to Washington for last-ditch negotiations, preceded by behind-the-scenes efforts by Prime Minister Takeshita and other senior LDP leaders with close ties to the industry to smooth the way for concessions.[89]

In intensive negotiations with Deputy USTR Mike Smith, Ozawa reached a settlement on March 29, 1988, just prior to the expiration of the American-imposed deadline. The agreement essentially provided for the KIA procedures to be applied to more than double the number of projects previously offered, including terminal buildings at the airports. The problem of "private" components of public works was resolved by the Japanese government promise to "encourage" private firms to treat U.S. bidders without discrimination on such projects.[90]

OUTCOMES

Semiconductors as a Case of "Involuntary Defection"

One of the semiconductor case's main features was the broad coalition supporting American demands put together by SIA, leading to a very specific win-set. The Japanese win-set never completely overlapped the American, primarily because of the industry's strong resistance to third-country monitoring and provision of proprietary data to the U.S. government. MITI nevertheless agreed to the American demands, probably in part because of the tremendous political pressure on the government to avoid the stigma of anti-dumping penalties or Section 301 retaliation. As one Japanese official intimately involved in the negotiations put it to me in retrospect, "Maybe [our] desire to keep [our] relationship with the U.S. overwhelmed [us]."[91] Another consideration was probably that aspects of the agreement were in MITI's interest, as it gave the ministry the opportunity to expand its control over the domestic industry.

Despite the fact that MITI may have tried to live up to the agreement, Japanese companies did not like it; "industry got mad," and probably a majority of the firms disagreed with the pact.[92] Although some of the largest firms cooperated with MITI, some Japanese producers did not take the agreement seriously or were overly zealous in their pursuit of other markets, and violated the pricing agreement in third countries.[93] According to one Japanese writer, during the negotiations MITI had neither consulted with nor reported fully to industry on the anti-dumping aspects of the negotiation.[94] A few of the companies that violated the agreement were those that MITI had not fully persuaded at the time of the agreement, or with whom MITI had not completely shared information during negotiations.[95] Therefore, at least some of the Japanese companies had never completely "ratified" the agreement, leading to "involuntary defection" on the part of the Japanese when MITI could not impose its control over these companies in third-country markets.

Even the side-letter with its expectation of a 20-percent U.S. share of the Japanese market within five years may have been entered into precipitously; MITI may have caved in to the "lobbyist diplomacy" of U.S. negotiators. While the large Japanese firms with whom it usually dealt might possibly import 20 percent of their chips from the U.S., the electronics firm end-users would probably not be able to reach that goal; MITI nevertheless agreed to the overall 20-percent target.[96]

Construction as a Ratified Agreement

In the construction case, with the Prime Minister's prior consultations lining up industry's agreement to concessions, plus his own credibility and ties to the construction industry, the deal that Ozawa cut with the Americans was certain to be ratified, and was.

Despite continued criticism from U.S. industry and congressional sources that the settlement was too narrow and should be extended to more projects, and further USTR investigations on the subject, the agreement held. Even critics agreed that Japan was complying with its provisions. In the later "super 301" investigations of Japan as an "unfair trader," construction was *not* one of the areas for which Japan was cited. In the construction case, retaliation by Congress brought new actors and stakes into the Japanese decision process, and the Japanese COG used his political clout with industry to refashion a win-set that overlapped with the American one, making a stable agreement possible.

Substantive Outcomes

Evaluating how much each side "won" or "lost" is more difficult. Evaluated strictly in terms of the American goals of stopping "dumping" (as per its definition of such) in U.S. and foreign markets, the semi-conductor agreement was at least a partial success, although it took sanctions to gain adherence in third-country markets. The goal of a 20-percent market share is less clear. As Table 1 shows, American suppliers' share of worldwide markets did not improve in the few years after the agreement, and Japanese-based suppliers continued to surpass their American competitors. In the U.S. market, Japan-based chip manufacturers actually substantially increased their market share, while U.S. suppliers experienced only some improvement in the Japanese market—nowhere near the hoped-for increase by the termination of the five-year agreement.

In construction, the almost total lack of contracts the Japanese market prior to the agreement made it difficult for the United States not to improve its market share subsequently. By 1990, 14 American companies had obtained licenses, there had been 13 joint-venture agreements between American and Japanese construction firms, and 16 U.S. companies had been awarded contracts. The rewards of market access reaped by American firms were less impressive, however—as of the beginning of 1990, contracts worth only about 200 million dollars on the 14 projects covered under the agreement.[97] Additionally, supporters of the American construction industry claimed that significant barriers to access remained in the Japanese market.[98] It should be remembered too that the Japanese obtained one of their primary goals in the negotiations—preservation of their designated bidding system, with all its domestic political and economic consequences.

In 1991, both agreements were renegotiated. The new construction agreement opened an additional 17 public-works projects to foreign bidding, with the prospect of an additional 6 in the future.[99] The new three-year (with option to renew for an additional two years) semiconductor accord put the 20-percent market-access figure into the agreement, but made it clear it is a hope, not a firm target, thus ending controversy over the "secret" side-letter of the 1986 pact. Data-gathering and monitoring by the U.S. government concerning dumping in the American market was greatly reduced or streamlined under the new agreement, and the final sanctions against Japan from the 1987 retaliation were lifted.[100]

COMPARING CASES

These cases involved similar government actors, and often similar negotiating strategies, on both sides. On the Japanese side were tough negotiating stances, often much narrower than the actual domestic win-set; the attempts of the COG, MITI, and MOFA to settle the dispute without American retaliation, despite resistance from recalcitrant bureaucratic or industry actors; and last-minute concessions to gain an agreement. On the U.S. side were constant threats of executive retaliation; the use of the "bad cop" Congress and the trade law as negotiating levers; the COG and State's attempts to avoid retaliating (often placing them in transnational alliance with Japan's COG, MITI, and MOFA) against Japan; and ultimatums and deadlines to bring about agreement. On both sides were the functions of summit meetings in pressuring the Japanese to make concessions, but also providing the COG with a means to defer or deflect pressures for retaliation. These are common factors in both cases.

In part, these procedural similarities reflect domestic institutional continuities, such as systemic roles in the case of COGs and agencies charged with maintaining key economic and political alliances; or the exploitation by key actors of their government institutions, such as the American division-of-powers system, or the Japanese parliamentary system with a dominant party but also strong bureaucratic and industrial actors. In part these commonalities reflect the differing international positions of the two countries with Japan economically dependent on the U.S. market and politically and strategically an ally of the more hegemonic American power, giving the U.S. threats of sanctions, ultimatums, and summit embarrassment a great deal of leverage.

Domestic institutions or international position, however, may variously explain the continuities and commonalities of strategy and (partially) of process, but singly do not account for the difference in outcomes. Despite the similar actors and strategies, the outcomes—stable agreement versus defected agreement—were quite different. To explain these, we must look at how the semiconductor and construction negotiations reflect the interaction of domestic and international bargaining on both sides of the Pacific.

In the semiconductor case, a united U.S. side with a fixed and specific win-set faced a divided Japan whose win-set was incompatible, because of resistance of some Japanese manufacturers. American demands fit with MITI's domestic political interests to enhance its control over the industry—essentially both the U.S. and MITI implicitly agreed on the need for MITI to organize a government-led solution to resolve the dispute.[101] These parallel interests, combined with pressure the Americans could place on Japan because of the unusual combination of anti-dumping and Section 301 leverage, induced the Japanese government to enter an agreement against the wishes of some of its own industry. The result was defection, since MITI could not initially force its industry to adhere to the agreement outside its own borders, nor could it deliver on the pace of Japan's markets opening that Americans expected.

In the construction case, both sides were divided in similar ways, several transnational alliances (COGs, State-MITI/MOFA) occurred, and the two sides were far apart on a key aspect of the American demands (revising procedures in other projects besides KIA). In contrast to the SIA-fostered cohesion in the semiconductor dispute, the U.S. construction industry was divided, and the hard-line advocates of shutting Japan out of the U.S. market were not effectively franchised, as is reflected in Chapin's bitter statement quoted above. Further, the United States lacked the anti-dumping leverage it had in the semiconductor case. When State blocked Section 301 sanctions once too often, Congress intervened with its own form of retaliation. This raised the stakes to the Japanese COG and, using his own influence with industry, he fashioned a new win-set and a ratifiable agreement with the United States.

The patterns of resolution and the outcomes are quite different, but in neither case can the outcome be explained without looking at the way the domestic political arrangements and interests of each side interacted with the other's negotiating strategies.[102]

A pure domestic politics (Level II) explanation cannot account for the results. In the construction dispute, the close ties between the affected Japanese industry and the ruling LDP and government were threatened by agreement to American demands. Because the political and economic stakes of conceding to American demands were very high for Japanese policy-making and interest-group elites, compared to the semiconductor case, we would expect Japanese domestic political arrangements to have militated against agreement more than in the latter case. It was the construction negotiations, however, in which a stable agreement was reached without American executive sanctions. Only by looking at the countervailing international pressure of potential retaliation outside the construction area can we understand why Japan became more flexible.

Similarly, in the semiconductor conflict, domestic factors cannot alone explain why MITI would pressure a powerful industry like semiconductor manufacturers to enter an international agreement that they did not want and that could undermine the continued growth of their global market share. MITI's concern for the U.S.-Japan relationship must be taken into account.

An international unitary-actor (Level I) analysis alone also does not work. The threat of Japanese competition to the U.S. national interest and the potential damage of American sanctions to Japanese interests were much greater in the semiconductor case than in the construction dispute. Again, we would expect the semiconductor negotiations to be more efficaciously resolved with a stable agreement. Yet the opposite occurred.

The interaction of domestic factors with the negotiations explains these paradoxes. The ultimate American flexibility on construction can be understood only by considering the divisions on the American side and the weakened voice of industry. By contrast, the U.S. forcefulness on semiconductors, even unto retaliation, has a great deal to do with the effective lobbying of the SIA and the consequent U.S. cohesion behind the negotiators. The willingness of the Japanese to risk such retaliation by industry violations in third countries, and little movement on access, can be explained only by the lack of communication and consensus between MITI and Japanese industry.

GOVERNMENTS, INTEREST GROUPS, AND TWO-LEVEL GAMES

The complex interweaving of domestic and international levels of politics in these negotiations is most obvious at the level of governments. MITI's apparent use of the semiconductor negotiations to advance its own domestic agenda vis-à-vis producers is one example. Another, more complex example comes from Secretary of State George Shultz's abortive attempt to delay retaliation against Japan in the construction case. This effort backfired domestically, provoking Congress to retaliate with the Brooks-Murkowski Amendment, and this amendment in turn led MITI to weigh in at the domestic Japanese table, softening the Japanese negotiating position.

From the perspective of extending two-level game theory, however, perhaps these two cases are more interesting in terms of what they suggest about domestic interest groups and the international table.

First, domestic interest groups need not be merely "ratifiers or nonratifiers"—a static element in the win-set equation that COGs manipulate to gain a stable agreement. Manipulation extends two ways, for domestic interest groups are also capable of strategic action to mold win-sets. Certainly the American win-set in the semiconductor case was shaped as much by SIA's efforts as by Reagan's. This was less the result of the SIA's inherent influence—in fact, it has only a narrow constituency in a few regions (California especially), and can deliver few votes—than of its ability to craft a negotiating position that united a divided industry and that fit the interests of state actors and even opponents. As pointed out above, SIA forged a package that maintained a coalition between suppliers and users of chips. That same package dovetailed with the Reagan Administration's "free trade" ideology (no quotas or floor prices) and its conception of the "national interest" (importance of semiconductors to America's economic future).[103] The package even provided unintended benefits to the chief player on the other side of the international table, by giving MITI an opportunity to expand its influence over the industry in Japan.

At the same time, we must not assume that politically powerful interest groups can always exercise veto power over COGs and the outcomes of negotiations. If ever an industry had political clout and government leaders in their debt, the construction industry in Japan did. This did not prevent the COGs from making concessions the industry did not like to gain an international agreement. Indeed, those concessions were made possible by the political connections and credibility of the COG and his representative (Ozawa) because of their history as agents and patrons of the construction industry.[104] Perhaps just because the COG had always been helpful to the industry, it understood the domestic and international costs to him of failing to get an agreement. Not only can manipulation between COGs and domestic interest groups be a two-way street, so may their political obligations.

Thus, in semiconductors, U.S. domestic interests tailored their demands to fit the domestic and international needs and interests of state actors (especially the COGs); whereas in construction, the Japanese COG took advantage of his connections and leverage with domestic social interests to forge a ratifiable international agreement.

Finally, we must not think that only governments play at both levels. With the increasing interdependence of economies, major interest groups often have international interests, and may also make moves at an international table. In the semiconductor case, the international interests of the Japanese firms were so strong as to lead them to undermine their own government's bilaterally negotiated agreement. In construction, two large American firms entered into joint ventures with Japanese firms even as their government was insisting that U.S. firms should have independent access to the Japanese market.

These two trade cases validate the necessity of analyzing the international and domestic levels of politics simultaneously to understand the processes and outcomes of international negotiation. They also suggest we should refine and extend out analysis of two-level games by re-evaluating the roles of domestic actors.

I would like to thank the persons knowledgeable about these negotiations—many of whom preferred to remain anonymous—who gave their valuable time, information, and perspective during interviews and in personal correspondence. I am grateful to Glen Fukushima and Ellen Frost for their suggestions, especially on potential interveiwees. I would also like to thank the organizers, especially Peter Evans, and the other participants in the project who provided much-needed feedback, suggestions, and criticisms on the several original drafts of this chapter. I am also grateful to the Japan Council, University of Pittsburgh, which provided research money from its Japan Iron and Steel Federation endowment fund to conduct interviews in Washington, D.C., and Tokyo. Japanese family names are cited first, as is the custom.

NOTES

1. Other disputes during this period involved agricultural products (beef and oranges) and telecommunications (cellular telephones), among others.

2. See Robert S. Walters, "U.S. Negotiation of Voluntary Restraint Agreements in Steel, 1984: Domestic Sources of Economic Diplomacy;" and Simon Reich, "Between Production and Protection: Reagan and the Negotiation of the VER for the Automobile Industry," two case studies in the Pew Foundation-sponsored series, University of Pittsburgh Case Studies in International Negotiation (Pittsburgh, Pa.: Graduate School of Public and International Affairs, 1987).

3. Interview with former official close to the negotiations and knowledgeable about State and other departments, March 1, 1990, Washington, D.C.; on Shultz, see David B. Yoffie and John J. Coleman, "The Semiconductor Industry Association and the Trade Dispute with Japan (A)," Harvard Business School case no. 9-387-205 (Cambridge, Mass., 1987, rev. Nov. 3, 1989), p. 6.

4. Interview with former official cited in note 3, March 1, 1990.

5. See, e.g., the *Washington Post* (hereafter *WP*), Dec. 17, 1985, p. E3.

6. See Thomas R. Howell, William A. Noellert, Janet H. MacLaughlin, and Alan W. Wolff, *The Microelectronics Race: The Impact of Government Policy on International Competition* (Boulder, Colo.: Westview Press, 1988), pp. 196–197, including note 522. Also see Yoffie and Coleman, "The SIA (A)," p. 2. On the SIA as a lobbying group, see Philip A. Mundo, "The U.S. Semiconductor Industry Association and the Political Response to Competition in High-Tech Industries," paper presented at the 1990 Annual Meeting of the American Political Science Association, San Francisco, Aug. 30–Sept. 2, 1990, pp. 1–32.

7. Clyde V. Prestowitz, Jr., *Trading Places: How We Allowed Japan to Take the Lead* (New York: Basic Books, 1988), pp. 55–56.

8. These differences among its members, for example, had prevented the

SIA from acting on charges of alleged Japanese dumping of 64K DRAMs in the early 1980s. See Yoffie and Coleman, "The SIA (A)," pp. 3–4. For background on the two countries' industries and market competition as a preface to the negotiations, also see Malcolm Salter and Susan Sanabria, "Semiconductors: U.S. Response to Japanese Ascendency," Harvard Business School case no. 9-387-210 (Cambridge, Mass., 1987), pp. 1–21; Howell et al., *The Microelectronics Race*, chaps. 1–3; Prestowitz, *Trading Places*, pp. 26–46.

9. Personal communication from SIA official.

10. Interview with industry source close to SIA and the negotiations, March 1, 1990, Washington, D.C. On SIA's efforts to gain the support of end-users and their differences with SIA, but AEA's ultimate support in the market-access goals, see Yoffie and Coleman, "The SIA (A)," pp. 4–5.

11. Interview with expert on the industry, Feb. 28, 1990, Washington, D.C. See also *New York Times* (hereafter *NYT*), Sept. 7, 1989, p. 25, article on SIA, where it is called "one of the most effective lobbying groups in the nation" and "a model for other lobbying groups."

12. *WP*, Dec. 17, 1985, p. E3.

13. Yoffie and Coleman, "The SIA (A)," pp. 2–3, note 1.

14. Ibid., pp. 7 and 8.

15. Prestowitz, *Trading Places*, p. 62.

16. Yoffie and Coleman, "The SIA (A)," p. 5.

17. Interview with former official cited in note 3. According to this respondent, what started out primarily as a market-access problem soon became "convoluted." When SIA and the worsening trade deficit "cranked up Congress," enormous pressure built on State and other agencies, for which the only outlet was trade policy. Also, with negotiations taking on "a life of their own," the problem for State became one of how to "manage" the issue.

18. Interview with former U.S. trade official, March 2, 1990, Washington, D.C.

19. One U.S. company official is quoted as saying, "The key became that the Japanese had to guarantee a market share in the 20s. It had to have 'a two' in front of the number in order to be acceptable": see Yoffie and Coleman, "The SIA (A)," p. 8.

20. Interview with former U.S. trade official cited in note 18. The U.S. would also resist "floor pricing" levels, because this would not let prices reflect production efficiencies. See Howell et al., *The Microelectronics Race*, pp. 198–199.

21. Personal communication from SIA official.

22. Ibid.

23. The Ministry of Foreign Affairs (MOFA), however, would play some role, especially toward the end of the negotiations.

24. See Reich, "Between Production and Protection," pp. 14–15.

25. Interview with expert cited in note 11. As examples of how MITI used the excuse of enforcing the agreement with the Americans to expand its power and information capabilities over the industry, he cited requiring monthly and quarterly reports and using the export-licensing system it controlled in new ways under the agreement, and applying many of its monitoring mechanisms to all

semiconductors, not just those covered under the agreement. The auto case provides a prior example of a similar strategy; see Reich, "Between Production and Protection," p. 14.

26. On the early agreements and their limitations, see Prestowitz, *Trading Places*, pp. 46–53; also Howell et al., *The Microelectronics Race*, p. 102.

27. Prestowitz, *Trading Places*, pp. 55–56; Yoffie and Coleman, "The SIA (A)," pp. 4–5.

28. *NYT*, Nov. 11, 1985, p. D2.

29. *NYT*, Nov. 14, 1985, p. D2, and *WP*, Dec. 9, 1985, p. 10.

30. Prestowitz, *Trading Places*, p. 57.

31. *WP*, Dec. 17, 1985, p. E3.

32. *WP*, Dec. 10, 1985, p. E3.

33. "Japanese Proposed Settlement Offer for Semiconductors," pp. 1–2, an informal, unofficial memorandum, undated and with no source specified, prepared for the U.S. negotiating team and shown to the author by a former official involved in the negotiation.

34. Ibid., p. 3. If floor prices applied to the chips sold in the American but not the Japanese market, the U.S. feared it would raise prices in the United States while keeping them lower in Japan, making it even more difficult for American firms to sell there.

35. E.g., in January the ITC ruled unanimously that Japanese firms were dumping 256K chips in the U.S.; *NYT*, Jan. 23, 1985, p. D4.

36. See, e.g., *WP*, Feb. 21, 1986, p. A9.

37. Interview with former U.S. trade official cited in note 18. Also in March, prior to the Yeutter-Watanabe meeting, five Japanese producers and MITI representatives had met with American firms and offered to increase their purchases of U.S. chips, but only by about 3 percent, a figure unacceptable to the U.S. companies: *WP*, March 26, 1986, p. 61, and personal correspondence with a SIA official.

38. *Wall Street Journal* (hereafter *WSJ*), March 31, 1986, p. 2.

39. *NYT*, May 29, 1990, p. D4.

40. See, e.g., *WP*, April 25, 1986, p. B12, and May 28, 1986, p. G1.

41. Interview cited in note 18.

42. *WP*, July 1, 1986, p. D1, and *Nihon Keizai Shinbun* (hereafter *NKS*), July 1, p. 1, and July 4, 1986.

43. Interview with former U.S. trade official cited in note 18.

44. E.g., *WP*, July 1, 1986, p. D1.

45. Interview with Kuroda Makoto, former MITI Vice Minister for International Affairs, May 30, 1991. Kuroda made it clear that his "constituents" were the Japanese producers and parts of government and MITI that were "hawkish" on the agreement.

46. Carol A. Ryavec, Vice President of Japanese equity research for Salomon Bros., Asia, quoted in *WSJ*, July 5, 1986, p. 34. See other such reports: *NYT*, July 26, pp. 33 and 36, and *WP*, July 29, 1986, p. E10.

47. On the agreement, see Coleman and Yoffie, "The SIA (A)," pp. 8–9; Howell et al., *The Microelectronics Race*, pp. 198–199; and the various press reports for Aug. 1, 1986.

48. According to an article by a Japanese semiconductor industry executive, the side-letter states in part, "The Government of Japan recognizes the U.S. semiconductor industry's expectation that semiconductor sales in Japan of foreign capital-affiliated companies will grow to at least slightly above 20 percent of the Japanese market in five years," and that the Japanese government "will encourage Japanese users to purchase more foreign-based semiconductors." See Fujiwara Mikio, "Nihon handôtai kyôtei: kore ga mitsuyaku bunsho da" [The Japan-U.S. Semiconductor Agreement: This Is the Secret Agreement Document], *Bungeishunjû* (May 1988), p. 126. Some argue that the secret side-letter was at U.S. insistence (e.g., see *WSJ*, Aug. 1, 1986, p. 3), but American negotiators and others claim it was proposed by the Japanese: interview with former trade official involved in the negotiations; also Prestowitz, *Trading Places*, pp. 65–66.

49. Prestowitz, *Trading Places*, p. 66.

50. *WSJ*, Sept. 25, 1986, p. 8; and interview with former U.S. trade official cited in note 18.

51. *WSJ*, Oct. 15, 1986, p. 8.

52. *WSJ*, Oct. 10, 1986, p. 2.

53. Coleman and Yoffie, "The SIA (A)," p. 10.

54. *NYT*, Jan. 2, 1987, pp. D1 and D3.

55. *NKS*, Jan. 30, 1987, p. 4, and same-day evening edition, p. 1; *WSJ*, Jan. 30, 1987, p. 27.

56. Interview with Isayama Takeshi, former head of North American bureau of MITI, May 30, 1991.

57. Interviews with former U.S. officials cited in notes 3 and 18.

58. Interviews cited in note 57.

59. *NKS*, Feb. 18, 1987, p. 3; Feb. 19, 1987, p. 3; March 3, 1987, p. 1; and March 18, 1987, p. 5; *WP*, March 21, 1987, p. D11.

60. On the famous Oki Denki accusations, see *NKS*, March 21, 1987, p. 8.

61. Coleman and Yoffie, "The SIA (A)," p. 12, and "The Semiconductor Industry Association and the Trade Dispute with Japan (B)," (Cambridge, Mass.: Harvard College, 1987; rev. February 1988), pp. 1–2.

62. See *NKS*, March 27, 1987, evening, p. 1; March 28, 1987, evening, pp. 1, 2, 3; March 29, 1987, p. 3.

63. Interview with former U.S. trade official cited in note 18. Coleman and Yoffie, "The SIA (B)," pp. 1–2.

64. For specifics on improvement in the Japan market, see below.

65. For further details on the domestic and international politics of the construction issue, see Ellis S. Krauss, "Under Construction: U.S.-Japan Negotiations to Open Japan's Construction Markets to American Firms, 1985–1988," University of Pittsburgh Case Studies in International Negotiation (Pittsburgh, Pa.: Graduate School of Public and International Affairs, 1989).

66. On the basic issues in the dispute, see ibid., pp. 2–7; Ellis S. Krauss and Isobel Coles, "Built-in Impediments: The Political Economy of the U.S.-Japan Construction Dispute," in Kozo Yamamura, ed., *Japan's Economic Structure: Should It Change?* (Seattle: Society for Japanese Studies, 1990), pp. 336–347; and Robert Cutts, "What the Construction Wrangle Is Really About," *PHP Intersect* (September 1988).

67. Interview with U.S. expert on semiconductor industry, Feb. 28, 1990.

68. See "Japan Carves Niche in U.S. Construction," *Asian Wall Street Journal* (hereafter *AWSJ*), Jan. 19, 1988, p. 1; and *WP,* June 6, 1986, pp. B8 and B10.

69. On incestuous construction-industry relationships that underlay both the issue and process of the construction dispute with the U.S., see Krauss and Coles, "Built-in Impediments," pp. 336–347.

70. Ibid., pp. 337–338.

71. On the pre-Seminar talks, the Seminar, and post-Seminar press conferences and reactions, see *NKS,* Oct. 8, 1986, p. 5; Oct. 8, 1986 (ee), p. 1; Oct. 9, 1986, p. 1; Oct. 9, 1986 (ee), p. 1; Oct. 10, 1986, p. 5; and Oct. 11, 1986, p. 3.

72. One such instance was in August 1987 when, following a series of new proposals made by the Japanese, Commerce Undersecretary J. Michael Ferran publicly told them that their new offers were "a fair amount of progress" but "insufficient to persuade Congress and the industry."

73. I. M. Destler, *American Trade Politics: System Under Stress* (Washington, D.C.: Institute for International Economics, 1986), p. 28.

74. In September 1987, for example, MITI Minister Tamura, whose ministry did not even have jurisdiction in this dispute, was given the strong impression in talks in Washington that the application of Section 301 was imminent unless Japan made further concessions. Tamura returned to Tokyo and publicly argued for a more flexible stand toward American demands; see *Asahi Shinbum* (hereafter *AS*), Sept. 11, 1987, p. 1; Sept. 12, 1987, p. 2; Sept. 14, 1987, p. 3.

75. See Krauss, "Under Construction," p. 25.

76. E.g., see the publicly contradictory moves of various Japanese government officials during a few days prior to the April–May 1987 summit described in ibid. pp. 23–24.

77. On how MOT and MOC worked against MOFA efforts, however, see "Feud with U.S. Drains Japan's Diplomats," *WSJ,* Nov. 20, 1987, p. 24.

78. E.g., in December 1987, the sub-cabinet TPRG, which was to recommend for Section 301 retaliation in other instances, was persuaded to defer a retaliation until after Takeshita's first summit meeting with Reagan in January 1988.

79. *NYT,* Dec. 5, 1987, p. 37.

80. Robert D. Putnam, "Diplomacy and Domestic Politics: The Logic of Two-Level Games," *International Organization* 42 (Summer 1988), p. 451–452, and the appendix to this volume.

81. Krauss, "Under Construction," pp. 28–29.

82. Interview with Isayama Takeshi, May 30, 1991, confirmed that one reason MITI became involved in the construction dispute after Brooks-Murkowski because of fear that retaliation would be in their jurisdiction.

83. Krauss, "Under Construction," pp. 29–30.

84. Further talks with USTR and Commerce officials led to Secretary of State Shultz and Foreign Minister Uno announcing the framework as a new Japanese offer in Washington on Jan. 12, 1988, the day before the Takeshita-Reagan summit.

85. See Krauss, "Under Construction," pp. 29–31.

86. On this issue, see ibid., pp. 32–33.

87. Quoted in Keith M. Rockwell, "State Department Denies Overrating Tokyo Offer," *Journal of Commerce,* Jan. 21, 1988.
88. Ostensibly because Farren had been too tough a negotiator. The White House denied the charges, but they became a public embarrassment: Keith M. Rockwell, "Power of Japan's Trade Lobbies Raises Eyebrows in Washington," *Journal of Commerce,* March 4, 1988, p. 1; *AWSJ,* March 7, 1988, p. 3.
89. Interview with Aichi Kazuo, Director-General, Environment Agency, and member of Takeshita faction, May 22, 1991.
90. For details on the agreement, see Krauss, "Under Construction," pp. 34–35 and Appendix C.
91. Interview with Kuroda Makoto, former MITI Vice Minister for International Affairs at time of semiconductor negotiations, May 30, 1991.
92. Interview with Isayama Takeshi, former head of North American bureau of MITI, May 30, 1991.
93. This seems to be the consensus interpretation, by several of the former U.S. officials and industry spokesman I interviewed, of both MITI and the company's actions, confirmed by some Japanese officials I interviewed. According to Isayama Takeshi, one of the companies accused of dumping "[was] not dominant, so [they] felt they can do as they wish. . . . [Their] self-discipline was not well-established."
A different view of one of the most famous and strangest of these cases, the Oki case, from the perspective of one of the companies accused, is given in Ōtaki Takashi, "Waga sha o ochiireta Amerika no wana" [The American trap into which our company fell], *Bungei Shunjū* (June 1987), pp. 134–141. Japanese officials also believe that Oki was the victim of a "sting" operation by the United States.
94. Namiki Nobuyoshi, *Tsūsansho no shūen* [The Last Moments of MITI] (Tokyo: Daiyamondo-sha, 1989), pp. 167–168.
95. Interview with Isayama Takeshi; also interviews with former semiconductor industry source, March 1, 1990, and U.S. trade official, March 2, 1990.
Another interpretation was that MITI was forced to sign the agreement but did not believe the U.S. would retaliate even if Japan was unable to completely live up to its provisions. This still would not change the conclusion below about involuntary defection.
96. Namiki, *Tsūsansho no shūen,* p. 170. A MITI official confirmed to me that MITI never did the calculation of whether the 20-percent figure was possible, because they considered the side-letter merely an acknowledgment of the U.S. side's "desire": interview with Kuroda Makoto, former MITI Vice Minister for International Affairs, May 30, 1991.
97. The Japanese claim that American firms also have received an additional 250 million dollars on other projects. All figures on construction are from "Japanese Bend on Contract Barriers," *Financial Times,* Jan. 31, 1990, p. 6.
98. Testimony before the Section 301 Committee of Senator Frank H. Murkowski, March 13, 1989, United States Senate.
99. David E. Sanger, "Japan to Allow Foreigners to Bid on Construction Jobs," *NYT,* June 2, 1991, p. A13.

100. Keith Bradsher, "Chip Pact Set by U.S. and Japan," *WP,* June 4, 1991, p. C1; Eduardo Lachica and Jacob M. Schlesinger, "Washington, Tokyo Agree on Semiconductor Accord," *WSJ,* June 5, 1991, p. 2.

101. Kenneth Flamm, "Policy and Politics in the International Semiconductor Industry," paper presented at the SEMI ISS Seminar, Newport Beach, Calif., Jan. 16, 1989, p. 11, refers to this solution as similar to a MITI-led cartel. The U.S. side, however, would claim that it opposed a "cartel," and that when MITI imposed production controls on the industry it was a violation of the agreement: personal correspondence from SIA official.

102. These cases also incidentally negate the stereotype of the U.S. as a state that acts only as a result of interest-group pressure, and Japan as a powerful bureaucratic state that can always compel compliance from interest groups. Construction was a state-led issue on the U.S. side, and in semiconductors MITI was not able to impose its preferences for agreement on a recalcitrant industry without defections.

103. For a related model that tries to systematically explain the differing actions of the U.S. President in the semiconductor issue, construction, and several other U.S.-Japan cases as the result of the interaction of domestic political pressure, "national interest" concerns, and laissez-faire/free-trade ideology, see Ellis S. Krauss and Simon Reich, "Ideology, Interests, and the American Executive: Toward a Theory of Foreign Competition and Manufacturing Trade Policy," *International Organization* 46 (Autumn 1992), pp. 857–897.

104. On this point, also see Krauss and Coles, "Built-in Impediments," p. 356.

PART 4

North-South Tensions

The United States and Central America
Interlocking Debates

Robert A. Pastor

From the perspective of small, vulnerable Central American nations, the United States is awesome and impenetrable. It manipulates their politics and divides their nations to further U.S. interests. Given the disparity in size and power between the United States and the countries of Central America, one would expect the United States to dominate. Less evident, but no less important, has been the effect these small nations have had on the United States, even in cases where their interests diverged.

The Panama Canal Treaties, the Sandinistas, and the contras were among the most controversial, politically debilitating issues ever faced by U.S. policy-makers. Securing ratification of the Panama Canal Treaties was, in President Carter's words, "the toughest political fight of my life, including my election as president."[1] Carter paid a steep political price in order to reach a barely ratifiable accommodation. The Reagan Administration failed to reach any understanding with the Sandinista government, and both sides paid for that failure, albeit in different ways. The Bush Administration retreated from the confrontational policy of its predecessor, deciding neither to support nor to abandon the contras. It also showed no interest in seeking any accommodation with the Sandinista regime. Ironically, withdrawal proved more effective than the coercive strategy in changing the regime.

The purpose of this chapter is to try to explain why agreement was achieved on new Canal treaties but failed in Nicaragua. Realists would expect the United States to have its way on both issues, but the outcomes of both cases were politically harmful to the U.S. President, and thus contradict this prediction. Presidential preferences can partly explain the different outcomes, with Carter ready to compromise and President Reagan unwilling to modify his "acceptability-set," but too much of the story and the analysis is omitted by personalizing it. In fact, what was more important in both cases was the extent to which the debates in each country penetrated and affected the other in ways that either facilitated or precluded agreement.

In the case of the Panama Canal Treaties, the two chiefs of government (COGs)—Carter and General Omar Torrijos of Panama—can be considered moderates or "doves." They shared an interest in getting the two domestic constituencies to accept their agreement. In the case of the contras, the two COGs—Reagan and President Daniel Ortega of Nicaragua—were the intransigents or "hawks." Whereas Carter and Torrijos tried to get their domestic constituents to ratify their promises, Reagan and Ortega sought to get their domestic constituents to ratify their threats. In the Nicaraguan case, it proved more difficult for the COG of the more powerful country to obtain domestic support for threats than for the COG of the weaker nation, because the force of nationalism favored the smaller nation.

After the riots in the Panama Canal Zone in January 1964, every U.S. president understood the logic of new Canal treaties. The exclusive control by the United States of a ten-mile-wide strip of land through the middle of Panama was an outmoded relic of a bygone era. The longer the United States refused to correct this wrong, the greater the risk to the Canal. Most U.S. policy-makers understood that, but they also recognized that the American people did not want to give away "their" Canal.

Therefore, treaty negotiations dragged on from 1965 until 1977. Jimmy Carter was the first U.S. president to give the Canal treaties high priority, and they were signed in September 1977 and ratified the next spring. During the process, moderates in both countries helped each other, sometimes tacitly, other times deliberately, by persuading domestic constituents to relax their constraining influence. Extremists also helped each other, by making accommodation more difficult, but the moderates prevailed, and I will try to explain why and how that occurred.

In the case of Nicaragua, we will examine the period from the onset of the Sandinista revolutionary government on July 20, 1979, through civil war to its defeat in a free election on February 25, 1990. For the first fifteen months of the relationship, a tacit and awkward understanding existed between the two governments: the United States agreed to assist the revolution, and the Sandinistas agreed to refrain from supporting the Salvadoran insurgents (FMLN). That accommodation broke down in early January 1981 when the United States obtained conclusive evidence that the Sandinistas were supporting the FMLN. Ronald Reagan viewed the Sandinistas as Communists, and his Administration gradually escalated its pressures and expanded its objectives. The Sandinista National Liberation Front (FSLN) became more militaristic, and Reagan used that to justify the war.

By 1988, the United States and Nicaragua were engaged in an indirect war, which drained Nicaragua's economy, polarized its politics, and murdered and maimed its young. The contra war also hurt its American sponsor. The United States was condemned by its friends and by the International Court of Justice, and President Ronald Reagan was saved from possible impeachment by his National Security Advisor, John Poindexter, who told Congress that he had shielded the President from decisions to support the contras at a time when that was illegal. Though popular when he left office, President Reagan was viewed by a majority of the American people as having lied about his role in the Iran-contra scandal, and in federal court Poindexter's lawyer confirmed the accuracy of the public's perception.[2]

Whereas in Panama the moderate strategy prevailed and accommodation was the result, in Nicaragua the extremes dominated the issue and confrontation resulted. To understand why, we shall try to unravel the knots that tie domestic and international politics and Americans' conceptions of security with their idealistic self-image. American policy-makers have long been torn between realistic calculations and idealistic aspirations. In no region is this tension more evident than in Central America, where policy-makers have wrestled with the contradiction between Monroe's dictum to exclude foreign rivals and Woodrow Wilson's dream to respect self-determination and defend human rights. In this policy debate, Congress and the American public have always played a key role.

A foreign-policy analysis that fails to take account of either the domestic or the international side will be at best incomplete. More likely, such an analysis will mislead. Sole reliance on international negotiations (Level I) would fail to explain the formulation of U.S. policy, the effect that other nations' strategies have on U.S. policy, and thus the outcome. It is widely accepted that the United States is a potent independent variable in the formulation of Nicaraguan or Panamanian foreign policies, but the way in which domestic bargaining (Level II) within these countries influences and is influenced by the international bargain (Level I) is not as well understood.

The politics within and between the United States, Panama, and Nicaragua have given the relationship its unique and often unfathomable character. In trying to explore that, this chapter will first provide some background on the two cases and will then analyze them to discern whether, and if so how, the relationship between the two levels explains why accommodation succeeded in Panama and failed in Nicaragua.

A HISTORY OF DIVIDED BUT CONNECTED POLITICS

The United States has been deeply involved in the politics of Panama and Nicaragua since the Gold Rush in the late 1840s made the isthmus an important transportation link between the Atlantic and Pacific coasts. The nature of U.S. involvement has changed, but the motives have remained relatively constant: to secure and maintain access to the Panamanian isthmus, and to prevent Nicaraguan instability from being exploited by a foreign rival of the United States. Each period of U.S. involvement has engaged the President, Congress, and the American public. Each time, the U.S. President was compelled to deal on a domestic political level with one hand while using the other to influence isthmian politics.

Small and poor, the Central American states have lacked a tradition of peaceful, democratic change. To displace an incumbent, the opposition has sought outside help, either from the United States or its rival. Whether the United States intervened or not, it remained a formidable factor in local Panamanian and Nicaraguan politics. At the same time, nationalists in both countries, whether they defied the United States or sought its support, tried to expand their nations' autonomy. Thus, both the United States and its Central American counterparts tried to exploit domestic divisions abroad, even while trying to prevent foreign interference in their own internal affairs.

Negotiating Panama Canal Treaties

The image of the U.S.S. *Oregon* making its 16,000-mile voyage around Cape Horn during the Spanish-American War persuaded the American people that the time had come to build a canal. As Panama was then a province of Colombia, U.S. Secretary of State John Hay negotiated a treaty with Colombia's Foreign Minister. Soon after the Colombian Senate rejected the treaty, on November 3, 1903, the Panamanians declared independence. The United States had helped Colombia suppress many previous revolts; this time, it prevented Colombian troops from landing to put down the rebellion. The new republic gave Philippe Bunau-Varilla, a wily Frenchman with interests in the Panamanian railroad, authority to negotiate a canal treaty.

The Hay–Bunau-Varilla Treaty, signed on November 18, 1903, ceded "rights, power, and authority in perpetuity" to the United States to exercise jurisdiction "as if it were sovereign" over a zone ten miles wide in order to construct, operate, and defend a canal. When the Panamanian delegation arrived in Washington and raised concerns about the treaty, Bunau-Varilla warned them that the United States might withdraw its protection and make a new deal with Colombia, which wanted to recover both Panama and the proposed canal. The treaty was duly ratified by both sides, and the canal was built in a decade. It opened in 1914, on the eve of the First World War.

The Panamanians resented the treaty from its inception and protested its provisions regularly. In response to some of Panama's concerns, President Franklin Roosevelt revised the treaty in 1936 to repeal the provision permitting the United States the right to intervene in Panama's internal affairs, and in 1955 President Eisenhower accepted some other revisions to the treaty to increase Panama's share of jobs and economic benefits. But these changes did not address Panama's three main concerns: the clause that gave U.S. rights to operate the Canal "in perpetuity"; American jurisdiction over a ten-mile-wide strip of land through the middle of Panama; and unilateral operation and defense of the Canal without Panamanian participation.

In January 1964, Panamanian students rioted in Panama and the Canal Zone. Twenty Panamanians and four Americans died, hundreds were injured, diplomatic relations between the United States and Panama were broken, and the OAS sent a mission to investigate charges of U.S. aggression. By the end of the year, the two governments began negotiating a new treaty. The two sides almost signed a draft in 1967, but elections in both countries the next year prevented closure. Arnulfo Arias was elected President in Panama, but before he could replace the leaders of Panama's National Guard, the Guard, led by Omar Torrijos, replaced him.

After consolidating power, Torrijos embarked on a strategy to increase international pressure on the United States to negotiate Canal treaties. He invited the UN Security Council to meet in Panama in 1973 and then offered a resolution calling for new treaties; the United States vetoed it. Upset by Panamanian tactics, but aware of the need to respond to legitimate demands, Secretary of State Henry Kissinger negotiated a "Joint Statement of Eight Principles," an outline of a new treaty, with his counterpart, Juan Tack, on February 8, 1974.

The principles called for abrogation of the 1903 treaty, the termination of perpetual rights by the United States, a gradual transfer of jurisdiction and operation of the Canal to Panama, and a new formula for defending the Canal. Even before the negotiators set to work to translate these principles into a treaty, Congress stepped between them. Senator Strom Thurmond of South Carolina introduced a Senate resolution with 34 co-sponsors (enough to prevent ratification of a treaty), and Congressman Dan Flood and 120 representatives introduced similar resolutions in the House, urging the United States to stop negotiating and "retain continued undiluted sovereignty over the Canal Zone." Thurmond condemned the Kissinger-Tack declaration and argued that it could not be "reconciled with the Senate resolution."[3]

The initiatives by Thurmond and Flood were early warning signs of what President Gerald Ford later described as his "challenge from the right." Ronald Reagan articulated that perspective most forcefully, and the Panama issue was central to his message:

> Our State Department apparently believes the hints regularly dispensed by the leftist Torrijos regime that the Canal will be sabotaged if we don't hand it over. . . . I don't understand how the State Department can suggest we pay blackmail to this dictator. . . . When it comes to the Canal, we built it, we paid for it, it's ours, and we should tell Torrijos and Company that we are going to keep it.[4]

Ford criticized Reagan's comment as "inflammatory and irresponsible,"[5] but it was also effective in stopping the negotiations. During the presidential campaign of 1976, both Carter and Ford tried to sound tough on the issue for domestic political purpose, but neither said anything that would preclude future negotiations with Panama.[6]

After his election, despite the political cost, Jimmy Carter instructed the National Security Council (NSC) to do its first Presidential Review Memorandum (PRM-1; it was a term of reference for the bureaucracy to prepare an options paper for an NSC meeting) on Panama. Carter also appointed Sol M. Linowitz, a former Ambassador to the OAS, to be co-negotiator with Ellsworth Bunker. Linowitz had chaired a private commission on U.S.-Latin American relations that had issued a report in December 1976 recommending new Canal treaties as "the most urgent issue" in the hemisphere faced by the new Administration.[7] Partly to preempt a debate on the treaties, as would occur during confirmation hearings, Linowitz was appointed the President's special representative for six months. This then was a double signal to Panama—that Carter was serious about negotiating new Canal treaties, and that both sides had a deadline of six months to complete the negotiations.

The decision to negotiate rapidly was based on twin judgments on the international and domestic political climate. First, the Administration believed that the Canal's security would be jeopardized by delay, as the Panamanian "patience machine," in Omar Torrijos' pungent phrase, "was running out of gas" after 13 years of fruitless negotiations. Second, because ratification would be politically difficult, the Administration estimated that the treaty would have to be signed by the summer of 1977 in order to be ratified by the spring of 1978—sufficient time before November elections for Senators to vote without too much fear of popular retribution.

The domestic and international dimensions of the issue were considered simultaneously. The PRM had emphasized the importance of developing a strategy for persuading Congress and the American public, but the paper drafted by the State Department for the NSC contained an agenda of ten items, with the tenth being "Congress and the public," but only "if time permits." As the NSC staff on Latin America, I called this to the attention of Zbigniew Brzezinski, Carter's National Security Adviser, who phoned Secretary of State Cyrus Vance, and both agreed that the tenth item should be considered first. Carter concurred that the two negotiators should consult with the Senate while they negotiated with Panama.

The Canal Treaty negotiations pitted two contradictory interests: Panama wanted full control over the Canal as soon as possible, and the United States wanted to operate the Canal as long as feasible and to defend it in perpetuity. In 1977, the State and Defense departments began by negotiating between themselves, but the President directed the negotiators to the real task of brokering an agreement between Panama and the Senate. The challenge was to locate the narrow overlap between what Panama wanted, and the Senate was willing to accept.

On March 2, 1977, the President, his senior advisers, and the two negotiators met in the Oval Office to discuss how to overcome the central stumbling block in the negotiations: how to fix an end date on a new treaty while guaranteeing U.S. security interests in the Canal in perpetuity. One adviser mentioned the need for some gray language like that in UN Resolution 242 or the "Shanghai Communiqué." Vice President Walter Mondale, drawing on his experience in the Senate, argued persuasively against such an approach, insisting that the final agreement would have to be unambiguous to obtain Senate ratification. The formula for satisfying these two contrary concerns was two treaties: the main treaty transferred the Canal to Panama by the year 2000, and a second Neutrality Treaty gave both governments the permanent right to defend the Canal.

In July, the negotiations bogged down over Panama's insistence on large payments from the United States. As Carter wrote in his memoirs: "Neither I nor Congress would agree to any payments to Panama other than those that could come out of revenues from the Canal itself." Carter realized that he could not ask the Senate to give away the Canal and pay Panama at the same time. On July 29, he sent a letter to Torrijos saying that U.S. negotiators were making their last offer, and that time was running out for Senate ratification.[8] At the same time, the United States asked its Latin American friends to urge Torrijos to complete the deal. On August 5 Torrijos accepted the economic proposals, and on August 10, 1977—the last day of Linowitz's appointment—the two negotiators returned to the White House from Panama and announced the conclusion of the treaty.[9]

Carter immediately notified all the members of the Senate and invited

Ford, Kissinger, other national leaders, and all the presidents and prime ministers of the Americas for a signing ceremony at the OAS on September 7, 1977. The sole purpose of the gala event was to impress the American people with the broad national and deep international support for the treaties.

The two leaders signed two treaties. The Panama Canal Treaty abrogated the 1903 Treaty and set a date—2000—when Panama would have complete jurisdiction and operational authority over the Canal. From the implementation of the treaty to 2000, the United States would gradually turn over responsibility for the administration, operation, and defense of the Canal. But the second treaty, the Treaty on Permanent Neutrality, guaranteed that the United States would retain the right to defend the Canal after the year 2000.

On September 6, 1977, the day before they signed the treaties, Carter and Torrijos met in the White House and talked about the difficulties of ratifying them. "What can we do . . . to help you?" Carter asked. Torrijos requested a personal message from Carter to the Panamanian people, but noted: "Remember, we are selling the same product to two different audiences." Carter agreed and said that they would have to develop two different advertising campaigns, but that these should not contradict each other. "Obviously," Carter told him, "your public statements will have great effect here. And I will continue to consult with you to make sure that I don't make your task more difficult."

Other than Carter's message to the Panamanian people, the U.S. government played no direct role in the debate in Panama. Torrijos wanted it like that. U.S. government officials did not know the depth or nature of the opposition to the treaties in Panama, though Torrijos understood both very well. He realized that a number of compromises that he had made to complete the treaties created problems for him. Still, he concluded:

> I am satisfied. But we paid a price for liberation. Those who decolonize themselves through negotiations do not achieve full liberation. . . . We now have to walk for 23 years [the duration of the treaty] with a pebble in our shoe, but that's the price we have to pay for getting the dagger out of our heart. I did not concede any more than I can sell to my people.[10]

The Senate, however, was the principal arena; and Carter, with Torrijos' assistance, utilized the full range of strategies to try to change public opinion and perceptions: issue linkage, side-payments, cooptation. More than two-thirds of the Senate understood the need for the treaties, but all of them knew that a vote for ratification would hurt them politically. The issue was not how to change preferences, but rather how to provide them with sufficient political space to vote the right way. A seemingly endless train of about 50 senators traveled individually or in small groups to Panama to interrogate Torrijos. Senator Robert Byrd tried to explain to Torrijos why he needed to be patient:

> What you have to understand is that any Senator voting for these treaties will pay a high political price. He will gain absolutely nothing personally by doing so. Therefore, you have to be tolerant and patient in bringing people around to understanding these problems and to taking this difficult decision.[11]

A host of side issues—including expropriated property in Panama, human rights, drugs, water projects, tariffs on copper, and natural gas legislation—were linked to the treaties during the debate, along with more directly related issues. Using a national security argument to gain support for the treaties, Carter had to handle these other issues carefully, lest he open himself to charges that he traded water projects for votes.

Hearings began in the Senate Foreign Relations Committee on September 26. Only two genuinely substantive issues were debated: the unilateral right of the United States to defend the Canal; and the priority of American ships to go to "the head of the line" in time of emergency. Though U.S. negotiators believed the treaties dealt adequately with these two issues, key senators questioned that. To resolve the problem, Carter invited Torrijos to the White House on October 14, just before the Panamanian plebiscite on the Treaties. The two agreed to an "understanding" which removed any ambiguity from these two issues. The majority and minority leaders of the Senate, Robert Byrd and Howard Baker, later introduced this "understanding" as a treaty amendment.

The Senate ratification debate on the Canal Treaties was second in length only to that of the Versailles Treaty, and it was tense and difficult the entire time. The Senate voted first on the Treaty on the Permanent Neutrality of the Panama Canal. On March 16, 1978, this passed by one vote more than the required two-thirds: 68–32. On April 18, the Senate voted exactly the same way on the Panama Canal Treaty, which abrogated the 1903 treaty.

Though the Carter Administration used public opinion polls to show that opposition declined as people learned more about the treaties, a later analysis indicated that public opinion hardly changed. In polls taken by the Roper Organization in January and September 1977 and June 1978, 52–53 percent of the American people said that the United States should keep the 1903 treaties. In April 1978, a *New York Times*/CBS news poll showed precisely the same number—53 percent—opposed the 1977 pacts and 30 percent approved. A decade later, that figure had not changed, although 58 percent then said that the United States should adhere to the treaties, even though they continued to disapprove of them.[12]

In the United States, the treaties cost their supporters and benefited their opponents. Ronald Reagan used his opposition to the treaties very deliberately to position himself for a successful run for the presidency. Twenty senators who voted for the treaties were not re-elected in 1978 and 1980, and in every one of those cases the Canal treaties were an issue, often an important one. Jimmy Carter also lost his bid for re-election—and while other issues were probably more important, Panama hurt.

Confronting the Sandinista Government

In contrast to the successful negotiations between the United States and Panama on new Canal treaties, the U.S. and Nicaraguan governments failed repeatedly from 1979 to 1989 to reach any durable understanding. A long and troubled history explains the lack of agreement between the two governments.

Since the mid-1930s, Nicaragua had been run by the Somoza family almost like a fiefdom.[13] By the 1970s, the Somozas' greed and repression had alienated every group in the country not under their control, and the children of the middle class began joining the FSLN, a guerrilla group inspired by the Cuban revolution and established in 1961. When Somoza lifted the state of siege in September 1977 in response to pressure by the Carter Administration, the moderate opposition in Nicaragua used the political opening to denounce the regime's corruption. In January 1978, Pedro Joaquín Chamorro, the leader of the opposition and editor of *La Prensa*, was assassinated. This galvanized and later united both the moderate and the radical opposition to the Somoza regime.

There was a consensus in the administration that if the United States did nothing, Somoza would try to repress the popular movement against him, the country would polarize even further, and the Sandinistas would eventually win a military victory. While the Carter Administration recognized that the Sandinistas had broadened their base of support, it viewed the key leaders as Marxist-Leninists, who looked to Cuba and the Soviet Union as allies and saw the United States as the enemy. Caught between a dictator it refused to defend and a guerrilla movement that it would not support, the Administration tried to encourage a democratic transition in Nicaragua under the auspices of the OAS.

The OAS group recommended a plebiscite on Somoza's tenure, but the negotiations collapsed in late January 1979 when Somoza rejected the conditions that would have permitted a free election. The United States imposed sanctions against Somoza, who then doubled the size of the National Guard. However, by May 1979, with Castro's help, the three Sandinista factions had united and established a secure and ample arms flow from Cuba through Panama and Costa Rica. The United States did not know the magnitude of the arms flows, nor did it have conclusive evidence of the involvement of Panama, Costa Rica, or Cuba.

In early June, the FSLN launched a military offensive and, supported by Mexico, Panama, Costa Rica, and the Andean Pact, it mounted a political initiative designed to strip Somoza of formal legitimacy and transfer it to them. The United States proposed a ceasefire between the FSLN and the National Guard that would coincide with Somoza's departure and then lead toward a negotiated coalition government. An inter-American force would oversee the ceasefire and facilitate the integration of the armed forces. A broad coalition of Latin American governments blocked this proposal at the OAS, and on July 20, 1979, after Somoza fled, the Sandinistas arrived to a joyous welcome in Managua.

The United States then faced three options on how to relate to the revolution. It could confront the revolutionary government in the hope of destabilizing or overthrowing it; it could withdraw, acknowledging that the shape of Nicaraguan politics was probably beyond U.S. control; or it could try to assist the new regime in a manner that would increase the prospects for democratization and regional security. On July 20, 1979, in a secret NSC meeting, the Administration chose the third option and decided to request 75 million dollars in aid from Congress.

The request for aid submitted to Congress in November 1979 precipitated a heated and protracted debate over whether the United States should support a regime that was intensely anti-American in its rhetoric and appeared to prefer Cuba and the Soviet Union as political and military models. Congress held a secret session to examine reports that the Sandinista regime was supporting guerrillas in other countries, but the evidence was not persuasive, and the aid bill was approved by Congress in the summer of 1980, subject to a laundry list of conditions on human rights, labor union rights, free press, etc. The most important provision was one that required the President to certify to Congress that Nicaragua was not supporting insurgents abroad before any aid could be disbursed.

The Carter Administration had already pursued these interests in its contacts with the new regime, and there is evidence that the Sandinistas took these into account and modified their preferred policies. The Sandinistas initially resisted their desires to help the Salvadoran guerrillas (Farabundo Martí Front for National Liberation, FMLN) in order to preserve their relationship with the United States.[14] In the course of an administration review of reports of Sandinista support for insurgency in September of 1980, Deputy Assistant Secretary of State James Cheek was sent to communicate the depth of U.S. concern on this issue. Documents captured from the FMLN four months later reveal that Cheek's demarche led the Sandinistas to postpone transferring weapons that had been stockpiled and were about to be sent. The U.S. debate affected the debate within the Sandinista leadership; and on this crucial issue of aid to the FMLN, a tacit accommodation held until about November 1980. In that month, the pressure from Cuba and the FMLN intensified, and the Sandinistas finally permitted the arms transfers, fracturing the accommodation with the United States, even before Ronald Reagan was inaugurated.

The Reagan Administration attempted to negotiate another, more explicit understanding in August 1981.[15] The principal U.S. concerns remained Nicaraguan support for insurgencies and its military relationship with the Soviet Union and Cuba. Led by Assistant Secretary of State Thomas Enders, the United States terminated aid and escalated its threats toward the Sandinista regime by intimating that it might pursue a paramilitary option. Enders then proposed several security agreements. The Sandinistas interpreted these as limiting their sovereignty, and they never offered alternative proposals.

To get their attention, Enders proposed, and Reagan approved, a plan on November 17, 1981, to organize, fund, and train a group of Nicaraguans to attack the Sandinista government. In March 1982, this group, called the contras, or counter-revolutionaries, destroyed two bridges in Nicaragua. The Sandinista government responded by declaring a state of emergency, beginning a process that would systematically reduce the political space in the country. By the end of the year, many moderate leaders, including Adolfo Calero, Alfonso Robelo, and Alfredo Cesar left the country and widened the political base of the contras. The Reagan Administration and the Sandinistas each pursued strategies that had the same effect of polarizing Nicaragua.

The Congressional Intelligence Committees had initially accepted the contras because the Administration claimed that its goal was to interdict arms supplies to Salvadoran rebels. By the end of 1982, however, contra leaders stated clearly their intent to overthrow the Sandinista government.

In 1983, three contrary trends became visible. Congress grew more troubled with the contra program and began to attach conditions on the use and purpose of the funds. The Sandinistas felt the pressure internally and from a number of Latin American and European governments, and showed increasing interest in negotiating the kind of arrangements originally proposed by Enders. Third, some in the Reagan Administration began to think that the Sandinistas could be overthrown. Enders was fired, and his idea of using the contras to pressure the Sandinistas into a security arrangement was discarded.

These trends eventually converged to a tragedy. President Reagan was able to persuade Congress to provide some funding for the contras—but with continued public opposition, the program could not be sustained, certainly not in the way envisaged by the Administration. Moreover, as the Sandinistas grew more interested in negotiations, and the Reagan Administration less interested, Congressional reluctance was transformed into opposition to the contras. Officials on the NSC then devised a covert operation to aid the contras and circumvent legislative prohibitions.

This covert operation began when aid stopped in the fall of 1984 and continued until the downing of a plane carrying arms to the contras in October 1986. Within a month, news reports linked this project to the selling of arms to Iran. As numerous investigations began, NSC Advisor John Poindexter resigned, and his aide Lt. Col. Oliver North was dismissed by Reagan. The Iran-Contra affair that grew out of this scandal threatened not only Reagan's policy toward Nicaragua but also his presidency.

In August 1987, the five Central American presidents met in Esquipulas, Guatemala, and signed a plan first proposed by Costa Rican President Oscar Arias Sanchez. The plan called for democratization through national reconciliation and an end to outside support for insurgencies. Prior to that meeting, and afterward, President Reagan requested military aid for the contras from Congress, arguing that only such aid would bring the Sandinistas to the bargaining table. The Central Americans, however, argued that peace would only become possible if the United States rejected military aid to the contras.

Congress had been almost evenly divided on aid to the contras, but the Central American Accord decisively shifted the balance in Congress against Reagan's request and in favor of helping to advance the peace plan. It was largely because Congress rejected military but approved humanitarian aid that the Sandinista government decided to negotiate directly with the contras, culminating in a cease-fire agreement signed in Sapoa, Nicaragua, on March 23, 1988.

Reagan's support for the contras and opposition to the peace plans remained unyielding. Every Sandinista misstep was used by the Administration to try to pry additional funding out of Congress for the contras. Congress and Central America looked for alternatives, but to the end, Ronald Reagan claimed that the contras offered the only path toward democracy in Nicaragua. "I make a solemn vow—as long as there is breath in my body," President Reagan told the hushed delegates at an OAS meeting, "I will speak and work, strive and struggle, for the cause of the Nicaraguan freedom fighters."[16]

Even though Congress refused to support the contras, Reagan refused to consider the possibility of accommodation with the Sandinistas or with the Democrats in Congress. Most of Congress, however, was tired of fighting this issue. On November 18, 1988, President-elect George Bush went to Capitol Hill to meet with Speaker of the House Jim Wright, who described Nicaragua as "the most implacable issue of the last eight years, and also the most politically polarizing and personally divisive question on the entire agenda." The President-elect agreed.[17]

Bush told Wright that after his inauguration he would send his newly designated Secretary of State James A. Baker III to work with Wright to forge a bipartisan approach to the issue. He was true to his word. On March 24, 1989, the President and the Speaker announced an agreement that supported the Central American Accord and approved humanitarian aid to the contras, but not military aid. It was a perfect compromise for Bush: he did not have to support the contras, but he also did not have to abandon them. The plan healed the divisions within Congress; it gave some leverage to the Central Americans to obtain Nicaraguan compliance with the Accord; and it gave room for the Nicaraguans and for international observers like former U.S. President Jimmy Carter and the Council of Freely Elected Heads of Government, which he chairs, to negotiate the terms of an election that would prove to be the freest and fairest in Nicaraguan history. In the end, the Bush retreat relaxed the pressure on Managua and permitted the development of a political climate that led to the Sandinista defeat at the polls *and* the acceptance by President Daniel Ortega of that defeat. The Bush Administration was neither able nor interested in reaching an accommodation with the Sandinista government, but it was delighted, at least initially, to work with the Chamorro government.

INTERNATIONAL NEGOTIATORS: LEVEL I

In examining the process by which accommodation was facilitated in Panama and precluded in Nicaragua (until the election, which will be addressed separately), we shall first explore the state-to-state (Level I) negotiations.

By 1977, both Panama and the United States were ready to commit themselves to a deal, and both knew that time was short and politics delicate in both countries. Both sides used and manipulated the international environment to try to influence the other. Panama effectively mobilized its neighbors first to put the issue on the U.S. agenda. Seven Latin American presidents sent a telegram to Carter on January 10, 1977, urging him to give the Canal treaties his highest priority. "The Panamanian cause is no longer the cause of that nation alone. Its intrinsic merits have made it the cause of all Latin America." Negotiations of new Panama Canal treaties were crucial, the presidents argued, if the United States wanted to establish good relations with Latin America. This symbolized the international support that affected the U.S. decision to negotiate. By demonstrating his commitment to negotiating new treaties,

Carter was able to use some of Torrijos' international allies as mediators to narrow the distance between the two governments and make accommodation possible.

Torrijos also effectively used Fidel Castro to secure his own political position. The Panamanian left was opposed to the treaties because they permitted the U.S. military to remain in Panama for 23 more years, but Torrijos undermined them by persuading Fidel Castro to endorse the treaties.

In the case of Nicaragua, direct negotiations between the United States and Nicaragua rarely occurred. Far more typical were exchanges of threats and covert actions. Both sides also tried frequently to influence the other through internal and international actors. The Sandinistas encouraged the Socialist International to establish a committee to defend Nicaragua. At the same time, the United States encouraged democratic governments in the area to try to persuade the Sandinistas to have free and fair elections. Four Latin American governments, which had started their efforts on Contadora Island in Panama in 1983, and subsequently the Central American governments, tried in vain to mediate between the United States and Nicaragua.

In brief, the same international strategies were employed in both cases, but only for Panama were there receptive partners. The preferences of the COGs were obviously important factors. Jimmy Carter and Omar Torrijos, though very different, had a great deal of sympathy and respect for each other; each continuously tried to look at the issue from the other's perspective as well as his own. In addition, they had excellent ambassadors and other interlocutors who could communicate instantly with the other and prevent misunderstandings from becoming serious problems.

Most important, their visions of the world were compatible. Carter's vision was a tolerant one that aimed to align the United States with changes that had occurred in the world, most notably the demand for respect in the Third World. He believed that the best way to preserve U.S. interests in the Canal, and to transform Panama from a resentful neighbor into a partner, was to demonstrate respect for Panama's aspiration for dignity. Carter suggested a broader definition of power: "We don't have to show our strength as a nation by running over a small nation."

Reagan's style and vision could not be more different. His picture was of a proud and assertive America, one that led the Third World rather than listened to it. He viewed new Canal treaties as another step backward in a continuing retreat of U.S. power. "Once again," Reagan said of the treaties, "Uncle Sam put his tail between his legs and crept away rather than face trouble."

It is not difficult to judge what would have happened if Reagan had been elected President in 1976; Omar Torrijos dictated a long, meandering discourse in November 1977 in which he discussed that possibility: "Because of his intransigence, had Reagan won, guerrilla warfare would have been mounted in the country.... Every possibility of negotiating would have been blocked, and in that case, the password would have been nationalization."[18] The extreme left, Torrijos knew, would exploit the violence. "They will start their own fires to gain their own goals," he said. "Three hundred thousand Latin Americans would be raising the anti-Yankee banner as they raised it when the Americans went in to fight Sandino [in Nicaragua in 1927].... If I had historical vanity," Torrijos continued, "I would have gone more for Sandino's place than for the real solution of our problem."

Torrijos did not let himself get carried away by his romantic impulses. "I do not delude myself.... Through a war ... there would be mourning in Panamanian homes. And hate, a profound feeling of hate for the United States." Because Carter recognized the justice of Panama's claim, the practical side of Omar Torrijos prevailed, and the treaties made the Canal more secure.

The allusion to Sandino was prophetic, of course. Ronald Reagan offered a real, not just a hypothetical test of the consequences of a different vision of the U.S. role in the region. The arena was Nicaragua (and in 1988, Panama). Reagan viewed the Sandinistas as Communists, who were incapable of negotiating seriously or permitting free elections. In a secret NSC meeting on June 25, 1984, President Reagan told his Cabinet that the only purpose of mentioning negotiations with Nicaragua was to try to convince Congress to give more aid to the contras:

> If we are just talking about negotiations with Nicaragua, that is too far-fetched to imagine that a Communist government like that would make any reasonable deal with us, but if it is to get Congress to support the anti-Sandinistas, then that can be helpful.[19]

Reagan believed that the Sandinistas only understood force. This is precisely the kind of strategy that brings out the worst in a Latin American nationalist, as Torrijos pointed out, and as the Sandinistas would demonstrate. Unlike Reagan, Enders was serious about negotiations, but in 1981 the Sandinistas saw him as arrogant; and after he was fired, there was simply no overlap between the win-sets of Reagan and Ortega. Both played the game in other arenas with the purpose of cornering or undermining the other to induce him to capitulate or withdraw. Bush did not have the attachment to the contras or antipathy to the Sandinistas that Reagan had, and that permitted a tacit accommodation.

A president's views are a powerful explanatory variable, but U.S. policy was not coincident and was sometimes at odds with those views in both the Panama and the Nicaraguan cases. The interactive perspective that we have outlined in trying to explain how the views of one affected the views of the other needs now to be expanded to include a second, domestic, bargaining level.

DOMESTIC FACTORS: LEVEL II

In both cases, the U.S. "domestic level" was Congress; the leading players were the President and Congress; the game (debate) focused more on the means than on the ends of U.S. policy; and interbranch politics explains the policy process.[20] The "rules of the game" were defined partly by the dependent variable—U.S. policy, or more specifically, the Canal treaties; aid to the Sandinista government; and then aid to the contras. Because the Senate or the full Congress had the power to approve or deny these policies, Capitol Hill functioned as the central decision-making arena. Carter's acceptability-set on Panama was much wider than the win-set necessary to obtain the approval of 67 Senators, and he instructed his negotiators to be sensitive to the Senate's preferences. Reagan's need to gain Congress' approval for aid to the contras also constrained his options and compelled him to respond to Congressional concerns in order to have Congress ratify his threats against the Sandinistas. But his preferences did not permit an overlap of win-sets with Nicaragua.

The rules of the ratification process were so taut as to make accommodation less likely and more difficult in both cases. The difference between them was that Carter's negotiations with Congress were a means to an end, a new treaty with Panama; Reagan's negotiations were a means of securing aid to the contras, which made accommodation with the Sandinistas less likely. On Nicaragua, Bush chose neither confrontation nor accommodation.

Each president retained the power to deal first, though in both cases he was handed a "stacked deck" of public opinion against him. In 1977, public opinion polls showed overwhelming opposition to the new Canal treaties, with between 78 and 87 percent of the public opposed.[21] Throughout the debate on aid to the contras in the 1980s, with the exception of a one-month shift after Oliver North's testimony in July 1987, public opinion ran steadily against the program by about 2 to 1, with 23–42 percent supporting it, and 46–70 percent opposing it.[22] Public opinion was the Sisyphean rock that Carter and Reagan had to push up Capitol Hill for each vote.

U.S. Level II on Panama Case

The debate on Panama did not center on whether the Canal should be secured or whether the United States should have good relations with

Latin America, but rather whether new Canal treaties would best accomplish both goals. Opponents were determined to prevent new treaties, and Senator Thurmond's resolution was a sign of their power. The Ford Administration had adopted a traditional approach: deciding to consult only *after* completing negotiations on a treaty. As a result, Congress preempted Ford. Carter moved early to prevent Thurmond from reintroducing his amendment. But Thurmond's ghost hovered over Carter's shoulder, keeping his win-set lean, leaving little margin for error. The negotiators were working within bounds set by the Senate's minimum conditions for ratification: a formula for the permanent defense of the Canal, and no payment to Panama to take back the Canal. All other issues—including the duration of the treaty—were negotiable.

Bureaucratic differences, primarily between the State and Defense departments, which had appeared so important during the Ford Administration and in the preparation for the first NSC meeting under Carter, virtually disappeared as a result of clear presidential direction and the cultivation of the Pentagon's senior officials, who were credited by Linowitz and Bunker for the language on the neutrality treaty. Because the executive branch was unified, it was stronger in its negotiations on Capitol Hill. Also, the Panamanian negotiators found no openings between the bureaucracies which they could use to contest their counterparts' assertions over what the Senate would accept.

To gain 67 votes, the Administration not only had to alter its negotiating strategies but also its political strategy. The principal vehicle was to help Senators find ways to vote for ratification by changing constituent preferences and assuring the Senate through regular consultations that the Administration was moving deliberately and responsibly. When Linowitz and Bunker testified before the Senate Foreign Relations Committee on behalf of the treaty in September 1977, Senator Howard Baker complimented the two for consulting so often and so completely: "You did much more than anybody I have ever known has done, and I congratulate both [of you] for doing that."[23]

In addition, about 20 senators were asked to invite 50 or more leaders from each of their states to the White House for a full day of briefings led by Carter. A deliberate strategy of locating and cultivating conservatives, including John Wayne and William F. Buckley, Jr., also helped. In brief, the President needed to use much of his power, resources, time, and prestige to get two-thirds of the Senate to ratify the treaties. The fact that the Senate only had to vote twice—once for each treaty—helped.

Panama's Domestic Level

The United States did not fully understand the nature of the Panamanian political landscape, partly because Torrijos had pulled the traditional political parties out by the roots, censored the press, and did not have elections. Only when the treaties were narrowly ratified by Panama did the Americans appreciate how narrow was Torrijos' win-set and how effective he had been at coopting *his* opposition.

Torrijos meticulously coopted both his left and his right. His two negotiators were a former Communist and a middle-class lawyer. He appointed a businessman as his Ambassador to Washington. Torrijos judged that ratification in Panama required, at a minimum, that the new treaties omit the phrase "in perpetuity" and have a fixed date for the U.S. departure. But to obtain that, he had to accept the United States' having a *permanent* right to defend the Canal. He accepted that provision only after Carter pledged that it would never use that right to interfere in Panama's internal affairs.

Second, Torrijos wanted the United States to compensate Panama for having used the Canal for 75 years. This again conflicted with Carter's need to avoid paying Panama, but it was resolved by ensuring that Panama would get a large proportion of the revenues from future tolls. Moreover, Torrijos, who personally was almost ascetic, was easily persuaded by Latin American leaders—like Carlos Andres Perez—that Panama's sovereignty could not be bought and should not be risked by asking for more than the U.S. could accept.

U.S. Level II on Nicaragua

On the issue of providing aid to the Sandinistas, President Carter's allies in Congress argued that if the U.S. didn't provide aid, "we will be abandoning the field to Castro and his Soviet bosses."[24] Opponents of the aid viewed Nicaragua as already lost. The evidence reviewed in a secret session did not persuade the majority of Congress. But to secure a majority in favor of the aid, Congressional leaders attached numerous conditions on its use, and while the Administration—like all administrations—preferred that its hands not be tied, it accepted the conditions. In fact, the conditions tended to strengthen the Administration in dealing with the Sandinistas. When Nicaragua violated the understanding, they broke the accommodation.

The issue and the nature of the interbranch bargain during the Reagan Administration were different. At the beginning, the President was powerful enough to obtain support for his program. Congress was almost evenly split between those who opposed and those who supported the contras. Between these two Congressional groups was a third that was prepared to support the President under certain conditions. This third group of about 30 congressmen and 10 senators played the pivotal role. In exchange for supporting contra aid, this group first expected the contras to interdict arms to Central American guerrilla groups, and later expected the Administration to use the leverage provided by the contras to negotiate a deal with the Sandinistas.

The Administration lost support on Capitol Hill when it showed little concern for interdiction or negotiations; it gathered support when the Sandinista leadership paraded its Soviet connections. In the end, the Administration was defeated when the Central Americans picked up the negotiating baton. Congress, as we have seen, will vote once or twice for an unpopular measure, but not repeatedly, and not when an alternative is available.

By Bush's inauguration, Congress was fatigued with Central America and interested in face-saving arrangements. At the same time, the increased costs of the war compelled the Sandinistas to seek an exit, and the one they chose was a free election monitored by respected international observers. Thus, both the United States and Nicaragua backed away from direct confrontation and provided the political space for others to redefine the issue. Based on the outcome of the election, a tacit accommodation emerged.

The Debate in Nicaragua

The Nicaraguan government at first accepted the conditions with the aid from the United States, but by November 1980 it decided to violate the key condition by giving massive military aid to the Salvadoran rebels. Probably the most important reason was that the Sandinista leaders were convinced that the Salvadoran rebels were about to win, and they wanted to be on the winners' side. A second reason was that they were feeling pressured by the Salvadorans, and more importantly the Cubans, who had sent large quantities of arms to Nicaragua to be transshipped to El Salvador. In addition, the Sandinistas knew that Reagan was about to replace Carter, and they might have judged that the relationship would end regardless of what they did, so they might as well support their friends. In any case, their decision to arm the FMLN broke their tacit accommodation with the United States.

The Sandinistas were not prepared to negotiate an explicit bargain on regional security when Enders approached them in August 1981; and when they were ready two years later, the United States had escalated its objectives from a concern with Nicaragua's external activities to a demand for internal political changes. As long as it was the U.S. government that was demanding these changes, the Sandinistas could not accept them—but when they were reformulated by Arias into a *Central American* proposal on democratization that would be binding on *all* the nations of the region, Ortega could accept them, and did, at Esquipulas in August 1987.

President Reagan never believed that Ortega was seriously interested in democracy, and Ortega never thought that Reagan was serious about accepting the Sandinista revolution, and so accommodation was not possible. By 1988, however, the economic situation in Nicaragua had deteriorated markedly, and Soviet support had become more uncertain. Ortega hoped that a free election would unlock aid from Western Europe, lift the U.S. embargo, and end the contra war, and he expected that he would win a free election. He therefore decided to advance the scheduled date for presidential elections to February 25, 1990, as part of a Central American package that included contra demobilization.

Ortega did not surmount his problem, however, because Bush did not trust Ortega and chose not to abandon the contras. Ortega realized that if he won a free election, the United States would not accept the results, and so he invited the UN, the OAS, and Jimmy Carter as head of the Council of Freely Elected Heads of Government to attest to the fairness of the election. Carter wound up mediating the election rules between Ortega and his rival Violeta Chamorro and, in the process, getting both sides to commit themselves to the results. During these negotiations, Ortega offered a series of proposals that would permit a gradual, moderate improvement in Nicaragua's relations with the United States, and Carter delivered these proposals to Bush and Baker, but neither were prepared to engage in negotiations.[25] U.S. policy was stalemated, and the Bush Administration remained on the sidelines for the duration of the election, which they feared could favor Ortega. On February 25, 1990, the Nicaraguan people elected Mrs. Chamorro by a landslide, with 54.7 percent for her and 40.8 percent for Ortega.

After the election, the Bush Administration normalized relations with Nicaragua, and after April 25 it asked Congress for a major aid program. Accommodation was possible because of the change in the Nicaraguan government—which, in turn, was possible because of Ortega's commitment to free elections and Bush's decision not to seek military aid for the contras.

EXPLAINING SUCCESS AND FAILURE: THEORETICAL IMPLICATIONS

In seeking explanations as to why the United States reached an agreement with Panama but not with Nicaragua, we already discussed the preferences of the heads of government, but we also need to understand the differences in the issues, the costs and benefits of agreement vs. no-agreement, and the way in which the debates on the two levels interacted.

First, the issues were different. The negotiations on Panama were classic negotiations between two sovereign governments on a treaty to define the responsibilities for operating and defending an international waterway. The issue in Nicaragua was its external and internal policies—a sensitive issue in any Latin American country, particularly one that had just liberated itself from the dominance of the United States. By the time the revolution had absorbed the impact of a truly hostile empire, and was prepared to negotiate its external policies, the United States had upped its ante to insist on internal changes. The Sandinistas would not negotiate their internal affairs with the United States, and even if they had, President Reagan would not have believed any commitments by Ortega anyway.

A second difference between the two cases relates to the calculations of the costs and benefits of agreement vs. no-agreement. The short-term political costs of new Panama Canal treaties were so high, and the long-term benefits so elusive, that Carter's predecessors were wary about reaching an agreement. The equation had changed by 1977. "This year," Torrijos said after signing the treaties, "all the chickens would have flown the coop if we had not reached this agreement. The U.S. would have run out of excuses, and we would have run out of patience. A catastrophe was averted by this treaty."[26]

International pressure had increased on the United States, and violent incidents had already begun in the Canal Zone. If they expanded in number or severity, the United States would have much more difficulty negotiating without appearing to be capitulating to a small country. Carter judged that the costs of postponement had, for the first time, exceeded the benefits, and that new treaties had to be negotiated soon. Having made Panama a priority, Carter could not afford to let the treaty be defeated.

On Nicaragua, the cost of failing to reach a tacit accommodation between the Carter Administration and the Sandinista government was the U.S. aid program with its conditions. That apparently was high enough to permit a temporary overlap between the two win-sets. Reagan and Ortega viewed each other as unchangeable enemies; the internal political benefit of attacking the other exceeded the cost of reaching an accommodation that neither thought would be respected. The calculations had changed somewhat by Bush's inauguration, but not so much that Bush wanted to explore the basis for an accommodation.

Finally, the two levels interacted in a manner that tolled the success of the Canal treaties and the failure of the contra policy. In Panama, both Carter and Torrijos were sensitive to tight win-sets and skillfully worked both the internal and international negotiations at the same time. By coordinating their approaches, they reinforced the prospects for a negotiated outcome that would be ratifiable in both countries.

In the case of Nicaragua, Carter and Ortega were able to find a tenuous accommodation both internally and between both countries. That fragile egg fell off the wall because of Nicaragua's decision to support the FMLN, and it proved impossible to put Humpty Dumpty together again. Reagan's doctrine then redefined the issue in a way—helping freedom-fighters to overthrow unfriendly governments—that Congress could not accept, and Nicaragua could not even consider. The Administration's need to gain repeated Congressional approval for his support of the contras, despite strong opposition, proved to be the policy's undoing. It is not true to say that Reagan did not want an agreement with the Sandinistas: he just wanted an agreement that was unacceptable to the Nicaraguans—and if they *had* accepted it, he might have reconsidered his own proposal. As he told reporters who asked him about a Sandinista proposal in the fall of 1983: "I haven't believed anything they've been saying since they got in charge, and you shouldn't either."[27]

Reagan was prepared to compromise with Congress to get his contra program, but he was not prepared to compromise with the Sandinistas, and ultimately he could not keep the two arenas separate. He accepted some Congressional conditions, including appointing new envoys to Central America, pledging to end the contras' human rights abuses, and promising negotiations. But Congress' principal condition was the last—negotiations; Reagan could feign interest in negotiations for just so long before a majority of Congress finally realized he was not sincere. Congress, in brief, was prepared to ratify Reagan's threat of the contras provided he shared their goal, which was to negotiate an arrangement with the Sandinistas along the lines of the Arias Plan. When the real plan came along, and the Sandinistas accepted it and the Reagan Administration rejected it, Congress followed Arias, not Reagan. No longer would they ratify his threat.

In contrast, the Senate was prepared to ratify Carter's promise because at least two-thirds accepted the rationale for the Canal treaties, and Carter and Torrijos made it easier, not harder, for additional Senators to show their constituents that they had defended the nation's security in the course of the debate.

HOW TO AFFECT THE DEBATE: POLICY IMPLICATIONS

Nations defend and advance their security, political, and economic interests by foreign policies aimed at influencing other nations' internal and external affairs. If direct force is not used, a nation must rely on threats, inducements, and incentives to increase the probability that other governments will change their policies to make them more compatible with one's interests. Using the metaphor of "two levels," one can describe a President's goal as securing one's internal position (Level II) and assisting tacit allies in your adversaries' internal debate. Specifically, the issue for the United States is how to influence the debate in Panama or Nicaragua while trying to prevent them from influencing the domestic debate in the United States.

The issue and the language matter. These small governments are very sensitive to interference by the United States and will devise numerous tactics to try to resist such influence. If the issue is a genuinely international one—like the Canal treaties—the prospect for successful negotiations is greater than if it is an internal issue.

The language of negotiations also matters, but much depends on who is talking and who is listening. There are certain regimes that will only respect threats or force, and others where such threats will preclude an accommodation. It is critical to be able to know how adversaries differ. If threats are necessary, they still need to be conveyed so as to leave the regime's leaders with an exit. Transnational alliances are necessary to judge which tactics and approaches might strengthen like-minded groups the most.

In considering ways to affect the debate, we need to distinguish between three kinds of external events or decisions. First are those that the COG invites from abroad because he lacks support in his government or country. Carter's use of the seven-presidents cable, and his invitation to all the heads of state in the hemisphere for the Panama Canal Treaties signing ceremony at the OAS, were two examples of how the President invited international leverage into the U.S. domestic debate to help his position.

Second are those foreign initiatives that are resisted by a COG because they could help his domestic opponents. An example of this was Esquipulas, as seen by Reagan. The Central American negotiations reinforced those who opposed military aid to the contras and induced the United States to adopt a more diplomatic approach.

Third are uninvited foreign efforts that do not have much impact on the domestic debate. This could occur because of poor timing, an ineffective lobbying effort, or one directed at the wrong target. The initiative by the four "Contadora" governments to change President Reagan's mind on the Sandinistas and the contras was as near a foolish use of time as anything they did. In these three sets of decisions, the transnational and transgovernmental linkages are evident, and in the first two they were very important in altering the domestic debate.

A second issue is how to use the debate in the United States to advantage. Diplomats are not trained to think in these terms, and therefore they fail to use a significant source of leverage. In fact, the domestic debate can, and often does, strengthen the hand of U.S. negotiators. This occurs frequently in trade policy, but this phenomenon was also present in the Panama Canal Treaties negotiations and with the Sandinistas in 1979–80.

Some have argued that the United States is a weak state because of checks and balances in the government, but such division offers opportunities for the U.S. to advance its interests more than centralized or parliamentary systems. The President can be much tougher in his negotiations by arguing that Congress will not accept what is being asked of him.[28]

Foreign policy is influenced by the nature of the policy instrument and the arena in which it is debated and decided. If the instrument is a treaty, the Senate and the President have great leverage, and the House none. If the instrument is pure diplomacy, the President has room to pursue his approach with minimal congressional influence; but if the instrument is aid, Congress has considerable power to define the outcome.

The pivotal questions are, first, how and why a government modifies its foreign policy because of a change in its internal calculus and, second, the extent to which that change can be attributed to negotiations or influence from the international level. In the case of Central America, the domestic and international levels have been welded so tightly that the reciprocal influence is now hard to separate. Focusing on a single level at a time is misleading and inadequate. With a fuller understanding of the interaction between domestic pressures and international realities, one is better positioned to influence the debate on foreign policy.

NOTES

1. Interview, *Washington Post*, October 12, 1981, p. 2.

2. A *New York Times*/CBS poll found that 52 percent believed Reagan had lied and 24 percent felt that he had told the truth. This poll was taken between January 12 and 15, 1989. Excerpts were published on January 18, 1989, but this figure is from the longer poll. In testimony before Congress, Poindexter said: "The buck stops here with me. I made the decision. . . ." But at his trial, Poindexter's lawyer said that "the President was the driving engine behind his [Poindexter's] actions," and his client was a victim of "a frame-up story." (David Johnston, "Poindexter Is Found Guilty of All Five Criminal Charges for Iran-Contra Cover-Up," *New York Times*, April 8, 1990, p. 1.)

3. For a discussion of Congress' role in precluding negotiations, and a strategy for how to prevent that, see Robert A. Pastor, "Coping with Congress's Foreign Policy," *Foreign Service Journal*, December 1975, pp. 15–18, 23.

4. Cited by Gerald Ford, *A Time To Heal* (New York: Harper and Row, 1979), p. 374.

5. Ibid.

6. For their statements during the campaign, see William J. Jorden, *Panama Odyssey* (Austin: University of Texas Press, 1984), p. 328.

7. Commission on U.S.-Latin American Relations, *The United States and Latin America: Next Steps* (New York: Center for Inter-American Relations, December 20, 1976), p. 5. I was the Executive Director of the Linowitz Commission and was subsequently appointed Director of Latin American Affairs on the National Security Council.

8. Jimmy Carter, *Keeping Faith: Memoirs of a President* (New York: Bantam Books, 1982), p. 158.

9. In fact, the treaties were not completed then, but the U.S. and Panamanian negotiators who remained in Panama knew they were working under a severe deadline to have it ready for signing within one month.

10. Cited in an interview with *Newsweek*, August 21, 1977.

11. In Jorden, *Panama Odyssey*, p. 483.

12. For an analysis of the polls, see George D. Moffett III, *The Limits of Victory: The Ratification of the Panama Canal Treaties* (Ithaca, N.Y.: Cornell University Press, 1985), p. 117. For the latter poll, see Adam Clymer, "Survey Finds Support for Panama Canal Pacts," *New York Times*, May 13, 1989, p. 6.

13. This subject is developed more fully in my book *Condemned to Repetition: The United States and Nicaragua* (Princeton, N.J.: Princeton University Press, 1987). See also Anthony Lake, *Somoza Falling* (Boston: Houghton, Mifflin, 1989).

14. For a detailed discussion of U.S. efforts to preclude Sandinista support for Salvadoran rebels, and the Sandinista response to these efforts, see Pastor, *Condemned to Repetition*, pp. 202–207, 216–228.

15. This section is based on my book *Condemned to Repetition*; Roy Gutman, *Banana Diplomacy: The Making of American Policy in Nicaragua, 1981–87* (New York: Simon and Schuster, 1988); the Iran-Contra reports of Congress; and an interview with Thomas Enders, in Ditchley Park, England, May 20, 1989.

16. His address was reprinted in the *New York Times*, October 8, 1987, p. 8.

17. Jim Wright, "Streams of Hope, Rivers of Blood: A Personal Narrative about Central America and the United States," ms., 1990, chap. 10, p. 4.

18. After a meeting with a group of senators on November 25, 1977, Torrijos unwound with his colleagues and dictated for about two hours a monologue on his conversations with the senators and on the state of Panama, Carter, Reagan, and many other topics. I quote from a transcript of that tape.

19. The minutes of this meeting were declassified during the trial of Oliver North. Excerpts were reprinted in *The New York Times*, April 14, 1989, p. 9.

20. For a description of the interbranch politics model, see Robert A. Pastor, *Whirlpool: U.S. Foreign Policy Toward Latin America and the Caribbean* (Princeton, N.J.: Princeton University Press, 1992), chap. 6.

21. For an excellent analysis of public opinion and the domestic debate on the Canal treaties, see Moffett, *The Limits of Victory*.

22. On public opinion on Nicaragua and a comparison of the two debates on Panama and Nicaragua, see Robert A. Pastor, "The Canal Treaties: The Other Debate on Central America," *Caribbean Review* 15 (Spring 1987). By 1988, even a majority of Republicans and conservatives opposed contra aid. The overall population opposed it 58 to 30 percent (*New York Times*, January 31, 1988, p. 4).

23. U.S. Senate, Committee on Foreign Relations, *Panama Canal Treaties: Hearings, Part I*, September 26, 1977, pp. 87–88.

24. This was the argument of Clement Zablocki, the Chairman of the House Foreign Affairs Committee; cited in Pastor, *Condemned to Repetition*, p. 209.

25. For a description and analysis of the electoral process and other proposals developed during that time, see Robert A. Pastor, "Nicaragua's Choice: The Making of a Free Election," *Journal of Democracy* 1 (Summer 1990): 13–25.

26. Interview, *Newsweek*, August 21, 1977.

27. Transcript of President Reagan's press conference, reprinted in the *New York Times*, November 4, 1983.

28. For an elaboration of the argument of Congress as an asset, see Robert A. Pastor, "Congress and U.S. Foreign Policy: Comparative Advantage or Disadvantage?" in *The Washington Quarterly* (Autumn 1991).

U.S. Policy and Human Rights in Argentina and Guatemala, 1973–1980

Lisa L. Martin and Kathryn Sikkink

During the 1970s, human rights became an important component of U.S. foreign policy toward Latin America. This chapter examines two countries targeted by this policy, Argentina and Guatemala. Using the concepts of the two-level game metaphor, we explain the divergent impact of U.S. human rights initiatives in these two countries. We conclude that U.S. efforts had, unexpectedly, a greater impact in Argentina than in Guatemala. This outcome results from a complex interaction of domestic politics and international negotiations, on which the two-level game metaphor casts some light.

Although they were given higher priority during the Carter Administration, human rights issues continue to be important elements in U.S. foreign policy. Thus, this analysis is relevant to contemporary debates about the use of sanctions to punish human rights violations, from Tiananmen Square to Sarajevo.

In September 1978, Vice President Walter Mondale and President Jorge Videla of Argentina reached a private agreement at a meeting in Rome: in exchange for Argentine agreement to let the Inter-American Commission on Human Rights (IACHR) make an on-site investigation of human rights practices in Argentina, the United States would release Export-Import Bank funds that had been blocked because of Argentine human rights abuses.[1] At the same time, U.S. legislation mandating an indefinite embargo on military assistance and arms sales to Argentina, because of gross violations of human rights, went into effect. These actions were the culmination of a series of U.S. steps aimed at improving Argentina's human rights record, following years of intense resistance by the Argentine government to international pressures. In December 1978, the Argentine government invited the IACHR to conduct an on-site investigation. In the period that followed this decision, the human rights situation in Argentina improved significantly; especially noteworthy was the decline in the incidence of involuntary disappearances, for which the Argentine regime had gained international notoriety.[2]

In June 1977 the Guatemalan government, enraged by a U.S. Human Rights report recording abuses in Guatemala, rejected U.S. military aid. The U.S. Congress, in response, reduced military assistance in 1977 and terminated military aid to Guatemala in 1978.[3] In the three-year period coinciding with the Carter Administration's human rights policy toward Guatemala, from June 1978 to February 1981, nearly 5,000 people were seized without warrant and killed in Guatemala, and another 615 people were missing, according to an Amnesty International report that linked the political assassinations directly to the government of President Fernando Lucas García. During this period the Guatemalan government refused to permit an on-site visit by the IACHR, to respond to U.S. human rights initiatives, or to cooperate with any international or regional human rights organization. The Guatemalan government rejected the legitimacy of the human rights issues as a topic for international negotiation.

These two cases of attempted international accommodation, one successful and the other a failure, provide an interesting paradox in the interaction of domestic and international politics. Why did the Videla military government, having engaged in the most brutal forms of human rights abuses in Argentine history over the previous two and one-half years, change its internal practices and invite international scrutiny by allowing a prestigious regional delegation to look into the situation in Argentina? At the same time, why did U.S. policy have so little impact on practices in Guatemala? How can we explain the intransigent refusal of the Guatemalan government to negotiate on the human rights issue?

This issue differs from most others in this book in a number of ways. First, informational uncertainties are endemic in the case of human rights negotiations. Essentially, negotiations are carried out over practices that the repressive government never formally admits occurred. Thus third-party information is essential to negotiations, both to initiate concern over the issue and to monitor changes in practices. "Negotiations" and "cooperation" in these two cases were not public affairs, except for congressional decisions to ban or limit military and economic assistance. No Latin American government could admit it was engaging in human rights violations or afford the apparent surrender of sovereignty inherent in admitting that it had controlled abuses in response to U.S. pressure. Although the U.S. Congress was a major player in this game, it never had the chance to formally ratify an agreement on human rights with either Argentina and Guatemala. Because of the nature of authoritarian rule, the structure of domestic interests and the ratification process in the repressive country are often unclear, so negotiators work with uncertainty in this realm as well.

Second, cross-issue linkage here between human rights practices and military and economic aid was the central dynamic of human rights policy. Such linkage does not merely facilitate agreements, it makes negotiations possible in the first place. Third, these were markedly asymmetrical negotiations—asymmetrical in terms of the relative power of the players, but also in the nature of the payoffs to the players. That is, if negotiations were successful, one side secured military and/or economic assistance, while the other side, the United States, merely secured the knowledge that its allies were respecting the rights of their citizens. Fourth, the unique "moral" nature of the issue leads to a different cast of characters, such as nongovernmental human rights organizations, than that in many other negotiations. In spite of these points of divergence from the original, we find the language and insights of the two-level games model applicable in these cases.

The greater U.S. influence on Argentina than on Guatemala is the empirical anomaly driving this study. Any theory that focuses on the power of individual states to explain outcomes would predict the opposite pattern. Robert Putnam argues that "all-purpose support for international agreements is probably greater in smaller, more dependent countries with more open economies."[4] Speaking about international human rights campaigns, Ernst Haas states that, "the more dependent the government is on aid, trade, and investments, the more often it is likely to yield to such pressure."[5] U.S. experience in Guatemala and Argentina belies these expectations. By any measure, Guatemala was far more dependent on the United States than was Argentina, but withstood pressure on human rights issues. One source refers to this as an "apparent paradox: that a military establishment umbilically tied to Washington can yet exercise its autonomy with such ruthless intransigence."[6]

Guatemala is a much smaller country than Argentina, with populations of 6.1 million and 25.4 million, respectively, in 1975.[7] In 1978, Argentina had a GNP of 53.4 billion dollars, while Guatemala's was only 6.1 billion.[8] Guatemala was also significantly poorer, with a GNP per capita in 1978 of only 930 dollars, while Argentina's was 2,030 dollars.[9] Argentina is far more industrialized, with only 13 percent of the labor force in agriculture in 1979, compared to Guatemala's 56 percent.[10] The differences between the two countries are also stark as measured by social indicators: in 1989 Argentina had a 94-percent adult literacy rate, 71 years life expectancy at birth, and an infant mortality rate of 32.2 per 1,000, while Guatemala's literacy rate was 57 percent, life expectancy at birth 62.6, and its infant mortality rate 53.6.[11] Guatemala's economy is more open, with foreign trade in 1975 equaling 37.8 percent of GNP, while it accounted for only 17.6 percent (the ninth-lowest figure in the world) in Argentina.[12] Finally, Guatemala is far more dependent on economic and military aid from the United States, receiving 91.7 million dollars in assistance from 1970 to 1973.[13] By any of these criteria, Guatemala should have been more susceptible to U.S. pressure than Argentina, and we should therefore see a greater improvement in human rights practices there during the period of U.S. activism on this issue in the late 1970s.

We explain this anomaly by locating four factors that led to the more successful negotiation on this issue: a small win-set, U.S. presidential preference for a vigorous human rights strategy, transnational cross-table lobbying by international and domestic human rights organizations, and the existence within the target government of a faction willing to consider a reduction in human rights violations as a means of pursuing its own internal strategy. Not only was the U.S. win-set smaller for Argentina than for Guatemala, but Washington also pursued its human rights strategy toward Argentina more intensely, and with fewer competing goals. In September 1978 these factors temporarily converged, enabling Vice President Mondale to achieve the agreement with President Videla to allow the IACHR to visit Argentina. In the Guatemalan case all such factors were missing, providing no opportunity for a successful agreement on human rights. In addition to this cross-country comparison, inter-temporal comparisons within the Argentine case allow us to identify the causal role of these factors.

This analysis begins with a brief chronology, outlining the progress of U.S. human rights policy in the 1970s. The following section discusses domestic coalitions on both sides and specifies the nature of the win-sets and the chief negotiators' preferences. We next turn to international negotiations, with particular reference to the 1978 Mondale-Videla agreement. And last, we present our explanation of these outcomes and speculate on insights generated by these cases for the two-level game model in general.

CHRONOLOGY

Congressional activism on human rights issues began in 1973, and both general and country-specific legislation in 1974 and 1975 tied U.S. security assistance to recipients' records in this area. However, until 1977, legislation merely expressed the "sense of the Congress" and "policy of the United States," and thus was not binding on the executive branch. Resistance from the Nixon and Ford administrations prevented any serious negotiations on human rights before 1977.

Argentina

On March 24, 1976, a military junta overthrew the government of President María Estela Martínez de Perón in Buenos Aires, and General Jorge Videla assumed the presidency. The coup was preceded by an upsurge in activities by right-wing death squads and armed guerrilla movements. The military government initiated a program of brutal repression of the opposition, including mass kidnappings, imprisonment without charges, torture, and murder. Amnesty International estimated in 1977 that 6,000 people were being held as political prisoners, most without being charged, and that between 2,000 and 10,000 had been abducted.[14] The organization also began to publish information demonstrating that the disappearances were part of a concerted government policy by which perceived opponents were kidnapped by the military and the police and taken to secret detention centers where they were routinely tortured and interrogated.[15] Most of the "disappeared" were eventually murdered and their bodies buried in unmarked mass graves, incinerated, or thrown into the sea.[16] Human rights organizations and the press increasingly brought this situation to the attention of U.S. policy-makers. A State Department report released at the end of 1976 admitted that human rights abuses were taking place in Argentina, but argued that continuation of security assistance, including 48.4 million dollars in military sales credits, would be in the U.S. national interest.[17]

After Jimmy Carter's inauguration, the government quickly adopted a more aggressive approach to human rights in Argentina. Carter appointed Patricia Derian, a civil rights activist, as Assistant Secretary of State for Humanitarian Affairs and Human Rights. Derian visited Argentina three times during 1977 to discuss human rights issues, especially disappearances and torture, with the government.

On February 24, 1977, Secretary of State Vance announced that the administration was reducing the planned level of military aid for Argentina from the 32 million dollars requested in the Ford Administration's budget for the next fiscal year to 15 million dollars, because of human rights abuses. Argentina, together with Uruguay and Ethiopia, was one of the three countries targeted early in the Carter Administration to emphasize its commitment to human rights. Argentina reacted angrily, claiming that this action was undue interference in its internal affairs, and rejected remaining U.S. military aid.[18]

In July 1977, Congress followed these actions by passing a bill eliminating all military assistance and terminating private sales of military goods as of September 30, 1978.[19] This allowed one year for evidence of improvement in the human rights situation in Argentina. President Videla met with President Carter in Washington in September 1977, during the ceremonies for signing the Panama Canal Treaties. At this meeting Videla first indicated that he would be willing to invite the IACHR to Argentina as a means of improving U.S.-Argentine relations.[20] Nevertheless, Videla did not follow through on this commitment until more than a year later, after the arms embargo had gone into effect and an Eximbank loan had been blocked. A number of high-level delegations, including a group led by Secretary of State Cyrus Vance, met with the junta during this period to discuss human rights.[21] However, there was no evidence of improvement by September 1978, and an indefinite embargo on arms sales went into effect. Argentina rushed to purchase military equipment during the year-long grace period, but on September 30, the last day of fiscal year 1978, Argentine military attachés were called to the Pentagon and told that the State Department had denied pending requests for licenses for nearly 100 million dollars of U.S. military equipment.[22]

At the same time, human rights considerations also pervaded decisions regarding economic assistance, loans from multilateral financial institutions, and Eximbank credits. The United States voted against approximately 25 Argentine loan applications in the multilateral financial institutions, but none of these votes actually led to denial of the loans.[23] In late summer 1978, the administration attempted to increase its economic pressure on Argentina by blocking a major Eximbank loan for nonmilitary equipment sales. This was the first move that would inhibit nonmilitary trade, and U.S. business responded by mounting a major lobbying effort for its repeal. Congress looked likely to overturn the decision. However, while the threat of denial was in place the administration achieved its clearest victory on the human rights front, the agreement to allow the IACHR to visit and prepare a report on human rights conditions in Argentina. This is an example of tactical issue linkage which led to a narrowing of the U.S. win-set.

In 1979 the Argentine government allowed the IACHR, an arm of the Organization of American States, into the country. In expectation of the visit, the junta took steps to improve human rights conditions. The IACHR report provided the most in-depth, well researched information on the situation in Argentina, documenting that the Argentine government had engaged in a systematic campaign of gross abuses of human rights.[24] In 1980 the State Department's annual human rights report called the situation in Argentina the "worst in the hemisphere," but noted that the number of disappearances had dropped significantly. By 1978 the practice was used much less frequently than before, and by 1980 it was virtually no longer used, although no explanation was given for previous disappearances.[25] U.S. policy toward Argentina during 1980 was complicated by efforts to gain its cooperation in imposing a grain embargo on the Soviet Union, and pressure on the human rights front seems to have been relaxed, although the ban on arms sales remained in effect. Two other key international events served to keep the case of Argentine human rights in the minds of U.S. policy-makers. In 1979 the Argentine authorities released noted journalist Jacobo Timerman, and the publication of his powerful memoir detailing his disappearance and torture by Argentine military, which he describes as fascist and viciously anti-Semitic, had a major impact in U.S. policy circles.[26] Second, in 1980 the Nobel Peace Prize was awarded to Argentine human rights activist Adolfo Pérez Esquivel, who used his public position to speak out against the continuing abuses in Argentina.

Guatemala

The history of the violation of basic human rights in Guatemala is even longer and more sordid than that in Argentina. The military maintained control of the government from 1954 (except for 1966–1970), with the U.S.-supported overthrow of the government of Jacobo Arbenz. During the period 1954–1976, Guatemala was a major recipient of U.S. military and economic assistance, including substantial training and equipment for military and police officers.[27] Police brutality and military repression against civilians have been commonplace since the late 1960s, when the military was joined by private death squads organized under the patronage and approval of the government and the army.[28] Within this general framework of repression, however, the human rights situation deteriorated in the 1970s. A Guatemalan organization, the Committee for Disappeared Persons, estimated that 15,325 deaths or disappearances occurred between 1970 and mid-1975.[29]

It is even more difficult to chart the pattern of human rights abuses in Guatemala than in Argentina. This is partly the result of a deliberate government policy to eliminate evidence. One Guatemalan colonel told a U.S. journalist, "In Argentina there are witnesses, there are books, there are films, there is proof. Here in Guatemala there is none of that. Here there are no survivors."[30]

General Kjell Laugerud, who held the presidency from 1974 to 1978, took steps to moderate the level of human rights abuses, disbanding some of the death squads. Kidnapping and other violations continued, however, although at a somewhat lower level. After the U.S. State Department released a March 1977 report on human rights abuses in Guatemala, but also noting that President Laugerud appeared to be improving the situation, Guatemala rejected all U.S. military aid. Congress then eliminated all military aid to Guatemala for fiscal year 1978.[31] Human rights organizations presented information on abuses and recommended contacts to give testimony at hearings that provided the basis for the congressional decision.[32] However, military supplies already in the pipeline continued to flow, and the administration continued shipments of military supplies by reclassifying them as nonmilitary items. Foreign Military Sales (FMS) credits totaled 2.8 million dollars in 1977, 2.5 million in 1978, and 3.6 million in 1979.[33] Commercial sales to the Guatemalan government and private businesses were the primary means Guatemala used during this period to obtain military equipment and technology from the United States. These export sales were licensed by either the Department of Commerce or the State Department; the Commerce Department approved licenses during this period for the sale of shotguns, handcuffs, and military aircraft to Guatemala.[34] Economic aid continued unabated. In October 1979 and May 1980 the United States voted against two Multilateral Development Bank (MDB) loans to Guatemala on human rights grounds, but approved five others during this period.[35]

Although human rights violations in Guatemala were as serious as anywhere in the hemisphere, less congressional and administrative pressure was put on Guatemala than on Argentina. Congress held no hearings specifically on Guatemala from 1976 until 1981. Neither the administration nor Congress took any steps toward cutting economic aid or imposing trade sanctions. In particular, the continuation of military sales during this period is evidence of a lack of commitment to fully implement human rights policy in the case of Guatemala.

This is explained in part by the absence of domestic human rights organizations in Guatemala, which limited the dissemination of information on abuses. The different timing of cycles of repression also helps explain differences in the forcefulness of U.S. human rights policy. In Argentina, the height of repression (1976–1978) coincided with the height of human rights activism in the Carter Administration. This period of activism coincided with a temporary decrease in what still was a very high level of human rights violations in Guatemala. The reforms of the Laugerud government (1974–1978)—"so modest in another setting, yet uncharacteristic of post-1954 Guatemala—afforded hope to elements of the political center and moderate left of an incipient opening."[36] It seems that this hope led U.S. policy-makers to exert less forceful pressures on the Laugerud Administration.

By 1979, under the new administration of General Lucas García, human rights abuses reached levels unprecedented even for Guatemala. International awareness of human rights violations in Guatemala became widespread. Amnesty International described disappearances as "epidemic," and reported over 2,000 people killed between mid-1978 and early 1980. The Guatemalan press contained reports of 3,252 disappearances in the first ten months of 1979.[37] In 1980 evidence surfaced of a specialized agency, under the control of President Lucas García and located in an annex to the National Palace, that coordinated the actions of various "private" death squads and regular army and policy units.[38]

By the time that awareness of Guatemalan human rights abuses became a matter of general concern, however, the attention of activists and policy-makers alike was focused on Nicaragua. Carter's human rights policy toward Central America was undermined by the perceived urgency of counterinsurgency in the wake of the Nicaraguan revolution.

Even before the 1980 elections, as Guatemalan military and local business associations became convinced that the Reagan Administration would move quickly to reinstate military assistance and training, they increasingly refused to deal with representatives of the Carter Administration. But U.S. policy on Guatemala did not change as quickly as the Guatemalan elite had hoped. By the early 1980s, and especially with release of the Amnesty International report linking death-squad activity directly to President Lucas García, congressmen were hesitant to be seen as advocates of a murderous regime. Second, the new administration's Central American policies focused on the priority issues of aid to El Salvador and support for the Nicaraguan contras. Some administration insiders feared that any attempt to reinstate military aid to Guatemala would undermine congressional support for the administration's priority goals in Central America.[39] As a result, the Reagan Administration did not lift the embargo on military aid to Guatemala until 1983, after General José Efraín Ríos Montt had come to power.

DOMESTIC COALITIONS

On the U.S. side, an unusual coalition of liberals and conservatives supported reductions in foreign aid due to human rights violations. In Congress, votes in favor of cutting assistance came both from liberals dedicated to reducing U.S. ties to repressive regimes and conservatives with a more general interest in reducing U.S. expenditures on foreign aid. However, this consensus did not extend to measures that would be costly for the United States, such as denial of Eximbank loans. Congressmen in favor of imposing sanctions on Argentina received support from human rights lobbying groups. Opposition to sanctions came from a number of sources: administration officials in favor of "flexibility"; career Latin American specialists, especially in the State Department; members of Congress who believed such actions were contrary to traditional interpretations of U.S. national security; and business interests operating in Argentina.

Congressional Alignments

Washington's interest in human rights as a foreign policy issue originated in Congress rather than the executive branch.[40] In a backlash to the foreign and domestic policies of the Nixon/Kissinger years, perceived by many as amoral or immoral—including the fallout from Vietnam and Watergate—Congressional activism in foreign affairs increased substantially, particularly in the area of human rights. This issue provided a vehicle for Congress to attack the executive and regain more control over foreign policy issues. The conditions permitting such activism arose in part from institutional changes within Congress that allowed junior representatives and senators to play an unusually important role in the formation of foreign policy. The ability of new members to influence foreign policy was especially pronounced with respect to Latin America, where few congressmen professed much knowledge or interest.[41] With the immediate heritage of Vietnam and the recent experience of the domestic civil rights movement, international human rights became a cause with significant public and congressional support. Domestic groups with an interest in human rights issues found receptive ground in Congress for their arguments, and testified at dozens of hearings.

Representative Donald Fraser took the lead in introducing numerous human rights amendments in Congress. Other active members included Senator Edward Kennedy and Representatives Tom Harkin, Ed Koch, and Don Bonker, who took over Fraser's chairmanship of the International Organizations Subcommittee in 1979. Studies of congressional voting patterns on human rights legislation show that the most consistent support for initiatives aimed at Latin American countries came from liberal Democrats. Opposition came from members with high scores on the National Security Index (NSI) developed by the American Security Council, a conservative pressure group.[42]

Coalitions in the Executive Branch

During the Nixon and Ford administrations, the executive sharply opposed this human rights activism and resisted enforcing such measures passed by Congress. This led Congress gradually to reduce the executive's freedom of action, for example by moving away from "sense of the Congress" resolutions and general legislation toward binding, country-specific measures. Because of strong opposition at the top, few individual ambassadors appear to have put much emphasis on the topic of human rights violations in their day-to-day diplomacy under Nixon and Ford. However, the Ford Administration's final report on human rights in various countries claimed that the subject of human rights was raised frequently with the Argentine government, more often than any other substantive issue.[43]

In spite of this report, the overwhelming body of evidence suggests that Henry Kissinger's "quiet diplomacy" on human rights largely amounted to silence.[44] Congress reacted to this attitude by creating within the State Department a Bureau of Humanitarian Affairs and Human Rights (HA), which bore responsibility not for maintaining good relations with any specific region, but for assuring that human rights concerns were brought into all aspects of U.S. foreign policy. In 1977 the head of this bureau was made an assistant secretary, providing HA with essential access to information, and under Pat Derian's leadership HA grew into an important, active participant in foreign policy decisions. The regional bureaus, however, tended to remain focused on their traditional task of maintaining a warm relationship with their host governments. While some individual ambassadors gave higher priority to human rights issues than they had previously, Derian encountered significant resistance to backing traditional diplomacy with actual cutoffs of U.S. assistance.[45]

Jimmy Carter's approach to human rights issues contrasted sharply with the previous administration's. From an electoral viewpoint, a general emphasis on human rights was one of the few issues that could (temporarily) unite a deeply divided Democratic Party in 1976. The right wing of the party, including Jeane Kirkpatrick and Patrick Moynihan, favored an active human rights policy directed against "totalitarian" regimes such as Vietnam and Cambodia. The left wing supported a campaign directed against "authoritarian" regimes such as those in Latin America. This fragile coalition reflected the "unholy alliance" of conservatives and liberals voting for human rights sanctions in Congress.

The issue of human rights originally gave Carter tangible political benefits, as well as fitting in with his own view of the proper purposes of U.S. foreign policy. As his National Security Adviser Zbigniew Brzezinski explained:

> The commitment to human rights reflected Carter's own religious beliefs, as well as his political acumen. He deeply believed in human rights. . . . At the same time, he sensed . . . that the issue was an appealing one, for it drew a sharp contrast between himself and the policies of Nixon and Kissinger.[46]

This contrast became evident in the new administration's approach to the implementation of congressional directives on human rights. For the first time, the executive branch took the lead in imposing sanctions for human rights reasons, such as making the February 1977 announcement about reduction of military aid to Argentina.

During the Carter Administration, a special committee was created to decide specific human rights issues, such as whether to approve loans from multilateral development banks. On the Interagency Committee on Human Rights and Foreign Assistance, more commonly known as the Christopher Committee, representatives from Treasury, Commerce, and the Agency for International Development (AID) tended to resist the "politicization" of their work implied by human rights considerations, while Derian argued strongly in favor of taking such considerations into account. Human rights issues dominated the diplomatic agenda of the Carter Administration toward Argentina; no human rights situation created greater concern in Washington in the 1970s.[47] The administration's attitude toward human rights in Guatemala revealed a greater degree of ambivalence. Both the State and Commerce departments continued to approve some licenses for commercial military sales to Guatemala during the entire period.

The case of U.S. Ambassador to Guatemala Frank Ortiz illustrates the conflicts within the administration over U.S. policy toward Guatemala. Ortiz, widely seen as a conservative without a strong commitment to human rights issues, was appointed U.S. Ambassador in Guatemala City in July 1979, during a period of intense human rights abuses. Ortiz developed close relations with the Lucas García government and argued that government-condoned violence was abating. He approved the March 1980 visit of a U.S. destroyer to a Guatemalan port, apparently without prior State Department knowledge, which many observers took as a sign of support for the Guatemalan government.[48] Pressures from human rights organizations and Congress contributed to the decision to replace Ortiz less than a year after he took office.

Coalitions in Argentina

The bureaucratic authoritarian regime in power in Argentina during this period was highly insulated from civil society, with a concentration of power and decision-making within the Military Junta and high command. Initially, President Videla did not have great autonomy from the rest of the Junta, and was constrained by the need to negotiate with the other forces in the military as well as with hard-liners within the Army. The informal process of ratification took place within the military government, and the contours of the win-set depended on internal negotiations among the branches of the military and within each of the branches, especially the more powerful Army.[49]

Putnam suggests that the greater the autonomy of central decision-makers from their Level II constituents, the larger the win-set and thus the greater likelihood of achieving international agreement. In both Guatemala and Argentina, however, the relative autonomy of the military government from civil society did not increase the size of the win-set on human rights issues. Since such issues often imply a direct accusa-tion of the military in power, the leeway for negotiation on such a topic would always be narrow, regardless of the degree of autonomy of the military government from civil society. In the case of Argentina, how-ever, Videla's increased autonomy vis-à-vis the Junta by late 1978 did appear to increase his ability to deliver on his promise to invite the IACHR to Argentina.[50]

Although it is difficult to know all the details of domestic negotiations on human rights in Argentina, there is no doubt, based on substantial documentation provided by the military themselves and uncovered by the judiciary in the trials of the military juntas, that the decisions to engage in repression were made at the highest levels of the Argentine government.[51] Thus the eventual decision to diminish that repression was also made by top-level government officials. The day-by-day imple-mentation of the "dirty war" was carried out by decentralized military units, each responsible for a particular geographical area and under the control of different branches of the military. These units, however, coordinated their activities with each other, and were ultimately under the control of the commander in chief of each branch.[52]

The "counter-revolutionary war" carried out by the military served to promote unity in the armed forces. The military had differences about the way in which the "dirty war" was carried out, but no substantial differences as to whether the repressive activity was necessary and justi-fied. The unity of the military forces on this issue, and the need to negoti-ate agreements among their various factions, including extreme hard-liners in the Army and Navy, meant that in the period 1976–77 there was no overlap between the win-sets of the Argentine military govern-ment and the U.S. government on the human rights issue.

Although by the military's claim 90 percent of the armed opposition had been eliminated by April 1977, this did not lead to an immediate change in human rights practices.[53] By 1978, one can distinguish differ-ent groups within the armed forces with different positions on what the military government should do in the future. One faction was led by Admiral Emilio Massera, a right-wing populist; another by Generals Car-los Suárez Mason and Luciano Menéndez, who supported indefinite mili-tary dictatorship and unrelenting war against the left; and a third, led by Generals Videla and Roberto Viola, who hoped for eventual political liberalization under a military president. Over time the Videla-Viola fac-tion emerged supreme within the Junta, and by late 1978 Videla had gained more control over the Ministry of Foreign Affairs, which had previously been in the Navy's sphere of influence.[54] The general strengthening of Videla's position in the fall of 1978, and his ascendancy in the foreign policy realm, combined with U.S. pressure, helps explain his ability to deliver on his promise to allow the IACHR to visit by December 1978. The Argentine acceptability-set and win-set both changed over this period, as Videla came to see advantages to moderating human rights abuses *and* gained autonomy from the rest of the Junta.

Even with the emergence of Videla and Viola as the dominant figures in the military government, the win-set for human rights policy within the Argentine military remained very small. The great majority had come to believe that they were fighting (and winning) an irregular war against international subversion, and that they should be thanked, not condemned by domestic and international groups. International human rights pressures also created some negative reverberations in Argentina that the military used to their advantage.[55] In the late 1970s, many Argentine citizens accepted the government line that human rights concerns were part of an international leftist plot to discredit Argentina in world opinion.

Only through the tactical linkage of human rights issues with international assistance did the United States manage to redefine the Argentine win-set so that it overlapped with its own. Even so, the size of the overlap between the win-sets was minimal, and the Carter Administration may have hit upon one of the few face-saving alternatives that allowed the Videla Administration to respond to human rights pressures. Because the Mondale-Videla agreement involved a private understanding, the two decisions were not publicly linked and Videla did not have to admit that he was caving in to U.S. pressure. By involving the IACHR, the Carter Administration interposed a regional organization that was more legitimate in the eyes of the Argentine government and public. To invite a panel of other Latin American jurists was less compromising than to permit direct interference from the U.S. government. Videla and Viola understood that as part of the process of military-led political liberalization they were advocating, some kind of explanation of past repression would have to be provided. It appears that they saw the visit and report of the IACHR not only as a means of improving relations with the United States, but also as a potential means of drawing a curtain on the past by providing a minimal explanation of abuses, while emphasizing the limited process of liberalization they were initiating.[56] It was not until the strong IACHR report was published one year after the visit that Videla and Viola realized they had seriously misjudged the Commission. In the words of one observer, the Commission's report "boomeranged" on Videla.

The only significant civilian allies of the government whose opinions appear to have contributed to the definition of the win-set were the civilian technocrats, especially the economic policy-makers. The economic program of the military regime constituted one of the two main goals of the government: the re-establishment of "order" and reinvigoration of the economy through a program of liberalization, expansion of exports, and foreign assistance and investment. The civilian technocrats and their closest allies in the military, the Videla-Viola faction, were concerned with the international image of Argentina, and the damage done to that image by the widespread reports of human rights violations. Nevertheless, neither the economic policy team nor domestic entrepreneurs became strong internal advocates of changing human rights practices, in part because the repression was perceived as a "taboo" topic by civilian allies of the military.[57] Also, because businessmen and members of the economic team had been targets of left-wing kidnapping and assassination attempts, they tended to support the repressive measures of the military.[58] In other words, the effects of issue linkage of human rights and economic aid were very diffuse, creating a general sense among the military that human rights issues might be costly, rather than leading specific targeted groups to lobby for policy change.

The military initially hoped that a veil of secrecy and repression could keep the outside world from recognizing the extent of human rights abuses. General Ramón Camps, Chief of Police of the Province of Buenos Aires, explained the importance of secrecy for the military: "On the orders of the highest military leadership, no one told the truth, so as not to affect international economic aid."[59] By 1978 it was clear that the strategy of secrecy had not worked. The scale of denunciations of human rights violations had become generalized and international.

One important reason for international awareness of Argentine human rights abuses was the presence, by 1977–78, of a wide range of domestic human rights organizations with significant external contacts. Thus, organizations like Mothers of the Plaza de Mayo, Grandmothers of the Plaza de Mayo, the Center for Legal and Social Studies, the Permanent Assembly for Human Rights, Commission of the Family Members of the Disappeared and Detained, the League for Human Rights, the Service for Peace and Justice, and the Ecumenical Commission for Human Rights, worked to document and publicize the abuses of human rights in Argentina. It is not clear whether these groups eventually had a direct impact on the decision-making of the Argentine military. They were often the target of abuse; their members were disappeared, their offices sacked and documents confiscated. These groups sought external contacts to publicize the human rights situation and to help protect themselves against further repression by their government. They were a crucial link in providing documentation and information to spur the interests and concern of U.S. policy-makers.[60]

Coalitions in Guatemala

In the Guatemalan case, the situation was quite different. Although the United States made some efforts to link military assistance and sales to the improvement of human rights practices, U.S. policy toward Guatemalan was much less comprehensive and forceful than its policy toward Argentina. The period following the cutoff of U.S. assistance witnessed not only no decline in human rights abuses, but an escalation in outright killings and disappearances. While estimates of human rights abuses differ for the period, there is agreement that 1978 marked the beginning of an escalation of repression that continued for the next five years, during the administrations of Generals Lucas García and Ríos Montt. An Amnesty International document says of this period, "Untold numbers died during the Lucas García and Ríos Montt administrations. Estimates vary, but all put the victims in the tens of thousands."[61] All the key human rights organizations concur that there was widespread military violence against civilians in this period, either directed by or condoned by the government.[62]

The government united behind a stance of blaming all political violence on groups for which they had no responsibility. As the Guatemalan government responded to testimony in congressional hearings in 1976, "This violence is due to the perpetration of criminal acts by groups of extremist ideology obliging the Government of the Republic to make superhuman efforts for the control and punishment of the terrorists."[63] The government, however, made no attempt to bring any of those responsible for violence against opposition leaders, peasants, and other "potential subversives" to justice. Those who opposed this strategy—opposition leaders and much of the rural population—were completely disenfranchised by brutal repression, including the routine killing of opposition organizers.[64]

What made the Guatemalan domestic situation different from the situation in Argentina? Four conditions seem important: (1) U.S. policy was less forceful and comprehensive, and thus the costs of no-agreement were lower. (2) There was no powerful group within the Guatemalan military that could perceive a tactical advantage in responding to U.S. human rights pressures. (3) The late 1970s witnessed a dramatic upsurge in the numbers and success of the rural armed insurgent movement. (4) Few Guatemalan human rights organizations existed to document abuses and establish transnational linkages with international human rights organizations.

The Guatemalan military and elite groups of civilians were unified in their conservative world view and absolute opposition to the human rights policies of the Carter Administration. They fancied themselves the upholders of free-world values now that the United States was governed by the "moderate Marxists" of the Carter Administration. Contrary to the situation in Argentina, where many commentators speak of "moderates" (albeit murderous ones) within the military, by the 1970s in Guatemala reformist groups within the military had been virtually eliminated.[65] Divisions existed among the Guatemalan armed forces on a variety of issues, but these did not lead to the emergence of a faction typically prepared to respond to human rights pressures.[66] The Guatemalan military had received substantial U.S. assistance and training over 20 years. While the two-level model is not well suited to incorporate the impact of history into the game, it is important to note that past U.S. influence (especially during the coup in 1954) contributed to the structure of the Guatemalan military that later blocked human rights pressures.

Historically, the Guatemalan military came to see rural Guatemala as its particular preserve. Any attempt to alter that position and organize peasants or rural workers into independent associations was perceived as threatening to the central concerns of the military. Revolutionary forces gained strength in Guatemala, during the period 1975–1980. It is estimated that by 1979 the guerrillas had at least 1,800 armed men and substantial civilian support.[67] The upsurge of rural insurgence in the late 1970s served to unify the military ideologically and focus them on the shared task of counter-insurgence. In this context, the military viewed U.S. human rights policy as interventionist, divisive to the military as an institution, and an interference in the strategy of counter-insurgence. Even more than in the case of Argentina, the military and important groups of elites believed that counter-insurgence was necessary to protect their very way of life, and that it was not possible without substantial repression. The Guatemalan military was also able to use negative reverberations to its advantage, creating the self-image of a country able to sustain itself without outside support. Chief of Staff Rodolfo Lobos Zamora declared, "We Guatemalans can feel satisfied at being the first country in the world that has managed to inflict a substantial defeat on subversion by means of our own eminently nationalistic strategy and tactics, without outside assistance." President Lucas García put it more succinctly: "Gringos are not going to teach us what democracy is."[68] International human rights activities were denounced as part of an international campaign in support of subversion and against the government and military of Guatemala.

Guatemalan business organizations were uniformly conservative and supportive of the repressive policies of the government during the 1970s. Right-wing business lobbies like Amigos del País and the Guatemalan Freedom Foundation had close connections with the government, and with the resident U.S. business community, united by a common conservative ideology. The former head of the American Chamber of Commerce in Guatemala, for example, was strongly opposed to the Carter Administration's human rights policy.[69] Private-enterprise lobbies also engaged in cross-table lobbying, devoting considerable money and energies to wooing Republican politicians even before the Reagan Administration took office.[70]

Eventually the extreme corruption of the Lucas García government, and the sense of increasing international isolation, led to its ouster in March 1982. U.S. military aid cutbacks were among the multiple factors that contributed to the coup against the Lucas García regime. As government reserves declined, junior officers became increasingly concerned about the lack of adequate supplies, and some even called for a reduced level of human rights violations to improve the military's image.[71] This regime change, with General Ríos Montt taking power in a coup, did not lead to an improvement in human rights practices.

INTERNATIONAL NEGOTIATIONS

No government wants to admit publicly that it violates the basic human rights of its citizens, or that improvements in their treatment are due to the pressures of another government. Thus, diplomacy on human rights issues rarely becomes public knowledge. As Assistant Secretary Derian said, making public such actions as denying loans for human rights reasons reflects a failure of negotiations, rather than a measure of success.[72] Governments engage in what we might call "opaque negotiations," with no public or formal agreements to signify cooperation. We can, nevertheless, examine which officials attempted to discuss human rights issues with the Argentine and Guatemalan governments, and the use of reductions and threats of reductions in assistance as bargaining tools. Tactical linkage between foreign assistance and human rights conditions provided the U.S. government with a source of leverage that eventually, in the Argentine case, led to a measure of success.

Argentina

The Carter Administration's first major approach toward the Argentine government was the reduction in military aid announced in February 1977. However, Argentina responded by rejecting all remaining U.S. military aid. The link to security assistance did not provide sufficient leverage in and of itself to gain an agreement on human rights. In the Argentine case, it was the convergence of multiple forceful human rights pressures that led to a successful outcome.

Ongoing diplomatic pressures reinforced the perception that the U.S.

government was committed to pursuing human rights issues. A human rights officer in the U.S. Embassy in Buenos Aires regularly discussed both general human rights policy and specific cases of disappearances with the Argentine government. Higher-level officials, including the Secretary of State and the President, contacted the Argentine government on human rights issues, taking actions such as furnishing lists of the disappeared and pressing the government to allow visits by nongovernmental organizations.[73] In 1977, U.S. Treasury Secretary Michael Blumenthal met with Argentine Economic Minister José Martínez de Hoz in June, Patricia Derian visited Foreign Minister Oscar Montes in August, Assistant Secretary Todman met with President Videla in August, President Carter met with President Videla in September, and Secretary of State Vance met with Videla in November.[74] Human rights organizations argued that these initiatives contributed to a slight improvement in the situation even before the invitation to the IACHR.

A major attempt, and probably the most successful, to increase pressure on the Junta occurred during the summer of 1978. On July 20, the Eximbank announced that it had decided to withhold a 270 million dollar loan for construction of a hydroelectric plant on the Yacireta River. Allis-Chalmers, which was to supply the parts for this plant, mounted a massive lobbying campaign, which gained widespread support from business interests, to reverse the administration's decision. Members of Congress who had supported the termination of military supplies to Argentina worried that the extension of sanctions to nonmilitary items could prove extremely costly to U.S. trade at a time when the trade deficit was increasingly troublesome. Within the administration, Secretary of Commerce Juanita Kreps argued against the decision to block the Eximbank loan. At the same time, the congressional embargo on military assistance and sales was scheduled to go into effect on September 30, and the Pentagon denied pending license requests.

When President Videla requested a meeting with Mondale, each country faced a unique situation. In the United States, the pressures on Argentina to change its human rights practices had reached a high point, but the coalition supporting such pressures was breaking down over the trade issue. As business became enfranchised because of the threat to export financing, congressional support for stringent sanctions declined. Mondale's use of the loan denial threat was thus somewhat risky, since if he had tried to carry through on this threat he might have been overridden by Congress. However, this risk was mitigated by the private nature of the negotiations, and by the fact that the Eximbank loan was only one part of a package of improved relations. In Argentina, Videla had solidified his internal position vis-à-vis other groups in the government and the military, but faced difficulties in the general realm of foreign relations. U.S.-Argentine relations, and to a lesser extent Argentine relations with European countries, had deteriorated over the human rights issue. The conflict with Chile over the Beagle Canal had intensified in mid-1978, while relations with Brazil remained troubled.[75] In this context, the agreements reached at the Mondale-Videla meeting offered both countries options for resolving the problems they faced. In September 1978, we find the temporary convergence of a small win-set in the United States, administration willingness to push hard on the human rights issue, and a faction within the Argentine government willing and able to use such pressure to pursue its own preferred policies.

Guatemala

The history of human rights negotiations with Guatemala is much shorter than that with Argentina, since the Guatemalan government successfully refused to meet with U.S. representatives to discuss this issue. The Guatemalan military government adopted a simple, if brutal, strategy. It did not attempt to deny that widespread politically motivated murder took place in the country. As Vice President Francisco Villagrán Kramer (later exiled) stated in 1980, "There are no political prisoners in Guatemala—only political murders."[76] The government kept its own toll of those killed, which sometimes exceeded that collected by Amnesty International. However, the government argued that it had no control over the groups responsible for these murders, claiming "involuntary defection." Therefore, it claimed that it had nothing to discuss with the United States.

Unlike the situation in Argentina, Congress and the administration took no further steps to cut aid to Guatemala after the fiscal 1978 FMS legislation. The only high-level meetings were between Vice President Mondale and President Laugerud during the Panama Canal Treaty ceremonies, and one with Mrs. Carter and Laugerud and President-elect Lucas García in May 1978.[77] After this, Lucas García refused to meet with other administration officials, and the United States did not send many representatives to the country. Assistant Secretary of State William Bowdler did visit in September 1979, but was not able to meet with Guatemalan officials.[78] Overall, what limited attempts the United States did make to engage Guatemala in negotiations on human rights issues were failures. The limited sanctions embodied in the military assistance legislation were insufficient to induce Guatemala to negotiate, especially since the administration partially circumvented these restrictions.

ANALYSIS

Explaining Argentine Success

Two puzzles deserve explanation at this point: Why pressure on Argentina succeeded in September 1978 while it had failed earlier, and why U.S. initiatives had a greater impact in Argentina than in Guatemala. As we discussed at the beginning of this chapter, a systemic perspective would lead us to expect greater success in Guatemala, a smaller, poorer nation more dependent on the United States. We argue that in September 1978, four necessary conditions for successful cooperation were temporarily met in the Argentine case. Implementation of the congressional military aid embargo and the denial of Eximbank funding narrowed the win-set in the United States; the President was genuinely interested in pursuing a human rights policy and had few competing objectives in Argentina; a dominant faction in the Argentine Junta thought it might be able to use the visit of the IACHR to prepare the way for political liberalization; and transnational lobbying had put the issue on both governments' agendas.

As we discussed above, Congress had gradually shrunk the win-set after 1973, putting tighter restrictions on foreign assistance to Argentina and eventually authorizing the administration to take human rights into account on Eximbank decisions. Each tactical issue-linkage removed potential "bargains" from the realm of ratifiable outcomes, and thus narrowed the win-set. The cutoff of Eximbank financing was costly to Argentina, as was the denial of military assistance and commercial sales. Unfortunately, cutting off Eximbank funding would also be quite costly to the United States, and Congress seemed likely to repeal the legislation authorizing the denial in the near future. Thus, Carter had only a short time-span in which to use the threat of a small win-set to achieve an agreement with the Argentine government. Coercive issue-linkage, in general, involves costs to both sides, and thus governments find it difficult to make credible threats such as cutting off Eximbank funding. This is in contrast to synergistic issue-linkage, where both sides benefit.[79]

Congressional pressure alone would have been insufficient, however. Nixon and Ford had shown that the executive branch could find ways to circumvent the intent of Congress. Carter's ability to continue military deliveries to Guatemala makes the same point. In addition, the coalition in Congress supporting a vigorous human rights policy was not strong enough to support costly trade sanctions in the face of presidential opposition. Thus, only a chief negotiator genuinely committed to improving human rights and facing few competing foreign policy objectives would use the opportunity of a small win-set to gain cooperation from Argentina. Mondale's meeting with Videla exploited a temporary shrinking of the win-set to reach such an agreement.

However, even these two factors would have been insufficient to gain cooperation from Argentina if there had existed no faction prepared to invite the IACHR and reduce human rights violations. By September 1978, President Videla saw advantages in such a policy, but needed some way to convince the hard-line factions to agree. Externally, Videla understood that the invitation to the IACHR was a precondition not only for the Eximbank loan, but also more generally for improved relations with the United States and a lessening of Argentine "pariah" status in the international community. Internally, Videla hoped to use the report to support a limited process of political liberalization under military tutelage.[80] The strengthening of Videla's position within the military government, the final cutoff of military assistance and sales, the threat of cutting Eximbank financing, and Mondale's promise of improved relations in exchange for the IACHR visit apparently provided the necessary levers to gain the agreement of the hard-liners. As Putnam has suggested, international negotiations allowed the chief negotiator, Videla, to shift the balance of power in the Level II game in favor of a policy he preferred for exogenous reasons.[81]

The situation in Guatemala was the opposite of that in Argentina as of September 1978. Congress allowed a larger win-set for Guatemala, never threatening to reduce economic aid or impose any kind of trade sanctions except denial of military assistance. Within the United States, the win-set for Guatemala included an outcome involving a continuation of economic aid with no corresponding improvement in human rights; this outcome did not lie within the U.S. win-set for Argentina. The Guatemalan case therefore does not actually reflect a "failed agreement," but is instead an instance of cooperation on the part of the United States with regard to economic aid, but defection by Guatemala. Because of the use of tactical issue-linkage in this case, the analytical focus shifts from reaching agreements to the implementation of threats. Nevertheless, consideration of overlapping win-sets provides a useful analytic tool. The President, facing competing policy objectives in Guatemala, never engaged in the same kind of high-level arm-twisting that he, Mondale, Vance, and Derian used with Videla. On top of these limitations, there were no factions within the Guatemalan regime looking for an excuse to bring the death squads under control. Thus, there was no scope for cooperation in the Guatemalan case, and we find that U.S. human rights policy failed there. Any of these conditions alone would have prevented significant success; in conjunction, they guaranteed failure.

Insights for the Two-Level Games Model: Institutions and Iteration

The case of human rights in Argentina highlights two aspects of the two-level game model in particular. First, it draws attention to the different types of "ratification processes" that domestic constituencies might use to approve or reject negotiated agreements, and the implications of these processes for the contours of the win-set. Second, it calls into question the hypothesis that small win-sets should, ceteris paribus, increase a country's bargaining power in international negotiations. In the final part of this chapter, we suggest a typology for thinking about ratification processes and a tentative explanation for constant executive arguments in favor of flexibility, or large win-sets.

The process by which Congress approved executive human rights policies differed from the formal process of treaty ratification. However, if the two-level game model is to work in a wide range of cases, "ratification" cannot be limited to formal up-or-down votes of completed agreements.[82] U.S. human rights policy suggests some of the different processes that Congress might use to "ratify" an agreement, which we call approval, authorization, and acquiescence. Although the American context has suggested this typology, it should be general enough to apply to other national policy environments as well.

> *Approval* refers to a process in which the principal negotiator arrives at an agreement with other Level I negotiators, and presents this agreement as a *fait accompli* to his Level II constituents. Congress then subjects the agreement to an up-or-down vote. We usually understand ratification this way; treaty ratification by the Senate presents a paradigmatic case.
>
> *Authorization* represents an alternative institutional process in which Congress acts before the principal negotiators begin bargaining. A well-known example of such a process is U.S. involvement in GATT negotiations. Prior to each major round of trade talks, the executive receives congressional authorization to negotiate within certain substantive or procedural constraints.
>
> In *acquiescence,* the institutional process does not mandate that Congress play a role in negotiations, either before or after the fact. Suggestive examples might include "gentlemen's agreements," such as that between the United States and Japan on immigration in the early twentieth century, or bilateral trade negotiations on Voluntary Export Restraints. In such cases, Congress has no voice in the negotiations, and the agreement is not submitted automatically for congressional approval. Thus, Congress generally acquiesces in the executive agreement, but can overturn it, as it did the gentlemen's agreement with Japan on immigration.

The ratification process has a double effect on the shape of the win-set, affecting both the apparent size and degree of uncertainty about what agreements can be ratified. As the process moves from acquiescence to authorization to approval, the legislature is likely to overturn more agreements, since they will regularly arise on its agenda. Thus, the effective size of the win-set will decrease. At the same time, movement to a more formal ratification process should decrease negotiators' uncertainty about what agreements will be approved. Under approval, any agreement is assured a formal vote, and the preferences of members of Congress should be sufficient to provide a good idea of its outcome. Under acquiescence and authorization, however, an additional element of uncertainty arises, since the executive may be able to evade formal congressional evaluation. With less formal ratification processes, the intensity of members' interest in the agreement will determine whether the issue actually comes before Congress.

In the course of U.S. policy-making on human rights in Argentina, Congress gradually moved to restrict the executive's effective win-set. One way it did this was through passing first general, then country-specific legislation. However, the legislature also changed the relevant ratification process, moving from acquiescence to authorization. Authorization of the Eximbank denial provided the necessary leverage to reach an agreement. This movement restricted the range of agreements the administration was likely to get past Congress, shrinking the effective win-set.

President Carter, despite his strong commitment to international human rights, lobbied actively against congressional actions that would tie his hands when discussing these issues with other countries.[83] For example, when Senator Kennedy introduced an amendment in 1977 that would mandate termination of military sales to Argentina, the administration opposed him. With Carter's blessing, Senator Humphrey introduced an alternative amendment which gave the administration more room to maneuver, and Congress approved Humphrey's version. In addition, many members of the administration, including Patricia Derian and the President, argued against congressional proposals to tie U.S. approval of loans by international financial institutions (IFIs) to recipients' respect for human rights. Officials argued that such requirements would *reduce* their bargaining power, although the Christopher Committee instructed U.S. representatives to the IFIs to oppose or abstain on most loans to Argentina, even without congressional requirements.[84]

The two-level game logic leads us to expect that a president genuinely committed to influencing the human rights policies of other states should *favor* formal congressional constraints on acceptable agreements. All else being equal, such restriction of the win-set should tend to bring the final agreements closer to the president's "ideal point."[85] One possible way to reconcile this apparent contradiction between logic and evidence might lie in a distinction between the "bargaining" and "implementation" phases of international negotiations.

Every negotiation goes through two phases. In the first, the bargaining phase, the two sides attempt to reach an agreement acceptable to both. It is during this phase that we should expect to find principal negotiators claiming that their "hands are tied," and that only agreements favorable to their side will gain approval from their domestic constituencies. In the second phase, the two sides must implement this agreement, with the cooperation of relevant domestic actors.

U.S.-Argentine discussions on human rights did not take the form of a one-shot bargain/implement procedure. Instead, we find a series of day-to-day agreements on the release of particular prisoners, approval of specific licenses for military sales, etc. In this kind of disaggregated negotiation process, the implementation phase of one agreement overlaps with the bargaining phase of the next. In such a situation, the bargaining advantages derived from limits on the principal negotiator's flexibility might be outweighed by the negative impact these limits will have on the next negotiation. If, in response to failed early negotiations, Congress were to cut off all aid, the executive would have reduced leverage in remaining talks.

In early discussions, the executive branch may want to carry out threats to deny particular loans, for example, in order to establish credibility. However, the executive will prefer to maintain control over the decision to go ahead with sanctions, rather than ceding it to the legislative branch. Executive preferences for flexibility might be explained by the fact that discussions on human rights were disaggregated, broken down into a series of smaller agreements. In this kind of negotiation process, sweeping limitations on U.S. assistance, leaving no room at all for executive flexibility, could be counterproductive, by cutting off on-going bargaining-phase talks. If the effects of disaggregation do account for the executive preference for flexibility, we should find a pattern in negotiators' arguments for it. Flexibility is a much greater asset when negotiations are disaggregated than when they are not. If the negotiation is a one-shot deal, flexibility is actually a disadvantage, as it reduces the negotiator's bargaining power. In September 1978, for example, Mondale was able to exploit the perception of *inflexibility* to gain an agreement with Videla. Greater executive flexibility in and of itself, however, in the case of Guatemala, did not lead to a more effective policy.

CONCLUSION

Many analysts have concluded that U.S. human rights policy was a failure, that it had almost no impact on the practices of governments that violated their citizen's basic rights.[86] This chapter refutes that contention, arguing that in at least one case, Argentina in late 1978, U.S. pressure did contribute to a decrease in the phenomenon of disappearances. However, we find that cooperation in this case resulted from the temporary convergence of four necessary conditions: a small win-set in the United States, a sympathetic chief negotiator, a faction in the Argentine government willing to use outside pressures to pursue its own political goals internally, and the existence and active involvement of nongovernmental human rights organizations. Lacking any one of these four factors, cooperation would almost certainly not have occurred. Given these stringent conditions, it is not surprising that, in general, the United States met with few comparable successes on the human rights front.

Prior to the Carter Administration's taking office, the executive branch was antagonistic to the vigorous pursuit of human rights policies, and frustrated congressional initiatives in this area. Congress responded by gradually tightening restrictions on various forms of foreign aid, and found a more sympathetic agent in the Carter Administration. These two processes coincided with domestic changes in Argentina that created conditions permitting a change in human rights policy. This change finally occurred in late 1978. In Guatemala, we find none of these conditions. There were no similar factions within the Guatemalan government; the U.S. win-set for this country was larger; the President was more reluctant to push human rights concerns, due to competing policy objectives; and no domestic human rights organizations existed in Guatemala. Surprisingly, "dependence" on the United States in an aggregate sense does not appear to have any relation to the level of cooperation achieved.

To say that U.S. policy "failed" in the case of Guatemala, however, is not to suggest that the aid cutoff was counter-productive, or that "quiet diplomacy" would have proved more successful. The case of Argentina suggests that the combination of severe pressures (military and economic aid, "no" votes in the IFIs, and the denial of Eximbank loans), plus the willingness to bargain on one important sanction (the Eximbank funds), contributed to change. This suggests that if the United States had made human rights a higher priority in its bilateral relations with Guatemala, and brought more pressure to bear, the chances of success might have been greater. But even forceful human rights pressures cannot guarantee success, since the necessary preconditions must exist within the repressive country to allow negotiations to succeed.

This pair of cases demonstrates the utility of the two-level game metaphor for sorting out the complex interactions of domestic and international factors in situations that diverge in many ways from the paradigmatic formal negotiation case. Negotiations were private, with no formal agreements reached. Congress never faced a formal ratification decision on any agreement. Negotiations themselves resulted only from tactical issue-linkage between human rights and foreign assistance, since no "automatic" interdependence existed here. Yet the metaphor provides significant insight into the conditions that led to success in one case, at a particular time, and failure in the other.

In addition, we find that this example enhances the two-level game model in a number of respects. It suggests that an answer to the anomaly of executive preferences for flexibility lies in the iteration of negotiations, and emphasizes the importance of formal ratification requirements for determining the size of the win-set. It also suggests the importance of transnational linkages in influencing the size and the contours of the win-set. In this instance, the activities of domestic and international human rights organizations provided the essential information that led to emergence of the issue and permitted monitoring of change.[87] Where information uncertainties were pronounced and few powerful interest groups competed for influence, relatively small nongovernmental organizations armed with information were able to have a substantial effect on policy.

NOTES

1. Interview with Walter Mondale, Minneapolis, June 20, 1989.

2. This interpretation differs from that of Carlos Escudé, who claims that U.S. human rights policy was unsuccessful in Argentina. First, although Escudé is correct that U.S. human rights policy was sometimes applied in a contradictory fashion to Argentina, he does not discuss the fact that it was applied more consistently in the case of Argentina than for any other country except Uruguay. Second, he does not discuss the granting of blocked Eximbank credits in exchange for the Argentine invitation to the IACHR, which is key to the argument we make here. Third, Escudé underestimates the importance of diplomatic pressures on the Argentine military government. While it is true that initially the Argentine government reacted nationalistically against the campaigns, by 1978 they were profoundly concerned about the international isolation of the military regime. Carlos Escudé, "Argentina: The Costs of Contradiction," in Abraham F. Lowenthal, ed., *Exporting Democracy: The United States and Latin America: Case Studies* (Baltimore: Johns Hopkins University Press, 1991).

3. Although the ban on U.S. military assistance to Guatemala was in effect until 1983, commercial military sales and economic assistance continued throughout the 1978–1983 period. U.S. General Accounting Office, *Military Sales: The United States' Continuing Munitions Supply Relationship with Guatemala*, report to the Chairman, Subcommittee on Western Hemisphere Affairs, Committee on Foreign Affairs, U.S. House of Representatives, January 1986.

4. Robert D. Putnam, "Diplomacy and Domestic Politics: The Logic of Two-Level Games," appendix to this volume, p. 444.

5. Ernst B. Haas, *When Knowledge Is Power: Three Models of Change in International Organizations* (Berkeley: University of California Press, 1990), p. 184.

6. George Black et al., *Garrison Guatemala* (New York: Monthly Review Press, 1984), p. 5.

7. Charles Lewis Taylor and David A. Jodice, *World Handbook of Political and Social Indicators*, 3rd ed., vol. 1 (New Haven, Conn.: Yale University Press, 1983), pp. 91–92.

8. Ibid., pp. 106–107.

9. Ibid., pp. 110–111.

10. World Bank, *World Development Report, 1981*, pp. 170–171.

11. Inter-American Development Bank, *Economic and Social Progress in Latin America: 1989 Report* (Washington, D.C., 1989), pp. 252, 340.

12. Ibid., pp. 226–228.

13. U.S. House Committee on Foreign Affairs, Subcommittees on Human Rights and International Organizations and on Inter-American Affairs, *Human Rights in Guatemala*, 97th Cong., 1st sess., hearing July 30, 1981, p. 38.

14. Amnesty International, *Amnesty International Report, 1977* (London, 1977), pp. 118–123.

15. Amnesty International, *Report of an Amnesty International Mission to Argentina* (London, March 1977).

16. *Nunca Más: The Report of the Argentine National Commission on the Disappeared* (New York: Farrar, Straus, and Giroux, 1986), pp. 209–234.

17. U.S. Department of State, *Human Rights and U.S. Policy: Argentina, Haiti, Indonesia, Iran, Peru, and the Philippines,* report to the U.S. House Committee on International Relations, Dec. 31, 1976, p. 6.

18. "Security Links Cited: Assistance Is Reduced to Argentina, Uruguay, and Ethiopia, Vance Says," *New York Times (NYT),* Feb. 25, 1977, p. A1; "Argentina and Uruguay Reject U.S. Assistance Linked to Human Rights," *NYT,* March 2, 1977, p. A10.

19. Congressional Research Service, Foreign Affairs and National Defense Division, *Human Rights and U.S. Foreign Assistance: Experiences and Issues in Policy Implementation, 1977–1978,* report prepared for U.S. Senate Committee on Foreign Relations, November 1979, p. 106.

20. Interview with Robert Pastor, June 28, 1990, Wianno, Massachusetts.

21. High-level diplomatic efforts were assisted in Buenos Aires by F. Allen (Tex) Harris, a full-time Human Rights Officer in the U.S. Embassy. Harris provided liaison with Argentine human rights groups and protested specific violations; in two years the embassy made more than 1200 representations to the Argentine government on cases of abuse. Americas Watch, *With Friends Like These: The Americas Watch Report on Human Rights and U.S. Policy in Latin America* (New York: Pantheon Books, 1985), pp. 99–100.

22. Lars Schoultz, *Human Rights and United States Foreign Policy Toward Latin America* (Princeton, N.J.: Princeton University Press, 1981), pp. 331–332.

23. Escudé, "Argentina," p. 21, argues that because none of these multilateral loans were denied to Argentina, and total multilateral lending to Argentina actually increased during the period 1978–1980, the U.S. human rights policy was

ineffectual. However, this unrealistically faults U.S. policy for the failure of Western allies to accept human rights considerations in the determination of multilateral aid.

24. "It appears evident that the decision to form the command units that were involved in the disappearance and possible extermination of these thousands of persons was adopted at the highest level of the Armed Forces. . . ." Organization of American States, Inter-American Commission on Human Rights, *Report on the Situation of Human Rights in Argentina* (Washington, D.C.: General Secretariat, OAS, 1980), p. 134.

25. Asamblea Permanente por los Derechos Humanos, *Las Cifras de la Guerra Sucia* (Buenos Aires, August 1988); and United Nations Working Group on Enforced or Involuntary Disappearances, UN doc. E/CN 4/1986/18 (1986), p. 21, reported in Maria Bartolomei and David Weissbrodt, "The Impact of Fact-Finding and International Pressures on the Human Rights Situation in Argentina, 1977–1983," unpub. ms.

26. Jacobo Timerman, *Prisoner Without a Name, Cell Without a Number* (New York: Random House, 1981).

27. From 1950 to 1980, 3,360 Guatemalan military officers were trained by the U.S. as a part of the International Military Education and Training Program (IMET). U.S. Department of Defense, *Foreign Military Sales, Foreign Military Construction, Sales, and Military Assistance Facts as of September 30, 1984*.

28. For a discussion of U.S. support for counter-insurgency campaigns in Guatemala in the 1960s, see Susanne Jonas, *The Battle for Guatemala: Rebels, Death Squads, and U.S. Power* (Boulder, Col.: Westview Press, 1991), pp. 69–71.

29. U.S. House Committee on International Relations, Subcommittee on International Organizations, *Human Rights in Nicaragua, Guatemala, and El Salvador: Implications for U.S. Policy*, 94th Cong., 2d sess., hearings June 8 and 9, 1976, p. 86.

30. Allan Nairn and Jean-Marie Simon, "Bureaucracy of Death," *New Republic*, June 30, 1986, p. 14.

31. Stephen B. Cohen, "Conditioning U.S. Security Assistance on Human Rights Practices," *American Journal of International Law* 76 (1982): 255.

32. For example, the Washington Office on Latin America, a church-sponsored human rights organization, helped the staff of the House Subcommittee on International Organizations select witnesses to testify in congressional hearings, and later helped brief the witnesses in preparation for their testimony. "Memo from the Washington Office on Latin America, Washington, D.C., May 11, 1976" in App. 1 of *Human Rights: Implications*, p. 155.

33. Lars Schoultz, "Guatemala," in Martin Diskin, ed., *Trouble in Our Backyard: Central America and the United States in the Eighties* (New York: Pantheon Books, 1983), p. 188.

34. U.S. GAO, *Military Sales*, p. 4. Approval of export licenses to Guatemala varied widely over this period: the State Department disapproved 2.1 percent in 1979 and 68 percent in 1980; ibid., p. 21.

35. Schoultz, "Guatemala," p. 187.

36. Peiro Gleijeses, "Guatemala: Crisis and Response," in *Report on Guatemala: Findings of the Study Group on United States-Guatemalan Relations*, p. 54.

37. Amnesty International, *Annual Report, 1980* (London, 1980), pp. 139–144.

38. Amnesty International, *Guatemala: A Government Program of Murder* (London, 1981), p. 7.

39. Gleijeses, "Guatemala: Crisis and Response," pp. 60–61.

40. In 1973, Congressman Donald Fraser (Democrat, Minnesota) began a series of hearings on the subject of human rights in the Subcommittee on International Organizations of the House Committee on International Relations. In 1974 these hearings culminated in a report entitled *Human Rights in the World Community: A Call for U.S. Leadership.*

41. It is noteworthy that some of the most activist members of Congress on the issue of human rights in Latin America never had related committee assignments, while members formally responsible for Latin American affairs, such as Representative Dante Fascell, chair of the House Foreign Affairs Subcommittee on Inter-American Affairs, typically voted against legislation tying U.S. assistance to human rights in Latin America. See Schoultz, *Human Rights,* pp. 146–148. This situation changed in 1981, when Representative Michael Barnes was named chairman of this subcommittee.

42. A high score on the NSI indicates that the congressman votes frequently in favor of "pro-security" legislation, such as increases in the defense budget and support for major weapons systems. See William P. Avery and David P. Forsythe, "Human Rights, National Security, and the U.S. Senate: Who Votes for What, and Why," *International Studies Quarterly* 23 (June 1979): 312; and David P. Forsythe, *Human Rights and U.S. Foreign Policy: Congress Reconsidered* (Gainesville: University of Florida Press, 1988), p. 37.

43. U.S. State Dept., *Human Rights and U.S. Policy,* p. 4.

44. See, for example, the statement of Patrick Breslin in U.S. Senate Committee on Foreign Relations, Subcommittee on Foreign Assistance, *Human Rights,* 95th Cong., 1st sess., hearing March 4, 1977, p. 12.

45. See U.S. House Committee on Foreign Affairs, Subcommittee on International Organizations, *Human Rights and the Phenomenon of Disappearances,* 96th Cong., 1st sess., hearing Oct. 18, 1979, p. 331.

46. Zbigniew Brzezinski, *Power and Principle* (New York: Farrar, Straus, and Giroux, 1983), p. 49.

47. Patrick J. Flood, "U.S. Human Rights Initiatives Concerning Argentina," in David D. Newsom, ed., *The Diplomacy of Human Rights* (New York: University Press of America, 1986), p. 129.

48. "Navy Ship's Visit to Guatemala Reveals U.S. Split on Policy," *Washington Post,* April 21, 1980, p. A14.

49. In the Argentine military regime, the Military Junta, made up of the commanders in chief of the Army, Navy, and Air Force, was the supreme authority. While decisions could be made by majority within the Junta, strong pressures existed for unanimity among its members, and unanimous approval was the general rule. Andrés Miguel Fontana, "Political Decision-Making by a Military Corporation: Argentina, 1976–1983" (Ph.D. diss., University of Texas at Austin, 1987), pp. 27–30.

50. Videla's position strengthened in May–September 1978 when he was reappointed to a term as President of the Republic; his ally, General Roberto Viola, was named Commander in Chief of the Army; and his chief internal opponent, Admiral Emilio Massera, resigned from the Junta.

51. "Se demostró que optaron por la clandestinidad y la ilegalidad," *El Diario del Juicio,* Dec. 11, 1985, pp. 1–2.

52. OAS, IACHR, *Report on . . . Human Rights in Argentina,* pp. 134–135.

53. According to a memorandum signed by Videla, the objectives of the military government "go well beyond the simple defeat of subversion." The memorandum called for a continuation and intensification of the "general offensive against subversion," including "intense military action." "Directivo 504," April 20, 1977, signed by General Videla, reproduced in "La orden secreta de Videla," *El Diario del Juicio,* December 3, 1985, pp. 5–8.

54. David Rock, *Argentina, 1516–1987: From Spanish Colonization to Alfonsín* (Berkeley: University of California Press, 1987), pp. 370–371. This understanding of divisions within the military was reinforced by interviews with military officers and civilian policy-makers of the Videla government, conducted in Buenos Aires in July and August 1990. Other observers, such as Jacobo Timerman, who saw the functioning of concentration camps from the inside, describe a conflict between the "moderates" led by Videla and Viola (eventually responsible for Timerman's release, after an intense international pressure campaign) and the hard-liners, such as Menéndez. The tension between the two groups was still so great in late 1979 that Timerman was released in the utmost secrecy, in order to prevent other groups within the Army from blocking his release. Menéndez, to protest Timerman's release, attempted a rebellion against the Videla faction. Timerman, *Prisoner,* p. 163.

55. In Argentina, the military effectively turned the slogan of human rights to their advantage when, during the 1979 World Cup held in Argentina, citizens sported bumper-stickers in the blue and white colors of the Argentine flag with the slogan "Los Argentinos Somos Derechos y Humanos" (a play on words with the term "human rights"—"derechos humanos"; it translates roughly as "We Argentines are upright and humane").

56. Interview May 13, 1990, with Tom J. Farer, member of the Special Commission of IACHR that conducted the on-site observation in Argentina in September 1979. Also, interview with Ambassador Arnoldo Listre, Buenos Aires, July 20, 1990.

57. Interview, Buenos Aires, July 31, 1990. This interviewee requested absolute anonymity.

58. Interview with José A. Martínez de Hoz, Minister of Economics in the Videla Administration, August 6, 1990, Buenos Aires.

59. Rock, *Argentina,* p. 385.

60. Members of these organizations traveled frequently to the United States and Europe, where they met with human rights organizations, talked to the press, testified before Congress, and met with members of Congress and their staffs and with State Department officials. Alison Brysk, "The Political Impact of Argentina's Human Rights Movement: Social Movements, Transition, and Democratization" (Ph.D. diss., Stanford University, 1990).

61. In March 1984, the juvenile division of the Guatemalan Supreme Court asked the country's mayors to draw up lists of how many children had lost parents since 1980 as a result of political violence. In September 1984, the Guatemalan press reported that the court's preliminary findings suggested that some 100,000 children (and perhaps as many as 200,000) had lost at least one parent, and that some 20 percent of them were orphans. Amnesty International, *Guatemala: The Human Rights Record* (London, 1984), p. 7.

62. Amnesty International, *Guatemala: A Government Program of Murder;* and Americas Watch, *Human Rights in Guatemala: No Neutrals Allowed* (New York, 1982).

63. U.S. House Committee on International Relations, *Human Rights in Nicaragua, Guatemala, and El Salvador,* p. 132.

64. Shelton H. Davis, "State Violence and Agrarian Crisis in Guatemala," in Diskin, ed., *Trouble,* pp. 155–171.

65. Gabriel Aguilera Peralta, "El Proceso de Militarización en el Estado Guatemalteco," *Polemica* no. 1 (September–October 1981), p. 39; Marlise Simons, "Guatemala: The Coming Danger," *Foreign Policy* no. 43 (1981), p. 103.

66. One historical division was between the younger, "modern" military who had been trained in the Escuela Politécnica and the older line officers who had not attended the military academy. The older officers tended to be more conservative, to have closer links to the rural elite, and to be more apt to respond violently to rural unrest. After the overthrow of Arbenz in 1954, most of the progressive officers were purged, but some divisions still remained within the military between different officers with political ambitions. Jim Handy, "Resurgent Democracy and the Guatemalan Military," *Journal of Latin American Studies* 18 (November 1986). On the Escuela Politécnica, see Franklin Patterson, "The Guatemalan Military and the Escuela Politécnica," *Armed Forces and Society* 14 (Spring 1988).

67. Peralta, "El Proceso de Militarización," p. 35.

68. "Lucas Criticizes Carter at Rally After Bombing," *Foreign Broadcast Information Service,* Latin America, September 8, 1980, p. 9.

69. Allan Nairn, "To Defend Our Way of Life: An Interview with a U.S. Businessman," excerpts from interview with Fred Sherwood, in Jonathan Fried et al., eds., *Guatemala in Rebellion* (New York: Grove Press, 1983), pp. 89–92.

70. Amigos del País hired the Washington public relations firm Deaver and Hannaford to improve Guatemala's international image and divert attention from its human rights record. "Guatemala: A Sharp Twist to the Right," *Latin American Regional Report: Mexico and Central America,* Nov. 28, 1980, p. 3.

71. Jim Handy, *Gift of the Devil: A History of Guatemala* (Toronto: Between the Lines Press, 1984), p. 182.

72. U.S. House Committee on Appropriations, Subcommittee on Foreign Operations and Related Agencies, *Foreign Assistance and Related Agencies Appropriations for 1978,* 95th Cong., 1st sess., hearings April 5, 1977, p. 305.

73. U.S. House Committee on Foreign Affairs, *Human Rights and the Phenomenon of Disappearances,* p. 331.

74. "U.S. Links Aid to Argentina Rights," *NYT,* June 1, 1977, p. A12; "Carter

Aide Again in Argentina for Assessment of Human Rights," *NYT*, Aug. 9, 1977, p. A4; "U.S. Official Has Talks in Argentina," *NYT*, Aug. 16, 1977, p. A6; and "Vance Wins Argentine Pledge on Nuclear Arms," *NYT*, Nov. 22, 1977, p. A3.

75. "Cuadro de Situación," *Carta Política*, October 1978, p. 5.

76. Amnesty International, *Guatemala*, p. 5.

77. "Notes on People," *NYT*, May 13, 1978, p. A12.

78. Schoultz, "Guatemala," p. 187.

79. For additional discussions of coercive issue-linkage, see the chapter by John Odell in this volume; and Lisa L. Martin, *Coercive Cooperation: Explaining Multilateral Economic Sanctions* (Princeton, N.J.: Princeton University Press, 1992).

80. Interviews with Ambassador Arnoldo Listre, July 20, 1990, and with Dr. Ricardo Yofre, August 1, 1990, Buenos Aires.

81. Putnam, Appendix, p. 457.

82. Ibid., p. 438.

83. "House Bars U.S. Aid to Seven Countries in Rebuff to Carter," *NYT*, June 24, 1977, p. A1.

84. U.S. House Committee on Foreign Affairs, *Resolution of Inquiry Concerning Human Rights Policies*, 96th Cong., 2d sess., hearing Feb. 6, 1980, p. 8.

85. Putnam, Appendix, p. 441.

86. See, for example, Gracia Berg, "Human Rights Sanctions as Leverage: Argentina, A Case Study," *Journal of Legislation* 7 (1980): 93–112.

87. The importance of human-rights organizations is reflected in the opening statement of Representative Bonker in the hearings considering reinstatement of military aid to Argentina in 1981. "Review of United States Policy on Military Assistance to Argentina," hearing before the Subcommittee on Human Rights and International Organization and on Inter-American Affairs of the Committee on Foreign Affairs, U.S. House of Representatives, April 1, 1981, p. 3.

12

Bargaining with the IMF
Two-Level Strategies and Developing Countries

Miles Kahler

Negotiations between international financial actors and developing countries were a constant during the 1980s: banks negotiating the restructuring of their debt, aid donors bargaining over the terms of grants and loans, and international financial institutions (principally the International Monetary Fund [IMF] and the World Bank) backing economic policy changes with their financial resources. In each of these situations, the bargaining power of the creditor coalition (the financial institutions and aid donors) has apparently been far greater than that of the developing countries. The virtual disappearance of sovereign lending by commercial banks, the collapse of commodity prices, recession and then slow growth in much of the industrialized world—all suggest a heightened dependence of developing countries on those few sources of external finance that remained.

Despite the dismal economic prospects facing many developing countries, the record of debt repayment and policy change only roughly approximated this image of bargaining asymmetry. Many sovereign debtors did struggle to maintain their payments on a restructured debt—but by the end of the decade, the list of those in arrears to their creditors had expanded from a handful of poor and pariah nations to a lengthening list that extended to the largest debtors. This pattern can be explained by the failure of commercial-bank lending to revive, even to those countries that had maintained their repayments. The mixed record on policy changes negotiated by the creditors—conditionality broadly defined—is more difficult to account for. Not only did developing countries—even poor and financially dependent ones—often delay entering into negotiations with the international financial institutions (IFIs: the IMF and the World Bank), but the negotiations often failed and agreements reached were often not implemented.[1] The behavior of the IFIs also did not match the estimates of their bargaining power: rather than punishing defection in this iterated game and thereby enforcing the bargains reached, they typically re-entered the bargaining or continued to disburse after program adjustments.

Reluctance to reach agreement on IFI terms, on the part of developing countries for whom the costs of no-agreement seem very high, is the central puzzle here. At least a part of the explanation lies in the internal politics of each bargainer. The politics of resistance to IFI prescriptions shape the cost-benefit calculus of elites in the developing world. Organizational and coalitional politics within the IMF and the World Bank push those institutions to continue to lend when suspension of financial assistance might seem the more rational strategy.

The outcome of interest, "agreement," seems relatively easy to identify in these cases. The IFIs, like the commercial banks, have designed elaborate conventions and contract-like arrangements to lower the risk of their lending. The IMF's stand-by and extended arrangements include a commitment on the part of the government in question to implement certain policy measures; finance is provided in tranches as the agreement is implemented. The structure of World Bank structural-adjustment and sectoral-adjustment lending is roughly the same: conclusion of a stand-by arrangement (or one of the other variants of lending) can be taken to mean "agreement."

Although this definition of "agreement" will inform the remainder of this chapter, it offers too clear-cut a picture of the meaning of "agreement" in these negotiations. The first qualification undermines the simple view of a series of discrete agreements followed by implementation. In fact, a particular letter of intent (the policy changes agreed to in an IMF stand-by) is only one in a long series of negotiating points for developing countries, a stream of negotiations dotted with waivers, breakdowns, and renegotiations. The IMF (and other creditors) has a strong interest in portraying the negotiations as one-shot, with a very low probability of financial assistance for defectors. Developing countries, reading the history of the IFIs and the dynamics of those organizations' internal politics, know that tomorrow is another day. Iteration, as suggested below, does have effects, but they often tend to strengthen the hand of the apparently weaker party.

Since agreements with the IFIs do not have the status of international treaties, either internally or externally, breaches of such agreements do not carry the same reputational consequences as do breaches of other international agreements. Outsiders have particular difficulty in assessing the reasons for defection and distinguishing between intentional and involuntary defection. Some governments may enter into these agreements with no intention to implement them, believing (or hoping) that their financial or political situation may improve in the near future. Others may intend to implement, but miscalculate the level of political resistance. An even more important increment of ambiguity is added by the importance of exogenous international economic changes in reinforcing agreement or providing excuses for defecting from it. Such international change provides a legitimate (from the point of view of both sides) reason for periodic review.

The following analysis examines negotiations between one IFI, the IMF, and two developing countries, Somalia and Jamaica, during the 1980s. The IMF in this instance is treated as another "country" with its own internal politics that constrain its bargaining strategies. Somalia and Jamaica have been chosen for their similarities on many dimensions—economic openness, relatively small size, dependence on the international economy and external finance, ties to American foreign policy—and their differences on key political dimensions. Jamaica is a long-standing, competitive, parliamentary democracy and, as a middle-income developing country, possesses a well articulated and organized cluster of economic interests. Somalia, one of the poorest developing countries, is best characterized as a weak authoritarian state embedded in a clan-based political order. Following an account of the ways in which "domestic" politics impinge on international behavior between the IMF and these two countries and on the broad strategic options for either side, I will examine the negotiations, which resulted in failure with Somalia and "successful" agreement with Jamaica, in light of the relative weight of second-level bargaining necessities.

DOMESTIC POLITICS AND WIN-SETS: THE INTERNATIONAL MONETARY FUND

Many observers have criticized the IMF for the consistency of its prescriptions for developing countries, the application of cookie-cutter programs to countries whose economic structures and political realities vary greatly. The "acceptability-set" of policies for the Fund in negotiations with developing countries appears very constricted. Although this perception is not wholly inaccurate, the variation in Fund programs is greater than often realized, and explanations for its stance in negotiations are often incomplete.

The Fund's reputed orthodoxy—the belief that adjustment measures are selected from a standard list of monetary and fiscal restraint, external liberalization, and devaluation—is grounded in part in the beliefs of the organization's staff, uniformly economists of the Western (European and North American) economics mainstream.[2] Heterodox solutions to balance-of-payments problems are likely to be scrutinized very carefully or ruled out entirely by the organization. Nevertheless, the appearance of such an acceptability-set for IMF programs is also a useful bargaining advantage. The image of this "kinky" set (in Putnam's phrase) offers additional leverage to the Fund in negotiations with developing countries: a program presented by a national government seems to stand a much higher chance of approval by the Fund and its Executive Board if it contains measures on that list, and high probability of failure if it does not.

This simple and essentially ideological explanation for IMF preferences must be heavily qualified by two other explanations that take into account the organizational and political dynamics of the organization. Among international organizations, the IMF has managed to extract a relatively high degree of autonomy from its members. Unlike the GATT, it was established as an organization, headed by a Managing Director and Deputy Managing Director, composed of a growing number of departments. Unlike many other international organizations, the Fund controls real resources that are important to its members. The analogy to a government, with its division between "spending" ministries and "auditing" or "controlling" ministries, is a reasonable one. Despite the prevailing image of the Fund as extremely tight-fisted with its resources, there is some tension within the organization between the Fund "missionaries" (the negotiating team) and their superiors. There are strong incentives for mission chiefs to return from negotiations with a developing country with an agreed program. An ambitious staff member must negotiate and oversee programs to advance in the organization. Programs in larger and more developed countries win more spurs than those in smaller and less developed countries. Particularly intractable cases, such as Tanzania or Jamaica (in the 1970s), also award higher status if negotiations are successful.

The Managing Director, who must win "ratification" of a program from the Executive Board of the IMF, has a different set of incentives. Although the Fund management has a strong interest in both expanding the scope of activities of the organization (hence its forceful support for the substitution account and special drawing rights) and expanding its membership (hence the special treatment awarded Rumania in the 1970s and the scarcely concealed fascination with China), the Executive Board will apply the principle of uniformity of treatment to most programs, scrutinizing them carefully to detect radically better deals for one country or class of countries than others. To ensure that the organization follows this rough standard, and to guarantee that its resources are used in accord with its prescribed goals, the IMF has established mechanisms of oversight, particularly in the Exchange and Trade Relations Department, which has historically checked the consistency of programs across area departments, and the Treasurer's Department, which has made sure that Fund resources are adequate to its lending program. An initial line of checks is also established in the heads of area departments (Africa or Western Hemisphere, for example), who are appointed by the Managing Director and often described as the toughest overseers of programs negotiated by IMF missions.

More important than these organizational determinants of the IMF's acceptability-set in negotiations are its internal politics of ratification. If the Managing Director of the IMF presides over a mini-"state," with its own conflicts between those with an interest in lending and those with an interest in checking those tendencies, it is a very weak state in relation to its constituents: the national governments that collectively direct the organization through the Board of Governors and, more immediately, the Executive Board.[3]

The Executive Board of the IMF represents a complicated set of national constituencies; only the largest economies have their own representatives on the Board. Several features of Fund organization weigh on the relationship between the Board and the Managing Director and staff. Since all IMF members are represented on it, the Board serves to establish an outer boundary to negotiations and agreements that appear to treat one member more favorably than others—the principle of uniformity of treatment mentioned earlier. This "democratic" principle is, however, highly qualified by two other features of IMF governance: weighted voting and special majorities.

Unlike organizations within the United Nations system, Fund members each possess a quota, roughly correlated with their weight in the world economy. This quota determines how much a member must contribute to the IMF's resources on joining the organization, how much it may draw when borrowing, and what percentage of votes it casts on the Executive Board. Voting weights range from the United States, with just under 20 percent of the votes, to the smallest members, with a fraction of one percent. The effect of weighted voting is that the dominant coalition is that of the industrialized countries, particularly the Group of Five (G-5): the United States, Japan, France, Germany, and the United Kingdom.

Their influence is only slightly qualified (and in some instances reinforced) by a system of special majorities that requires more than a simple majority of votes in deciding certain issues.[4] Special majorities do increase the incentives for bloc voting (e.g., developing countries, industrialized countries), and they certainly increase the veto power of the United States and the Europeans (as a group) on certain crucial issues (one of the special majorities is 85 percent).[5]

Industrialized country power is a constant in the exercise of influence by the Executive Board, not only through weighted voting on particular matters, but also in selection of the Managing Director and decisions regarding the resources available to the IMF. That influence, however, is not exerted through formal votes, which are rare, or through the frequent rejection (failure to ratify) of individual country programs. Programs negotiated by the IMF staff and approved by the Managing Director are almost never rejected outright by the Board. In their extensive comments, however, board members signal to the Managing Director and staff their qualms about program design and their wishes for the future direction of Fund relations with particular countries. Programs are shaped and reshaped over time as a result of Board comments: the anticipated reactions of this key constituency lead to staff redesign of programs to meet Board objections and criticism. The Executive Board has typically supported the convention that the IMF staff and management are the only avenue to financial resources: direct appeals to the Executive Board have never succeeded. The autonomy granted to the staff is useful for the industrialized countries in particular, since the IMF serves as an institutional buffer with their developing country clients on sensitive issues of economic policy.

"Ratification" of country programs within the IMF, then, appears virtually automatic, but in fact is the result of a constant process of discussion and comment by the IMF's most powerful members. The task of the Managing Director, the "chief of government," is to read the preferences of these key constituencies correctly, while at the same time expanding the scope and scale of the IMF's activities. In the 1980s, the preferences of the key industrialized countries regarding IMF programs clearly turned toward tighter conditionality, i.e., increasing the ratio of policy changes required for the level of finance offered by the IMF. John Williamson has convincingly documented this shift in IMF orientation in mid-1981, soon after the beginning of the Reagan Administration; interviews support his finding of a change at this time, led by the United States but supported by the other members of the G-5 (excepting France).[6] For most of the 1980s, then, the industrialized countries as a group reduced the size of the win-set in any negotiations with the Fund. The debt crisis, which began in late 1982, only heightened G-5 support of sharp adjustment in order to guarantee repayment to commercial creditors. These preferences in the design of IMF programs matched those of the bureaucratic actors who stood behind the Executive Board: usually the finance ministries and central banks of the industrialized countries.

At the same time, some of the industrialized countries, particularly the United States, Britain, and France, had developing country clients heavily dependent on finance from external sources, including the IMF. In particular cases, the influence of those powerful members was directed toward ensuring the approval of programs that were not as rigorous as those negotiated with other members. Board members, representing the finance ministry's point of view, usually attempted to shield the Fund from overt intervention on the basis of foreign policy interests; in cases of central strategic or foreign policy importance, however, they could be overridden. In these instances of favoritism, responding to constituency pressures meant that the win-set of the Fund was widened.

The "domestic politics" of the IMF has yet another layer, beyond those of its organization and its principal shareholders. During the 1980s the IMF became, even more clearly than in the past, a core member of a creditor coalition that coordinated its bargaining stance and the design of its financial packages. The other key members of this coalition were the World Bank, which instituted its own program of adjustment lending; the major industrialized countries, as both aid donors and creditors in their own right (organized in the Paris Club); and the commercial banks.

The multiple objectives of the creditors often produced conflict and division in their dealings with particular developing countries. The IMF's perspective was relatively short-term and driven by balance-of-payments crises; the World Bank took a longer-term and more structural approach to economic reform; the commercial banks were interested in having other financial players protect their enormous outstanding debt; and the industrialized countries, as described above, had conflicting interests as great powers, as creditors, and as guarantors of their national financial systems. Although cross-conditionality—the coordination and mutual dependence of bargains struck by the various creditors and sources of finance—could be seen as increasing the bargaining leverage of the creditor coalition, the possibilities for division within the coalition were often more apparent. The politics of the creditor coalition and the other "domestic politics" that determined the IMF's negotiating stance provided some possibility for reverse leverage by developing countries.

DOMESTIC POLITICS AND WIN-SETS: THE DEVELOPING COUNTRIES

The domestic politics of a developing country negotiating with the IMF are likely to impinge upon the process; negotiations over adjustment programs are often politicized along at least three dimensions. First, ideological resistance to IMF prescriptions may surface: objections to the Fund's model of the economy, to its market-oriented prescriptions, or to its emphasis on balance-of-payments adjustment rather than other goals, such as growth or equity. Such resistance is likely to arise in societies in which parties organized along ideological lines are a prominent element in political life. Ideological opposition may also be voiced within the state bureaucracy, particularly by those ministries engaged in planning or overseeing large budgets.

The second line of resistance lies along the nationalist fault line, opposing the apparent subordination of national policy to external forces and portraying the government as an agent of the industrialized countries and international capitalism more broadly. Nationalist resistance may emerge from any number of quarters in the society; it may, like other forms of ideological resistance, provide a useful screen for the defense of economic interests. Mobilized nationalist appeals may directly affect negotiations and be affected by them: one of the principal examples of negative reverberation is a nationalist response to apparent international pressures. The IMF has often aroused such negative reverberation.

Economic interests are the third and most readily analyzed dimension of political resistance to stabilization and adjustment programs. Much of the existing research on the political economy of such programs has centered on groups whose political standing or economic well-being are likely to be affected by the agreed policy changes.[7] Organized labor and, more broadly, the "urban popular classes" (a less clearly defined category) are generally conceded to have the most to lose in the short term from stabilization and adjustment programs. Most orthodox stabilization programs produce a decline in real wages, in the short run, and the dismantling or decontrol of state enterprises, prices, and subsidies, many of which benefit the organized sectors.[8] The resistance of these sectors of the economy often figures into the calculus of politicians who survey the Level II bargaining required for implementation, if not formal ratification, of an IMF program.

The position of other sectors in the economy is less well defined. Business is often thought to benefit from orthodox stabilization measures supported by the IMF, but import-substitution manufacturing and firms closely tied to the state sector or benefiting from state subsidies are likely to form part of the opposition to a program of exchange decontrol, import liberalization, and budgetary cutbacks. In similar fashion, the agricultural sector, which is also presumed to back export-promoting measures such as devaluation, may find its short-term interests endangered by a dismantling of subsidies and price supports. Many of the interests affected by an adjustment program will define their political position in terms of short-term economic costs that they are likely to suffer; those costs are computed from the "original position" of each sector or set of interests, not from some idealized picture of where their economic interests should lie following the program's implementation.

The interest group checklist approach to assessing the array of interests that will affect negotiation and ratification of an IMF stand-by has more serious weaknesses, however. Many of the plausible interests that might support an adjustment program and benefit from some of its most bitterly resisted measures, such as devaluation, are not organized to exert influence on the bargaining or ratification of such an agreement. Peasants in sub-Saharan Africa are a case in point: although the tough stabilization program undertaken in Ghana has undoubtedly increased the economic well-being of many cocoa farmers, they have not organized in support of either the economic program or the government. Even organized groups may not be enfranchised to participate in the ratification of an IMF agreement or economic policy decisions. In developing countries, enfranchisement is often ill defined: some powerful groups without formal status may exercise effective vetoes over such agreements. A final weakness of a purely interest-based approach relates to the way in which interests are incorporated into the political process. As Haggard and Kaufman point out, even organized labor, usually assumed to be bitterly opposed to stabilization programs, may react differently in different contexts of incorporation: "The most immediate political challenges to stabilization are likely to emerge in intermediate situations, where unions or informal sector workers possess sufficient resources for defensive mobilization but are still vulnerable to periodic repression and lack secure access to decision making or clear rights to organize."[9] Simply defining the costs borne by different groups need not imply that those costs will be expressed immediately in the domestic politics of ratification.

These qualifications to an approach based purely on the structure of economic interests point to the importance of political institutions in shaping the negotiation and ratification process. Two dimensions seem particularly important in the politics of IMF programs: the presence within a state of a coherent technocratic core to which the political elite has delegated substantial power; and periodic political tests (often electoral) that must be surmounted by those in power. In the model of a strong authoritarian state, the technocratic core is shielded from capture by economic interests in the society. Such a presence often plays a key role in negotiating and implementing adjustment programs: the IMF and other external agencies pressing for orthodox solutions typically rely on a transnational alliance with such technocrats to reach agreement on a program and its implementation.

The degree to which a political elite expects to face regular political tests will influence its "acceptable" set of outcomes in negotiations with the IMF. The most formal of such tests is regular elections: studies suggest a strong relationship between new governments and the successful implementation of such programs; governments facing a political test in the near future are less likely to undertake politically risky international agreements. Even authoritarian regimes may face less formal (or more imperfect) tests of their political standing with key groups or the population as a whole.

The domestic politics of win-sets in developing countries that are negotiating IMF agreements incorporate the topology of resistance among economic interests as well as the presence or absence of certain key political institutions. The final element is the chief of government (COG). Outlining domestic interests and institutions may in fact determine the acceptability-set for the COG in negotiations with the IMF. The closeness of fit between this leader's own acceptability-set and the ratification winsets in a society is determined by two key characteristics of the COG: preferences regarding economic policy and political entrepreneurship. The COG may not have strong preferences regarding economic policy and may simply represent a vector of contending domestic forces (read from a particular vantage point). Such a COG might be labeled a "political maximizer"—in contrast to an "economic strategist," who has at least certain broad views as to where the economy should be heading and how to get there (if only in the form of such nostrums as "no new taxes" or "government is the problem"). Equally significant in the fit between acceptability-set and the reading of *existing* interests, as expressed through *existing* institutions, is the degree to which the COG is a political entrepreneur who does not see the pattern of interests as fixed in the short run. Some COGs view apparent political givens as in fact malleable; others will interpret them as fixed, and bargain as if they cannot be changed. Of course, the degree of malleability is difficult to determine at the outset of a program of change, and even more difficult to assess by outsiders, such as the IMF.

SOMALIA AND JAMAICA: WIN-SETS AND DOMESTIC POLITICS OF ADJUSTMENT

Somalia and Jamaica provide two cases of negotiations with the IMF that are similar on certain economic and political dimensions but vary on the political determinants of win-sets described above. Both are small, open, developing economies. During the 1980s, both were highly dependent on external finance from aid donors and the IFIs, but they had not been important borrowers from the commercial banks: the creditor coalition with which they had to deal awarded a major role to the IMF and the World Bank. Both countries faced serious structural economic problems that had no easy solutions. Somalia's largely pastoral economy was subject to the vagaries of drought and market access, compounded in the 1980s by a large refugee population. Jamaica's bauxite industry, historically its major export sector, was in decline, although successive governments refused to accept this fact and the urgent need for diversification.

Both had strong links to the United States that were based on strategic calculations. During the Ogaden War against Ethiopia in 1977–78, Somalia's former great-power protector, the Soviet Union, switched its support (and its military assistance) to the new Marxist regime of Ethiopia. Rather than risk isolation and defeat, Somalia performed its own reversal of alliances, drawing closer to the United States, the European Community, and the Arab states that were its major markets.

Jamaica was also awarded major geopolitical and ideological significance by the United States. During the Carter Administration, the populist government of Michael Manley was regarded by some in the administration (such as Andrew Young) as a test of American willingness to come to terms with non-Communist, left-wing governments. After Manley's defeat by Edward Seaga in 1980, Seaga's rhetoric of free markets and anti-Communism was endorsed and financially supported by the Reagan Administration as a counter to a perceived Soviet-Cuban threat in the Caribbean and a symbol of capitalist development strategies. The U.S. presence was in many respects more overwhelming in Jamaica than in Somalia: as with other Caribbean nations, the United States was Jamaica's major trading partner, "the major source of investment and concessional assistance, and the primary destination of outmigration and (in times of uncertainty) capital flight."[10]

Despite these similarities, Somalia and Jamaica had very different political economies that would shape their negotiating stance and their respective win-sets in ratifiable agreements with the IMF. On any indicator of economic development and social well-being, Somalia was among the poorest countries in the world. The economic life of most of its population was pastoral, based on the herding and sale (often for export) of camels, goats, sheep, and cattle. Following the military coup that brought General Muhammad Siyaad Barre to power in 1969, the political economy was set on a course of "scientific socialism": state control was extended to segments of the urban economy, such as banks and insurance companies, but the key sector of livestock remained private. Other agricultural sectors, such as bananas, which had been important exports, gradually declined; economic diversification was reversed, and by the early 1980s livestock exports represented over 70 percent of total export earnings. Manufacturing was a relatively minor segment of the economy, even by African standards, representing only 6 percent of the gross domestic product (GDP) in the early 1980s. Most manufacturing was carried out by state-owned enterprises that were generally regarded as inefficient.

Somalia is one of the most ethnically homogeneous societies in sub-

Saharan Africa: Somali nationalism lay behind its conflict with Ethiopia and its claims to portions of Kenya and the former French colony of Djibouti. Despite this overarching national identity, politics in Somalia is embedded in a complicated clan and lineage structure; after colonial rule and two decades of scientific socialism, "most Somalis continue to give greater political and emotional loyalty to their lineages."[11] Overlying this resilient clan structure was a highly centralized and militarized authoritarian state. Following the 1969 coup and the embrace of scientific socialism, political power lay with a Supreme Revolutionary Council (SRC), essentially a military junta, headed by Siyaad Barre. In 1976, to add greater legitimacy to the regime, the Somali Socialist Revolutionary Party (SSRP) was established, and Siyaad Barre was named Secretary General of the Party. In 1980, in the aftermath of the Ogaden War and the resulting refugee crisis, the SRC was resurrected; by the early 1980s Somalia had three overlapping political structures, the SRC, the politburo and Central Party Committee of the SSRP, and the Council of Ministers (which Siyaad Barre, as President, also chaired). As one historian remarked, it was "doubtful whether many populations of comparable size to Somalia can have had more top-heavy or grandiose forms of government. It was certainly a labyrinthine structure which promoted confusion amongst the governed and discouraged decision-making outside the President's immediate circle."[12] Despite this elaborate formal structure, however, Siyaad Barre's power was based on his masterful manipulation of clan loyalties, basing his regime on three key clans linked to his family (the so-called MOD complex), making appointments from minor branches of opposition clans, and using economic patronage to buy off dissidence on the part of yet other clans that might threaten this delicate balance.[13]

Jamaica, in contrast to Somalia, is a middle-income developing country; its GNP per capita is more than three times that of the African country. Despite its heavy dependence on bauxite and aluminum for export earnings before 1980, its economy is far more diversified and, of particular political importance, urbanized. Like most Caribbean economies, its manufacturing sector (representing about 15 percent of GDP) developed under an import-substitution regime, "heavily protected and heavily import dependent."[14] Over the course of the 1980s, as traditional sugar and mineral exports have declined, tourism and nontraditional manufactures (such as garment assembling) have grown in importance.

Like Somalia, Jamaica was awarded a competitive parliamentary regime by its colonial masters; unlike Somalia, Jamaica has maintained that system: power has alternated between two major parties at two-term intervals. These parties, the People's National Party, led by Michael Manley, and the Jamaica Labour Party, led by Edward Seaga, have been compared to political "clans" that engage in regular electoral tests, appeal to cross-class coalitions, and incorporate such groups as the peasantry, the unemployed, and the labor movement. Support is maintained by the distribution of particularistic benefits, such as housing, jobs, government contracts, and business concessions. Although the parties emphasize ideological differences—Manley's PNP espousing populism in the 1970s, and Seaga campaigning against the PNP in 1980 on a pro-capitalist, anti-Communist line—in fact, the two parties are best seen as catch-all parties, appealing to the median Jamaican voter. And that median voter has particular political and economic preferences that both parties find difficult to violate.

Underlying the party structure, and once again in contrast to Somalia, is a well-developed set of interest groups. Each political party is attached to a labor federation: the PNP to the National Workers Union; the JLP to the Bustamante Industrial Trade Union (BITU). (About one-quarter to one-third of the workforce is unionized.) Business had established its own peak association in the 1970s to respond to the Manley government: the Private Sector Organization of Jamaica. In contrast to the weak urban sector in Somalia, Jamaican policy-making confronted a highly organized and volatile urban sector, one that had a history of turning to protests and demonstrations (sometimes violent) when its interests were threatened.

In both political systems during the 1980s, the role of the COG was central to policy-making and to negotiations with the IMF. Both Siyaad Barre and Edward Seaga centralized power. Siyaad Barre's overlapping roles were recounted above: nothing of importance happened in the Somali government without his approval. His own preferences on economic policy are not clear, but seemed to be dictated by political pragmatism (despite his earlier support for scientific socialism). Indeed, he is alleged to have declared, "I believe neither in Islam, nor socialism nor tribalism, nor Somali nationalism, nor pan-Africanism. The only ideology to which I am committed is the ideology of political survival."[15]

Edward Seaga has greater claim to being an economic strategist rather than simply a political maximizer. Certainly the public image that he cultivated, that of a skilled technocrat, was reinforced by the highly ideological 1980 election campaign that brought him to power. The prime minister in the Jamaican political system, closely modeled on the British parliamentary system, is awarded considerable power, and party leaders have traditionally had long tenures. Seaga further centralized control over economic policy by assuming the portfolio of Finance Minister in addition to Prime Minister after 1980, and by a style of governance that avoided consultation with fellow cabinet ministers or organized groups. Despite his public image, however, Seaga would prove to be more a political maximizer than his admirers outside Jamaica at first believed.

NEGOTIATING STRATEGY:
INCORPORATING THE TWO-LEVEL GAME

Up to this point, domestic interests and political institutions have been portrayed as constraints on the COG, or even determinants of the acceptability-set of the political leadership. The image of a two-level game suggests, however, that these constraints are not fixed and that international bargaining may profitably be directed toward loosening them, expanding the win-set of the opposing side. Both the IMF and the developing countries have in the course of their negotiations employed an array of strategies, some of which take into account this dimension of international bargaining.

Whatever its financial leverage, the IMF cannot implement its own programs. A core strategy of the IMF is to structure financial rewards in such a way as to foster compliance with a negotiated agreement with a minimum of slippage. For example, the IMF may impose behavioral conditions of government commitment or "ownership" of a program. Such prior conditions (prior to approval of the stand-by) might include a devaluation or some other politically sensitive measure assuring that the government is willing to incur some political costs for the program. Even more central to policy-based lending by both the IMF and the World Bank is the phasing of financing as agreed policy changes are implemented, to guarantee that a government does not accept the financing and then renege on the stand-by agreement.

Each of these strategies uses finance as a lever to influence national governments, while "black-boxing" the national government and the second (domestic) level of bargaining. The IMF and other external agencies also engage in strategies that attempt to shape the incentives of their counterparts by influencing the domestic level of bargaining that surrounds an agreement. Fund missionaries often undertake a campaign of suasion within a government to encourage the formation of a supportive domestic coalition or shore up an existing one. The IMF staff displays considerable variation on this score, but as one staff member involved in a number of programs put it: "If you want the program to succeed, then you must work for it." Such strategies might include briefing ministers outside the usual circle of the finance ministry and the central bank, if they will be essential to the success of the program. Coalition-building may mean sparing budgetary sacred cows that permit senior politicians to support an adjustment program: chief among these politically sensitive items are food subsidies and military spending. Principally, this strategy means frequent visits to cabinet ministers and even the COG to allay fears of political repercussions from the program and to begin the next round of persuasion for further adjustment steps. As one mission chief for a successful African program put it, "You do a lot of talking and write a lot of short memos."

By far the most significant coalition-building by the IMF is the construction of transnational alliances with technocrats in government ministries that share IMF policy preferences, typically the finance ministry and the central bank. These ministries, responsible for macroeconomic and budgetary oversight, are often in agreement with the prescriptions of the IMF, whose programs provide them with valuable ammunition.[16] The career paths of these technocrats have also predisposed them toward transnational alignment with the IFIs, since many have spent time as staff members at one of them.[17] The Fund and the Bank also attempt to *create* such interlocutors and allies in the longer run through programs of technical assistance, ensuring that this critical transnational link is sustained over time.

More controversial, and much rarer, have been active efforts to build a coalition in support of a program outside a government. Typically, the Fund mission will see anyone requested by a government. Robert Putnam notes the example of Italian negotiations for a stand-by in 1977, in which the IMF consulted directly with unions and the Left, and revised its proposal in an effort to win their support.[18] Another such episode occurred in Jamaica during the Manley government's negotiations with the Fund, when the Fund mission agreed to explain the program to interest groups whose resistance might be expected to endanger an agreement. With the exception of bureaucratic players within the government itself, the IMF seems to respect the gatekeeper role of the national government, as any international organization must.

The final coalition-building role of the IMF is indirect and "negative": serving as a "lightning rod" for governments that do not wish to bear the political costs of an adjustment program. In the past, the IMF has tacitly accepted such a role as a price that it would sometimes pay to obtain an agreement that would otherwise be impossible. Governments believed (and the IMF was willing to accept) that the win-set would be larger if the stabilization program could be associated with an unpopular outside actor. The costs of such a role included increased negative reverberation during future negotiations in the country and reduced commitment to implementation of the agreed program. Although the IMF may still unwittingly play the lightning rod, the present Managing Director has made clear that the organization will no longer willingly accept such a role as a matter of negotiating strategy. The lightning-rod strategy is one variant of a strategy of compensation; another, which has rarely been employed explicitly by the IMF or World Bank, would offer compensation not to the government, but to those groups whose short-term economic interests are most likely to be negatively affected by the adjustment program.

By offering compensation to such groups, their resistance to the agreement would be reduced; with reduced domestic resistance, commitment to the program by politicians would increase.[19]

The IMF, despite the limits imposed on an international organization, has developed a repertoire of negotiating strategies that play on the second level of bargaining. Its developing country interlocutors have also attempted to play upon the "internal" politics of the IMF itself and its creditor coalition. Each of three strategies—divide, delay, and decline—puts pressure on the internal bargain that supports a small and orthodox win-set on the creditor side.

Developing country governments may actively attempt to divide the demanding members of the coalition from more sympathetic ones. Often this means that the "good cop" World Bank, with its larger win-set, is pulled into the negotiations over adjustment; both the IMF and the World Bank have attempted to coordinate their bargaining positions (cross-conditionality) to counter this strategy. The other "good cop" may be a major aid donor with strategic interests in the developing country. In such cases, issue-linkage (security to finance) is employed in order to make gains in bargaining with the Fund. The gate-keeping role of the finance ministries (guarding access to Fund decision-making) makes it difficult for developing countries to exploit such linkages. Their allies—the military or foreign affairs bureaucracies in the industrialized countries—are often excluded from commenting on Fund programs. (This is a perennial source of frustration for area specialists in the U.S. State Department.)

Delay in the course of negotiations may be risky for the developing country, particularly if its reserves are rapidly declining and alternative sources of finance are not available. Nevertheless, delay puts pressure on the internal coalition within the IMF that has been mobilized to support a particular negotiating position or outcome. The threat of overturning an intricately balanced set of internal compromises and forcing the IMF to return to the bargaining table may cause IMF management to concede some part of the developing country's wishes in program design. Delay may also mobilize other members of the creditor coalition, particularly if other negotiations are placed at risk (such as restructuring of commercial bank debt).

Finally, decline is yet another "passive" strategy (often coupled with delay) that places a different sort of pressure on the creditor coalition. The threat of economic collapse (or disorderly adjustment) may once again bring rich-country allies to the rescue of their geopolitical charges. That pressure from the IMF's most powerful members may be coupled to internal IMF concerns for countries that are of particular symbolic importance. Such symbols may be economic failures (such as Tanzania) that need to be brought back into the fold of orthodoxy, or they may be economic successes of considerable importance to the credibility of either IMF or World Bank prescriptions. Ghana is a good example of such a "success," generously rewarded to see that it stays a success.

NEGOTIATING WITH THE IMF, SOMALIA, 1983–1984

Somalia in late 1983 was another example of an IMF "success" in a continent that boasted few economic success stories. In the aftermath of the Ogaden war, the loss of Soviet military assistance, and the economic crisis spawned by the war, the Somali government of Siyaad Barre entered into three stand-by arrangements with the International Monetary Fund. The terms of these agreements had grown increasingly comprehensive and tough. The second stand-by had entailed a substantial devaluation of the Somali shilling, a move that was highly unusual in Africa at the time and often bore considerable political risks. The third stand-by (1982–83) emphasized further supply-side measures, such as additional devaluation and liberalization of trade restrictions and pricing policies.[20]

The apparent success of these agreements in reviving the Somali economy led both the Fund staff and the technocratic team that guided Somali economic policy to begin discussions in 1983 for an extended arrangement.[21] The Extended Fund Facility (EFF) was instituted by the IMF in 1974 in response to criticisms that the Fund approach to adjustment was too short-term in outlook and too sparing in the resources committed to a particular country's adjustment effort. An extended arrangement still involved an underlying exchange of financial support for policy change, but the policies emphasized were tilted toward measures to increase production through external and internal liberalization. Since these measures were often more difficult to implement than the traditional monetary and fiscal policies at the core of the Fund stand-by, the Fund made a multi-year rather than single-year commitment to the adjustment effort, thereby (in theory) encouraging the political elite to persist in the program.

Since its establishment in 1974, however, the EFF had become a source of some skepticism at the IMF and, particularly after the shift in industrialized country attitudes toward tougher conditionality in mid-1981, such programs were scrutinized very carefully to ensure that financial resources were only committed in exchange for major policy changes. At the time of the EFF negotiations with Somalia, the Executive Board had just considered an extended arrangement for Malawi, which had been criticized on just these grounds. The Fund management was inclined to regard an EFF arrangement as a "prize," to be considered only after two conditions were met: a successful "track record" with Fund programs and approval of the country's public investment program by the World Bank. Because of the history of the EFF program and the industrialized countries' influence, the win-set for an EFF program was narrower than most stand-bys.

Somalia's economic policy team, led by the energetic Finance Minister Abdillahi Ahmad Addow (former Ambassador to the United States and son-in-law of President Siyaad Barre) and central bank governor Mohamud Jama Ahmed, had their own reasons for wishing an extended arrangement: better terms and larger sums committed by the IMF, as well as a means of extracting a medium-term commitment from the Somali government for the reforms that the economic ministers believed necessary. Both the IMF and Somali teams seemed to believe that economic crisis provided an opportunity to push further and harder with sweeping reforms. Although Somalia's economy had recovered from war and drought in the early 1980s, a new and severe setback emerged in 1983 with the imposition of a ban on cattle imports from Somalia by Saudi Arabia, Somalia's chief market. The reason given for the ban by the Saudis was concern over rinderpest, a deadly livestock disease, although there was no evidence of such infection in the Somali herds. The Saudi move shocked the Somalis into a recognition of their extreme dependence on a single export, livestock, and a single market, Saudi Arabia. (Somali livestock proved to be uncompetitive in alternative markets, such as Egypt.) The case for economic policies that would spur diversification seemed particularly strong.

The negotiations between the IMF and the Somali team were intensive, and the program that was tentatively agreed was sweeping in its liberalizing scope: a removal of most trade restrictions, abolition of remaining price controls, further privatization of public sector enterprises (a relatively small sector in Somalia), sharp reduction in the fiscal deficit, and most important, measures to remove government control over foreign exchange and institute a market-determined exchange rate. The negotiated EFF was clearly, as one participant put it, "a major shift in policy with major economic and political implications," and the provisions for liberating the foreign-exchange market and the exchange rate would have been "revolutionary" in Africa at that time. Two features of the negotiations would have important consequences for later events. The Somali negotiating team included no members from the party central committee or the military. In the course of obtaining approval from the World Bank for the public investment program, the Bank refused to support the Bardera Dam project, a pet project of Minister of Planning Ahmed Habib Ahmed. The cost of World Bank approval was the unwillingness of a key minister to support the agreement negotiated by Finance Minister Addow.

At the final negotiating sessions in December 1983, the IMF team and Addow had apparently agreed that Addow would "get everyone behind him," the IMF mission chief would bring a draft letter of intent to Washington, and a formal signing would be held in Washington (a shrewd effort on the part of the Fund negotiators to guarantee management commitment to the arrangement). Although the course of events at this point is unclear, Addow, reading the structure of the Somali regime, seemed to interpret "everyone" as Siyaad Barre, who was fully briefed on the agreement and seemed poised to enact the necessary measures for the EFF program, but not the other members of the Council of Ministers. The IMF agreed to delay implementation of the core measures from the end of January until the middle of February, and that delay proved to be fatal to the agreement.

The mid-February deadline passed, and it became clear that there was a struggle in the Somali government over compliance with the agreement: its opponents had had time to mobilize and to cause the President to equivocate. The next three weeks saw a contest for the President's mind between the economic ministries, led by Addow and supported by the IMF staff and parts of the Somali business sector, and the party and military members of the Council of Ministers. Those members made it clear that, despite Addow's efforts to disenfranchise them in the ratification process, they were intent on inclusion. The basis of resistance within the Council of Ministers was fairly clear. There may have been some resentment at Addow's attempt at a policy "coup," circumventing the Council of Ministers and going directly to the President, although such secretive and segmented decision-making seems to have been preferred by Siyaad Barre. Although opposition may have been phrased in the vocabulary of socialist ideology, its principal source was the radical revision of the foreign-exchange system. In many African countries the control of foreign exchange and the rents that could be extracted from it were major instruments of political patronage and influence (as well as a means of considerable personal enrichment). The extended arrangement as negotiated would end that particular policy, at the same time threatening a sharp weakening of the power of senior members of the government who had access to foreign exchange.

The political struggle over the IMF agreement remained an elite battle: there was little evidence of the mobilization of other groups (with the exception of business) in this authoritarian regime. As the deadline for key policy actions passed, the possibility of resurrecting the extended arrangement grew more and more remote: the IMF staff argued that the EFF arrangement had been framed for a particular point in time in a deteriorating economy. Aid donors, particularly the United States, exerted their own pressure in favor of carrying out the agreement. The

Somali government hastily attempted to offer implementation of the EFF program with the exception of a "few points" that would be phased in more gradually, but the IMF was not willing to budge from its position. The IMF mission chief was invited back to Mogadishu for a final interview with Siyaad Barre, but it was clear that the President had made up his mind: the EFF arrangement would not be implemented in its negotiated form. His unwillingness was only confirmed in the Council of Ministers vote of 15 to 14 against the program. All of the ministers with economic portfolios voted for the program, the party and military members voted against, and the alienated Minister of Planning (Habib) abstained.

Why had the COG, fully briefed and apparently supportive of a further reform effort, finally decided that early 1984 was not the time for sweeping policy changes? First, the economic crisis and uncertainty produced by the Saudi cattle ban seemed to induce caution and equivocation on the part of the President, rather than commitment to plunge even faster and further into market-oriented reforms. Although the President mentioned at the time his concern for the "poor man on the street," there were few signs of urban popular resistance to the IMF program, and Siyaad Barre's ideological preconceptions were by this time inconsequential.

The President's stance can also be explained by the implications of policy change for his political survival. Dismantling the foreign-exchange system in Somalia would weaken a major instrument with which Siyaad Barre and his allies could manipulate the intricate game of clan politics: that concern motivated part of the ministerial resistance. More broadly, liberalizing economic reforms might strengthen his political opponents over time. The livestock trade that provided most of the country's export earnings was based in the north, where commerce with the Persian Gulf states flourished. Some of the Isaaq clans of that region had long been frustrated by the economic controls imposed by the Somali government and by a perceived neglect of economic development in the north. The northern region and its clans, most likely to benefit from a widened economic liberalization, was also the base of one of the organized resistance movements to the Barre regime, the Somali National Movement.[22] The President had skillfully used foreign exchange in an effort to coopt Isaaq politicians; to his politically attuned eye, ending foreign-exchange controls and further economic liberalization may have appeared to remove a reliable instrument for controlling political opposition, while shifting resources to those who could be at the core of that opposition. The IMF program offered, in this view, substantial political costs with few concrete benefits. This interpretation of presidential calculations is supported by arguments made by opponents of the extended arrangement with the IMF: liberalizing foreign exchange would permit the regime's opponents to mount opposition and even to buy arms. One final aspect of Siyaad Barre's decision: at certain points, the President seemed to attempt a linkage between acceptance of the IMF program and more military assistance from the United States. One individual close to the negotiations suggested in jest that if the IMF had opened a "military facility" and offered to dispense a few tanks, it might have had better luck with the program. The U.S. government did nothing during the negotiations or their aftermath to encourage Somali beliefs in the possibility of such a linkage, but it suggests the central concerns of political survival that pervaded the final decision.

These conclusions regarding Barre's calculus of decision are only inferences from indirect evidence. If this reading of Barre's political calculus is correct, however, the question of whether failure to agree on the EFF program was a failure of ratification—whether Barre changed his mind because of the opposition that surfaced within the regime—is less puzzling. Asking the question in this way obscures the sources of Barre's decision. The ratification struggle was probably most important for crystallizing Barre's doubts about the political wisdom of accepting the IMF agreement. Its opponents did not pose a short-term political threat to Barre, or even to the IMF agreement—Barre's position within the system was too dominant for them to do so—but they did serve as proxies for the long-run political costs that Barre himself feared. The vocal opposition to the agreement was an early alarm over the possible erosion in political leverage and support that Barre would risk if he accepted the policy changes contained in the EFF program.

Failure of the EFF agreement produced a significant reshaping of the Somali government in which the IMF's allies were removed from key economic ministries. Addow was shifted to the Ministry for Presidential Affairs (a minister without portfolio). The new finance minister was the former economic spokesman for the party, and the other members of the new economic team were also from party circles. The Somali government had responded to economic crisis by a reorientation of policy away from IMF and World Bank prescriptions and programs, at least in the near term.

NEGOTIATING WITH THE IMF, JAMAICA, 1981–1988

Following the landslide defeat of Michael Manley and the PNP at the general election of 1980 (the "IMF election"), Jamaica had a clear track record with the IMF: repeated negotiations, failed agreements with a very mixed record of implementation, large commitment of IMF resources, and a political system in which IMF programs had been major political issues. The contention and conflict of the Manley years marked both Jamaican politics and the attitudes of external actors such as the IMF. Because of the Fund's uncomfortable role as a political target, the Manley experience seemed to reinforce the IMF's initial tendencies to cooperate closely with the successor government of Edward Seaga. By the time of the February 1989 election that returned Michael Manley to power, however, the IMF and other external actors could look back on a decade marked until 1987 by a similar pattern of failed agreements, although a better record (from the IMF's point of view) of policy change.[23]

The conflictual course of relations between the IMF and the Seaga government that held power from 1980 until 1989 began with a fundamental misperception of the election and Seaga by outsiders. The highly ideological tone of the election, as well as Seaga's technocratic background, caused the IMF, the World Bank, and the U.S. government to see in him a resolute ally in the cause of policy reform. The new government had won the election with 58 percent of the vote, a result that seemed to offer a mandate for externally supported policy change. This outside view was distorted, however. The Jamaican electorate in 1980 was voting against economic mismanagement on the part of the Manley government, not in favor of a program of austerity or market-oriented reform. The policy preferences of Seaga himself did not align that closely with the desires of the IMF: as Joan Nelson notes, Seaga's analysis of Jamaica's prospects in 1980 was more nearly structuralist than radically market-oriented. Import compression under Manley needed to be removed, stimulating the removal of bottlenecks and the use of surplus capacity, supported by a buoyant international economic environment and renewed inflows of foreign investment.[24] Perhaps most important, external agencies did not realize that Seaga's acceptability-set in negotiations (and his perception of the win-set for Jamaican society) ran parallel to the set of policies acceptable to the preceding Manley government. *Any* Jamaican government, whatever its ideological rhetoric, confronted similar political resistance to policies of the sort pressed by the IMF. Any Jamaican politician would perceive a win-set in negotiations with the IMF that excluded many of the policy changes demanded by its creditors.

The first phase of IMF (and World Bank and USAID) relations with Jamaica (1981–1982) was characterized by easy agreement on programs that made few politically difficult demands on the Jamaican government, and most notably, no "negative features"—devaluation or layoffs of public-sector employees. By April 1981 an extended arrangement, plus additional finance from the Compensatory Financing Facility, had been arranged with the IMF. Agreement was relatively easy for two reasons: the IMF, the World Bank, and USAID all shared the optimistic forecasts on which the Seaga government based its expansionist program.[25] In addition (and in contrast to Somalia), the U.S. government weakened the bargaining position of the IMF through two avenues: directly, through occasional direct intervention to shift Fund bargaining positions; and indirectly, through a massive infusion of aid that made IMF and World Bank lending appear "expensive" in terms of the policy conditions that were attached.[26]

The era of expansion and easy agreement drew to a close in late 1982. The international economy failed to match the bright predictions of the Seaga government, as the United States slid into a deep recession, the debt crisis produced a withdrawal of new private finance, and bauxite prices and production slumped. The IMF began to urge austerity on the Seaga government, and in January 1983 Seaga announced a change in policy course as external imbalance worsened. Over the course of 1983, Jamaica moved from a de facto dual exchange rate (which the IMF had accepted tacitly) to a unified rate with biweekly auctions to allocate foreign exchange. As Jane Harrigan points out, however, the Jamaican government continued its efforts to manipulate the exchange rate. Over the next two years, its preferences in terms of policy instruments were clearly and increasingly at odds with the preferences of the IMF and World Bank. The Seaga government accepted the need for devaluation only reluctantly, and attempted to cushion its impact on the urban population through increasing subsidies (increasing the pressure on the fiscal deficit). Its chosen instrument of austerity became monetary policy, which, as Harrigan notes, distributes the costs of adjustment away from the public sector and the organized urban population and toward the business sector:

> Resistance centered on the government's concern at the manner in which devaluation, in such an open economy, rapidly translated into domestic price increases, implying a concomitant reduction in real wage levels, particularly for the poorer members of Jamaican society not protected by the institutional wage-bargaining of the strong Trade Union Movements. This predominantly political concern continued to prevail throughout the 1980s.[27]

From late 1983 until October 1985, however, the government accepted the auction device and the devaluation that it implied. The countervailing measures that it undertook to offset the impact of devaluation, however, caused it to fall out of compliance with successive IMF agreements: the EFF program was finally abandoned in September 1983. A new stand-by agreement negotiated in July 1984 reflected Seaga's weakened bargaining position, and his temporarily enhanced freedom of action to pursue adjustment policies domestically. A major feature in the

strengthened hand of the IMF and the World Bank was Jamaica's worsening financial situation. The import-led expansion of the early 1980s
had left the country with a mountain of debt and a worsening outlook
for continued support. Net bilateral aid had peaked in 1981 and had
been declining since; World Bank funding had peaked in 1982 and then
dropped sharply; in 1985, net flows from the IMF to Jamaica became
negative. The worsening financial picture also increased government
resistance to further devaluation, however, since it increased the burden
of debt-servicing.

At the same time, Seaga's already strong position in conducting Jamaican economic policy, reinforced by the parliamentary institutions described above and by his political style, was further strengthened by a
political fluke. Following the Grenada invasion in October 1983, Seaga,
benefiting from his support of the U.S. action, decided to call a snap
election. In doing so, he violated an agreement with the opposition PNP
that no election would be called until the electoral rolls had been revised
(a move that was likely to benefit the PNP). The PNP boycotted the
election, and Seaga was presented in December 1983 with a one-party
parliament. By strengthening his hand internally, the election may have
weakened his bargaining position with the IFIs. Of course, it also encouraged those opposed to his economic programs to seek extra-parliamen-
tary avenues of action.

The economy continued to worsen in 1984 and 1985, as inflation
rose and the national product slumped. Political resistance to the Seaga
government's economic program increased in 1985, after the removal of
food subsidies and a sharp increase in gasoline prices. In January, a
national demonstration was held that could only be controlled through
the intervention of the opposition PNP. Strikes continued during the
spring of 1985, culminating in an unprecedented general strike in June.
The strike was supported by unions from both federations, including the
BITU, linked to Seaga's own political party.[28]

PNP pressure on the government continued into the autumn. In September 1985, Jamaica once again failed to meet IMF targets and the
stand-by arrangement was suspended. The Jamaican dollar came under
pressure in October 1985, and Michael Manley led a march on the Bank
of Jamaica. Despite the latitude offered by the absence of a parliamentary
opposition, an electoral test loomed before Seaga: municipal elections
were scheduled for mid-1986, and they would clearly be treated as a
referendum on his government.

Growing political pressures and increasing policy fatigue within the
government led to a sharp change of course toward confrontation with
the IMF. As might have been expected, it focused on the exchange rate:
the central bank intervened in the foreign-exchange auction to revalue

the Jamaican dollar and then pegged it against the U.S. dollar. This rejection of the IMF prescriptions for a flexible exchange rate was coupled by an aggressive strategy by Seaga to obtain a new bargain from the creditor coalition. At the Joint IMF-World Bank meetings in October 1985, he made a pointed plea for new policies that would renew growth in the developing countries, an appeal that echoed the rhetoric of the Baker Plan announced at the same time. In addition, Seaga called for a tripartite "fresh look" mission, composed of IMF, World Bank, and USAID representatives, to re-evaluate the policy recommendations that were pressed on his government. Whether his request for this mission was an effort to open divisions within the creditor coalition (and it was clear at this time that the World Bank agreed with many of the criticisms that the Seaga government was making), or whether it was a genuine effort to open a new dialogue with the IFIs, Seaga's strategy only partially succeeded. The "fresh look" report was presented in April 1986 and promptly rejected by the government, since its recommendations were close to those pressed by the IFIs over the preceding three years: less reliance on tight monetary policy and flexible management of the exchange rate.[29]

In response to the failure of its "fresh look" initiative, the Seaga government prepared its own alternative program, differing once again on the importance of devaluation. Since it confronted a creditor coalition that would not be divided, its strategy now moved to a combination of suasion and delay. Political pressures to reach a resolution were increased by the lopsided PNP victory in the municipal elections. Negotiations with the Fund stalled on the perennial issue of an early devaluation. Given the restricted win-sets on either side concerning that issue—a program with a substantial devaluation was not within the acceptability-set of the Seaga government, and a program without a devaluation seemed unlikely to be acceptable to the IMF or its dominant members—the two sides seemed unlikely to agree.

Nevertheless, in March 1987 a new stand-by was approved that included many of the recommendations of the "fresh look" mission but did not require a devaluation. The explanation for this agreement on Jamaica's terms lie less in domestic changes on either side than on important shifts in the international economic environment. Political cycles on either side may have encouraged the IMF to expand its win-set in the negotiations. The Managing Director was stepping down at the end of 1986, and this internal "electoral cycle" may have argued for clearing up troublesome loose ends, rather than leaving them for his successor. The growing strength of the PNP could not have gone unnoticed by the IMF, given its unhappy history of negotiations with Manley in the 1970s.

(There is no direct evidence, however, that assisting Seaga politically was part of the IMF's calculations.)

More important, the collapse of oil prices in 1986 strengthened the Jamaican bargaining position by relieving pressure on the balance of payments and improving the government's fiscal position (savings which were not passed on to consumers).[30] In addition, the decline of the United States dollar made the Jamaican claims concerning devaluation seem less implausible. Equally important, Jamaica's huge debt, largely owed to the IFIs, had now become a bargaining advantage: "The leverage of the donors' policy bargaining position was weakened by the growing pressure to disburse in order to avoid default on the part of the recipient."[31]

CONCLUSIONS: DOMESTIC AND INTERNATIONAL CONSTRAINTS IN IMF NEGOTIATIONS

Although the criterion of "agreement" has been employed throughout this chapter in evaluating the outcome of negotiations, it is clear that negotiations with the IMF seldom end with a clear and unrevised agreement that is implemented without delay or slippage. Somalia's "failure" in 1984 had been preceded by several successful stand-by arrangements; Jamaica's "success" in 1987 followed a very uneven record of implementation over two governments. The formal treaty model of negotiation, agreement, ratification fits poorly with the reality of these negotiations. One could also argue, in the case of IMF stand-bys or extended arrangements, that genuine ratification only comes in implementation. Other international negotiations may resemble the IMF model more closely than the formal image of agreement presented by a treaty.

The *pattern of domestic interests* clearly narrowed the range of win-sets that both the IMF and the developing country negotiators and COGs perceived in these negotiations. In Somalia, the rent-seeking interests of the political and military elite made any agreement that encompassed the end of state control over foreign exchange extremely difficult to ratify and implement. For Jamaica, with its democratic political system and more highly articulated interest groups, the response of the organized and volatile urban population offered the principal obstacle to an agreement that included steep devaluation or a flexible exchange rate, even for a government that seemed to face few immediate political constraints. The acceptability-set of the Seaga government, if not the win-set, was narrowed by concern over the political response to devaluation.

For the IMF, win-sets were more often defined formulaically, but behind the formulas (such as the prerequisites for an EFF program, or the requirement for an up-front devaluation) lay the interests of the Fund's key constituents, the industrialized countries. On one hand, during the 1980s an agreement that was perceived as "loose" in its conditionality was unlikely to survive IMF Board scrutiny. On the other hand, individual countries, such as the United States, would also attempt to modify programs that were viewed as too tough on their favored clients.

The *rules of ratification*—approval by the Executive Board and its most powerful members—were clear in the case of the IMF. For the developing countries, however, the issue of enfranchisement is often ambiguous. In the weak authoritarian state of Somalia, both the IMF and the technocrats seemed to assume that ratification meant approval by President Siyaad Barre. Barre seemed to decide that ratification would require a degree of consensus between technocrats on the one hand and party and military representatives on the other. Given Jamaica's high degree of policy-making centralization under Prime Minister Seaga, one could argue that ratification in Jamaica also meant approval by the COG. Nevertheless, Seaga's concern over future political tests made it clear that true ratification would come at the time of parliamentary elections.

Difficulty in reading the rules of ratification in many countries complicates the task of outsiders who are attempting to influence the process. Since authoritarian governments may not know which political actors will force their enfranchisement during the ratification process, the lack of clear institutional rules may lead to paralysis and the possibility of unpredictable backlash against the agreement. External actors will often assume that those bargaining with them know the preferences of the principals, but a dualistic power structure (as in Somalia) may mean that information about preferences in other parts of the government is highly imperfect.

In each of these developing countries, the role of the *chief of government* was critical: both Siyaad Barre and Seaga presided over highly centralized policy-making systems. No agreement as significant as an IMF program could be implemented without their approval. Ironically, despite this centralization of power, both COGs behaved much more as political maximizers than as economic strategists. Neither appeared willing to attempt to shape perceived domestic constraints to reach an agreement. Both behaved in a curiously passive way in the face of political controversy over these agreements.

For Siyaad Barre, the gains from agreement were probably not worth upsetting the intricate balance of clan interests on which his regime rested. Seaga, however, had much stronger views on economic strategy, and Jamaica's less brittle democratic setting appeared to offer better prospects for forging a political coalition in favor of economic policy change. Seaga's political style hindered the consultation and suasion required by a more entrepreneurial strategy, however. As both Harrigan and Nelson point out, Seaga "utilized a highly centralized, nonparticipatory, system of government in an attempt to subvert opposition to policy changes."[32] The Prime Minister declined measures (such as targeted welfare programs) that might have reduced domestic political resistance to agreements and neglected to mobilize sectors of the population that were likely to benefit from the policy reforms embodied in IMF and World Bank agreements. Even if Seaga had been less accepting of the existing political landscape and more willing to assume political risks, the highly organized character of Jamaican politics provided a strong bias in favor of the status quo. The losers from economic policy change were well organized and acutely aware of their prospective losses; the winners (consumers, the informal sector, small farmers) were typically unorganized until well after policy changes were implemented. For a politician facing a fixed electoral cycle, the incentives pointed toward retaining an existing constituent base rather than trying to develop a new one.

The *strategies* attempted on either side to shape the second level of bargaining were by and large unsuccessful. The IMF in these two cases was unable to pursue its preferred strategy of technocratic alignment. In Somalia, an energetic band of economic liberalizers were, in the end, isolated and repudiated by the President. In Jamaica, Seaga had so centralized policy-making that very little independence was delegated to the IMF's technocratic interlocutors. In addition, on key points such as devaluation, the Jamaican technocrats disagreed with the IMF.

One developing-country strategy was to play on the influence of the United States within the politics of the IMF. Jamaica was far more successful than Somalia in implementing that strategy. In both cases, these clients did not have the central geopolitical or economic importance to align the United States on their side of the IMF bargaining in every case. The United States refused to budge from its support of the IMF position during the Somalia negotiations; although it intervened to soften the IMF line toward Jamaica, the United States offered the strongest resistance to approval of the March 1987 stand-by.

The carefully focused functional expertise of the IMF made *issue linkage* a difficult strategy for any of the participants. Siyaad Barre seemed to hope for a bargain that would exchange approval of the EFF program for additional U.S. military assistance, but the IMF, supported by the United States, refused to be drawn into such a trade. The narrow definition of its role offered by the IMF—short-term balance-of-payments support—is one way of protecting itself against such linkage attempts.

Uncertainty and perceived economic "crisis" did not induce these governments to agree more readily to IMF programs. In both Somalia and Jamaica, outsiders tended to assume that economic crisis would lead to acceptance of IMF prescriptions, because of financial desperation or will-

TABLE 1. The Ambiguous Effects of "Crisis"

Somalia: Trade and Current Account Balances							
	1981	1982	1983	1984[a]	1985	1986	1987
	(millions of shillings)						
Exports (live animals)	1143	1748	1244	514	2604	4420	7300
	(millions of U.S. dollars)						
Exports	175	171	98	55	91	89	104
Trade balance	−195	−301	−264	−411	−240	−295	−382
Current account	−83	−177	−142	−132	−97	−88	−100

Jamaica: Trade and Current Account Balances							
	1981	1982	1983	1984	1985	1986	1987[b]
	(millions of U.S. dollars)						
Trade balance	−323	−442	−439	−335	−436	−248	−362
Current account	−337	−409	−359	−335	−304	−40	−91

[a] Failed IMF negotiations
[b] Agreement on IMF stand-by

ingness to take a reformist leap in the dark. There is little evidence in these two cases that crisis is uniformly defined, or that economic uncertainty encourages governments to undertake politically risky economic programs. As Table 1 illustrates, agreement in these two cases was not linked to periods of economic crisis, when the bargaining advantages of the IMF were at their peak. The negotiations between Somalia and the IMF for an extended arrangement broke down in a year when Somalia's principal export industry had collapsed and its trade balance had deteriorated sharply. Seaga's government made successive failed agreements with the IMF during the 1980s, a decade of long-running economic crisis for Jamaica. The 1987 agreement on a stand-by occurred at a time when its current account showed substantial improvement.

Two reasons can be offered for resistance to agreement in the face of an apparent crisis. First, decline itself is a bargaining weapon: Jamaica's heavy indebtedness had become by 1986 a threat to the IMF and the World Bank, encouraging further lending to protect their existing commitments. Second, the weighting of alternatives may appear quite different to politicians facing political risks than it does to the staff of international organizations. Siyaad Barre declined substantial financial assistance and a sweeping reform program because of those political risks; he probably realized that Somalia would adjust, as it ultimately did, through growth of the black market and increasing economic hard-

ship. That process, however wasteful, could be managed without threatening his political survival, as it had been managed in the past.

The surrounding *international economic environment* was central to
agreement of non-agreement in these negotiations. For these small, open
economies, the political and economic payoffs from agreement were
more dependent on international economic conditions than they were
for larger countries. International developments served to widen or narrow the win-set on either side. For the IMF, the virtual cessation of
private lending to most developing countries served to narrow its win-
set, particularly given the unwillingness of industrialized country governments to increase public sources of finance. At the same time, the inability
of the IMF to have its "catalytic" effect on private capital flows created
a narrower win-set in the countries with which it bargained. An IMF
agreement accompanied by bilateral aid and favorable international economic circumstances was likely to be followed by others (as occurred in
Somalia in the early 1980s). Bleak economic prospects later in the decade
(Jamaica in 1984–85) served to undermine agreements that were expected to deliver economic improvement in the medium term. A perverse pattern of failed agreements resulted, as the IMF was compelled
to ask for tougher and politically more risky programs, and domestic
actors necessary for ratification in the developing countries came to view
an IMF agreement as a promise of economic stagnation. A poor external
outlook also influenced the interpretation of "crisis," lending support to
those who argued that domestic policy change would be ineffectual. As
Jamaica's international prospects improved in 1986–87, not only did its
bargaining leverage increase, but the chances for domestic consolidation
of the policy changes undertaken also increased. In these cases and many
other examples of IMF bargaining in the 1980s, constraints on agreement at the domestic level were shaped in turn by the international economy in which both levels of bargaining were embedded.

The author wishes to thank David Laitin for his comments on this chapter.

NOTES

1. Most studies on the record of IMF or World Bank conditionality are concerned with the economic effects of those programs rather than their effects on
policy change and implementation. For examples of those who have looked at
this aspect, see Tony Killick et al., *The Quest for Economic Stabilization* (London:
Heinemann, 1984), pp. 251–255, 260–261; Stephan Haggard, "The Politics of
Adjustment: Lessons from the IMF's Extended Fund Facility," in Miles Kahler,
ed., *The Politics of International Debt* (Ithaca, N.Y.: Cornell University Press, 1986).
A recent World Bank survey of policy-based lending in the 1980s found an

overall compliance rate of about 60 percent: *Adjustment Lending: An Evaluation of Ten Years of Experience* (Washington, D.C.: World Bank, 1988, p. 7.)

2. A succinct account of IMF conditionality as interpreted by a senior staff member is given in Manuel Guitian, *Fund Conditionality: Evolution of Principles and Practices* (Washington, D.C.: International Monetary Fund, 1981). A more critical view is offered by Sidney Dell, *On Being Grandmotherly: The Evolution of IMF Conditionality* (Princeton, N.J.: Princeton University Dept. of Economics, 1981).

3. An excellent account of the evolution of the IMF's internal governance is given by Frank A. Southard, Jr., *The Evolution of the International Monetary Fund* (Princeton, N.J.: Princeton University Dept. of Economics, 1979).

4. Individual country programs, the subject of this chapter, are not subject to the requirement of a special majority.

5. On weighted voting and special majorities, see Frederick K. Lister, *Decision-Making Strategies for International Organizations: The IMF Model* (Denver, Colo.: University of Denver Graduate School of International Studies, 1984), pp. 43–99; Joseph Gold, *Voting Majorities in the Fund* (Washington, D.C.: International Monetary Fund, 1977).

6. John Williamson, *The Lending Policies of the International Monetary Fund* (Washington, D.C.: Institute for International Economics, 1982), pp. 43–51.

7. An excellent rendering of those findings is Stephan Haggard and Robert Kaufman, "The Politics of Stabilization and Structural Adjustment," in Jeffrey D. Sachs, ed., *Developing Country Debt and Economic Performance* (Chicago: University of Chicago Press, 1989), pp. 209–254. Also see Joan M. Nelson, "Conclusions," in Joan Nelson, ed., *Economic Crisis and Policy Choice* (Princeton, N.J.: Princeton University Press, 1990), pp. 348–358.

8. On the urban popular sectors and their ability to resist adjustment programs, see Joan Nelson, "Poverty, Equity, and the Politics of Adjustment," in Stephan Haggard and Robert Kaufman, eds., *The Politics of Economic Adjustment* (Princeton: Princeton University Press, 1992), pp. 244–258.

9. Haggard and Kaufman, "Politics of Stabilization," p. 226.

10. Joan Nelson, "The Politics of Adjustment in Small Democracies: Costa Rica, the Dominican Republic, Jamaica," in Nelson, ed., *Economic Crisis*, p. 172.

11. David D. Laitin and Said S. Samatar, *Somalia: Nation in Search of a State* (Boulder, Colo.: Westview Press, 1987), p. 30.

12. I. M. Lewis, *A Modern History of Somalia* (Boulder, Colo.: Westview Press, 1988), p. 249. A model of the Somali political structure as established in the 1970s is given in Ahmed I. Samatar, *Socialist Somalia* (London: Zed Books, 1988), p. 112.

13. Laitin and Samatar, *Somalia*, pp. 156–157.

14. Nelson, "The Politics of Adjustment," p. 172.

15. Laitin and Samatar, *Somalia*, p. 159.

16. David Finch, a member of the Fund staff from 1950 until 1987, emphasizes the IMF role in supporting internal allies in *The IMF: The Record and the Prospect* (Princeton, N.J.: Princeton University, Dept. of Economics, 1989), pp. 7–11.

17. Joan Nelson, "Conclusions," in Nelson, ed., *Economic Crisis*, pp. 330–331.

18. Robert D. Putnam, "Diplomacy and Domestic Politics: The Logic of Two-Level Games," Appendix to this volume.

19. Arguments in favor of explicit compensation are offered in Paul Mosley, Jane Harrigan, and John Toye, *Aid and Power: The World Bank and Policy-Based Lending* (London: Routledge, 1991), vol. 1, chap. 5.

20. The content of these agreements is given in "Somalia's Adjustment Program Shows Success in Promoting Growth, Building External Sector," *IMF Survey* (August 30, 1982), pp. 271–273.

21. This account of the EFF negotiations in 1983–84 is drawn from interviews in Washington, D.C. Unfortunately, I was unable to interview any of the Somali participants in these negotiations.

22. Lewis, *A Modern History of Somalia*, pp. 251–252, describes the political economy of northern resistance in the early 1980s.

23. This account of IMF-Jamaican relations in the 1980s is based on Joan Nelson, "The Politics of Adjustment in Small Democracies," in Nelson, ed., *Economic Crisis*, pp. 189–213, on earlier drafts of the Nelson chapter, and on Jane Harrigan, "Jamaica," in Mosley, Harrigan, and Toye, *Aid and Power*, vol. 2, pp. 311–361.

24. Nelson, "The Politics of Adjustment," p. 190.

25. Harrigan, "Jamaica," p. 329.

26. Ibid., p. 332. The United States government reportedly intervened to obtain a waiver of Jamaica's performance criteria when Jamaica did not meet IMF targets in March 1983.

27. Ibid., p. 327.

28. Nelson, "Politics," pp. 192–193; Harrigan, "Jamaica," p. 340.

29. Nelson, "Politics," p. 193; Harrigan, "Jamaica," p. 345.

30. Harrigan, "Jamaica," p. 349.

31. Ibid., p. 350.

32. Ibid., p. 340.

PART 5

Conclusion

13

Building an Integrative Approach to International and Domestic Politics

Reflections and Projections

Peter B. Evans

International bargains are not simply about relations between nations. They are also about the distribution of costs and benefits among domestic groups and about domestic opinion divided on the best way of relating to the external environment. The possibility of international accords, as well as their content, are jointly determined by domestic and international factors. This basic perspective underlies an integrative approach to thinking about international relations and domestic politics, but an integrative perspective must go beyond adding domestic constraints to international equations. If negotiators act strategically, then bargaining is an inter-active process, simultaneously shaped by the pursuit of international gains and the political dynamics of domestic ratification.

International negotiation must be seen as a double-edged process in which every actor tries to take into account expected reactions on both the domestic and international levels. Deals at the international level change the character of domestic constraints, while the movement of domestic politics opens up new possibilities for international accords. Domestic goals are pursued via international moves, and domestic politicking is central to international negotiation. The role of international and domestic factors in the determination of outcomes is simultaneous and mutual.

As Andrew Moravcsik points out in the Introduction to this volume an integrative perspective has come increasingly to dominate contemporary theorizing on diplomacy and domestic politics. In his words, the question is no longer *whether* to combine domestic and international explanations in order to understand conflicts and accords among nations, but *how* to combine them. This volume is one answer to the question "How?" Building on a wide range of earlier efforts to integrate international and domestic explanations, it applies a new version of the integrative approach to a systematically diverse set of cases.

The framework put forward in Robert Putnam's 1988 article provided a conceptual springboard, but it was used in a way that would exploit the ideas that authors brought with them. The project did not, for example, focus on the more formal aspects of Putnam's presentation. This was in part because existing formal techniques seemed unlikely to uncover the kinds of complex interactive patterns that we were interested in (see the Introduction, note 61), but it was also because the project was not conceived of as a "testing" operation. Each author cut into ongoing theoretical debates in a different way, yet the chapters ended up sharing new ways of talking about how domestic and international explanations could be integrated. New concepts spread from one case to another as the cases came to build on each other. A central aim of this final chapter is to emphasize the way the perspective cumulates across cases and the added gains that came from looking at the cases as a set.

The cases work well as a set because each reflects a common organizational "template"; they also work well together because of the way the set as a whole was designed. Cases were deliberately chosen to stretch the set of issues and countries that Putnam used to develop his original ideas by including security as well as economic issues, coercive as well as cooperative bargaining, and a full range of country interactions—West-West, East-West, and North-South. Nested within this "most different" design was a second layer of contrasts built around "most similar" comparisons. With one exception,[1] all of the analyses juxtapose two or more cases with similar contexts and parameters but contrasting outcomes.

The nested design made it possible to answer two quite different kinds of questions with the same set of cases. The "most different" comparisons respond to questions regarding the approach's range of applicability. What kinds of negotiations lend themselves to an integrative analysis? Does the approach suggested by Putnam elucidate coercive as well as cooperative negotiations? Does the same integrative logic apply to security issues and trade issues? Are North-South negotiations different from West-West negotiations? The fine-grained "most similar" comparisons attack the question, "What factors really make the difference between success and failure in efforts to complete a particular type of agreement?" The two kinds of questions complement and reinforce each other.

Two dozen cases, no matter how elegantly structured, cannot rigorously test the propositions they generate. This is especially true here because our elegantly nested cases have biases if they are thought of as a sample. Focusing on cases where interactive dynamics play a role leaves instances of unremitting bilateral hostility or xenophobia under-represented relative to those where differences were negotiable. Controversy in the domestic political economy of at least one of the countries involved, making two-level strategies more transparent, also increased the likelihood of a case's inclusion. In short, Sadat and Begin were more likely to appear than Saddam Hussein and Shamir. Questions of representativeness suggest that the universe to which the findings apply should be defined carefully. Nonetheless, the set is still very diverse, and the array of propositions that emerged from analyzing it have wide-ranging implications for existing theories of international and domestic politics.

RESULTS AND REFLECTIONS

A comprehensive survey of the welter of potential propositions that emerged would make for an indigestible final chapter. What follows, therefore, is a selection of some intriguing and suggestive results. It focuses on results that resonate across several different cases and emphasizes those which grew out of the project itself, rather than those fully anticipated in the original Putnam article. Thus, ratification of threats and changes in leaders' autonomy over time are highlighted, while linkages, targeting, and reverberation are stressed less. I have divided the substantive discussion into three sections.

The first deals first with variations in the relative autonomy of the COG (chief of government, a.k.a. statesman, chief executive, or leader)[2] vis-à-vis domestic constituencies.[3] Four points are emphasized:

1. The strategy of "tying hands"—deliberately shrinking the win-set in pursuit of an agreement closer to the COG's preferred outcome—is infrequently attempted and usually not effective. The "tying hands" strategy, suggested by Thomas Schelling's work,[4] is logically plausible but lacks efficacy in practice. Perhaps because they are aware of its limited efficacy, statesmen prefer not to have their "hands tied" by constituents, even when they share the constituents' preferences.

2. The relative autonomy of international leaders decreases continuously and substantially over the course of most negotiations. State leaders are in the driver's seat as international agendas are being formulated. The more clearly international options become defined, the more leaders are constrained by mobilized interest groups and trapped by personal investment in the on-going negotiations.

3. Leaders who are more "hawkish" relative to their constituents have less autonomy than those who are more "dovish." Hawks have difficulty making threats credible because they impose costs on domestic as well as foreign groups. The option of "COG collusion" with those on the other side of the international table gives doves more room to maneuver.

4. Manipulation of foreign perceptions of ratifiability is *not* an effective strategy, even for those who head authoritarian regimes. Cross-national informational asymmetries are less prevalent than we at first supposed, and mis-estimations within domestic polities are more prevalent. COGs not only have surprising difficulty in convincing those on the other side of the international table that their "hands are tied," but are also surprisingly likely to misjudge what is ratifiable in their own polities.

The second section deals with how the possibilities of reaching an agreement depend, not on COG strategy, but on configurations of domestic and international interests.[5] Four findings are highlighted in this area as well:

1. When the costs are concentrated and the benefits diffuse, agreements are usually, though not invariably, doomed. The certitude of failure depends on the extent to which negatively affected groups are "disproportionately enfranchised." Enfranchisement depends in turn on the institutional mechanisms through which interests become part of the political process.

2. Interests that create intractable obstacles to international agreements in the short run, whether domestic or transnational, are likely to be the object of restructuring efforts in the long run. Confronting vested interests that impede desired agreements, COGs have strong incentives to undermine the bases of their domestic opponents' power. Even in the long run such structural change is difficult to accomplish, but two-level strategies give chief executives substantial leverage.

3. There is no relationship between the extent of enfranchisement and the propensity to conclude agreements. Democracy does not seem to be an impediment to constructing international accords, as Morgenthau and Kennan feared (see the Introduction, note 30). Authoritarian disenfranchisement is associated with small win-sets that are as great an obstacle to agreement as the boisterous pluralism of undisciplined democracies.

4. There is no relationship between the presence of transnational actors in a particular arena and the likelihood that an attempted agreement will succeed. Even though the existence of transnational alliances enhances the possibility of synergistic strategies, actors with transnational ties are as likely to view state-to-state agreements as threatening to their own private transnational alliances as they are to find them supportive. Specifying when transnational actors will be supportive rather than hostile is not easy, but our cases allow us to make a start.

Since the pairs each author compared were selected to share a similar historical context, the issue of longitudinal change at the global level was hard for individual authors to attack. The third section explores this issue. How have historical changes in the context of international politics over time affected possibilities for synergistic strategies? The basic proposition of this section is straightforward: Over the course of the past five or six decades, and especially in the last ten to fifteen years, the growing proliferation of transnational alliances and the increasing dominance of economic as opposed to security concerns have conspired, along with learning effects, to make synergistic strategies more prevalent and an integrative approach to international politics more essential. Coercive bargaining is still important, but even when threats are central to the negotiations there are increasing possibilities for synergistic issue linkage.

These three substantive sections are followed by a final section intended to emphasize the project's open-endedness. It sets out one clear opportunity and one obvious challenge presented to future researchers by the participants' findings. The clear opportunity is created by the longitudinal lacuna in our research design. Because the case set was not designed to provide systematic evidence on questions of historical change, our very suggestive findings about the effects of the changing global context beg for reinforcement (or refutation). Recent dramatic shifts in the global context add impetus to this agenda. The obvious challenge is created by the vision of the constrained but still relatively autonomous chief executive as the fulcrum for an integrative analysis. This "state-centric" vision emerged out of the cases almost in spite of the project's preconceptions.[6] Even among those who accept the importance of developing an integrative approach, many will want to challenge this COG-centered view, suggesting instead ways of linking domestic and international factors more directly, with less intermediation through the pinnacles of the state apparatus.

These four sections together should provide more than a summary of interesting propositions. They should provide a convincing cumulative vision, a demonstration of how findings reverberate and build momentum across the 11 sets of cases. The place to start is obviously with our favorite character—the ubiquitously pivotal "COG."

AUTONOMY AND CONSTRAINT

The image of the state leaders as "Janus-faced," forced to balance domestic and international concerns, stands at the core of the integrative approach, making it "state-centric," not in the realist sense of emphasizing nation-states as units but in the sense of seeing chief executives, and state bureaucracies more generally, as actors whose aims cannot be reduced to reflections of domestic constituent pressure. The cases produced a number of propositions that map out important aspects of where, when, and how simultaneous participation at international and domestic tables can be used to pursue preferences that are in some sense the COG's "own." Four effects will be explored in this section: the preference for flexibility, sequence effects, the consequences of a "hawkish" positioning of COGs vis-à-vis their constituents, and the effects of uncertainty and asymmetrical access to information.

Tying Hands and Cutting Slack

Not all statesmen have enough latitude to make arguments about their autonomy interesting. Daladier, the French premier at the time of the 1933 world economic conference, is perhaps the best example of a COG with no maneuvering room at all (see Eichengreen and Uzan). According to Thomas Schelling's logic,[7] this might have been advantageous, risking no-agreement but increasing the chance that Daladier, whose "hands were tied," would get an agreement he liked. In fact, it proved to be no advantage at all, since the negotiations failed.

Statesmen may sometimes see "tied hands" as giving them advantage, but little support for this proposition emerged from these cases. Leaders like Brezhnev (see Snyder) and Sadat (see Stein) invoked "tied hands" to no avail. Their adversaries simply did not buy the argument. The only case in which a "tied hands" argument seemed to be effective was in negotiations "among friends" that involved disagreements over means instead of conflicting interests. Recognizing that his German allies' hands were in fact "tied" by domestic public opinion, Reagan moderated his demands on Schmidt and Kohl in the early 1980s (see Eichenberg).

Even more striking are cases in which leaders try to escape the opportunity of coming to the table with "tied hands," even when it might seem to give them a bargaining advantage. The Carter Administration's attempt to avoid being tied down by Congress on human rights, even though the administration was in full substantive agreement with the thrust of Congress' position, is the best case in point. Martin and Sikkink explain this apparent anomaly by emphasizing that in an iterative bargaining situation, where implementation is as problematic as attaining initial agreement, executives value flexibility much more than whatever initial advantage "tied hands" might confer. (Theoretically, the ideal situation might be to preserve "slack" in fact, while convincing international adversaries that the COG's hands were tied by domestic forces—but, as we shall see below, this strategy is generally ineffective.)

Both because it turns out to be difficult to reap the rewards Schelling postulates for "tied hands," and because there are returns to "slack" that

Schelling's logic does not take into account, COGs prefer slack to tied hands. This does not, however, mean that slack is necessarily associated with successful agreements. Roosevelt, who was the "tied-handed" Daladier's American counterpart in the 1933 negotiations, had an exceptional degree of autonomy, but he used it to scuttle the agreement (Eichengreen and Uzan). Finally, it should be emphasized that, COG preferences notwithstanding, preserving autonomy over the entire course of a negotiation is a very difficult thing to do.

Agenda-Setting and Mobilization

Surveying the cases, there is little doubt that agenda-setting usually reflects leaders' preferences. International initiatives in direct response to constituency pressure were surprisingly uncommon. This is especially clear in the case of security issues. If we look at our four security-related comparisons in Eichenberg, Stein, Snyder, and Moravcsik[8] and the two North-South comparisons that are noneconomic (in Pastor and Martin and Sikkink), it is hard to find a clear constituency-driven logic at the stage when negotiations are conceived or initiated. It is not that the reactions of domestic constituents were not considered by initiating leaders, or that potential for domestic political gain was uniformly absent. What is missing, as we look over these cases, is a systematic connection between either constituency pressure or domestic political gain and the initiation of negotiations.

Helmut Schmidt was certainly not responding to constituency pressure when he pushed the INF onto the international agenda in 1977 (Eichenberg). Nor was there any domestic constituency behind Jimmy Carter's determination to resolve the future of the Panama Canal (Pastor). It is not that chief executives are pursuing personal interests in these cases. Calculation of individual benefit, either material or even political, would not consistently explain Schmidt's or Carter's initiatives. Executive initiative in these cases must be seen not so much in terms of leeway to pursue individual ends but as indicative of the privileged position of chief executives and their advisors when it comes to defining what specifically constitutes the "national interest." In other cases, such as Snyder's analysis of Soviet policy toward Berlin, the pursuit of domestic political benefit is clear, but, even in these cases, the content of initiatives is still driven by each leader's creative attempts to redefine the correspondence between international bargains and domestic interests, rather than a straightforward vector of constituency interests.

If executive definitions of the national interest corresponded neatly to systemic exigencies, we might argue for a division of explanatory labor: a systemic logic explains initiative in security cases; when specific economic interests are involved, as in trade cases, then constituency pressure kicks in. Unfortunately for such a view, evidence for systemic determinism at the initiation stage is cloudy. The immanent logic of the international system is ambiguous at best. That an intermediate nuclear force was the proper response to the build-up of Soviet missiles in 1977 was apparently not obvious to U.S. security specialists like Zbignew Brzezinski, or for that matter to others in Schmidt's own party (Eichenberg). That U.S. national interest demanded Carter's efforts to turn over control of the Panama Canal was even less obvious to Ronald Reagan and his advisors (Pastor). In both cases, the logic of the international system was interpreted quite differently by different chief executives and their advisors, despite the absence of significant changes in objective features at the systemic level. Which COG was in command was the primary determinant of the initial bargaining agenda. As Snyder points out, there is a stark difference between "an objective, Martians'-eye view" of security interests and the assessments that flow from statesmen's "strategic ideologies."

A constituency-driven logic is easier to discover in sector-specific trade cases, but even in these cases constituency initiation was not the rule. In some cases, domestic groups definitely pushed their grievances onto the international table. U.S. semiconductor producers (in Krauss) and corn growers (in Odell) are the best examples. In others, they clearly were not responsible for initiation. The construction industry (Krauss) was too split to take the initiative, and the U.S. actions to open the Brazilian computer market caught its supposed constituency by surprise (Odell). In still other cases, COGs initiated negotiations that were in direct conflict with what the most relevant domestic interests wanted. Neither the majors nor domestic oil liked either the thrust of the Anglo-U.S. negotiations initiated by Hull or Ickes' alternative agenda (see Milner). Likewise, Milner's analysis shows the U.S. government initiating negotiations on civilian aviation, not at the behest of the country's dominant international carrier but precisely in order to limit that carrier's economic power.

The greater relevance of systemic arguments in security cases, and of constituency-driven arguments when economic issues are involved, makes sense. What is surprising is the overriding prevalence of COG initiative in both kinds of cases. Equally striking is the degree to which autonomy decreases as negotiations progress. Two different logics work to increase constraint. First there is the simple processual logic of the negotiations themselves; then there is the more complex political logic through which domestic constituencies become mobilized and, in many cases, take the driver's seat as the question of ratification begins to loom.

In our cases, the processual logic works generally to turn leaders into internationalists with a vested interest in producing agreements. Initiating a set of negotiations and becoming publicly identified with them creates a political investment which will be lost if no agreement results. COGs therefore develop an interest in agreement per se which is independent of the costs and benefits implied by the content of the agreement. As Stein emphasizes, Sadat, Begin, and Carter all saw themselves as paying a heavy price in the event of no-agreement, a price sufficiently heavy to outweigh marginal changes in the degree to which the agreement reflected their relative preferences. Likewise, signing some agreement became the principal preoccupation of Carter and Torrijos (Pastor). The rising cost of no-agreement based on participation in the negotiations themselves creates COG preferences that clearly cannot be reduced to some sum of constituent interests.

By the very act of putting new issues on the international agenda, COGs and their negotiators cannot help but awaken and mobilize constituencies with the potential of undercutting the attempted agreement. One important reason why diplomacy is double-edged is that diplomatic initiatives can awaken dormant domestic constituencies. The debate over INF mobilized a massive constituency in favor of the "double zero," an outcome quite different from the one Schmidt had in mind (Eichenberg). Ickes' efforts to restructure international oil awakened a domestic oil lobby sufficiently powerful to bury the administration's international initiative (see Milner). Not all executive initiatives are redirected. Carter and Torrijos triumphed over the opposition that was mobilized by their initiative (Pastor). Sadat got the treaty and the U.S. aid that went with it, despite the panoply of forces, both internal and regional, that were arrayed against it (Stein). Still, final outcomes depend fundamentally on domestic interest groups, just as Putnam's original focus on ratification suggests.

Over the whole course of negotiations, the differences between COGs and their constituencies produces a "constrained autonomy" in which tension between executive aims and constituency desires are fundamental to the dynamics that produce a final agreement (or no-agreement). Once this tension is seen as fundamental to the process of bargaining, it is impossible to avoid considering the content of the differences that separate COGs and constituents.

Hawks and Doves

Heroically simplifying the myriad possibilities that emerge once COG preferences are allowed some independence from those of constituents, we assumed that preferences might be ordered along a single dimension. Preferences of COGs and constituents can then take on the three possible configurations that are laid out in the Introduction: dove, agent, and hawk.[9] The dove is more sympathetic than his or her constituents to the position of the other state; the agent's aims correspond to those of constituents; and the hawk is more hostile. Being an effective agent may require great political acumen and full utilization of the tools that Putnam describes, but the COG as agent still has the passive option of letting the ratification play itself out in response to the existing correlation of domestic forces. Success in the role of dove or hawk requires manipulation of the domestic win-set. Doves and hawks have no choice but to take a more active stance vis-à-vis their constituents, which is why only politically secure leaders are likely to risk the role of hawk or dove.[10]

Precisely because "COG as dove" shares interests with those on the other side of the international table, such leaders are in a domestically vulnerable position. When specific domestic interests are involved, "COG as dove" may be indistinguishable from COG as traitor in the eyes of the interests involved. The plaintive accusations of the U.S. construction industry against the State Department during negotiations over access to Japanese construction markets is a prime example (Krauss).[11] Such vulnerability creates, of course, additional incentives for the COG to formulate an active strategy designed to reshape domestic attitudes toward potential agreements.

The position of COG as dove also opens up special possibilities for two-level strategies. Depending on the degree of "dovishness" involved, the COG may be in the curious position of sharing more acceptable agreements with those on the other side of the international table than with the majority of enfranchised domestic constituents, creating the possibility of a transnational alliance between statesmen, which we came to call "COG collusion." Torrijos' efforts in helping Carter expand the definition of what was ratifiable in the United States were as important as his efforts in his own domestic arena (Pastor). European chief executives and their defense ministries were allies vis-à-vis their own "nationalistic" firms (Moravcsik). Gorbachev (Snyder), Sadat and Begin (Stein), Sarney (Odell), and even Videla (Martin and Sikkink) were all able to use COG collusion to increase their autonomy vis-à-vis domestic constituencies.

"COG as hawk" raises a different set of issues. The agreements that the COG would find acceptable are even less acceptable to the other side than those preferred by domestic constituents. Since the prerogative of setting the agenda rests with the COG, no mutually acceptable agreements are likely to emerge at the international level. If the statesmen as hawks were content with simply preserving the status quo by making sure that no agreement is completed, they would almost inevitably "win," but the posture of hawk implies discontent with the status quo. In order to produce an agreement that changes the status quo, the COG as hawk must expand the other side's definition of what it will accept by raising the cost of no-agreement. This, in turn, requires linking failure to agree with negative changes in the status quo, i.e., making threats.

Superficially it might appear that threats (since they do not involve formal "agreements" with other states) could be imposed without domestic ratification, thereby associating truculence with greater autonomy for the COG. In fact, our cases show that ratifiability is equally important for threats, and that the COG is constrained in the use of threats just as in the use of promises. Even if it is possible in principle to impose a threat without a prior process of formal ratification, such threats turn out to lack credibility.

Odell's analysis of the U.S.-Brazil computer dispute makes the logic clear. The U.S. tried to overcome Brazilian recalcitrance with threats, but its initiative was not supported by the most affected domestic constituency (U.S. computer companies) and was therefore not credible to the Brazilians. U.S. policies toward Nicaragua (Pastor) are a second case in point. Again, the executive's differences with the other side were greater than those of the majority of domestic constituents, so much so that no plausible agreement could be suggested for ratification and, again, the attempt to threaten the other side (by aiding the contras) foundered because lack of ratification undermined credibility. In both cases, the other side assumed that the domestic political costs of implementing the threats were too great, either because they would alienate a key constituency (computers) or because the majority of the enfranchised would not support them (Nicaragua).

Overall, the role of COG as hawk seems more difficult than that of COG as dove. "COG collusion" gives doves the international table itself as a resource. From the international table they can get "linkable issues" and suasive transnational allies to assist in efforts at reshaping the domestic win-set. The international table offers no possibility of synergy to hawks, leaving them to rely on other strategies (sometimes even dubious ones like Contragate) to escape the constraints imposed by the process of ratification. Hawks are not always losers. Carter did succeed in convincing Argentina of the credibility of his threat to cut off credits before it became obvious that his constituency was unlikely to ratify this threat (Martin and Sikkink). Reagan did manage at least to prevent accommodation with the Sandinistas (Pastor) and eventually to squeeze some concessions out of the Brazilians (Odell). Nonetheless, our cases suggest that problems of ratifying threats create serious obstacles for the COG as hawk.

All of this undermines traditional Spencerian visions of the pinnacles of state power as intrinsically more bellicose than their peaceable civilian constituents. While there are a few instances of leaders embarking on hostile adventures as a way of escaping desperate domestic dilem-mas—(e.g., Sadat in 1973, see Stein)—they are surprisingly few. By 1978, Sadat had become a principal architect of a peaceful solution. With the possible exception of Stalin during the first Berlin crisis (Snyder), our sample is almost devoid of cases where major statesmen are consistently successful in using hawkish tactics to improve their domestic political position. Even Reagan, who might be analyzed in these terms in Central America (Pastor), is the dovish advocate of double zero in the European arena (Eichenberg).

Ironically, threats are most credible when delivered by the COG as agent or, better still, as dove. In the disputes over agriculture (Odell), semiconductors (Krauss), and construction (Krauss), U.S. negotiators were able convincingly to portray themselves as reining in rabid domestic constituencies. The domestic political costs of implementing the threat were therefore less than those of implementing an accord within the other side's (pre-threat) win-set. Ratification of the threat was not only unproblematic, it was arguably a process likely to result in escalation.

The possibility of COG as hawk being able to take on the guise of dove at the international table raises again the issue of "tied hands." COGs could prefer slack to tied hands but still try to portray their hands as tied. How effective it is for the COG to falsely claim "tied hands," to portray the "win-set" as smaller and less manageable than it really is depends on how well information about domestic political realities travels across national borders.

Uncertainty and Misinformation

In contemplating the generalizations that might emerge from these cases, our initial expectation was that the quality of available information would deteriorate sharply across national boundaries. Ignorance of the domestic polities of others would be a major source of blunders, possibly an important reason for the failure to achieve agreements. Conversely, the ability to strategically manipulate information about the true prefer-ences of one's own polity would be an important asset, increasing the relative gains of those able to make use of it. We expected that statesmen would use their access to information about the domestic ratification process to enhance both their autonomy vis-à-vis constituents and their bargaining power at the international table.

We were right about some things. Levels of ignorance and uncertainty were high, as we expected. Problems of mis-estimating which agreements were in the win-set were rife, as we expected. We did find some attempts to strategically manipulate external perceptions of what was ratifiable domestically. We also saw some dramatic effects from the provision of new information. Questions of biased interpretation, ideologically generated misunderstandings, and conflicting models of how the world worked were all important in explaining failed agreements.

Our mistake was not in overestimating the importance of information; it was in overestimating the informational consequences of national boundaries. COGs' estimates of what was ratifiable in their own domestic polities were often wrong, and even successful domestic strategies prevailed in spite of a high degree of uncertainty. Estimates of the other side's domestic polities were often mistaken as well, but not dramatically more often than estimates of one's own polity. COGs did try to strategically misrepresent their own polities in order to gain bargaining advantage, but not as often as we expected, and with much less success. Highlighting genuine uncertainty with respect to ratifiability seemed more effective than concocting portrayals of the domestic polity.

The U.S. domestic arena provides the best examples of the usefulness of genuine uncertainty. In all of the trade cases, negotiators raised the spector of nationalist domestic interests, represented by Congress, overrunning the (relatively) conciliatory state apparatus.[12] The team of executive "soft cop" and congressional "hard cop" appears fundamental to the U.S. negotiating stance. The intransigence of Congress may be presented in an exaggerated way, but, because of the genuine difficulty of estimating the ability of domestic groups to mobilize and win allies, even the best-informed, carefully discounted versions (such as those provided by Japanese lobbyists in Krauss' trade cases) constitute an effective threat.

The very transparency of U.S. ratification procedures helps makes genuine threats credible. Conversely, of course, transparency makes spurious threats hard to sustain, undercutting COG as hawk. The best example here is the computer case (Odell). When the administration was on shaky ground in the Brazilian computer case, the Brazilians discounted bellicose statements from Congress and the U.S. Trade Representative, estimated the credibility of the threat quite accurately, and responded accordingly.

There is only one case in which the United States seems to have succeeded in extracting concessions by controlling information about prospects for ratification rather than by using actual uncertainties. In the Videla-Mondale human rights negotiations (Martin and Sikkink), it appears that Mondale successfully withheld the fact that sanctions were unlikely to be renewed by Congress, and Videla's concessions were based on the assumption that they would be. This case is an exception good for proving the rule. Prior congressional action had been consistent with the perception that they were hawkish on the issue, so transparency made the prediction plausible. The Mondale-Videla talks were secret, so Mondale did not offer his interpretation publicly, opening it to possible contradiction by other U.S. actors. Perhaps most important, Videla had domestic reasons for wanting to "concede" on the issue, and was therefore motivated to collude by accepting the view that Mondale was offering.

Just as borders provided less formidable barriers to political information than we had thought they might be, the quality of information within domestic boundaries was lower than we had expected. Estimates from the other side of the international table are not always accurate, but there is no evidence in our cases that negotiators' estimates about their own domestic tables are substantially more accurate. British skeptics perceived the French win-set on arms collaboration more accurately than the French themselves (Moravcsik). Gorbachev's estimate of which arms proposals would be most attractive to the German electorate seems to have been as accurate as Kohl's (Eichenberg). American skeptics of semiconductor implementation were closer to the mark than the Japanese Ministry of International Trade and Industry (Krauss). The Brazilians did about as well as the USTR in estimating U.S. computer firms sentiments (Odell). Overall, the proposition that the quality of information falls off sharply at national borders garners no support from our cases.

As the IMF's misjudgment of both Siyaad Barre and Edward Seaga (see Kahler) illustrates, estimating the preferences of other COGs may be more difficult than estimating domestic ratifiability. Nonetheless, even here it is not clear that a drop-off in accuracy occurs at the national border. Ahmad Addow seems to have misjudged his father-in-law as badly as the IMF did (Kahler). Ickes misjudged Roosevelt's willingness to back his plans for oil (Milner). Gorbachev took the Soviet foreign policy establishment by surprise (Snyder).

Complementing the surprising absence of evidence for an international information gradient is an equally surprising dearth of cases of efficacious misrepresentation of the domestic win-set. Cases in which substantial misrepresentation was attempted are reasonably rare in our sample and, with the possible exception of Mondale and Videla, none of them succeeded. Even more surprising is the fact that authoritarian regimes did not seem to have the advantage in this area that one would intuitively expect. Snyder's analysis of Soviet attempts is the best case in point: he claims, for example, that far from giving Brezhnev an advantage in negotiations, the "opacity" of Soviet politics made it impossible for him to argue convincingly that his "hands were tied" by hardliners like Suslov. In general, Snyder sees counterproductive misrepresentation of bargaining positions on the Berlin issue by all sides as undercutting the possibility of joint gains, and finds no examples of relative gain through misrepresentation.

Why weren't foreign ignorance and misrepresentation more common in our sample? Two complementary explanations are plausible. First, because the contemporary world is empirically one in which the flow of information across borders is not easily controlled. The Brazilians can hire a former U.S. Ambassador to Brazil to canvass congressional opinion for them. Gorbachev can read many of the same German public opinion polls that Kohl does. Equally critical is the analytical point made earlier in the discussion of "tied hands." Negotiations are highly iterated, not one-shot games. When potential gains based on misinformation in one round must be balanced against loss of credibility in future rounds, credibility usually weighs more heavily.

None of this makes information less important. If our cases were characterized by a relative availability of factual information, they were also characterized by strong interpretive effects. Snyder's emphasis on the potential costs of trying to negotiate on the basis of perceptions generated by politically constructed "strategic ideologies" has already been emphasized. Eichengreen considers differences in cognitive models about how economies work a central reason for the failure of 1933 World Economic Conference. Kahler points out that the views of the IMF and Jamaica concerning the consequences of devaluation were simply incompatible, making agreement almost impossible.

The returns from breaking through these ideologically constructed worldviews can be large. Sadat's famous trip to Jerusalem is perhaps the best example (Stein). By publicly and irrevocably tying his own hands, Sadat gained credibility in both Israel and the United States and broke through stereotypical views of the range of positions possible for an Arab leader. The human rights cases mentioned earlier (in Martin and Sikkink) also demonstrate the returns to be had from increasing information flows. Without the information on Argentine violations provided by international human rights organizations, it would have been very difficult to construct a credible congressional threat. Even in the Guatemalan case, tracing death squads back to Lucas García's office was crucial in maintaining international pressure on the regime.

Analytically, it is clear that increased information enhances the possibility of successful agreements only in certain kinds of negotiations. When negotiations are purely distributional, accurate information may only increase the losers' intransigence. Only insofar as "coordination problems" are involved is information likely to increase the chances of agreement. What our cases show is that most negotiations have a sufficient element of "coordination problems" to make global increases in the availability of information an important contextual variable in shaping both negotiating strategies and overall expectations of success. What they also show, however, is the importance of domestic information gradients for international agreements. Local misreadings of domestic politics are as likely to be responsible for failed agreements as cross-border ignorance.

From the relative autonomy of leaders in setting agendas to the surprising inability of COGs to exploit information asymmetries, there is systematic and consistent variation in the balance of autonomy and constraint that shapes the COG's pivotal role in forging agreements. While illuminating that balance is one of our project's major accomplishments, the role of the COG cannot be understood in isolation. The success or failure of agreements depends upon their impact on pre-existing structures of interest, both national and transnational. Statesmen may be the most prominent players of two-level games, but other players' agendas often triumph nonetheless. Understanding when and why is essential to an integrative approach.

INTERESTS AND AGREEMENTS

Agreement may flow naturally from the prospect of joint gain. Initial win-sets may overlap, and the agreements in their intersection find favor with the chief executives involved. In most cases, however, distributional issues divide domestic interests. Not everyone participates in the joint gains, and the losers have an interest in blocking prospective agreements. This does not necessarily condemn agreements to failure. Sometimes COGs as doves succeed in finding or producing a non-obvious intersection, as with Carter and Torrijos (Pastor). Sometimes divisions are overcome even though COGs are relatively passive, as in the case of Reagan and the construction accord (Krauss). Is there anything systematic about the structure of domestic interests as they relate to the issues under negotiation that separates successful agreements like the Panama Canal Treaties or the construction accord from failures like Ickes' oil initiative (Milner) or European collaboration on tanks and fighters (Moravcsik)?

Concentrated Costs Versus Diffuse Benefits

The conditions of failure are easier to specify than those of success. If we look at the 1943 oil case (Milner), the semiconductor case (Krauss), and tanks and fighters (Moravcsik), the similarities are striking. In each case, potential gains are diffuse, but costs are borne by a concentrated group which is highly organized. Each of these groups is also "disproportionately enfranchised," either because they have politically privileged positions in the ratification process or because their cooperation is essential to the implementation of the agreement itself.

In 1943, domestic oil was vitally threatened, not just by the prospect of immediate material losses (through greater competition from foreign oil) but also by the prospect of diminished long-term ability to control the rules under which oil was produced and sold (Milner). The problem was compounded by the fact that single-party rule in Texas and the other oil-producing states combined with the congressional seniority system to give domestic oil a strategic place in the ratification process. Whatever diffuse benefits might have accrued to oil consumers through lower prices could not balance domestic oil-producers' concentrated interest and clout. Moravcsik's defense contractors were not just organized by monopolized control over the specialized production capacities involved. They were essential players in both the formulation and implementation of any agreement, and could therefore exercise veto power despite clear gains from a "national interest" point of view. The sabotage of the semi-conductor agreement by the Japanese producers had a similar logic. They were paying a concentrated cost (loss of markets), in return for which Japanese industry as a whole was presumably reaping the diffuse benefits of easier entry into the U.S. market. National interest might have been served by agreement, but without the cooperation of those paying the cost no agreement could be implemented.

The structure of domestic interests in these cases stands in contrast to the structure of similar sectorial disputes where agreements were reached. In the European Community case (Odell), costs of agreement were concentrated and specific (falling on French maize farmers), but other, equally enfranchised groups could see clear costs of *no*-agreement. French brandy and wine producers saw their immediate interests threatened. Volkswagen and other German manufacturers were equally (if less immediately) threatened. Lacking the kind of power over implementation that protected the defense contractors and semiconductor producers, the maize growers lost and the agreement went through.

The construction case (Krauss) offers a variation on the same theme. It shows that even within sectors, the question of compactness and concentration is crucial. Differentiation within the U.S. industry made it possible to target one segment—large firms with hopes of securing contracts in Japan—and separate it from the rest of the industry—small firms fearful of Japanese competition in the U.S. market. Because the agreement produced concentrated benefits for the most politically powerful components of the industry, it was ratifiable.

Sectorally specific cases are not the only ones in which the structure of domestic interests make a difference. Somali rejection of the IMF agreement (Kahler) followed a logic quite similar to that advanced by Moravcsik to explain the failure of arms collaboration. Benefits from the proposed monetary reform were primarily collective and diffusely distributed. The existing system of currency control had, in effect, privatized returns, allocating them to a very concentrated group. The group that would pay the costs of changing it—military and political elites—were, to put it mildly, disproportionately enfranchised. Failure was predictable.

The Guatemala case (Martin and Sikkink) adds a new variation. Again, costs to a concentrated, disproportionately enfranchised group were balanced against more diffusely distributed benefits and, as expected, there was no-agreement. In this case, however, both costs and benefits were collective. For the military and the tiny landowning elite, human rights were a "collective bad." Those who saw it as a collective good were numerous but not enfranchised. The result was again predictable. In Argentina (Martin and Sikkink), a slightly more differentiated state apparatus, which included civilian technocrats who did not view their interests as coincident with those of the repressive wing of the military, expanded the possibilities for agreement. There was space for targeted issue-linkage to complement the calculus of costs and benefits with regard to the collective good (again, human rights). The threat of blocked credits created unease within the ruling group, strengthening Videla's hand enough to make agreement possible.

As these cases make clear, mapping the incidence of costs and benefits yields, in itself, no prediction whatsoever independent of the institutional arrangements that define enfranchisement. The political consequences of costs and benefits are always considered by the institutions that define enfranchisement and ratification procedures. An analysis of the former must always be accompanied by an analysis of the latter.

Institutions and Enfranchisement

The question of enfranchisement can be raised at two levels. At the most general level is the question of how the extent of enfranchisement affects the propensity of countries to enter into agreements. Does the inclusion of a larger proportion of the population among the enfranchised (democracy) reduce the size of the typical win-set and thereby increase the difficulty of entering into agreements? Then there is the issue of the specific institutional rules that translate interests into a role in the process of ratification, and how this influences the prospects of specific agreements.

Despite a number of provocative specific findings, the overall consequences of specific institutional rules are ambiguous. Eichengreen and Uzan, for example, stress the role of proportional representation in exaggerating the veto power of the French peasants in 1933. Conversely, the fact that the U.S. was negotiating with the European Community Commission rather than a body in which French farmers were directly enfranchised helped create the possibility of agreement in the maize war (Odell). Yet the constraints normally imposed by Israel's system of proportional representation were finessed with apparent ease by Begin (Stein).

The issue is further complicated by the fact that ratification procedures cannot be taken as fixed. In the human rights cases, the U.S. Congress gradually shifted procedures from informal acquiescence to formal authorization or approval (Martin and Sikkink). In the oil case, the independent domestic producers' ability to shift to a formal ratification procedure enabled them to kill the agreement (Milner). For Gorbachev, exclusion from the ratification process of concentrated interest groups with prior veto power was essential to his ability to undertake international initiatives (Snyder). In short, ratification procedures help determine the balance of power among different domestic groups and between COGs and constituents, but ratification procedures are also determined by the balance of power.

On the question of the general effects of the scope of enfranchisement, the literature seems to support the idea that polities with broad enfranchisement ("democracies," roughly speaking) will characteristically have smaller win-sets, and therefore a harder time ratifying agreements, than countries with severe restrictions on effective franchise. The classic Morgenthau/Kennan vision of the disabilities of democratic foreign policy seems consistent with this assumption (see Introduction). Putnam's assumption that democratic leaders have smaller win-sets than dictatorships follows in the same vein.

Our cases, however, question the existence of an inverse relation between scope of enfranchisement and the size of the win-set. Guatemala is the archetype of generalized disenfranchisement, yet its win-set proved both small and resistant to enlargement (Martin and Sikkink). In this case, restricted enfranchisement seems to have created compact, disciplined unity in support of a narrow set of interests, defined largely in contrast to those of the disenfranchised majority. The compact, enfranchised minority is difficult to split by means of targeted issue-linkage and sufficiently vested in its positions to be immune to suasion. The possibility of relative losses vis-à-vis the disenfranchised majority, especially in terms of autonomy and political control, outweighs the joint gains that might be achieved through accords with other countries.

In other cases the effects of restricted franchise seemed less clear-cut, but there was still little evidence of an inverse relation between restricted franchise and the size of the win-set. Far from being blessed with a large win-set by the undemocratic character of the Soviet system, Khrushchev and Brezhnev seemed to scramble continually to find agreements that might satisfy the conflicting demands of their restricted set of constituents (Snyder). The win-set created by the small number of clan and political leaders that constituted the enfranchised population of Siyaad Barre's regime was also very restricted, making agreement with the IMF more difficult than in the more democratic Seaga Administration (Kahler).

These assumptions about the institutionally mediated impact of domestic interest-group structures on the prospects for agreement must obviously be set in the context of our earlier consideration of the relative autonomy of the COG. An active "COG as dove" may be able to strategically manipulate ratification procedures, combine suasion and targeting, and achieve accords that would have seemed doomed from an ex-ante analysis of the structure of domestic interests.

Sadat is a case in point (Stein). Insofar as the goods involved were collective (peace and security), he exploited the full potential of suasion. At the same time, he maximized the opportunities for targeting provided by the limited differentiation of those enfranchised within Egypt's authoritarian system. Finally, he exploited his power vis-à-vis a weakly institutionalized set of ratification procedures to push through an agreement that, even when sweetened by linking peace with U.S. aid, was still probably opposed by a majority of domestic interest groups. Gorbachev's ability to break through the constraints imposed by the domestic interest structure is similar (Snyder).

Domestic Restructuring

The cases of both Gorbachev and Sadat suggest an important complement to any analysis of the effects of domestic interest structures. The causal relation between domestic interests and the prospects for international accord is not unidirectional. Another reason why diplomacy is double-edged is that it can reshape domestic interests as well as responding to them. Existing domestic interest structures help determine the probability of agreements, but international agreements may provide the opportunity to restructure domestic interests. Indeed, the hope of domestic restructuring may provide the underlying impetus for ostensibly international agreements, as is arguably true for both Gorbachev and Sadat.

Neither Sadat nor Gorbachev arrived at the international table simply in search of an agreement. Both were hoping to use the results of international bargains to strengthen the political and economic position of supportive domestic groups and weaken that of opponents, with the ultimate aim of permanently changing domestic interest structures. By linking a collective good (peace, disarmament) with a good that could be privately appropriated (American aid, or Western trade and technology), they sought to introduce new resources into what would otherwise have been a hard-to-win, zero-sum game (extracting resources from the military in order to have something to distribute to civilian supporters). Thus, they aimed to transform resources under their control as COGs (suasive ability and access to the international table) into resources that could actually be distributed to domestic supporters.

The successful blocking of agreements by domestic interest groups may create an impetus for restructuring. Confronting a domestic interest structure that is clearly intractable on the issue of arms collaboration, French and German negotiators are, in Moravcsik's view, likely to try restructuring the domestic industry in order to diminish industrialists' power to block future accords. Milner's analysis shows the potential of such a strategy. Pre-emptive restructuring of the U.S. aviation industry in order to increase the international involvement of previously domestic airlines was crucial to the construction of support for the eventual IATA accord.

Whether at the national or sectoral level, domestic restructuring has more fundamental implications than the successful implementation of specific policies. Restructuring implies the construction of a "new game," with new odds for the ratifiability of a range of specific policies. By the same token, of course, the time and resources required to overcome the inertia of an established social and political structure may make even the most crafty efforts at restructuring quixotic. Even with 2 billion dollars in U.S. aid, Sadat achieved only the most marginal success in changing the character of Egyptian society. History may eventually judge Gorbachev a success, but the consequences of his restructuring efforts may also be seen as one of the world's most colossal failures.

Domestic restructuring may also be an aim for those on the other side of the international table. Statesmen often make restructuring an international adversary's domestic polity part of their agenda at the international table. IMF demands are only the most obvious example (Kahler). Carter's human rights agenda was about other countries' domestic institutions and power rather than their international behavior, as was Reagan's underlying agenda vis-à-vis Nicaragua. The initial successes of Gorbachev and Sadat were due in no small measure to the fact that their restructuring agendas corresponded to the preferences of those on the other side of the international table. Even at the sectoral level, restructuring other people's domestic arenas is often a central issue. Restructuring Japanese industrial organization was a central U.S. aim in both the semiconductor and construction cases (Krauss), as well as in the U.S. fight with Brazil over its computer policies.

As these sectoral examples make clear, however, "domestic restructuring" is not always the appropriate label. In many cases the restructuring involves creating or expanding transnational ties. Indeed, any analysis of domestic interests and their relation to international agreements must be complemented by consideration of transnational interests, ties, and alliances.

Transnational Interests and Alliances

Purely domestic interest groups cannot play two-level games, but actors with transnational ties share the statesmen's privilege, even if in an attenuated way, of participating internationally as well as domestically. They may be formally enfranchised in only one country and excluded from formal participation at the international table, but the transnational alliances they form have an indirect impact on both sides of the international game. The calculus of domestic costs and benefits is insufficient to define the interests of a transnational alliance. Such alliances are likely to have a direct, immediate stake in the content of international agreements. Yet they are also more likely to be able to achieve international goals in the absence of intergovernmental accords. How is the existence of a transnational alliance likely to affect the chances of successful agreement?

Before attempting a general answer to this question, it is first worth noting the stark contrast between the security cases and the economically oriented cases on the issue of transnational alliances. The only instance among our security cases in which transnational alliances play a role is the arms-collaboration case (Moravcsik) in which the economics of satisfying security needs rather than territorial control were what really was at stake. Snyder stresses the absence of transnational alliances in U.S.-Soviet relations, and postulates that relations focused on security issues stifle transnational alliances. There may be, he notes, transnational collusion in the form of parallel pursuit of a common interest in increasing tension and military spending by hard-liners on both sides of the Iron Curtain, but there are not alliances.

The only noneconomic issue in our sample which generates an interesting transnational alliance is human rights (Martin and Sikkink). Here, the role of international human rights groups is different from that of "normal" private transnational actors. The primary function of these groups was informational, subverting the attempts of states to control information about their domestic polities. They provide one more reminder that transnational alliances diminish the effectiveness of statesmens' dissembling, and are part of the reason for diminished international information asymmetries, but hardly undercut the general proposition that transnational alliances come into play primarily where economic issues are at stake.

Narrowing the focus to economic issues, does it make sense to argue that where transnational alliances exist, and their participants take an interest in an issue, international agreements are more likely? The proposition sounds plausible. It overlooks, however, the fact that transnational actors, unlike purely domestic ones, have the organizational and informational resources necessary to construct private alternatives to governmental accords, alternatives which may well correspond more closely to their interests. Intergovernmental accords may even encroach on spheres previously organized by means of private alliances, thereby threatening transnational interests. In this case, the presence of transnational alliances would make international agreements *less* likely.

The issue is not only: "How do transnational alliances affect the chances of successful agreement?" The reverse causality is equally interesting. Do consummated agreements stimulate the creation of new private transnational alliances? Or does the existence of formal accords diminish the necessity for them? Finally, transnational effects must be added to the calculation of distributive consequences of international agreements. Do governments act nationalistically, constructing accords primarily to protect domestic interest groups against the economic power of transnational actors? Or are accords more likely to be constructed at the behest of transnational actors and at the expense of domestic interest groups?

Our cases offer an opportunity for a preliminary adjudication of these contradictory propositions concerning the relations between transnational alliances and international agreements. The cases included analyses of traditional transnational actors with organizational ties that connect the two sides of an international negotiation, like IBM,[13] as well as less conventional ones like the international human rights organizations. They included examples of alliances between organizations with bases in different countries but shared transnational interests, like Pan American Airways (PAA) and BOAC or the international oil companies, as well as actors for whom strong international interests did not (at first) result in transnational alliances, like Krauss' semiconductor firms. Together they produce a complex but quite intriguing picture of interplay between transnational alliances and international agreements.

The complexity of the relation between private transnational alliances and international accords is nicely illustrated in Milner's analysis of oil and aviation. Oil began with private alliances, but U.S. oil companies felt that reinforcement from the U.S. state was the best avenue for improving their relative position in the private transnational alliance that bound together the oil majors. When Ickes' efforts ran aground, however, they reconstructed the private alliance. Likewise, the civil aviation story began with an attempted private alliance between BOAC and PAA.[14] This attempt was undercut by states that felt their stake was too great to allow private control, but the final result was a more open and institutionalized version of a private alliance (IATA) created, at least in part, through governmental efforts.

A very different kind of ambivalence about accords is illustrated by the U.S.-Brazil computer case (Odell). IBM and most of the other largest American producers had the toughest kind of transnational linkage with Brazilian production—their 100-percent-owned subsidiaries dominated the Brazilian market for large machines. Precisely for this reason, they were at first reluctant to ratify the Reagan Administration's threats. As Odell points out, their transnational linkages provided a quite comfortable alternative to the openness sought by the United States. U.S. transnational corporations were not averse to having the Reagan Administration's help in changing Brazil's regulatory rules (as they showed in the later fight on software), but they were not about to risk this position in pursuit of a compliance which seemed unlikely to succeed and likely to lead to generalized conflict if pursued too aggressively.

In all these examples, states and private transnational actors are uneasy allies, each desiring both a predictable environment for undertaking activities beyond national borders and control over these activities. Each prefers that a greater share of the control accrue to itself, but can accept less, providing concession achieves a more predictable international environment. Often their preferred strategies for organizing transnational economic activities are in competition. No-agreement in state-to-state terms may create room for a preferable private arrangement. For those with established positions in global markets, the status quo may well look better than a new, officially sanctioned regime. Overall, it is clear why there is no consistent relation between the interest of transnational actors in an issue and the probability of successful agreement.

One way of reducing the apparent confusion is to focus more closely on international market position, as Moravcsik suggests in his discussion of the arms case. We need to distinguish between three kinds of private actors: established participants in transnational alliances, "wannabes" who are potential players in international markets but lack an established position, and domestic actors who lack the capacity to exploit international market opportunities. Looking through the lens of this tripartite division, attitudes toward agreements make more sense.

In both the oil case and the U.S.-Brazil computer case, established transnational actors failed to support accords because their "cost of no-agreement" was low or nonexistent. Almost by definition, established participants in transnational alliances already enjoy satisfactory means of pursuing their interests across national boundaries. An official accord may improve the terms of that arrangement (as the U.S. oil companies were hoping in 1943), but pursuit of a generalized solution through an international agreement may also stimulate the mobilization of hostile domestic interest groups (in either country) and raise the level of conflict.

Potential transnational actors, "wannabes," are less ambivalent than established members of transnational alliances. They may see international accords as a means of gaining access to international markets. In the IATA example (Milner), it was the U.S. domestic carriers trying to break into international markets that expected the most gains from international accords, not the established international giants (PAA, BOAC). Likewise, it was the U.S. computer firms that did *not* have subsidiaries in Brazil who saw value in the U.S. efforts at securing an agreement from the Brazilians.

Most likely to be opposed to international accords are private actors whose returns accrue from their own domestic markets and who lack the economic or organizational resources necessary to benefit from transnational alliances. Joint gains at the national level may well be losses, from their point of view. For U.S. domestic oil producers, the possibility of greater access to Mideast oil was a cost, not a gain (Milner). Exchanging new access to Japanese construction contracts for continued Japanese access to U.S. contracts might mean joint gains at the national level, but from the point of view of small U.S. firms, ill-equipped to take advantage of the new market and vulnerable to competition at home, the agreement was all loss and no gain (Krauss). Brazilian computer producers were in a similar position, especially small firms unlikely to attract transnational allies. In all these cases, the characteristics of the firms themselves made them vulnerable to competition from transnational actors and incapable, at least in the short run, of forging alliances that might allow them to join a transnational game.

Despite their participation in international markets, exporters are closer to domestic producers than to either established or "wannabe" transnational actors. Domestic production for sale abroad does not necessarily create transnational alliances. In fact, it may make transnational alliances threatening, as in the cases of Dasault and Krauss-Mafei (Moravcsik). French maize exporters did their best to prevent the European Community from reaching an agreement with the United States—and even U.S. maize exporters, the agreement's principal beneficiaries, argued that the U.S. should have imposed much tougher conditions rather than signing the compromise agreement (Odell). It was precisely the export strength of Japanese semiconductor firms that led them to undermine the U.S.-Japanese agreement (Krauss).

Once different kinds of transnational actors are distinguished, the modal tendency of the connections between transnational alliances and international agreements is relatively clear-cut. Agreements tend to favor those able to pursue transnational interests, creating mutually supportive relations between state actors and private transnational actors. Nonetheless, private actors who have already constructed effective transnational alliances may not support prospective agreements, considering them less rewarding and more risky than the private arrangements they already have in place.

Despite the ambivalent relation between transnational alliances and agreements, state actors rarely seem to side with purely domestic interests. In our cases, at least, they never offered unqualified support to producers with purely domestic interests. Relative to such producers they are always doves. Even in the most extreme case, Brazil's support of its local computer industry, the Ministry of Foreign Relations consistently searched for compromise solutions and the COG supported a software policy that was closer to the U.S. position than that of local firms (Odell).

The construction case (Krauss) is not atypical. Just as the U.S. domestic firms claimed, there was a tacit transgovernmental alliance designed to reach an agreement favoring transnational producers at the expense of domestic ones. In the arms case (Moravcsik), the symbiotic relation between transgovernmental alliances and private transnational alliances was explicit. Collaboration in the helicopter industry (Moravcsik) was saved in alternating fashion, first by the institutional innovations of the private actors and later by the willingness of COGs to link this particular issue to the larger institutionalized relationship between the two countries. If projected state efforts to restructure other segments of defense production succeed in spreading transnational alliances to them, the public-private transnational "conspiracy" will be complete.

State actors as they appear in our economic cases are far from the truculent chauvinists of liberal nightmares. Their "internationalist" position should not, however, be misread as being simply pro-market. Even the Reagan Administration, the most adamantly market-oriented of all the governments in our sample, could not escape constructing agreements that promote "managed trade" rather than market rules. As Krauss notes in his discussion of the semiconductor case, one of the main institutional effects of U.S. pressure within Japan was to strengthen MITI's ability to monitor and control the industry. The overall consequence of the agreement was not to increase the sway of market forces, but to fix prices for the benefit of producers at the expense of consumers.

What then are the consequences of agreements for the growth of private transnational alliances? Both successful and failed agreements are associated with the subsequent formation of new transnational alliances. In helicopter collaboration (Moravcsik), the success of the alliance was directly dependent on an international accord. In oil, reconstruction of the private alliance was the result of the accord's failure (Milner). In construction, the success of the accord stimulated new alliances between

U.S. and Japanese firms, but the failure of the semiconductor agreement did the same thing (Krauss). The real difference that separates the consequences of successful and failed agreements parallels the logic of support for agreements that has already been laid out. Failed agreements (e.g., see Milner on oil) are likely to strengthen the hand of established transnational alliances. Successful agreements (e.g., see Krauss on construction, Milner on aviation) are likely to stimulate potential transnational actors ("wannabes") to enter the international arena. What successful agreements are *not* likely to do is to strengthen the hand of purely domestic actors. The symbiosis between statesmen and private transnational actors may be an ambivalent one, but it is a symbiosis nonetheless, one that seems likely over the longer term to shift the background of interests and alliances against which specific agreements are negotiated.

THE CHANGING GLOBAL CONTEXT

In 1988, when the project was conceived, the possibility that the end of a bipolar international system was around the corner seemed fanciful. Nor was the question of long-term changes in the international order directly addressed in Putnam's original article. So it is not surprising that contrasting historical contexts were not part of our "most different" design. With three exceptions (Eichengreen and Uzan, Milner, and Snyder), all of the cases focus on negotiations conducted during the past twenty years. Nonetheless, several authors produced arguments pertinent to the trajectory of change over time, some of them quite relevant to the more specific issue of what the features of a "new world order" might be if one were to emerge.

The general longitudinal proposition suggested by our cases (and only hinted at in Putnam's article) is that synergistic strategies have become, and are likely to continue becoming, more common over time. The obvious corollary of this proposition is that the need for an integrative approach is likely to increase. Some might go further, suggesting that increased opportunities for synergistic bargaining imply in turn agreements that are "better" from a welfare point of view—but evidence for this second corollary is more mixed.

Reflecting on our only pre–World War II case, the 1933 World Economic Conference (Eichengreen and Uzan), is a good way to begin a consideration of historic trends. In the context of our other cases, the thoroughness of the failure of the 1933 conference is striking. Objectively, the issues in 1933 were more tractable than those which formed the basis of bargaining in many of our later examples. Some of the issues were "coordination problems" with clear possibilities for joint gains. Even the distributive conflicts were amenable in principle to "targeting," and there were a number of opportunities to construct "synergistic linkages" across issues.

The absence of creative responses to these opportunities stands in sharp contrast to the 1978 Bonn Summit. Since failure to neutralize the French peasantry was a key element in the general failure of 1933, the contrast to the successful resolution of the 1986 "corn wars" (Odell) is also striking. These contrasts are certainly consistent with the idea that the half-century since 1933 has seen the emergence of a cognitive and institutional environment that makes synergistic strategies more possible and more likely.

Eichengreen and Uzan highlight two factors in the 1933 failure that seem likely to have changed over time. The first is a lack of shared conceptual frameworks. With the British convinced that deflation was the primary problem and the French convinced that it was exchange rate instability, agreeing on a mutually beneficial strategy was difficult. Either theory could have been a basis for a mutually beneficial agreement, but neither side was capable of seeing the world the way the other saw it. Post–World War II economic negotiations are often characterized by differences over the relative importance of different factors, but 1933-style stark disagreements on the roots of economic problems have become increasingly unusual, first in West-West negotiations and more recently in East-West and North-South bargaining. A shared diagnosis is a good first step in finding a synergistic deal that will allow the emergence of an agreement.

Eichengreen and Uzan also connect the 1933 economic failure to the absence of transnational alliances. They argue that transnational linkages among interest groups, while not entirely absent, were much less important than in the post–World War II world. A denser network of transnational alliances could have facilitated the emergence of conceptual frameworks shared across international boundaries. The presence of a network of transnational alliances also increases the array of possible synergistic bargains. (Though, as we have seen, specific transnational actors are not automatically supporters of agreements that impinge on their interests.) In the global context of 1933, private transnational actors could neither play a role in the emergence of common conceptual frameworks nor contribute to the construction of synergistic bargains.

Insofar as transnational networks help create opportunities for synergistic issue-linkage, a shift in the relative frequency of negotiations focused on economic as opposed to territorial-security issues will increase such opportunities. Our cases show clearly that territorial conflicts between long-term military adversaries are least likely to evoke the complex domestic divisions that make synergistic issue-linkage possible. Issues of sovereignty and national security generate few transnational alliances.

Bargains about trade, investment, and labor flows may evoke bitter distributional contention, but they create opportunities for synergistic linkages. If it is true, as seems plausible, that adversarial negotiations over territory and formal sovereignty represent a declining proportion of current negotiations, the tendency toward an increasing role for synergistic strategies follows.

Snyder's analysis of the evolution of the Berlin crisis dovetails nicely with this analysis. He shows that even in an arena where transnational alliances were absent, and bargaining was dominated by hostile competing claims to territorial sovereignty, there has been a shift toward greater use of synergistic issue-linkage. In the immediate post–World War II period, questions of territory and sovereignty completely dominated Berlin negotiations. Synergistic strategies were primitive or nonexistent, whereas the denouement in the Gorbachev era saw the integration of economic and security issues and intensified (though not necessarily successful) efforts to discover synergistic linkages.

If these arguments are sound, the rise of an integrative perspective reflects the growing proportion of negotiations which in fact require such a perspective as much as it reflects enhanced perceptiveness on the part of analysts. The demise of bipolarity should accelerate this trend, further shrinking the domain of international negotiations to which an analysis that brackets domestic politics can legitimately be applied.

One important caveat must be added to this picture of the evolution of a global bargaining context. Increased opportunities for synergistic issue-linkage may mean fewer purely zero-sum negotiating situations, but our cases certainly do not paint a Panglossian picture of movement toward an ever more benign global context. A world dominated by economic negotiations, shaped by the interaction of state leaders and private transnational alliances and aimed at discovering synergistic linkages, is definitely preferable to a world of zero-sum confrontations over security issues. It is also a world with a better chance of securing the collective goods that international regimes can provide and realizing welfare gains through the resolution of "coordination problems." But it is not a world free of coercive outcomes and welfare losses. As French maize-growers, small American construction firms, and Brazilian computer manufacturers are acutely aware, even a world of synergistic bargaining has losers.

Losers are inevitable, whether or not bargaining is synergistic, and agreements with losers can have welfare-enhancing effects overall. Still, there are two features of the distribution of losers that give a slightly ominous tinge to the "new world order" as projected from our cases. First, even within our sample, which was biased toward the underrepresentation of cases lacking a cooperative element, North-South cases, both economic and noneconomic, were dominated by coercive bargaining.[15]

Being "tough" may be laudable in some cases (e.g., Carter's coercive pursuit of human rights), but the possibility that coercive bargaining will predominate in North-South negotiations cannot be ignored and may well have negative welfare implications in the long run.

The tendency toward the increasing marginalization of domestically-oriented economic interests, noted in the previous section, while it increases the probability of successful agreements, may be a negative trend from a welfare point of view. Given that labor is inherently more domestic in its orientation than capital, agreements that marginalize domestic interests may well have regressive distributional effects. Since none of our cases analyze the impact of agreements on the interests of labor per se, this aspect of the world of synergistic bargains remains to be explored.

The ambiguous welfare implications of synergistic bargaining need to be clarified, but they do not change our main conclusion. The recent evolution of the global context of international bargaining makes the task of building an integrative approach to diplomacy and domestic politics more urgent. It is not just that diplomacy is increasingly perceived as double-edged, it has become so in reality. The rise of integrative perspectives is not simply a result of the development of more sophisticated intellectual models, it also results from real changes in the world we are trying to explain.

CHALLENGES AND OPPORTUNITIES

Projecting the implications of our findings for future research is as important as reflecting on what was accomplished. These findings demonstrate the value of building an integrative approach. Moreover, the version of the integrative approach explored here works. Even Lakatos would have to consider it a progressive research program.[16] It elucidates otherwise confusing outcomes, extends the scope of the empirical evidence for which it is possible to provide an account, and, most important, generates additional puzzles. How should the suggestive and often counter-intuitive findings that flow from a cumulative look at these cases affect future research? What general avenues of investigation might the approach and finding call forth?

The "puzzle-generating" capacity of the approach is easy to illustrate concretely. The specific propositions discussed in this chapter offer myriad leads to be followed up and numerous ambiguities to be resolved. They present themselves as a set of specific challenges to those interested in pushing ahead with the construction of an integrative approach. None of the propositions generated by the project are "cut and dried"; all point to further inquiry; all offer scope for refinement and extension. Three illustrations should suffice:

1. Sometimes the interests of transnational actors lay in the success of agreements, but often they did not. A differentiation of transnational actors was suggested to help account for this ambiguity, but the relationship still begs for further specification. The question has now become: What kinds of transnational alliances enhance the probability of forging state-to-state agreements? Or, under what conditions do state-to-state agreements generate opposition from transnational actors?

2. The necessity for ratification and lack of opportunities for "COG collusion" put statesmen at a disadvantage when they took the role of hawk. But hawks are sometimes successful in imposing the agreements they seek. This suggests a new set of questions; for example: What configurations of domestic interests enable statesmen to pursue "hawkish" aims despite the domestic costs of foreign threats?

3. Synergistic linkages have been identified as a potential source of leverage for promoting domestic restructuring, especially at the sectoral levels. Yet, with the exception of the airline case (Milner), the evidence for domestic restructuring was hardly conclusive. Following some of our cases further (e.g., Moravcsik's arms collaboration), and adding others, could help answer the question: When are synergistic linkages a sufficient condition for the promotion of domestic restructuring?

The project's potential heuristic contribution is as great at the level of general research strategy as it is at the level of specific findings. General implications for future research strategies can be illustrated nicely by two examples: the clear opportunity for adding systematic longitudinal comparisons and the obvious challenge posed by the "COG-centric" focus will be used to make the point.

The absence of a systematic historical dimension in construction of the project's case-set begs for complementary research bringing comparative evidence to bear on the longitudinal questions that we could only answer in a speculative way. Is there really a twentieth-century trajectory leading in the direction of greater opportunities for synergistic linkage? Does this imply greater ease in overcoming "coordination problems" and corresponding greater scope for positive-sum solutions in international negotiations? Serious exploration of the issue of longitudinal change would require more than a few additional cases. A diverse set of "most similar" pairs, divided not by success and failure but by time period, would allow future researchers to attack this issue directly. Exploring the consequences of the end of bipolarity from an integrative, two-level perspective would be a particularly rewarding version of this agenda. Given the greater prominence of coercive bargaining in our North-South as opposed to West-West cases, regional diversity would be one essential element in the design of a case-set.

The persistence with which the COG is portrayed by the project's findings as an independent factor linking international and domestic politics poses a challenge for other researchers that is hard to ignore. The results reported here begin and end with that assumption. Others should challenge it, just as the work reported here challenged the assumption that the outcomes of international bargaining can be accounted for without recourse to an integrative analysis. Has the focus on leadership gone too far, pointing research uncritically down a slippery slope that leads to the idiosyncratic, personalistic "first-image" explanations rejected by systemic realists a generation ago? Is it possible to integrate international and domestic dynamics more directly and parsimoniously, without delving into the strategies undertaken by chief executives in pursuit of goals generated by their own political histories, structural positions, and ideological visions? Such a challenge could be mounted initially simply by reanalyzing the cases that have been presented here. Demonstrating that a "directly integrative" paradigm could explain these results more parsimoniously would be an achievement. If the same paradigm could explain additional cases as well, it would establish the challenge as successful.

Whether these results stimulate longitudinal extensions or whether they provoke a successful challenge, they will have served their function. Building an integrative approach to international and domestic politics is not a task that can be disposed of by one set of scholars—several generations are a more likely measure of the required investment. An integrative approach is the right tack; ignoring the links that bind together international and domestic considerations would be intellectually disastrous. That much is hard to deny. Beyond that, all results must be considered vulnerable hypotheses, not consecrated canon.

This chapter is really a collective product. It not only grew out of the work of individual chapter writers, but is based more specifically on the ideas that emerged in an intensive week-long meeting of all the project participants in June of 1990, after individual contributions had been drafted. The synthesis of this discussion provided in Robert Putnam's notes was essential in shaping this chapter's structure. Jeff Frieden's contribution during the meeting should also be underlined. Earlier versions were revised in the light of critical comments by Miles Kahler, Lisa Martin, Andy Moravcsik, John Odell, and, of course, my fellow editors. The keen eye and careful comments of Brian Folk were crucial in sharpening the final draft.

NOTES

1. Eichengreen and Uzan on the 1933 World Economic Conference.
2. While in many cases the referent for "COG" is an individual leader, it often

makes sense to conceptualize the COG as a (relatively small) group of central decision-makers within which particular decisions are generated with varying degrees of collective input.

3. The issues dealt with in this first section are selected from the set of issues outlined in the Introduction under the headings "The Manipulation of Domestic Constraints" and "The Preferences of Statesmen."

4. Thomas C. Schelling, *The Strategy of Conflict* (Cambridge, Mass: Harvard University Press, 1960).

5. This section deals with a selection of the issues covered in the Introduction under the headings "Domestic Politics and International Bargaining" and "Strategies Employed by Domestic Groups."

6. The "state-centric" character of the vision that emerged from this project may seem ironic in view of Putnam's criticisms of this approach, but it should be emphasized that "state strength," which is the concept Putnam specifically criticizes, did *not* in fact prove useful in our version of the integrative approach.

7. See Appendix and Introduction to this volume, and Schelling, *The Strategy of Conflict.*

8. Even in the armaments case (Moravcsik), which mixes economics and security, it is once again the state apparatus, not domestic companies, that sets the agenda in pursuit of international agreement.

9. Obviously the assumption that constituency preferences can be summed to a "median preference" does considerable violence to the realities of coalition politics, as, e.g., Snyder's analysis of Khrushchev's attempts to construct a coalition out of groups with contradictory interests illustrates.

10. Eichenberg makes this point very clearly in his analysis of the twists and turns of U.S. and German leaders on the INF issue.

11. "Why should State consult us?" the head of the industry association complained. "They represent the Japanese. . . . They're the enemy for us just as the Japanese are." (Krauss, p. 286.)

12. Highlighting domestic hostility to the agreement and consequent uncertainty about what is ratifiable is obviously a variant on "tied hands." The fact that uncertainty, especially when it can be independently verified across boundaries, seems more effective than a flat assertion of tied hands is a subtlety worth pursuing further.

13. When actors like IBM are in question, the distinction between a "transnational actor" and a "transnational alliance" becomes moot. As the traditional term "multinational corporation" implies, such firms contain transnational alliances inside their own organizational skin. They may be alliances in which the part of the organization based in the country of the firm's origin exercises hegemony, but parts of the company are nonetheless actors in many different polities.

14. Since BOAC is state-owned, the alliance was not strictly speaking private, but BOAC acted essentially as a private actor rather than as an agent of government.

15. Both of Martin and Sikkink's cases (Argentina and Guatemala), the U.S. and Nicaragua (Pastor), and the U.S. and Brazil (Odell) were all clearly examples of coercive bargaining. Most would also consider IMF bargaining with Somalia

and Jamaica (see Kahler) as coercive. This leaves only Carter and Torrijos (Pastor) as an example of cooperative bargaining. Camp David (see Stein) is of course also an example of cooperative bargaining, but from the U.S. side negotiations were driven by bipolar security concerns more than by North-South issues.

16. Imre Lakatos, *The Methodology of Scientific Research Programmes* (Cambridge, Eng.: Cambridge University Press, 1978).

APPENDIX

Diplomacy and Domestic Politics
The Logic of Two-Level Games

Robert D. Putnam

INTRODUCTION: THE ENTANGLEMENTS OF DOMESTIC AND INTERNATIONAL POLITICS

Domestic politics and international relations are often somehow entangled, but our theories have not yet sorted out the puzzling tangle. It is fruitless to debate whether domestic politics really determine international relations, or the reverse. The answer to that question is clearly "Both, sometimes." The more interesting questions are "When?" and "How?" This paper offers a theoretical approach to this issue, but I begin with a story that illustrates the puzzle.

One illuminating example of how diplomacy and domestic politics can become entangled culminated at the Bonn Summit Conference of 1978.[1] In the mid-1970s, a coordinated program of global reflation, led by the "locomotive" economies of the United States, Germany, and Japan, had been proposed to foster Western recovery from the first oil shock.[2] This proposal had received a powerful boost from the incoming Carter Administration and was warmly supported by the weaker countries, as well as the Organization for Economic Cooperation and Development and many private economists, who argued that it would overcome international payments imbalances and speed growth all around. On the other hand, the Germans and the Japanese protested that prudent and successful economic managers should not be asked to bail out spendthrifts. Meanwhile, Jimmy Carter's ambitious National Energy Program remained deadlocked in Congress, while Helmut Schmidt led a chorus of complaints about the Americans' uncontrolled appetite for imported oil and their apparent unconcern about the falling dollar. All sides conceded that the world economy was in serious trouble, but it was not clear which

431

was more to blame—tight-fisted German and Japanese fiscal policies, or slack-jawed U.S. energy and monetary policies.

At the Bonn Summit, however, a comprehensive package deal was approved, the clearest case yet of a summit that left all participants happier than when they arrived. Helmut Schmidt agreed to additional fiscal stimulus, amounting to 1 percent of GNP; Jimmy Carter committed himself to decontrol domestic oil prices by the end of 1980; and Takeo Fukuda pledged new efforts to reach a 7-percent growth rate. Secondary elements in the Bonn accord included French and British acquiescence in the Tokyo Round trade negotiations; Japanese undertakings to foster import growth and restrain exports; and a generic American promise to fight inflation. All in all, the Bonn Summit produced a balanced agreement of unparalleled breadth and specificity. More remarkably, virtually all parts of the package were actually implemented.

Most observers at the time welcomed the policies agreed to at Bonn, although in retrospect there has been much debate about the economic wisdom of this package deal. However, my concern here is not whether the deal was wise economically, but how it became possible politically. My research suggests, first, that the key governments at Bonn adopted policies different from those that they would have pursued in the absence of international negotiations—but second, that agreement was possible only because a powerful minority within each government actually favored on domestic grounds the policy being demanded internationally.

Within Germany, a political process catalyzed by foreign pressures was surreptitiously orchestrated by expansionists inside the Schmidt government. Contrary to the public mythology, the Bonn deal was not forced on a reluctant or "altruistic" Germany. In fact, officials in the Chancellor's Office and the Economics Ministry, as well as in the Social Democratic Party and the trade unions, had argued privately in early 1978 that further stimulus was domestically desirable, particularly in view of the approaching 1980 elections. However, they had little hope of overcoming the opposition of the Finance Ministry, the Free Democratic Party (part of the government coalition), and the business and banking community, especially the leadership of the Bundesbank. Publicly, Helmut Schmidt posed as reluctant to the end. Only his closest advisors suspected the truth: that the Chancellor "let himself be pushed" into a policy that he privately favored, but would have found costly and perhaps impossible to enact without the summit's package deal.

Analogously, in Japan a coalition of business interests, the Ministry of International Trade and Industry (MITI), the Economic Planning Agency, and some expansion-minded politicians within the Liberal Democratic Party pushed for additional domestic stimulus, using U.S. pressure as one of their prime arguments against the stubborn resistance of the Ministry of Finance (MOF). Without internal divisions in Tokyo, it is unlikely that the foreign demands would have been met; but without the external pressure, it is even more unlikely that the expansionists could have overridden the powerful MOF: "Seventy percent foreign pressure, 30 percent internal politics," was the disgruntled judgment of one MOF insider; "Fifty-fifty," guessed an official from MITI.[3]

In the American case, too, internal politicking reinforced, and was reinforced by, the international pressure. During the summit preparations, American negotiators occasionally invited their foreign counterparts to put more pressure on the Americans to reduce oil imports. Key economic officials within the administration favored a tougher energy policy, but they were opposed by the President's closest political aides, even after the summit. Moreover, Congressional opponents continued to stymie oil price decontrol, as they had under both Nixon and Ford. Finally, in April 1979, the President decided on gradual administrative decontrol, bringing U.S. prices up to world levels by October 1981. His domestic advisors thus won a postponement of this politically costly move until after the 1980 presidential election, but in the end, virtually every one of the pledges made at Bonn was fulfilled. Both proponents and opponents of decontrol agree that the summit commitment was at the center of the administration's heated intramural debate during the winter of 1978–79, and instrumental in the final decision.[4]

In short, the Bonn accord represented genuine international policy coordination. Significant policy changes were pledged and implemented by the key participants. Moreover—although this counterfactual claim is necessarily harder to establish—those policy changes would very probably not have been pursued (certainly not on the same scale and within the same time frame) in the absence of the international agreement. Within each country, one faction supported the policy shift being demanded of its country internationally, but that faction was initially outnumbered. Thus, international pressure was a necessary condition for these policy shifts. On the other hand, without domestic resonance, international forces would not have sufficed to produce the accord, no matter how balanced and intellectually persuasive the overall package. In the end, each leader believed that what he was doing was in his nation's interest—and probably in his own political interest, too, even though not all his aides agreed.[5] Yet without the summit accord, he probably would not (or could not) have changed policies so easily. In that sense, the Bonn deal successfully meshed domestic and international pressures.

Neither a purely domestic nor a purely international analysis could account for this episode. Interpretations cast in terms either of domestic causes and international effects ("second-image")[6] or of international causes and domestic effects ("second-image-reversed")[7] would represent merely "partial equilibrium" analyses and would miss an important part of the story, namely, how the domestic politics of several countries became entangled via an international negotiation. The events of 1978 illustrate that we must aim instead for "general equilibrium" theories that account simultaneously for the interaction of domestic and international factors. This paper suggests a conceptual framework for understanding how diplomacy and domestic politics interact.

DOMESTIC-INTERNATIONAL ENTANGLEMENTS: THE STATE OF THE ART

Much of the existing literature on relations between domestic and international affairs consists either of ad hoc lists of countless "domestic influences" on foreign policy or of generic observations that national and international affairs are somehow "linked."[8] James Rosenau was one of the first scholars to call attention to this area, but his elaborate taxonomy of "linkage politics" generated little cumulative research, except for a flurry of work correlating domestic and international "conflict behavior."[9]

A second stream of relevant theorizing began with the work by Karl Deutsch and Ernst Haas on regional integration.[10] Haas, in particular, emphasized the impact of parties and interest groups on the process of European integration, and his notion of "spillover" recognized the feedback between domestic and international developments. However, the central dependent variable in this work was the hypothesized evolution of new supranational institutions, rather than specific policy developments, and when European integration stalled, so did this literature. The intellectual heirs of this tradition, such as Joseph Nye and Robert Keohane, emphasized interdependence and transnationalism, but the role of domestic factors slipped more and more out of focus, particularly as the concept of international regimes came to dominate the subfield.[11]

The "bureaucratic politics" school of foreign-policy analysis initiated another promising attack on the problem of domestic-international interaction. As Graham Allison noted, "Applied to relations between nations, the bureaucratic politics model directs attention to intra-national games, the overlap of which constitutes international relations."[12] Nevertheless, the nature of this "overlap" remained unclarified, and the theoretical contribution of this literature did not evolve much beyond the principle that bureaucratic interests matter in foreign-policy-making.

More recently, the most sophisticated work on the domestic determinants of foreign policy has focused on "structural" factors, particularly "state strength." The landmark works of Peter Katzenstein and Stephen Krasner, for example, showed the importance of domestic factors in foreign economic policy. Katzenstein captured the essence of the problem: "The main purpose of all strategies of foreign economic policy is to make domestic policies compatible with the international political economy."[13] Both authors stressed the crucial point that central decision-makers ("the state") must be concerned simultaneously with domestic and international pressures.

More debatable, however, is their identification of "state strength" as the key variable of interest. Given the difficulties of measuring "state strength," this approach courts tautology,[14] and efforts to locate individual countries on this ambiguous continuum have proved problematic.[15] "State strength," if reinterpreted as merely the opposite of governmental fragmentation, is no doubt of some interest in the comparative study of foreign policy. However, Gourevitch is quite correct to complain that "the strong state-weak state argument suggests that . . . the identity of the governing coalition does not matter. This is a very apolitical argument."[16] Moreover, because "state structures" (as conceived in this literature) vary little from issue to issue or from year to year, such explanations are ill-suited for explaining differences across issues or across time (unless "time" is measured in decades or centuries). A more adequate account of the domestic determinants of foreign policy and international relations must stress *politics*: parties, social classes, interest groups (both economic and non-economic), legislators, and even public opinion and elections, not simply executive officials and institutional arrangements.[17]

Some work in the "state-centric" genre represents a unitary-actor model run amok. "The central proposition of this paper," notes one recent study, "is that the state derives its interests from and advocates policies consistent with the international system at all times and under all circumstances."[18] In fact, on nearly all important issues "central decision-makers" disagree about what the national interest and the international context demand. Even if we arbitrarily exclude the legislature from "the state" (as much of this literature does), it is wrong to assume that the executive is unified in its views. Certainly this was true in *none* of the states involved in the 1978 negotiations. What was "the" position of the German or Japanese state on macroeconomic policy in 1978, or of the American state on energy policy? If the term "state" is to be used to mean "central decision-makers," we should treat it as a plural noun: not "the state, it . . ." but "the state, they. . . ." Central executives have a special role in mediating domestic and international pressures precisely because they are directly exposed to both spheres, not because they are united on all issues nor because they are insulated from domestic politics.

Thus the state-centric literature is an uncertain foundation for theorizing about how domestic and international politics interact. More interesting are recent works about the impact of the international economy on domestic politics and domestic economic policy, such as those by Alt, Evans, Gourevitch, and Katzenstein.[19] These case studies, representing diverse methodological approaches, display a theoretical sophistication on the international-to-domestic causal connection far greater than is characteristic of comparable studies on the domestic-to-international half of the loop. Nevertheless, these works do not purport to account for instances of reciprocal causation, nor do they examine cases in which the domestic politics of several countries became entangled internationally.

In short, we need to move beyond the mere observation that domestic factors influence international affairs and vice versa, and beyond simple catalogs of instances of such influence, to seek theories that integrate both spheres, accounting for the areas of entanglement between them.

TWO-LEVEL GAMES: A METAPHOR FOR DOMESTIC-INTERNATIONAL INTERACTIONS

Over two decades ago, Richard Walton and Robert McKersie offered a "behavioral theory" of social negotiations that is strikingly applicable to international conflict and cooperation.[20] They pointed out, as all experienced negotiators know, that the unitary-actor assumption is often radically misleading. As Robert Strauss said of the Tokyo Round trade negotiations: "During my tenure as Special Trade Representative, I spent as much time negotiating with domestic constituents (both industry and labor) and members of the U.S. Congress as I did negotiating with our foreign trading partners."[21]

The politics of many international negotiations can usefully be conceived as a two-level game. At the national level, domestic groups pursue their interests by pressuring the government to adopt favorable policies, and politicians seek power by constructing coalitions among those groups. At the international level, national governments seek to maximize their own ability to satisfy domestic pressures, while minimizing the adverse consequences of foreign developments. Neither of the two games can be ignored by central decision-makers, so long as their countries remain interdependent, yet sovereign.

Each national political leader appears at both game boards. Across the international table sit his foreign counterparts, and at his elbows sit diplomats and other international advisors. Around the domestic table behind him sit party and parliamentary figures, spokesmen for domestic agencies, representatives of key interest groups, and the leader's own political advisors. The unusual complexity of this two-level game is that moves that are rational for a player at one board (such as raising energy prices, conceding territory, or limiting auto imports) may be impolitic for that same player at the other board. Nevertheless, there are powerful incentives for consistency between the two games. Players (and kibitzers) will tolerate some differences in rhetoric between the two games, but in the end either energy prices rise or they don't.

The political complexities for the players in this two-level game are staggering. Any key player at the international table who is dissatisfied with the outcome may upset the game board; and conversely, any leader who fails to satisfy his fellow players at the domestic table risks being evicted from his seat. On occasion, however, clever players will spot a move on one board that will trigger realignments on other boards, enabling them to achieve otherwise unattainable objectives. This "two-table" metaphor captures the dynamics of the 1978 negotiations better than any model based on unitary national actors.

Other scholars have noted the multiple-game nature of international relations. Like Walton and McKersie, Daniel Druckman has observed that a negotiator "attempts to build a package that will be acceptable both to the other side and to his bureaucracy." However, Druckman models the domestic and international processes separately and concludes that "the interaction between the processes . . . remains a topic for investigation."[22] Robert Axelrod has proposed a "Gamma paradigm," in which the U.S. president pursues policies vis-à-vis the Soviet Union with an eye toward maximizing his popularity at home. However, this model disregards domestic cleavages, and it postulates that one of the international actors—the Soviet leadership—cares only about international gains and faces no domestic constraint, while the other—the U.S. president—cares only about domestic gains, except insofar as his public evaluates the international competition.[23] Probably the most interesting empirically based theorizing about the connection between domestic and international bargaining is that of Glenn Snyder and Paul Diesing. Though working in the neo-realist tradition with its conventional assumption of unitary actors, they found that, in fully half of the crises they studied, top decision-makers were *not* unified. They concluded that prediction of international outcomes is significantly improved by understanding internal bargaining, especially with respect to minimally acceptable compromises.[24]

Metaphors are not theories, but I am comforted by Max Black's observation that "perhaps every science must start with metaphor and end with algebra; and perhaps without the metaphor there would never have been any algebra."[25] Formal analysis of any game requires well-defined rules, choices, payoffs, players, and information—and even then, many simple two-person, mixed-motive games have no determinate solution. Deriving analytic solutions for two-level games will be a difficult challenge. In what follows I hope to motivate further work on that problem.

TOWARD A THEORY OF RATIFICATION:
THE IMPORTANCE OF "WIN-SETS"

Consider the following stylized scenario that might apply to any two-level game. Negotiators representing two organizations meet to reach an agreement between them, subject to the constraint that any tentative agreement must be ratified by their respective organizations. The negotiators might be heads of government representing nations, for example, or labor and management representatives, or party leaders in a multi-party coalition, or a finance minister negotiating with an IMF team, or leaders of a House-Senate conference committee, or ethnic-group leaders in a consociational democracy. For the moment, we shall presume that each side is represented by a single leader or "chief negotiator," and that this individual has no independent policy preferences, but seeks simply to achieve an agreement that will be attractive to his constituents.[26]

It is convenient analytically to decompose the process into two stages:

1. Bargaining between the negotiators, leading to a tentative agreement; call that Level I.
2. Separate discussions within each group of constituents about whether to ratify the agreement; call that Level II.

This sequential decomposition into a negotiation phase and a ratification phase is useful for purposes of exposition, although it is not descriptively accurate. In practice, expectational effects will be quite important. There are likely to be prior consultations and bargaining at Level II to hammer out an initial position for the Level I negotiations. Conversely, the need for Level II ratification is certain to affect the Level I bargaining. In fact, expectations of rejection at Level II may abort negotiations at Level I without any formal action at Level II. For example, even though both the American and Iranian governments seem to have favored an arms-for-hostages deal, negotiations collapsed as soon as they became public and thus liable to de facto "ratification." In many negotiations, the two-level process may be iterative, as the negotiators try out possible agreements and probe their constituents' views. In more complicated cases, as we shall see later, the constituents' views may themselves evolve in the course of the negotiations. Nevertheless, the requirement that any Level I agreement must, in the end, be ratified at Level II imposes a crucial theoretical link between the two levels.

"Ratification" may entail a formal voting procedure at Level II, such as the constitutionally required two-thirds vote of the U.S. Senate for ratifying treaties, but I use the term generically to refer to any decision-process at Level II that is required to endorse or implement a Level I agreement, whether formally or informally. It is sometimes convenient to think of ratification as a parliamentary function, but that is not essential. The actors at Level II may represent bureaucratic agencies, interest groups, social classes, or even "public opinion." For example, if labor unions in a debtor country withhold necessary cooperation from an austerity program that the government has negotiated with the IMF, Level II ratification of the agreement may be said to have failed; ex ante expectations about that prospect will surely influence the Level I negotiations between the government and the IMF.

Domestic ratification of international agreements might seem peculiar to democracies. As the German Finance Minister recently observed, "The limit of expanded cooperation lies in the fact that we are democracies, and we need to secure electoral majorities at home."[27] However, ratification need not be "democratic" in any normal sense. For example, in 1930 the Meiji Constitution was interpreted as giving a special role to the Japanese military in the ratification of the London Naval Treaty;[28] and during the ratification of any agreement between Catholics and Protestants in Northern Ireland, presumably the IRA would throw its power onto the scales. We need only stipulate that, for purposes of counting "votes" in the ratification process, different forms of political power can be reduced to some common denominator.

The only formal constraint on the ratification process is that since the identical agreement must be ratified by both sides, a preliminary Level I agreement cannot be amended at Level II without reopening the Level I negotiations. In other words, final ratification must be simply "voted" up or down; any modification to the Level I agreement counts as a rejection, unless that modification is approved by all other parties to the agreement.[29] Congresswoman Lynn Martin captured the logic of ratification when explaining her support for the 1986 tax-reform bill as it emerged from the conference committee: "As worried as I am about what this bill does, I am even more worried about the current code. The choice today is not between this bill and a perfect bill; the choice is between this bill and the death of tax reform."[30]

Given this set of arrangements, we may define the "win-set" for a given Level II constituency as the set of all possible Level I agreements that would "win"—that is, gain the necessary majority among the constituents—when simply voted up or down.[31] For two quite different reasons, the contours of the Level II win-sets are very important for understanding Level I agreements.

First, *larger win-sets make Level I agreement more likely,* ceteris paribus.[32] By definition, any successful agreement must fall within the Level II win-sets of each of the parties to the accord. Thus, agreement is possible only if those win-sets overlap; and the larger each win-set, the more likely they are to overlap. Conversely, the smaller the win-sets, the greater the risk that the negotiations will break down. For example, during the prolonged prewar Anglo-Argentine negotiations over the Falklands/Malvinas, several tentative agreements were rejected in one capital or the other for domestic political reasons; when it became clear that the initial British and Argentine win-sets did not overlap at all, war became virtually inevitable.[33]

A brief, but important, digression: *The possibility of failed ratification suggests that game-theoretical analyses should distinguish between* voluntary *and* involuntary *defection.* Voluntary defection refers to reneging by a rational egoist in the absence of enforceable contracts—the much-analyzed problem posed, for example, in the prisoner's dilemma and other dilemmas of collective action. Involuntary defection instead reflects the behavior of an agent who is unable to deliver on a promise because of failed ratification. Even though these two types of behavior may be difficult to disentangle in some instances, the underlying logic is quite different.

The prospects for international cooperation in an anarchic, "self-help" world are often said to be poor because "unfortunately, policy-makers generally have an incentive to cheat."[34] However, as Axelrod, Keohane, and others have pointed out, the temptation to defect can be dramatically reduced among players who expect to meet again.[35] If policy-makers in an anarchic world were in fact constantly tempted to cheat, certain features of the 1978 story would be very anomalous. For example, even though the Bonn agreement was negotiated with exquisite care, it contained no provisions for temporal balance, sequencing, or partial conditionality that might have protected the parties from unexpected defection. Moreover, the Germans and the Japanese irretrievably enacted their parts of the bargain more than six months before the President's action on oil price decontrol and nearly two years before that decision was implemented. Once they had done so, the temptation to the President to renege should have been overpowering, but in fact virtually no one on either side of the decontrol debate within the administration dismissed the Bonn pledge as irrelevant. In short, the Bonn "promise" had political weight, because reneging would have had high political and diplomatic costs.

However, in any two-level game, the credibility of an official commitment may be low, even if the reputational costs of reneging are high, for the negotiator may be unable to guarantee ratification. The failure of Congress to ratify abolition of the "American Selling Price" as previously agreed during the Kennedy Round of trade negotiations is one classic instance; another is the inability of Japanese Prime Minister Sato to deliver on a promise made to President Nixon during the "Textile Wrangle."[36] A key obstacle to Western economic coordination in 1985–87 was the Germans' fear that the Reagan Administration would be politically unable to carry out any commitment it might make to cut the U.S. budget deficit, no matter how well-intentioned the President.

Unlike concerns about voluntary defection, concern about "deliverability" was a prominent element in the Bonn negotiations. In the postsummit press conference, President Carter stressed that "Each of us has been careful not to promise more than he can deliver." A major issue throughout the negotiations was Carter's own ability to deliver on his energy commitments. The Americans worked hard to convince the others, first, that the President was under severe domestic political constraints on energy issues, which limited what he could promise; but second, that he could deliver what he was prepared to promise. The negotiators in 1978 seemed to follow this presumption about one another: "He will do what he has promised, so long as what he has promised is clear and within his power."

Involuntary defection, and the fear of it, can be just as fatal to prospects for cooperation as voluntary defection. Moreover, in some cases, it may be difficult, both for the other side and for outside analysts, to distinguish voluntary and involuntary defection, particularly since a strategic negotiator might seek to misrepresent a voluntary defection as involuntary. Such behavior is itself presumably subject to some reputational constraints, although it is an important empirical question how far reputations generalize from collectivities to negotiators, and vice versa. Credibility (and thus the ability to strike deals) at Level I is enhanced by a negotiator's (demonstrated) ability to "deliver" at Level II; this was a major strength of Robert Strauss in the Tokyo Round negotiations.[37]

Involuntary defection can only be understood within the framework of a two-level game. Thus, to return to the issue of win-sets, the smaller the win-sets, the greater the risk of involuntary defection, and hence the more applicable the literature about dilemmas of collective action.[38]

The second reason why win-set size is important is that *the relative size of the respective Level II win-sets will affect the distribution of the joint gains from the international bargain.* The larger the perceived win-set of a negotiator, the more he can be "pushed around" by the other Level I negotiators. Conversely, a small domestic win-set can be a bargaining advantage: "I'd like to accept your proposal, but I could never get it accepted at home." Lamenting the domestic constraints under which one must operate is (in the words of one experienced British diplomat) "the natural thing to say at the beginning of a tough negotiation."[39]

This general principle was, of course, first noted by Thomas Schelling nearly thirty years ago:

> The power of a negotiator often rests on a manifest inability to make concessions and meet demands. . . . When the United States Government negotiates with other governments . . . if the executive branch negotiates under legislative authority, with its position constrained by law, . . . then the executive branch has a firm position that is visible to its negotiating partners. . . . [Of course, strategies such as this] run the risk of establishing an immovable position that goes beyond the ability of the other to concede, and thereby provoke the likelihood of stalemate or breakdown.[40]

Writing from a strategist's point of view, Schelling stressed ways in which win-sets may be manipulated; but even when the win-set itself is beyond the negotiator's control, he may exploit its leverage. A Third World leader whose domestic position is relatively weak (Argentina's Alfonsin?) should be able to drive a better bargain with his international creditors, other things being equal, than one whose domestic standing is more solid (Mexico's de la Madrid?).[41] The difficulties of winning Congressional ratification are often exploited by American negotiators. During the negotiation of the Panama Canal Treaty, for example, "the Secretary of State warned the Panamanians several times . . . that the new treaty would have to be acceptable to at least sixty-seven senators," and "Carter, in a personal letter to Torrijos, warned that further concessions by the United States would seriously threaten chances for Senate ratification."[42] Precisely to forestall such tactics, opponents may demand that a negotiator ensure himself "negotiating room" at Level II before opening the Level I negotiations.

The "sweet-and-sour" implications of win-set size are summarized in Figure 1, representing a simple zero-sum game between X and Y. X_M and Y_M represent the maximum outcomes for X and Y, respectively, while X_1 and Y_1 represent the minimal outcomes that could be ratified. At this stage, any agreement in the range between X_1 and Y_1 could be ratified by both parties. If the win-set of Y were contracted to, say, Y_2 (perhaps by requiring a larger majority for ratification), outcomes between Y_1 and Y_2 would no longer be feasible, and the range of feasible agreements would thus be truncated in Y's favor. However, if Y, emboldened by this success, were to reduce its win-set still further to Y_3 (perhaps

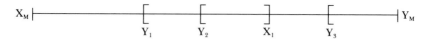

Figure 1. Effects of reducing win-set size

by requiring unanimity for ratification), the negotiators would suddenly find themselves deadlocked, for the win-sets no longer overlap at all.[43]

DETERMINANTS OF THE WIN-SET

It is important to understand what circumstances affect win-set size. Three sets of factors are especially important:

Level II preferences and coalitions
Level II institutions
Level I negotiators' strategies

Let us consider each in turn.

1. The Size of the Win-set Depends on the Distribution of Power, Preferences, and Possible Coalitions among Level II Constituents

Any testable two-level theory of international negotiation must be rooted in a theory of domestic politics, that is, a theory about the power and preferences of the major actors at Level II. This is not the occasion for even a cursory evaluation of the relevant alternatives, except to note that the two-level conceptual framework could in principle be married to such diverse perspectives as Marxism, interest-group pluralism, bureaucratic politics, and neo-corporatism. For example, arms negotiations might be interpreted in terms of a bureaucratic politics model of Level II politicking, while class analysis or neo-corporation might be appropriate for analyzing international macroeconomic coordination.

Abstracting from the details of Level II politics, however, it is possible to sketch certain principles that govern the size of the win-sets. For example, the lower cost of "no-agreement" to constituents, the smaller the win-set.[44] Recall that ratification pits the proposed agreement, *not* against an array of other (possibly attractive) alternatives, but only against "no-agreement."[45] No-agreement often represents the status quo, although in some cases no-agreement may in fact lead to a worsening situation; that might be a reasonable description of the failed ratification of the Versailles Treaty.

Some constituents may face low costs from no-agreement, and others high costs, and the former will be more skeptical of Level I agreements than the latter. Members of two-wage-earner families should be readier to strike, for example, than sole breadwinners, and small-town barbers should be more isolationist than international bankers. In this sense, some constituents may offer either generic opposition to, or generic support for, Level I agreements, more or less independently of the specific content of the agreement, although naturally other constituents' decisions about ratification will be closely conditioned on the specifics. The size of the win-set (and thus the negotiating room of the Level I negotiator) depends on the relative size of the "isolationist" forces (who oppose international cooperation in general) and the "internationalists" (who offer "all-purpose" support). All-purpose support for international agreements is probably greater in smaller, more dependent countries with more open economies, as compared to more self-sufficient countries, like the United States, for most of whose citizens the costs of no-agreement are generally lower. Ceteris paribus, more self-sufficient states with smaller win-sets should make fewer international agreements and drive harder bargains in those that they do make.

In some cases, evaluation of no-agreement may be the *only* significant disagreement among the Level II constituents, because their interests are relatively homogeneous. For example, if oil imports are to be limited by an agreement among the consuming nations—the sort of accord sought at the Tokyo summit of 1979, for example—then presumably every constituent would prefer to maximize his nation's share of the available supply, although some constituents may be more reluctant than others to push too hard, for fear of losing the agreement entirely. Similarly, in most wage negotiations, the interests of constituents (either workers or shareholders) are relatively homogeneous, and the most significant cleavage within the Level II constituencies is likely to be between "hawks" and "doves," depending on their willingness to risk a strike. (Walton and McKersie refer to these as "boundary" conflicts, in which the negotiator is caught between his constituency and the external organization.) Other international examples in which domestic interests are relatively homogeneous except for the evaluation of no-agreement might include the SALT talks, the Panama Canal Treaty negotiations, and the Arab-Israeli conflict. A negotiator is unlikely to face criticism at home that a proposed agreement reduces the opponents' arms too much, offers too little compensation for foreign concessions, or contains too few security guarantees for the other side, although in each case opinions may differ on how much to risk a negotiating deadlock in order to achieve these objectives.

The distinctive nature of such "homogeneous" issues is thrown into sharp relief by contrasting them to cases in which constituents' preferences are more heterogeneous, so that any Level I agreement bears unevenly on them. Thus, an internationally coordinated reflation may encounter domestic opposition *both* from those who think it goes too far (bankers, for example) *and* from those who think it does not go far enough (unions, for example). In 1919, some Americans opposed the Versailles Treaty because it was too harsh on the defeated powers, and others because it was too lenient.[46] Such patterns are even more common, as we shall shortly see, where the negotiation involves multiple issues, such as an arms agreement that involves tradeoffs between seaborne and airborne weapons, or a labor agreement that involves tradeoffs between take-home pay and pensions. (Walton and McKersie term these "factional" conflicts, because the negotiator is caught between contending factions within his own organization.)

The problems facing Level I negotiators dealing with a *homogeneous* (or "boundary") conflict are quite different from those facing negotiators dealing with a *heterogeneous* (or "factional") conflict. In the former case, the more the negotiator can win at Level I—the higher his national oil allocation, the deeper the cuts in Soviet throw-weight, the lower the rent he promises for the Canal, and so on—the better his odds of winning ratification. In such cases, the negotiator may use the implicit threat from his own hawks to maximize his gains (or minimize his losses) at Level I, as Carter and Vance did in dealing with the Panamanians. Glancing over his shoulder at Level II, the negotiator's main problem in a homogeneous conflict is to manage the discrepancy between his constituents' expectations and the negotiable outcome. Neither negotiator is likely to find much sympathy for the enemy's demands among his own constituents, or much support for his constituents' positions in the enemy camp. The effect of domestic division, embodied in hard-line opposition from hawks, is to raise the risk of involuntary defection and thus to impede agreement at Level I. The common belief that domestic politics is inimical to international cooperation no doubt derives from such cases.

The task of a negotiator grappling instead with a *heterogeneous* conflict is more complicated, but potentially more interesting. Seeking to maximize the chances of ratification, he cannot follow a simple "the more, the better" rule of thumb; imposing more severe reparations on the Germans in 1919 would have gained some votes at Level II, but lost others, as would hastening the decontrol of domestic oil prices in 1978. In some cases, these lines of cleavage within the Level II constituencies will cut across the Level I division, and the Level I negotiator may find silent allies at his opponent's domestic table. German labor unions might welcome foreign pressure on their own government to adopt a more expansive fiscal policy, and Italian bankers might welcome international demands for a more austere Italian monetary policy. Thus transnational alignments may emerge, tacit or explicit, in which domestic interests pressure their respective governments to adopt mutually supportive policies. This is, of course, my interpretation of the 1978 Bonn Summit accord.

In such cases, domestic divisions may actually improve the prospects for international cooperation. For example, consider two different distributions of constituents' preferences as between three alternatives: A, B, and no-agreement. If 45 percent of the constituents rank these A > no-agreement > B, 45 percent rank them B > no-agreement > A, and 10 percent rank them B > A > no-agreement, then both A and B are in the win-set, even though B would win in a simple Level-II-only game. On the other hand, if 90 percent rank the alternatives A > no-agreement > B, while 10 percent still rank them B > A > no-agreement, then only A is in the win-set. In this sense, a government that is internally divided is more likely to be able to strike a deal internationally than one that is firmly committed to a single policy.[47] Conversely, to impose binding *ex ante* instructions on the negotiators in such a case might exclude some Level I outcomes that would, in fact, be ratifiable in both nations.[48]

Thus far we have implicitly assumed that all eligible constituents will participate in the ratification process. In fact, however, participation rates vary across groups and across issues, and this variation often has implications for the size of the win-set. For example, when the costs and/ or benefits of a proposed agreement are relatively concentrated, it is reasonable to expect that those constituents whose interests are most affected will exert special influence on the ratification process.[49] One reason why Level II games are more important for trade negotiations than in monetary matters is that the "abstention rate" is higher on international monetary issues than on trade issues.[50]

The composition of the active Level II constituency (and hence the character of the win-set) also varies with the politicization of the issue. Politicization often activates groups who are less worried about the costs of no-agreement, thus reducing the effective win-set. For example, politicization of the Panama Canal issue seems to have reduced the negotiating flexibility on both sides of the diplomatic table.[51] This is one reason why most professional diplomats emphasize the value of secrecy to successful negotiations. However, Woodrow Wilson's transcontinental tour in 1919 reflected the opposite calculation, namely, that by expanding the active constituency he could ensure ratification of the Versailles Treaty, although in the end this strategy proved fruitless.[52]

Another important restriction of our discussion thus far has been the assumption that the negotiations involve only one issue. Relaxing this assumption has powerful consequences for the play at both levels.[53] Various groups at Level II are likely to have quite different preferences on the several issues involved in a multi-issue negotiation. As a general rule, the group with the greatest interest in a specific issue is also likely to hold the most extreme position on that issue. In the Law of the Sea negotiations, for example, the Defense Department felt most strongly about sea-lanes, the Department of the Interior about sea-bed mining rights, and so on.[54] If each group is allowed to fix the Level I negotiating position for "its" issue, the resulting package is almost sure to be "non-negotiable" (that is, non-ratifiable in opposing capitals).[55]

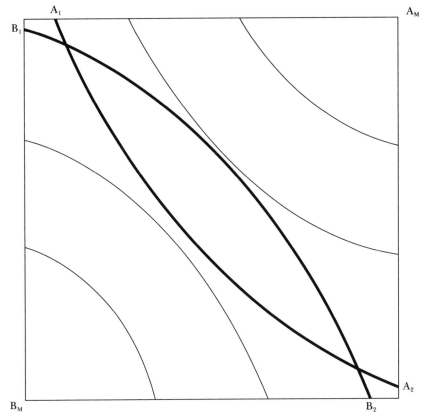

Figure 2. Political indifference curves for two-issue negotiation

Thus, the chief negotiator is faced with tradeoffs across different issues: how much to yield on mining rights in order to get sea-lane protection, how much to yield on citrus exports to get a better deal on beef, and so on. The implication of these tradeoffs for the respective win-sets can be analyzed in terms of iso-vote or "political indifference" curves. This technique is analogous to conventional indifference-curve analysis, except that the operational measure is vote loss, not utility loss. Figure 2 provides an illustrative Edgeworth box analysis.[56] The most-preferred outcome for A (the outcome which wins unanimous approval from both the beef industry and the citrus industry) is the upper right-hand corner (A_M), and each curve concave to point A_M represents the locus of all possible tradeoffs between the interests of ranchers and farmers, such that the net vote in favor of ratification at A's Level II is constant. The bold contour A_1-A_2 represents the minimal vote necessary for ratification by A, and the wedge-shaped area northeast of A_1-A_2 represents A's win-set. Similarly, B_1-B_2 represents the outcomes that are minimally ratifiable by B, and the lens-shaped area between A_1-A_2 and B_1-B_2 represents the set of feasible agreements. Although additional subtleties (such as the nature of the "contract curve") might be extracted from this sort of analysis, the central point is simple: the possibility of package deals open up a rich array of strategic alternatives for negotiators in a two-level game.

One kind of issue linkage is absolutely crucial to understanding how domestic and international politics can become entangled.[57] Suppose that a majority of constituents at Level II oppose a given policy (say, oil price decontrol), but that some members of that majority would be willing to switch their vote on that issue in return for more jobs (say, in export industries). If bargaining is limited to Level II, that tradeoff is not technically feasible, but if the chief negotiator can broker an international deal that delivers more jobs (say, via faster growth abroad), he can, in effect, overturn the initial outcome at the domestic table. Such a transnational issue linkage was a crucial element in the 1978 Bonn accord.

Note that this strategy works not by changing the preferences of any domestic constituents, but rather by creating a policy option (such as faster export growth) that was previously beyond domestic control. Hence, I refer to this type of issue linkage at Level I that alters the feasible outcomes at Level II as *synergistic linkage*. For example, "In the Tokyo Round, . . . nations used negotiation to achieve internal reform in situations where constituency pressures would otherwise prevent action without the pressure (and tradeoff benefits) that an external partner could provide."[58] Economic interdependence multiplies the opportunities for altering domestic coalitions (and thus policy outcomes) by expanding the set of feasible alternatives in this way—in effect, creating political entanglements across national boundaries. Thus, we should expect synergistic linkage (which is, by definition, explicable only in terms of two-level analysis) to become more frequent as interdependence grows.

2. The Size of the Win-set Depends on the Level II Political Institutions

Ratification procedures clearly affect the size of the win-set. For example, if a two-thirds vote is required for ratification, the win-set will almost certainly be smaller than if only a simple majority is required. As one experienced observer has written: "Under the Constitution, thirty-four of the one hundred senators can block ratification of any treaty. This is an unhappy and unique feature of our democracy. Because of the effective veto power of a small group, many worthy agreements have been rejected, and many treaties are never considered for ratification."[59] As noted earlier, the U.S. separation of powers imposes a tighter constraint on the American win-set than is true in many other countries. This increases the bargaining power of American negotiators, but it also reduces the scope for international cooperation. It raises the odds for involuntary defection and makes potential partners warier about dealing with the Americans.

The Trade Expansion Act of 1974 modified U.S. ratification procedures in an effort to reduce the likelihood of Congressional tampering with the final deal and hence to reassure America's negotiating partners. After the American Selling Price fiasco, it was widely recognized that piecemeal Congressional ratification of any new agreement would inhibit international negotiation. Hence, the 1974 act guaranteed a straight up-or-down vote in Congress. However, to satisfy Congressional sensitivities, an elaborate system of private-sector committees was established to improve communication between the Level I negotiators and their Level II constituents, in effect coopting the interest groups by exposing them directly to the implications of their demands.[60] Precisely this tactic is described in the labor-management case by Walton and McKersie: "Instead of taking responsibility for directly persuading the principals [Level II constituents] to reduce their expectations, [the Level I negotiator] structures the situation so that they (or their more immediate representatives) will persuade themselves."[61]

Not all significant ratification practices are formalized; for example, the Japanese propensity for seeking the broadest possible domestic consensus before acting constricts the Japanese win-set, as contrasted with majoritarian political cultures. Other domestic political practices, too, can affect the size of the win-set. Strong discipline within the governing party, for example, increases the win-set by widening the range of agreements for which the Level I negotiator can expect to receive backing. For example, in the 1986 House-Senate conference committee on tax reform, the final bill was closer to the Senate version, despite (or rather, *because of*) Congressman Rostenkowski's greater control of his delegation, which increased the House win-set. Conversely, a weakening of party discipline across the major Western nations would, ceteris paribus, reduce the scope for international cooperation.

The recent discussion of "state strength" and "state autonomy" is relevant here. The greater the autonomy of central decision-makers from their Level II constituents, the larger their win-set and thus the greater the likelihood of achieving international agreement. For example, central bank insulation from domestic political pressures in effect increases the win-set and thus the odds for international monetary cooperation; recent proposals for an enhanced role for central bankers in international policy coordination rest on this point.[62] However, two-level analysis also implies that, ceteris paribus, the stronger a state is in terms of autonomy from domestic pressures, the *weaker* its relative bargaining position internationally. For example, diplomats representing an entrenched dictatorship are less able than representatives of a democracy to claim credibly that domestic pressures preclude some disadvantageous deal.[63] This is yet another facet of the disconcerting ambiguity of the notion of "state strength."

For simplicity of exposition, my argument is phrased throughout in terms of only two levels. However, many institutional arrangements require several levels of ratification, thus multiplying the complexity (but perhaps also the importance) of win-set analysis. Consider, for example, negotiations between the United States and the European Community over agricultural trade. According to the Treaty of Rome, modifications of the Common Agricultural Policy require unanimous ratification by the Council of Ministers, representing each of the member states. In turn, each of those governments must, in effect, win ratification for its decision within its own national arena; and in coalition governments, that process might also require ratification within each of the parties. Similarly, on the American side, ratification would (informally, at least) necessitate support from most, if not all, of the major agricultural organizations; and within those organizations, further ratification by key interests and regions might be required. At each stage, cleavage patterns, issue linkages, ratification procedures, side-payments, negotiator strategies, and so on, would need to be considered. At some point in this analytic regress the complexity of further decomposition would outweigh the advantages, but the example illustrates the need for careful thought about the logic of multiple-level games.

3. The Size of the Win-set Depends on the Strategies of the Level I Negotiators

Each Level I negotiator has an unequivocal interest in maximizing the other side's win-set, but with respect to his own win-set, his motives are mixed. The larger his win-set, the more easily he can conclude an agreement, but also the weaker his bargaining position vis-à-vis the other negotiator. This fact often poses a tactical dilemma. For example, one effective way to demonstrate commitment to a given position in Level I bargaining is to rally support from one's constituents (for example, holding a strike vote, talking about a "missile gap," or denouncing "unfair trading practices" abroad). On the other hand, such tactics may have irreversible effects on constituents' attitudes, hampering subsequent ratification of a compromise agreement.[64] Conversely, preliminary consultations at home, aimed at "softening up" one's constituents in anticipation of a ratification struggle, can undercut a negotiator's ability to project an implacable image abroad.

Nevertheless, disregarding these dilemmas for the moment, and assuming that a negotiator wishes to expand his win-set in order to encourage ratification of an agreement, he may exploit both conventional side-payments and generic "good will." The use of side-payments to attract marginal supporters is, of course, quite familiar in game theory, as well as in practical politics. For example, the Carter White House offered many inducements (such as public works projects) to help persuade wavering senators to ratify the Panama Canal Treaty.[65] In a two-level game, the side-payments may come from unrelated domestic sources, as in this case, or they may be received as part of the international negotiation.

The role of side-payments in international negotiations is well known. However, the two-level approach emphasizes that the value of an international side-payment should be calculated in terms of its marginal contribution to the likelihood of ratification rather than in terms of its overall value to the recipient nation. What counts at Level II is not total national costs and benefits, but their incidence, relative to existing coalitions and proto-coalitions. An across-the-board trade concession (or still worse, a concession on a product of interest to a committed free-trade congressman) is less effective than a concession (even one of lesser intrinsic value) that tips the balance with a swing-voter. Conversely, trade retaliation should be targeted neither at free-traders nor at confirmed protectionists, but at the uncommitted.

An experienced negotiator familiar with the respective domestic tables should be able to maximize the cost-effectiveness (to him and his constituents) of the concessions that he must make to ensure ratification abroad, as well as the cost-effectiveness of his own demands and threats, by targeting his initiatives with an eye to their Level II incidence, both at home and abroad. In this endeavor Level I negotiators are often in collusion, since each has an interest in helping the other to get the final deal ratified. In effect, they are moving jointly toward points of tangency between their respective political indifference curves. The empirical frequency of such targeting in trade negotiations and trade wars, as well as in other international negotiations, would be a crucial test of the relative merits of conventional unitary-actor analysis and the two-level approach proposed here.[66]

In addition to the use of specific side-payments, a chief negotiator whose political standing at home is high can more easily win ratification of his foreign initiatives. Although generic good will cannot guarantee ratification, as Woodrow Wilson discovered, it is useful in expanding the win-set and thus fostering Level I agreement, for it constitutes a kind of "all-purpose glue" for his supporting coalition. Walton and McKersie cite members of the United Auto Workers who, speaking of their revered leader, Walter Reuther, said, "I don't understand or agree with this profit-sharing idea, but if the Red Head wants it, I will go along."[67] The Yugoslav negotiator in the Trieste dispute later discounted the difficulty of persuading irredentist Slovenes to accept the agreement, since "the government [i.e., Tito] can always influence public opinion if it wants to."[68]

Note that each Level I negotiator has a strong interest in the popularity of his opposite number, since Party A's popularity increases the size of his win-set, and thus increases both the odds of success and the relative bargaining leverage of Party B. Thus, negotiators should normally be expected to try to reinforce one another's standing with their respective constituents.

Partly for this reason, and partly because of media attention, participation on the world stage normally gives a head of government a special advantage vis-à-vis his or her domestic opposition. Thus, although international policy coordination is hampered by high transaction costs, heads of government may also reap what we might term "transaction benefits." Indeed, the recent evolution of Western summitry, which has placed greater emphasis on publicity than on substance, seems designed to appropriate these "transaction benefits" without actually seeking the sort of agreements that might entail transaction costs.[69]

Higher-status negotiators are likely to dispose of more side-payments and more "good will" at home, and hence foreigners prefer to negotiate with a head of government rather than with a lower official. In purely distributive terms, a nation might have a bargaining advantage if its chief negotiator were a mere clerk. Diplomats are acting rationally, not merely symbolically, when they refuse to negotiate with a counterpart of inferior rank. America's negotiating partners have reason for concern whenever the American president is domestically weakened.

UNCERTAINTY AND BARGAINING TACTICS

Level I negotiators are often badly misinformed about Level II politics, particularly on the opposing side. In 1978 the Bonn negotiators were usually wrong in their assessments of domestic politics abroad; for example, most American officials did not appreciate the complex domestic game that Chancellor Schmidt was playing over the issue of German reflation. Similarly, Snyder and Diesing report that "decision-makers in our cases only occasionally attempted such assessments, and when they tried they did pretty miserably. . . . Governments generally do not do well in analyzing each other's internal politics in crises [and, I would add, in normal times], and indeed it is inherently difficult."[70] Relaxing the assumption of perfect information to allow for uncertainty has many implications for our understanding of two-level games. Let me illustrate a few of these implications.

Uncertainty about the size of a win-set can be both a bargaining device and a stumbling block in two-level negotiation. In purely distributive Level I bargaining, negotiators have an incentive to understate their own win-sets. Since each negotiator is likely to know more about his own Level II table than his opponent does, the claim has some plausibility. This is akin to a tactic that Snyder and Diesing describe, when negotiators seek to exploit divisions within their own government by saying, in effect, "You'd better make a deal with me, because the alternative to me is even worse."[71]

On the other hand, uncertainty about the opponent's win-set increases one's concern about the risk of involuntary defection. Deals can only be struck if each negotiator is convinced that the proposed deal lies within his opposite number's win-set, and thus will be ratified. Uncertainty about Party A's ratification lowers the expected value of the agreement to Party B, and thus Party B will demand more generous side-payments from Party A than would be needed under conditions of certainty. In fact, Party B has an incentive to feign doubt about Party A's ability to deliver, precisely in order to extract a more generous offer.[72]

Thus, a utility-maximizing negotiator must seek to convince his opposite number that his own win-set is "kinky," that is, that the proposed deal is certain to be ratified, but that a deal slightly more favorable to the opponent is unlikely to be ratified. For example, on the energy issue in 1978, by sending Senator Byrd on a personal mission to Bonn before the summit, and then by discussing his political problems in a lengthy tete-à-tete with the Chancellor, Carter sought successfully to convince Schmidt that immediate decontrol was politically impossible, but that decontrol by 1981 was politically do-able. Kinky win-sets may be more credible if they pivot on what Schelling calls a "prominent" solution, such as a 50-50 split, for such outcomes may be distinctly more "salable" at home. Another relevant tactic is for the negotiator actually to submit a trial agreement for ratification, in order to demonstrate that it is not in his win-set.

Uncertainty about the contours of the respective "political indifference curves" thus has strategic uses. On the other hand, when the negotiators are seeking novel packages that might improve both sides' positions, misrepresentation of one's win-set can be counterproductive. Creative solutions that expand the scope for joint gain and improve the odds of ratification are likely to require fairly accurate information about constituents' preferences and points of specific neuralgia. The analysis of two-level games offers many illustrations of Zartman's observation that all negotiation involves "the controlled exchange of partial information."[73]

RESTRUCTURING AND REVERBERATION

Formally speaking, game-theoretic analysis requires that the structure of issues and payoffs be specified in advance. In reality, however, much of what happens in any bargaining situation involves attempts by the players to restructure the game and to alter one another's perceptions of the costs of no-agreement and the benefits of proposed agreements. Such tactics are more difficult in two-level games than in conventional negotiations, because it is harder to reach constituents on the other side with persuasive messages. Nevertheless, governments do seek to expand one another's win-sets. Much ambassadorial activity—wooing opinion leaders, establishing contact with opposition parties, offering foreign aid to a friendly, but unstable, government, and so on—has precisely this function. When Japanese officials visit Capitol Hill, or British diplomats lobby Irish-American leaders, they are seeking to relax domestic constraints that might otherwise prevent the administration from cooperating with their governments.

Another illuminating example of actions by a negotiator at the opposing Level II to improve the odds of ratification occurred during the 1977 negotiations between the International Monetary Fund and the Italian government. Initial IMF demands for austerity triggered strong opposition from the unions and left-wing parties. Although the IMF's bargaining position at Level I appeared strong, the Fund's negotiator sought to achieve a broader consensus within Italy in support of an agreement, in order to forestall involuntary defection. Accordingly, after direct consultations with the unions and leftist leaders, the IMF restructured its proposal to focus on long-term investment and economic recovery (incidentally, an interesting example of targeting), without backing off from its short-term demands. Ironically, the initial Communist support for this revised agreement subsequently collapsed because of conflicts between moderate and doctrinaire factions within the party, illustrating the importance of multilevel analysis.[74]

In some instances, perhaps even unintendedly, international pressures "reverberate" within domestic politics, tipping the domestic balance and thus influencing the international negotiations. Exactly this kind of reverberation characterized the 1978 Summit negotiations. Dieter Hiss, the German sherpa and one of those who believed that a stimulus program was in Germany's own interest, later wrote that summits change national policy

> only insofar as they mobilize and/or change public opinion and the attitude of political groups. . . . Often that is enough, if the balance of opinion is shifted, providing a bare majority for the previously stymied actions of a strong minority. . . . No country violates its own interests, but certainly the definition of its interests can change through a summit with its possible tradeoffs and give-and-take.[75]

From the point of view of orthodox social-choice theory, reverberation is problematic, for it implies a certain interconnectedness among the utility functions of independent actors, albeit across different levels of the game. Two rationales may be offered to explain reverberation among utility-maximizing egoists. First, in a complex, interdependent, but often unfriendly world, offending foreigners may be costly in the long run. "To get along, go along" may be a rational maxim. This rationale is likely to be more common the more dependent (or interdependent) a nation, and it is likely to be more persuasive to Level II actors who are more exposed internationally, such as multinational corporations and international banks.

A second rationale takes into account cognitive factors and uncertainty. It would be a mistake for political scientists to mimic most economists' disregard for the suasive element in negotiations.[76] Given the pervasive uncertainty that surrounds many international issues, messages from abroad can change minds, move the undecided, and hearten those in the domestic minority. As one reluctant late-comer to the "locomotive" cause in 1978 explained his conversion, "In the end, even the Bank for International Settlements [the cautious Basel organization of central bankers] supported the idea of coordinated reflation." Similarly, an enthusiastic advocate of the program welcomed the international pressure as providing a useful "tailwind" in German domestic politics.

Suasive reverberation is more likely among countries with close relations, and is probably more frequent in economic than in political-military negotiations. Communiqués from the Western summits are often cited by participants to domestic audiences as a way of legitimizing their policies. After one such statement by Chancellor Schmidt, one of his aides privately characterized the argument as "not intellectually valid, but politically useful." Conversely, it is widely believed by summit participants that a declaration contrary to a government's current policy could be used profitably by its opponents. Recent Congressional proposals to ensure greater domestic publicity for international commentary on national economic policies (including hitherto confidential IMF recommendations) turn on the idea that reverberation might increase international cooperation.[77]

Reverberation as discussed thus far implies that international pressure expands the domestic win-set and facilitates agreement. However, reverberation can also be negative, in the sense that foreign pressure may create a domestic backlash. Negative reverberation is probably less common empirically than positive reverberation, simply because foreigners are likely to forgo public pressure if it is recognized to be counterproductive. Cognitive balance theory suggests that international pressure is more likely to reverberate negatively if its source is generally viewed by domestic audiences as an adversary rather than an ally. Nevertheless, predicting the precise effect of foreign pressure is admittedly difficult, although empirically, reverberation seems to occur frequently in two-level games.

The phenomenon of reverberation (along with synergistic issue linkage of the sort described earlier) precludes one attractive short-cut to modeling two-level games. If national preferences were exogenous from the point of view of international relations, then the domestic political game could be modeled separately, and the "outputs" from that game could be used as the "inputs" to the international game.[78] The division of labor between comparative politics and international relations could continue, though a few curious observers might wish to keep track of the play on both tables. But if international pressures reverberate within domestic politics, or if issues can be linked synergistically, then domestic outcomes are not exogenous, and the two levels cannot be modeled independently.

THE ROLE OF THE CHIEF NEGOTIATOR

In the stylized model of two-level negotiations outlined here, the chief negotiator is the only formal link between Level I and Level II. Thus far, I have assumed that the chief negotiator has no independent policy views, but acts merely as an honest broker, or rather as an agent on behalf of his constituents. That assumption powerfully simplifies the analysis of two-level games. However, as principal-agent theory reminds us, this assumption is unrealistic.[79] Empirically, the preferences of the chief negotiator may well diverge from those of his constituents. Two-level negotiations are costly and risky for the chief negotiator, and they often interfere with his other priorities, so it is reasonable to ask what is in it for him.

The motives of the chief negotiator include:

1. Enhancing his standing in the Level II game by increasing his political resources or by minimizing potential losses. For example, a head of government may seek the popularity that he expects to

accrue to him if he concludes a successful international agreement, or he may anticipate that the results of the agreement (for example, faster growth or lower defense spending) will be politically rewarding.

2. Shifting the balance of power at Level II in favor of domestic policies that he prefers for exogenous reasons. International negotiations sometimes enable government leaders to do what they privately wish to do, but are powerless to do domestically. Beyond the now-familiar 1978 case, this pattern characterizes many stabilization programs that are (misleadingly) said to be "imposed" by the IMF. For example, in the 1974 and 1977 negotiations between Italy and the IMF, domestic conservative forces exploited IMF pressure to facilitate policy moves that were otherwise infeasible internally.[80]

3. To pursue his own conception of the national interest in the international context. This seems the best explanation of Jimmy Carter's prodigious efforts on behalf of the Panama Canal Treaty, as well as of Woodrow Wilson's ultimately fatal commitment to the Versailles Treaty.

It is reasonable to presume, at least in the international case of two-level bargaining, that the chief negotiator will normally give primacy to his domestic calculus, if a choice must be made, not least because his own incumbency often depends on his standing at Level II. Hence, he is more likely to present an international agreement for ratification, the less of his own political capital he expects to have to invest to win approval, and the greater the likely political returns from a ratified agreement.

This expanded conception of the role of the chief negotiator implies that he has, in effect, a veto over possible agreements. Even if a proposed deal lies within his Level II win-set, that deal is unlikely to be struck if he opposes it.[81] Since this proviso applies on both sides of the Level I table, the actual international bargaining set may be narrower—perhaps much narrower—than the overlap between the Level II win-sets. Empirically, this additional constraint is often crucial to the outcome of two-level games. One momentous example is the fate of the Versailles Treaty. The best evidence suggests, first, that perhaps 80 percent of the American public *and* of the Senate in 1919 favored ratification of the treaty, if certain reservations were attached; and second, that those reservations were acceptable to the other key signatories, especially Britain and France. In effect, it was Wilson himself who vetoed this otherwise ratifiable package, telling the dismayed French Ambassador, "I shall consent to nothing."[82]

Yet another constraint on successful two-level negotiation derives from the leader's existing domestic coalition. Any political entrepreneur has a fixed investment in a particular pattern of policy positions and a particular supporting coalition. If a proposed international deal threatens that investment, or if ratification would require him to construct a different coalition, the chief negotiator will be reluctant to endorse it, even if (judged abstractly) it could be ratified. Politicians may be willing to risk a few of their normal supporters in the cause of ratifying an international agreement, but the greater the potential loss, the greater their reluctance.

In effect, the fixed costs of coalition-building thus imply this constraint on the win-set: How great a realignment of prevailing coalitions at Level II would be required to ratify a particular proposal? For example, a trade deal may expand export opportunities for Silicon Valley, but harm Aliquippa. This is fine for a chief negotiator (for example, Reagan?) who can easily add Northern California yuppies to his support coalition and who has no hope of winning Aliquippa steelworkers anyhow. But a different chief negotiator with a different support coalition (for example, Mondale?) might find it costly or even impossible to convert the gains from the same agreement into politically usable form. Similarly, in the 1978 "neutron bomb" negotiations between Bonn and Washington, "asking the United States to deploy [these weapons] in West Germany might have been possible for a Christian Democratic government; for a Social Democratic government, it was nearly impossible."[83] Under such circumstances, simple "median-voter" models of domestic influences on foreign policy may be quite misleading.

Relaxing the assumption that the chief negotiator is merely an honest broker, negotiating on behalf of his constituents, opens the possibility that the constituents may be more eager for an agreement (or more worried about "no-agreement") than he is. Empirical instances are not hard to find: in early 1987, European publics were readier to accept Gorbachev's "double-zero" arms-control proposal than European leaders, just as in the early 1970s the American public (or at least the politically active public) was more eager for a negotiated end to the Vietnam War than was the Nixon Administration. As a rule, the negotiator retains a veto over any proposed agreement in such cases. However, if the negotiator's own domestic standing (or indeed, his incumbency) would be threatened if he were to reject an agreement that falls within his Level II win-set, and if this is known to all parties, then the other side at Level I gains considerable leverage. Domestic U.S. discontent about the Vietnam War clearly affected the agreement reached at the Paris talks.[84] Conversely, if the constituents are (believed to be) hard-line, then a leader's domestic weakness becomes a diplomatic asset. In 1977, for example, the Americans calculated that "a delay in negotiating a treaty . . . endangered [Panamanian President Omar] Torrijos' position; and Panama without Torrijos most likely would have been an impossible negotiating partner."[85] Similarly, in the 1954 Trieste negotiations, the weak Italian government claimed that "'Unless something is done in our favor in Trieste, we can lose the election.' That card was played two or three times [reported the British negotiator later], and it almost always took a trick."[86]

My emphasis on the special responsibility of central executives is a point of affinity between the two-level game model and the "state-centric" literature, even though the underlying logic is different. In this "Janus" model of domestic-international interactions, transnational politics are less prominent than in some theories of interdependence.[87] However, to disregard "cross-table" alliances at Level II is a considerable simplification, and it is more misleading the lower the political visibility of the issue, and the more frequent the negotiations between the governments involved.[88] Empirically, for example, two-level games in the European Community are influenced by many direct ties among Level II participants, such as national agricultural spokesmen. In some cases, the same multinational actor may actually appear at more than one Level II table. In negotiations over mining concessions in some less developed countries, for example, the same multinational corporation may be consulted privately by both the home and host governments. In subsequent work on the two-level model, the strategic implications of direct communication between Level II players should be explored.

CONCLUSION

The most portentous development in the fields of comparative politics and international relations in recent years is the dawning recognition among practitioners in each field of the need to take into account entanglements between the two. Empirical illustrations of reciprocal influence between domestic and international affairs abound. What we need now are concepts and theories that will help us organize and extend our empirical observations.

Analysis in terms of two-level games offers a promising response to this challenge. Unlike state-centric theories, the two-level approach recognizes the inevitability of domestic conflict about what the "national interest" requires. Unlike the "second-image" or the "second-image-reversed," the two-level approach recognizes that central decision-makers strive to reconcile domestic and international imperatives simultaneously. As we have seen, statesmen in this predicament face distinctive strategic opportunities and strategic dilemmas.

This theoretical approach highlights several significant features of the links between diplomacy and domestic politics, including:

the important distinction between voluntary and involuntary defection from international agreements;

the contrast between issues on which domestic interests are homogeneous, simply pitting hawks against doves, and issues on which domestic interests are more heterogeneous, so that domestic cleavage may actually foster international cooperation;

the possibility of synergistic issue linkage, in which strategic moves at one game-table facilitate unexpected coalitions at the second table;

the paradoxical fact that institutional arrangements which strengthen decision-makers at home may weaken their international bargaining position, and vice versa;

the importance of targeting international threats, offers, and side-payments with an eye toward their domestic incidence at home and abroad;

the strategic uses of uncertainty about domestic politics, and the special utility of "kinky win-sets";

the potential reverberation of international pressures within the domestic arena;

the divergences of interest between a national leader and those on whose behalf he is negotiating—and in particular, the international implications of his fixed investments in domestic politics.

Two level games seem a ubiquitous feature of social life, from Western economic summitry to diplomacy in the Balkans, and from coalition politics in Sri Lanka to legislative maneuvering on Capitol Hill. Far-ranging empirical research is needed now to test and deepen our understanding of how such games are played.

This essay was first published in *International Organization* 42 (Summer 1988): 427–460. An earlier version was delivered at the 1986 Annual Meeting of the American Political Science Association. For criticisms and suggestions, I am indebted to Robert Axelrod, Nicholas Bayne, Henry Brady, James A. Caporaso, Barbara Crane, Ernst B. Haas, Stephan Haggard, C. Randall Henning, Peter B. Kenen, Robert O. Keohane, Stephen D. Krasner, Jacek Kugler, Lisa Martin, John Odell, Robert Powell, Kenneth A. Shepsle, Steven Stedman, Peter Yu, members of research seminars at the Universities of Iowa, Michigan, and Harvard, and two anonymous reviewers. I am grateful to the Rockefeller Foundation for enabling me to complete this research.

NOTES

1. The following account is drawn from Robert D. Putnam and C. Randall Henning, "The Bonn Summit of 1978: A Case Study in Coordination" in

Richard N. Cooper et al., *Can Nations Agree? Issues in International Economic Cooperation* (Washington, D.C.: The Brookings Institution, October 1989), pp. 12–140; and Robert D. Putnam and Nicholas Bayne, *Hanging Together: Cooperation and Conflict in the Seven-Power Summits,* rev. ed. (Cambridge, Mass.: Harvard University Press, 1987), pp. 62–94.

2. Among interdependent economies, most economists believe, policies can often be more effective if they are internationally coordinated. For relevant citations, see Putnam and Bayne, *Hanging Together,* p. 24.

3. For a comprehensive account of the Japanese story, see I. M. Destler and Hisao Mitsuyu, "Locomotives on Different Tracks: Macroeconomic Diplomacy, 1977–1979," in I. M. Destler and Hideo Sato, eds., *Coping with U.S.-Japanese Economic Conflicts* (Lexington, Mass.: D. C. Heath, 1982).

4. For an excellent account of U.S. energy policy during this period, see G. John Ikenberry, "Market Solutions for State Problems: The International and Domestic Politics of American Oil Decontrol," *International Organization* 42 (Winter 1988): 151–177.

5. It is not clear whether Jimmy Carter fully understood the domestic implications of his Bonn pledge at the time. See Putnam and Henning, "The Bonn Summit," and Ikenberry, "Market Solutions."

6. Kenneth N. Waltz, *Man, the State, and War: A Theoretical Analysis* (New York: Columbia University Press, 1959).

7. Peter Gourevitch, "The Second Image Reversed: The International Sources of Domestic Politics," *International Organization* 32 (Autumn 1978): 881–911.

8. I am indebted to Stephan Haggard for enlightening discussions about domestic influences on international relations.

9. James Rosenau, "Toward the Study of National-International Linkages," in his *Linkage Politics: Essays on the Convergence of National and International Systems* (New York: Free Press, 1969); as well as his "Theorizing Across Systems: Linkage Politics Revisited," in Jonathan Wilkenfeld, ed., *Conflict Behavior and Linkage Politics* (New York: David McKay, 1973), esp. p. 49.

10. Karl W. Deutsch et al., *Political Community in the North Atlantic Area: International Organization in the Light of Historical Experience* (Princeton, N.J.: Princeton University Press, 1957); and Ernst B. Haas, *The Uniting of Europe: Political, Social, and Economic Forces, 1950–1957* (Stanford, Calif.: Stanford University Press, 1958).

11. Robert O. Keohane and Joseph S. Nye, *Power and Interdependence* (Boston: Little, Brown, 1977). On the regime literature, including its neglect of domestic factors, see Stephan Haggard and Beth Simmons, "Theories of International Regimes," *International Organization* 41 (Summer 1987): 491–517.

12. Graham T. Allison, *Essence of Decision: Explaining the Cuban Missile Crisis* (Boston: Little, Brown, 1971), p. 149.

13. Peter J. Katzenstein, ed., *Between Power and Plenty: Foreign Economic Policies of Advanced Industrial States* (Madison: University of Wisconsin Press, 1978), p. 4. See also Katzenstein, "International Relations and Domestic Structures: Foreign Economic Policies of Advanced Industrial States," *International Organization* 30

(Winter 1976): 1–45; Stephen D. Krasner, "United States Commercial and Monetary Policy: Unravelling the Paradox of External Strength and Internal Weakness," in Katzenstein, *Between Power and Plenty,* pp. 51–87; and Krasner, *Defending the National Interest: Raw Materials Investments and U.S. Foreign Policy* (Princeton, N.J.: Princeton University Press, 1978).

14. For example, see Krasner in Katzenstein, p. 55: "The central analytic characteristic that determines the ability of a state to overcome domestic resistance is its strength in relation to its own society."

15. Helen Milner, "Resisting the Protectionist Temptation: Industry and the Making of Trade Policy in France and the United States during the 1970s," *International Organization* 41 (Autumn 1987): 639–665.

16. Gourevitch, "The Second Image Reversed," p. 903.

17. In their more descriptive work, "state-centric" scholars are often sensitive to the impact of social and political conflicts, such as those between industry and finance, labor and business, and export-oriented versus import-competing sectors. See Katzenstein, *Between Power and Plenty,* pp. 333–336, for example.

18. David A. Lake, "The State as Conduit: The International Sources of National Political Action," paper delivered at the 1984 Annual Meeting of the American Political Science Association, p. 13.

19. James E. Alt, "Crude Politics: Oil and the Political Economy of Unemployment in Britain and Norway, 1970–1985," *British Journal of Political Science* 17 (April 1987): 149–199; Peter B. Evans, *Dependent Development: The Alliance of Multinational, State, and Local Capital in Brazil* (Princeton, N.J.: Princeton University Press, 1979); Peter Gourevitch, *Politics in Hard Times: Comparative Responses to International Economic Crises* (Ithaca, N.Y.: Cornell University Press, 1986); Peter J. Katzenstein, *Small States in World Markets: Industrial Policy in Europe* (Ithaca, N.Y.: Cornell University Press, 1985).

20. Richard E. Walton and Robert B. McKersie, *A Behavioral Theory of Labor Negotiations: An Analysis of a Social Interaction System* (New York: McGraw-Hill, 1965).

21. Robert S. Strauss, "Foreword," in Joan E. Twiggs, *The Tokyo Round of Multilateral Trade Negotiations: A Case Study in Building Domestic Support for Diplomacy* (Washington, D.C.: Georgetown University Institute for the Study of Diplomacy, 1987), p. vii. Former Secretary of Labor John Dunlop is said to have remarked that "Bilateral negotiations usually require three agreements—one across the table and one on each side of the table," as cited in Howard Raiffa, *The Art and Science of Negotiation* (Cambridge, Mass.: Harvard University Press, 1982), p. 166.

22. Daniel Druckman, "Boundary Role Conflict: Negotiation as Dual Responsiveness," in I. William Zartman, ed., *The Negotiation Process: Theories and Applications* (Beverly Hills, Calif.: Sage, 1978), vol. 1, pp. 100–101, 109. For a review of the social-psychological literature on bargainers as representatives, see Dean G. Pruitt, *Negotiation Behavior* (New York: Academic Press, 1981), pp. 41–43.

23. Robert Axelrod, "The Gamma Paradigm for Studying the Domestic Influence on Foreign Policy," paper delivered at the 1987 Annual Meeting of the International Studies Association.

24. Glenn H. Snyder and Paul Diesing, *Conflict Among Nations: Bargaining, Decision Making, and System Structure in International Crises* (Princeton, N.J.: Princeton University Press, 1977), pp. 510–525.

25. Max Black, *Models and Metaphors* (Ithaca, N.Y.: Cornell University Press, 1962), p. 242, as cited in Duncan Snidal, "The Game *Theory* of International Politics," *World Politics* 38 (October 1985): 36n.

26. To avoid unnecessary complexity, my argument throughout is phrased in terms of a single chief negotiator, although in many cases some of his responsibilities may be delegated to aides. Later in this paper I relax the assumption that the negotiator has no independent preferences.

27. Gerhardt Stoltenberg, *Wall Street Journal Europe*, Oct. 2, 1986, as cited in C. Randall Henning, *Macroeconomic Diplomacy in the 1980s: Domestic Politics and International Conflict Among the United States, Japan, and Europe*, Atlantic Paper no. 65 (New York: Croom Helm, for the Atlantic Institute for International Affairs, 1987), p. 1.

28. Ito Takashi, "Conflicts and Coalition in Japan, 1930: Political Groups and the London Naval Disarmament Conference," in Sven Groennings et al., eds., *The Study of Coalition Behavior* (New York: Holt, Rinehart, and Winston, 1970); Kobayashi Tatsuo, "The London Naval Treaty, 1930," in James W. Morley, ed., *Japan Erupts: The London Naval Conference and the Manchurian Incident, 1928–1932* (New York: Columbia University Press, 1984), pp. 11–117. I am indebted to William Jarosz for this example.

29. This stipulation is, in fact, characteristic of most real-world ratification procedures, such as House and Senate action on conference committee reports, although it is somewhat violated by the occasional practice of appending "reservations" to the ratification of treaties.

30. *New York Times*, Sept. 26, 1986.

31. For the conception of "win-set," see Kenneth A. Shepsle and Barry R. Weingast, "The Institutional Foundations of Committee Power," *American Political Science Review* 81 (March 1987): 85–104. I am indebted to Professor Shepsle for much help on this topic.

32. To avoid tedium, I do not repeat the "other things being equal" proviso in each of the propositions that follow. Under some circumstances, an expanded win-set might actually make practicable some outcome that could trigger a dilemma of collective action. See Vincent P. Crawford, "A Theory of Disagreement in Bargaining," *Econometrica* 50 (May 1982): 607–637.

33. The Sunday Times Insight Team, *The Falklands War* (London: Sphere, 1982); Max Hastings and Simon Jenkins, *The Battle for the Falklands* (New York: Norton, 1984); Alejandro Dabat and Luis Lorenzano, *Argentina: The Malvinas and the End of Military Rule* (London: Verso, 1984). I am indebted to Louise Richardson for these citations.

34. Matthew E. Canzoneri and Jo Anna Gray, "Two Essays on Monetary Policy in an Interdependent World," International Finance Discussion Paper no. 219 (Board of Governors of the Federal Reserve System, February 1983).

35. Robert Axelrod, *The Evolution of Cooperation* (New York: Basic Books, 1984); Robert O. Keohane, *After Hegemony: Cooperation and Discord in the World*

Political Economy (Princeton, N.J.: Princeton University Press, 1984), esp. p. 116; and the special issue of *World Politics*, "Cooperation Under Anarchy" (Kenneth A. Oye, ed.), 38 (October 1985): 1–254.

36. I. M. Destler, Haruhiro Fukui, and Hideo Sato, *The Textile Wrangle: Conflict in Japanese-American Relations, 1969–1971* (Ithaca, N.Y.: Cornell University Press, 1979), pp. 121–157.

37. Gilbert R. Winham, "Robert Strauss, the MTN, and the Control of Faction," *Journal of World Trade Law* 14 (September/October 1980): 377–397; and Winham, *International Trade and the Tokyo Round* (Princeton, N.J.: Princeton University Press, 1986).

38. This discussion implicitly assumes uncertainty about the contours of the win-sets on the part of the Level I negotiators—for if the win-sets were known with certainty, the negotiators would never propose for ratification an agreement that would be rejected.

39. Geoffrey W. Harrison, in John C. Campbell, ed., *Successful Negotiation: Trieste 1954* ((Princeton, N.J.: Princeton University Press, 1976), p. 62.

40. Thomas C. Schelling, *The Strategy of Conflict* (Cambridge, Mass.: Harvard University Press, 1960), pp. 19–28.

41. I am grateful to Lara Putnam for this example. For supporting evidence, see Robert R. Kaufman, "Democratic and Authoritarian Responses to the Debt Issue: Argentina, Brazil, Mexico," *International Organization* 39 (Summer 1985): 473–503.

42. William Mark Habeeb and I. William Zartman, *The Panama Canal Negotiations* (Washington, D.C.: Johns Hopkins Foreign Policy Institute, 1986), pp. 40, 42.

43. Several investigators in other fields have recently proposed models of linked games akin to this "two-level" game. Kenneth A. Shepsle and his colleagues have used the notion of "interconnected games" to analyze, for example, the strategy of a legislator simultaneously embedded in two games, one in the legislative arena and the other in the electoral arena. In this model, a given action is simultaneously a move in two different games, and one player maximizes the sum of his payoffs from the two games. See Arthur Denzau, William Riker, and Kenneth Shepsle, "Farquharson and Fenno: Sophisticated Voting and Home Style," *American Political Science Review* 79 (December 1985): 1117–1134; and Kenneth Shepsle, "Cooperation and Institutional Arrangements," paper delivered the Harvard–M.I.T. Conference on Institutional Change (Dedham, Mass., February 1986). This approach is similar to models recently developed by economists working in the "rational expectations" genre. In these models, a government contends simultaneously against other governments and against domestic trade unions over monetary policy. See, for example, Kenneth Rogoff, "Can International Monetary Policy Cooperation be Counterproductive?" *Journal of International Economics* 18 (May 1985): 199–217; and Roland Vaubel, "A Public Choice Approach to International Organization," *Public Choice* 51 (1986): 39–57. George Tsebelis ("Nested Games: The Cohesion of French Coalitions," *British Journal of Political Science* 18 [April 1988]: 145–170) has developed a theory of "nested games" in which two alliances play a competitive game to determine

total payoffs, while the individual players within each alliance contend over their shares. Fritz Sharpf ("A Game-Theoretical Interpretation of Inflation and Unemployment in Western Europe," *Journal of Public Policy* 7 [1988]: 227–257) interprets macroeconomic policy as the joint outcome of two simultaneous games; in one, the government plays against the unions, while in the other it responds to the anticipated reactions of the electorate. James E. Alt and Barry Eichengreen ("Parallel and Overlapping Games: Theory and an Application to the European Gas Trade," *Economics and Politics* 1 [1989]: 119–144) offer a broader typology of linked games, distinguishing between "parallel" games, in which "the same opponents play against one another at the same time in more than one arena," and "overlapping" games, which arise "when a particular player is engaged at the same time in games against distinct opponents, and when the strategy pursued in one game limits the strategies available in the other." Detailed comparison of these various linked-game models is a task for the future.

44. Thomas Romer and Howard Rosenthal, "Political Resource Allocation, Controlled Agendas, and the Status Quo," *Public Choice* 33 (1978): 27–44.

45. In more formal treatments, the no-agreement outcome is called the "reversion point." A given constituent's evaluation of no-agreement corresponds to what Raiffa, in *Negotiation*, terms a seller's "walk-away price," that is, the price below which he would prefer "no-deal." No-agreement is equivalent to what Snyder and Diesing, in *Conflict Among Nations*, term "breakdown," or the expected cost of war.

46. Thomas A. Bailey, *Woodrow Wilson and the Great Betrayal* (New York: Macmillan, 1945), pp. 16–37.

47. Raiffa, (*Negotiation*, p. 12) notes that "the more diffuse the positions are within each side, the easier it might be to achieve external agreement." For the conventional view, by contrast, that domestic unity is generally a precondition for international agreement, see Michael Artis and Sylvia Ostry, *International Economic Policy Coordination* (Chatham House Papers no. 30; London: Routledge and Kegan Paul, 1986), pp. 75–76.

48. "Meaningful consultation with other nations becomes very difficult when the internal process of decision-making already has some of the characteristics of compacts between quasi-sovereign entities. There is an increasing reluctance to hazard a hard-won domestic consensus in an international forum." Henry A. Kissinger, "Domestic Structure and Foreign Policy," in James N. Rosenau, ed., *International Politics and Foreign Policy* (New York: Free Press, 1969), p. 266.

49. See James Q. Wilson, *Political Organization* (New York: Basic Books, 1975), on how the politics of an issue are affected by whether the costs and the benefits are concentrated or diffuse.

50. Another factor fostering abstention is the greater complexity and opacity of monetary issues; as Gilbert R. Winham ("Complexity in International Negotiation," in Daniel Druckman, ed., *Negotiations: A Social-Psychological Perspective* [Beverly Hills, Calif.: Sage, 1977], p. 363) observes, "Complexity can strengthen the hand of a negotiator vis-à-vis the organization he represents."

51. Habeeb and Zartman, *The Panama Canal Negotiations*.

52. Bailey, *Woodrow Wilson*.

53. I am grateful to Ernst B. Haas and Robert O. Keohane for helpful advice on this point.

54. Ann L. Hollick, *U.S. Foreign Policy and the Law of the Sea* (Princeton, N.J.: Princeton University Press, 1981), esp. pp. 208–237; and James K. Sebenius, *Negotiating the Law of the Sea* (Cambridge, Mass.: Harvard University Press, 1984), esp. pp. 74–78.

55. Raiffa, *Negotiation*, p. 175.

56. I am indebted to Lisa Martin and Kenneth Shepsle for suggesting this approach, although they are not responsible for my application of it. Note that this construction assumes that each issue, taken individually, is a "homogeneous" type, not a "heterogeneous" type. Constructing iso-vote curves for heterogeneous-type issues is more complicated.

57. I am grateful to Henry Brady for clarifying this point for me.

58. Gilbert R. Winham, "The Relevance of Clausewitz to a Theory of International Negotiation," delivered at the 1987 annual meeting of the American Political Science Association.

59. Jimmy Carter, *Keeping Faith: Memoirs of a President* (New York: Bantam Books, 1982), p. 225.

60. Winham, "Robert Strauss" and *International Trade;* and Twiggs, *The Tokyo Round*.

61. Walton and McKersie, *A Behavioral Theory*, p. 321.

62. Artis and Ostry, *International . . . Coordination*. Of course, whether this is desirable in terms of democratic values is quite another matter.

63. Schelling, *Strategy*, p. 28.

64. Walton and McKersie, *A Behavioral Theory*, p. 345.

65. Carter, *Keeping Faith*, p. 172. See also Raiffa, *Negotiation*, p. 183.

66. The strategic significance of targeting at Level II is illustrated in John Conybeare, "Trade Wars: A Comparative Study of Anglo-Hanse, Franco-Italian, and Hawley-Smoot Conflicts," *World Politics* 38 (October 1985): 157: retaliation in the Anglo-Hanse trade wars did not have the intended deterrent effect, because it was not (and perhaps could not have been) targeted at the crucial members of the opposing Level II coalition. Compare Snyder and Diesing, *Conflict Among Nations*, p. 552: "If one faces a coercive opponent, but the opponent's majority coalition includes a few wavering members inclined to compromise, a compromise proposal that suits their views may cause their defection and the formation of a different majority coalition. Or if the opponent's strategy is accommodative, based on a tenuous soft-line coalition, one knows that care is required in implementing one's own coercive strategy to avoid the opposite kind of shift in the other state."

67. Walton and McKersie, *A Behavioral Theory*, p. 319.

68. Vladimir Velebit, in Campbell, *Successful Negotiation*, p. 97. As noted earlier, our discussion here assumes that the Level I negotiator wishes to reach a ratifiable agreement; in cases (alluded to later) when the negotiator's own preferences are more hard-line than his constituents', his domestic popularity might allow him to resist Level I agreements.

69. Transaction benefits may be enhanced if a substantive agreement is

reached, although sometimes leaders can benefit domestically by loudly rejecting a proffered international deal.

70. Snyder and Diesing, *Conflict*, pp. 516, 522–523. Analogous misperceptions in Anglo-American diplomacy are the focus of Richard E. Neustadt, *Alliance Politics* (New York: Columbia University Press, 1970).

71. Snyder and Diesing, *Conflict*, p. 517.

72. I am grateful to Robert O. Keohane for pointing out the impact of uncertainty on the expected value of proposals.

73. I. William Zartman, *The Fifty-Percent Solution* (Garden City, N.Y.: Anchor Books, 1976), p. 14. The present analysis assumes that constituents are myopic about the other side's Level II, an assumption that is not unrealistic empirically. However, a fully informed constituent would consider the preferences of key players on the other side—for if the current proposal lies well within the other side's win-set, then it would be rational for the constituent to vote against it, hoping for a second-round proposal that was more favorable to him and still ratifiable abroad; this might be a reasonable interpretation of Senator Lodge's position in 1919 (see Bailey, *Woodrow Wilson*). Consideration of such strategic voting at Level II is beyond the scope of this paper.

74. John R. Hillman, "The Mutual Influence of Italian Domestic Politics and the International Monetary Fund," *The Fletcher Forum* 4 (Winter 1980): 1–22. Luigi Spaventa (in "Two Letters of Intent: External Crises and Stabilization Policy, Italy, 1973–77," in John Williamson, ed., *IMF Conditionality*, [Washington, D.C.: Institute for International Economics, 1983], pp. 441–473) argues that the unions and the Communists actually favored the austerity measures, but found the IMF demands helpful in dealing with their own internal Level II constituents.

75. Dieter Hiss, "Weltwirtschaftsgipfel: Betrachtungen eines Insiders" [World Economic Summit: Observations of an Insider], in Joachim Frohn and Reiner Staeglin, eds., *Empirische Wirtschaftsforschung* (Berlin: Duncker and Humblot, 1980), pp. 286–287.

76. On cognitive and communications explanations of international cooperation, see, for example, Ernst B. Haas, "Why Collaborate? Issue-Linkage and International Regimes," *World Politics* 32 (April 1980): 357–405; Richard N. Cooper, "International Cooperation in Public Health as a Prologue to Macroeconomic Cooperation," in Cooper et al., *Can Nations Agree?*, pp. 178–254; and Zartman, *The Fifty-Percent Solution*, esp. part 4.

77. Henning, *Macroeconomic Diplomacy*, pp. 62–63.

78. This is the approach used to analyze the Anglo–Chinese negotiations over Hong Kong in Bruce Bueno de Mesquita, David Newman, and Alvin Rabushka, *Forecasting Political Events: The Future of Hong Kong* (New Haven, Conn.: Yale University Press, 1985).

79. For overviews of this literature, see Terry M. Moe, "The New Economics of Organization," *American Journal of Political Science* 28 (November 1984): 739–777; John W. Pratt and Richard J. Zeckhauser, eds., *Principals and Agents: The Structure of Business* (Boston: Harvard Business School Press, 1985); and Barry M. Mitnick, "The Theory of Agency and Organizational Analysis," paper delivered at the 1986 Annual Meeting of the American Political Science Associa-

tion. This literature is only indirectly relevant to our concerns here, for it has not yet adequately addressed the problems posed by multiple principals (or constituents, in our terms). For one highly formal approach to the problem of multiple principals, see R. Douglas Bernheim and Michael D. Whinston, "Common Agency," *Econometrica* 54 (July 1986): 923–942.

80. Hillman, "Mutual Influence," and Spaventa, "Two Letters."

81. This power of the chief negotiator is analogous to what Shepsle and Weingast, "Institutional Foundations," term the "penultimate" or "ex post veto" power of the members of a Senate-House conference committee.

82. Bailey, *Woodrow Wilson*, quotation at p. 15.

83. Robert A. Strong and Marshal Zeringue, "The Neutron Bomb and the Atlantic Alliance," paper delivered at the 1986 Annual Meeting of the American Political Science Association, p. 9.

84. I. William Zartman, "Reality, Image, and Detail: The Paris Negotiations, 1969–1973," in Zartman, *The Fifty-Percent Solution*, pp. 372–398.

85. Zbigniew Brzezinski, *Power and Principle* (New York: Farrar, Strauss, and Giroux, 1983), p. 136, as quoted in Habeeb and Zartman, *Panama Canal Negotiations*, pp. 39–40.

86. Harrison, in Campbell, *Successful Negotiation*, p. 67.

87. Samuel P. Huntington, "Transnational Organizations in World Politics," *World Politics* 25 (April 1973): 333–368; Keohane and Nye, *Power and Interdependence;* Neustadt, *Alliance Politics.*

88. Barbara Crane, "Policy Coordination by Major Western Powers in Bargaining with the Third World: Debt Relief and the Common Fund," *International Organization* 38 (Summer 1984): 399–428.

CONTRIBUTORS

Richard C. Eichenberg is Associate Professor of Political Science at Tufts University, where he is also Director of the International Relations Program.

Barry Eichengreen is Professor of Economics at the University of California at Berkeley and Research Associate of the National Bureau of Economic Research.

Peter B. Evans is Professor of Sociology at the University of California at Berkeley.

Harold K. Jacobson is Jesse S. Reeves Professor of Political Science and Director, Center for Political Studies, Institute for Social Research at the University of Michigan.

Miles Kahler is Professor of International Relations at the Graduate School of International Relations and Pacific Studies at the University of California at San Diego.

Ellis S. Krauss is Professor of Political Science at the University of Pittsburgh.

Lisa Martin is Associate Professor of Government at Harvard University.

Helen Milner is Associate Professor of Political Science at Columbia University.

Andrew Moravcsik is Assistant Professor of Government at Harvard University and Research Associate, Program on International Politics, Economics and Security at the University of Chicago.

John S. Odell is Professor of International Relations, University of Southern California.

Robert A. Pastor is Professor of Political Science at Emory University and Fellow at Emory's Carter Center.

Robert D. Putnam is Gurney Professor of Political Science and Associate Dean of Arts and Sciences at Harvard University.

Kathryn Sikkink is Assistant Professor of Political Science at the University of Minnesota.

Jack Snyder is Professor of Political Science at the Institute of War and Peace Studies at Columbia University.

Janice Gross Stein is Professor of Political Science at the University of Toronto, and a Fellow of the Royal Society of Canada.

Marc Uzan is an economic adviser in New York. He coauthored chapter 6 while visiting in the Department of Economics at the University of California at Berkeley.

INDEX

In the text of the book, organizations are often referred to by their abbreviations. In the index, entries with only a few page references are listed by both name and abbreviation. Organizations and institutions having extensive page references are listed by their abbreviation:

> COG (chief of government)
> INF negotiations

These are also listed by name, referring the reader to the proper location:

> Intermediate Nuclear Force (INF) negotiations. *See* INF negotiations.

In the index subheadings, abbreviations are used for both countries and organizations:

> U.S. role in
> actions of OAS

A list of abbreviations and accompanying names appears on pp. xii–xv.

ABICOMP (Brazilian computer industry association), 249

Acceptability-set, 30, 197–98; COG's diverging from constituencies', 289, 458–59, 460; COG shifts toward constituencies', 66, 78, 90, 94; COG unwilling to modify, 303; of developing countries, 371–72; domestic interests affecting, 135, 172, 217–18, 324; relation to win-set, 30–31

Acheson, Dean, 112–13

Addow, Abdillahi Ahmad, 380–81, 410

Adenauer, Konrad, 110, 113

AEA (American Electronics Association), 240–41, 254, 269

Afghanistan War, 4, 60

Agenda-setting, COG autonomy in, 25, 68, 155, 403–5, 457

Agent-structure problem, 96n.1

AGPM (French Association of Maize Producers), 246

Agreement: costs of no-agreement, 79, 87–90, 230, 234–35, 350, 405; defined in terms of IFI lending negotiations, 364–65; factors affecting likelihood of, 54, 324, 400, 412, 421–22, 427, 445–46; failure to reach, 84–86,

171–72, 177–80, 423; high costs of, 218, 233, 324, 364, 382–83; resistance to agreement with IMF by developing countries, 26, 369–70, 391–92; of value to COG with eroding support, 72–73. *See also* Negotiation process; Ratification

Agricultural and farm subsidies. *See* Common Agricultural Policy (CAP)

Agricultural interests, 192–95, 246, 370; actions in EC-U.S. feedgrain dispute, 242, 245, 264n.44; French farmers, 3, 26, 192, 204n.45, 414–15

Aid, foreign or international, 85, 98n.19

Air Transit Agreement of Chicago. *See* International Air Transit Agreement

Air Transport Agreement of Chicago. *See* International Air Transport Agreement

Allison, Graham, theories of bureaucratic politics, 10, 434

American Electronics Association (AEA), 240–41, 254, 269

American Jewish community, 84

American Selling Price fiasco, 449

Amnesty International reports on human rights, 331, 334, 338

Side payments, 25, 162n.16, 199, 228–29, 448; cost effectiveness of, 451; from IMF, 377–78; from USSR to Third World, 119; in Panama Canal Treaty negotiations, 310, 311; to foreign constituencies, 29
Sikkink, Kathryn, 20, 27, 30, 330, 415, 418, 469. *See also* Human rights policies, U.S.-Latin American negotiations over
"Silverites" and silver inflation, 195–96, 205n.61. *See also* Gold standard
Singer, J. David, 6
"Single-zero" option, 51, 61, 62, 64t, 64, 75n.16
Smith, Mike, 286
Smoot-Hawley Tariff (1930), 174, 196, 205n.63
SNECMA (Société Nationale...de Moteurs d'Aviation), 138, 140
Snidal, Duncan, 11
Snyder, Glenn H., 437, 452
Snyder, Jack, 18–19, 25, 26, 104, 403, 410, 415, 470
Social Democratic Party (SPD) (FRG), 52, 118
Société Nationale d'Etude et de Construction de Moteurs d'Aviation (SNECMA), 138, 140
Society-centered theories, 6
"Soft-cop, hard-cop" ploy, 283, 289, 409
Somali Socialist Revolutionary Party (SSRP), 374
Somalia: domestic constraints affecting negotiations, 389–92; negotiations with and resistance to IMF, 21, 379–83, 413–14; political economy of, 372–75, 380, 383, 390–91, 391t; refugee crisis in, 374
Somoza government of Nicaragua, 312–13
Sovereignty, 424. *See also* Security issues
Soviet Union (USSR), 4, 19, 373; collapse of, 73, 122; Communist Party of, 111, 120; under Brezhnev, 19, 105, 116–19; under Gorbachev, 19, 119–21, 122; under Khrushchev, 19, 105, 110, 111, 114–15; under Stalin, 19, 109, 408
SPD (Social Democratic Party) (FRG), 52, 118

Sprague, Oliver, 187
Spurious reverberation, 108, 125n.9
SSRP (Somali Socialist Revolutionary Party), 374
Stable state preferences assumption, 11–13
Stalin, Joseph, 18, 109, 408
State, Department of (U.S.), 267–68, 277, 278, 320, 340
State bureaucracies, 6, 10, 69, 99n.22, 339–41; Allison's theories on, 10; infighting among, 210–11, 214–15, 281, 320, 381; Japanese, 271, 272, 274–75, 279–81; MoDs, 130, 131–32, 142, 149, 152; relation to executive, 343–45; Soviet, 111; U.S., 267–68, 273, 277, 278, 320; U.S. defense, 130, 131–32, 320, 446
State-centered theories, 6, 401–2, 429n.6, 435–36, 459, 462n.17; COG as fulcrum in, 401, 427–28, 456–58, 459
States, 10–11, 16; democratic, 6, 9–10; domestic versus foreign policy motives of, 7–9, 13–14; loans to, 363; as non-unitary actors, 155; self-sufficiency of, 19–20, 163n.21; systemic theoretical assumptions about, 9–13; threats to, 12, 111, 129; as unitary actors (critiqued), 236–37, 291, 436. *See also* Nationalism; Nondemocratic regimes; "State-strength"
Statesman. *See* COG (chief of government); Negotiators
State-society relations, 6
"State-strength," 434–35, 449–50; critique of theory, 40n.59, 206n.70, 327
Stein, Janice Gross, 77, 402, 403, 415, 470. *See also* Camp David accords
"Sterling oil" issue, 217
Structural realist approach, 434; to Arab-Israeli dispute, 77–79, 94; to East-West bargaining over Germany, 18–19, 113–14. *See also* "State-strength"
Structuralist vs. market economics, 384
"Suasive reverberation," 86–87, 93, 455
Subnational actors. *See* Domestic-level constraints
Swing groups, 26
Symbolic role of particular countries for IMF, 378–79

Compositor:	Maryland Composition Co.
Text:	10/12 Baskerville
Display:	Baskerville
Printer:	Maple-Vail Book Manufacturing Group
Binder:	Maple-Vail Book Manufacturing Group